T0399215

The Collected Works
of John Ford

VOLUME IV

The Collected Works of John Ford

VOLUME IV

Edited by

BRIAN VICKERS

TOM CAIN

LISA HOPKINS

ELEANOR LOWE

KATSUHIKO NOGAMI

MARTIN WIGGINS

CLARENDON PRESS · OXFORD

2023

OXFORD
UNIVERSITY PRESS

Great Clarendon Street, Oxford, OX2 6DP,
United Kingdom

Oxford University Press is a department of the University of Oxford.
It furthers the University's objective of excellence in research, scholarship,
and education by publishing worldwide. Oxford is a registered trade mark of
Oxford University Press in the UK and in certain other countries

Published in the United States of America by Oxford University Press
198 Madison Avenue, New York, NY 10016, United States of America

British Library Cataloguing in Publication Data
Data available

Library of Congress Control Number: 2022943538

ISBN 978–0–19–286561–8

Printed and bound in the UK by
Clays Ltd, Elcograf S.p.A.

Acknowledgements

TOM CAIN would like to thank the Leverhulme Trust for an Emeritus Fellowship; Exeter University for a Visiting Fellowship; Brian Vickers, Gilles Monsarrat, and JoanBeal; the late Alistair Elliot and Tom Craik; and many helpful librarians, in particular the staff of the Guildhall Library, London, the Bodleian Library, the British Library, the New York Public Library, and the college libraries of St. John's, Oxford, Magdalen, Brasenose, Lincoln, Eton, and Haverford, Pennsylvania.

LISA HOPKINS would like to thank Carter Hailey for contributing the textual analysis, also Matthew Steggle, Tom Rutter, and Chris Hopkins.

ELEANOR LOWE AND MARTIN WIGGINS would like to acknowledge their debt to previous editors of the play, and to thank Brian Vickers, Patrick Spottiswoode, Kate Welch, and Karin Brown of the Shakespeare Institute Library, and each other. Their thanks are also due to the British Library for reproducing the play's title page and Oxford Brookes University for funding.

KATSUHIKO NOGAMI would like to express special thanks to Professor Brian Vickers, former Professors Noriko Koike, Masahiro Kubodera, Kazuhiko Ōshima, Sōzo Umemiya and Akihiro Yamada, late Professors Kenji Naitō and Shōichi Oguro, and Dr. Antony Telford Moore.

BRIAN VICKERS would like to thank Tom Cain and Katsuhiko Nogami for commenting on early drafts of his Introduction, Annie Duarte for editorial checking, and Valerie Hall for timely help with the typescript.

Contents

Illustrations

Abbreviations and short titles

The place of publication is London unless otherwise stated.

(1) General Abbreviations

BL   British Library

EB   *Encyclopedia Britannica*

EEBO   *Early English Books Online (https://www.proquest.com/eebo/litera-
          ture)*

ODNB   *The Oxford Dictionary of National Biography* (online edn.)

OED   *The Oxford English Dictionary*, 2nd edn.

Q   *1633 Quarto*

SD   stage direction

SP   speech prefix

STC   A. W. Pollard and G. R. Redgrave, *A Short-Title Catalogue of Books
          Printed in England, Scotland, and Ireland . . . 1475–1640*, 2nd edn.,
          revised and enlarged, begun by W. A. Jackson and F. S. Ferguson,
          completed by Katharine F. Pantzer, 3 vols (1976–91)

TLN   through line number

(2) Abbreviations of Primary Works

BH   *The Broken Heart*, Ford (1629)

CBS   *Christ's Bloody Sweat*, Ford (1613)

CWJF 1   *The Collected Works of John Ford*, eds. Gilles Monsarrat, Brian
          Vickers, and R. J. C. Watt (Oxford, 2012), Vol. I

CWJF 2   *The Collected Works of John Ford*, ed. Brian Vickers (Oxford, 2017),
          Vol. II

CWJF 3   *The Collected Works of John Ford*, ed. Brian Vickers (Oxford, 2017),
          Vol. III

FCN   *The Fancies, Chaste and Noble*, Ford (1635)

FE   *A Funeral Elegy for William Peter*, Ford (1612)

FM   *Fame's Memorial*, Ford (1606)

FMI   *The Fair Maid of the Inn*, Massinger, Ford, Webster (1626)

GM   *The Golden Mean*, Ford (1613 and 1614)

HT	*Honor Triumphant*, Ford
JC	*Julius Caesar*, Shakespeare
LC	*Love's Cure*, Massinger, Fletcher (1615)
LL	*A Line of Life*, Ford (1620)
LLL	*Love's Labour's Lost*, Shakespeare
LM	*The Lover's Melancholy*, Ford (1628)
LoC	*The Laws of Candy*, Massinger, Ford (1620)
LS	*Love's Sacrifice*, Ford (1632)
LT	*The Ladies' Trial*, Ford (1638)
PW	*The Chronicle History of Perkin Warbeck*, Ford (1633)
R&J	*Romeo & Juliet*, Shakespeare
SD	*The Sun's Darling*, Ford, Dekker (1621)
SG	*The Spanish Gypsy*, Ford, Dekker, Middleton, Rowley (1623)
WoE	*The Witch of Edmonton*, Ford, Dekker, Rowley (1621)

Periodicals

ELR	*English Literary Renaissance*
EMLS	*Early Modern Literary Studies*
MLR	*Modern Language Review*
MP	*Modern Philology*
NQ	*Notes and Queries*
PMLA	*Publications of the Modern Language Association of America*
RenD	*Renaissance Drama*
SEL	*Studies in English Literature 1500–1900*
ShakS	*Shakespeare Studies*
ShS	*Shakespeare Survey*
SP	*Studies in Philology*

Works cited by more than one play

Anderson	Donald K. Anderson, Jr. (ed.), *Concord in Discord: The Plays of John Ford, 1586–1986* (New York, 1986)
Dyce	*The Works of John Ford, with Notes . . . by William Gifford, Esq. A New Edition, carefully Revised . . . by the Rev. Alexander Dyce* (London: James Toovey, 1869), 3 vols
Ellis	*John Ford*, ed. Havelock Ellis (Mermaid Series) (The Best Plays of The Old Dramatists) (London: Vizetelly & Co., 1888)

Ewing	Ewing, S. Blaine Jr., *Burtonian Melancholy in the Plays of John Ford* (Princeton, NJ, 1940)
Gifford	*The Dramatic Works of John Ford*, ed. William Gifford (London: John Murray, 1827), 2 vols
Hopkins, *Political*	Hopkins, Lisa, *Ford's Political Theatre* (Manchester, 1994)
Huebert	Huebert, Ronald, *John Ford, Baroque English Dramatist* (Montreal and London, 1977)
JCS	Bentley, Gerald Eades, *The Jacobean and Caroline Stage*, 6 vols (Oxford, 1941–68)
Lomax	*John Ford: 'Tis Pity She's a Whore and Other Plays: The Lover's Melancholy / The Broken Heart / 'Tis Pity She's a Whore / Perkin Warbeck*, ed. Marion Lomax (Oxford World's Classics) (London: Oxford University Press, 1995)
Madelaine, "Sensationalism"	Madelaine, Richard, ' "Sensationalism" and "Melodrama" in Ford's Plays', in Neill (ed.), pp. 29–53
Neill (ed.)	Neill, Michael (ed.), *John Ford: Critical Re-Visions* (Cambridge, 1988)
Oliver	Oliver, H. J., *The Problem of John Ford* (Melbourne and London, 1955)
Sargeaunt	Sargeaunt, M. J., *John Ford* (Oxford, 1935)
Sensabaugh	Sensabaugh, G. F., *The Tragic Muse of John Ford* (Stanford, CA, 1944)
Stavig	Stavig, Mark, *John Ford and the Traditional Moral Order* (Madison, WI, 1968)
Tilley	M. P. Tilley, ed., *A Dictionary of Proverbs in the Sixteenth and Seventeenth Centuries in England* (Ann Arbor, MI, 1950)
Weber	*The Dramatic Works of John Ford*, ed. Henry Weber (Edinburgh: printed by George Ramsay & Company, 1811), 2 vols
Wymer	Wymer, Rowland, *Webster and Ford* (London, 1995)

'Tis Pity She's a Whore

Footnotes, textual notes, and commentary

Abbott	Abbott, E. A., ed., *A Shakespearian Grammar* (London, 1869; rpt. 1929, 1980)

Barker	*'Tis Pity She's a Whore*, ed. Simon Barker (London and New York: Routledge, 1997)
Bawcutt	*'Tis Pity She's a Whore*, ed. N. W. Bawcutt (Regents Renaissance Drama Series) (Lincoln, NE: University of Nebraska Press, 1966)
Bevington	*English Renaissance Drama: A Norton Anthology*, eds. David Bevington, Lars Eagle, Katherine Eisaman, Maus and Eric Rasmussen (New York and London: W. W. Norton, 2002)
Brewer	*Brewer's Dictionary of Phrase & Fable*, ed. Adrian Room (London, 1963; revised, 2002)
Burton, *Anatomy*	Robert Burton, *The Anatomy of Melancholy*, intr. Holbrook Jackson (London, 1936; rpt. 1978)
Catholic Encyclopaedia	*The Catholic Encyclopaedia* (New York), accessed 2009 from New Advent: http://www.newadvent.org/cathen/06082a.htm
Crystal	David and Ben Crystal, *Shakespeare's Words: A Glossary and Language Companion* (2002)
Dodsley	*A Select Collection of Old Plays*, ed. Robert Dodsley (London: Dodsley, 1744), 12 vols, Vol. V
EDD	*The English Dialect Dictionary*, ed. Joseph Wright (1898), 6 vols
Gibson	Gibson, Colin, ed., *The Selected Plays of John Ford: The Broken Heart, 'Tis Pity She's a Whore, Perkin Warbeck* (Cambridge: Cambridge University Press, 1986)
Hopkins	*'Tis Pity She's a Whore*, ed. Lisa Hopkins (London: Nick Hern Books, 2002)
McIlwraith	*Five Stuart Tragedies*, ed. A. K. McIlwraith (World Classics) (London: Oxford University Press, 1953)
March	March, Jenny, ed., *Cassell's Dictionary of Classical Mythology* (2001)
Massai	*'Tis Pity She's a Whore*, ed. Sonia Massai (Arden Early Modern Drama) (London: Methuen Drama, Bloomsbury Publishing Plc., 2011)
Moore	*Love's Sacrifice*, ed. A. T. Moore (Revels Plays; Manchester University Press, Manchester, 2008)
Morris	*'Tis Pity She's a Whore*, ed. Brian Morris (New Mermaid Series) (London and New York: Ernest Benn and W. W. Norton and Co., 1968)
Nashe	*The Works of Thomas Nashe*, ed. Ronald B. McKerrow (Oxford, 1958), 5 vols

Neill, 'Strange Riddle'	Neill, Michael, 'What Strange Riddle's This?': Deciphering *'Tis Pity She's a Whore'*, in Neill (ed.), pp. 153–79
NOCM	*The New Oxford Companion of Music,* gen. ed. Denis Arnold, 2 vols (Oxford, 1996)
Reed	*A Select Collection of Old Plays, The Second Edition, Corrected and Collated with the Old Copies,* ed. Isaac Reed (London: printed by H. Hughs, 1780), 12 vols, Vol. VIII
Roper	*'Tis Pity She's a Whore,* ed. Derek Roper (The Revels Plays Series) (Manchester: Manchester University Press, 1975)
Schmitz	'A Critical Edition of John Ford's 'Tis Pitty Shee's a Whore', ed. Elsie Kemp Schmitz (unpublished MPhil typescript prepared at Cambridge, England, 1956–9)
Sherman	*'Tis Pity She's a Whore and The Broken Heart,* ed. Stuart P. Sherman (Belles-Lettres Series) (Boston and London: D. C. Heath & Co., Publishers, 1915)
Simpson & Roud	*A Dictionary of English Folklore,* eds. Steve Roud and Jacqueline Simpson (Oxford, 2000)
Sturgess	*John Ford: Three Plays,* ed. Keith Sturgess (Penguin English Library) (Harmonsworth: Penguin Books, 1970)
Walley	*Early Seventeenth-Century Plays, 1600–1642,* eds. Harold Reinoehl Walley and John Harold Wilson (New York: Harcourt, Brace and Company, 1930)
Wiggins	*'Tis Pity She's a Whore,* ed. Martin Wiggins, 2nd Edn. (New Mermaids) (London and New York: A & C Black, and W. W. Norton, 2003)

Lover's Melancholy

Footnotes, textual notes, and commentary

Bright, *Treatise*	Bright, Timothy, *A Treatise of Melancholie* (London, 1586)
Craik	Notes communicated privately by the late Prof. Tom Craik
Hill	*The Lover's Melancholy,* ed. R. F. Hill (Revels Plays; Manchester University Press, Manchester, 1985)
Linthicum, *Costume*	Linthicum, M. C., *Costume in the Drama of Shakespeare and his Contemporaries* (Oxford, 1936)

Williams, *Dictionary*   Williams, Gordon, *A Dictionary of Sexual Language and Imagery in Shakespearean and Stuart Literature* (1994)

The Broken Heart

Footnotes, textual notes, and commentary

Brooke and Paradise   C. F. Tucker Brooke and N. B. Paradise, eds., *English Drama 1580–1627* (New York, 1933)

Harrier   Richard C. Harrier, ed., *The Anchor Anthology of Jacobean Drama* (New York, 1863), vol. I

Lamb   Charles Lamb, *Specimens of English Dramatic Poets who lived about the time of Shakespeare* (London, 1808; reprinted 1901)

Merivale   J. H. Merivale in *The Monthly Review*, series 2, 67 (April 1812), p. 373

Mitford   [John Mitford], *A Letter to Richard Heber, Esq. containing some observations of the merits of Mr. Weber's late edition of Ford's Dramatic Works* (London, 1812)

Modern British Drama   *Modern British Drama*, 5 vols (London: printed for William Miller, 1811), vol. I, *Tragedies*

Spencer   *The Broken Heart*, ed. T. J. B. Spencer (Revels Plays; Manchester University Press, Manchester 1980)

The Queen

Footnotes, textual notes, and commentary

Bang   Bang, W. (ed.), *The Queen or The Excellency of Her Sex, Materialien zur Kunde des älteren Englischen Dramas*, I. 13 (Louvain, 1906) [Kraus reprint, Vanduz, 1963]

Sedge   Sedge, Douglas, 'An Edition of *The Queen, or The Excellency of Her Sex*' (University of Birmingham, MA thesis, 1963)

Introduction

BRIAN VICKERS

The first volume of this edition (Oxford, 2012) was devoted to Ford's non-dramatic works. Gilles Monsarrat edited Ford's early chivalric celebration of the Danish King's visit to England, *Honor Triumphant* and *The Monarches Meeting* (1606). Rob Watt and Brian Vickers edited Ford's two long poems: his tribute to a military hero, *Fames Memoriall, or The Earle of Devonshire Deceased* (1606) and his long meditation on the Passion, *Christes Bloodie Sweat* (1613). Gilles Monsarrat edited Ford's two prose works in the genre of Christian Stoicism, *The Golden Meane* (1613–14), and *A Line of Life* (1620). Brian Vickers edited two newly attributed shorter poems: the first, *A Funerall Elegye for William Peter* (1612), had been previously misassigned to Shakespeare.[1] The second, Ford's eulogy to a fellow-dramatist and co-author, *Elegy on John Fletcher* (*c.*1625), was discovered by the gifted manuscript scholar, Jeremy Maule, shortly before his untimely death.

The second and third volumes (Oxford, 2017) were devoted to Ford's co-authored plays. Volume II, edited and written by Brian Vickers, consisted of detailed discussions of the widely practised method of joint authorship in Jacobean and Caroline drama. Given the absence of external evidence, the resulting scholarly problem is how to identify the playwrights involved on internal evidence alone. By using modern techniques of data-processing I was able to show that *The Laws of Candy* (1619–20), previously attributed to Ford alone, was in fact a collaboration, with the senior dramatist Philip Massinger playing the major role. Volume II also included separate analyses of the authorship division in the other collaborative plays, the texts of which appeared in Volume III, namely *The Laws of Candy*, edited by Christopher Adams and Brian Vickers; *The Witch of Edmonton* (1621), which Ford wrote with Dekker and William Rowley, edited by Rowland Wymer; *The Welsh Ambassador* (1623), written with Dekker, edited by Nigel Bawcutt; *The Spanish Gipsy* (1623), written with Dekker (with a few additions by Middleton and Rowley), edited by Marcus Dahl, Christopher Adams, and Brian Vickers; and *The*

[1] See Brian Vickers, *'Counterfeiting' Shakespeare. Evidence, Authorship, and John Ford's Funerall Elegye* (Cambridge, 2002).

Sun's Darling (1624), written with Dekker, edited by Christopher Adams and Brian Vickers. Finally, in *The Fair Maid of the Inn* (1626), edited by Martin Wiggins and Eleanor Lowe, the contributions of Massinger, Webster, and Ford are clearly distinguishable. Previous attribution scholars had attributed one scene (4.1) to Fletcher, who died in 1625, during the play's composition (see Ford's *Elegy* for him in Vol. I). Using modern attribution methods, however, I found only two slight echoes of Fletcher but over thirty close matches with Ford. Authorship attribution studies can adopt the Roman definition of justice, *suum cuique tribuere*, 'Give to each one his due'.[2]

The present volume is the first of two containing Ford's sole-authored plays, to which he owes his past and present fame. His first work for the stage, as I argue in my Introduction to the play, was *'Tis Pity She's a Whore*, not published until 1633. My esteemed colleague Martin Wiggins, in his ground-breaking *British Drama 1533–1642: A Catalogue*, working from external evidence only, dated *'Tis Pity* to 1621–31, with a 'best guess' of 1631.[3] But specialist studies of its prosody, from the late nineteenth century to the present day, using a variety of tests, have defined it as Ford's first play, earlier than the co-authored *Laws of Candy* (1619–20), and I date it to 1617–18. As I show there, it contains several features of dramatic structure that differentiate it from his co-authored plays of the mid-1620s.

In structure and plotting it has more in common with earlier Jacobean plays, especially the Italianate revenge tragedies of Webster and Middleton, which also end with multiple deaths and the breakdown of social order. In subject matter it is closest to Tourneur's *The Atheist's Tragedy* (1610). D'Amville, the main character, like Giovanni, is both an atheist and a hedonist. This may seem an unusual combination in the modern world, where most exponents of atheism are serious thinkers with no investment in the voluptuary arts, but Robert Ornstein, in an overlooked essay, showed that Renaissance critics of atheism bracketed them together.[4] Early in the play D'Amville expresses his desire to

> have all my senses feasted in
> Th'abundant fulness of delight at once,
> And with a sweet insensible increase
> Of pleasing surfeit melt into my dust. (1.1.18–21)[5]

[2] Justinian, *Institutes*, 1.1.

[3] Martin Wiggins, *British Drama 1533-1642: A Catalogue*, 10 vols (Oxford, 2012–2021), 4.481.

[4] See Ornstein, '*The Atheist's Tragedy* and Renaissance Naturalism', *Studies in Philology*, 51 (1954): 194–207.

[5] Quotation are from Irving Ribner (ed.), *The Atheist's Tragedy or, The Honest Man's Revenge* (London, 1964). In both plays a male character accuses a woman of suffering from 'a pleurisy of

Ornstein made this comment on D'Amville's 'sensuality': 'We might call him an atheistic epicure, but this would be redundant as "atheist" and "epicure" were practically synonymous terms to the apologists' for religion, such as Hooker, who argued that 'atheism is merely the excuse of those who devote their lives to sensual pleasure'.[6] In Hooker's own words,

> The fountain and wellspring of which impiety is a resolved purpose of mind to reap in this world what sensual profit or pleasure soever the world yields, and not to be barred from any whatsoever means available thereto.[7]

William R. Elton, in his survey of the philosophical background of *King Lear*,[8] noted the influence of Epicurus—not the true Epicurean philosophy but the corrupted version created by Plutarch and other rival schools of philosophy, according to which its followers worshipped the baser senses, opting out of society and the public good for their own pleasures. Elton cited a treatise by John Véron (*c.*1561), which included an *Apology of the Same, against Swynyshe Grunting of the Epicures and Atheyestes of Our Time* (17). Many moralists opposing Epicurus united the two targets. In France, Pierre Viret, in *L'Instruction chrétienne* (1564), fulminated against ' "epicuriens et atheistes" ' who deny providence, regarding human life as governed by fortune or fate. Similar attitudes were common in England. In 1594, Thomas Bowes' translation of La Primaudaye's *The Second Part of the French Academy* warned that ' "there are as many, yea moe at this day that do openly shew themselves to be Atheists & Epicures, than there are of those that are taken for good Christians" ' (22). In *The Golden-Grove* (1600) William Vaughan expressed the same view more pungently, 'condemn[ing] "Atheists, and the hoggish sect of the Epicures" ' (24). The common factor in both perversions was a concern with the self, very evident in Giovanni's behaviour.

Ford's play shares several features with Tourneur's. In both plays the atheist justifies his unbelief.[9] D'Amville rejects providence and asserts

lust'. In Tourneur's tragedy Charlemont accuses Castabella of a 'strange incontinence! Why, was thy blood | Increas'd to such a pleurisy of lust' (3.1.112–13); in Ford's Soranzo denounces Annabella: 'Must your hot ytch and plurisie of lust, | The heyday of your luxury be fedd | Up to a surfeite?' (4.3.8–10). Ford reused the phrase in *The Queen*, where Alphonso rebuffs his Queen: 'the tyde | Of thy luxurious blood is at the full; | And . . . thy raging plurisie of lust | Cannot be sated' (2.2.123–6).

   [6] Ornstein, '*The Atheist's Tragedy* and Renaissance Naturalism', p. 198.

   [7] See Richard Hooker, *Of the Laws of Ecclesiastical Polity: A Critical Edition with Modern Spelling*, 3 vols, ed. Arthur Stephen McGrade (Oxford, 2013), 2.14.

   [8] Elton, *King Lear and the Gods* (San Marino, CA, 1966; enlarged edn., Lexington, KY, 1988).

   [9] In his essay 'Of Atheism', Bacon took such self-justifications as a sign of weakness: 'It appeareth in nothing more, that atheism is rather in the lip than in the heart of man, than by this;

that fate rules all things (1.1.4–14, 1.2.47–51). He is frank about his self-centredness: 'Let all men lose, so I increase my gain: | I have no feeling of another's pain' (1.1.128–9; 1.2.142–3). In a crucial scene D'Amville makes an incestuous proposal to his daughter-in-law (Castabella) to have sex with him, expounding the hedonist's belief that 'All the purposes of man | Aim but at one of these two ends, pleasure | Or profit' (4.3.110–12). Disgusted, she replies that neither goal would tempt her to incest, enabling D'Amville to produce the atheist's argument that the degrees of 'kindred and affinity' governing permitted marriages displayed in churches are 'Articles of bondage', since 'Nature allows a gen'ral liberty | Of generation' to all other creatures (4.3.125–8). Tourneur gives Castabella the classic response of Renaissance moralists, that

> if you argue merely out
> Of Nature, do you not degenerate
> From that, and are you not unworthy the
> Prerogative of Nature's masterpiece (4.3.134–7)

The divine creation gave humanity reason and language, setting us above the animals.[10] The only reply that D'Amville can offer is to attempt rape: 'Tereus-like, | Thus will I force my passage to—' (173–4): but, fortunately, Castabella's husband Charlemont can intervene. Having routed D'Amville in argument, at the play's climax Tourneur makes him seize the executioner's axe in order to kill Charlemont and Castabella, but—in the dramatist's stage-direction, 'As he raises up the axe [he] strikes out his own brains, [and then] staggers off the scaffold' (5.2.241.1–2). Tourneur leaves him enough breath before dying to reject atheism, and to assert the power of providence.

Ford also allows Giovanni to expound his hedonism and to rehearse the atheist's attack on socio-religious custom in favour of Nature. But his dramatic design has no place for a challenging opponent like Castabella. Giovanni expounds his values to the Friar, who, from the outset, refuses to take part in such discussions (but listens uncomfortably), and to Annabella, who accepts them without argument. But whereas Tourneur makes it clear that the balance of sympathy lies with

that atheist will ever be talking of that their opinion, as if they fainted in it within themselves, and would be glad to be strengthened by the consent of others' (Francis Bacon, *A Critical Edition of the Major Works*, ed. Brian Vickers (Oxford, 1996), p. 371).

[10] Cf. Bacon: 'They that deny a God destroy man's nobility; for certainly man is of kin to the beasts by his body; and, if he be not of kin to God by his spirit, he is a base and ignoble creature. It likewise destroys magnanimity, and the raising of human nature' (p. 372).

Castabella, and is prepared to subvert his dramatic climax to affirm the-odicy, Ford withholds judgement. He allows Giovanni to present him-self at his own self-worth, for the audience to judge him accordingly. By all normal ethical, religious, and social norms of seventeenth-century Europe Giovanni condemns himself out of his own mouth. When words change to deeds as the action develops, seemingly depriving him of his sister as a sexual partner, Giovanni's increasingly desperate behaviour brings out the destructive egoism and megalomania that Ford has hinted at in earlier scenes. (It is strange that commentators think that he presented Giovanni sympathetically.) As I argue, it is if Ford had asked himself, what kind of person would practice and justify incest?—and then, what that does that tell us about their attitude to themselves and others? It is almost a clinical study of abnormal psychology.

When Ford could return to sole authorship in the late 1620s, having shared six joint compositions, he continued this exploration of human psychology in two of the plays included here, *The Lover's Melancholy* and *The Broken Heart*. For the first he publicly acknowledged his debt to Robert Burton's *The Anatomy of Melancholy*, in its longer 1628 ver-sion. As Tom Cain shows in his edition, like any conscientious scholar, 'Ford sought to invoke his authority for the psychologies he depicts. His own profound insights are usually based on Burton, and there are over eighty references in the commentary in this edition to passages from the *Anatomy* which shaped Ford's discourse, often in very direct ways.' *The Lover's Melancholy* is neither a simplistic dramatization of Burton, nor does it have any didactic designs on the audience. Unlike some other contemporary plays, which displayed 'morbid and extreme states' in melodramatic terms, Ford's primary interest is in 'the psy-chological effects of passion and sorrow on his main protagonists, and on their cure'. Critics have complained that this almost clinical focus on their psychologies resulted in a 'static plot structure'. Cain accepts the criticism but justifies Ford's choice to prioritize psychology by focussing on the cures for destructive grief and love. The plot

> provides Ford with a series of scenes within which he explores not
> *a* lover's melancholy, but three case histories, in which he brings
> to the fore in successive episodes the disabling, grief-stricken love
> melancholy of Palador, the equally disabling irrational 'heroic'
> love of Thamasta, and the paternal grief of Meleander.

As Cain noted, if we were to add the missing apostrophe to the play's title it should be placed after, not before, the 's': these are lovers' melancholies.

Of the three 'case histories', Ford gives most space to Meleander, grief-stricken by the reported death of his daughter, Eroclea, as we can see from his first utterance, a groan, 'able to roote up heart, liver, lungs and all' (2.2.8–9). His grief is more deep-rooted than that of young lovers, and Cain makes an illuminating reference to Burton's 'long discourse on grief for the "Death of Friends" (which at this date includes relatives such as daughters) which "may challenge a first place" as a cause of melancholy'. Burton points out that a temporary absence can have 'violent effects', but nothing compared to death, ' "when they must eternally be seperated, never here to meet againe? This is so grievous a torment for the time, that it takes away all appetite, desire of life, and extinguisheth all delights, it causeth deepe sighes and groanes, teares, exclamations, howling, roaring".' Such profound disturbances cannot be cured at once but need gradual treatment. Cain describes Corax's ministrations as 'preparatory therapy', first awakening him from his stupor, then administering a 'Nectar' or sleeping draught (4.2.176), continuing his thoughtful regimen in the final act, so that when Meleander wakes from his therapeutic sleep 'he may by degrees, digest | The present blessings in a moderate Joy' (5.1.13–14). This may sound like a textbook treatment of curing severe melancholy—as indeed it is—but Ford makes the process gradual, and as Cain describes it, 'appropriately theatrical, staged first in a series of tableaux, with the restoration and augmentation of various offices of state, and the presentation of [a] miniature of Eroclea'. Meleander is at first shocked at seeing her image, suspecting magic, but then wishing he could see her alive (Ford happily echoes the statue scene in *The Winter's Tale*). Cain comments that Meleander's 'willingness to entertain the idea of a miraculously recreated Eroclea functions as psychological preparation for the subsequent introduction of the real thing, her presentation orchestrated by Corax'. Whatever the plot's deficiencies, we can admire the tact and timing with which Ford integrated these case studies into a satisfying play.

Meleander's first reaction to Eroclea's reappearance is to thank her for taking 'so much paines | To live, till I might once more looke upon thee, | Before I broke my heart' (116–18), a phrase that looks back to the opening scene, where Ford alluded to a poem by Strada describing the death of a nightingale from a broken heart. It is no accident that he returned to the psychology of grief in his next play, *The Broken Heart* (1628), which, like *The Lover's Melancholy*, was performed at the Blackfriars indoor theatre rather than the Cockpit, and may have been commissioned to repeat the latter's success. The title seemingly refers to Calantha, who in the final scene, crowned Queen of Sparta, announces that she will choose a husband. Her only love had been Ithocles, recently murdered, whose hearse is present on stage, and at the play's climax Calantha places the wedding ring upon the corpse's finger and orders the musicians to 'sing the song | I fitted for my end.' Its concluding lines are:

> Love only reignes in death: though Art
> Can find no comfort for a broken heart. (5.3.93–4)

As the song ends, the queen has died—'Her heart is broke indeed'—so fulfilling the prophecy made earlier by the philosopher Tecnicus:

> When youth is ripe and age from time doth part,
> The livelesse Trunke shall wed the broken heart. (4.1.133–4)

This is undeniably the main instance of this malady, but Lisa Hopkins suggests in her edition here that it is not the only one: 'Penthea and Orgilus also suffer from broken hearts, as presumably do Ithocles when he realises that he is about to die and be parted from Calantha, Euphranea when she has to watch her brother bleed to death, and Bassanes when he learns that Penthea is dead.'

Although that description might seem to echo the multiple case histories of *The Lover's Melancholy*—'the disabling, grief-stricken love melancholy of Palador, the equally disabling irrational "heroic" love of Thamasta, and the paternal grief of Meleander'—in this play there can be no possibility of a cure. The conflicts are fixed, deriving from an ancient family feud which was meant to be healed by the marriage between the children from each family, Orgilus and Penthea. But Penthea's father dies before the marriage can take place, and her brother, Ithocles, wanting revenge on an enemy, blocks Penthea's marriage to Orgilus, forcing her to marry the insanely jealous Bassanes. Her life an unending misery, Penthea starves herself to death, but before dying she tells Calantha of Ithocles' love for her. Calantha's father approves their betrothal, but after Penthea's death Orgilus has his revenge by killing Ithocles.

The Broken Heart has a much more coherent plot than its predecessor but shares with it a similar authorial attitude towards his creation. As Terence Spencer observed,

> Shakespeare's characters are constantly engaged in assessing each other on moral grounds. They constantly talk about moral laws; and this certainly encourages the audience or reader to deduce moral conclusions from the play. But Ford does not encourage us

to take a moral point of view. He is non-committal. He seems ethically neutral. He has the detachment of the psychiatrist, it can be claimed, rather than the responsibility of the moralist. Compassion and curiosity are his characteristics. His plays reveal a passionate concern with cases of deep distress, which derive not from unknown but from known causes: especially, the agony of thwarted or misguided love.[11]

Ford gave the agonies of love a new twist in *The Queen*, the fourth play in this volume, which Eleanor Lowe and Martin Wiggins describe as 'a quirky political tragicomedy in the mode of late Fletcher'. It is set in Arragon and begins with Alphonso, sentenced to death by the Queen (who is never named), facing execution. He is a rebel found guilty of trying to overturn, as he puts it, the government of a 'fond' (foolish) woman, 'this female Mistriss of the Crown', which threatens the country's ruin (1.1.143–8). Unexpectedly, the Queen enters, enquiring whether he is 'sorry . . . for [his] late desperate rudenes'. Alphonso, having addressed her as 'a brave she tyrant', explains that

> I hate your sex in general, not you
> As y'are a Queen, but as y'are a woman (224–5)

Surprisingly, the Queen proposes mercy, if he'll be 'a new man', an option that Alphonso accepts with a deeply ironic speech (233–51). Apparently oblivious to his irony, the Queen pardons him. Moreover, having apparently fallen in love with Alphonso at first sight, she declares her intention to reform this woman-hater:

> And more to purchase kinde opinion of thy Sex,
> Our self will lend our help. (275–6)

Whereas other bystanders have described Alphonso as possessing 'a high Saturnal spirit', being 'drown'd | In melancholy and sowre discontent', the Queen sees prospects for reformation:

> here kiss our hand, we dare conceive
> That 'twas thy hight of youth, not hate of us
> Drew thee to those attempts, and both we pardon. (280–3)

By the end of this opening scene we are invited to the Court, where we 'may happily see [Alphonso] crowned King' (329).

With remarkable speed, and with little concern for narrative or psychological coherence, Ford has established a situation reminiscent of

---

[11] T. J. B. Spencer (ed.), *The Broken Heart* (Manchester, 1980), p. 49.

the paradoxical starting point of the rhetorical *controversiae* so popular with Massinger and Fletcher.[12] This one could be summed up as 'A Queen chooses to marry a misogynist'. No sooner has Alphonso been married and crowned than he sets his Queen a condition. Needing more time 'to redeem a while some serious thoughts | Which have misdeem'd your sex,' they should live separately for a week, which the Queen accepts (1.2.56–72). This interdiction is a form of contract and is simultaneously a test of the Queen's love. The week having been extended to a month, the Queen—who naively believes that 'the King | Made our division but a proof of faith' (2.2.127–8)—breaks the contract by visiting Alphonso. He rejects her as a 'monstrous enchantress' who, unable to control her 'raging plurisie of lust', is trying to 'raise | A wanton devil up in our chaste breast' (139–46). It seems as if the 'serious thoughts' that bother Alphonso stem from his hatred of women's sexuality, for he tells her to 'live chast' or otherwise never see him again: 'From this time forth | I hate thy sex; of all thy sex, thee worst' (170–3). The only character who emerges to resolve this deadlock is Muretto, one of the king's servants, who praises the Queen's beauty but insinuates that she is familiar with a young Lord, Petruchi (3.1.39–76). This arouses Alphonso's anger but also his jealousy.

Muretto in effect plays a similar role to Corax in *The Lover's Melancholy*, in curing a psychological imbalance so that a man and woman can restore their love. But his cure of a woman-hater differs from the remedy for curing hatred and other passions that Burton prescribed: 'To balance our hearts with love, charity, meeknesse, patience, and counterpoise those irregular motions of envy, livor, spleene, hatred, with their opposite vertues . . . to oppose . . . meeknesse to anger', and so to 'arme our selves against all such violent excursions, which may invade our minds.'[13] This therapeutic advice, partly derived from Epictetus, would be sensible if we were dealing with normal emotional disturbance. But Ford has realized that the 'opposite vertue' to Alphonso's distrust of women's sexuality is to arouse, or restore, his sexual desire. To pick out some stages in this lengthy cure: Alphonso acknowledges that 'my judgment | Still prompts my senses, that my Queen is fair' (4.2.11–12), a belief that Muretto enthusiastically amplifies while warning him that he will be 'a noted cuckold' if she persists

---

[12] See Eugene Waith, *The Pattern of Tragicomedy in Beaumont and Fletcher* (New Haven, CT, 1952), pp. 135–7. Ford aided Massinger in adapting the Senecan *controversia* 10.2 in *LoC* (1619–20): see my commentary in *CWJF* II.87–9, III.1–21.

[13] Burton, *The Anatomy of Melancholy*, Book 2, 3.6, subsection 1; eds. Nicolas K. Keeling, Thomas C. Faulkner, and Rhonda L. Blair, 6 vols (Oxford, 1990–2000), II.187.

in this (wholly imaginary) relationship with Petruchi. Muretto arranges a meeting between the three of them, in which Alphonso is divided between ecstatic admiration of his wife and hatred of her supposed lover (4.2.68–179). After the meeting disperses in frustration, Muretto expresses his satisfaction:

Fare ye well King, this is admirable, I will be chronicled, all my business ripens to my wishes. (180–1)

This comment resembles Prospero's, after he has observed Miranda and Sebastian's first view of each other: 'It goes on, I see, | As my soul prompts it' (*Tempest* 1.2.420–1). Readers and spectators are reassured that everything will end well, as it does.

In the final scene Muretto draws attention to Alphonso's internal struggle: 'I know my Lord your jealousy and your affections wrestle together for the mastery' (5.2.28–9). After a series of denouements confirming the Queen's chastity and Petruchi's innocence, Alphonso accuses Muretto of having planted and fed the suspicion of jealousy. Muretto admits that, having seen 'with what violence [Alphonso] pursude his . . . detestation of the Queen [and] all her sex', he studied how he might cure his 'distraction'.

And having felt his disposition in every pulse, I found him most addicted to this pestilence of jealosy with a strong persuasion of which, I from time to time ever fed him by degrees, till I brought the Queen and the noble Petruchi into the dangers they yet stand in. But with all . . . I season'd my words with such an intermixing the praises of the Queens bewty, that from jealosy I drew the King into a serious examination of her perfections. . . . At length having found him indeed surely affected, I perceav'd that nothing but the suppos'd blemish of her dishonour could work a second divorce between them. (160–72)

By mixing praise of the Queen's beauty and virtue with suspicion of her behaviour Muretto knew that, once the suspicion was dispelled, the other feelings would grow and prosper. The reunion of man and wife is brief but moving (191–207), and in one respect Burton would have approved, for he conceded that 'The last and best Cure of Love-Melancholy, is, to let them have their Desire'.[14]

---

[14] *Anatomy*, Book 3, 2.5. title of subsection 5; ed. cit., III. 242; or, as Burton expatiated in the text: 'The last refuge, and surest remedy . . . is to let them goe together, and enjoy one another . . . They may then kisse and coll, lye and look babies in one anothers eyes, as their Syres before them did, they may then satiate themselves with loves pleasures, which they have so long wished and expected' (242–3).

I have used the privilege of a general editor with an overview of the contents of this volume to pick out some of the features they share. In all four plays Ford preserves his detachment as a dramatist and his keen interest in human behaviour. But there is a great distance between the unsparing treatment of abnormal psychology in *'Tis Pity She's a Whore*, set against the background of a wholly corrupt society, in a tragedy offering no consolation, and the series of disasters that punctuate *The Broken Heart*. In this play the 'agony of thwarted or misguided love' that Terence Spencer defined as one of Ford's major preoccupations is caused by human malice, petty revenge, the envy that tries to prevent other people's happiness. Some of its personages are destructive and unredeemable, such as the insanely jealous Bassanes, but others retain their human dignity in the face of injustice. Penthea is not diminished by suffering, Ithocles and Orgilus arouse admiration for the courage with which they face death, and Calantha's life and death transcend adversity. There is just as great a distance between these tragedies and the tragicomedies *The Lover's Melancholy* and *The Queen*, with their happy endings. In both plays psychological imbalance can be cured. In the former, drawing on Burton, Ford produced a textbook example of the best contemporary medical remedies for melancholy. In the latter Ford devised an unorthodox way of curing misogyny that may owe something to a tradition in romantic comedy, in which 'Even as one heat another heat expels, | Or as one nail drives out another.'[15] In both plays those who regard Ford as a tragedian may be surprised to learn that his range included a concern for human health and happiness.

---

[15] *The Two Gentleman of Verona*, 2.4.190–1.

'Tis Pity She's a Whore

Edited by KATSUHIKO NOGAMI

With an Introduction by BRIAN VICKERS

INTRODUCTION

Date

'Tis Pity She's a Whore was published in 1633, as 'Acted by the Queenes Maiesties seruants at the Phoenix in Drury-Lane', but it may have been written long before that date. It was not entered in the Stationers' Register—along with about one-third of all books published in this period[1]—and we have no records of its first performance. The named theatre and theatre-company might seem a positive clue to its date, but the theatre had been in existence for many years. The Phoenix, a small indoor theatre, 'was the first professional playhouse in the so-called West End'. Its owner was Christopher Beeston, who in 1616 leased buildings near Drury Lane that had previously been used for cockfighting and converted them into a theatre. John Orrell argued that two drawings by Inigo Jones of a rectangular neo-classical theatre, with an apse, having no trace of the original circular cockfight structure, represent the designs he made for Beeston in 1616.[2] However, as Herbert Berry noted in his authoritative survey, Leslie Hotson had discovered 'more persuasive evidence' in the Public Record Office of a three-gabled structure clearly visible in Wenceslaus Hollar's great Map of London (1657).[3] That location, corresponding to present-day 135 Drury Lane, has recently been confirmed by Graham Barlow in a meticulous analysis of surviving building records.[4] As for Beeston, G. E. Bentley described him as having been, 'From his erection

---

[1] See Leo Kirschbaum, *Shakespeare and the Stationers* (Columbus, OH, 1953), p. 61.
[2] See John Orrell, *The Theatres of Inigo Jones and John Webb* (London, 1985).
[3] See Herbert Berry, 'The Phoenix', in Glynne Wickham, Herbert Berry, and William Ingram (eds.), *English Professional Theatre, 1530–1600* (Cambridge, 2000), pp. 623–37.
[4] See Graham F. Barlow, 'Wenceslaus Hollar and Christopher Beeston's Phoenix Theatre in Drury Lane', *Theatre Research International*, 13 (1988): 30–44.

of the Phoenix in 1617 to his death in 1638 . . . probably the most important theatrical figure in London.'[5] He was a member of Queen Anne's Company from 1603 to her death in 1619, and acted in all the companies that he formed for the Phoenix, Prince Charles's Men from 1619 to 1622, Lady Elizabeth's Men from 1622 to 1625, and Queen Henrietta's Men from 1625 to 1637. Since Beeston retained the 'Booke', or official manuscript of a play, 'Tis Pity could have been written for any of these companies from 1617 onwards.

Bentley points out that in the plays that Beeston released for printing, 'the company named on the title-page is usually the one that produced the play most recently, not originally, and a number of the plays in the repertory of Queen Henrietta's company are known to have been originally written for Lady Elizabeth's men' (JCS 4.560). Of two other Phoenix plays published in 1633, Derek Roper notes that Rowley's All Lost by Lust had been acted in 1619 or 1620, while Massinger's A New Way to Pay Old Debts 'had been written as early as 1621 or 1622'.[6] Ford's dedication describes the play as 'these first fruits of my leisure'. That enigmatic remark could refer to some otherwise unrecorded task he had undertaken, or to the publication of Christes Bloodie Sweat in 1613, followed by two editions of his moral treatise, The Golden Meane (1613, 1614).[7]

Martin Wiggins dates 'Tis Pity to 1621–31, with a 'best guess' of 1631,[8] but many scholars have suggested earlier dates. Following Bentley's objection to the 'huddling of [Ford's] dramatic development into the short period between 1628 and 1633', Derek Roper argued that it 'may have been written at any time between 1617 and 1628'.[9] Previous scholars saw it as an early play. In 1957 Clifford Leech described it as 'the last Jacobean tragedy', in which Ford 'manage[d] to re-create in one play, perhaps the first that he wrote independently, the Jacobean tragic spirit'.[10]

In 1960 Robert Ornstein endorsed the traditional assumption that 'Tis Pity was 'the earliest of the tragedies'.[11] Lisa Hopkins, in her survey of this topic, listed several scholars who argued that it was an early play: Una Ellis-Fermor, writing in 1936, G. F. Sensabaugh (1939),

---

[5] See JCS, 2.363–70.
[6] Roper, p. xciv. This is still the best scholarly edition.
[7] Cf. Monsarrat's edition of A Line of Life (CWJF 1.537–657).
[8] Martin Wiggins, British Drama, 1533–1642: A Catalogue, 10 vols (Oxford, 2012–21), 4.481.
[9] Roper, p. xxv; JCS 3.441–2.
[10] Clifford Leech, John Ford and the Drama of his Time (London, 1957), pp. 41–64 (37).
[11] Robert Ornstein, The Moral Vision of Jacobean Tragedy (Madison, WI 1960), pp. 203, 291 n.

H. J. Oliver (1955), Irving Ribner (1962), N. W. Bawcutt (1966), Kenneth Muir (1976), and R. F. Hill (1985).[12]

Pioneering students of Ford's versification also agreed as to its early date. In 1888 Eduard Hannemann documented Ford's metrical practices in considerable detail, including his use of feminine (disyllabic) and trisyllabic endings. The two plays with the lowest frequencies are *Love's Sacrifice* (15 per cent disyllabic, 0.5 per cent trisyllabic), and *'Tis Pity* (14 and 1 per cent, respectively), far below those for *The Broken Heart* (50 and 9 per cent) and *Perkin Warbeck* (43 and 6 per cent).[13] In 1912 Frederick Pierce, unaware of Hannemann's work, provided his own computations, which included raw counts of the number of rhyming pentameter lines and the number of triple endings. The early plays have many rhymes and few triple endings: *Love's Sacrifice* 90 and 4, respectively, *'Tis Pity* 104 and 12. As Ford's style matured, the later plays reversed this preference: *The Broken Heart* has 42 rhymes and 187 triple endings, *Perkin Warbeck* 22 and 148.[14] Pierce also calculated the percentage of double endings in unrhymed lines, where both *Love's Sacrifice* and *'Tis Pity* scored 15 per cent, compared to *The Broken Heart* (49 per cent) and *Perkin Warbeck* (43 per cent). All three of Pierce's tests, and both of Hannemann's, clearly distinguish the earlier from the later plays. That great authorship scholar E. H. C. Oliphant, in his pioneering work on the Beaumont and Fletcher canon, accepted Pierce's figures, concluding that '*Love's Sacrifice* and *'Tis Pity* were considerably earlier in date than 1622, when *The Witch of Edmonton* was written,' from when 'Ford's later style' can be traced.[15] Joan Sargeaunt, in the first modern study of Ford, also accepts Pierce's conclusion, that *Love's Sacrifice* and *'Tis Pity* were 'the two earliest of his plays written independently'.[16]

This whole topic was placed on a far more accurate basis by Marina Tarlinskaja, who introduced Russian computational prosody.[17] Where the traditional study of English verse attempts, unsuccessfully, to apply the methods of classical metrics, which distinguishes between long and

---

[12] See Hopkins, pp. 4–5.

[13] See Eduard Hannemann, *Metrische Untersuchungen zu John Ford* (Halle, 1888), p. 37. See pp. 32–5 for a list of hundreds of trisyllabic endings in Ford.

[14] See Frederick Pierce, 'The Collaboration of Dekker and Ford', *Anglia*, N.F. 36 (1912): 141–68 (143).

[15] See E. H. C. Oliphant, *The Plays of Beaumont and Fletcher: An Attempt to Determine Their Respective Shares and the Shares of Others* (New Haven, CT, 1927), pp. 87–90.

[16] See Sargeaunt, pp. 161–3. She rightly criticizes Pierce's unreliable figures for run-on lines (40 per cent in both plays) as 'far too high'.

[17] See Marina Tarlinskaja, *Shakespeare and the Versification of English Drama, 1561–1642* (Farnham and Burlington, VT, 2019).

short syllables, the Russian school of prosody simply identifies metrical stresses, strong and weak, represented as 'S' and 'W'. A regular blank verse line (iambic) alternates weak and strong syllables as here:

Now is the winter of our discontent
W S W   S W S   W   S W S

1   2   3   4   5   6   7   8   9   10

A line having an extra syllable (the so-called 'feminine ending') has this scheme:

To be, or not to be, that is the quest'ion
W   S   W S   W S   W S   W   S W

1   2   3   4   5   6   7   8   9   10 11

In quantitative prosody each line of verse is analysed in this way and the total stresses (weak or strong) for each metrical foot are computed. In the mature period of professional English drama, between 1579 and 1642, the comparative metrical regularity of Marlowe and the dramatists of the 1580s gave way to a greater variety, where the stresses shifted unpredictably. There are theoretically nine places where a syllable can be weak or strong, and a verse line often includes an internal pause. Chronological studies have shown that in earlier Elizabethan drama the pause occurred after the fourth syllable, in lines that often consisted of a whole semantic unit, that is, a sentence or a clause closed with a full-stop or semi-colon ('end-stopped'). The later Jacobean and Caroline dramas placed the pause more often after the sixth syllable, encouraging a run-on line ('enjambement'). Studies of Shakespeare's verse since the Victorian period have familiarized scholars with this sequence of dramatists first adopting the regular ten-syllable line and gradually loosening it.

The value of Tarlinskaja's historical prosody is that she has analysed the plays of every English Renaissance dramatist, whether sole- or co-authored, and established their prosodic identity over time. In addition to the main metrical characteristics summarized here she has developed a range of smaller, supplementary markers. Ford's late play *The Broken Heart* (1629) 'stands out with 60 per cent of feminine endings', while *'Tis Pity* has 'only 15.8 per cent':[18] this is an enormous difference, suggesting a much earlier date. Tarlinskaja distinguished between 'simple'

---

[18] See ibid., pp. 238–44. Her book has an appendix following p. 286, containing tables collecting all her prosodic data, running to 90 pages. Unfortunately, these pages are unnumbered.

line endings, such as '*the LESson*' and '*much BETTer*', and 'compound endings', such as '*adMIRE him*' and '*shall FIND us*'. The incidence of compound (or 'heavy') endings in *The Broken Heart* is 3.4 per cent; *'Tis Pity* 'contains a meagre 0.5 per cent'. As for run-on lines,

> Though *'Tis Pity She's a Whore* contains many masculine endings, it has fewer, not more, run-on lines than Ford's other plays. [25.0 per cent] This is strange: masculine endings should stimulate run-on lines, particularly in a later play. (240)

Another prosodic feature that argues against a later date is the stressing on strong positions. All of Ford's plays conform to the Jacobean–Caroline pattern of stressing position 6 more often than 4, but *'Tis Pity* is a 'striking exception: position 4 not only bears more stresses than 6, it is stressed in over 80 per cent of the lines, quite unexpected in a Ford play, particularly in a drama of 1632' (241). I have synthesized Tarlinskaja's data into a table:

Prosodic data for four Ford plays[19]

	1	2	3	4	5	6
TPW	82, 79	23, 26, 19	25	53	16	0.5
LC	77, 79	15, 25, 20	38	67	43	2
BH	74, 78	14, 23, 20	35	96	59	3
PW	75, 79	13, 20, 20	44	93	51	7

Key: Column 1: stress on syllabic positions 4, 6 (all percentages rounded up) 2: strong syntactic breaks after syllabic positions 4, 6, 7 3: run-on lines 4: enclitic phrases 5: feminine endings 6: heavy feminine endings

Finally, in a category that Tarlinskaja calls 'Rhythmical italics', that is, 'rhythmical deviations from the metrical scheme to support meaning', where Ford's last play, *Perkin Warbeck* (1633) has 162 cases per 1,000 lines', *'Tis Pity* 'contains only 86.4 per 1,000 lines' (243). Tarlinskaja's methods and results will be new to many readers but they have been carefully calculated and can be regarded as reliable. She places *'Tis Pity* in 1617–18, as Ford's first play.

---

[19] Ibid., pp. 238–45; Appendix B (my manual numbering), pp. 303–4, 313, 323, 343–4.

The Play

'Tis Pity She's a Whore is a play of transgressions against social *mores*, principles of natural justice and human behaviour, especially trust. These multiple transgressions involve all the characters. Most of their transgressions are exposed, and some of them have fatal consequences, generally deserved. But we cannot talk of punishments, for that would need a just society and legitimate agents of justice, who are signally lacking in this play. The main transgression is the incestuous love between Giovanni and Annabella, the children of Florio, a 'Citizen of Parma', as the list of characters identifies him. But Ford embedded that relationship in a plot structure of unrelieved violence and intrigue.

At the play's beginning it is generally known that Annabella has three suitors: Soranzo, 'a Nobleman'; Grimaldi, 'A Roman Gentleman'; and Bergetto, nephew to Donado, 'Another Citizen'. Bergetto is a simpleton, one of the type of failed suitors often found in comedies, such as Simple in *The Merry Wives of Windsor*, Andrew Aguecheek in *Twelfth Night*, and Bartholomew Cokes in *Bartholomew Fair*. The most important suitor is the rich nobleman Soranzo, but his status is compromised by a known previous relationship with Hippolita, whom he has treated badly. In early modern drama, as in many forms of literature, people who feel harmed seek compensation, or revenge. In Act 2 scene 2 Soranzo is discovered in his study, reading the love-poetry of Sannazaro, when Hippolita bursts in, angry at the news that he is now a suitor for Annabella's hand. As she reminds him, she had been a respectable wife to Richardetto when Soranzo had seduced her.

> Doe you know mee now? looke perjurd man on her
> Whom thou and thy distracted lust have wrong'd,
> Thy sensuall rage of blood hath made my youth
> A scorne to men and Angels (2.2.26–9)

Unusually in such recriminations, Ford—bent on exposing all the vices in this society—makes Hippolita admit that she was also to blame for yielding to lust, 'The Devill in my blood'. Soranzo had promised to marry her if or when her husband died, on which basis she agreed to Richardetto undertaking a dangerous sea voyage to Leghorn [Livorno], where his niece had been left 'young and unfriended' by his brother's death (74–7). Richardetto has not been heard of since, and it is generally assumed that he is dead. Soranzo protests that he was not responsible for Richardetto's fate, and as for Hippolita's admission of sensuality he declares himself equally to blame:

> The vowes I made, (if you remember well)
> Were wicked and unlawfull; 'twere more sinne
> To keepe them, then to breake them; as for mee
> I cannot maske my penitence . . . (2.2.84–7)

This is from a man we have just seen reading fashionable love poetry and having erotic thoughts about Annabella. His tactical self-accusation neutralizes hers (another unusual reaction) and Soranzo leaves with a hypocritical denunciation of her 'monstrous life' and 'lust' (95–9), increasing her anger and wish for revenge.

The finality of Soranzo's exit is only apparent, for Ford now shows us the wiles of his servant Vasques, a resourceful and ruthless Machiavellian. Whenever Vasques offers help, as a loyal servant he only does so to protect his master and to harm anyone who could be a threat. He ostentatiously sympathizes with Hippolita, who offers him financial and sexual rewards in return for his help with her revenge plot. He agrees to help and swears a solemn oath:

VASQUES . . . whatsoever your designes are, or against whomsoever, I will
    not onely be a speciall actor therein, but never disclose it till it be effected.
HIPPOLITA I take thy word, and with that, thee for mine:
    Come then, let's more conferre of this anon.
    On this delicious bane my thoughts shall banquet,
    Revenge shall sweeten what my griefes have tasted. (2.2.155–61)

Hippolita indulges her expectation of this 'delicious bane' (an oxymoron, sweet for her, fatal for Soranzo), imagining that she is the agent; in fact, she is already Vasques' dupe.

It is a convention in drama that whenever a character is mentioned as missing, they are not far away. In fact, we have already met Richardetto, posing as a 'learnèd doctor, | Much skilled in physic', whom Soranzo has engaged to treat Annabella's sickness. Richardetto is accompanied by his niece Philotis, carrying a lute to add music to his therapy. Two scenes later Ford reveals that the 'doctor' is in fact Hippolita's supposedly dead husband, who reveals to Philotis the reason for 'this borrowed shape':

> Thy wanton Aunt in her lascivious riots
> Lives now secure, thinkes I am surely dead
> In my late Journey to Ligorne for you;
> (As I have caus'd it to be rumord out)
> Now would I see with what an impudence
> Shee gives scope to her loose adultery (2.3.7–12)

Ford has economically linked the Richardetto–Hippolita plot to that of Soranzo by introducing the second suitor for Annabella, Grimaldi, 'A Roman and a soldier'. Grimaldi has secured a post with the Pope's nuncio in Parma, in order 'to get the love of Annabella'. Grimaldi visits the doctor to obtain a love potion, but Richardetto misinforms him that Annabella loves Soranzo, who, as we know from an earlier scene (1.2) is Grimaldi's enemy, 'The Man I hate | Worse than confusion; I'll kill him straight' (2.3.53–4). Suddenly the scene is transformed into another plot of revenge and murder. Richardetto offers to notify Grimaldi when Annabella meets Soranzo, and to make his revenge certain:

> I'le finde a time when hee and shee doe meete,
> Of which I'le give you notice, and to be sure
> Hee shall not scape you, I'le provide a poyson
> To dip your Rapiers poynt in, if hee had
> As many heads as Hidra had, he dyes.
> GRIMALDI   But shall I trust thee Doctor?
> RICHARDETTO   As your selfe,
> Doubt not in ought. [*Aside*] Thus shall the Fates decree,
> By me Soranzo falls, that ruin'd mee. *Exeunt*. (2.3.57–64)

This is the second scene to end with a contract between a revenger and an accomplice, this time for a double revenge.

The third suitor for Annabella, as we saw from an earlier scene, is Bergetto, 'this ideot', as she describes him (1.2.113), 'such another Dunce', as his uncle says (1.3.24). Ford gives Bergetto several opportunities to display his unsuitability, culminating in the scene where he tells Annabella of how, having foolishly got into a quarrel with 'a swaggering fellow' and been given a bloody pate, he was tended by 'the doctor's niece', Philotis, whom he intends to love 'as long as I live' (2.6.68–83). At this point Bergetto moves from being a tedious comic figure to being the innocent victim of Grimaldi's planned revenge on Soranzo. As arranged, Grimaldi visits Richardetto, who tells him that Soranzo will be 'affied' to Annabella 'this very night' at Friar Bonaventure's cell. (The information is mistaken.) Richardetto is now taking on a role analogous to Vasques, the fixer who sets up violent encounters. He has the poison he has promised Grimaldi, and sends him off to kill Soranzo—'be quicke and sure' (3.5.19), exchanging affectionate partings:

> RICHARDETTO Ever my love!
> GRIMALDI   And mine to you. (20–1)

No sooner has Grimaldi left than Richardetto gloats:

> So, if this hitt, I'le laugh and hug revenge;
> And they that now dreame of a wedding-feast,
> May chance to mourne the lusty Bridegromes ruine.
> But to my other businesse (3.5.22–5)

His 'other businesse' is the instruction he has given Philotis to encourage Bergetto as a suitor. She reports that Bergetto wants to marry her
that night, and Richardetto is forced to think of a new device: 'in dis-
guise | Wee'le earely to the Fryars' (3.2.33–4). Ford does not provide
Richardetto with an explanation for bringing Grimaldi and Bergetto
together. In the event, Grimaldi enters *with his rapier drawn, and a
dark lantern'* (3.7.0), and lies down to await Soranzo. Hearing someone approaching, he invokes 'some angry *Justice*', unwittingly stabs
Bergetto, and runs away. Richardetto rouses the officers to pursue the
murderer. When we next see him, with Donado weeping for his nephew's death, Richardetto professes sorrow: 'His Fortune grieves me as
it were mine own' (3.9.7). But this seemingly unprepared-for plot
development allows Ford to give us a first sight of how justice is executed in Parma.

The officers of the watch who pursued Grimaldi had seen him 'get
into my lord Cardinal's house' and Richardetto expresses his hope in
the workings of law and order: 'The Cardinal is noble; he no doubt |
Will give true justice' (3.9.21–2). But in another reversal of expectations, the Cardinal rebukes the 'saucy mates' who have dared to knock
at his gate, looking for justice, and announces that he already knows
about Bergetto's death. Grimaldi explains that he had wanted revenge
on Soranzo, who had treated him with scorn, and

> (For that I could not win him else to fight)
> Had thought by way of ambush to have killed him.
> But was unluckily therein mistook. (3.9.45–7)

An admission of intending to ambush an unarmed man, 'unluckily'
killing someone else, would in any normal society have resulted in
Grimaldi's prosecution and punishment. The Cardinal, however,
informs these law-abiding citizens that a higher power has taken over:

> You Cittizens of Parma, if you seeke
> For Justice; Know as Nuntio from the Pope,
> For this offence I here receive Grimaldi
> Into his holinesse protection.
> Hee is no Common man, but nobly borne . . .

    *   *   *   *   *   *   *

> If more you seeke for, you must goe to Rome,
> For hee shall thither; learne more wit for shame.
> Bury your dead—away Grimaldi—leave 'em. [*Exeunt* (3.9.52–61)

The shock to their expectations of civic justice leaves the citizens making impotent complaints:

> DONADO Is this a churchman's voice? Dwells Justice here?
> FLORIO Justice is fled to Heaven and comes no nearer.

All that they can do is to 'obey', with the faint hope that 'Heaven will judge them for't another day'. In this play Ford has fashioned a society without love or concern for other people, where characters pursue their own pleasures indifferent to other's losses, where promises are easily made and easily broken, and where justice is an empty word.

Ford has organised his plot strands so that two of Annabella's suitors have been disposed of, leaving Soranzo triumphant. We see him presiding at the banquet celebrating his marriage to Annabella that opens Act 4. A masque takes place, adorned with garlands of willows, symbols 'of grief for unrequited love or the loss of a mate' (*OED*), as knowledgeable spectators will have known. Hippolita was among the dancers and when she unmasks, audience and readers may have anticipated some violent act. Ford has not revealed what form the revenge that she has plotted with Vasques will take, and we are pleasantly surprised to find her in an apparently benevolent mood. She is aware that people might expect her to 'claim | Some interest in Soranzo', but she makes him a magnanimous gesture:

>   One thing more.
> That you may know my single charity,
> Freely I here remit all interest
> I ere could clayme: and give you backe your vowes,
> And to confirm't, reach me a Cup of wine.
> My Lord Soranzo, in this draught I drinke,
> Long rest t'ee. [*Aside*] Looke to it Vasques.
> VASQUES [*Aside*] Feare nothing— *He gives her a poysond Cup.*
> *She drinks.*   (4.1.55–62)

In another of Ford's shocking reversals, Vasques denounces Hippolita: 'Know now, mistress she-devil, your own mischievous treachery hath killed you. I must not marry you' (68–9). As he explains to the bystanders:

This thing of malice, this woman had privately corrupted mee
with promise of marriage, under this politique reconciliation to
poyson my Lord, whiles shee might laugh at his Confusion on his
marriage-day; I promis'd her faire, but I knew what my reward
should have beene, and would willingly have spar'd her life, but
that I was acquainted with the danger of her disposition, and now
have fitted her a just payment in her owne coyne, there shee is,
shee hath yet—and end thy dayes in peace vild woman, as for life
there's no hope, thinke not on't.

OMNES   Wonderfull Justice!
RICHARDETTO   Heaven thou art righteous. (4.1.77–88)

Readers and spectators may feel glad that Soranzo has not been
poisoned, but it is difficult to endorse either Vasques' inversion of
her murderous intention as 'a just payment' (whose justice?), or
Richardetto's hypocritical praise of heavenly righteousness. Ford
clearly regards Richardetto as a sympathetic character, despite being
guilty of procuring poison for Grimaldi to kill Soranzo, for in
the scene following he allows him to give a charitable verdict
on Hippolita:

> My wretched wife, more wretched in her shame
> Than in her wrongs to me, hath paid too soon
> The forfeit of her modesty and life. (4.2.1–3)

Ford has given Richardetto another function here, as commentator on
the vice permeating this society. He speaks with moral authority in
advising his niece to 'free your years | From hazard of these woes' by
joining a convent, where her 'chast and single life shall crown your
birth' (27). In this vicious environment, 'chaste vows' seem a better
choice.

We have no difficulty understanding the reactions of Hippolita,
deceived and rejected by Soranzo, or Richardetto, deceived and
rejected by Hippolita. But the motives of Giovanni are far more complex, taking on different forms as the play progresses. In my view, in
creating Giovanni Ford presents him with clarity and detachment.
Some commentators argue that Ford treats him with sympathy, which
would involve endorsing his defence of incest.

Among the early critics, in 1933 G. B. Harrison opined that 'Ford's
sympathies are clearly with the defiant, not the repentant sinner'; in
1934 Hazelton Spencer referred to 'the poet's doctrinaire sympathy
with the lovers as such'; in 1947 Wallace Bacon accused Ford of 'having allowed a Neoplatonic attitude towards love to draw him into

sympathy with the most sinful of his characters'.[20] In 1959 R. J. Kaufmann recorded his experience that 'While watching the play one grows strangely tolerant of the unaccommodated Giovanni.'[21] In 1968 Mark Stavig stated that 'Ford portrays Giovanni as a talented, virtuous man who is overcome by a tumultuous passion that brings about his destruction.'[22] In 1969 Juliet McMaster felt that 'Giovanni and Annabella monopolize our sympathy', by 'contrast with the figures in the subplot'.[23] In 1977 A. P. Hogan believed that 'Giovanni's weak argument does not strip him of all sympathy . . . His youthful iconoclasm, his ardent championship of individualism and pleasure against the Friar's crabbed and frozen orthodoxy, are seductive qualities.'[24] In 1989 Charles Forker argued that, 'until the tragic climax, Ford treats the incestuous relationship with considerable sympathy—not as a bestial abomination but as a tragic but humanly comprehensible error'.[25] In his monograph on incest in early modern drama (1993) Richard McCabe found that 'Set against the decadent backdrop of Parmese society, the incestuous couple generate a degree of sympathy which might otherwise elude them.'[26] In a later article (2006) he repeated his verdict: 'That the lovers remain sympathetic despite such excesses is largely owing to the remarkable mutuality of their love and the repellent corruption of the surrounding community.'[27]

For over seventy years scholars have felt that Ford shows or creates sympathy for Giovanni. By contrast, I argue that Ford presents Giovanni at his own self-estimate, setting himself against society's values from the outset, and that as the play develops, he becomes increasingly self-indulgent until he puts himself outside all shared norms of human behaviour. It is as if Ford had asked himself, 'What kind of person would advocate incest with his sister?'; and—having broken that barrier—'What effect would it have on his personality?'

---

[20] For Harrison, Spencer, and Wells see Hopkins, pp. 23–4.

[21] See R. J. Kaufmann, 'Ford's Tragic Perspective', *Texas Studies in Language and Literature*, I (1959): 522–37 (534–5).

[22] See Stavig, p. 95.

[23] See Juliet McMaster, 'Love, Lust, and Sham: Structural Patterns in the Plays of John Ford', *Renaissance Drama* 2 (1969): 157–66 (164).

[24] See A. P. Hogan, '*'Tis Pity She's a Whore*: The Overall Design', *Studies in English Literature, 1500–1700*, 17 (1977): 303–16 (305).

[25] See Charles Forker, '"A Little More Than Kin, and Less Than Kind": Incest, Intimacy, Narcissism, and Identity in Elizabethan and Stuart Drama', *Medieval and Renaissance Drama in England*, 4 (1989): 13–51 (24).

[26] See Richard McCabe, *Incest, Drama and Nature's Law 1550–1700* (Cambridge, 1993), p. 234.

[27] See Richard McCabe, '*'Tis Pity She's a Whore* and Incest', in Garrett A. Sullivan et al. (eds.), *Early Modern English Drama: A Critical Companion* (Oxford, 2006), pp. 309–20 (314).

To return to the opening scene, its function is to show Giovanni challenging moral norms in a dialogue with Friar Bonaventura, his former teacher at the university. The action begins in mid-flow, with the Friar telling Giovanni to 'Dispute no more' on an issue that is too serious for scholastic discussion, the existence of God (1.1.1–8). Elsewhere, Giovanni proclaims his disbelief in heaven and hell, and it is significant that his first reference to Annabella's beauty is a hyperbole claiming that, 'if framed anew', the pagan gods would kneel to her, 'as I do kneel to them' (20–4)—so much for Christianity. The self-confessed atheist then dismisses the interdictions against incest:

> Shall a peevish sound,
> A customary forme, from man to man,
> Of brother and of sister, be a barre
> Twixt my perpetuall happinesse and mee? (1.1.24–7)

Giovanni's first sophistic argument is familiar from Falstaff's dismissal of honour:

> What is honour? A word. What is in that word 'honour'? What is that 'honour'? Air. A trim reckoning. (1 Henry IV, 5.1.133–5)

Alice Arden uses the same trick to dismiss her husband, who, she claims, 'usurps' her hearth,

> having nought but this,
> That I am tied to him by marriage.
> Love is a god, and marriage is but words.[28] (1.99–101)

With this 'trim reckoning' (fine accounting) any human value can be reduced to nothingness. Every reader or theatregoer can see the sophistry of such arguments. Giovanni's next attempt is more expansive:

> Say that we had one father, say one wombe,
> (Curse to my joyes) gave both us life, and birth;
> Are wee not therefore each to other bound
> So much the more by Nature; by the links
> Of blood, of reason; Nay if you will hav't,
> Even of Religion, to be ever one,
> One soule, one flesh, one love, one heart, one All?[29] (1.1.28–34)

In Giovanni's reasoning 'nature' is an unqualified absolute, a key reference point in libertine discourse, such as Comus's

---

[28] See M. L. Wine (ed.), *Arden of Faversham* (London, 1954), p. 11.
[29] As Roper observed, the italics in the Quarto record Ford's own emphases.

> Wherefore should Nature pour her bounties forth
> With such a full and unwithdrawing hand,
> Covering the earth with odours, fruits and flocks,
> Thronging the Seas with spawn innumerable,
> But all to please and sate the curious taste?[30]

But Ford has given Giovanni a deliberately inadequate argument. Centuries of philosophical and religious doctrine had taught the need for reason and self-control to monitor natural impulses: nature needs culture. Giovanni's language is evidently dubious as he invokes 'blood'—as Massai notes,[31] then meaning 'both consanguinity and lust, blood being one of the four humours associated with "a courageous, hopeful, and amorous disposition" (*OED*)'. Giovanni attempts to link 'blood' with 'reason' and 'religion', the civic and religious resources that should control lust. His arguments are hopelessly muddled, summed up in this attempt to deny plurality: 'one womb . . . One soul, one flesh, one love, one heart, one *All*'. Obviously, there are two souls, two bodies, two hearts, two people. Nothing binds the siblings in the sense that Giovanni urges. The real focus of Giovanni's concern is, as always, himself. He vents his displeasure that the social and religious 'positions' against incest could be 'a bar | 'Twixt *my* perpetual happiness and *me*', could be a 'curse to *my* joys', and that, 'for that *I* am her brother born, | *My* joys be ever banished from her bed' (my italics). Giovanni's feeble attempts at general argument serve his personal sexual pleasure. Nobody in the audience at the performances by Queen Henrietta's Men would have had any difficulty recognizing his real motives.

Ford leaves us in no doubt that Giovanni's goal is personal sexual fulfilment. The soliloquy he gives at his next appearance describes his frustrated desires, in the crisis mode of Petrarchan love poetry:

> Lost, I am lost: my fates have doom'd my death:
> The more I strive, I love, the more I love,
> The lesse I hope: I see my ruine certaine.
> What Judgement, or endevors could apply
> To my incurable and restlesse wounds,
> I throughly have examin'd, but in vaine:
> O that it were not in Religion sinne,
> To make our love a God, and worship it. (1.2.139–46)

---

[30] See *Comus*, 710–24, in John Milton, *Complete Poems and Major Prose*, ed. Merritt Y. Hughes (New York, 1957), pp. 106–7.

[31] See Massai, p. 101.

Before he became a dramatist, Ford had published two prose essays on civic virtue and moderation, *The Golden Meane* (1614) and *A Line of Life* (1620), following his substantial poem, *Christes Bloodie Sweat* (1613).[32] As Gilles Monsarrat has shown, there are multiple parallels between the poem and *'Tis Pity She's a Whore* which show a common set of attitudes to personal and public life.[33] One passage explicitly denounces the secular idolization of love:

> Love is no god, as some of wicked times
> (Led with the dreaming dotage of their folly)
> Have set him foorth in their lascivious rimes,
> Bewitch'd with errors, and conceits unholy:
> It is a raging blood, affections blind,
> Which boiles both in the body and the mind.
>
> (*CBS* 1081–6)

Giovanni inverts this denunciation, wishing 'that it were not in Religion sinne', but the grammatical construction (a conditional) reminds us that it is a sin. Nonetheless he dismisses religion, revealing the self-focused nature of his arguments:

> I find all these but dreames, and old mens tales
> To fright unsteedy youth; I'me still the same,
> Or I must speake, or burst; 'tis not I know,
> My lust; but 'tis my fate that leads me on.
> Keepe feare and low faint hearted shame with slaves,
> Ile tell her that I love her, though my heart
> Were rated at the price of that attempt (1.2.151–7)

The first-person forms *I* and *my* punctuate the speech ('*my* fates . . . *my* death . . . *my* ruine . . . *my* incurable and restlesse wounds . . . *my* continuall teares . . . *my* veines . . . *my* lust . . . *my* fate'). The sequence begins and ends by blaming 'fate' for his predicament, but the sense of stifled energy—'I'me still the same, | Or I must speake, or burst'—suggests that the force driving him on is internal, and makes us doubt his assertion ''tis not I know, | My lust'. (We recall the French saying 'Qui s'excuse, s'accuse'.)

Ford achieves a complex effect by placing Annabella and her 'Tutresse' (Guardian) Putana on the upper stage early in this scene, viewing events below. Having observed the rivalry between Grimaldi

---

[32] See Gilles Monsarrat, Brian Vickers, and R. J. C. Watt (eds.), *The Collected Works of John Ford*, vol. I (Oxford, 2012), for *Christes Bloodie Sweat*, ed. Watt and Vickers (pp. 294–428).

[33] Gilles Monsarrat, 'The Unity of John Ford: *'Tis Pity She's a Whore* and *Christ's Bloody Sweat*', *Studies in Philology*, 77 (1980): 247–70.

and Soranzo as competitors for Annabella's hand, Putana evaluates their respective attractions, a stock feature in romantic drama (1.2.62–96).[34] Then Bergetto appears, well described by Putana as 'another of your ciphers to fill up the number' (100). Annabella has remained silent during Putana's 'prating', but seeing Giovanni below, she is struck by the 'blessed shape | Of some celestiall creature' (126–7), before recognizing him as her brother. Distressed by Giovanni's evident 'griefe' and wanting to share 'his sadnesse', she starts the descent to the main stage while Giovanni is describing his frustrated sexual love for her and summoning the courage to risk revealing it. The audience and readers know that this will be a crucial exchange, for Giovanni's happiness depends on him persuading his sister to take part in an incestuous relationship. What arguments can he use? How will she react? When Putana has left, their conversation begins slowly, and we see it from their two separate perspectives. We know that for Giovanni words that might be misconstrued ('blush', 'harme') carry a weight of significance of which Annabella is unaware. He broaches the real subject with the hesitant remark, 'I thinke you love me Sister' (184). Having received a confirmation, he begins to praise her beauty using the traditional love formula of a *blason* (1.2.188–203).[35] In Renaissance poetry (mostly written by men) this form uses the third-person pronoun to list a woman's attractive qualities, often from head to foot or vice versa. The more daring versions ended with an erotic allusion to the mid-parts of her body, 'hidden by an envious veil'. When used in drama by a lover in the wooing process, the form shifts to the second-person pronoun, hoping for a sympathetic audience. Giovanni praises Annabella, starting with her face. Where Juno had the most beautiful forehead of all the goddesses, 'Your forehead exceeds hers'; 'a pair of stars | As are thine eyes, would (like *Promethean* fire)' draw sparks from 'senselesse stones'. Ascending to rhyme,

> The Lilly and the Rose most sweetly strange
> Upon your dimpled Cheekes doe strive for change.

Annabella thinks he is joking until—like Richard III to Anne—he pulls out a dagger, bares his breast, and in effect gives her a choice: ''tis my destiny, | That you must eyther love, or I must dye' (224–5). Ford

---

[34] Cf. *The Merchant of Venice*, 1.2.33–121; and *Troilus and Cressida*, 1.2.177–257 (an ironic treatment).

[35] A convention in Petrarchan poetry (formalized by Clement Marot in the 1530s). Cf., e.g., Spenser, *Amoretti*, sonnet 64.

takes care to remind us that they are not the normal stage couple. Giovanni makes an absolute hyperbolic assertion:

> O Annabella I am quite undone,
> The love of thee (my sister) and the view
> Of thy immortall beauty hath untun'd
> All harmony both of my rest and life (1.2.211–15)

Annabella's response is laconic, reminding him of their blood relationship:

> ANNABELLA You are my brother Giovanni.
> GIOVANNI   You,
>   My Sister Annabella; I know this:
>   And could afford you instance why to love
>   So much the more for this (228–31)

At this point Giovanni begins to cite 'instances', drawing on his repertoire of 'Persuasions to Incest', and reverting to rhyme (an alert producer might play the next lines for comedy):

>   to which intent
> Wise Nature first in your Creation ment
> To make you *mine*: else't had beene sinne and foule,
> To share one beauty to a double soule.
> Neerenesse in birth or blood, doth but perswade
> A neerer neerenesse in affection. (231–6; my italics)

To increase emphasis, Giovanni shifts from logic (or his version of it) to rhetoric, using the figure *polyptoton*, which repeats words derived from the same root, 'near' ('a neerer neerenesse' is an extreme formulation, typical of Giovanni). The ending of his speech, however, is undignified, as he visibly runs out of patience. We know that the Friar (or 'holy Church') has not given him permission,[36] but he seizes on the ambiguous modal verb '*may*' to form a *sorites* of other verbs, '*may . . . should . . . will*'

> I have askt Counsell of the holy Church,
> Who tells mee I may love you, and 'tis just,
> That since I may, I should; and will, yes will:
> Must I now live, or dye? (237–40)

The repetition of '*will, yes will*' makes him sound like a petulant child insisting on getting its way. Giovanni has put a great deal of effort into

---

[36] In the opening scene Giovanni had secured the Friar's agreement—'Yes, you may love, fair son' (1.1.20), but that was a generalized permission, before Annabella had been mentioned.

this speech, but Annabella's surprising reply shows that he need not have bothered:

> Live, thou hast wonne
> The field, and never fought; what thou hast urg'd,
> My captive heart had long agoe resolv'd.   (240–2)

In the 1620s, as today, many readers and theatregoers would have expected, and some may have hoped, that Annabella would have refused an incestuous relationship. If so, her immediate acceptance of his proposal would be a shocking violation of social and religious norms. Ford makes this no casual decision: brother and sister kneel, as to a solemn ritual; their speeches have the same form of words, as in a liturgy; and they confirm their vows with a kiss. If one of Ford's aims was to affront or provoke audience members who respected social and religious conventions, in this instance he offended believers from both confessions. In the 1569 *Book of Common Prayer* the 'Forme of Solempnizacion of Matrimonie' specifies that, after the congregation has sung either Psalm 128 or 67, '*The Psalme ended, and the man and the woman knelyng afore the Lordes table: The Priest standyng at* the *Table, and turnyng hys face towarde them, shal saie*, "Lorde have mercie upon us. . . . Our Father which art" &c.' The 1614 *Roman Ritual* had the exchange of consent before the nuptial Mass, sometimes actually outside of the church on the porch, or gathering area. The rubric stated that the couple should kneel before the altar with the priest facing them.

The scene ends with one of those relatively rare signals in early modern drama (very rare in Shakespeare) that a couple leaving the stage is about to make love:

GIOVANNI After so many teares as wee have wept,
        Let's learne to court in smiles, to kisse and sleepe. *Exeunt*

Some dramatists would have closed this plot line here, leaving the incestuous union as a *fait accompli*. But Ford has more targets in view. One brief scene (85 lines) later, the stage direction of 2.1, '*Enter GIOVANNI and ANNABELLA, as from their Chamber*', sets a highly unusual scene in early modern drama, showing post-coital happiness. We may have expected that Giovanni would express his satisfaction by reviving an old metaphor—'yeelding thou hast conquer'd', but it comes as a surprise to find Annabella unembarrassedly expressing her happiness to have enjoyed 'these stolne contents' with her 'hearts delight' (2.1.6–8). But Ford strikes a discordant note with her phrase 'stolne' for their pleasures: stolen from whom? Neither has been bound to anyone else, so they have not violated any personal contract. Perhaps we are meant to be reminded that they have offended the social and religious taboo on incest? If so, it is not the only discordant tone in this scene. Giovanni begs a kiss off her and compares himself to the supreme pagan god:

> Kisse me, so; thus hung *Jove* on *Laeda's* necke,
> And suck't divine *Ambrosia* from her lips:
> I envy not the mightiest man alive,
> But hold my selfe in being King of thee,
> More great, then were I King of all the world (2.1.16–20)

As we shall see, this is not an isolated expression of Giovanni's sense of his own self-worth and superiority ('in being King of thee'). More shocking, perhaps, is his concluding line to this exchange:

> GIOVANNI   But I shall lose you *Sweet-heart.*
> ANNABELLA But you shall not.
> GIOVANNI   You must be married Mistres.
> ANNABELLA Yes, to whome?
> GIOVANNI   Some one must have you.
> ANNABELLA You must.
> GIOVANNI   Nay some other.
> ANNABELLA Now prithee do not speake so, without jesting
>   You'le make mee weepe in earnest. (2.1.21–5)

We share Annabella's shock that Giovanni can be so cold-blooded as to plan disposing of her to 'some other' man. Having had 'this pretty toye called *Maiden-head'*, is that all he wants from her?

Ford now pursues several other plot-strands: the arrival of Richardetto disguised as a physician (2.1); the angry scene between Hippolita and Soranzo, calmed by Vasques (2.2); Richardetto's disclosure to his niece of his real intention in moving to Parma, followed by his offer to Grimaldi of poison with which to kill Grimaldi (2.3); and Poggio reading aloud a fatuous love letter from Bergetto to Annabella (2.4). Ford brings Giovanni back in 2.5, once again with the Friar, to whom he has just revealed that he and Annabella have become lovers, which the Friar describes as 'a tale, whose every word | Threatens eternall slaughter to the soule' (2.5.1–2). It has not often been noted that Ford makes Giovanni try three times to justify his practice of incest: to the Friar (1.1), to Annabella (1.2), and again here, to the Friar. But this third attempt seems badly timed, superfluous. Having achieved his desire to sleep with Annabella, he has no need to justify it. The repetition suggests that he is less confident in his decisions than he would like to seem. Moreover, on each occasion Ford undermines Giovanni by making him rely on sophistry. The Friar warns him that he is marked down 'to taste a mischiefe', but Giovanni offers to defend himself in another set-piece argument, again beginning with a formal principle

> What I have done, I'le prove both fit and good.
> It is a principall (which you have taught
> When I was yet your Scholler) that the Frame
> And Composition of the *Minde* doth follow
> The Frame and Composition of *Body*:
> So where the *Bodies* furniture is *Beauty*,
> The *Mindes* must needs be *Vertue*: which allowed,
> *Vertue* it selfe is *Reason but refin'd*,
> And *Love* the Quintessence of that, this proves
> My Sisters *Beauty* being rarely *Faire*,
> Is rarely *Vertuous*; chiefely in her love,
> And chiefely in that *Love*, her love to me.
> If *hers to me*, then so is *mine to her*,
> Since in like Causes are effects alike. (2.5.13–26)

Several commentators have noticed the similarity between this passage and one in Ford's first published work, *Honor Triumphant. Or The Peeres Challenge, by Armes defensible, at Tilt, Turney, and Barrier*. Late medieval chivalric combats were still popular in Renaissance England, notably the tilts marking the Monarch's Accession Day, which continued till 1622, and were sometimes memorialized by poets.[37] Planned to celebrate the visit to England in 1606 of Christian IV, King of Denmark, this tournament never took place, but Ford's text was published in 1606, together with his poem, *The Monarchs Meeting*.[38] The title page described *Honor Triumphant* as being *In Honor of all faire Ladies, and in defence of . . . four positions* [theses], *Maintained by Arguments*, of which the third is '*Faire Lady was never false*'. Gilles Monsarrat has rejected the view held by some critics that Ford was being ironic, or even parodying the genre (p. 60), but describes his approach as 'uncertain, almost divided, shifting between,

---

[37] See A. B. Ferguson, *The Chivalric Tradition in Renaissance England* (Washington, DC, 1986). For an example of tilt poetry see Peele, 'The Honour of the Garter', celebrating The Earl of Northumberland's installation in 1593 as a Knight of the Garter, in David H, Horne, *The Life and Minor Works of George Peele* (New Haven and London, 1952), pp. 244–59.

[38] All quotations are from Gilles Monsarrat (ed.), *Honor Triumphant* and *The Monarchs Meeting*, in *CWJF* I, pp. 39–168.

on the one hand, facetious or preposterous arguments and, on the other, apparently serious ones' (p. 71). The Third Position begins, as does Giovanni's speech, by stating a 'principall': '*The temperature of the mind follows the temperature of the bodie*. Which certaine axiome (says that sage Prince of Philosophers *Aristotle*) is ever more infallible'.[39] If that axiom is accepted, 'then without controversie, as the outward shape is more singular, so the inward vertues must be most exquisite' (p. 96). Monsarrat noted that Ford returned to this axiom in his prose treatise, *A Line of Life. Pointing at the Immortalitie of a Vertuous Name* (1620), but he failed to quote the whole passage, which places Giovanni's arguments in a more critical light:

> A mans minde is the man himself (said the Romane Orator) and the chiefest of the Grecian Naturalists was confident to averre, that *the temperature of the minde followed the temperature of the body*, It were a Lesson worthie to bee cond, if eyther of those rules may be positively received. (*CWJF* 1, p. 577)

That is, 'it is worth studying if either point can be accepted with confidence'. Ford has no quarrel with Cicero's dictum, but sees the danger of Aristotle's: 'Out of the latter it may be gathered, how easie it were, for everie man to be his owne Schoolemaster, in the conformation or reformation of his life, without other Tutour then himselfe' (ibid.). Having been 'his own priest', officiating at his own wedding, Giovanni is now set to be 'his owne Schoolemaster'. He rejects all forms of authority, all principles of belief or conduct, apart from those that can be made to fulfil his desires.

In *Honor Triumphant*, as in Giovanni's argument, Ford used the opposition between 'the outward shape' and 'the inward vertues' as ground for a transition to Neoplatonic love-theory, familiar in England since Hoby's translation of Baldassare Castiglione's *The Book of the Courtier* (1561) and Spenser's *Fowre Hymnes* (1596).[40] Ford argues that, 'if the sawes of authority be authenticall, nothing can be more precious, nothing in itself so vertuous' as beauty (p. 96). Beauty 'is the greatest *good* in itself, that heart of humanitie can wish for' (p. 97). Affirmation is followed by deduction: 'Then it followes, that *firmest*

---

[39] In fact, as Monsarrat shows, this 'certaine axiome' is 'the title of a work by Galen, usually translated into Latin as "*Animi mores corporis temperaturam sequuntur*"'. In his *Examen de Ingenios. The Examination of Mens Wits* (tr. R. Carew, 1594), 'Juan Huarte says, "Galen writ a booke, where he prooveth, That the manners of the soule, follow the temperature of the body"' (*CWJF* 1, p. 66 and note, pp. 149–50).

[40] See, e.g., Enid Welsford (ed.), *Spenser, Fowre Hymnes, Epithalamium: A Study of Edmund Spenser's Doctrine of Love* (Oxford, 1967).

vertues are shrowded in the fairest complexions' (ibid.), and that 'the *exterior beauty, is assurance of the interior quality*' (p. 99). Ford uses italics as if to establish stages in an argument, a self-conscious use of logical techniques which is aware of taking extreme positions. He rehearses 'three particularities . . . that stand firm for this argument', the third being

> *ground of troth*, now to be verefi'de.—Verefi'de said I? the self assurance of the subject, is a testimonie most probable, if *vice* be the nourisher of *vice*, *vertue* must be the effect of *vertue*. That is sincerely a *vertue*, which is *good*, and that *good* is *Beauty*, so herein *fictions* comprehend *truth*, as forma *bonum*. (ibid.)

At this point Ford breaks off his argument with a self-deprecating apology: 'yet ere I wade further, and be gravel'd in the ouze, and quicksand of my own intention, I am . . . to make an Apology' (p. 99). Ford punned on the verb 'gravel', which also means 'to bring to a standstill, to confound or nonplus', confirming Monsarrat's judgement that the young author welcomed this 'opportunity to display . . . his wit and debating skills' (p. 59). Ford knowingly broke off his argument, having patently subverted logic in such sequences as 'the self assurance of the subject, is a testimonie most probable', and the succession of tautologous statements leading to the designedly ridiculous statement that 'herein *fictions* comprehend *truth*'. There is no mistaking the self-parody here.

The persona of this speech misuses logic in jest, but Giovanni is totally serious. Few modern critics have a first-hand knowledge of Renaissance logic, but many years ago Allan H. Gilbert demonstrated its remarkable impact on Elizabethan drama.[41] Citing profuse examples from the 1580s to the 1630s, he showed that dramatists used logical terminology with a freedom and accuracy suggesting that at least some spectators and readers could distinguish between a sound argument and a specious one. Gilbert described this speech by Giovanni as 'perhaps the most astonishing use of logic in the drama'. Giovanni begins with a principle, and 'then proceeds to prove by a series of steps that his sister's [incestuous] love is virtuous. By another principle, serving as the major premise of an abridged syllogism, he proves that his own love is also virtuous. The Friar is horrified by Giovanni's conclusion' (541). The false logic is evident: it may be that a person's body

---

[41] See Allan H. Gilbert, 'Logic in the Elizabethan drama', *Studies in Philology*, 32 (1935): 527–45. His examples are drawn from plays by Lyly, Middleton, Dekker, Heywood, Jonson, Massinger, Marston, and Chapman.

is beautiful, but that does not guarantee beauty or virtue in the mind. *Virtus* is a category including several attributes. Civic virtue was traditionally divided into the cardinal virtues (wisdom, temperance, bravery, and justice), which are revealed over a period of time. The mind's 'furniture', in Giovanni's terms, may well be virtue, but the exercise of choice between good and evil is only seen in practice—as Kierkegaard said, 'a man lives his values'. While beauty can be assessed at a glance, virtue cannot.

Ford makes Giovanni a hasty and unscrupulous arguer. He uses the traditional transition at the end of a stage in an argument—'which allowed'—having left no space for discussion, and pushes on with a new claim: 'Virtue itself is reason but refined, | And love the quintessence of that'. Giovanni jumps from point to point like a flea, or a frog.[42] In traditional philosophy, reason is the faculty of controlled analysis and judgement in all cognitive processes. Reason cannot be 'refined' into virtue, or anything else. The word 'refined' implies some purifying process, as in alchemy or chemistry, but there are no impurities in reason, it cannot be reduced to something more 'pure' or more concentrated than itself. Ford shows Giovanni moving from one unsound position to the next. How can 'love' be 'the quintessence of *that*'—does the ambivalent pronoun refer to 'virtue' or 'reason'? Giovanni claims victory in this part of his argument—'This proves', and then creates a dazzling but purely verbal sequence, shifting from one repetition to the next: 'rarely fair . . . hers to me . . . mine to her . . . like causes . . . affects alike', a tissue of rhetorical repetitions given a semblance of coherence by skeletal terms of logic: 'If . . . then . . . Since'. Ford creates a brilliant parody of logic-chopping, reminiscent of Polonius's self-pleasing cleverness:

> Madam, I swear I use no art at all.
> That he is made 'tis true; 'tis true 'tis pity;
> And pity 'tis 'tis true. A foolish figure—
> But farewell it, for I will use no art. (2.2.96–9)

The comparison shows that both dramatists intended their characters to appear ridiculous.

The Friar's response is brief but telling: 'O ignorance in knowledge!' His only advice is to 'persuade thy sister to some marriage', but Giovanni indignantly replies: 'Why, that's to damn her!' He seems

---

[42] Cf. Monsarrat's comment on *Honor Triumphant*: 'Ford skips from one idea to another without attempting to connect them' (p. 64).

unaware that, by the Church's standards, Annabella is already damned. He is concerned, however, about her reputation: such behaviour would 'prove | Her greedy of variety of lust' (2.5.41–2). Yet we remember that, after their first night of love, he had brusquely informed Annabella: 'You must be married Mistres . . . Some one must have you' (2.1.22–3). Perhaps Giovanni is embarrassed to hear the Friar describe in public a remedy he had proposed in private. He certainly seems confused, for when the Friar requests permission to hear Annabella's confession, 'lest shee should dye un-absolv'd', Giovanni suggests that she will certainly vouch for their love, seemingly unaware that this is irrelevant to the spiritual crisis the Friar has described. Giovanni even moves from logic to rhetoric, launching another *blason* of his sister:

> View well her face, and in that little round,
> You may observe a world of variety;
> For Colour, lips; for sweet perfumes, her breath;
> For Jewels, eyes; for threds of purest gold,
> Hayre; for delicious choyce of Flowers, cheekes (2.5.49–53)

An alert audience will wonder what Giovanni hopes to achieve by addressing this catalogue of feminine attraction to the Friar. It is clearly inappropriate, but worse is to come. I mentioned earlier that in more erotic versions of the blazon the poet would draw attention to the parts of a woman's body he had omitted (the rhetorical figure *occupatio*), sometimes blaming an envious veil. Giovanni does this in more direct terms:

> But Father, *what is else for pleasure fram'd*,
> Least I offend your eares shall goe un-nam'd. (57–8; my italics)

If it is inappropriate for Giovanni to be addressing this blazon to the Friar, it is doubly so to include that final gesture, which shows that he is so absorbed in his own passions that he is oblivious to the person to whom he is expressing them.

But Ford has included it for the insight it gives into Giovanni's conception of Annabella as a woman 'for pleasure fram'd'. We may deplore him reducing her to an object for his gratification; Ford's contemporaries would also know that in classical and Renaissance moral philosophy, *voluptas* was the antithesis to *virtus*. They were familiar with the fable of Hercules at the crossroads, where he meets two goddesses, one soberly dressed, pointing him up the steep and stony path to virtue, the other sexily attired, enticing him down the flowery way to pleasure.[43] Hercules follows virtue, the hero's choice. Modern readers may not appreciate the absolute nature of this opposition, an either/or choice. Many contemporary sources warned about the dangers of pleasure. John Bodenham's *Bel-vedére or The Garden of the Muses* (1600), contains *sententiae* from a wide range of authors. 'To vaine delight, a man may easily goe: | But safely to returne, may much be fear'd'; 'Uncertaine pleasures, bring a certain paine'; 'Oft pleasures past, doe way to woe prepare'; 'Unlawfull pleasures, haste destruction'; 'Banke-rupts in pleasure can but pay with woe'; 'Demetrius being all to vaine pleasures given, | Was by the Macedonians quite expulst'; 'Demosthenes in his Orations, | Always forbad Voluptuous vaine delights'.[44]

The word 'pleasure' and related terms, such as 'delight', 'joyes', recur in the mouths of the other sensualists in this play. In our first view of Soranzo he quotes a verse from 'the smooth licentious Poet' Sannazaro, which describes the life of a lover as 'unrest, and the reward disdaine'. Soranzo contradicts it with his own version: '[Love's] pleasures life, and his reward all joyes' (2.2.1–11). Hippolita, deceived into thinking that Vasques will be her lover, anticipates happiness: 'let *My youth* | Revell in these new pleasures' (3.8.18–19; Ford's ironic italics). In her unreformed life, Annabella briefly uses the language of hedonism. After her first experience of sex she tells her guardian: 'what a Paradise of joy | Have I past over!', and Ford gives Putana a bawdy gloss: 'Nay what a Paradise of joy have you past under?' (2.1.38–40). After her scene with the Friar (3.6) we see Annabella's complete reversal to the principles of virtue: 'Pleasures farewell, and all yee thriftlesse minutes, | Wherein False joyes have spun a weary life, | To these my Fortunes now I take my leave' (5.1.1–3). The language of hedonism occurs most often in the mouth of Giovanni. The fact that he and Annabella had the same mother was a 'Curse to my ioyes' (1.1.29), a misfortune that he protests against: 'Shall then, (for that I am her brother borne) | My joyes be ever banisht from her bed?' (1.1.36–7), and from that part of Annabella's body that 'is . . . for pleasure fram'd' (2.5.57). In a soliloquy he records his surprise that, despite Annabella's marriage, his sexual pleasure is undiminished, 'and every kisse | As

---

[43] The fable 'The Choice of Herakles', ascribed to the Sophist Prodicus, became well known through Xenophon, *Memorabilia*, 2.1.21–34. See the classic study by Erwin Panofsky, *Hercules am Scheidewege und andere antike Bildstoffe in der neueren Kunst* (Leipzig/Berlin, 1930) and, most recently, Andrea Harbach, *Die Wahl des Lebens in der antiken Literatur* (Berlin, 2010).

[44] See Lukas Erne and Devani Singh (eds.), *Bel-vedére or The Garden of the Muses. An Early Modern Printed Commonplace Book* (Cambridge, 2020), pp. 281–5.

sweet and as delicious as the first' (5.3.4–9). When the Friar enters Giovanni greets him as if at a ceremony: 'Father, you enter on the Jubile | Of my retyr'd delights' (5.3.17–18)—that is, the joyful celebration of my private pleasures. But the Friar brings news that (thanks to Vasques having tricked Putana into identifying Annabella's lover) their sexual relationship has been discovered. Giovanni first suspects Annabella: 'Are wee growne Traytours to our owne delights?' (5.3.38). He proudly (or vindictively) tells his father that Annabella's pregnancy witnesses 'The happy passage of our stolne delights' (5.6.48), *deliciae* being a euphemism for sexual pleasure. Ford makes Giovanni's preference clear from the outset. When the Friar tells him that God's mercy is ever present and that 'time is left you both—' to repent, he might have said, if Giovanni had not interrupted him with his Choice of Life: 'To embrace each other' (63–5).

Ford soon places Annabella in the same situation, being lectured by the Friar. In a previous scene, Giovanni overhears Annabella reject Soranzo's marriage proposal (3.2.42–55), with satisfaction: 'Why now I see she loves me'. But at this point the whole balance of the play changes as she feels her first birth pains: 'O, I begin to sicken' (64). Immediately afterwards, Giovanni learns from Putana that his sister is pregnant and realises the crisis they face: '*oh mee, I have a world of businesse in my head,* | . . . *how doe this newes perplex me*' (3.3.22–4; Ford's italics). Earlier Giovanni had mockingly rejected the Friar's offer to 'shrive' Annabella, but he now fetches him:

> To visit my sicke sister, that with words
> Of ghostly comfort in this time of neede,
> Hee might absolve her, whether she live or dye (3.4.28–30)

As the audience will realize, it is doubly ironic that Giovanni should have sought the Friar's help: first, it contradicts his rejection of religion and notions of heaven and hell; secondly, Bonaventura's 'ghostly' (spiritual) comfort exposes to Annabella most forcefully the sufferings that await her in Hell. His 'Lecture' is a terrifying description of how she will be 'Almost condemn'd alive' in 'a black and hollow Vault' . . . | Of an infeckted darknesse', where 'the damned soules | Roare without pitty' (3.6.9–16). The Friar itemizes the punishments devised to fit the crimes committed by Gluttons and Drunkards, the Usurer and the Murtherer, with a special place for the likes of Giovanni and Annabella:

> there lies the wanton
> On Racks of burning steele, whiles in his soule

>   Hee feeles the torment of his raging lust.
> ANNABELLA Mercy, oh mercy.
> FRYAR   There stands these wretched things,
>   Who have dream't out whole yeares in lawless sheets
>   And secret incests, cursing one another;
>   Then you will wish, each kisse your brother gave,
>   Had beene a Daggers poynt; then you shall heare
>   How hee will cry, oh would my wicked sister
>   Had first beene damn'd, when shee did yeeld to lust. (3.6.21–30)

This devastating description, culminating in a premonition of Giovanni blaming her, visibly affects Annabella, arousing 'new motions' to repentance. She reaches the same defeated position that Giovanni had reached in his interview.

> ANNABELLA Is there no way left to redeeme my miseries?
> FRYAR   There is, despaire not; Heaven is mercifull,
>   And offers grace even now (33–5)

Annabella accepts the Friar's plan to marry Soranzo, as Giovanni guesses when he returns (47–8). At the wedding banquet he reveals his anguish in an aside:

> Oh Torture, were the marriage yet undone,
> Ere I'de endure this sight, to see *my Love*
> Clipt by another, I would dare Confusion,
> And stand the horror of ten thousand deaths. (4.1.15–19; my italics)

For the possessive lover there is no worse fate than to think of anyone but himself embracing his beloved.

As we have seen, Ford springs a surprise on us by making this banquet turn to tragedy. Hippolita presents her masque while planning to murder Soranzo but is duped by Vasques into drinking the poisoned cup. As the company disperses, Soranzo leads Annabella away with a show of marital harmony: 'come *My Love*, | Wee'le home and thank the Heavens for this escape' (4.1.103–4; Ford's italics). But after a short scene between Richardetto and Philotis, we see the couple again in a shocking reversal:

> *Enter* SORANZO *unbrac't, and* ANNABELLA *dragg'd in.*

> SORANZO Come strumpet, famous whoore, were every drop
>   Of blood that runs in thy adulterous veynes
>   A life, this Sword, (dost see't) should in one blowe
>   Confound them all. Harlot, rare, notable Harlot,
>   That with thy brazen face maintainst thy sinne (4.3.1–5)

Annabella, unrepentant to this 'Beastly man', this '*Over-Loving Lordship*', refuses to reveal the father of her child other than describing him as a '*Noble Creature* . . . so angel-like, so glorious' (36–7). Provoked by her defiance, Soranzo pulls her hair and throws her to the ground, threatening death. Vasques enters from an adjacent room (he has the gift of popping up whenever needed) to deter his master from the 'un-manlike' action of killing his wife in his rage, calming Soranzo with the promise to identify her lover. This he does at once by cajoling Putana to confirm his suspicion that it was 'her brother Giovanni' who is the father (213). Once she does so, Vasques unexpectedly calls in some 'Banditti', ordering them to take 'This old Damnable hagge, gag her instantly, and put out her eyes, quickly, quickly' (225–7). In 1827 Henry Gifford, Ford's early editor, rightly objected that Vasques cannot have had time to assemble a group of outlaws to help him and Soranzo carry out their revenge plot. However, as Sonia Massai observed, 'their entrance is a sensational *coup de théâtre* and makes Vasques's power to perpetrate evil seem almost superhuman' (ed. cit., 213). It also builds up our sense of the precariousness of life in this society, where you can be killed or pardoned in an instant, according to the whim of a powerful man.

Many scenes in *'Tis Pity She's a Whore* follow on from preceding events, and arrive predictably, but occasionally Ford introduces a scene that has not been anticipated. We saw Soranzo denouncing Annabella; now we see her alone, on the upper stage, imprisoned in her room and moved by the Friar's 'Hell-fire sermon' to abandon *voluptas*, that libertine life of sensual satisfaction: 'Pleasures farewell, and . . . False joyes' (5.1.1–3). She can now formulate the two opposite impulses that are present throughout the play:

> My Conscience now stands up against my lust
> With depositions charactred in guilt,
> And tells mee I am lost: (5.1.9–11)

Despite lamenting her 'vild unhappinesse', Annabella is able for the first time to put another person's suffering ahead of her own:

> O Giovanni, that hast had the spoyle
> Of thine owne vertues and my modest fame,
> Would thou hadst beene lesse subject to those Stars
> That luckelesse raign'd at my Nativity:
> O would the scourge due to my blacke offence
> Might passe from thee, that I alone might feele
> The torment of an uncontrouled flame. (17–23)

In those lines Ford gives her a balanced estimate of Giovanni's destructive effect ('spoil') on both his own virtues and her 'modest' reputation, but she attaches the blame to the inauspicious stars at her nativity, not his. The most moving passage is her wish that she alone might suffer. The two plays are different in scope, but this is a moment akin to Lear's self-accusation: 'O I have ta'en too little care of this'. Annabella is unaware that the Friar (standing below on the main stage) has overheard her remorse; he now has the satisfaction of hearing her recall his warnings that the 'Lethargies of Lust' lead to damnation. Ford gives the Friar a double role, as an authentic witness of 'this free confession twixt your peace and you' (42) and as a messenger. Annabella asks him to deliver a letter she has written to Giovanni telling him to 'repent', for she has had time 'To blush at what hath past' (51). As a Latin saying put it, '*Rubor est color virtutis*': to show shame by blushing is the sign of virtue. Ford ends the scene with Annabella's peace and readiness for death.

A matching scene (5.3) presents Giovanni in soliloquy, before the Friar delivers Annabella's letter. Ford shows her brother unchanged by experience. He still rejects all barriers to personal liberty:

> Busie opinion is an idle Foole,
> That as a Schoole-rod keepes a child in awe,
> Frights the unexperienc't temper of the mind (5.3.1–3)

This time Giovanni is not rejecting a constituent element in moral principles but a human characteristic which had been often criticized. In classical and Renaissance thought *opinio* often connoted uninformed popular ideas, suppositions, or conjectures, an easy target. The popular commonplace books of the early seventeenth century contain many denunciations of 'opinion'. Robert Allott's *Englands Parnassus* (1600) includes warnings by Chapman: 'We must in matters moral, quite reject | Vulgar Opinion, ever led amisse: | And let autenticke reason be our guide'; by Everard Guilpin: 'Shee is the echo of inconstancie'; and Gervase Markham: 'This syren of Opinion . . . adjiudgeth nothing it doth see, | By what it is, but what it seemes to bee'.[45]

The problem is that the 'opinion' Giovanni attacks is by no means a popular belief but one unique to him,

> So did it mee; who ere My precious Sister
> Was married, thought all tast of love would dye
> In such a Contract; but I finde no change

---

[45] See Charles Crawford (ed.), *Englands Parnassus* (Oxford, 1913), p. 166.

> Of pleasure in this formall law of sports.
> Shee is still one to mee, and every kisse
> As sweet, and as delicious as the first
> I reap't   (5.3.4–10)

In other words, 'I used to think sex with my sister would be less enjoy-able once she was married, but it's as good as when I first had her!' To put it into modern terms makes it inescapably provocative, intention-ally shocking in the casual way Giovanni informs us. Ford is consistent in making his libertine challenge all restrictive social and sexual norms, but he also creates a counter-narrative in which the values that Giovanni holds are increasingly questionable. Since Annabella has just rejected them ('Pleasures farewell'), his continued use of such words as 'pleasure', 'sports', 'delicious', and 'delights' make him seem shallow and superficial. Ford builds up to a self-satisfied climax as he celebrates the 'all of happinesse' that he enjoys:

> And I'de not change it for the best to come,
> A *life of pleasure* is Elyzeum. (15–16)

It is a moot point whether Giovanni knows that in classical mythology Elyzium was the region where the souls of the blessed reside after death. At all events, readers and theatregoers will realize the incongru-ity of comparing that reward for virtue to his state of sexual satisfac-tion in an incestuous relationship. Ford draws on a long tradition of casting *voluptas* as the greatest danger to the good life—in ethical terms—to undermine Giovanni's complacency. The letter from Annabella, and the Friar's warnings, show him that there is no 'best to come', and in the Friar's absence his ranting against the 'relligion-maskd sorceries' of this 'peevish chattering weake old man' (27–9, 35–6, 39–40) sounds like empty bluster.

The arrival of Vasques with an invitation to Soranzo's birthday feast strikes a chill note: at the height of celebrating the victory of sexual pleasures, Giovanni may be about to lose them. The Friar warns him that the feast is a murderous plot but Giovanni is resolved to 'Be all a man', to have 'a glorious death' in which he will harm his enemies. Ford gives him the language of a general rousing his army to battle, but Giovanni is rousing himself, calling on his 'gall'[46] to produce the anger he will need:

---

[46] Roper notes that in Renaissance physiology the gall bladder was thought to receive the 'fiery superfluity' of choler from the liver (ed. cit., 106).

> Now, now, worke serious thoughts on banefull plots,
> Be all a man my soule; let not the Curse
> Of old prescription rent from mee the gall
> Of Courage, which inrolls a glorious death.
> If I must totter like a well-growne Oake,
> Some under shrubs shall in my weighty fall
> Be crusht to splitts: with me they all shall perish. *Exit.* (5.3.73–9)

As ever, he will have been the outstanding figure, scattering destruction as he falls. This resolve links him to other narcissistic figures who want to take many others to death, e.g. Ovid's Medea and Shakespeare's Macbeth.

Ford now springs the most surprising of many reversals. Soranzo and Vasques have plotted to kill Giovanni at the banquet, and, being confident of their ability to do so (with the help of their hired *banditti*), they unguardedly agree to his seemingly innocent requests. Just after Putana's blinding, Giovanni enters with a question to Vasques: 'Where's my Sister?', who generously replies 'In her chamber; please you visit her; she is alone'. Having been rewarded for his pains Vasques professes himself 'doubly' Giovanni's servant (4.3.243–50), not realizing that for once he is the dupe. In a later scene Soranzo, having instructed and paid the *Banditti*, feels equally generous when Giovanni asks him, 'how's my sister?'

SORANZO   Like a good huswife, scarcely ready yet,
                Y'are best walke to her chamber.
GIOVANNI   If you will.
SORANZO   I must expect my honourable Friends,
                Good brother get her forth.
GIOVANNI   You are busie Sir.   *Exit* GIOVANNI
VASQUES   Even as the great Devill himselfe would have it, let him
                goe and glut himselfe in his owne destruction.   (5.4.40–6)

Confident in the success of his latest plot, Soranzo complacently imagines him having incestuous sex with Annabella, the wife whom he also plans to murder. He has failed to anticipate that Giovanni might have something else in mind.

A few moments later we see Annabella, lying on her bed wearing her wedding dress, as Soranzo had ordered (5.2.10–11). Giovanni has used his licence to visit Annabella, but rather than 'glut himselfe in his owne destruction', as Vasques imagined, he is indeed blaming Annabella, as the Friar had foretold, accusing her of being 'treacherous' to her 'past vowes and oaths', of being 'a faithlesse sister' guilty of a 'revolt'

(5.5.4–9). After his angry rant, Annabella's words seem in grim touch with reality:

> Brother, deare brother, know what I have beene,
> And know that now there's but a dying time
> Twixt us and our Confusion. (16–18)

Like the Friar, she warns him that 'This Banquet is an harbinger of Death' (24), but Giovanni replies with an unrelated consideration of whether the world will end in a conflagration and whether they will meet in some 'other world' (30–41), as Ford swiftly darkens the tone of their conversation. Giovanni is evidently thinking of her death, weeping what he describes as 'the funerall teares | Shed on your grave'. He pronounces a valedictory eulogy on Annabella as if she were already dead:

> Never till now did Nature doe her best,
> To shew a matchlesse beauty to the world,
> Which in an instant, ere it scarce was seene,
> The jealous Destinies required againe. (59–62)

Once more, Giovanni attempts to shift responsibility to some external force; but he himself embodies the pagan 'Destinies', who have power over life and death. Moreover, he is claiming not only that power but also a high religious office—that of Christ at the Day of Judgment—to decide the destination of her soul:

> Pray Annabella, pray; since wee must part,
> Goe thou white in thy soule, to fill a Throne
> Of Innocence and Sanctity in Heaven. (63–5)

These words contradict Giovanni's defiant atheism, as he casts himself in his most important role so far. Yet a sister whom he has seduced to commit incest can hardly be 'white' in her soul, and by the Friar's standards, to which she has been converted, she knows that her soul will not be going to heaven.

Throughout this scene Ford produces great tension by juxtaposing Annabella's helplessness, not knowing what her brother is planning, with Giovanni's vatic exultation. He calls on the sun to disappear, 'And make this mid-day night', as if he has the power to re-enact the cosmic confusion that attended Christ's Crucifixion. Now he claims to be acting for her sake, to preserve her reputation, working by a perverted scale of values by which 'Honour'—or good standing in society—is more important than love:

ANNABELLA What meanes this?
GIOVANNI   To save thy fame and kill thee in a kisse. *Stabs her.*
           Thus dye, and dye *by mee*, and *by my* hand,
           Revenge is *mine*; Honour doth love Command. (84–6;
           my italics)

Ford makes Giovanni repeat the first-person pronoun to show that he
is claiming ownership of this deed. He has possessed her during her
life and will now possess her death. Annabella's dying words show that
her first thought is for him, not herself, but then she realizes that he
has been 'unkind', unnatural:

ANNABELLA Forgive him Heaven!—and me my sinnes; farewell.
           Brother unkind, unkind! Mercy great Heaven! Oh! Oh!
           Dyes. (92–3)

Compared to the hyperboles he showered on Annabella earlier,
Giovanni pronounces one of the most perfunctory epitaphs in early
modern drama: 'Shee's dead, alas good soule.' It is hard to imagine
a more unfeeling reaction, which must call in question critics'
impression that Ford presented Giovanni sympathetically. But it is
completely in character for this complete egoist, who is more concerned to chart the stages by which he dominated her life and
death:

          The haplesse Fruite
    That in her wombe receiv'd its life *from mee*,
    Hath had *from mee* a Cradle and a Grave. (94–6; my italics)

Ford has consistently shown that Giovanni's concerns are always for
himself. He is always the centre of attention, getting himself psyched
up to play his greatest role:

    Shrinke not Couragious hand, stand up my heart,
    And boldly act *my last, and greater part.*
        Exit with the Body. (105–6; Ford's italics)

Now we see for what purpose Giovanni had urged himself to 'Be all a
man': to kill his sister, an unarmed woman. What is 'glorious' here?

I have argued that Ford conceived Giovanni's readiness to flout religious and social norms as a form of egoism, setting himself above
timorous normality. At strategic points throughout the play Ford has
given instances of his sense of power. In his first scene with the Friar
he compared himself to the greatest power in nature:

> It were more ease to stop the Ocean
> From floates and ebbs, than to disswade my vowes. (1.1.64–5)

Not even Tamburlaine claimed such a power. In the scene where he spied on Annabella's behaviour when Soranzo was wooing her, she said that her choice of a lover would be 'as the Fates inferre'; from his eavesdropping position Giovanni declared, 'Of those I'me regient now' (3.2.119–20). Giovanni repeats this claim in his final scene with Annabella:

> why I hold Fate
> Clasp't in my fist, and could Command the Course
> Of times eternall motion   (5.5.11–13)[47]

In his extraordinary final appearance ('*Enter Giovanni with a heart upon his Dagger*)' he asserts that

> Fate or all the Powers
> That guide the motions of Immortall Soules
> Could not prevent mee. (5.6.9–13)

He sees himself as some higher power 'That tryumphs over death'. Yet all he has done is to kill Annabella; to cause the death of a defenceless woman is not to triumph over it. Ford creates Giovanni's boastful claims in a form that allows us to see their hollowness. It is true that neither 'Fate' nor 'the Powers | That guide the motions of Immortal Soules' (a strange mixture of pagan and Christian ideas) could prevent him, but these abstractions cannot influence the actions of any human being. A person bent on murder can only be prevented by a superior human force who is aware of their intention. Ford gives Giovanni delusions of grandeur, as if he had caused a second crucifixion (which would equate him with Pontius Pilate):

> The Glory of my Deed
> Darkned the mid-day Sunne, made Noone as Night. (20–1)

Contemporaries of Ford would have been more aware than we are that one of the root meanings of 'glory' is 'an effulgence of light', even 'the circle of light depicted around the head or whole figure of Jesus' (*OED*). To claim that power is to have megalomaniac delusions.

The climax of Giovanni's glorification of his own agency and power is reached when he explains to the startled company that he has 'dig'd

---

[47] Ford surely intended his audience and readers to recognize the allusion to Tamburlaine's boast: 'I hold the Fates fast bound in iron chains, | And with my hand turn Fortune's wheel about' (*1 Tamburlaine*, 1.2.173–4).

for food | In a much richer Myne' than gold or precious stones—another confused metaphor. Giovanni puzzles the bystanders even more by asking if they recognize the piece of bleeding flesh speared on his dagger's point (as if one could):

>   'tis a Heart,
>   A Heart my Lords, in which is mine intomb'd,
>   Looke well upon't; d'ee know't?
> VASQUES   What strange ridle's this?
> GIOVANNI   'Tis Annabella's Heart, 'tis ; why d'ee startle?
>   I vow 'tis hers, this Daggers poynt plow'd up
>   Her fruitfull wombe, and left to mee the fame
>   Of a most glorious executioner. (25–32)

Giovanni's father describes him as 'a frantick mad man' (41), as do many modern critics, but the precision of Ford's language adds another dimension to this strange character. If his heart is 'intomb'd' in Annabella's, then by ripping it out he is reclaiming part of himself while possessing what's left of her. Ford knows that it is difficult to remove the heart from the body, due to the protective ribcage. As Macbeth did to the rebel Macdonald, Giovanni has had to 'unseam' Annabella 'from the nave' ['navel, or perhaps crotch'] upwards.[48] Ford adds another unnatural element by making Giovanni present the deed in sexual terms. As Derek Roper pointed out, 'In the context of "fruitful womb" the ploughing could normally be a sexual metaphor, as might the dagger: cf. "she made great Antony lay his sword to bed. He ploughed her and she cropped" (*Antony and Cleopatra*). Their effect here is to make the murder seem a sadistic version of the sexual acts' (ed. cit., 117). This is true, but it also brings out the physicality of incest, an issue that Ford has avoided until now.

The reader is disadvantaged at this point, but the theatre director can bring out the shocked reaction of everyone on stage as Giovanni glories in having achieved 'the fame | Of a most glorious executioner'—in reality, executioners held a menial post in a ruler's employ. Ford takes the opportunity of Giovanni directly addressing his father for the last time to shock him with the details of their long sexual relationship, carried on under his nose:

> GIOVANNI   Nine Moones have had their changes,
>   Since I first throughly view'd and truely lov'd
>   *Your Daughter* and *my Sister*.

[48] See *Macbeth*, ed. Sandra Clark and Pamela Mason (London, 2015), p. 132.

FLORIO   How! alas,
          My Lords, hee's a frantick mad-man!
GIOVANNI   Father no;
          For nine Moneths space, in secret I enjoy'd
          Sweete *Annabella's* sheetes; Nine Moneths I liv'd
          A happy Monarch of her heart and her.
          Soranzo, thou know'st this; thy paler cheeke
          Beares the Confounding print of thy disgrace,
          For her too fruitfull wombe too soone bewray'd
          The happy passage of our stolne delights,
          And made her Mother to a Child unborne.
CARDINAL Incestuous Villaine. (38–49; Ford's italics)

This is a gratuitously cruel speech, the most hurtful words that Giovanni could ever have spoken to his father. It is additionally shocking that, far from showing remorse or shame, Giovanni revels in the graphic details that he 'enjoyd | Sweet Annabella's sheetes' for nine months, 'happy Monarch of her heart and her', until her womb revealed the fruits of 'our stolne delights'. (Annabella previously described the pleasures of their first night together as 'stolne contents'.) When his father accuses him of lying, Giovanni proclaims that he has spoken 'the Oracle of truth', attacking others of lacking the 'faith | To credit yet my Triumphs'. Once again Ford gives him the language of a victorious general or a messianic leader, but there is a massive contrast between those aspirations and the perverse deed for which Giovanni demands recognition and admiration:

                              here I sweare
          By all that you call sacred, by the love
          I bore my *Annabella* whil'st she liv'd,
          These hands have from her bosome ript *this heart.* (55–8; Ford's italics)

Vasques had been sent to fetch Annabella, and when he returns Giovanni demands, 'Is't true or no sir?' Having only found her butchered corpse, Vasques can confirm: ''Tis most strangely [unnaturally] true', at which point Florio collapses. When the Cardinal rebukes him, 'Monster of Children', for having broken his father's heart, Giovanni exults in having achieved another 'triumph':

                              oh my Father,
          How well his death becomes him in his griefes!
          Why this was done with Courage; now survives
          None of our house but I, guilt in the blood
          Of a *Fayre sister* and a *Haplesse Father.* (63–7; Ford's italics)

That is a curious aesthetic reaction—'How well his death becomes him'—as if Florio were an actor in a play, but it is followed by what seems equally inappropriate self-approval: 'Why this was done with Courage'. Who is Giovanni praising? Florio showed no courage in dying from a heart-attack, so perhaps Giovanni is praising himself? If so, then he has perverted another of the cardinal virtues. Modern editors must emend 'guilt' to the dominant metaphor, 'gilt', but the unregularized spelling of the 1630s happily preserves both spellings. Giovanni regularly takes stock of his own achievements and is always 'well pleased' with what he has done, but here he finds a rationale after the event, since he hardly set out to destroy his 'house'. True, he has killed his sister and brought about the death of his father, but those were reactions to circumstances, not an intention reasoned in advance. In the concluding scenes of the play Ford gives Giovanni all the space he needs to wreak destruction and justify it.[49] But he is now challenged for the first time by a threatening opponent who has every motive to kill him. Soranzo exclaims:

> Inhumane scorne of men, hast thou a thought
> T' out live thy murthers?

Ford had placed Giovanni in the same class as Tamburlaine. Now he elevates himself to the status of one of the three classical Fates:

GIOVANNI   Yes, I tell thee yes;
  For in my fists I beare the twists of life.
  Soranzo, see this heart which was thy wife's;
  Thus I exchange it royally for thine,
  And thus and thus, now brave revenge is mine. (69–73)

Giovanni gives Soranzo his death wound, but that hardly validates his grandiose claim, and his pretensions are destroyed a few moments later, when Vasques and the Banditti stab him to death.

  We receive so many conflicting impressions about Giovanni in this final scene that it becomes difficult to integrate them into any coherent sense of his personality. The delusions of grandeur that Ford has given him throughout the play, ranking himself on a par with massive sources of power—Jove, the ocean, Tamburlaine, finally Atropos—converge into a kind of megalomania. It is a staggering performance, fascinating spectators and readers with his confidence that whatever he

---

[49] In 5.3 he speaks 56 of 78 lines; in 5.4 only 5 lines, but they are his crucial request to visit his sister; in 5.5 his part runs to 91 of 106 lines, and in 5.6 he speaks 70 of the first 105 lines. He dominates the action in his switches of mood and unpredictable violence.

chooses to do is right. All the way through, however, he never gives a thought to anyone else's welfare. He is in the class of destructive ego-ists, such as Falstaff, Iago, Edmund. The one exception is Annabella, for whom he declares his love on numerous occasions. Yet his words do not match his deeds, from the cold calculation that she must marry 'some man' so that he can continue to enjoy his pleasure, to his mur-der of Annabella so that Soranzo can't have her:

> I must not dally, this sad Marriage-bed
> In all her best, bore her alive and dead.
> *Soranzo* thou hast mist thy ayme in this,
> I have prevented [anticipated] now thy reaching plots,
> And kil'd a Love, for whose each drop of blood
> I would have pawn'd my heart   (5.5.97–102)

Perhaps he would have done, but there was one person more important than Annabella, Giovanni himself. Modern culture has delivered so many examples of possessive love becoming destructive that we can understand his behaviour without feeling sympathy for him. Writing to budding dramatists, Horace had advised them to 'keep a character to the end even as it came forth at first, and have it self-consistent'.[50] Ford followed that advice, ensuring that Giovanni's final words leave one impression dominant:

> Oh, my last minute comes.
> Where e're I goe, let mee enjoy this grace,
> Freely to view *My Annabella's face. Dyes.* (104–6; Ford's italics)

In this climax of destruction Vasques is the only surviving agent from the play's beginning. The forces of law and order are represented by the Cardinal, whom we saw earlier sheltering the murderer Grimaldi by taking him into the Pope's protection. The Cardinal begins to question Vasques about his deeds as a faithful servant to Soranzo, and then touches on what seems to be a marginal issue: 'know'st thou any yet unnam'd | Of Counsell in this incest?' (120–1). Vasques reveals the name of Putana, 'whose eyes after her confession I caus'd to be put out' (125–6). The Cardinal instantly orders Putana to be burned at the stake. He then confronts Vasques, whose crimes include the murder of Hippolita, and delivers his judgement:

---

[50] Horace, *Ars Poetica*, 126–7; *Satires, Epistles and Ars Poetica* tr. H. R. Fairclough (London and Cambridge, MA, 1970), 486–7.

> Fellow, for thee; since what thou did'st, was done
> Not for thy selfe, being no Italian,
> Wee banish thee for ever, to depart
> Within three dayes, in this wee doe dispense
> With grounds of reason, not of thine offence. (138–42)

That seems a strange 'reason' to let Vasques go free, that he didn't commit these crimes to benefit himself, but Ford prepared for this judgement in an earlier scene between Vasques and Soranzo (5.4.20–7). Having placed the Banditti in hiding, the servant assures his master that 'nothing is unready to this *Great worke*, but a great mind in you'. The master declares that he needs no encouragement to taking his revenge:

> 'Tis well; the lesse I speake, the more I burne,
> And blood shall quench that flame.

Vasques expresses his approval: 'Now you begin to turne Italian', meaning that he (Soranzo) is now burning with desire for blood like a typical Italian, unlike Vasques, who is cooler and more cunning, like a typical Spaniard. Vasques tells the Cardinal that he did what he did out of loyalty to Soranzo and his father, implying that his was not a hot-blooded selfish desire for revenge. As Tom Cain has put it, 'Vasques wasn't acting for himself but for—if you can call them that—"better" motives.'[51] Vasques is duly gratified: ''Tis well; this Conquest is mine, and I rejoice that a *Spaniard* out-went an *Italian in revenge*.'

The cardinal's final act is to confiscate 'all the Gold and Jewells, or whatsoever' of all the deceased for the Pope's own use, confirming an English audience's view of the Catholic church's indiscriminate greed. To complete this travesty of justice, Ford gives the Cardinal the last words:

> never yet
> Incest and Murther have so strangely met.
> Of one so young, so rich in Natures store,
> Who could not say, 'Tis pitty shee's a Whoore? *Exeunt.* (154–7)

We now realize that Putana was killed in order to quell any rumours of incest, so that the Cardinal can report to Rome that the recent disturbances in Padua were caused by a woman's uncontrolled sexuality. As Lisa Hopkins has observed: 'despite the gross inappropriateness of [the Cardinal's] bald judgement on events . . . it is nevertheless his

---

[51] I thank Tom Cain for a helpful discussion (email 28 April 2021).

privilege to have not only the last but also the official word on the subject.'[52] In the earlier scene the citizens who had been defeated in attempting to bring the murderer to justice had expressed their indignation: 'dwels *Justice* here?'—'*Justice* is fledd to heaven and comes no nearer!' (3.9.62–3). Theatregoers and readers may wish they could at least make some protest. The action is completed but we do not have closure, as all the issues it has raised are left unresolved.

Ford chose to end his play on this troubling note to complete his analysis of the society that produced Giovanni. Some critics have argued that Ford's bleak portrait of Padua was intended to make the lovers seem more admirable. To me the larger truth is that Giovanni shares his faults with several of the main characters. He only ever cares for his own interests, as do Soranzo, Hippolita, Vasques, Grimaldi, and the Cardinal. Like them, he is prepared to act ruthlessly to gain what he desires, or to have his revenge on anyone who might prevent him. The only character who puts another person's interests ahead of her own is Annabella, after the Friar has converted her to a Christian worldview, in which sins will be punished in hell but those who repent can earn God's forgiveness. From that point on she always thinks first of Giovanni's well-being before her own. Although she is soon swept up by her brother's wish to possess her to the point of destruction, this sequence of repentance and forgiveness is further evidence that the moral-theological structure of *'Tis Pity She's a Whore* is essentially that of *Christ's Bloody Sweat*.

The only other character to show concern for another's welfare is Richardetto, who saves Philotis from the world's evils by sending her to a convent. Otherwise, he is used by Ford as an observer,[53] who nonetheless gets caught up in the prevailing patterns of revenge and violence, but without committing a crime. Bergetto has no harmfulness but not much virtue either.

The intense focus on human evils, with very few redeeming qualities, sets this play apart in Ford's canon. One further characteristic of *'Tis Pity* that differentiates it from other Ford plays, and argues for an earlier date, is its intense activity and its negative ending. As Rowland Wymer observes, '*'Tis Pity* achieves a ferocious intensity unique in

[52] Hopkins, *Political*, p. 101.

[53] In his first scene with Philotis Richardetto explains that he has returned to Padua in disguise to spy on Hippolita's 'lascivious riots' and 'loose adultery' (2.3.7–13). When Hippolita dies, having drunk the poison she'd prepared for Soranzo, Richardetto comments: 'Here's the end | Of lust and pride' (4.1.101); in the final scene he repeats his motive for returning to Padua: 'To see the effect of Pride and Lust at once | Brought both to shamefull ends' (5.6.150–1).

Caroline theatre', one reason why it has been 'seen as a Jacobean tragedy'.[54] That intensity is created by a closely intertwined plot structure which gives priority to swift action, driven at each level by characters who are determined to obtain their goals fully and quickly: Giovanni, Soranzo, Vasques, Hippolita, Grimaldi, Richardetto. Critics have commented on Ford's 'casualness of plot-development' in other plays, where 'dramatic incidents are casually introduced',[55] but this cannot be said of *'Tis Pity*. The furious pace of the plotting and counterplotting leaves no time for reflection or for the sympathetic portrayal of suffering found in other plays. Clifford Leech observes that *'Tis Pity She's a Whore*

> is not Ford's most characteristic play. What we shall find in *Perkin Warbeck* and *The Broken Heart* and *Love's Sacrifice* is a presentation of exalted human beings whose actions never come within the scope of censure. Suffering, not action, is the dominant strain in their world, the suffering of melancholy or of deprivation.[56]

'Tis Pity, by contrast, contains no 'exalted human being', apart from Giovanni's personal image of Annabella, and every character in the play comes 'within the scope of censure', apart from the harmless appearance of Philotis before she is despatched to the 'chaste and single life' of the cloister (4.2.13–30) to preserve her from this evil society. Ford caps the chaos and violence of the closing scene with the amoral acts of the Cardinal. The Jacobean tragedy with the closest similarity to the ending of this play is Middleton's *Women Beware Women* (1621). As R. B. Parker commented, the weaknesses of Bianca, Leantio, and Isabella

> leave these characters at the mercy of their degenerate environment. Except for the Cardinal, all the other characters are either consciously wicked, or bestial, or stupidly cynical, mercenary, and proud of their wordly wisdom.[57]

In a further subversion of morality, 'the standards which society sets up to guide its members, moreover, are shown to be completely inadequate and easily perverted to serve the very vices they are designed to combat' (ibid.). The social context in Middleton's play is more fully realized than in Ford's, but the end effect is equally negative.

---

[54] Rowland Wymer, *Webster and Ford* (London, 1995), p. 101.
[55] Clifford Leech, *John Ford and the Drama of his Time* (London, 1957), pp. 76–7.
[56] Ibid., p. 11.
[57] See R. B. Parker, 'Middleton's experiments with comedy and judgement', in J.R. Brown and B. Harris (eds.), *Jacobean Theatre* (London, 1964), pp. 179–99 (192–3).

The other Ford plays present admirable human qualities, even in the men who harm women. Leech notes this characteristic in the early co-authored plays. In *The Spanish Gipsy* (1625) Roderigo's revulsion from his offence, having raped Clara, is intense, matching the remorse of Frank in *The Witch of Edmonton*.[58] Ford gives Orgilus a steadiness and resolve in his final minutes (*Broken Heart*, 5.2.100–55), qualities shared by Perkin Warbeck, illegitimate pretender to the throne, who nonetheless achieves nobility in his last scene before execution (5.3.52–74, 88–101, 120–49). But the focus of sympathy in those closing scenes is more often on a female character. In *The Broken Heart* Penthea, forced by her brother Ithocles to marry the insanely jealous Bassanes, retains her constancy through a miserable life despite temptations, and finally escapes by starving herself to death. Ford created her as a model of feminine dignity and resolve under intolerable pressure. He did the same with Lady Katherine Gordon in *Perkin Warbeck*, who displays unyielding 'constancy in suffering' (5.1.4). Clifford Leech made the appropriate comment that, apart from *'Tis Pity*, Ford's dramatic world is dominated by women characters, who are exalted for their beauty, their devotion and their exquisite command of speech and gesture' (112). By comparison, Giovanni's brutal silencing of Annabella belongs to an earlier, more violent age.

---

[58] Leech, *John Ford*, p. 34. See *The Spanish Tragedy*, 3.1.1–29, and *The Witch of Edmonton*, 5.3.74–80, respectively.

'TIS
Pitty Shee's a Whore

Acted by the *Queenes* Maiesties Seruants, at *The Phænix in*
Drury-Lane.

LONDON.
Printed by *Nicholas Okes* for *Richard*
Collins, and are to be fold at his fhop
in *Pauls* Church-yard, at the figne
of the three Kings. 1633.

Title page of *'Tis Pity She's a Whore* (1633). By permission of the Bodleian Library, Oxford.

'Tis Pitty She's a Whore

Edited by KATSUHIKO NOGAMI

The Sceane
PARMA.

The Actors Names.

BONAVENTURA, *A Fryar.*
A CARDINAL, *Nuntio to the Pope.*
SORANZO, *A Nobleman.*
FLORIO, *A Cittizen of Parma.*
DONADO, *Another Cittizen.*
GRIMALDI, *A Roman Gentleman.*
GIOVANNI, *Sonne to Florio.*
BERGETTO, *Nephew to Donado.*
RICHARDETTO, *A Suppos'd Phisitian.*
VASQUES, *Servant to Soranzo.*
POGGIO, *Servant to Bergetto.*
BANDITTI

Woemen.

ANNABELLA, *Daughter to Florio.*
HIPPOLITA, *Wife to Richardetto.*
PHILOTIS, *Neece to Richardetto.*
PUTANA, *Tutresse to Annabella.*

(OFFICERS, ATTENDANTS, SERVANTS, *etc.*)

To my Friend, the Author.
With admiration I behel'd This Whore
Adorn'd with Beauty, such as might restore

[Title] 'Tis] Dodsley; T'is *Q*   [**The Actors Names**] 11 VASQUES] *Q*; VASQUEZ *Massai*
18 PUTANA] *Q*; PUTTANA *Massai*   19 OFFICERS, ATTENDANTS, SERVANTS, *etc.*] *Gifford*;
not in *Q*

(If ever being as Thy Muse hath fam'd)
Her Giovanni, in his love unblam'd: 5
The ready Graces lent their willing ayd,
Pallas her selfe now playd the Chamber-maide
And help't to put her Dressings on: secure
Rest Thou, that Thy Name herein shall endure
To th'end of Age; and Annabella bee   10
Gloriously Faire, even in her Infamie.

A2ʳ   THOMAS ELLICE.

To the truely Noble, *John*,
Earle of *Peterborough*, Lord Mordant,
Baron of *Turvey*.

My LORD,

Where a Truth of *Meritt* hath a generall warrant, There *Love* is   5
but a *Debt, Acknowledgement a Justice*. Greatnesse cannot often
claime *Virtue* by Inheritance; Yet in this, YOURS appeares most
Eminent, for that you are not more rightly Heyre to your
Fortunes, then Glory shalbe to your *Memory*. Sweetnesse of
disposition ennobles a freedome of Birth; in BOTH, your lawfull   10
Interest adds Honour to your owne Name, and mercy to my
presumption. Your Noble allowance of *These First Fruites* of my
leasure in the Action, emboldens my confidence, of your as noble
construction in this Presentment: especially since my Service
must ever owe particular duty to your Fa-|vours, by a particular   15
A2ᵛ Ingagement. The Gravity of the *Subject* may easily excuse the
leightnesse of the *Title*: otherwise, I had beene a severe Judge
against mine owne guilt. Princes have vouchsaf't Grace to trifles,
offred from a purity of Devotion, your Lordship may likewise
please, to admit into your good opinion, with these weake   20
endevours, the constancy of Affection from the sincere *Lover* of
your Deserts in Honour,

IOHN FORD.

[**Epistle Dedicatory**]ᴧ 22 Honour,] *Weber (honour,)*; ~ᴧ *Q*   23 IOHN] *Q*; JOHN *Dodsley*
23 FORD.] *Weber*, ~: *Q*; ~ᴧ *Bawcutt*

I.1   *Enter* FRYAR *and* GIOVANNI.   B1ʳ

FRYAR Dispute no more in this, for know (young man)
These are no Schoole-points; nice Philosophy
May tolerate unlikely arguments,
But Heaven admits no jest; wits that presum'd
On wit too much, by striving how to prove   5
There was no God; with foolish grounds of Art,
Discover'd first the neerest way to Hell;
And fild the world with develish Atheisme:
Such questions youth are fond; For better 'tis,
To blesse the Sunne, then reason why it shines;   10
Yet hee thou talk'st of, is above the Sun,
No more; I may not heare it.

GIOVANNI   Gentle Father,
To you I have unclasp't my burthened soule,
Empty'd the store-house of my thoughts and heart,
Made my selfe poore of secrets; have not left   15
Another word untold, which hath not spoke
All what I ever durst, or thinke, or know;
And yet is here the comfort I shall have?
Must I not doe, what all men else may, love?

FRYAR Yes, you may love faire sonne.

GIOVANNI   Must I not praise   20
That beauty, which if fram'd a new, the gods
Would make a god of, if they had it there;
And kneele to it, as I doe kneele to them?   B1ᵛ

FRYAR Why foolish mad-man!

I.1] *this edn; no act or scene heading in Q;* Actus primus. *Dodsley;* SCENE I.—*Friar*
BONAVENTURA'S *Cell.* | *Weber, Dyce;* [I.1] *Massai*   6 God;] *Q; ~, Dodsley; ~ₐ*
Dyce   6 Art,] *Q; ~ₐ Sherman* (art)   9 fond; For] *Q; ~: far Dodsley; ~: ~ Weber* (for);
~; ~ Bawcutt (for)   10 then] *Q;* than *Dodsley*   12] *Weber;* No . . . it. | Gentle Father, *Q*
18 have?] *Dodsley; ~, Q*   19 may,] *Q; ~ₐ— Roper; ~,— Dyce*   20] *Weber;* Yes . . .
sonne. | Must . . . praise *Q*   20 Yes,] *Dodsley; ~. Q; ~ₐ Weber*   20 love] *Q; ~,*
Dodsley   21 a new] *Q; a-new Dodsley;* anew *Weber*   24] *Weber;* Why . . . madman! |
Shall . . . sound, *Q*   24 Why] *Q; ~, Dodsley*   24 mad-man!] *Dodsley; ~? Q; ~,— Dyce*
(madman)

GIOVANNI   Shall a peevish sound,
  A customary forme, from man to man,   25
  Of brother and of sister, be a barre
  Twixt my perpetuall happinesse and mee?
  Say that we had one father, say one wombe,
  (Curse to my ioyes) gave both us life, and birth;
  Are wee not therefore each to other bound   30
  So much the more by Nature; by the links
  Of blood, of reason; Nay if you will hav't,
  Even of Religion, to be ever one,
  One soule, one flesh, one love, one heart, one *All?*

FRYAR   Have done unhappy youth, for thou art lost.   35

GIOVANNI   Shall then, (for that I am her brother borne)
  My joyes be ever banisht from her bed?
  No Father; in your eyes I see the change
  Of pitty and compassion: from your age
  As from a sacred *Oracle* distills   40
  The life of Counsell: tell mee holy man,
  What Cure shall give me ease in these extreames.

FRYAR   Repentance (sonne) and sorrow for this sinne:
  For thou hast mov'd a Majesty above
  With thy un-raunged (almost) Blasphemy.   45

GIOVANNI   O doe not speake of that (dear Confessor).

FRYAR   Art thou (my sonne) that miracle of Wit,
  Who once within these three Moneths wert esteem'd
  A wonder of thine age, throughout *Bononia?*
  How did the University applaud   50
  Thy Government, Behaviour, Learning, Speech,

29 ioys] *Q;* joys *Dodsley*   31 Nature;] *Q;* ~? *Gifford*   31 the links] *Q* (corrected); the
the links *Q* (uncorrected)   32 reason;] *Q;* ~? *Gifford*   34 *All*] *Q;* all
Dodsley   39 compassion:]*Q*~; *Weber*   40 *Oracle*]*Q;*oracle *Dodsley*   41 Counsell:
tell] *Q;* ~. ~ *Weber* (Tell)   42 extreames.] *Q;* ~? *Weber*   44 above] *Q;* ~,
Gifford   45 un-raunged (almost)] *Q;* unguarded, ~, *Dodsley;* unranged, ~ *Reed;* unranged
~ *Dyce;* unrang̀ed almost *Ellis;* unranged-almost *Bawcutt*   46[Confessor).] *Q;* ~! *Dodsley*
(confessor); ~. *Reed* (confessor)   49 *Bononia*] *Q;* Bologna *Wiggins*

Sweetnesse, and all that could make up a man?
I was proud of my Tutellage, and chose
Rather to leave my Bookes, then part with thee,
I did so: but the fruites of all my hopes   55
Are lost in thee, as thou art in thy selfe.
O *Giovanni*: hast thou left the Schooles
Of Knowledge, to converse with Lust and Death?
(For Death waites on thy Lust) looke through the world,   B2ʳ
And thou shalt see a thousand faces shine   60
More glorious, then this Idoll thou ador'st:
Leave her, and take thy choyce, 'tis much lesse sinne,
Though in such games as those, they lose that winne.

GIOVANNI   It were more ease to stop the *Ocean*
From floates and ebbs, then to disswade my vowes.   65

FRYAR   Then I have done, and in thy wilfull flames
Already see thy ruine; Heaven is just,
Yet heare my counsell.

GIOVANNI   As a voyce of life.

FRYAR   Hye to thy Fathers house, there locke thee fast
Alone within thy Chamber, then fall downe   70
On both thy knees, and grovell on the ground:
Cry to thy heart, wash every word thou utter'st
In teares, (and if't bee possible) of blood:
Begge Heaven to cleanse the leprosie of Lust
That rots thy Soule, acknowledge what thou art,   75
A wretch, a worme, a nothing: weepe, sigh, pray
Three times a day, and three times every night:
For seven dayes space doe this, then if thou find'st
No change in thy desires, returne to me:
I'le thinke on remedy, pray for thy selfe   80
At home, whil'st I pray for thee here—away,
My blessing with thee, wee have neede to pray.

---

52 man?] *Q; ~! Weber*   54 thee,] *Q; ~. Weber; ~; Gifford*   64 *Ocean] Q;* ocean
Dodsley   65 floates] *Q;* flows *Dodsley*   66 flames] *Q (corrected);* flame *Q (uncorrected);*
flaws *Sturgess*   68] *Weber;* Yet . . . counsell. | As . . . life. *Q*   68 counsell.] *Q; ~!*
Dodsley (counsel)   80 remedy, pray] *Q; ~. ~ Dodsley* (Pray)

GIOVANNI   All this I'le doe, to free mee from the rod
Of vengeance, else I'le sweare, my Fate's my God.

Exeunt.

1.2   *Enter* GRIMALDI *and* VASQUES *ready to fight.*

VASQUES   Come sir, stand to your tackling, if you prove *Craven,*
I'le make you run quickly.

GRIMALDI   Thou art no equall match for mee.

VASQUES   Indeed I never went to the warres to bring home
newes, nor cannot play the Mountibanke for a meales   5
meate, and sweare I got my wounds in the field: see you
these gray haires, they'le not flinch for a bloody nose, wilt
thou to this geere?

B2ᵛ   GRIMALDI.   Why slave, think'st thou I'le ballance my reputation
With a Cast-suite? Call thy Maister, he shall know that I dare—   10

VASQUES   Scold like a Cot-queane (that's your Profession)
thou poore shaddow of a Souldier, I will make thee know,
my Maister keeps Servants, thy betters in quality and
performance; Com'st thou to fight or prate?

GRIMALDI   Neither with thee. I am a Romane and a Gentleman,   15
one that have got mine honour with expence of blood.

VASQUES   You are a lying Coward, and a foole; fight, or by
these Hilts I'le kill thee—brave my Lord—you'le fight.

GRIMALDI   Provoake me not, for if thou dost——

1.2] *this edn; not in Q;* SCENE II.—*The Street, before the house of* FLORIO, *which has a Balcony.* | *Weber;* SCENE II.—*The street before* FLORIO*'s house.* | *Dyce;* [1.2] *Massai* 0.1 SD *Enter* GRIMALDI *and* VASQUES *ready to fight.*] Q; ~ ~ ~ ~, *with their swords drawn.* | *Gifford* 5 newes, nor cannot] Q; ~. Nor can I *Dodsley* (news); ~; nor I cannot *Gifford* (news) 6 field: see] Q; ~. ~ *Dodsley* (See) 10 Cast-suite?] *Weber* (cast-suit?); ~; Q; ~. *Dodsley* (cast-suit) 10 Maister;] Q; master; *Dyce* 14 performance;] Q; ~. *Weber* 15–16 Neither . . . blood.] *after Weber,* Neither . . . thee, | I . . . got | Mine . . . blood. Q 15 thee.] *Dyce;* ~, Q; ~; *Dodsley* 15 Romaneₐ] *Dodsley;* ~. Q 17 foole; fight] *Dodsley;* ~, ~ Q; ~! ~ *Weber* (Fight) 18 thee—] Q; ~:— *Gifford* 18 braveₐ my Lord—you'le fight.] *this edn;* ~ ~ ~,—— ~. Q; ~ ~ lord—you'll ~. *Dodesley;* ~ ~ lord! *Gifford;* ~ ~ lord! You'll ~? *Roper* (Brave); ~, ~ ~! You'll ~. *Wiggins* (Brave) 18] *Roper adds* SD [*Grimaldi draws.*] *after* thee; *Wiggins,* SD [GRIMALDI *draws his sword*].

VASQUES   Have at you.   20

They fight, GRIMALDI *hath the worst.*

Enter FLORIO, DONADO, SORANZO.

FLORIO What meane these sudden broyles so neare my dores?
Have you not other places, but my house
To vent the spleene of your disordered bloods?
Must I be haunted still with such unrest,
As not to eate, or sleepe in peace at home?   25
Is this your love *Grimaldi?* Fie, 'tis naught.

DONADO   And *Vasques.* I may tell thee 'tis not well
To broach these quarrels; you are ever forward
In seconding contentions.

Enter above ANNABELLA *and* PUTANA.

FLORIO   What's the ground?

SORANZO   That with your patience Signiors, I'le resolve: 30
This Gentleman, whom fame reports a souldier,
(For else I know not) rivals mee in love
To Signior *Florio's* Daughter; to whose eares
He still preferrs his suite to my disgrace,
Thinking the way to recommend himselfe,   35
Is to disparage me in his report:
But know *Grimaldi,* though (may be) thou art
My equall in thy blood, yet this bewrayes
A lownesse in thy minde; which wer't thou Noble
Thou would'st as much disdaine, as I doe thee   40
For this unworthinesse; [*to* DONADO *and* FLORIO] and on
     this ground
I will'd my Servant to correct this tongue,   B3ʳ
Holding a man, so base, no match for me.

20.1 SD1 *They fight,* GRIMALDI *hath the worst.*] *set against lines 19–20.2* Q; *They fight,* GRIMALDI
is worsted. | *Gifford* 20.2 SD2 SORANZO] Q; *and ~ Weber; ~ from opposite Sides.* | *Gifford*
21 meane] Q (*corrected*); meaned Q (*uncorrected*)   26 'tis] *Dodsley;* t'is Q   28 quar-
rels;] *Dodsley;* ~, Q   29] *Weber;* In . . . contentions. | What's . . . ground? Q   29.1 SD
Enter above ANNABELLA *and* PUTANA.] Q; *Enter* ANNABELLA *and* PUTANA, *on the Balcony.* |
Weber   29.1 SD PUTANA] Q; PUTTANA *Massai*   36 report:] Q; ~. *Weber;* ~.— *Gifford*
41 and] Q; And *Wiggins*   41 SD [*to* DONADO *and* FLORIO]] *Lomax, not in* Q; [*To*
FLORIO] *Wiggins*   42 will'd] Q; willed *Weber*   42 this] Q; his *Dodsley;* thy *Sturgess*

VASQUES   And had not your suddaine comming prevented us,
I had let my Gentleman blood under the gilles. [*to* GRIMALDI]   45
I should have worm'd you Sir, for running madde.

GRIMALDI   Ile be reveng'd *Soranzo*.

VASQUES   On a dish of warme-broth to stay your stomack, doe
honest Innocence, doe; spone-meat is a wholesomer dyet then
a spannish blade.   50

GRIMALDI   Remember this.

SORANZO   I feare thee not, *Grimaldi*.
                              Exit GRIMALDI.

FLORIO   My Lord *Soranzo*, this is strange to me,
Why you should storme, having my word engag'd:
Owing her heart, what neede you doubt her eare?
Loosers may talke by law of any game.   55

VASQUES   Yet the villainie of words, signior *Florio* may be such,
As would make any unspleen'd Dove Chollerick,
Blame not my Lord in this.

FLORIO   Be you more silent,
I would not for my wealth, my daughters love
Should cause the spilling of one drop of blood.   60
Vasques put up; let's end this fray in wine.
              Exeunt [*omnes, except* PUTANA *and* ANNABELLA]

PUTANA   How like you this child? here's threatning, challenging,
quarrelling, and fighting, on every side, and all is for your
sake; you had neede looke to your selfe (*Chardge*) you'le be
stolen away sleeping else shortly.   65

44 had not] *Dodsley;* had ∧ Q   45 SD [*to* GRIMALDI]] *Lomax; not in* Q
51] *Weber;* remember this | I . . . *Grimaldi.* Q   51 Remember this.] Q (remember this.); ~
~! *Dodsley;* I'll ~ ~. *Sturgess* (remember)   51 SD *Exit* GRIMALDI.] Q (*Ex. Gri.*); *Exit Gri.*
Dodsley   56 villainie] *Dodsley* (villainy *subst.*); villaine Q   57 Dove∧] *Dodsley* (dove); ~,
Q   61 put up:] *Gifford;* ~ ~, Q; ~ ~! *Weber*   61.1 SD *Exeunt* [*omnes, except* PUTANA
and ANNABELLA] *this edn; Exeunt.* Q; [*Exeunt all but* ANNABELLA *and* PUTANA, *above.* |
Walley; Exeunt [FLORIO, DONADO, SORANZO *and* VASQUES] *Bawcutt*   62 threatning,]
Dodsley; ~∧ Q; threatening, *Reed*

ANNABELLA   But (*Tutresse*) such a life gives no content
  To me, my thoughts are fixt on other ends;
  Would you would leave me.

PUTANA   Leave you? no marvaile else; leave me, no leaving
  (Chardge) this is love outright; indeede I blame you not,   70
  you have choyce fit for the best Lady in *Italy*.

ANNABELLA   Pray doe not talke so much.

PUTANA   Take the worst with the best, there's *Grimaldi* the
  souldier a very well-timbred fellow: they say he is a Roman,
  Nephew to the Duke *Mount Ferratto*, they say he did good   75
  service in the warrs against the *Millanoys*, but faith (*Chardge*)
  I doe not like him, and be for nothing, but for being a
  souldier. Not one a-| mongst twenty of your skirmishing   B3ᵛ
  Captaines, but have some pryvie mayme or other, that marres
  their standing upright, I like him the worse, hee crinckles so   80
  much in the hams; though hee might serve, if there were no
  more men, yet hee's not the man I would choose.

ANNABELLA   Fye how thou prat'st.

PUTANA   As I am a very woman, I like *Signiour Soranzo* well; hee
  is wise, and what is more, rich; and what is more then that,   85
  kind, and what is more then all this, a Noble-man; such a one
  were I the faire *Annabella*, my selfe, I would wish and pray for;
  then hee is bountifull; besides hee is handsome, and, by my
  troth, I thinke wholesome: (and that's newes in a gallant of
  three and twenty;) liberall that I know; loving, that you know; 90
  and a man sure, else hee could never ha' purchast such a good
  name, with *Hippolita* the lustie Widdow in her husbands
  life time. And t'were but for that report (sweet heart) would

66 life∧] *Dodsley*; ~, *Q*   68 me.] *Q*; ~! *Reed*   69–71] *this edn*; Leave . . . (Chardge) |
This . . . haue | Choyce . . . *Italy*. | *Q*   69 me,] *Q*; ~∧ *Reed*   69 leaving (Chardge)]
Q; ~, ~, *Dodsley* (charge); ~, ~; *Reed* (Charge)   70 this] *Reed*; This *Q*   70 outright;
indeede] *Q*; ~. ~ *Reed* (Indeed)   74 fellow: they] *Q*; ~. ~ *Dodsley* (They)   75 the
Duke] *Q*; Duke *Dodsley*   75 *Mount Ferratto*] *Q*; Montferrato *Dodsley*   75] they say]
Q; ~ ~ too, *Dodsley*   76 *Millanoys*] *Q*; Milaneze *Dodsley*; Milanese *Weber*   77 and] *Q*;
an't *Weber*   78 souldier.] *Gibson* (soldier); ~; *Q*   78 Not one] *Dodsley*; one *Q*
81 there] *Dodsley*; their *Q*   84 *Soranzo*∧] *Dodsley* (Soranzo); ~, *Q*   87–8 for; then]
this edn; ~. ~ *Dodsley* (Then); ~: ~ *Q*   90 three and twenty;)] *this edn*; ~ ~ ~.) *Q*; ~ ~ ~);
Hopkins; ~ ~ ~; *Dodsley*; ~~·~~; *Reed*; ~~·~~. *Wiggins*   90 I know;] *Dodsley*; ~ ~: *Q*
93 life time.] *Dodsley* (lifetime); ~~. *Reed*; ~ ~: *Q*   93 And] *Q*; An *Weber*

'a were thine. Commend a man for his qualities, but take a
husband as he is a plaine-sufficient, *naked man*: such a one is for   95
your bed, and such a one is *Signior Soranzo,* my life for't.

ANNABELLA   Sure the woman tooke her mornings Draught to
soone.

Enter BERGETTO *and* POGGIO [*below*].

PUTANA   But looke (sweet heart) looke what thinge comes
now: here's another of your cyphers to fill up the number;   100
Oh brave old Ape in a silken Coate, observe.

BERGETTO   Did'st thou thinke *Poggio,* that I would spoyle my
new cloathes, and leave my dinner to fight?

POGGIO   No Sir, I did not take you for so arrant a babie.

BERGETTO   I am wyser then so: for I hope *Poggio,* thou never   105
heard'st of an elder brother, that was a Coxcomb, did'st *Poggio?*

POGGIO   Never indeede Sir, as long as they had either land or
mony left them to inherit.

BERGETTO   Is it possible *Poggio?* oh monstruous! why Ile
undertake, with a handfull of silver, to buy a headfull of wit   110
at any tyme, but sirrah, I have another purchase in hand, I
shall have the wench myne unckle sayes, I will but wash my
face, and shift socks, and then have at her yfaith——Marke
B4ʳ   my pace *Poggio.*

94 'a] *Q;* he *Weber*   94 thine.] *Dodsley;* ~: *Q;* ~! *Dyce*   95 plaine-sufficient,] *Q;* ~ ~ₐ
Dodsley (two words); ~, ~, *Weber*   96 *Soranzo,*] *Dodsley* (Soranzo); ~ₐ *Q*   97 to] *Q;*
too *Dodsley*   98.1 SD [*below*]] *this edn; not in Q*   99–101] *this edn;* But looke (sweet
heart,) . . . now: | Here's . . . number: | Oh . . . Coates, observe. *Q;* But looke, sweet heart, . . .
now! | Here's . . . number: | Oh, . . . coat! Observe. *Weber*   100 number;] *Dodsley;* ~: *Q*
102–103] *after Dodsley;* Did'st . . . my | New . . . fight. *Q*   102 thinkeₐ] *Q;* ~,
Dodsley   103 dinnerₐ] *Q;* ~, *Dodsley*   103 fight?] *Weber;* ~. *Q*   105–106] *after
Weber;* I . . . thou | Neuer . . . Coxcomb, | Did'st *Poggio? Q*   105 hopeₐ] *Q;* ~,
Reed   106 Coxcomb, didst] *Q* (Did'st); ~; ~ *Dodsley* (coxcomb); ~. ~ *Reed* (coxcomb)
(Didst)   109 possibleₐ] *Q;* ~, *Reed*   114 paceₐ] *Q;* ~, *Dodsley*   114 *Poggio.*]
Dodsley (Poggio.); ~: *Q*   114] *Dyce adds* SD [*Passes over the stage, and exit.*] *after* 'Poggio';
McIlwraith, SD [*Exit.*]; *Bawcutt,* SD [*Walks affectedly*]; *Wiggins,* SD [*He walks affectedly*]; *not in Q*

POGGIO   Sir I have seene an Asse, and a Mule trot the Spannish   115
    pavin with a better grace, I know not how often.
                                Exeunt [BERGETTO *and* POGGIO].

ANNABELLA   This Ideot haunts me too.

PUTANA   I, I, he needes no description, the rich *Magnifico*, that is
    below with your Father (*Chardge*) *Signior Donado* his
    Unckle, for that he meanes to make this his Cozen a golden   120
    calfe, thinkes that you wil be a right *Isralite*, and fall downe
    to him presently: but I hope I have tuterd you better: they
    say a fooles bable is a Ladies playfellow: yet you having
    wealth enough, you neede not cast upon the dearth of flesh
    at any rate: hang him, Innocent!   125

                    Enter GIOVANNI [*below*].

ANNABELLA But see *Putana*, see: what blessèd shape
    Of some cælestiall Creature now appears?
    What man is hee, that with such sad aspect
    Walkes carelesse of him selfe?

PUTANA   Where?

ANNABELLA   Looke below.

PUTANA   Oh, 'tis your brother sweet—

ANNABELLA   Ha!

PUTANA   'Tis your brother.   130

ANNABELLA   Sure 'tis not hee, this is some woefull thinge
    Wrapt up in griefe, some shaddow of a man.
    Alas hee beats his brest, and wipes his eyes

---

115 Sir∧] *Q*; ~, *Dodsley*   115 Mule∧] *Q*; ~, *Dodsley*(mule)   116.1 SD *Exeunt* [BERGETTO
and POGGIO]] *Bawcutt*; [*Exeunt.* | *Q*; [*Aside.–Exeunt.*] *Weber*; [*Aside, and following him*]
Gifford; [*Aside, and follows him.* | *Dyce*; [*Exit.*] *McIlwraith*   118 description; the] *this edn*;
~, ~ *Q*; ~. ~ *Dodsley* (The)   120 Unckle,] *Dodsley* (unckle,), *Reed* (uncle,); ~; *Q*
122 better: they] *Q*; ~. ~ *Dodsley* (They)   124–5 flesh∧ at] *Q*; ~, ~ *Dodsley*   125 him,
Innocent!] *Dodsley*; ~∧ ~. *Q*   125.1 SD *Enter* GIOVANNI] *Q*; Giovanni *passes over the Stage.*
| *Gifford*   125.1 SD [*below*].] *this edn*; *not in Q*   126 blessèd] *Dyce*; blessed
Q   126–7] *Weber*; prose in *Q*   129 Looke∧ below] *Q*; ~, ~ *Dodsley* (Look)

Drown'd all in teares: me thinkes I heare him sigh.
Lets downe *Putana*, and pertake the cause,   135
I know my Brother in the Love he beares me,
Will not denye me partage in his sadnesse,
My soule is full of heavinesse and feare.

                    Exeunt [ANNABELLA *and* PUTANA].

GIOVANNI   Lost, I am lost: my fates have doom'd my death:
The more I strive, I love, the more I love,   140
The lesse I hope: I see my ruine certaine.
What Judgement, or endevors could apply
To my incurable and restlesse wounds,
I throughly have examin'd, but in vaine:
O that it were not in Religion sinne,   145
To make our love a God, and worship it.
I have even wearied heaven with prayers, dryed up
The spring of my continuall teares, even sterv'd
My veines with dayly fasts: what wit or Art
Could Counsaile, I have practiz'd; but alas   150
I find all these but dreames, and old mens tales
To fright unsteedy youth; I'me still the same,
Or I must speake, or burst; 'tis not I know,
My lust; but 'tis my fate that leads me on.
Keepe feare and low faint hearted shame with slaves,   155
Ile tell her that I love her, though my heart
Were rated at the price of that attempt.
Oh me! she comes.

                    Enter ANNABELLA *and* PUTANA.

ANNABELLA   Brother.

GIOVANNI   If such a thing

134 me thinks] *Q*; methinks *Dodsley*   138] *Dyce adds* SD [*Aside.* | *after* feare.   138.1 SD
Exeunt [ANNABELLA *and* PUTANA]] *Roper*, *Exeunt* [*from above* ANNABELLA *and* PUTANA]]
Wiggins; *Exit.* | *Q*; [*Exeunt from the Balcony.* | *Weber*; [*Aside, and exit with* PUT. *Gifford*; [*Exit
above with Put.* | *Dyce*; *Exit* [*with* PUTANA] *Barker*, *Exeunt* [*Annabella and Puttana above*]
Massai.   139] *Dyce starts the scene three here, giving* SD '—*A Hall in* FLORIO'*S House.*'
139 Lost, I am lost:] *Q*; ~! ~ ~ ~! *Dodsley*   140 strive, I love,] *Q*; ~, ~ ~: *Dodsley*; ~, ~ ~; *Dyce*
141 hope:] *Q*; ~. *Dodsley*   145 sinne,] *Q*; sin∧ *Dodsley*   150 alas∧] *Q*; ~! *Dodsley*; ~, *Dyce*
152 same,] *Q*; ~; *Dodsley*; ~: *Dyce*   153 Or] *Q*; O *Dodsley*   155 faint hearted] *Q*; ~-~
Dodsley   156 tell her∧] *Dodsley*; ~ ~, *Q*   158] *Weber*; Oh . . . comes. | SD | Brother. | If . . .
thing *Q*   158 SD *Enter* ANNABELLA *and* PUTANA.] *Q*; *Wiggins places* SD *after* attempt
157.   158 Brother.] *Q*; ~! *Dodsley*

As Courage dwell in men, (yee heavenly powers)
Now double all that vertue in my tongue.   160

ANNABELLA   Why Brother, will you not speake to me?

GIOVANNI   Yes; how d'ee Sister?

ANNABELLA   Howsoever I am, me thinks you are not well.

PUTANA   Blesse us; why are you so sad Sir.

GIOVANNI   Let me intreat you leave us awhile, *Putana*.   165
Sister, I would be pryvate with you.

ANNABELLA   With-drawe *Putana*.

PUTANA   I will.
[*Aside*] If this were any other Company for her, I should thinke
my absence an office of some credit; but I will leave them   170
together.

                                                    Exit PUTANA.

GIOVANNI   Come Sister lend your hand, let's walke together.
I hope you neede not blush to walke with mee,
Here's none but you and I.

ANNABELLA   How's this?   175

GIOVANNI   Faith I meane no harme.

ANNABELLA   Harme?

GIOVANNI   No good faith; how ist with'ee?

158 *Dyce adds* SD2 [*aside*] *after* SP GIOVANNI; *Wiggins*, SD2 [*aside*] *before* If.   160 tongue.]
Q; ~! *Reed*   160] *Gifford adds* SD [*Aside*.] *after* tongue.   161 Why∧] *Q*; ~,
Dodsley   161–2] *Q*, Why, brother, | Will . . . sister? | Howe'er . . . well *Gifford*; Why . . . me?
| Yes . . . sister? | Howsoever I am, | Methinks . . . well. *Roper*   162 d'ee∧] *Q*; do ye, *Dodsley*,
d'ye∧ *Dyce*   163 Howsoever] *Q*; Howsoe'er *Weber*; Howe'er *Gifford*; However
McIlwraith   163] *Q*; Howsoever . . . am, | Methinks . . . well. *Roper*   163 me thinks]
Q; methinks *Dodsley*; Methinks *Roper*   164 us;] *this edn*; ~∧ *Q*; ~, *Dodsley*, ~! *Dyce*
164 Sir.] *Q*; ~? *Dodsley* (sir)   165 *Putana*.] *Dodsley, Bawcutt* (Putana.); ~, *Q*; ~,— *Dyce*;
~∧,— *Gibson, Roper* (Putana)   167 With-drawe∧] *Q*; ~, *Dodsley* (Withdraw)   168–70
will. | If] *Q* (will,); ~. ~ *Weber*   170 will.] *Weber*; ~, *Q*   171 SD [*Aside*]] *Weber*; not in
Q; *Bawcutt places* SD [*Aside*.] *after* will 165.   171.1 SD *Exit* PUTANA.] *Q*; [*Aside, and exit*.]
Gifford; *Exit* | *Roper*   172 Come Sister] *Q*; ~, ~, *Dodsley* (sister)   172 together.] *Q*; ~;
Dodsley, ~! *Dyce*   173 mee,] *Q*; ~; *Dodsley*   174–6 Here's . . . franticke] *Q*; Here's . . .
this? | Faith . . . faith: | How . . . frantic— *verse in Weber*; Here's . . . [I]'faith, | I . . . faith. | How . . .
ye? SD [*Aside*.] I . . . frantic.— *verse in Dyce*   176 Faith] *Q*; ~, *Dodsley*; I'faith∧ *Gifford*
178] *Q*; No . . . with'ee? | I trust . . . brother] *Dyce*; No . . . faith | How . . . franticke— | I am . . .
brother *Weber*   178 No∧] *Q*; ~, *Dodsley*   178 faith; how ist] *Q*; ~; ~ is it *Dodsley*, ~: ~
~ *Reed* (How)   178 with'ee] *Q*; with thee *Dodsley*

C1ʳ ANNABELLA [*Aside*] I trust hee be not franticke——
     I am very well, brother.   180

GIOVANNI Trust me but I am sicke, I feare so sicke,
     'Twill cost my life.

ANNABELLA Mercy forbid it: 'tis not so I hope.

GIOVANNI I thinke you love me Sister.

ANNABELLA Yes you know, I doe.   185

GIOVANNI I know't indeed——y'are very faire.

ANNABELLA Nay then I see you have a merry sicknesse.

GIOVANNI That's as it proves: the Poets faigne (I read)
     That *Juno* for her forehead did exceede
     All other goddesses: but I durst sweare,   190
     Your forehead exceeds hers, as hers did theirs.

ANNABELLA Troth, this is pretty.

GIOVANNI   Such a paire of stares
     As are thine eyes, would (like *Promethean* fire)
     (If gently glaun'st) give life to senselesse stones.

ANNABELLA Fie upon 'ee.   195

GIOVANNI The Lilly and the Rose most sweetly strange
     Upon your dimpled Cheekes doe strive for change.
     Such lippes would tempt a Saint; such hands as those
     Would make an *Anchoret* Lascivious.

ANNABELLA D'ee mock mee, or flatter mee?   200

---

179 SD [*Aside*]] *Dyce; not in Q; Gifford places* SD *after* franticke.   179] *Bawcutt adds* SD
[*To him.*] *before* I.   180 well,] *Dodsley;* ~ₐ *Q*   181 meₐ] *Q;* ~, *Dodsley*   181 am
sicke,] *Q;* ~ ~; *Dodsley*   181 so sicke,] *Q* (sick); ~ sickₐ *Dodsley*   183 it:] *Q;* ~! *Dodsley*
183 soₐ] *Q;* ~, *Dodsley*   184–5] *Q;* I think . . . doe. | I know't . . . faire. *Weber;* I think . . .
know | I do . . . fair. *Dyce*   184 meₐ] *Q;* ~, *Dodsley*   185 know,] *Q;* ~ₐ *Dodsley*
186 indeed—] *Q;* ~,— *Dodsley*   186 y'are] *Q;* you are *Dodsley;* you're *Weber*   187 Nayₐ]
Q; ~, *Dodsley*   188 proves:] *Q;* ~. *Dodsley*   188 the] *Dodsley;* they *Q*   190 goddesses:] *Q;* ~; *Dodsley*   191 theirs] *Q;* their *Dyce*   192 Troth . . . stares] *Weber; prose in Q*
192 Troth,] *Dodsley;* ~ₐ *Q*   192 pretty.] *Q;* ~! *Roper*   195 'ee] *Q;* thee *Dodsley*
196 strange] *Q;* strain'd *Dodsley*   200 D'ee] *Q;* Do you *Dodsley;* d'ye *Dyce*   200 mee?]
Dodsley (me); ~, *Q*

GIOVANNI   If you would see a beauty more exact
Then Art can counterfit, or nature frame,
Looke in your glasse, and there behold your owne.

ANNABELLA   O you are a trime youth.

GIOVANNI   Here.   *Offers his Dagger to her.*

ANNABELLA   What to doe?

GIOVANNI   And here's my breast, strick home.   205
Rip up my bosome, there thou shalt behold
A heart, in which is writ the truth I speake.
Why stand 'ee?

ANNABELLA   Are you earnest?

GIOVANNI   Yes most earnest.
You cannot love?

ANNABELLA   Whom?

GIOVANNI   Me; my tortur'd soule
Hath felt affliction in the heat of Death.   210
O *Annabella* I am quite undone,   C1ᵛ
The love of thee (my sister) and the view
Of thy immortall beauty hath untun'd
All harmony both of my rest and life.
Why d'ee not strike?

ANNABELLA   Forbid it my just feares,   215
If this be true, 'twere fitter I were dead.

GIOVANNI   True, *Annabella?* 'tis no time to jest,
I have too long supprest the hidden flames
That almost have consum'd me; I have spent

205] *Weber;* Here. | What . . . doe? | And . . . home. *Q*   205 SD *his Dagger*] *Q; a dagger* |
Reed   205 doe?] *Dodsley;* ~. *Q*   205 strick] *Q;* strike *Dodsley*   208 Why . . . ear-
nest.] *Weber;* Why . . . earnest? | Yes earnest *Q*   205 Why . . . earnest?] *Weber, one line in Q;*
prose in Dodsley   208 'ee] *Q;* you *Dodsley;* ye *Dyce*   208 Yesₐ most earnest] *Q;* ~, ~ ~
Dodsley   209] *Weber;* You . . . Whom? | Me . . . soule *Q;* You . . . love? | Whom? | Me; . . .
soule] *Dodsley*   209 You . . . Whom?] *Weber, one line in Q*   209 love?] *Q;* ~. *Dodsley;*
~— *Roper*   209 Me; my] *this edn;* ~, ~ *Q;* ~. ~ *Dodsley* (My)   211 O *Annabella*] *Q;*
~, ~, *Dodsley* (Annabella)   211 undone,] *Q;* ~! *Dodsley*   213 beautyₐ] *Q;* ~,
Dodsley   213 hath] *Q;* have *Dodsley*   214 life.] *Dodsley;* ~, *Q*   215] *Weber;* Why .
. . strike? | Forbid . . . feares *Q*   215 d'ee] *Q;* do you *Dodsley;* d'ye *Dyce*   215 itₐ] *Q;* ~,
Dodsley   215 feares,] *Q;* ~! *Dodsley* (fears)   217 True, *Annabella?*] *Dodsley* (Annabella);
~ₐ ~; *Q;* ~, ~! *Reed*   217 jest,] *Q;* ~; *Dodsley;* ~. *Dyce*   218 the] *Q;* my *Dodsley*

Many a silent night in sighes and groanes,   220
Ran over all my thoughts, despis'd my Fate,
Reason'd against the reasons of my love,
Done all that smooth-cheeked Vertue could advise,
But found all bootelesse; 'tis my destiny,
That you must eyther love, or I must dye.   225

ANNABELLA   Comes this in sadnesse from you?

GIOVANNI   Let some mischiefe
Befall me soone, if I dissemble ought.

ANNABELLA   You are my brother *Giovanni*.

GIOVANNI   You,
My Sister *Annabella*; I know this:
And could afford you instance why to love   230
So much the more for this; to which intent
Wise Nature first in your Creation ment
To make you mine: else't had beene sinne and foule,
To share one beauty to a double soule.
Neerenesse in birth or blood, doth but perswade   235
A neerer neerenesse in affection.
I have askt Counsell of the holy Church,
Who tells mee I may love you, and 'tis just,
That since I may, I should; and will, yes will:
Must I now live, or dye?

ANNABELLA   Live, thou hast wonne   240
The field, and never fought; what thou hast urg'd,
My captive heart had long agoe resolv'd.
I blush to tell thee, (but I'le tell thee now)
C2ʳ   For every sigh that thou hast spent for me,
I have sigh'd ten; for every teare shed twenty: 245
And not so much for that I lov'd, as that
I durst not say I lov'd, nor scarcely thinke it.

220 groanes,] *Q*; ~; *Dodsley* (groans)   223 smooth-cheeked] *Dodsley*; smooth'd-cheeke *Q*
226] *after Weber*; Comes . . . you? | Let . . . mischiefe *Q*   226] *after Weber*; You . . .
Giovanni | You *Q*   228 brotherᴧ] *Q*; ~, *Dodsley*   228 You,] *Sherman*; ~ᴧ *Q*
229 Sisterᴧ] *Q*; ~, *Dodsley* (sister)   233 mine:] *Q*; ~; *Dodsley*   235 or] *Q*; and *Weber*
238 you,] *Q*; ~; *Dodsley*   238 just,] *Q*; ~. *Dodsley*   240] *Weber*; Must . . . dye? | Live . . .
wonne *Q*   240 Live,] *Q*; ~; *Dodsley*   245 teareᴧ shed] *Q*; ~, ~ *Reed*   247 lov'd,]
Dodsley; ~; *Q*

GIOVANNI   Let not this Musicke be a dreame (yee gods)
  For pitties sake I begge 'ee.

ANNABELLA   On my knees,   *Shee kneeles.*
  Brother, even by our Mothers dust, I charge you,   250
  Doe not betray mee to your mirth or hate,
  Love mee, or kill me Brother.

GIOVANNI   On my knees,   *He kneeles.*
  Sister, even by my Mothers dust, I charge you,
  Doe not betray mee to your mirth or hate,
  Love mee, or kill mee Sister.   255

ANNABELLA   You meane good sooth then?

GIOVANNI   In good troth I doe,
  And so doe you I hope: say, I'm in earnest.

ANNABELLA   I'le swear't and I.

GIOVANNI   And I, and by this kisse,   *Kisses her.*
  (Once more, yet once more, now let's rise, by this)
  I would not change this minute for *Elyzium*,   260
  What must we now doe?

ANNABELLA   What you will.

GIOVANNI   Come then,
  After so many teares as wee have wept,
  Let's learne to court in smiles. to kisse and sleepe.

                                              Exeunt.

249] *Weber;* For . . . 'ee. | On . . . knees, *Q*   249 pitties sake] *this edn;* pitties-sake *Q;* pity's sake *Dodsley*   249 'ee] *Q;* ye *Dodsley*   249 SD *Shee kneels.*] *Q; Wiggins places after* 'ee. 251 hate,] *Q;* ~; *Dodsley;* ~: *Dyce*   252] *Weber;* Love . . . Brother. | On . . . knees. *Q* 252 SD *He kneels.*] *Q; Wiggins places after* Brother.   253 dust,] *Dyce;* ~ʌ *Q*   254 hate,] *Q;* ~; *Dodsley*   256] *Weber;* You . . . then? | In . . . doe. *Q*   257 youʌ] *Q;* ~, *Dodsley* 258] *Weber;* I'le . . . I. | And . . . kisse, *Q*   258 swear't ʌ and I] *Q;* swear it, ~ ~ *Dodsley;* ~, I *Gifford* ('and' *omitted*); swear it, I *Dyce* ('and' *omitted*)   258 kisse,] *Q;* ~,— *Dyce;* ~— *Roper* (kiss)   259] *Wiggins adds* SD1 [*Kisses her*] *after* Once more,   259] *Wiggins adds* SD2 [*Kisses her*] *after* yet once more.   259 yet once more,] *Q;* ~ ~ ~; *Reed*   259 rise, by this)] *Q;* ~) ~ ~ *Weber*   259] *Q; Gifford adds* SD [*they rise.*] *between* 'rise)' *and* 'by'; *Wiggins,* SD [*They rise*] *after* this; *Massai,* SD [*Kisses her and they rise.*] *after* 'this'. 261] *Weber;* What . . . doe? | What you . . . then, *Q;* What . . . doe? | What you will. | Come then,] *Dodsley*

1.3   *Enter* FLORIO *and* DONADO.

FLORIO   *Signior Donado*, you have sayd enough,
I understand you, but would have you know,
I will not force my Daughter 'gainst her will.
You see I have but two, a Sonne and Her;
And hee is so devoted to his Booke,   5
As I must tell you true, I doubt his health:
Should he miscarry, all my hopes rely
Upon my Girle; as for worldly Fortune,
I am, I thanke my Starres, blest with enough:
My Care is how to match her to her liking,   10
I would not have her marry Wealth, but Love,
C2ᵛ   And if she like your Nephew, let him have her,
Here's all that I can say.

DONADO   Sir you say well,
Like a true father, and for my part, I,
If the young folkes can like, (twixt you and me)   15
Will promise to assure my Nephew presently,
Three thousand *Florrens* yeerely during life,
And after I am dead, my whole estate.

FLORIO   'Tis a faire proffer sir, meane time your Nephew
Shall have free passage to commence his suite;   20
If hee can thrive, hee shall have my consent,
So for this time I'le leave you *Signior*.

                                                    Exit.

DONADO   Well,
Here's hope yet, if my Nephew would have wit,
But hee is such another Dunce, I feare
Hee'le never winne the Wench; when I was young   25
I could have done't yfaith, and so shall hee

1.3] *this edn; not in* Q; SCENE III. –*An Apartment in* Florio's *House.* | *Weber,* SCENE IV. *A Street.* | *Gifford, Dyce;* [1.3] *Massai*   1 enough,] Q; ~; *Dodsley*   8 Girle; as] Q; ~. ~ *Dodsley* (girl) (As)   9 am,] *Dodsley,* ~∧ Q   9 enough:] Q; ~. *Dodsley*   10 liking,] Q; ~; *Dodsley,* ~: *Dyce*   12 her,] Q; ~; *Dodsley*   13] *Weber,* Here's . . . say. | Sir . . . well, Q   13 Sir∧] Q; ~, *Dodsley*   14 father,] Q; ~; *Dodsley*   14 I,] *Dodsley,* ~∧ Q   16 presently,] Q; ~∧ *Dodsley*   17 *Florrens*] Q; florins *Massai*   17 yeerely∧] Q; ~, *Reed* (yearly)   19 proffer sir,] Q; ~, ~; *Dodsley*   19 meane time] Q; meantime *Reed*   21 consent,] Q; ~. *Dodsley*   22] *Weber,* So . . . *Signior.* | Well, Q   22 you∧] Q; ~, *Dodsley*   23 wit,] Q; ~; *Dodsley*   25 Wench; when] Q; ~. ~ *Dodsley* (wench) (When)   26 done't∧ yfaith] Q; ~, ~ *Dodsley* (ifaith)   26 hee∧] Q; ~, *Dodsley* (he)

If hee will learne of mee; and in good time
Hee comes himselfe.

Enter BERGETTO *and* POGGIO.

How now *Bergetto*, whether away so fast?

BERGETTO   Oh Unckle, I have heard the strangest newes that   30
ever came out of the Mynt, have I not *Poggio*?

POGGIO   Yes indeede Sir.

DONADO   What newes *Bergetto*?

BERGETTO   Why looke yee Unkle! my Barber told me just
now that there is a fellow come to Towne, who undertakes   35
to make a Mill goe without the mortall helpe of any water
or winde, onely with Sand-bags: and this fellow hath a
strange Horse, a most excellent beast, I'le assure you
Unkle, (my Barber sayes) whose head to the wonder of all
Christian people, stands just behind where his tayle is, is't   40
not true *Poggio*?

POGGIO   So the Barber swore forsooth.

DONADO   And you are running thither?

BERGETTO   I, forsooth, Unkle.

DONADO   Wilt thou be a Foole stil? come sir, you shall not goe,   45
you have more mind of a Puppet-play, then on the businesse
I told y'ee: why thou great Baby, wu't never have wit, wu't
make thy selfe a May-game to all the world?

POGGIO   Answere for your selfe Maister.   C3ʳ

27 mee; and∧] *Q*; ~; ~, *Dyce*   28.1 SD *Enter* BERGETTO *and* POGGIO.] *Q*; *Wiggins places*
SD *after* mee 27.   29] *Q gives this line to* Poggio.   29 now∧] *Q*; ~, *Dodsley*
31 Mynt,] *Q*; ~! *Dodsley* (mint)   31 not∧] *Q*; ~, *Dodsley*   32–3] *one line in Q*
32 indeede∧] *Q*; ~, *Dodsley* (indeed)   33 newes∧] *Q*; ~, *Dodsley* (news)   34 Unkle!] *this*
edn; ~, *Dodsley* (uncle); ~? *Q* (Vnkle)   37 Sand-bags:] *Q*; ~; *Dodsley* (sand-bags); ~! *Roper*
(sand-bags)   38 you∧] *Q*; ~, *Dodsley*   39 head∧] *Q*; ~, *Dodsley*   40 is, is't] *Q*; ~. ~
Dodsley (Is't); ~.—~ *Dyce*; ~—~ *Roper*   41 true∧] *Q*; ~, *Dodsley*   42 swore∧] *Q*; ~,
Dodsley   43–4] *Dodsley, one line in Q*   43 thither] *Gifford*; hither *Q*   44 I, forsooth, Unkle] *Dodsley* (Ay); ~∧ ~∧ *Q*   45 come∧] *Q*; ~, *Dodsley*   46 Puppet-play,] *Q*;
~∧ *Dodsley* (puppet-play)   47 y'ee] *Q*; you *Dodsley*; ye *Dyce*   47 why∧] *Q*; ~, *Dodsley*
47 Baby, wu't] *Q*; ~, will't *Dodsley* (baby); ~, wilt *Weber*; ~, wouldst *Massai*   47 wit, wu't]
Q; ~, will't *Dodsley*; ~? Wilt *Weber*; ~, woudst *Massai*   49 your selfe∧] *Q*; ~, *Dodsley* (yourself)

BERGETTO   Why Unkle, shu'd I sit at home still, and not goe   50
abroad to see fashions like other gallants?

DONADO   To see hobby-horses: what wise talke I pray had you
with *Annabella*, when you were at *Signior Florio's* house?

BERGETTO   Oh the wench: uds sa'me, Unkle, I tickled her with a
rare speech, that I made her almost burst her belly with laughing.   55

DONADO   Nay I thinke so, and what speech was't?

BERGETTO   What did I say *Poggio*?

POGGIO   Forsooth my Maister said, that hee loved her almost
aswell as he loved Parmasent, and swore (I'le be sworne for
him) that shee wanted but such a Nose as his was, to be as   60
pretty a young woeman, as any was in *Parma*.

DONADO   Oh grose!

BERGETTO   Nay Unkle, then shee ask't mee, whether my Father
had any more children then my selfe: and I sayd no, 'twere
better hee should have had his braynes knockt out first.   65

DONADO   This is intolerable.

BERGETTO   Then sayd shee, will *Signior Donado* your Unkle
leave you all his wealth?

DONADO   Ha! that was good, did she harpe upon that string?

BERGETTO   Did she harpe upon that string, I, that she did: 70
I answered, leave me all his wealth? why woeman, hee hath
no other wit, if hee had, he should heare on't to his
everlasting glory and confusion: I know (quoth I) I am his

51 to see fashions] *Q*; *not in Weber*   51 fashions∧] *Q*; ~, *Dodsley*   52 hobby-horses:
what] *Q*; ~! ~ *Roper* (What)   52 talke∧ I pray∧] *Q*; ~, ~ ~, *Dodsley* (talk)   56 Nay∧]
Q; ~, *Dodsley*   57 say∧] *Q*; ~, *Dodsley*   58 Forsooth∧] *Q*; ~, *Dodsley*   59 aswell]
this edn; as-well *Q*; as well *Dodsley*   60 was,] *Q*; ~∧ *Dodsley*   61 young . . . *Parma* |
SP DONADO Oh grose!] *Dodsley, one line in Q*   61 woeman,] *Q*; ~∧ *Dodsley* (woman)
63 Nay∧] *Q*; ~, *Dodsley*   64 my selfe:] *Q*; ~? *Dodsley* (myself); ~; *Dyce*   67 Donado∧]
Q; ~, *Dodsley* (Donado)   67 Unkle∧] *Q*; ~, *Dodsley* (uncle)   70 string, I,] *this edn*; ~,
~∧ *Q*; ~? ~, *Dodsley* (Ay); ~! Ay∧ *Dyce*   72 wit] *Q*; will *Dodsley*   73 confusion:] *Q*; ~.
Dodsley, ~; *Roper*

white boy, and will not be guld: and with that she fell into a
great smile, and went away. Nay I did fit her.   75

DONADO   Ah sirrah, then I see there is no changing of nature,
Well *Bergetto*, I feare thou wilt be a very Asse still.

BERGETTO   I should be sorry for that Unkle.

DONADO   Come, come you home with me, since you are no
better a speaker, I'le have you write to her after some courtly   80
manner, and inclose some rich Jewell in the Letter.

BERGETTO   I, marry, that will be excellent.

DONADO   Peace Innocent,
Once in my time I'le set my wits to schoole,
If all faile, 'tis but the fortune of a foole.   85

BERGETTO   *Poggio*, 'twill doe *Poggio*.   *Exeunt.*   C3ᵛ

2.1   *Enter* GIOVANNI *and* ANNABELLA, *as from their Chamber.*

GIOVANNI   Come *Annabella*, no more Sister now,
But Love; a name more Gracious, doe not blush,
(Beauties sweete wonder) but be proud, to know
That yeelding thou hast conquer'd, and inflam'd
A heart whose tribute is thy brothers life.   5

ANNABELLA   And mine is his, oh how these stolne contents
Would print a modest Crymson on my cheekes,
Had any but my hearts delight prevail'd.

GIOVANNI   I marvaile why the chaster of your sex
Should thinke this pretty toye call'd *Maiden-head*,   10
So strange a losse, when being lost, 'tis nothing,
And you are still the same.

ANNABELLA   'Tis well for you,
Now you can talke.

75 Nay∧] Q; ~, Dodsley   76–7] Q; prose in Weber   76 Ah∧] Q; ~,
Dodsley   76 nature,] Q; ~: Dodsley; ~. Weber; ~; Roper   77 Well∧] Q; ~,
Dodsley   78 that∧] Q; ~, Dodsley   78 I,] this edn; ~∧ Q; Ay∧ Dodsley   83 Peace∧]
Q; ~, Dodsley   86 doe∧] Q; ~, Dodsley (do)   2.1] this edn; Actus Secundus. Q;
SCENE I. —An Apartment in the same. | Weber; SCENE I.—An Apartment in FLORIO'S House. |
Dyce; 2[.1] Massai   1 Come∧] Q; ~, Dodsley   12] Dyce; one line in Q

GIOVANNI   Musicke as well consists
In th'eare, as in the playing.

ANNABELLA   Oh y'are wanton,
Tell on't, y'are best, doe.

GIOVANNII   Thou wilt chide me then,   15
Kisse me, so; thus hung *Jove* on *Laeda's* necke,
And suck't divine *Ambrosia* from her lips:
I envy not the mightiest man alive,
But hold my selfe in being King of thee,
More great, then were I King of all the world: 20
But I shall lose you *Sweet-heart.*

ANNABELLA   But you shall not.

GIOVANNI   You must be married Mistres.

ANNABELLA   Yes, to whome?

GIOVANNI   Some one must have you.

ANNABELLA   You must.

GIOVANNI   Nay some other.

ANNABELLA   Now prithee do not speake so, without jesting
You'le make mee weepe in earnest.

GIOVANNI   What, you will not.   25
But tell me sweete, can'st thou be dar'd to sweare
That thou wilt live to mee, and to no other?

ANNABELLA   By both our loves I dare, for didst thou know
My Giovanni how all suiters seeme
C4ʳ   To my eyes hatefull, thou wouldst trust mee then.   30

GIOVANNI   Enough, I take thy word; Sweete, we must part,
Remember what thou vow'st, keepe well my heart.

13] *Weber, one line in Q*   14] *Weber, one line in Q*   14 y'are] *Q;* you're *Dodsley;* your
Weber   14] *Weber,* Tell . . . doe! | Thou . . . then, *Q*   14 y'are] *Q;* you're *Dodsley;* you
were *Gifford*   15 then,] *Q;* ~. *Dodsley;* ~? *Roper*   16] *Wiggins adds SD [They kiss.]
after* me.   21–2 But you . . . not | You . . . Mistres] *Weber, one line in Q*   22–3 Yes . . .
whom? | Some . . . you] *Dodsley, one line in Q*   23 You must. Nay . . . other.] *Dodsley, one
line in Q*   24 so, without jesting∧] *Q;* ~, ~ ~. *Dodsley;* ~; ~ ~∧ *Gifford;* ~: ~ ~∧ *Dyce;* ~ ~ ~;
Roper   25] *Weber;* You'le . . . earnest. | What . . . not. *Q*   25 What,] *Dodsley;* ~∧ *Q*
26 me∧] *Q;* ~, *Dodsley*   31 Sweete,] *Weber* (sweet); ~∧ *Q*

ANNABELLA   Will you be gon?

GIOVANNI   I must.

ANNABELLA   When to returne?

GIOVANNII   Soone.

ANNABELLA   Looke you doe.

GIOVANNI   Farewell.

Exit.

ANNABELLA   Goe where thou wilt, in mind I'le keepe thee here,   35
And where thou art, I know I shall be there. *Guardian!*

Enter PUTANA.

PUTANA   Child, how is't child? well, thanke Heaven, ha!

ANNABELLA   O *Guardian*, what a Paradise of joy
Have I past over!

PUTANA   Nay what a Paradise of joy have you past under?   40
why now, I commend thee (*Chardge*) feare nothing,
(sweeteheart) what though hee be your Brother; your
Brother's a man I hope, and I say still, if a young Wench
feele the fitt upon her, let her take any body, Father or
Brother, all is one.   45

ANNABELLA   I would not have it knowne for all the world.

PUTANA   Nor I indeed, for the speech of the people; else 'twere
nothing.

FLORIO   (*within*) Daughter *Annabella.*

ANNABELLA   O mee! my Father,—here Sir,—reach my worke.   50

33 Will . . . gone? I must] *Weber, one line in Q;* Will . . . gone? | I must *Dyce*   34 When . . .
returne? Soon.] *Dyce, one line in Q*   34 Looke . . . doe. Farewll] *Weber, one line in Q*
34 SD *Exit.*] *Q; Dyce places* SD [*Exit Gio.* | *after* there. 36.   36 there.] *Dodsley;* ~∧ *Q*
36 *Guardian!*] *Dodsley* (Guardian); ~. *Q*   36] *Massai adds* SD [*Calls.*] *before* 'Guardian!'
40 Nay . . . under? why] *Dodsley,* Nay . . . under? | why *Q*   41 now,] *Dodsley,* ~∧ *Q*
42 though] *Q;* tho' *Dodsley*   43 hope,] *Q;* ~; *Dodsley*   49 SD (*within*)] *Weber,*∧~∧
Q; ~ — *Dodsley;* [~ | *Dyce*   50 Father,—here] *Q;* ~! ~ *Wiggins* (Here)   50] *Wiggins
adds* SD1 [*Calls off-stage*] *before* here; *Massai,* SD1 [*to Florio*] *before* here.   50] *Lomax adds*
SD [*To Putana*] *after* Sir; *Massai,* SD 2 [*to Puttana*]   50] *Wiggins adds* SD [PUTANA *passes
her a needlework*] *after* worke.

FLORIO   (*within*) What are you doeing?

ANNABELLA   So, let him come now.

Enter FLORIO, RICHARDETTO, *like a Doctor of Phisicke,
and* PHILOTIS *with a Lute in her hand.*

Florio So hard at worke, that's well; you lose no time,
Looke, I have brought you company, here's one,
A learned Doctor, lately come from *Padua*,
Much skild in Physicke, and for that I see   55
You have of late beene sickly, I entreated
This reverend man to visit you some time.

ANNABELLA   Y'are very welcome Sir.

RICHARDETTO   I thanke you Mistresse,
Loud Fame in large report hath spoke your praise,
Aswell for Vertue as perfection: 60
For which I have beene bold to bring with mee
A Kins-woeman of mine, a maide, for song
And musicke, one perhaps will give content,
Please you to know her.

ANNABELLA   They are parts I love,
And shee for them most welcome.

PHILOTIS   Thanke you Lady.   65

FLORIO   Sir now you know my house, pray make not strange,
And if you finde my Daughter neede your Art,
I'le be your pay-master.

RICHARDETTO   Sir, what I am
Shee shall command.

FLORIO   You shall bind me to you,
Daughter, I must have conference with you,   70

C4ᵛ is printed in the left margin beside line 62–63.

51] *Dyce; one line in* Q; What . . . doeing? | So, . . . now *Weber*
Q; —— *Dodsley*, [~ | *Dyce*   51 now.] *Dodsley*, ~, Q
52 worke,] Q; ~! *Dodsley* (work)   56 sickly,] Q; ~; *Dodsley*
ent Q   58] *Weber*, Y'are . . . Sir. | I . . . Mistresse, Q
59 youₐ] Q; ~, *Dodsley*   60 Aswell] Q; As well *Dodsley*
woman *Dodsley*   62 songₐ] *Dodsley*, ~, Q   64–5] *Weber*, Please . . . her. | They . . .
love, | And . . . welcome. | Thanke . . . Lady. Q   64 her.] Q; ~? *Dodsley*   65 youₐ] Q;
~, *Dodsley*   66 Sirₐ] Q; ~, *Dodsley*   68–9] *Weber*, I'le . . . pay-master. | Sir, . . .
Command. | You . . . you. Q   68 pay-master] Q; paymaster *Bawcutt*   69] *Dyce adds*
'[Sir]' *before* You.
51 SD (*within*)] *Weber*, ^~^.
52–7] *Weber*, *prose in* Q
57 reverend] *Reed*; rever-
58 Y'are] Q; You're *Weber*
62 Kins-woeman] Q; kins-

About some matters that concernes us both.
Good Maister Doctor, please you but walke in,
Wee'le crave a little of your Cozens cunning:
I thinke my Girle hath not quite forgot
To touch an Instrument, she could have don't,   75
Wee'le heare them both.

RICHARDETTO   I'le waite upon you sir.   *Exeunt.*

   2.2   *Enter* SORANZO *in his study reading a Booke*

SORANZO   *Loves measure is extreame, the comfort, paine:*
The life unrest, and the reward disdaine.
What's here? lookt o're againe, 'tis so, so writes
This smooth licentious Poet in his rymes.
But *Sannazar* thou lyest, for had thy bosome   5
Felt such oppression as is laid on mine,
Thou wouldst have kist the rod that made the smart.
To worke then, happy Muse, and contradict
What *Sannazar* hath in his envy writ.
Loves measure is the meane, sweet his annoyes,   10
His pleasures life, and his reward all joyes.
Had *Annabella* liv'd when *Sannazar*
Did in his briefe *Encomium* celebrate
Venice that Queene of Citties, he had left
That Verse which gaind him such a sume of Gold,   15
And for one onely looke from *Annabell*
Had writ of her, and her diviner cheekes,
O how my thoughts are—

VASQUES   (*within*) Pray forbeare, in rules of Civility, let me give
notice on't: I shall be tax't of my neglect of duty and service.   20   D1ʳ

---

71 concernes] *Q*; concern *Weber*   73–6] *Weber*; Wee'le . . . both. | I'le . . . sir. *Q*
76 youₐ] *Q*; ~, *Dodsley*   2.2] *this edn*; *not in Q, Dodsley*; SCENE II.—Study in the House
of SORANZO. *Weber*; SCENE II.—*A room in* SORANZO's *house.* | *Dyce*; [2.2] *Massai*   0.1 SD]
Q; *Enter* SORANZO, *reading a book.* | *Weber*   1 SP SORANZO] *Ellis*; *not in Q, Dyce places*
SD [*Reads.*] *after* SP SORANZO.   3–4] *so Q*; *roman with quotation marks in Dyce*
3 lookt] *Q*; look *Hopkins*   3 againe, 'tis so,] *Q*; ~; ~ ~, *Dodsley* (again); ~. ~ ~; *Reed* (again)
('Tis)   5 *Sannazar*] *Dyce*; *Sanazar Q*   5 lyest, forₐ] *Q*; ~; ~, *Reed*   7 the smart]
Q; thee smart *Dodsley*   8 then,] *Dodsley*; ~ ₐ *Q*   9] *Gifford adds* SD [*Writes.*] *after*
writ.   10–11] *so Q*; *roman with quotation marks in Dyce*   11 pleasures] *Q*; pleasure's
Dodsley   13 *Encomium*] *Reed* (Encomium); *Eucomium Q*   14 *Venice*ₐ] *Q*; ~, *Dodsley*
(Venice)   19 SD (*within*)] *Weber*; ₐ~ₐ— *Q*; ~~ *Dodsley*; [*Within* | *Dyce*   19 for-
beare,] *Q*; ~: *Reed* (forbear); ~; *Dyce*

SORANZO What rude intrusion interrupts my peace,
 Can I be no where private?

VASQUES (*within*) Troth you wrong your modesty.

SORANZO What's the matter *Vasques*, who is't?

  Enter HIPPOLITA [*wearing mourning*] *and* VASQUES.

HIPPOLITA 'Tis I: 25
 Doe you know mee now? looke perjurd man on her
 Whom thou and thy distracted lust have wrong'd,
 Thy sensuall rage of blood hath made my youth
 A scorne to men and Angels, and shall I
 Be now a foyle to thy unsated change?   30
 Thou knowst (false wanton) when my modest fame
 Stood free from staine or scandall, all the charmes
 Of Hell or sorcery could not prevaile
 Against the honour of my chaster bosome.
 Thyne eyes did pleade in teares, thy tongue in oaths, 35
 Such and so many, that a heart of steele
 Would have beene wrought to pitty, as was mine:
 And shall the Conquest of my lawfull bed,
 My husbands death urg'd on by his disgrace,
 My losse of woeman-hood be ill rewarded   40
 With hatred and contempt? No, know *Soranzo*,
 I have a spirit doth as much distast
 The slavery of fearing thee, as thou
 Dost loath the memory of what hath past.

SORANZO Nay deare *Hippolita*.

HIPPOLITA   Call me not deare, 45
 Nor thinke with supple words to smooth the grosenesse
 Of my abuses; 'tis not your new Mistresse,
 Your goodly *Madame Merchant* shall triumph

---

21 peace,] *Q*; ~? *Dodsley* 23 SD (*within*)] *Weber* ; ∧~∧.*Q*; ~— *Dodsley*, [*Within* | *Dyce*
23 Troth∧] *Q*; ~, *Weber* (Truth) 24 *Vasques*,] *Q*; ~? *Reed* (Vasques) 24.1 SD
[*wearing mourning*]] *this edn*; *not in Q*; [*dressed in black*] *Wiggins* 24–5 What's . . . is't? |
'Tis I] *Q*; *verse in Weber* 26 looke∧] *Q*; ~, *Dodsley* (looke) 26 ma∧] *Q*; ~, *Dodsley*
27 wrong'd,] *Q*; ~; *Dodsley*; ~. *Dyce* (wronged) 29 Angels,] *Q*; ~; *Dodsley* (angels)
32 staine∧] *Reed*; ~, *Q* 35 oaths,] *Dodsley*; ~∧*Q* 40 woeman-hood∧] *Q*; ~, *Reed*
(womanhood) 45] *Weber*, Nay . . . *Hippolita*. | Call . . . deare. *Q* 45 *Hippolita*.] *Q*;
~! *Dodsley* (Hippolita); ~— *Gifford* (Hippolita); ~,— *Dyce*

On my dejection; tell her thus from mee,
My byrth was Nobler, and by much more Free.   50

SORANZO   You are too violent.

HIPPOLITA   You are too double
In your dissimulation; see'st thou this,
This habit, these blacke mourning weedes of Care?
'Tis thou art cause of this, and hast divorc't   D1ᵛ
My husband from his life and me from him,   55
And made me Widdow in my widow-hood.

SORANZO   Will you yet heare?

HIPPOLITA   More of thy perjuries?
Thy soule is drown'd too deeply in those sinnes,
Thou need'st not add to th' number.

SORANZO   Then I'le leave you,
You are past all rules of sence.

HIPPOLITA   And thou of grace.   60

VASQUES   Fy Mistresse, you are not neere the limits of reason; if
my Lord had a resolution as noble as Vertue it selfe, you take
the course to unedge it all. Sir, I beseech you doe not perplexe
her; griefes (alas) will have a vent; I dare undertake Madam
Hippolita will now freely heare you.   65

SORANZO   Talke to a woman frantick, are these the fruits of your
love?

HIPPOLITA   They are the fruites of thy untruth, false man,
Didst thou not sweare, whil'st yet my husband liv'd,
That thou wouldst wish no happinesse on earth
More then to call me wife? didst thou not vow   70
When hee should dye to marry mee? for which
The Devill in my blood, and thy protests

49 dejection] *Q*; defection *Dodsley*   49 mee,] *Q*; ~: *Reed* (me)   51] *Weber*; You . . .
violent | You . . . double *Q*   52 dissimulation; see'st] *this edn*; ~, ~ *Q*; ~. ~ *Dodsley*
(Seest)   53 Care?] *Dodsley* (care); ~ₐ*Q*   57] *Weber*; Will . . . heare? | More . . . perju-
ries? *Q*   57 thy] *Q* (corrected); the *Q* (uncorrected)   58 sinnes,] *Q*; ~; *Dodsley*
(sins)   59–60] *Weber*; Thou . . . number. | Then . . . you, | You . . . sence. | And . . . grace.
Q   59 you,] *Q*; ~; *Dodsley*   60 sence] *Q*; sense *Dodsley*   61 reason;] *Dodsley*; ~ₐ
Q; ~: *Dyce*   63 Sir,] *Dodsley*; ~ₐ*Q*   64 her;] *Dodsley*; ~, *Q*   64 vent;] *Dodsley*; ~,
Q; ~: *Dyce*   66 frantick, are] *Q*; ~!—~ *Reed* (Are)   67 man,] *Q*; ~? *Dodsley*; ~! *Reed*

Caus'd mee to Counsaile him to undertake
A voyage to *Ligorne*, for that we heard,
His Brother there was dead, and left a Daughter   75
Young and unfriended, who with much adoe
I wish't him to bring hither; hee did so,
And went; and as thou know'st dyed on the way.
Unhappy man to buy his death so deare
With my advice; yet thou for whom I did it,   80
Forget'st thy vowes, and leav'st me to my shame.

SORANZO   Who could helpe this?

HIPPOLITA   Who? perjur'd man thou couldst,
   If thou hadst faith or love.

SORANZO   You are deceiv'd,
   The vowes I made, (if you remember well)
   Were wicked and unlawfull; 'twere more sinne   85
D2ʳ To keepe them, then to breake them; as for mee
   I cannot maske my penitence; thinke thou
   How much thou hast digrest from honest shame,
   In bringing of a gentleman to death
   Who was thy husband, such a one as hee,   90
   So noble in his quality, condition,
   Learning, behaviour, entertainment, love,
   As *Parma* could not shew a braver man.

VASQUES   You doe not well; this was not your promise.

SORANZO   I care not; let her know her monstrous life,   95
   Ere I'le be servile to so blacke a sinne,
   I'le be a Coarse; woeman, come here no more,
   Learne to repent and dye; for by my honour
   I hate thee and thy lust; you have beene too foule.   [*Exit.*

VASQUES   This part has beene scurvily playd.   100

74 *Ligorne*] *Q*; Leghorn *Dodsley*   77 hither;] *Q*; ~: *Dyce*   80 advice;] *Q*; ~! *Reed*
82–3] *Weber*; Who . . . this? | Who? . . . couldst, | If . . . love. | You . . . deceiv'd, *Q*   85 unlaw-
full;] *Reed*; ~, *Q*   86 them,] *Q*; ~: *Reed*   87 penitence; thinke] *this edn*; ~, ~ *Q*; ~. ~
Reed (Think)   94 well;] *Reed*; ~, *Q*   95 not;] *Reed*; ~, *Q*   96 I'le be] *Q*; I ~
Dodsley ("le' *omitted*)   97 a Coarse] *Q* (uncorrected); ~ Curse *Q* (corrected); ~ curse
Dodsley, accurs'd *Bawcutt*, conj. *Schmitz*; ~ corse *Roper*, accursed *Massai*   99 SD [*Exit.*]]
Dyce; Exit Soranzo. | *Dodsley*, not in *Q*   100] *Dyce adds* SD [*aside*] *before* This; *Gifford*, SD
[*Aside.*] *after* playd.

HIPPOLITA   How foolishly this beast contemnes his Fate,
And shuns the use of that, which I more scorne
Then I once lov'd, his love; but let him goe,
My vengeance shall give comfort to his woe.

She offers to goe away.

VASQUES   Mistresse, Mistresse, Madam *Hippolita*, Pray a word   105
or two.

HIPPOLITA   With mee Sir?

VASQUES   With you if you please.

HIPPOLITA   What is't?

VASQUES   I know you are infinitely mov'd now, and you thinke   110
you have cause; some I confesse you have, but sure not so
much as you imagine.

HIPPOLITA   Indeed.

VASQUES   O you were miserably bitter, which you followed even
to the last sillable; Faith you were somewhat too shrewd, by   115
my life you could not have tooke my Lord in a worse time,
since I first knew him: to morrow you shall finde him a new man.

HIPPOLITA   Well, I shall waite his leasure.

VASQUES   Fie, this is not a hearty patience; it comes sowerly from
you; troth let me perswade you for once.   120

HIPPOLITA   [*Aside*] I have it and it shall be so; thanks opportunity!
——[*Aloud*] Perswade me to what?——

103 lov'd,] *Weber;* ~; *Reed;* ~ˌ *Q*   104 his] *Q;* this *Shcmitz*   104 SD *She offers to goe away.*] *Q,* set against lines 103–4 in two lines, [*Going.* | *Weber, She starts to go away.* | *Hopkins*
105 Mistresse, Madam] *Q* ('mistresse' corrected); ~ˌ ~ *Q* (uncorrected)   105–6] *Weber,*
Mistresse, . . . Hippolita | Pray . . . two. *Q*   105–7 Pray . . . or | two. | With . . . Sir?] *Weber,*
one line in Q   108–9] *Dodsley, one line in Q*   108 yoˌ] *Q;* ~, *Dodsley*   III cause;]
Dodsley; ~, *Q;* ~: *Dyce*   112–13 as . . . imagine. | Indeed.] *Dodsley, one line in Q*
113 Indeed.] *Q;* ~! *Dodsley*   115 sillable;] *Q;* ~: *Dodsley* (syllable)   115 Faith] *Q;* 'faith
Weber   115 shrewd,] *Q;* ~; *Dodsley;* ~: *Dyce*   117 I first] *Q;* first I *Dodsley*   117 to
morrow] *Q;* to-morrow *Reed*   117–18 man. | Well . . . leasure.] *Dodsley, one line in Q*
119 patience;] *Dodsley;* ~, *Q*   120 you; troth,] *Dodsley;* ~, ~ˌ *Q;* ~; 'troth *Weber,* ~: ~, *Dyce*
121 SD [*Aside*]] *Dyce; not in Q; Dodsley places* SD [*Aside*] *after* opportunity.   121 opportunity!] *Dyce;* ~ˌ *Q;* —— *Dodsley*   122 SD [*Aloud*]] *Roper, not in Q;* [*To him*] *Lomax; Bawcutt
places* SD [*To him*] *after* opportunity 121.   122 Perswade] *Weber* (Persuade); perswade *Q*
122 meˌ] *Q;* ~! *Gifford*

VASQUES   Visit him in some milder temper. O if you could but
master a little your female spleene, how might you winne him!

HIPPOLITA   Hee wil never love me: *Vasques*, thou hast beene a   125
too trusty servant to such a master, and I beleeve thy reward
D2ᵛ   in the end wil fal-| out like mine.

VASQUES   So perhaps too.

HIPPOLITA   Resolve thy selfe it will; had I one so true, so truly
honest, so secret to my Counsels, as thou hast beene to him   130
and his, I should thinke it a slight acquittance, not onely to
make him Maister of all I have, but even of my selfe.

VASQUES   O you are a noble Gentlewoman.

HIPPOLITA   Wu't thou feede alwayes upon hopes? well, I know
thou art wise, and see'st the reward of an old servant daily   135
what it is.

VASQUES   Beggery and neglect.

HIPPOLITA   True, but *Vasques*, wer't thou mine, and wouldst
bee private to me and my designes; I here protest my selfe,
and all what I can else call myne, should be at thy dispose.   140

VASQUES   [*Aside*] Worke you that way old moule? then I have
the wind of you—[*Aloud*] I were not worthy of it, by any
desert that could lye within my compasse; if I could—

HIPPOLITA   What then?

VASQUES   I should then hope to live in these my old yeares with   145
rest and security.

HIPPOLITA   Give me thy hand, now promise but thy silence,
And helpe to bring to passe a plot I have;
And here in sight of Heaven, (that being done).
I make thee Lord of mee and mine estate.   150

---

123 temper.] *Dodsley*, ~, *Q*   124 female] *Dodsley*, femall *Q*   127–8 out . . . mine. | So . . .
too.] *Dodsley*; *one line in Q*   134 Wu't] *Q*; Wilt *Dodsley*; Wou't *Roper*; Woudst *Massai*
136–7 it is. | Beggery . . . neglect.] *Dodsley*; *one line in Q*   141 SD [*Aside*]] *Dyce* [*aside*];
not in Q; *Weber places* SD [*Aside*] *after* you.   142 SD [*Aloud*]] *this edn*; [*Aside*.] *Dodsley*,
[*To her*] *Bawcutt*; *not in Q*   143 lye within] *Dyce* (lie); ~—~ *Q*   147 hand,] *Q*; ~;
Dodsley, ~: *Reed*

VASQUES   Come you are merry, this is such a happinesse that I
 can neither thinke or beleeve.

HIPPOLITA   Promise thy secresie, and 'tis confirm'd.

VASQUES   Then here I call our good *Genii* forwitnesses,
 whatsoever your designes are, or against whomsoever, I will   155
 not onely be a speciall actor therein, but never disclose it till
 it be effected.

HIPPOLITA   I take thy word, and with that, thee for mine:
 Come then, let's more conferre of this anon.
 On this delicious bane my thoughts shall banquet,   160
 Revenge shall sweeten what my griefes have tasted.   *Exeunt.*

2.3 *Enter* RICHARDETTO *and* PHILOTIS.

RICHARDETTO   Thou see'st (my lovely Neece) these strange mishaps,
 How all my fortunes turne to my disgrace,
 Wherein I am but as a looker on,   D3r
 Whiles others act my shame, and I am silent.

PHILOTIS   But Unkle, wherein can this borrowed shape   5
 Give you content?

RICHARDETTO   I'le tell thee gentle Neece,
 Thy wanton Aunt in her lascivious riots
 Lives now secure, thinkes I am surely dead
 In my late Journey to *Ligorne* for you;
 (As I have caus'd it to be rumord out)   10
 Now would I see with what an impudence
 Shee gives scope to her loose adultery
 And how the Common voyce allowes hereof:
 Thus farre I have prevail'd.

151–2] *Weber,* Come . . . merry | This . . . can | Neither . . . belieue. *Q*   151 Come∧] *Q;* ~,
Dodsley   151 merry,] *this edn;* ~∧ *Q;* ~; *Dyce;* ~. *Reed*   154 *Genii*] *Dodsley,* Genij *Q*
154 forwitnesses] *Dyce;* foe-witnesses *Q;* for-witnesses *Sherman;* for ~ *Dodsley*   159 anon.]
Q; ~.— *Gifford*   161 SD Exeunt.] *Q;* *Aside, and exit with* VAS. *Gifford*   **2.3**] *this edn;*
not in Q; SCENE III.—*The Street.* | *Weber, Dyce;* [2.3] *Massai*   6] *Weber,* Give . . . content?
| I'le . . . Neece, *Q*   9 *Ligorne*] *Q;* Leghorn *Dodsley*   10 (As . . . out)] *Q;* ~ . . . ~,
Dodsley

PHILOTIS   Alas, I feare
You meane some strange revenge.

RICHARDETTO   O be not troubled,   15
Your ignorance shall pleade for you in all,
But to our businesse; what, you learnt for certaine
How *Signior Florio* meanes to give his Daughter
In marriage to *Soranzo*?

PHILOTIS   Yes for certaine.

RICHARDETTO   But how finde you young *Annabella's* love,   20
Inclind to him?

PHILOTIS   For ought I could perceive,
Shee neyther fancies him or any else.

RICHARDETTO   There's Mystery in that, which time must shew.
Shee us'd you kindly.

PHILOTIS   Yes.

RICHARDETTO   And crav'd your company?

PHILOTIS   Often.   25

RICHARDETTO   'Tis well, it goes as I could wish,
I am the Doctor now, and as for you,
None knowes you; if all faile not we shall thrive.
But who comes here?

Enter GRIMALDI.

I know him, 'tis *Grimaldi*,
A Roman and a souldier, neere allyed   30
Unto the Duke of *Montferrato*, one
Attending on the *Nuntio* of the Pope
That now resides in *Parma*, by which meanes
D 3ᵛ   He hopes to get the love of *Annabella*.

GRIMALDI   Save you Sir.

14–15] *Weber*; Thus . . . prevail'd. | Alas . . . feare | You . . . revenge. | O . . . troubled, *Q*
17 businesse; what,] *Dodsley*; ~, ~, *Q*; ~: ~! *Reed*; ~. ——~! *Dyce*   19] *Weber*; In . . . *Soranzo?* |
Yes, . . . certaine *Q*   19 Yes∧] *Q*; ~, *Dodsley*   20] *Weber*; Inclind . . . him? | For . . .
perceive, *Q*   22 that,] *Reed*; ~∧ *Q*   22 shew.] *Dodsley* (show); ~, *Q*   22 Shee . . .
kindly? Yes.] *Dodsley*, *one line in Q*   24–5 And . . . company? | Often.] *Dodsley*, *one line in*
Q   29] *Weber*; But . . . here? | I . . . *Grimaldi*, *Q*   29 SD *Enter* GRIMALDI] *Q*; *Gifford*
places SD after line 34; *Massai, after line* 28.

RICHARDETTO   And you Sir.

GRIMALDI   I have heard   35
  Of your approv'd skill, which through the City
  Is freely talkt of, and would crave your ayd.

RICHARDETTO   For what Sir?

GRIMALDI   Marry sir for this —
  But I would speake in Private.

RICHARDETTO   Leave us Cozen.   *Exit* PHILOTIS.

GRIMALDI   I love faire *Annabella*, and would know   40
  Whether in Arts there may not be receipts
  To move affection.

RICHARDETTO   Sir perhaps there may,
  But these will nothing profit you.

GRIMALDI   Not mee?

RICHARDETTO   Unlesse I be mistooke, you are a man
  Greatly in favour with the Cardinal.   45

GRIMALDI   What of that?

RICHARDETTO   In duty to his Grace,
  I will be bold to tell you, if you seeke
  To marry *Florio's* daughter, you must first
  Remove a barre twixt you and her.

GRIMALDI   Who's that?

RICHARDETTO   *Soranzo* is the man that hath her heart,   50
  And while hee lives, be sure you cannot speed.

GRIMALDI   *Soranzo*, what mine Enemy, is't hee?

RICHARDETTO   Is hee your Enemy?

35 Save . . . Sir. And . . . Sir.] *Weber; one line in Q;* ~ . . . ~ | ~ . . . ~. *Dodsley*   35 And . . .
Sir. I . . . heard] *Weber; prose in Q*   36 approv'd] *Q;* approved *Weber;* approvèd *Dyce*
38–9] *Weber;* For . . . sir? | Marry . . . this— | But . . . Private. | Leave . . . Cozen. *Q*   39 SD
Exit PHILOTIS.] *Q; PHI. retires.* | *Gifford*   41 Arts] *Q;* art *Dyce*   41 receipts] *Q;* reci-
pes *Massai*   42–3] *Weber;* To ... affection. | Sir . . . may, | But . . . you. | Not mee? *Q*
45–6 Greatly . . . Cardinal | What . . . that?] *Q;* Greatly . . . that? *Weber*   46] *Dyce;* What . . .
that? | In . . . Grace, *Q*   49] *Weber;* Remove . . . her | Who's that? *Q*   49 Who's]
Dodsley, Whose *Q*   52 Soranzo,] *Q;* ~! *Reed* (Soranzo)   53 Enemy?] *Dodsley* (enemy);
~, *Q*   53] *Weber,* Is . . . Enemy? | The . . . hate *Q*

GRIMALDI   The man I hate,
Worse then Confusion; I'le kill him streight.

RICHARDETTO   Nay, then take mine advice,   55
(Even for his Graces sake the Cardinal)
I'le finde a time when hee and shee doe meete,
Of which I'le give you notice, and to be sure
Hee shall not scape you, I'le provide a poyson
To dip your Rapiers poynt in; if hee had   60
As many heads as *Hidra* had, he dyes.

D4ʳ GRIMALDI   But shall I trust thee Doctor?

RICHARDETTO   As your selfe,
Doubt not in ought. [*Aside*] Thus shall the Fates decree,
By mee *Soranzo* falls, that ruin'd mee.   *Exeunt.*

2.4   *Enter* DONADO, BERGETTO *and* POGGIO.

DONADO   Well Sir, I must bee content to be both your Secretary
and your Messenger my selfe; I cannot tell what this Letter may
worke; but as sure as I am alive, if thou come once to talke with
her, I feare thou wu't marre whatsoever I make.

BERGETTO   You make Unkle? Why, am not I bigge enought to   5
carry mine owne Letter I pray?

DONADO   I, I, carry a fooles head o'thy owne; why, thou Dunce,
wouldst thou write a letter, and carry it thy selfe?

BERGETTO   Yes that I wud, and reade it to her with my owne
mouth, for you must thinke, if shee will not beleeve me my selfe   10

54 kill] *Q* (corrected); tell *Q* (uncorrected); to *Dyce* (*conj. Gifford*)   55 mine] *Q*; my
Dodsley   56 Cardinall)] *Q*; ~: *Reed* (cardinal)   58 notice;] *Dodsley*; ~, *Q*   60 in;]
Dodsley, ~, *Q*; ~: *Dyce*   62] *Weber*; But . . . Doctor? | As your selfe, *Q*   63 ought] *Q*;
aught *Reed*   63 ought.] *Reed* (aught); ~; *Q*   63 SD [*Aside*]] *Bawcutt*; not in *Q*; *Dyce*
places SD [*Exit Grim.*] *before* Thus. *Gifford*, SD [*Exit Grim.*] *after* decree.   63 Thus] ~
Dyce; thus *Q*   63 decree,] *Q*; ~. *Gifford*   64 Bymee] *Q*; ~ thee *Sturgess*   64 ruin'd]
Q (corrected); min'd *Q* (uncorrected)   64 SD Exeunt.] *Q*; not in *Weber*, [*Exit.* | *Dyce*
2.4] *this edn*; not in *Q*; SCENE IV.—*An Apartment in* DONADO's *House.* | *Weber*, SCENE
IV.—*Another part of the street.* | *Dyce*; [2.4] *Massai*   0.1 SD DONADO,] *Q*; ~, *with a Letter,*
Gifford   3 worke;] *Dodsley* (work); ~, *Q*   4 wu't] *Q*; wilt *Dodsley*, *Weber*, wouldst
Massai   5 make∧] *Q*; ~, *Dodsley*   5 Unkle?] *Q*; ~! *Dyce* (unkle)   5 Why,] *Dyce*
(why); ~∧ *Q* (why)   7 I, I,] *Q*; Ay, ay, *Dodsley*   7 o'thy] *Q*; of thy *Dodsley*, o' thy *Dyce*
7 why,] *Dodsley*; ~∧ *Q*   9 wud] *Q*; would *Dodsley*, woud'st *Weber*, woudst *Dyce*

when she heares me speake, she will not beleeve anothers hand-writing. O you thinke I am a blocke-head Unkle; no sir, *Poggio* knowes I have indited a letter my selfe, so I have.

POGGIO   Yes truely sir, I have it in my pocket.

DONADO   A sweete one no doubt, pray let's see't.   15

BERGETTO   I cannot reade my owne hand very well; *Poggio,* reade it, *Poggio.*

DONADO   Begin.

POGGIO reades.

POGGIO   *Most dainty and honey-sweete Mistresse, I could call you faire, and lie as fast as any that loves you; but my Unkle being*   20
         the elder man, I leave it to him, as more fit for his age, and the colour of his beard; I am wise enough to tell you I can board where I see occasion, or if you like my Unkles wit better then mine, you shall marry mee; if you like mine better then his, I will marry you in spight of your teeth; So commending my best   25
         parts to you, I rest. Yours upwards and downewards,
or you may chose, Bergetto.

BERGETTO   Ah ha, here's stuffe Unkle.

DONADO   Here's stuffe indeed to shame us all; pray whose advice did you take in this learned Letter?   30

POGGIO   None upon my word, but mine owne.   D4ᵛ

BERGETTO   And mine Unkle, beleeve it, no bodies else; 'twas mine owne brayne, I thanke a good wit for't.

DONADO   Get you home sir, and looke yon keepe within doors till I returne.   35

BERGETTO   How? that were a jest indeede; I scorne it yfaith.

<hr>

11 speake,] *Dodsley* (speak); ~; *Q*   12 Unkle;] *this edn*; ~, *Q*; ~: *Dodsley* (uncle); ~. *Gifford* (uncle)   15] *Wiggins adds* SD [POGGIO *gives* BERGETTO *the letter*] *after* see't.   16 well; *Poggio,*] *Gifford*; ~ₐ ~, *Q*; ~, ~. *Dodsley* (Poggio)   16–17] *Gifford*; I . . . *Poggio* | Reade it *Poggio. Q*   19] *Weber adds* SD [*Reads.*] *after* SP POGGIO.   20 *you; but*] *Dodsley*; ~, ~ *Q*   22 *board*] *Q*; bourd *Weber* (*conj. Reed*)   28 stuffeₐ] *Q*; ~, *Dodsley*   29–30] *Weber*; Here's . . . all, | Pray . . . Letter? *Q*   31 Noneₐ] *Q* ~, *Dodsley*   32 mineₐ] *Q*; ~, *Weber*   34 homeₐ] *Q*; ~, *Dodsley*   36 itₐ yfaith.] *Q*; ~, ~ *Gifford* (I'faith)

DONADO   What, you doe not?

BERGETTO   Iudge me, but I doe now.

POGGIO   Indeede sir 'tis very unhealthy.

DONADO   Well sir, if I heare any of your apish running to   40
motions, and fopperies till I come backe, you were as good
no; looke too't.   *Exit* DONADO.

BERGETTO   *Poggio*, shall's steale to see this Horse with the head
in's tayle?

POGGIO   I, but you must take heede of whipping.   45

BERGETTO   Dost take me for a Child *Poggio*? Come
honest *Poggio*.

                                                    Exeunt.

        2.5   *Enter* FRYAR *and* GIOVANNI.

FRYAR   Peace, thou hast told a tale, whose every word
Threatens eternall slaughter to the soule:
I'me sorry I have heard it; would mine eares
Had beene one minute deafe, before the houre
That thou cam'st to mee: *O young man* cast-away,   5
By the rellingious number of mine order,
I day and night have wak't my aged eyes,
Above my strength, to weepe on thy behalfe:
But Heaven is angry, and be thou resolv'd,
Thou art a man remark't to tast a mischiefe,   10
Looke for't; though it come late, it will come sure.

GIOVANNI   Father, in this you are uncharitable;
What I have done, I'le prove both fit and good.
It is a principall (which you have taught
When I was yet your Scholler) that the Frame   15
And Composition of the *Minde* doth follow

37 What,] *Dodsley*; ∼∧ Q   38 Iudge] Q; Judge *Dodsley*   42 no] Q; not *Dodsley*
42 too't] Q; to't *Dodsley*   42 SD *Exit* DONADO.] Q (*Exit Do.*); [*Exit.* | *Dyce*; *Exit.* |
Roper   45 I,] *this edn*; ∼ Q; Ay, *Dodsley*   46] *Weber*; Dost . . . *Poggio*, | Come honest
Poggio. Q   2.5] *this edn; not in* Q; SCENE V. —*The* FRIAR'S *Cell.* | *Weber*; SCENE V.—*Friar*
BONAVENTURA'S *Cell.* | *Dyce*; [2.5] *Massai*   2 the] Q; thy *Reed*   5 man cast-away,]
Q; ∼ cast away∧] *Gibson*;∼ ∼! *Dodsley* (cast-away); ∼, ∼, *Dyce* (castaway); ∼ ∼, *Bawcutt* (castaway);
∼ ∼ ∼, *Roper*; ∼, ∼ ∼ *Lomax* (*conj. Morris*)   6 number] Q; founder *conj. Gifford*   8 my]
Dodsley; thy Q   15 Frame] *Dodsley* (frame); Fame Q

The Frame and Composition of *Body*:
So where the *Bodies* furniture is *Beauty*,
The *Mindes* must needs be *Vertue*: which allowed,
Vertue it selfe is *Reason but refin'd*,   20
And *Love* the Quintessence of that; this proves   E1ʳ
My Sisters *Beauty* being rarely *Faire*,
Is rarely *Vertuous*; chiefely in her love,
And chiefely in that *Love, her love to me*.
If *hers to me*, then so is *mine to her*;   25
Since in like Causes are effects alike.

FRYAR   O ignorance in knowledge! Long agoe,
How often have I warn'd thee this before?
Indeede if we were sure there were no *Deity*,
Nor *Heaven* nor *Hell*, then to be lead alone,   30
By Natures light (as were Philosophers
Of elder times) might instance some defence.
But 'tis not so; then Madman, thou wilt finde,
That *Nature* is in Heavens positions blind.

GIOVANNI   Your age o're rules you, had you youth like mine,   35
You'd make her love your heaven, and her divine.

FRYAR   Nay then I see th'art too farre sold to Hell,
It lies not in the Compasse of my prayers
To call thee backe; yet let me Counsell thee:
Perswade thy sister to some marriage.   40

GIOVANNI   Marriage? why that's to dambe her; that's to prove
Her greedy of variety of lust.

FRYAR   O fearefull! if thou wilt not, give me leave
To shrive her; lest shee should dye un-absolv'd.

GIOVANNI   At your best leasure Father, then shee'le tell you,   45
How dearely shee doth prize my Matchlesse love,
Then you will know what pitty 'twere we two
Should have beene sundred from each others armes.
View well her face, and in that little round,

17 *Body*.] *Q*; ~; *Dodsley* (body); [the] ~. *Gifford* (body)   19 *Mindes*] *Q*; mind's *Dodsley*
21 that;] *this edn*; ~, *Q*; ~: *Dodsley*   27 knowledge!] *Dodsley*; ~, *Q*   27 Long] *Dyce*;
long *Q*   30 *Hell*,] *Q*; ~; *Reed* (hell)   35 o're rules] *Q*; o'rerules *Dodsley*   37 th'art]
Q; thou'rt *Dodsley*   37 Hell,] *Q*; ~: *Reed* (hell)   41 dambe] *Q*; damn *Dodsley*

You may observe a world of variety;   50
For Colour, lips; for sweet perfumes, her breath;
For Jewels, eyes; for threds of purest gold,
Hayre; for delicious choyce of Flowers, cheekes;
Wonder in every portion of that Throne:
Heare her but speake, and you will sweare the Sphaeres   55
Make Musicke to the Cittizens in Heaven:
But Father, what is else for pleasure fram'd,
Least I offend your eares shall goe un-nam'd.

E1ᵛ

FRYAR   The more I heare, I pitty thee the more,
That one so excellent should give those parts   60
All to a second Death; what I can doe
Is but to pray; and yet I could advise thee,
Wouldst thou be rul'd.

GIOVANNI   In what?

FRYAR   Why leave her yet,
The Throne of *Mercy* is above your trespasse,
Yet time is left you both—

GIOVANNI   To embrace each other,   65
Else let all time be strucke quite out of number;
Shee is like mee, and I like her resolv'd.

FRYAR   No more, I'le visit her; this grieves me most,
Things being thus, a paire of soules are lost.

                                        Exeunt.

2.6   *Enter* FLORIO, DONADO, ANNABELLA, PUTANA.

FLORIO   Where's Giovanni?

ANNABELLA   Newly walk't abroad,
And (as I heard him say) gon to the Fryer
His reverend Tutor.

---

50 world of variety] *Q*; world's variety *Gifford*   51 Colour] *Q*; coral *Dodsley*   51 lips;]
Dodsley; ~, *Q*   54 Throne] *Q*; form *Dodsley*   59 more,] *Q*; ~; *Dodsley*   63] *Weber*;
Wouldst . . . rul'd. | In what? | Why . . . yet, *Q*   63 yet,] *Q*; ~; *Dodsley*; ~: *Dyce*; ~.
Hopkins   65] *Weber*; Yet . . . both— | To . . . other, *Q*   65 other,] *Q*; ~; *Dodsley*
2.6] *this edn; not in Q*; SCENE VI.—*An Apatment in* FLORIO'*S House.* | *Weber*; SCENE VI. *A
room in* FLORIO *'s house.* | *Dyce*; [2.6] *Massai*   0.1 SD PUTANA] *Q*; *and* ~ *Weber*, [*and*]
PUTTANA *Massai*   1] *Weber*; Where's Giovanni? | Newly . . . abroad *Q*   1 Where's] *Q*;
Where is *Weber*   3] *Weber*; His . . . Tutor. | That's . . . man, *Q*   3 reverend] *Dodsley*;
reverent *Q*

FLORIO   That's a blessed man,
A man made up of holinesse; I hope
Hee'le teach him how to gaine another world.   5

DONADO   Faire Gentlewoman, here's a letter sent
To you from my young Cozen; I dare sweare
He loves you in his soule; would you could heare
Sometimes, what I see dayly, sighes and teares,
As if his breast were prison to his heart.   10

FLORIO   Recieve it *Annabella*.

ANNABELLA   Alas good man.

DONADO   What's that she said ?

PUTANA   And please you sir, she sayd, alas good man; truely I
doe commend him to her every night before her first sleepe,
because I would have her dreame of him, and shee harkens   15
to that most relligiously.

DONADO   Say'st so; godamercy *Putana*, there's something for
thee, and prythee doe what thou canst on his behalfe; sha'
not be lost labour, take my word for't.   E2ʳ

PUTANA   Thanke you most heartily sir; now I have a *Feeling* of   20
your mind, let mee alone to worke.

ANNABELLA   *Guardian*!

PUTANA   Did you call?

ANNABELLA   Keepe this letter.

DONADO   *Signior Florio*, in any case bid her reade it instantly.   25

FLORIO   Keepe it for what? pray reade it mee here right.

---

3 man,] *Q;* ~! *Dodsley*   4 holinesse;] *Weber* (holiness); ~, *Q*   7 Cozen;] *Dodsley*
(cousin); ~, *Q*   8 soule;] *Dodsley* (soul); ~, *Q;* ~: *Dyce* (soul)   11] *Weber;* Receive . . .
Annabella. | Alas . . . man. *Q*   11] *Gifford adds* SD [*Takes the letter.*] *after* man; *Wiggins,*
SD [*She takes the letter, but does not read it*] *after* man; *Massai,* SD [*Takes the letter.*] *before* Alas.
11 Alas∧ good man.] *Q;* ~, ~ ~! *Dodsley*   13 And] *Q;* An't *Weber*   13 man;] *this edn;* ~,
Q   13] *Roper adds* SD [*Aside to Don.*] *before* truly.   16] *Roper adds* SD [*Aside to Put.*]
before Say'st.   17 so;] *Dodsley;* ~, *Q;* ~? *Dyce*   17 *Putana,*] *Dodsley* (Putana); ~! *Dyce*
(Putana); ~∧ *Q*   18] *Gifford adds* SD [*Gives her money*] *after* thee.   18 sha'] *Q;* it shall
Dodsley; 'shall *Gifford*   20] *Roper adds* SD [*Aside to Don.*] *before* Thanke.   20 heart-
ily sir;] *this edn;* ~ ~, *Q;* ~, ~; *Dodsley*   24 letter.] *Dodsley;* ~, *Q*   26 Keep it for what?]
Q; ~ ~; ~ ~? *Dodsley;* ~ ~! ~ ~? *Gifford* (For)

ANNABELLA   I shall sir,   *She reades.*

DONADO   How d'ee finde her inclin'd *Signior*?

FLORIO   Troth sir I know not how; not all so well
   As I could wish.   30

ANNABELLA   Sir I am bound to rest your Cozens debter,
   The Jewell I'le returne; for if he love,
   I'le count that love a Iewell.

DONADO   Marke you that?
   Nay keepe them both sweete Maide.

ANNABELLA   You must excuse mee,
   Indeed I will not keepe it.

FLORIO   Where's the Ring,   35
   That which your Mother in her will bequeath'd,
   And charg'd you on her blessing not to give't
   To any but your Husband? send backe that.

ANNABELLA   I have it not.

FLORIO   Ha! have it not, where is't?

ANNABELLA   My brother in the morning tooke it from me,   40
   Said he would wear't to Day.

FLORIO   Well, what doe you say
   To young *Bergetto's* love? are you content
   To match with him? speake.

DONADO   There's the poynt indeed.

ANNABELLA   [*Aside*] What shal I doe, I must say something now.

FLORIO   What say, why d'ee not speake?

ANNABELLA   Sir with your leave   45
   Please you to give me freedome.

28 d'ee] *Q*; do you *Dodsley*; d'ye *Dyce*   33–5] *Weber*; I'le . . . Iewell. | Mark . . . that? | Nay
. . . Maide. | You . . . mee, | Indeed . . . it | Where's . . . Ring, *Q*   33 Iewell] *Q*; jewel *Dodsley*
35 Ring,] *Dyce* (ring); ~. *Q*; ~? *Dodsley* (ring)   39] *Weber*; I . . . not, | Ha! . . . is't? *Q*
38 is't?] *Q*; is it? *Dodsley*   41] *Weber*; Said . . . Day | Well, . . . say *Q*   41 to Day] *Q*;
to-day *Reed*   43] *Weber*; To . . . speake. | There's . . . indeed. *Q*   44 SD [*Aside*]] *Dyce*
(*aside*); not in *Q*; *Gifford* placed SD [*Aside*. | *after* doe.   44 doe,] *Q*; ~! *Dodsley* (do); ~?
Dyce   45–6] *Weber*; What . . . speake? | Sir . . . leave, | Please . . . freedome. | Yes . . . it. *Q*
45 d'ee] *Q*; do you *Dodsley*; d'you *Weber*   46] *Weber*; Please . . . freedome | Yes . . . 't
Q   46 freedome.] *Q*; ~? *Gifford* (freedom)   46 have 't] *Roper*; have *Q*; have it *Gifford*

FLORIO   Yes you have 't.

ANNABELLA   *Signior Donado*, if your Nephew meane   E2ᵛ
    To raise his better Fortunes in his match,
    The hope of mee will hinder such a hope;
    Sir if you love him, as I know you doe;   50
    Find one more worthy of his choyce then mee,
    In short, I'me sure, I sha'not be his wife.

DONADO   Why here's plaine dealing, I commend thee for't,
    And all the worst I wish thee, is heaven blesse thee,
    Your Father yet and I will still be friends,   55
    Shall we not *Signior Florio*?

FLORIO   Yes, why not?
    Looke here your Cozen comes.

              Enter BERGETTO *and* POGGIO.

DONADO   [*Aside*] Oh Coxcombe, what doth he make here?

BERGETTO   Where's my Unkle sirs.

DONADO   What's the newes now?   60

BERGETTO   Save you Unkle, save you, you must not thinke I
    come for nothing Maisters, and how and how is't? what you
    have read my letter, ah, there I—tickled you yfaith.

POGGIO   But 'twere better you had tickled her in another place.

BERGETTO   Sirrah *Sweet-heart*, I'le tell thee a good iest, and riddle   65
    what 'tis.

ANNABELLA   You say you'd tell mee.

BERGETTO   As I was walking just now in the Streete, I mett a
    swaggering fellow would needs take the wall of me, and
    because hee did thrust me, I very valiantly cal'd him *Rogue*, hee   70

---

49 hope;] *Q*; ~. *Dodsley*; ~: *Dyce*   49 mee,] *Q*; ~; *Dodsley* (me); ~: *Dyce* (me)   55 friends,] *Q*; ~. *Dodsley*; ~:— *Dyce*   56] *Weber*; Shall . . . *Florio*? | Yes . . . not? *Q*   58 SD [*Aside*]] *Dyce* (aside); *not in Q*   58 Oh∧] *Q*; O, *Dyce*   58 he make] *Q*; make him *Dodsley*   62] *Bevington adds* SD [*to Annabella*] *after* Maisters.   64] *Dyce adds* SD [*Aside to Ber.*] *after* SP POGGIO.   65] *Wiggins adds* SD [*To* ANNABELLA] *after* Sirrah.   66 'tis] *Q*; it is *Dodsley*   67 you'd] *Q*; you'll *Gifford*   70 *Rogue*, hee] *Q*; ~. ~ *Dodsley* (rogue) (He)

hereupon bad me drawe, I told him I had more wit then so,
but when hee saw that I would not, hee did so maule me
with the hilts of his Rapier, that my head sung whil'st my
feete caper'd in the kennell.

DONADO   [*Aside*] Was ever the like asse seene?   75

ANNABELLA   And what did you all this while?

BERGETTO   Laugh at him for a gull, till I see the blood runne
about mine eares, and then I could not choose but finde in
my heart to cry; till a fellow with a broad beard, (they say
hee is a new-come Doctor) cald mee into this house, and   80
gave me a playster, looke you here 'tis; and sir there was a
young wench washt my face and hands most excellently, yfaith
E3ʳ   I shall love her as long as I live for't, did she not *Poggio* ?

POGGIO   Yes and kist him too.

BERGETTO   Why la now, you thinke I tell a lye Unkle I warrant.   85

DONADO   Would hee that beate thy blood out of thy head, had
beaten some wit into it; For I feare thou never wilt have any.

BERGETTO   Oh Unkle, but there was a wench, would have done a
mans heart good to have lookt on her, by this light shee had
a face mee-thinks worth twenty of you Mistresse *Annabella*.   90

DONADO   [*Aside*] Was ever such a foole borne?

ANNABELLA   I am glad shee lik't you sir.

BERGETTO   Are you so, by my troth I thanke you forsooth.

FLORIO   Sure 't was the Doctors neece, that was last day with
us here: 95

BERGETTO   'Twas shee, 'twas shee.

DONADO   How doe you know that simplicity?

BERGETTO   Why doe's not hee say so? if I should have sayd no, I
should have given him the lye Unkle, and so have deserv'd a dry
beating againe; I'le none of that.   100

---

71 him] Q; *not in.* Weber   75 SD [*Aside*]] *Dyce* (aside); *not in* Q   77 see] Q; saw
Gifford   80 this] Q; his *Gifford*   90 mee-thinks] Q; methinks *Dodsley*   91 SD
[*Aside*]] *Dyce* (aside); *not in* Q   93 so,] Q; ~? *Dodsley*

FLORIO   A very modest, well-behav'd young Maide as I have
seene.

DONADO   Is shee indeed?

FLORIO   Indeed shee is, if I have any Iudgement.

DONADO   Well sir, now you are free, you need not care for   105
sending letters, now you are dismist, your Mistresse here
will none of you.

BERGETTO   No; why what care I for that, I can have Wenches
enough in *Parma* for halfe a Crowne a peece, cannot I *Poggio*?

POGGIO   I'le warrant you sir.   110

DONADO   *Signior Florio*,
I thanke you for your free recourse you gave
For my admittance; and to you faire Maide
That Jewell I will give you 'gainst your marriage,
Come will you goe sir?   115

BERGETTO   I marry will I Mistres, farwell Mistres, I'le come
againe to morrow—farwell Mistres.
                    Exeuntt DONADO, BERGETTO, *and* POGGIO.

                    Enter GIOVANNI.

FLORIO   Sonne, where have you beene? what alone, alone, still,
still?
I would not have it so, you must forsake
This over bookish humour. Well, your Sister
Hath shooke the Foole off.   F3ᵛ

GIOVANNI   'Twas no match for her.   120

FLORIO   'Twas not indeed I ment it nothing lesse,
Soranzo is the man I onely like;

101–3] *Weber*; A . . . seene | Is . . . indeed? | Indeed | Shee . . . Iudgement *Q*; A . . . seen | Is . . .
indeed? | Indeed . . . judgement *Gifford*; A . . . maid, | As . . . seen . . . she is, | If . . . judgement.
Massai   106 letters, now] *Q*; ~; ~ *Dodsley*; ~∧ ~ *Gifford*   108 that,] *Q*; ~; *Dodsley*, ~:
Reed; ~? *Dyce*   112 you] *Q*; ~, *Dodsley*   113 Maide] *Q*; ~, *Ddodsley* (maid)
115] *Wiggins adds* SD [*To* BERGETTO] *before* Come.   115 Come∧] *Q*; ~, *Dodsley* (come)
116 farwell] *Q*; farewell *Dodsley*   116 SD *Exeunt* DONADO, BERGETTO *and* POGGIO]
Gifford; Exit ~, ~ ~ ~ *Q*   116–19] *Weber*; prose in *Q*   116 what∧] *Q*; ~, *Gifford*
117 alone, alone, still, still?] *Q*, *Roper* (*noting possibility of dittography*); alone, alone, still?
Gifford   119 over bookish] *Q*; over-bookish *Weber*   120] *Weber*; Hath . . . off. | 'Twas
. . . her. *Q*

Looke on him *Annabella*, come, 'tis supper-time,
And it growes late.   *Exit* FLORIO.

GIOVANNI   Whose Jewell's that?   125

ANNABELLA   Some Sweet-hearts.

GIOVANNI   So I thinke.

ANNABELLA   A lusty youth,
Signior Donado gave it me to weare
Against my Marriage.

GIOVANNI   But you shall not weare it,
Send it him backe againe.

ANNABELLA   What, you are jealous?

GIOVANNI   That you shall know anon, at better leasure: 130
Welcome sweete night, the Evening crownes the Day.
                                        Exeunt.

            3.1   *Enter* BERGETTO *and* POGGIO.

BERGETTO   Do'es my Unkle thinke to make mee a Baby still?
   no, *Poggio*, he shall know, I have a skonce now.

POGGIO   I, let him not bobbe you off like an Ape with an apple.

BERGETTO   Sfoot, I will have the wench, if he were tenne Unkles,
   in despight of his nose *Poggio*.   5

POGGIO   Hold him to the Grynd-stone, and give not a jot of
   ground, shee hath in a manner promised you already.

BERGETTO   True *Poggio*, and her Unkle the Doctor swore I should
   marry her.

124 SD *Exit* FLORIO.] *Q*; [*Exit.*| *Dyce*   125–6 Whose . . . that? | Some Sweet-heart. | So . . .
thinke] *Q*; *verse in Weber*   126 Some . . . youth,] *Dyce*; Some Sweet-hearts. | So . . . thinke
| A . . . youth *Q*   126–8 A . . . youth | Signiour . . . weare | Against . . . Marriage] *Dyce*; A . . .
me | to . . . Marriage *Q*   126–7 A . . . youth | Signior . . . me] *Dyce*; A . . . me *Q, Weber*
127–8 to weare | Against . . . Marriage] *Dyce*; to . . . Marriage *Q, Weber*   128] *Dyce*; Against . . .
Marriage | But . . . it *Q*   128–9 But . . . it, | Send . . . jealous?] *Dyce*; But . . . again | What . . .
jelous? *Q*;   **3.1**] *this edn*; *Actus Tertius. Q*; SCENE I.—*The Street.* | *Weber,* —*A room in*
DONADO'S *house.* | *Dyce*; 3[.1] *Massai*   3 I,] *this edn*; ~∧*Q*; Ay, *Dosdley*   5 nose∧] *Q*;
~, *Dodsley*   6–9] *Weber*; Hold . . . ground, | Shee . . . already. True . . . Doctor | Swore . .
. her. *Q*   8 SP BERGETTO] *Dodsley (Ber.)*; *Pog. Q*

POGGIO   He swore I remember.   10

BERGETTO   And I will have her, that's more; did'st see the
codpeice-poynt she gave me, and the box of Mermalade?

POGGIO   Very well, and kist you, that my chopps watred at the
sight on't; there's no way but to clap up a marriage in hugger
mugger.   15

BERGETTO   I will do't; for I tell thee *Poggio*, I begin to grow
valiant methinkes, and my courage begins to rise.   E4ʳ

POGGIO   Should you be afraid of your Unkle?

BERGETTO   Hang him old doating Rascall, no, I say I will have her.

POGGIO   Lose no time then.   20

BERGETTO   I will beget a race of Wise men and Constables, that
shall cart whoores at their owne charges, and breake the Dukes
peace ere I have done my selfe. —Come away.

                                                            Exeunt.

     3.2   *Enter* FLORIO, GIOVANNI, SORANZO, ANNABELLA,
                    PUTANA *and* VASQUES.

FLORIO   My Lord *Soranzo*, though I must confesse,
The proffers that are made me, have beene great
In marriage of my daughter; yet the hope
Of your still rising honours, have prevaild
Above all other Joynctures; here shee is,   5
She knowes my minde, speake for your selfe to her,
And heare you daughter, see you use him nobly,
For any private speech, I'le give you time:
Come sonne and you, the rest let them alone,
Agree as they may.

SORANZO   I thanke you sir.   10

10 swore] *Q;* ~, *Dodsley;* ~; *Dyce*   11 her,] *Dodsley;* ~ₐ *Q*   16 do't;] *Dyce;* ~ₐ *Q;* do it;
Dodsley   22-3 charges, . . . done] *Q;* ~ . . . ~, *Gifford;* ~; . . . ~ *Dyce*   23 my selfe.] *Q;*
myself, *Dodsley*   23 —Come] *Reed;* —— *Q* (come); ~ *Dyce*   **3.2**] *this edn; not in Q;*
SCENE II.—*A Room in* FLORIO'*s House, with a Gallery.* | *Weber;* SCENE II. *A room in* FLORIO'*s
house.* | *Dyce;* [3.2] *Massai*   5 Joynctures] *Q;* junctures *Dodsley;* jointures *Reed*   6 her,]
Q; ~. *Dodsley;* ~,— *Dyce*   9 sonne and you, the rest let] *Q;* ~, ~ ~ ~ ~, ~ *Dodsley* (son); ~; ~
~ ~ ~, ~ *Reed* (son), *Weber;* ~, ~ ~ ~ ~; ~ *Gifford* (son); ~, ~, ~ ~ ~, ~ *Bawcutt;* ~, ~ you; ~ ~, ~
Lomax; ~, ~ ~ ~, ~ ~; ~ *Massai*   9] *Lomax adds* SD [*to Putana*] *after* you.   10] *Weber;*
Agree . . . may. | I . . . sir. *Q*   10 Agree] *Q;* Agree [they] *Gifford*

GIOVANNI   [*Aside*] Sister be not all woeman, thinke on me.

SORANZO   *Vasques?*

VASQUES   My Lord.

SORANZO   Attend me without—
            Exeunt omnes, manent SORANZO *&* ANNABELLA.

ANNABELLA   Sir what's your will with me?

SORANZO   Doe you not know what I should tell you?   15

ANNABELLA   Yes, you'le say you love mee.

SORANZO   And I'le sweare it too;
        Will you beleeve it?

ANNABELLA   'Tis not poynt of faith.

            Enter GIOVANNI *above.*

SORANZO   Have you not will to love?

ANNABELLA   Not you.

SORANZO   Whom then ?

ANNABELLA   That's as the Fates inferre.

GIOVANNI   [*Aside*] Of those I'me regient now.

SORANZO   What meane you sweete?   20

E4ᵛ ANNABELLA   To live and dye a Maide.

SORANZO   Oh that's unfit.

11 SD [*Aside*]] *Dyce* [*aside to Ann.*]; *Dodsley places* SD [*Aside to her.*] *after* me.; *not in* Q
11 Sisterₐ] Q; ~, *Dodsley*   12–13] *Vasques?* | My Lord.] *Dodsley, one line in* Q; *verse in Weber*
14–14.1 Attend . . . without—SD] *one line in* Q; *verse in Weber*   14] *Weber,* Attend . . .
without— | Sir . . . me? Q   14 SD *Exeunt omnes, manent* SORANZO *and* ANNBELLA]
Roper, ~ ~, *manent* SORAN *&* ANNA Q (*set against* 'without' *and* 'me' *at ll.* 14); ~ ~, *preter*
SORANZO *and* ANNABELLA *Reed;* ~ ~, *excepting* SORANZO *and* ANNABELLA *Weber,* [~ *all but*
ORANZO *and* ANNABELLA *Gifford*   14–15 Sir . . . me? | Doe . . . . . . you?] Q; Sir. . .know |
what   .   .   .   you? *Weber*   15] Q; Doe   .   .   .   know | what   .   .   .   you? *Weber*
16–17 Yes . . . believe it?] *this edn;* Yes; . . . mee. | And . . . believe it? Q; Yes; . . . me. | *Sor.* And
I will . . . it? *Weber;* Yes, | You'll . . . me. *Sor.* And . . . too; | Will . . . believe it? *Roper*
16–17 And . . . too; | Will . . . it?] *Roper, one line in* Q   17 Will . . . faith.] *Roper,* Will . . .
it? | 'Tis . . . faith Q   17 not] Q; no *Gifford*   17 SD *above*] Q; *above, unseen* | *Weber;*
in the Gallery, above.| *Gifford*   18] *Roper,* Have . . . love? | ANNABELLA Not you. SORANZO
Whom then? Q   18 not] Q; no *Gifford*   20 SD [*Aside*]] *Dyce* (*aside*); *not in* Q
20–1] *Weber,* Of . . . now. | What . . . sweete? | To . . . Maide. | Oh . . . unfit. Q

GIOVANNI   [*Aside*] Here's one can say that' s but a womans noate.

SORANZO   Did you but see my heart, then would you sweare—

ANNABELLA   That you were dead.

GIOVANNI   [*Aside*]   That's true, or somewhat neere it.

SORANZO   See you these true loves teares?

ANNABELLA   No.

GIOVANNI   [*Aside*]   Now shee winkes. 25

SORANZO   They plead to you for grace.

ANNABELLA   Yet nothing speake.

SORANZO   Oh grant my suite.

ANNABELLA   What is't?

SORANZO   To let mee live.

ANNABELLA   Take it.—

SORANZO   Still yours.—

ANNABELLA   That is not mine to give.

GIOVANNI   [*Aside*] One such another word would kil his hopes.

SORANZO   Mistres, to leave those fruitlesse strifes of wit,   30
I know I have lov'd you long, and lov'd you truely;
Not hope of what you have, but what you are
Have drawne me on, then let mee not in vaine
Still feele the rigour of your chast disdaine.
I'me sicke, and sicke to th'heart.

22 SD [*Aside*]] *Dyce* (*aside*); *not in* Q   24–8] *Weber*, That . . . dead. | That's . . . it. | See . . . teares? | ANNABELLA No. GIOVANNI Now . . . winkes. | They . . . grace. | Yet . . . speake. | Oh . . . suite. | ANNABELLA What is't? SORANNZO To . . . live. | Take it.—| Still yours.— | That . . . give. Q   24 SD [*Aside*]] *Dyce* (*aside*); *not in* Q   24] *Massai adds* SD [*Closes her eyes.*] *after* SP ANNABELLA.   25 SD [*Aside*]] *Dyce* (*aside*); *not in* Q   27 What is't? To . . . live] *one line in* Q   27 is't?] *Weber*, ~∧ Q, is it? *Dodsley*   28 it.—] *Dodsley*, ~∧— Q, ~. *Dyce*   29 SD [*Aside*]] *Dyce* (*aside*); *not in* Q   31 I know] Q, Know *Dodsley* 33 Have] Q, Hath *Gifford*

ANNABELLA   Helpe, *Aqua vitae.*   35

SORANZO   What meane you?

ANNABELLA   Why I thought you had beene sicke.

SORANZO   Doe you mocke my love?

GIOVANNI   [*Aside*]   There sir shee was too nimble.

SORANZO   'Tis plaine; shee laughes at me, these scornefull taunts
Neither become your modesty, or yeares.

ANNABELLA   You are no looking-glasse, or if you were,   40
I'de dresse my language by you.

GIOVANNI   [*Aside*]   I'me confirm'd.—

ANNABELLA   To put you out of doubt, my Lord, mee-thinks
Your common sence should make you understand,
That if I lov'd you, or desir'd your love,
Some way I should have given you better tast: 45
But since you are a Noble man, and one
I would not wish should spend his youth in hopes,
Let mee advise you here, to forbeare your suite,
And thinke I wish you well, I tell you this.   Fɪʳ

SORANZO   Is't you speake this ?

ANNABELLA   Yes, I my selfe; yet know   50
Thus farre I give you comfort, if mine eyes
Could have pickt out a man (amongst all those
That sue'd to mee) to make a husband of,
You should have beene that man; let this suffice,
Be noble in your secresie and wise.   55

GIOVANNI   [*Aside*] Why now I see shee loves me.

ANNABELLA   One word more:
As ever Vertue liv'd within your mind,

35–7] *Weber*, I'me . . . heart. | Helpe . . . *vitae.* | What . . . you? | Why . . . sicke. | Do . . . love? |
There . . . nimble. *Q*   37 SD [*Aside*] *Dyce* (*aside*); *not in Q*   38–49] *Reed; prose in
Q*   38 'Tis] *Dyce adds* SD [*aside*] *before* 'Tis.   38 me] *Gifford adds* SD (*Aside.*) *after
me; Wiggins,* SD [*To* ANNABELLA].   40–1 You . . . were, | I'de . . . by you] *Weber, prose in
Q*   41] *Weber,* I'de . . . you. | I'me comfirm'd.— *Q*   41 SD [*Aside*]] *Dyce* (*aside*); *not
in Q*   41 confirm'd.—] *Dodsley;* ~ʌ— *Q;* ~. *Dyce*   42 mee-thinks] *Q;* methinks *Dodsley*
45 tast:] *Q;* ~; *Reed* (taste)   48 you here] *Q;* you *Gifford*   50] *Weber,* Is't . . . this? |
Yes, . . . know *Q*   51 Thus . . . comfort] *Q;* (~ . . . ~) *Gifford*   56 SD [*Aside*]] *Dyce*
(*aside*); *not in Q*   56] *Weber,* Why . . . me. | One . . . more: *Q*

As ever noble courses were your guide,
As ever you would have me know you lov'd me,
Let not my Father know hereof by you: 60
If I hereafter finde that I must marry,
It shall be you or none.

SORANZO   I take that promise.

ANNABELLA   Oh, oh my head.

SORANZO   What's the matter, not well?

ANNABELLA   Oh I begin to sicken.

GIOVANNI   [*Aside*]   Heaven forbid.   *Exit from above.*

SORANZO   Helpe, helpe, within there ho.   65
    Looke to your daughter *Signior Florio.*

            Enter FLORIO, GIOVANNI, PUTANA.

FLORIO   Hold her up, shee sounes.

GIOVANNI   Sister how d'ee?

ANNABELLA   Sicke, brother, are you there?

FLORIO   Convay her to her bed instantly, whil'st I send for a
    Physitian, quickly I say.

PUTANA   Alas poore Child.   *Exeunt, manet* SORANZO.   70

            Enter VASQUES.

VASQUES My Lord.

SORANZO   Oh *Vasques,* now I doubly am undone,
    Both in my present and my future hopes:
    Shee plainely told me, that shee could not love,
    And thereupon soone sickned, and I feare   75
    Her life's in danger.   F1ᵛ

62–4] *Weber,* It . . . none. | I . . . promise. | Oh, . . . head. | What's . . . well? | Oh . . . sicken. |
Heaven forbid. *Q*   63 head.] *Q;* ~! *Dodsley*   64 SD1 [*Aside*]] *Sherman (aside); not in
Q*   64 SD2 *Exit from above.*] *Q.* [*Aside, and exit from above.* | *Dyce*   65–7] *Q;* Help . . .
daughter | Signior . . . *Flo.* Hold . . . sounes. *Walley*   65 ho.] *Q;* ~! *Dodsley*   66 Looke]
Gifford (Look); 'Gio. Looke' *in Q*   66.1 SD *Enter*] *Q;* Re-enter | *Dyce*   66.1 SD
PUTANA] *Q; and* PUTANA *Weber*   66.1 SD] *Weber places SD after ho 65.*   68] *Dyce;*
Sister . . . d'ee? | Sicke . . . there? *Q*   68 d'ee] *Q;* do you *Dodsley*   68 brother, are] *Q;*
~. ~ *Reed* (Are)   70 Alas∧] *Q;* ~! *Dodsley*   70 SD1 *Exeunt, manet* SORANZO] *Q;*
Exeunt all but SORANZO *Weber, Exeunt* [FLORIO, ANNABELLA, GIOVANNI, PUTANA];
SORANZO *remains*| *Wiggins*   70.1 SD2 *Enter*] *Q;* Re-enter | *Dyce*   74 me,] *Q;* ~∧ *Dyce*

VASQUES   Byr lady Sir, and so is yours, if you knew all. —'las sir,
I am sorry for that, may bee 'tis but the *Maides sicknesse*, an
over-fluxe of youth—and then sir, there is no such present
remedy, as present Marriage. But hath shee given you an   80
absolute deniall?

SORANZO   She hath and shee hath not; I'me full of griefe,
But what she sayd, I'le tell thee as we goe.

Exeunt.

3.3   *Enter* GIOVANNI *and* PUTANA.

PUTANA   Oh sir, wee are all undone, quite undone, utterly
undone, and sham'd forever; your sister, oh your sister.

GIOVANNI   What of her? for Heavens sake speake, how do'es shee?

PUTANA   Oh that ever I was borne to see this day.

GIOVANNI   She is not dead, ha, is shee?   5

PUTANA   Dead? no, shee is quicke, 'tis worse, she is with childe.
You know what you have done; Heaven forgive 'ee, 'tis too
late to repent, now Heaven helpe us.

GIOVANNI   With child? how dost thou know't?

PUTANA   How doe I know't? am I at these yeeres ignorant, what 10
the meaninges of Quames, and Waterpangs be? of changing
of Colours, Quezinesse of stomacks, Pukings, and another
thing that I could name; doe not (for her and your Credits
sake) spend the time in asking how, and which way, 'tis so;
shee is quick upon my word, if you let a Physitian see her 15
water y'are undone.

GIOVANNI   But in what case is shee?

PUTANA   Prettily amended, 'twas but a fit which I soone espi'd,
and she must looke for often hence-forward.

77] *Dyce adds* SD [*aside*] *before* Byr.   77] *Massai adds* SD [*aside*] *after* Sir.   77] *Gifford adds* SD [*Aside*]. *before* 'las; *Bawcutt*, SD [*To him*]; *Roper*, SD [*Aloud*].   77 —'las∧] Q; —~, *Dodsley*, ~∧ *Weber* ('Las)   78 that,] Q; ~; *Reed*   78 an] Q; and *Weber*   83 sayd,] Q; ~∧ *Dyce* (said)   3.3] *this edn; not in* Q; SCENE III. —A *Chamber in the same.* | *Weber*, —*Another Room in the same.* | *Dyce*; [3.3] *Massai*   2 sister.] Q; ~! *Dodsley*   6 Dead?] Q; ~! *Gifford*   6 quicke,] Q; ~; *Reed* (quick)   6 childe.] *Dodsley*, ~, Q (childe) 7 'ee] Q; you *Dodsley*   8 repent, now] Q; ~∧ ~, *Gifford*   11 meaninges] *this edn*; meaning's Q; meaning *Dodsley*   11 Quames] Q; qualms *Dodsely*   11 Waterpangs] Q; water-pangs *Dodsley*   14 so;] Q; ~: *Reed*   16 y'are] Q; you are *Dodsley*

GIOVANNI   Commend me to her, bid her take no care,   20
Let not the Doctor visit her I charge you,
Make some excuse, til I returne; *oh mee,*
I have a world of businesse in my head,
Doe not discomfort her; how doe this newes perplex mee!
If my Father come to her, tell him shee's recover'd well,   25
Say 'twas but some ill dyet; d'ee heare *Woeman,*
Looke you to 't.

PUTANA   I will sir.   *Exeunt.*   F2ʳ

3.4   *Enter* FLORIO *and* RICHARDETTO.

FLORIO   And how d'ee finde her sir?

RICHARDETTO   Indifferent well,
I see no danger, scarse perceive shee's sicke,
But that shee told mee, shee had lately eaten
Mellownes, and as shee thought, those disagreed
With her young stomacke.

FLORIO   Did you give her ought?   5

RICHARDETTO   An easie surfeit water, nothing else,
You neede not doubt her health; I rather thinke
Her sicknese is a fulnesse of her blood,
You understand mee?

FLORIO   I doe; you counsell well,
And once within these few dayes, will so order't   10
She shall be married, ere shee know the time.

RICHARDETTO   Yet let not hast (sir) make unworthy choice,
That were dishonour.

FLORIO   Maister Doctor no,
I will not doe so neither, in plaine words

20 her,] *Q*; ~; *Reed*   20 care,] *Q*; ~; *Reed*   22 *mee,*] *Q*; ~! *Dodsley* (me)   24–6 Doe
. . . me | If . . . well | Say 'twas] *Q*; Do . . . her.— | How . . . Father | Come . . . well; | Say 'twas
Gifford; Do . . . news | Perplex . . . her, | Tell . . . well; say 'twas *Gibson*   24 her;] *Dodsley*;
~, *Q*   24 doe] *Q*; does *Dodsley*   26 d'ee] *Q*; Do you *Dodsley*; d'ye *Dyce*   28 will∧]
Q; ~, *Dodsley*   **3.4**] *this edn*; not in *Q*; SCENE IV.—*Another Room in the same House.* |
Weber; SECENE IV. *Another room in the same.* | *Dyce*; [3.4] *Massai*   0.1 RICHARDETTO.]
Q; ~ [*disguised as the Doctor*] *Wiggins*   1] *Weber*; And . . . sir? | Indifferent well, *Q*
1 d'ee] *Q*; do you *Dodsley*; d' you *Weber*; d'ye *Dyce*   5] *Weber*; With . . . stomacke. | Did . . .
ought? *Q*   5 ought] *Q*; aught *Reed*   6 else,] *Q*; ~; *Dodsley*   9] *Weber*; You . . .
mee? | I . . . well, *Q*   10 will] *Q*; we'll *conj. Roper*   13] *Weber*; That . . . dishonor. |
Maister . . . no, *Q*   13 no,] *Q*; ~; *Dodsley*   14 neither,] *Q*; ~; *Dodsley*, ~: *Dyce*

My Lord *Soranzo* is the man I meane.   15

RICHARDETTO   A noble and a vertuous Gentleman.

FLORIO   As any is in *Parma*; not farre hence,
Dwels Father *Bonaventure*, a grave Fryar,
Once Tutor to my Sonne; now at his Cell
I'le have 'em married.

RICHARDETTO   You have plotted wisely.   20

FLORIO   I'le send one straight to speake with him to night.

RICHARDETTO   *Soranzo's* wise, he will delay no time.

FLORIO   It shall be so.

Enter FRYAR *and* GIOVANNI.

FRYAR   Good peace be here and love.

FLORIO   Welcome relligious Fryar, you are one,
That still bring blessing to the place you come to.   25

GIOVANNI   Sir, with what speed I could, I did my best,
To draw this holy man from forth his Cell,
F2ᵛ   To visit my sicke sister, that with words
Of ghostly comfort in this time of neede,
Hee might absolve her, whether she live or dye.   30

FLORIO   'Twas well done *Giovanni*, thou herein
Hast shewed a Christians care, a Brothers love.
Come Father, I'le conduct you to her chamber,
And one thing would intreat you.

FRYAR   Say on sir.

FLORIO   I have a Fathers deare impression,   35
And wish before I fall into my grave,
That I might see her married, as 'tis fit;
A word from you *Grave man*, will winne her more,
Then all our best perswasions.

20] *Weber*, I'le . . . married. | You . . . wisely. *Q*   21] *Weber*, I'le . . . straight | To speake . . .
night. *Q*   23] *Weber*, It . . . so. | Good . . . love. *Q*   34] *Weber*, And . . . you. | Say . . .
sir. *Q*   39] *Weber*, Then . . . perswasions. | Gentle Sir, *Q*

FRYAR   Gentle Sir,
All this I'le say, that Heaven may prosper her.   40

                                        Exeunt.

              3.5   *Enter* GRIMALDI.

GRIMALDI   Now if the Doctor keepe his word, *Soranzo*,
      Twenty to one you misse your Bride; I know
      'Tis an unnoble act, and not becomes
      A Souldiers vallour; but in termes of love,
      Where Merite cannot sway, Policy must.   5
      I am resolv'd, if this Physitian
      Play not on both hands, then *Soranzo* falls.

                    Enter RICHARDETTO.

RICHARDETTO   You are come as I could wish, this very night
      Soranzo, 'tis ordain'd must bee affied
      To *Annabella*; and for ought I know,   10
      Married.

GRIMALDI   How!

RICHARDETTO   Yet your patience,
      The place, 'tis Fryar *Bonaventures* Cell.
      Now I would wish you to bestow this night,
      In watching thereabouts, 'tis but a night,
      If you misse now, to morrow I'le know all.   15

GRIMALDI   Have you the poyson?

RICHARDETTO   Here 'tis in this Box,
      Doubt nothing, this will doe't; in any case
      As you respect your life, be quicke and sure.

GRIMALDI   I'le speede him.

RICHARDETTO   Doe; away, for 'tis not safe   F3ʳ
      You should be seene much here—ever my love.   20

3.5] *this edn; not in Q:* SCENE V.—RICHARDETTO'S *Apartment in the same.* | *Weber; A room in* RICHARDETTO'*shouse.*| *Dyce*; [3.5] *Massai*   2 Bride;] *Q;~.Dodsley*(bride)   6 resolv'd,] *Q; ~; Sherman*   8–11] *Reed; prose in Q*   8 You are] *Q;* You're *Dyce*   8 wish,] *Q; ~; Dodsley*   9 ordain'd] *Q; ~, Dodsley*   10–11 I know, | Married. How!] *Weber; one line in Q*   11 patience,] *Q; ~; Dodsley*   12 Fryar] *Dodsley* (friar), *Gifford* (Friar); Fryars *Q*   14 thereabouts,] *Q; ~; Dodsley*   15 now, to morrow] *Q; ~!* Tomorrow *Weber; ~,* to-morrow *Dyce*   16] *Weber;* Have . . . poyson? | Here . . . Box. *Q*   19] *Weber;* I'll . . . him. | Doe; . . . safe *Q*

GRIMALDI   And mine to you.   *Exit* GRIMALDI.

RICHARDETTO   So, if this hitt, I'le laugh and hug revenge;
And they that now dreame of a wedding-feast,
May chance to mourne the lusty Bridegromes ruine.
But to my other businesse; Neece *Philotis.*   25

Enter PHILOTIS.

PHILOTIS   Unkle.

RICHARDETTO   My lovely Neece, you have bethought 'ee.

PHILOTIS   Yes, and as you counsel'd,
Fashion'd my heart to love him, but hee sweares
Hee will to night be married; for he feares
His Unkle else, if hee should know the drift,   30
Will hinder all, and call his Couze to shrift.

RICHARDETTO   To night? why best of all; but let me see,
I—ha—yes,—so it shall be; in disguise
Wee'le earely to the Fryars, I have thought on't.

Enter BERGETTO *and* POGGIO.

PHILOTIS   Unkle, hee comes.

RICHARDETTO   Welcome my worthy Couze.   35

BERGETTO   Lasse pretty Lasse, come busse Lasse, a ha Poggio.

PHILOTIS   There's hope of this yet.

RICHARDETTO   You shall have time enough, withdraw a little,
Wee must conferre at large.

BERGETTO.   Have you not sweete-meates, or dainty devices   40
for me?

PHILOTIS   You shall enough *Sweet-heart;*

21 SD *Exit* GRIMALDI.] *Dodsley; Exit. Q*   25–7 But . . . counsel'd] *Massai*; But . . . Philotis.
| Uncle. | My . . . ye? | Yes, . . . counselled *Q*; But . . . Philotis | Uncle. | My . . . niece | You . . .
you ('ee) | Yes, . . . counsell'd *Gifford*; But . . . Philotis! | Uncle? | My ~ niece! | You . . . ye? | Yes,
. . . counselled *Dyce*; But . . . business. | Niece . . . niece, | You have . . . counselled
Wiggins   25 businesse; Neece] *Q*; ~. ~ *Massai* (business) (Niece)   25] *Wiggins adds*
SD [*Calls*] *before* Neece.   26 'ee] *Q*; ye *Dodsley;* you *Gifford*   33 I—] *Q*; Ay— *Dodsley*
35] *Weber*; Uncle . . . comes. | Welcome . . . Couze. *Q*   36] *Weber adds* SD [*Kisses her.*]
before a ha; *Dyce*, SD [*Kisses her.* | *after* Poggio.   37 SP PHILOTIS] *Q* (*Phi.*); Richardetto
Gifford; Rich. | *Dyce*; POGGIO *Bawcutt*   37] *Dyce adds* SD [*aside.*] *before* There's; *not in Q*
42 shall] *Q*; shall have *Gifford*

BERGETTO   *Sweet-heart*, marke that *Poggio*; by my troth I
cannot choose but kisse thee once more for that word
Sweet-heart, *Poggio* I have a monstrous swelling about my   45
stomacke, whatsoever the matter be.

POGGIO   You shall have Phisick for't sir.

RICHARDETTO   Time runs apace.

BERGETTO   Time's a blockhead.

RICHARDETTO   Be rul'd, when wee have done what's fitt to doe,   50
Then you may kisse your fill, and bed her too.

                              Exeunt.   F3ᵛ

3.6   *Enter the* FRYAR *in his study, sitting in a chayre,*
ANNABELLA *kneeling and whispering to him, a Table before*
them and wax-lights, she weepes, and wring her hands.

FRYAR   I am glad to see this pennance; for beleeve me,
You have unript a soule, so foul and guilty,
As I must tell you true, I marvaile how
The earth hath borne you up; but weepe, weepe on,
These teares may doe you good; weepe faster yet,   5
Whiles I doe read a Lecture.

ANNABELLA   Wretched creature.

FRYAR   I, you are wretched, miserably wretched,
Almost condemn'd alive; there is *a place*
(List daughter) in a blacke and hollow Vault,
Where day is never seene; there shines no Sunne,   10
But flaming horrour of consuming Fires;
A lightlesse Sulphure, choakt with smoaky fogs
Of an infeckted darknesse; in *this place*
Dwell many thousand, thousand sundry sorts

45 *Sweet-heart*,] *Dodsley* (sweet-heart); ~, *Q*   45 *Poggio*ʌ] *Q*; ~! *Weber*   45] *Weber*
adds SD [*Kisses her.* | *after* POGGIO; *Roper*, SD [*Kisses her.*] *before* POGGIO.   49 block-
head.] *Q*; ~! *Roper*   49] *Roper adds* SD [*Kisses her.*] *after* blockhead.   **3.6**] *this edn*;
not in Q; SCENE VI.—*The* FRIAR'*s Cell.* | *Weber*; FLORIO'*s House.* | *Gifford*; SCENE VI.—
FLORIO'*s house.* | *Dyce*; [3.6] *Massai*   0.1–03] *Q*; *Sherman omits 'in his study', Dyce changes*
Q's SD *for* SD 'ANNABELLA'*s chamber. A table with wax lights;* ANNABELLA *at confession before*
the Friar; she weeps and wrings her hands.'   0.1 SD *Enter the* FRYAR] *Q*; [*Enter omitted*] ~ ~
| *Weber (The)*   4 up;] *Dodsley*; ~, *Q*; ~: *Dyce*   6] *Weber*, Whiles . . . Lecture. | Wretched
creature. *Q*   6 creature.] *Q*; ~! *Dodsley*   8 alive; there] *Q*; ~. ~ *Dodsley* (There)
12 Sulphure] *Dodsley* (sulphur); Suphure *Q*

Of never dying deaths; there damned soules   15
Roare without pitty, there are Gluttons fedd
With Toades and Addars; there is burning Oyle
Powr'd downe the Drunkards throate, the Usurer
Is forc't to supp whole draughts of molten Gold;
There is the Murtherer for-ever stab'd,   20
Yet can he never dye; there lies the wanton
On Racks of burning steele, whiles in his soule
Hee feeles the torment of his raging lust.

ANNABELLA   Mercy, oh mercy.

FRYAR   There stands these wretched things,
Who have dream't out whole yeares in lawless sheets   25
And secret incests, cursing one another;
Then you will wish, each kisse your brother gave,
Had beene a Daggers poynt; then you shall heare
How hee will cry, oh would my wicked sister
F4ʳ   Had first beene damn'd, when shee did yeeld to lust.   30
But soft, methinkes I see repentance worke
New motions in your heart, say? how is't with you?

ANNABELLA   Is there no way left to redeeme my miseries?

FRYAR   There is, despaire not; Heaven is mercifull,
And offers grace even now; 'tis thus agreed,   35
First, for your Honours safety that you marry
The Lord *Soranzo*, next, to save your soule,
Leave off this life, and henceforth live to him.

ANNABELLA   Ay mee.

FRYAR   Sigh not, I know the baytes of sinne
Are hard to leave, oh 'tis a death to doe't.   40
Remember what must come, are you content?

ANNABELLA   I am.

22 whiles] *Q;* whilst *Dodsley*   24] *Weber;* Mercy . . . mercy. | There . . . things, *Q*
24 stands] *Q;* stand *Reed*   32 heart,] *Q;* ~? *Dodsley,* ~: *Dyce*   35 now; 'tis] *Q;* ~. ~
Dodsley ('Tis)   37 *Soranzo,*] *Q;* ~; *Dodsley* (Soranzo)   39] *Weber;* Ay mee. | Sigh . . .
sinne *Q*   39 mee.] *Q;* ~! *Dodsley* (me)   40 leave,] *Q;* ~; *Dodsley*   40 doe't.] *Q;*
~! *Dodsley* (do't); ~: *Dyce* (do't)   42] *Weber;* I am. | I . . . time. *Q*

FRYAR   I like it well, wee'le take the time,
Who's neere us there?

Enter FLORIO *and* GIOVANNI.

FLORIO   Did you call Father?

FRYAR   Is Lord *Soranzo* come?

FLORIO   Hee stayes belowe.

FRYAR   Have you acquainted him at full?

FLORIO   I have   45
And hee is over-joy'd.

FRYAR   And so are wee:
Bid him come neere.

GIOVANNI [*Aside*]   My Sister weeping, ha?
I feare this *Fryars* falshood, I will call him.   *Exit.*

FLORIO   Daughter, are you resolv'd?

ANNABELLA   Father, I am.

Enter GIOVANNI, SORANZO, *and* VASQUES.

FLORIO   My Lord *Soranzo*, here.   50
Give mee your hand, for that I give you this.

SORANZO   Lady, say you so too?

ANNABELLA   I doe, and vow,
To live with you and yours.

FRYAR   Timely resolv'd:
My blessing rest on both, more to be done,
You may performe it on the Morning-sun   55
                                Exeunt.   F4ᵛ

43 SD *and*] *Weber*, *not in* Q   43] *Dyce*; Who's . . . there? | Did . . . Father? Q
44–9] *Weber*; Is . . . Come? | Hee . . . belowe. | Have . . . full? | I . . . over-ioy'd. | And . . . neere.
| My . . . falshood, | I . . . him. | Daughter . . . resolv'd? | Father . . . am. Q   45–6 I have |
And . . . over-ioy'd.] *one line in* Q   46–7 And . . . wee: | Bid . . . neere.] *one line in* Q
47–8] My . . . ha? | I . . . falshood.] *one line in* Q   47 SD [*Aside*]] *Gifford* (*aside*); *not in*
Q   47 ha?] Q; ~! *Weber* (Ha)   48] *Gifford adds* SD [*Aside.*] *before* I will; *Bawcutt*,
SD [*To him*]; *Roper*, SD [*To them*]; *Wiggins*, SD [*Aloud*].   49] *Weber*, Daughter . . .
resolv'd? | Father . . . am. Q   51 hand,] Q; ~; *Reed*   51 this.] Q; ~. *Gifford*
51 *Gifford adds* SD [*Joins their hands.*] *after* this; *Wiggins*, SD [*Joins* SORANZO's *and*
ANNABELLA's *hands*]; *Massai*, SD [*Joins Soranzo and Annabella hand in hand*].
52–3] *Weber*; Lady . . . too? | I . . . yours. | To . . . yours. | Timely resolv'd: Q   54 both,]
Q; ~; *Reed*; ~! *Dyce*

3.7   *Enter* GRIMALDI *with his Rapier drawne,*
and a Darke-lanthorne.

GRIMALDI   'Tis early night as yet, and yet too soone
To finish such a worke; here I will lye
To listen who comes next.   *Hee lies downe.*

Enter BERGETTO *and* PHILOTIS *disguis'd, and after·*
RICHARDETTO *and* POGGIO.

BERGETTO   Wee are almost at the place, I hope *Sweet-heart.*

GRIMALDI   I heare them neere, and heard one say *Sweet-heart,*   5
'Tis hee; now guide my hand some angry *Justice*
Home to his bosome. [*Aloud*] Now have at you sir!
                    Strikes BERGETTO *and Exit.*

BERGETTO   Oh helpe, helpe, here's a stich fallen in my gutts,
Oh for a Flesh-taylor quickly—*Poggio.*

PHILOTIS   What ayles my love?   10

BERGETTO   I am sure I cannot pisse forward and backward, and yet
I am wet before and behind, lights, lights, ho lights.

PHILOTIS   Alas, some Villaine here has slaine my love.

RICHARDETTO   Oh Heaven forbid it; raise up the next neighbours
Instantly *Poggio*, and bring lights.   *Exit* POGGIO.   15
How is't *Bergetto*? slaine?
It cannot be; are you sure y'are hurt?

BERGETTO   Oh my belly seeths like a Porriage-pot, some cold
water I shall boyle over else; my whole body is in a sweat,
that you may wring my shirt; feele here—why *Poggio.*   20

Enter POGGIO *with* OFFICERS, *and lights and Halberts.*

POGGIO   Here; alas, how doe you?

3.7] *this edn; not in Q;* SCENE VII.—*Before the Friar's Cell.* | *Weber;* SCENE VII. *The street before
the monastery.* | *Dyce;* [3.7] *Massai*   3.1 SD after] *Q; ~ him Weber; followed at a short dis-
tance by| Dyce*   3.2 SD RICHARDETTO] *Q; ~ [disguised as the Doctor] Wiggins*   5] *Dyce
adds* SD [*aside*] *before* I heare.   7 bosome.] *Dodsley; ~, Q*   7 SD [*Aloud*]] *Bawcutt,
not in Q*   7 Now] *Dodsley; now Q*   7 you₍] *Q; ~, Dodsley*   7 sir!] *Weber; ~.
Q;*   7 SD *Strikes*] *Q; Stabs | Dyce*   8–9] *Q; prose in Weber*   12 behind,] *Q; ~;
Dodsley*   12 lights, lights, ho lights.] *Q; ~! ~! ~ ~! Dodsley*   14–17] *Q; Oh . . . lights.
- SD [Exit POG. | How . . . be; | Are . . . hurt? Gifford; Oh . . . lights. | SD [Exit POGGIO.] | How
. . . hurt? Hopkins*   15 lights.] *Dodsley; ~, Q*   20 Poggio.] *Q; ~! Dodsley* (Poggio)
20.1 SD *Enter*] *Q; Re-enter Dyce*   20.1 SD *and Halberts.*] *Q; not in Dyce*

RICHARDETTO   Give me a light, what's here? all blood! O sirs,
Signior Donado's Nephew now is slaine,
Follow the murtherer with all the haste
Up to the Citty, hee cannot be farre hence,   25
Follow I beseech you.

OFFICERS   Follow, follow, follow.
                                                            Exeunt OFFICERS.   G1ʳ

RICHARDETTO   Teare off thy linnen Couz, to stop his wounds,
Be of good comfort man.

BERGETTO   Is all this mine owne blood? nay then good-night
with me, *Poggio*, commend me to my Unkle, dost heare? bid   30
him for my sake make much of this wench, oh—I am going
the wrong way sure, my belly akes so—oh farwell, *Poggio*—
oh—oh—

                                                            Dyes.

PHILOTIS   O hee is dead.

POGGIO   How! dead!

RICHARDETTO   Hee's dead indeed,
'Tis now to late to weepe, let's have him home,   35
And with what speed we may, finde out the Murtherer.

POGGIO   Oh my Maister, my Maister, my Maister.   *Exeunt.*

3.8   *Enter* VASQUES *and* HIPPOLITA.

HIPPOLITA Betroath'd?

VASQUES   I saw it.

HIPPOLITA   And when's the marriage-day?

VASQUES   Some two dayes hence.

24 the haste] *Q*; thy haste *conj. Roper*; thou hast *conj. Southall* (*cited by Roper*); despatch *Morris*
26] *Dyce*; Follow . . . you. | Follow . . . follow. *Q*   27] *Wiggins adds* SD [*To* PHILOTIS]
before Teare.   27 wounds,] *Q*; ~; *Dodsley*   28] *Wiggins adds* SD [*To* BERGETTO]
before Be.   30 me, *Poggio*] *Q*; ~. ~ *Dodsley*   30 heare?] *Q*; ~! *Dodsley* (hear)
32 farwell] *Q*; farewell *Dodsley*   34] *Weber*; O . . . dead. | How! Dead! | Hee's . . . indeed,
Q   35 to late] *Q*; too ~ *Dodsley*   37 Maister, my Maister, my Maister.] *Q*; ~! ~ ~! ~ ~!
Dodsley (master)   **3.8**] *this edn*; *not in Q*; SCENE VIII.—*The Street.* | *Weber*; SCENE VIII. *A*
room in HIPPOLITA's *house.* | *Dyce*; [3.8] *Massai*   1–4] *Q*; Betroth'd? | I . . . it. | And . . .
hence. *Dyce*; Betroth'd? . . . day? | Some . . . hence. *Massai*

HIPPOLITA   Two dayes? Why man I would but wish two houres   5
To send him to his last, and lasting sleepe.
And *Vasques* thou shalt see, I'le doe it bravely.

VASQUES   I doe not doubt your wisedome, nor (I trust) you my
secresie, I am infinitely yours.

HIPPOLITA   I wilbe thine in spight of my disgrace,   10
So soone? o wicked man, I durst be sworne,
Hee'd laugh to see mee weepe.

VASQUES   And that's a Villanous fault in him.

HIPPOLITA   No, let him laugh, I'me arm'd in my resolves,
Be thou still true.   15

VASQUES   I should get little by treachery against so hopefull a
preferment, as I am like to climbe to.

HIPPOLITA   Even to my bosome *Vasques,* let *My youth*
Revell in these new pleasures, if wee thrive,
Hee now hath but a paire of dayes to live.   *Exeunt.*   20

3.9   *Enter* FLORIO, DONADO, RICHARDETTO,
POGGIO *and* OFFICERS.

G1ᵛ   FLORIO   'Tis bootlesse now to shew your selfe a child
Signior Donado, what is done, is done;
Spend not the time in teares, but seeke for Justice.

RICHARDETTO   I must confesse, somewhat I was in fault,
That had not first acquainted you what love   5
Past twixt him and my Neece, but as I live,
His Fortune grieves me as it were mine owne.

DONADO   Alas poore creature, he ment no man harme,
That I am sure of.

FLORIO   I beleeve that too;

8–9] *this edn*; I . . . trust, | you . . . yours. *Weber*; I . . . secresie, | I . . . yours. *Q*   10 wilbe]
Q; will be *Dodsley*   18 bosomeʌ] *Q*; ~, *Dodsley* (bosom)   18 *Vasques,*] *Q*; ~: *Weber*
(Vasques); ~. *Dyce* (Vasques)   19 pleasures,] *Q*; ~; *Dodsley*; ~: *Dyce*   **3.9**] *this edn*; *not
in* Q; SCENE IX.—*The Street before the* CARDINAL'S *Gates.* | *Weber,* SCENE IX. *The street before
the* CARDINAL'*s gates.* | *Dyce*; [3.9] *Massai*   0.1 SD DONODO] ~ [*weeping*] *Lomax*
0.1 SD RICHARDETTO] ~ [*disguised as the Doctor*] *Wiggins*   2 done, is done;] *Q*; ~, ~ ~:
Dodsley   9] *Weber*; That . . . of. | I . . . too; *Q*

But stay my Maisters, are you sure you saw   10
The Murtherer passe here?

OFFICER   And it please you sir, wee are sure wee saw a Ruffian
with a naked weapon in his hand all bloody, get into my Lord
Cardinals Graces gate, that wee are sure of; but for feare of his
Grace (blesse us) we durst goe no further.   15

DONADO   Know you what manner of man hee was?

OFFICER   Yes sure I know the man, they say 'a is a souldier, hee
that lov'd your daughter Sir an't please y'ee, 'twas hee for
certaine.

FLORIO   *Grimaldi* on my life.

OFFICER   I, I, the same.   20

RICHARDETTO   The Cardinal is Noble, he no doubt
Will give true Justice.

DONADO   Knocke some one at the gate,

POGGIO   I'le knocke sir.   POGGIO *knocks.*

SERVANT   (*within*) What would'ee?   25

FLORIO   Wee require speech with the Lord Cardinal
About some present businesse, pray informe
His Grace, that we are here.

                Enter CARDINAL *and* GRIMALDI.

CARDINAL   Why how now friends? what sawcy mates are you
That know nor duty nor Civility?   30
Are we a person fit to be your hoast?
Or is our house become your common Inne
To beate our dores at pleasure? what such haste
Is yours as that it cannot waite fit times?   G2ʳ
Are you the Maisters of this Common-wealth,   35
And know no more discretion? oh your newes

12 And] *Q*; An *Weber*   15 (blesse us)] *Q*; ~ ~! *Roper* (bless)   15] *Roper adds* SD [*They
cross themselves.*] *before* we.   17 souldier, hee] *Q*; ~. ~ *Wiggins* (He)   17] *Wiggins adds*
SD [*To* FLORIO] *before* hee.   18 y'ee] *Q*; ye *Weber*   20] *Weber*; *Grimaldi . . .* life. |
I, . . . same. *Q*   20 I, I,] *Q*; Ay, ay, *Dodsley*   25 SD (*within*)] *Weber*, ~. *Q* [*within*]
Dyce   25 would'ee] *Q*; would ye *Dodsley*   27 businesse,] *Q*; ~; *Dodsley* (business); ~:
Dyce (business)   28.1 SD CARDINAL *and*] *Q*; ~, *followed by* | *Dyce*   36] *Massai adds*
SD [*Recognizes Donado.*] *after* discretion?   36 oh] *Q*; - ~, *Massai* (Oh)

Is here before you, you have lost a Nephew
Donado, last night by *Grimaldi* slaine:
Is that your businesse? well sir, we have knowledge on't,
Let that suffice.

GRIMALDI   In presence of your Grace,   40
In thought I never ment *Bergetto* harme,
But *Florio* you can tell, with how much scorne
Soranzo, backt with his Confederates,
Hath often wrong'd mee; I to be reveng'd,
(For that I could not win him else to fight)   45
Had thought by way of Ambush to have kild him,
But was unluckily, therein mistooke;
Else hee had felt what late *Bergetto* did:
And though my fault to him were meerely chance,
Yet humbly I submit me to your Grace,   50
To doe with mee as you please.

CARDINAL   Rise up *Grimaldi*,
You Cittizens of *Parma*, if you seeke
For Justice; Know as *Nuntio* from the Pope,
For this offence I here receive *Grimaldi*
Into his holinesse protection.   55
Hee is no Common man, but nobly borne;
Of Princes blood, though you Sir *Florio*,
Thought him to meane a husband for your daughter
If more you seeke for, you must goe to *Rome*,
For hee shall thither; learne more wit for shame.   60
Bury your dead—away *Grimaldi*—leave 'em.
                    Exeunt CARDINAL *and* GRIMALDI.

DONADO   Is this a Church-mans voyce? dwels *Justice* here?

FLORIO   *Justice* is fledd to heaven and comes no neerer.
Soranzo! Was't for him? O Impudence!
Had he the face to speake it, and not blush?   65

40] *Weber*; Let . . . suffice. | In . . . Grace, *Q*   40] *Wiggins adds* SD [*Kneeling*] *before* In presence; *Massai*, SD [*Kneels*.].   43 *Soranzo*,] *Dodsley* (Soranzo); ~∧ *Q*   47 unluckily] *Dodsley*; unluckely *Q*   49 though] *Q*; tho' *Dodsley*   50] *Gifford adds* SD [*Kneeling*. | *after* Grace.   51] *Weber*; To . . . please. | Rise . . . *Grimaldi*, | *Q*   51 *Grimaldi*,] *Q*; ~; *Dodsley*   51] *Gifford adds* SD [*He rises.* | *after* 'Grimaldi'; *Wiggins*, SD [GRIMALDI *rises*.].
55 holinesse] *Q*; holiness' *Dodsley*   57 Sir∧ *Florio*] *Q*; sir, Florio *Sturgess*   61.1 SD *Exeunt*] *Dodsley*; Exit | *Q*   63 neerer.] *Dodsley* (nearer); ~∧ *Q*   64 *Soranzo*! Was't] *this edn*, *Bawcutt* (Soranzo! ~); ~, ~ *Q* (was't); ~!—~ *Weber* (Soranzo)

Come, come *Donado*, there's no helpe in this,
When *Cardinals* thinke murder's not amisse,
Great men may doe their wills, we must obey,
But Heaven will judge them for't another day.

Exeunt.   G2ᵛ

4.1   *A Banquet. Hoboyes.*

Enter the FRYAR, GIOVANNI, ANNABELLA, PHILOTIS, SORANZO,
DONADO, FLORIO, RICHARDETTO, PUTANA *and* VASQUES.

FRYAR   These holy rights perform'd, now take your times,
To spend the remnant of the day in Feast;
Such fit repasts are pleasing to the Saints
Who are your guests, though not with mortall eyes
To be beheld; long prosper in this day   5
You happy Couple, to each others ioy.

SORANZO   Father, your prayer is heard, the hand of goodnesse
Hath beene a sheild for me against my death;
And more to blesse me, hath enrich my life
With this most precious Jewell; such a prize   10
As Earth hath not another like to this.
Cheere up my Love, and Gentlemen, my Friends,
Rejoyce with mee in mirth, this day wee'le crowne
With lusty Cups to *Annabella's* health.

GIOVANNI   Oh Torture, were the marriage yet undone,   *Aside.*   15
Ere I'de endure this sight, to see my Love
Clipt by another, I would dare Confusion,
And stand the horror of ten thousand deaths.

VASQUES   Are you not well Sir?

GIOVANNI   Prethee fellow wayte,
I neede not thy officious diligence.   20

FLORIO   *Signior Donado*, come you must forget
Your late mishaps, and drowne your cares in wine.

67 amisse,] *Q;* ~; *Gifford* (amiss); ~. *Dyce* (amiss)   68 their] *Dodsley;* there *Q*   **4.1**] *this edn; Actus Quartus.Q;* SCENE I.—*A Hall in* FLORIO'S *House. —A Banquet. —Hautboys.* | *Weber;* SCENE I. *A room in* FLORIO's *house. A banquet set out; hautboys.* | *Dyce;* 4[.1] *Massai* 0.3 SD RICHRDETTO] *Q;* ~ [*disguised as the Doctor*] *Wiggins*   0.3 SD *and* VASQUES.] *Q;* ~ VASQUEZ [*and Attendants*]. *Massai*   4 though] *Q;* tho' *Dodsley*   5 in] *Q;* from *Dodsley*   6 ioy.] *Dodsley* (joy); ~! *Reed;* ~: *Q*   15 Torture,] *Q;* ~! *Reed* (torture)   15 SD *Aside*.] *Q; Gifford places* SD [*aside*] *after* deaths 18; *Dyce,* SD [*aside*] *before* Oh 19] *Weber;* Are . . . Sir? | Pry'thee . . . wayte, *Q*

SORANZO *Vasques?*

VASQUES   My Lord.

SORANZO   Reach me that weighty bowle,

G3ʳ Here brother *Giovanni*, here's to you,
Your turne comes next, though now a Batchelour,   25
                  [*Drinks and offers him the bowle.*]

Here's to your sisters happinesse and mine.

GIOVANNI I cannot drinke.

SORANZO   What?

GIOVANNI   'Twill indeede offend me.

ANNABELLA Pray, doe not urge him if hee be not willing.

FLORIO How now, what noyse is this?

VASQUES O sir, I had forgot to tell you; certaine young Maidens   30
of *Parma* in honour to Madam *Annabella's* marriage, have
sent their loves to her in a Masque, for which they humbly
crave your patience and silence.

SORANZO Wee are much bound to them, so much the more
As it comes unexpected; guide them in.   35
                  Hoboyes.

Enter HIPPOLITA *and Ladies* [*masked*] *in white Roabes with
Garlands of Willowes.
Musicke and a Daunce.*   *Dance.*

23] *Weber; Vasques?* | My Lord. |Reach . . . bowle. *Q*   23 *Vasques?*] *Q; ~! Reed* (Vasques)
23 bowle,] *Q; ~; Dodsley* (bowl); ~. *Dyce* (bowl)   23] *Massai places* SD [*Vasques hands him
a bowl.*] *after* bowle.   25.1 SD] *this edn; not in Q; Gifford places* SD [*Drinks, and offers him
the bowl.*] *after* mine; *Wiggins,* SD [SORANZO *drinks, and offers* GIOVANNI *the goblet*] *after* mine.
27] *Weber;* I . . . drinke. | What? | 'Twill . . . me. *Q*   28] *Wiggins places* SD [*Sounds are
heard off-stage*] *after* willing; *Massai,* SD [*Noises within*] *after* willing.   29 now,] *Q; ~?
Reed; ~! Dyce*   30 young] *Dodsley,* youg *Q*   34–5] *Gifford; prose in Q*   35] *Massai
places* SD [*Exit Vasques*] *after* in.   35.1 SD 1 *Hoboyes.*] *Q,* Weber [*Hautboys.*]; *Gifford places*
SD [*Hautboys.*] *after* willing 28.   35.2 SD HIPPOLITA] *Q; Weber adds* 'masked' *after*
HIPPOLITA.   35.2 SD *and*] *Q; followed by* | *Gifford*   35.2 SD [*masked*]] *Massai; not in
Q*   35.2 in] *Q; ~* [*masks and*] | *Wiggins*   35.3 SD Willowes.] *Q; ~, all masked. Gifford*
(*willows*)

SORANZO   Thanks lovely Virgins; now might wee but know
To whom wee have beene beholding for this love,
Wee shall acknowledge it.

HIPPOLITA   Yes, you shall know.   [*Unmasks*]
What thinke you now?

OMNES   *Hippolita?*

HIPPOLITA   'Tis shee,
Bee not amaz'd; nor blush young louely Bride,   40
I come not to defraud you of your man,
'Tis now no time to reckon up the talke
What *Parma* long hath rumour'd of us both,
Let rash report run on; the breath that vents it
Will (like a bubble) breake it selfe at last.   45
But now to you *Sweet Creature*, lend's your hand,
Perhaps it hath beene said, that I would claime
Some interest in *Soranzo*, now your Lord,
What I have right to doe, his soule knowes best:
But in my duty to your Noble worth,   50
Sweete *Annabella*, and my care of you,   G3ᵛ
Here take *Soranzo*, take this hand from me.
                    [*She joins their hands.*]

I'le once more joyne, what by the holy Church
Is finish't and allow'd; have I done well?

SORANZO   You have too much ingag'd us.

HIPPOLITA   One thing more   55
That you may know my single charity,
Freely I here remit all interest
I ere could clayme: and give you backe your vowes,

36 Virgins;] *this edn*; ~, *Q*; ~: *Reed* (virgins); ~! *Dyce* (virgins)   37 this] *Q* (corrected); thy
Q (uncorrected)   38–9] *Weber*; Wee . . . it. | Yes, . . . know, |What . . . now? | *Hippolita?* |
'Tis shee, *Q*   38 SD [*Unmasks*] *Dyce*; not in *Q*; *Weber places* SD (*unmasks.*) *before* Yes;
Wiggins, SD [Unmasks] *before* What; *Massai*, SD [*Discloses herself.*] *before* Yes.   38 know.]
Dyce; ~, *Q*   41 man,] *Q* ~; *Dodsley*, ~: *Reed*   42] *Roper adds* SD [*To Sor.*] *before* 'Tis.
43 both,] *Q*; ~; *Dodsley*; ~: *Reed*   46] *Roper adds* SD [*To Ann.*] *before* But.   46 hand,]
Q; ~: *Dodsley*; ~; — *Dyce*; ~. *Massai*   46] *Massai adds* SD [*Takes Annabella's hand.*] *after*
hand.   48 Lord,] *Q*; ~; *Dodsley* (lord)   52 me.] *Roper*; ~, *Q*; ~; *Dyce*   52.1 SD]
Lomax; not in *Q*; *Massai places* SD [*joining Annabella and Soranzo hand in hand*] *after* Here.
54 allow'd; have] *Q*; ~. ~ *Reed* (Have); ~.— *Dyce* (Have)   55] *Weber*; You . . . us. | One . . .
more *Q*   55 more∧] *Q*; ~, *Dodsley*; ~; *Weber*; ~. *Gifford*   58 clayme:] *Q*; ~, *Dodsley*
(claim)   58 vowes,] *Q*; ~; *Dodsley* (vows)

And to confirm't, reach me a Cup of wine.
My Lord *Soranzo*, in this draught I drinke,   60
Long rest t'ee! [*Aside*] Looke to it *Vasques*.

VASQUES   [*Aside*] Feare nothing—

> *He gives her a poysond Cup.*
> *She drinks.*

SORANZO   *Hippolita*, I thanke you, and will pledge
This happy Union as another life,
Wine there.   65

VASQUES   You shall have none, neither shall you pledge her.

HIPPOLITA   How!

VASQUES   Know now Mistresse shee devill, your owne
mischievous treachery hath kild you, I must not marry you.

HIPPOLITA   Villaine.   70

OMNES   What's the matter?

VASQUES   Foolish woeman , thou art now like a Fire-brand ,
that hath kindled others and burnt thy selfe; *Troppo sperare*
inganna, thy vaine hope hath deceived thee, thou art but
dead, if thou hast any grace, pray.   75

HIPPOLITA   Monster.

VASQUES   Dye in charity for shame, This thing of malice, this
woman had privately corrupted mee with promise of
marriage, under this politique reconciliation to poyson my
Lord, whiles shee might laugh at his Confusion on his   80
marriage-day; I promis'd her faire, but I knew what my

---

59 confirm't, . . . wine.] *Q*; ~—~ . . . ~— *Gifford*   59] *Wiggins adds* SD [*To* VASQUES] *before*
reach.   59 wine.] *Dodsley*; ~∧ *Q*   59] *Dyce adds* SD [*Vas. gives her a poisoned cup.* | *after*
wine.   61 t'ee!] *Dyce* (t' ye); ~— *Q*; ~— *Dodsley* (t'ye)   61 SD [*Aside*]] *this edn; not in*
Q; *Weber places* SD [*Aside to him.*] *after* '*Vasques*'; *Dyce*, SD '[*She drinks*].— [*Aside to Vas.*]' *before*
Looke; *Massai*, SD [*aside to Vasquez*] *before* Looke.   62 SD1 [*Aside*]] *Dyce* (*aside to Hip.*);
not in Q   62 SD2 He . . . drinks.] *set against* ll. 62–3 *in Q*; *Dyce places* SD *after* wine
59.   64–5 This . . . life. | Wine there.] *Q*; *one line in Wiggins*   65] *Massai places* SD [*to*
Vasquez] *before* Wine.   68 now∧] *Q*; ~, *Dodsley*   69 hath] *Weber*; Hath *Q*
70 Villaine.] *Q*; ~! *Dodsley* (villain)   73 sprerare] *this edn; sperar Q*   74 inganna]
Weber; niganna *Q*   74 thee,] *Q*; ~; *Dodsley*   77–8 Dye . . . shame, | This] *Q*; Die . . .
shame—This *Weber*   77 shame,] *Q*; ~! *Dodsley*   77] *Wiggins adds* SD [*To the others*]
after shame.   79 marriage] *Dodsley*; malice *Q*   79 to poyson] *Dodsley* (~ poison); to to
~ *Q*   80 whiles] *Q*; whilst *Dodsley*   81 marriage-day;] *Q* (marriage day); ~. *Dyce*

reward should have beene, and would willingly have spar'd her
life, but that I was acquainted with the danger of her disposition,
and now have fitted her a just payment in her owne coyne,
there shee is, shee hath yet——and end thy dayes in peace vild   85
woman; as for life there's no hope, thinke not on't.

OMNES   Wonderfull Justice!

RICHARDETTO   Heaven thou art righteous.

HIPPOLITA   O 'tis true.
I feele my minute coming, had that slaue
Kept promise, (o my torment) thou this houre   90
Had'st dyed *Soranzo*—heate above hell fire—
Yet ere I passe away—Cruell, cruell flames—
Take here my curse amongst you; may thy bed
Of marriage be a racke unto thy heart,
Burne blood and boyle in Vengeance—o my heart,   95
My Flame's intolerable—maist thou live
To father Bastards, may her wombe bring forth
Monsters, and dye together in your sinnes
Hated, scorn'd and unpittied—oh—oh—   *Dyes.*

FLORIO   Was e're so vild a Creature?

RICHARDETTO   Here's the end   100
Of lust and pride.

ANNABELLA   It is a fearefull sight.

SORANZO   *Vasques*, I know thee now a trusty servant,
And never will forget thee—come *My Love*,
Wee'le home, and thanke the Heavens for this escape,
Father and Friends, wee must breake up this mirth,   105
It is too sad a Feast.

DONADO   Beare hence the body.

85] *Wiggins adds* SD [*To* HIPPOLITA] *before* and.   85 vild] *Q*, vile *Dodsley*   86 woman;]
Dodsley; ~, *Q*   87–8] *Dyce*; Wonderful justice! | Heaven . . . righteous | O . . . true. *Q*,
Wonderful . . . righteous. | O . . . true. *Weber*   88 righteous.] *Q*, ~! *Dodsley*   89 com-
ing,] *Q*, ~: *Reed*; ~. *Dyce*   90 torment)] *Q*, ~, *Dodsley*, ~! *Reed*; ~!— *Dyce*   92 flames∧]
Q, ~! *Reed*   94 unto] *Q*, upon *Dodsley*   94 heart] *Q*, 'heat' *conj. Roper*   94–5 heart
| Burn∧ . . . Vengeance—] *Q*, ~~ | Burn, . . . vengeance; *Roper*   96 Flame's] *Q*, shame's *conj.*
Sturgess   97 Bastards,] *Q*, ~; *Reed* (bastards)   100–1] *Weber*; Was . . . Creature? |
Here's . . . end | Of . . . pride. ANNABELLA It . . . sight. *Q*   100 vild] *Q*, vile
Dodsley   101] *Weber*, *one line in Q*   103 thee∧] *Q*, ~. *Reed*   106] *Weber*; It . . .
Feast. | Beare . . . body. *Q*   106] *Massai adds* SD [*to Vasquez*] *before* Bear.   106] *Massai*
adds SD2 [*Vasquez and Attendants carry Hippolita offstage.*] *after* body.

FRYAR   Here's an ominous change,
  Marke this my *Giovanni*, and take heed,
  I feare the event; that marriage seldome's good,
  Where the bride-banquet so begins in blood.

                    Exeunt [with HIPPOLITA's *body].*   110

4.2   *Enter* RICHARDETTO *and* PHILOTIS.

RICHARDETTO   My wretched wife more wretched in her shame
  Then in her wrongs to me, hath paid too soone
  The forfeit of her modesty and life.
  And I am sure (my Neece) though vengeance hover,
  Keeping aloofe yet from *Soranzo's* fall,   5
  Yet hee will fall, and sinke with his owne weight.
  I need not (now my heart perswades me so)
  To further his confusion; there is one
  Above begins to worke, for as I heare,
G4ᵛ Debate's already twixt his wife and him,   10
  Thicken and run to head; shee (as 'tis sayd)
  Sleightens his love, and he abandons hers
  Much talke I heare, since things goe thus (my Neece)
  In tender love and pitty of your youth,
  My counsell is, that you should free your yeeres   15
  From hazard of these woes; by flying hence
  To faire *Cremona*, there to vow your soule
  In holinesse a holy Votaresse,
  Leave me to see the end of these extreames;
  All humane worldly courses are uneven,   20
  No life is blessèd but the way to Heaven.

PHILOTIS   Unkle, shall I resolve to be a Nun?

RICHARDETTO   I gentle Neece, and in your hourely prayers
  Remember me your poore unhappy Unkle;
  Hie to *Cremona* now, as Fortune leades,   25

107] *Gifford adds* SD [*aside to Gio.*] *before* Here's.   107 change,] *Q;* ~! *Dodsley*   110 SD
Exeunt [with HIPPOLITA's *body*]] *Lomax, Exeunt. Q; Exeunt [with the body] Wiggins*   **4.2**] *this
edn; not in Q;* SCENE II. —*The Street.* | *Weber,* SCENE II. *A room in* RICHARDETTO's *house.* |
Dyce; [4.2] *Massai*   2 hath] *Q* (corrected); hath hath *Q* (uncorrected)   7 not (now]
Q; ~, ~ *Dodsley;* ~~~ *Gifford, Dyce;* ~ ~~ *Ellis*   7 so)] *Q;* ~, *Dodsley;* ~— *Dyce*   8 one]
Q; One *Gifford*   10 Debate's] *Q;* Debates *Dodsley*   13 heare,] *Q;* ~: *Reed* (hear); ~.
Gifford; ~; *Bawcutt*   19 extreames;] *Dodsley,* ~∧ *Q*   21 blessèd] *Dyce;* blessed *Q*

Your home, your cloyster, your best Friends, your beades,
Your chast and single life shall crowne your Birth;
Who dyes a Virgine, live a Saint on earth.

PHILOTIS   Then farwell world, and worldly thoughts adeiu,
Welcome chast vowes, my selfe I yeeld to you.   30

Exeunt.

4.3   *Enter* SORANZO *unbrac't, and* ANNABELLA *dragg'd in.*

SORANZO   Come strumpet, famous whoore, were every drop
Of blood that runs in thy adulterous veynes
A life, this Sword, (dost see't) should in one blowe
Confound them all. Harlot, rare, notable Harlot,
That with thy brazen face maintainst thy sinne.   5
Was there no man in *Parma* to be bawd
To your loose cunning whoredome else but I?
Must your hot ytch and plurisie of lust,
The heyday of your luxury be fedd
Up to a surfeite? and could none but I   10
Be pickt out to be cloake to your close tricks,
Your belly-sports? Now I must be the Dad
To all that gallymaufrey that's stuft
In thy Corrupted bastard-bearing wombe,   H1ʳ
Shey, must I?

ANNABELLA   Beastly man, why 'tis thy fate: 15
I sued not to thee, for, but that I thought
Your *Over-loving Lordship* would have runne
Madd on denyall, had yee lent me time,
I would have told 'ee in what case I was,
But you would needes be doing.

27 Birth;] *Sherman*; ~, *Q*; ~: *Weber* (birth)   28 live] *Q*; lives *Dodsley*   29 farwell] *Q*;
farewell *Dodsley*   29 adieu,] *Q*; ~; *Reed*   **4.3**] *this edn; not in* Q; SCENE III.—*A
Chamber in* SORANZO'S *House.* | *Weber*; SCENE III. *A chamber in* SORANZO'S *house.* | *Dyce*; [4.3]
Massai   0.1 SD *unbrac't*] *Q*; ~ [*with his Sword unsheathed*] *Weber*; ~ [*with his sword drawn*]
Wiggins   0.1 SD ANNABELLA *dragg'd in.*] *Q*; *dragging in* ANNABELLA. *Weber*   3 see't^]
Q; ~? *Dodsley*   4 all.] *Dodsley*; ~, *Q*   5 sinne.] *Dodsley* (sin.); ~^ *Q*; ~, *Dyce*   10 sur-
feite?] *Dodsley*; ~, *Q*   11 tricks,] *Q*; ~? *Dodsley*   13 that's] *Q*; that is *Reed*
14 wombe,] *Q*; ~; *Dodsley* (womb); ~! *Dyce* (womb)   14.1 'catchword' Say] *Q* (*uncor-
rected*); 'Why' *Q* (*corrected*)   15] *after Weber*; Shey . . . I? | Beastly . . . fate: *Q*   15 Shey]
Q; Why *Weber*; Say *Dodsley, for the discussion on this, see Commentary*   18 denyall, had] *Q*;
~. ~ *Dodsley* (denial) (Had)   18 yee] *Q*; you *Dodsley*   19 'ee] *Q*; you *Dodsley*; ye *Dyce*

SORANZO   Whore of whores!   20
   Dar'st thou tell mee this?

ANNABELLA   O yes. Why, art not?
   You were deceiv'd in mee; 'twas not for love
   I chose you, but for honour; yet know this,
   Would you be patient yet, and hide your shame,
   I'de see whether I could love you.

SORANZO   Excellent Queane!   25
   Why art thou not with Child?

ANNABELLA   What needs all this,
   When 'tis superfluous? I confesse I am.

SORANZO   Tell mee by whome.

ANNABELLA   Soft sir, 'twas not in my bargaine.
   Yet somewhat sir to stay your longing stomacke
   I'me content t'acquaint you with; *The man*,   30
   The more then *Man* that got this sprightly Boy,
   (For 'tis a Boy that for glory sir,
   Your heyre shalbe a Sonne.)

SORANZO   Damnable Monster.

ANNABELLA   Nay and you will not heare, I'le speake no more.

SORANZO   Yes speake, and speake thy last.

ANNABELLA   A match, a match;   35
   This *Noble Creature* was in every part
   So angell-like, so glorious, that a woeman,
   Who had not beene but human as was I,
   Would have kneel'd to him, and have beg'd for love.
   You, why you are not worthy once to name   40
   His name without true worship, or indeede,

20–1] *Weber*; But . . . doing. | Whore . . . whores! | Dar'st . . . this? | O . . . not? *Q*   21 yes.
Why, art not] *this edn*; yes, why not *Q*   25–6] *Weber*; I'de . . . you. | Excellent Queane! |
Why . . . Child? | What . . . this, *Q*   28] *Weber*, Tell . . . whome. | Soft . . . bargaine, *Q*
28 Soft∧ sir] *Q*; ~, *Weber*; ~ *Gifford* ('sir' *omitted*)   30 I'me] *Q*; I am *Gifford*   32 Boy∧
that for glory∧ sir] *Q*; ~, therefore glory, ~ *Dodsley* (boy); ~, and therefore glory, ~ *Reed* (boy);
Weber; ~, that's for your glory, ~ *Gifford* (boy); ~, [and] therefore glory, ~ *Dyce*; ~, that for your
glory, ~ *McIlwraith* (boy), *Roper*; ~; therefore glory that, ~ *Sturgess* (boy); ~; that for your glory,
~ *Gibson* (boy); ~, [and] that for glory, ~ *Barker* (boy)   33] *Weber*, Your . . . Sonne,) |
Damnable Monster. *Q*   33 Monster.] *Q*; ~! *Dodsley* (monster)   34 and] *Q*; an' *Weber*
35] *Weber*; Yes . . . last. | A . . . match; *Q*   40 You,] *Q*; ~! *Reed*

Unlesse you kneel'd, to heare another name him.

SORANZO   What was hee cal'd?   H1ᵛ

ANNABELLA   Wee are not come to that,
    Let it suffice, that you shall have the glory,
    To *Father* what so *Brave a Father got*.   45
    In briefe, had not this chance, falne out as't doth,
    I never had beene troubled with a thought
    That you had been *a Creature*; but for marriage,
    I scarce dreame yet of that.

SORANZO   Tell me his name.

ANNABELLA   Alas, alas, there's all!   50
    Will you beleeve?

SORANZO   What?

ANNABELLA   You shall never know.

SORANZO   How!

ANNABELLA   Never, If you doe, let mee be curst.

SORANZO   Not know it, Strumpet, I'le ripp up thy heart,
    And finde it there.

ANNABELLA   Doe, doe.

SORANZO   And with my teeth,
    Teare the prodigious leacher ioynt by joynt.   55

ANNABELLA   Ha, ha, ha, the man's merry.

SORANZO   Do'st thou laugh?
    Come *Whore*, tell mee your lover, or by Truth
    I'le hew thy flesh to shreds; who is't?

ANNABELLA   *Che morte più dolce che morire per amore?* (*sings.*)

43] *Weber*; What . . . cal'd? | Wee . . . that, *Q*   43 that,] *Q*; ~; *Reed*   49–53] *Bawcutt*;
I . . . that. | Tell . . . name. | Alas, . . . all | Will . . . beleeve? | What? | You . . . How! | Never. | If . . .
curst *Q*; I . . . name. | Alas . . . believe? | What . . . Never | If . . . curs'd *Weber*; I . . . name. | Alas . . .
Believe? |What . . . if | You . . . curs'd *Dyce*; I . . . that. | Tell . . . all. | Will . . . know. | How . . .
cursed *Wiggins*   50 all!] *Dodsley*; ~ *Q*   51–2 You . . . know | How!] *Bawcutt*; *one line
in Q*   52 Never, if . . . curst] *Bawcutt*; ~, | If . . . curst *Q*; ~, if | you . . . curs'd *Gifford*
52 be curst] *Q*; curd'd *Gifford* ('be' *omitted*)   54 *Weber*; And . . . there. | Doe, doe. | And . . .
teeth, *Q*   56] *Weber*; Ha, . . . merry. | Do'st . . . laugh? *Q*   58 is't?] *Dodsley*; ~ˌ *Q*
59 *più*] *Dyce*; *pluis* | *Q*; *piu* | *Weber*   59] SD (*sings*)] *Q* (without brackets); *Dyce places* SD
[*sings*] *before* 'Che'.

SORANZO   Thus will I pull thy hayre, and thus I'le drag   60
Thy lust be-leapred body through the dust.
Yet tell his name.

ANNABELLA   *Morendo in grazia a lui, morirei senza dolore. (sings.)*

SORANZO   Dost thou Triumph? the Treasure of the Earth
Shall not redeeme thee, were there kneeling Kings,   65
Did begge thy life, or Angells did come downe
To plead in teares, yet should not all prevayle
Against my rage; do'st thou not tremble yet?

ANNABELLA   At what? to dye; No, be a *Gallant hang-man;*
I dare thee to the worst; strike, and strike home,   70
H2ʳ   I leave revenge behind, and thou shalt feel't.

SORANZO   Yet tell mee ere thou dyest, and tell mee truely,
Knowes thy old Father this?

ANNABELLA   No by my life.

SORANZO   Wilt thou confesse, and I will spare thy life?

ANNABELLA   My life? I will not buy my life so deare.   75

SORANZO   I will not slacke my Vengeance.   [*Draws his sword.*]

Enter VASQUES.

VASQUES   What d'ee meane Sir?

SORANZO   Forbeare *Vasques,* such a damned *Whore*
Deserves no pitty.

VASQUES   Now the gods forefend!   80
And wud you be her executioner, and kill her in your rage too?
O 'twere most un-manlike; shee is your wife, what faults hath
beene done by her before she married you, were not against

61] *Dyce adds* SD [*Hales her up and down*] *after* dust 61.   63 *grazia*] *Dyce; gratia* | *Q*
63 *a lui*] *Roper; Lei* | *Q; Dei* | *Weber, dee* | *Gifford*   63 *morirei*] *Bawcutt; morirere* | *Q* (corrected); *morire* | *Q* (uncorrected)   63 SD (*sings.*)] *Q* (without brackets); *Dyce places* SD
[*sings*] *before* 'Morendo'.   65 thee,] *Q; ~; Dodsley*   68 rage; do'st] *Q; ~. ~ Reed* (Dost);
~: ~ *Dyce* (dost)   69 dye;] *Q; ~! Dodsley* (die)   69 *hang-man;*] *Reed* (hangman); ~ₐ
Q (*hang-man*)   70 worst;] *Dodsley; ~, Q; ~: Dyce*   71 I leave] *Q* (corrected); leave *Q*
(uncorrected)   73] *Weber, one line in Q*   76–7 I . . . Vengeance | What . . . Sir?] *Q;
verse in Weber*   76 SD [*Draws his sword*]] *Gifford; not in Q*   77 d'ee] *Q; do you
Dodsley, d'ye Dyce*   79–80 Deserves . . . pitty | Now . . . forefend!] *Q; verse in Dyce*
81 wud] *Q; wou'd Dodsley; would Dyce*   82 hath] *Q; have Gifford*

you; alas *Poore Lady*, what hath shee committed, which any
Lady in *Italy* in the like case would not? Sir, you must be   85
ruled by your reason, and not by your fury, that were unhu-
mane and beastly.

SORANZO   Shee shall not live.

VASQUES   Come shee must; you would have her confesse the
Authors of her present misfortunes I warrant 'ee; 'tis an   90
unconscionable demand, and shee should loose the estimation
that I (for my part) hold of her worth, if shee had done it; why
sir you ought not of all men living to know it: good sir bee
reconciled, alas good gentlewoman.

ANNABELLA   Pish, doe not beg for mee, I prize my life   95
As nothing; if *The man* will needs bee madd,
Why let him take it.

SORANZO   *Vasques*, hear'st thou this?

VASQUES   Yes, and commend her for it; in this shee shews the
noblenesse of a gallant spirit, and beshrew my heart, but
it becomes her rarely. [*Aside*] Sir, in any case smother   100
your revenge; leave the senting out your wrongs to mee,
bee rul'd as you respect your honour, or you marr all.
[*Aloud*] Sir, if ever my service were of any Credit with
you, be not so violent in your distractions: you are married
now; what a tryumph might the report of this give to   105
other neglected Sutors, 'tis as manlike to beare extremities,
as godlike to forgive.   H2ᵛ

SORANZO   O *Vasques, Vasques*, in this peece of flesh,
This faithlesse face of hers, had I layd up
The treasure of my heart; hadst thou beene virtuous   110
(Faire wicked woeman) not the matchlesse joyes

84 you; alas] *Q*; ~. ~! *Dodsley* (Alas); ~: ~, *Dyce*   90 Authors] *Q*; author *Dyce*   90 'ee;]
Bawcutt; ~, *Q*; you: *Dodsley*; ye: *Dyce*   94 gentlewoman.] *Q*; ~! *Dodsley*   96] *Weber*;
Why . . . it. | *Vasques*, . . . this? *Q*   100 rarely.] *Weber*; ~ₐ——] *Q*; ~, *Reed*   100 SD
[*Aside*]] *Weber* (*Aside to Soranzo.*); *not in Q*;   101 senting out] *Q*; scenting out *Weber*;
scenting-out *Gifford*   102 rul'dₐ] *Q*; ~, *Reed* (ruled)   102 your honour] *Dodsley*;
hour ~ *Q*   102 all.] *Reed*; ~ₐ *Q*   103 SD [*Aloud*]] *Weber*; *not in Q*   106 Sutors,
'tis] *Q*; suitors. 'Tis *Dodsley*; ~! ~ *Reed* (suitors)   110] *Wiggins adds* SD [*To* ANNABELLA]
before hadst.

Of Life it selfe had made mee wish to live
With any Saint but thee; *Deceitfull Creature*,
How hast thou mock't my hopes, and in the shame
Of thy lewd wombe, even buried mee alive?   115
I did too dearely love thee.

VASQUES   [*Aside*] This is well;
    Follow this temper with some passion, bee briefe and moving,
    'tis for the purpose.   *Aside*.

SORANZO   Be witnesse to my words thy soule and thoughts,   120
    And tell mee didst not thinke that in my heart,
    I did too superstitiously adore thee.

ANNABELLA   I must confesse, I know you lov'd mee well.

SORANZO   And wouldst thou use mee thus? O *Annabella*,
    Bee thou assur'd, whatsoe're the Villaine was,   125
    That thus hath tempted thee to *This disgrace*,
    Well hee might lust, but never lov'd like mee:
    Hee doated on the picture that hung out
    Upon thy cheekes, to please his humourous eye;
    Not on the part I lov'd, which was thy heart,   130
    And as I thought, thy Vertues.

ANNABELLA   O my Lord!
    These words wound deeper then your Sword could do.

VASQUES   Let mee not ever take comfort, but I begin to weepe my
    selfe, so much I pitty him; why *Madam* I knew when his rage
    was over-past, what it would come to.   135

SORANZO   Forgive mee *Annabella*, though thy youth
    Hath tempted thee above thy strength to folly,
    Yet will not I forget what I should bee,
    And what I am, a husband; in that name
    Is hid Devinity; if I doe finde   140
    That thou wilt yet be true, here I remit
    All former faults, and take thee to my bosome.

113 *Creature,*] *Q;* creature! *Dodsley*   115 alive?] *Q;* ~! *Reed*   115–16] *Q; verse in Roper;*
prose in Weber   117 SD [*Aside*]] *Dyce* [*aside to Sor.*]; *Weber places* SD [*Aside to Soranzo*]
after purpose 117; *Roper,* SD 'Aside [*to him.*]' *after* well.   119] *Wiggins adds* SD [*To*
ANNABELLA] *before* Be.   120 words∧ thy] *Q;* ~, my *Dodsley*   124 thou] *Gifford;* thus
Q   125 whatsoe're] *Q;* whoe'er *Gifford*   124–131] *Weber,* And . . . virtues. | O . . .
Lord! *Q*   136 *Annabella,* though] *Q;* Annabella. Though *Dodsley*

VASQUES.   By my troth, and that's a poynt of noble charity.   H3ʳ

ANNABELLA   Sir on my knees—

SORANZO   Rise up, you shall not kneele,
Get you to your chamber, see you make no shew   145
Of alteration, I'le be with you streight;
My reason tells mee now, that *'Tis as common*
To erre in frailty as to bee a woeman.
Goe to your chamber.   *Exit* ANNABELLA.

VASQUES   So, this was somewhat to the matter; what doe you   150
thinke of your heaven of happinesse now sir?

SORANZO   I carry hell about mee, all my blood
Is fir'd in swift revenge.

VASQUES   That may bee, but know you how, or on whom? alas, to
marry a great woeman, being made great in the stocke to your   155
hand, is a usuall sport in these dayes; but to know what *ferret*
it was that haunted your *Cunny-berry*, there's the cunning.

SORANZO   I'le make her tell her selfe, or —

VASQUES   Or what? you must not doe so; let me yet perswade
your sufferance a little while, goe to her, use her mildly,   160
winne her if it be possible to a Voluntary, to a weeping tune;
for the rest, if all hitt, I will not misse my marke; pray sir goe
in, the next news I tell you shall be wonders.

SORANZO   Delay in vengeance gives a heavyer blow.   *Exit.*

VASQUES   Ah sirrah, here's worke for the nonce; I had a   165
suspicion of a bad matter in my head a pretty whiles agoe;
but after *My Madams* scurvy lookes here at home, her
waspish perversnesse, and loud fault-finding, then I
remembred the Proverbe, that *Where Hens crowe, and*
Cocks hold their peace, there are sorry Houses; sfoot, if the   170
lower parts of a *Shee-taylors Cunning* can cover such a
swelling in the stomacke, I'le never blame a false stich in a

144] *Weber,* Sir, . . . knees— | Rise . . . kneele, *Q*   144] *Bawcutt adds* SD [*Kneels.*] *after*
knees—; *Wiggins,* SD [*Kneeling*].   147–8 'Tis . . . woeman.] *Q;* roman *in Dodsley*
154 bee,] *Q;* ~; *Dodsley* (be)   154 you] *Dodsley;* yoo *Q*   154 alas,] *Q;* ~! *Dodsley*
156 *ferret*] *Dodsley,* Secret *Q*   157 haunted] *Q;* hunted *Dodsley*   159 so;] *Dodsley;* ~, *Q*
160 while,] *Q;* ~; *Dodsley*   162 marke; pray] *Q;* ~. ~ *Dodsley* (mark) (Pray)   166 whiles]
Q; while *Dodsley*   169–170 *Where . . . sorry* | *Houses;*] *Q;* roman *in Dodsley*

shoe whiles I live againe; up and up so quicke? and so quickly
too? 'twere a fine policy to learne by whom this must be
knowne: and I have thought on't—here's the way or none—   175
what crying old Mistresse! alas, alas, I cannot blame 'ee, wee
have a Lord, Heaven helpe us, is so madde as the devil
himselfe, the more shame for him.

Enter PUTANA [*in tears*].

PUTANA   O *Vasques*, that ever I was borne to see this day! | Doth
H3ᵛ   hee use thee so too, sometimes *Vasques?*   180

VASQUES   Mee? why hee makes a dogge of mee; but if some
were of my minde, I know what wee would doe; as sure as I
am an honest man, hee will goe neere to kill my Lady with
unkindnesse; say shee be with-child, is that such a matter for
a young woeman of her yeeres to be blam'd for?   185

PUTANA   Alas good heart, it is against her will full sore.

VASQUES   I durst be sworne, all his madnesse is, for that shee will
not confesse whose 'tis, which hee will know, and when he doth
know it, I am so well acquainted with his humour, that hee
will forget all streight; well I could wish, shee would in   190
plaine termes tell all, for that's the way indeed.

PUTANA   Doe you thinke so?

VASQUES   Fo, I know't; provided that hee did not winne her to't
by force, hee was once in a mind, that you could tell, and
ment to have wrung it out of you, but I somewhat pacified   195
him for that; yet sure you know a great deale.

PUTANA   Heaven forgive us all, I know a little *Vasques*.

173 whiles] *Q*; whilst *Dodsley*   174 whomʌ this] *Q*; ~. ~ *Weber* (This); ~; ~ *Gifford, Dyce*
175 knowne] *Q*; done *Dodsley*   175 *Wiggins adds* SD [*To* PUTANA] *after* none.
176 'ee] *Q*; thee *Dodsley*   178.1 SD *Enter* PUTANA [*in tears*].] *this edn*; *Enter* PUTANA. *Q*;
Weber places SD '*Enter* PUTANA.' *after* on't 172; *Gifford*, SD '*Enter* PUTANA, *in tears*' *after* on't
172; *Wiggins*, SD '*Enter* PUTANA [*weeping*]' *after* knowne 172; *Massai*, SD '*Enter* PUTANA
[*weeping*]' *after* knowne 172.   179 day!] *Dodsley*; ~, *Q*   182 doe; as] *Q*; ~. ~ *Reed*
(do) (As)   185 yeeresʌ] *Dodsley* (years); ~, *Q*   190 streight; wellʌ I] *Q*; ~; ~, ~ *Dodsley*
(strait); ~: ~, ~ *Reed* (strait); ~. ~, ~ *Dyce* (straight) (Well)   193 Fo] *Q*; Faugh *Massai*
196 for] *Q*; from *Dodsley*

VASQUES   Why should you not? who else should? upon my
          Conscience shee loves you dearely, and you would not
          betray her to any affliction for the world.   200

PUTANA   Not for all the world by my Faith and troth *Vasques*.

VASQUES   'Twere pitty of your life if you should, but *In this* you
          should both releive her present discomforts, pacifie my Lord,
          and gaine your selfe everlasting love and preferment.

PUTANA   Do'st thinke so *Vasques?*   205

VASQUES   Nay I know't; sure 'twas some neere and entire friend.

PUTANA   'Twas a deare friend indeed; but —

VASQUES   But what? feare not to name him; my life betweene you
          and danger; faith I thinke 'twas no base Fellow.

PUTANA   Thou wilt stand betweene mee and harme?   210

VASQUES   U'ds pitty, what else; you shalbe rewarded too; trust me.

PUTANA   'Twas even no worse then her owne brother.

VASQUES   Her brother *Giouanni* I warrant 'ee?

PUTANA   Even hee *Vasques*: as brave a Gentleman as ever kist
          faire Lady; O they love most perpetually.   215

VASQUES   A brave Gentleman indeed; why therein I Commend   H4ʳ
          her choyce. [*Aside*] Better and better! You are sure 'twas hee?

PUTANA   Sure; and you shall see hee will not be long from her too.

VASQUES   He were to blame if he would: but may I beleeve thee?

PUTANA   Beleeve mee! why do'st thinke I am a Turke or a Jew?   220
          no *Vasques*, I have knowne their dealings too long to belie
          them now.

VASQUES   Where are you? there within sirs ?

                    Enter BANDITTI.

---

198 else;] *Q*; ~? *Dodsley*   213 'ee] *Q*; you *Dodsley*; ye *Dyce*   217 choyce.] *Gifford*; ~—
Q   217 SD [*Aside*]] *Gifford* (aside); not in *Q*   217 Better] *Gifford*; ——better *Q*
217 better!] *this edn*; ~—— *Q*; ~. *Gifford*;   217] *Gifford adds* SD [*to her.*] *after* better!
217 You] *Gifford*; you *Q*   223] *Massai adds* SD [*Calls.*] *before* Where.   223 you?
there∧] *Q*; ~? ~, *Dodsley*; ~ ~? *Gifford*

PUTANA.   How now, what are these?

VASQUES   You shall know presently; come sirs, take mee *This*   225
old Damnable hagge, gag her instantly, and put out her eyes,
quickly, quickly.

PUTANA   *Vasques, Vasques.*

VASQUES   Gag her I say, sfoot d'ee suffer her to prate? what d'ee
fumble about? let mee come to her, I'le helpe your old   230
gums, you Toad-bellied bitch! [*He gags* PUTANA.] Sirs,
carry her closely into the Coale-house, and put out her eyes
instantly, if shee roares, slitt her nose; d'ee heare, bee speedy
and sure. Why this is excellent and above expectation.

Exeunt [BANDITTI] *with* PUTANA.

Her owne brother? O horrible! to what a height of liberty   235
in damnation hath the Devill trayn'd our age, her Brother,
well; there's yet but a beginning; I must to my Lord, and
tutor him better in his points of vengeance; now I see how
a smooth tale goes beyond a smooth tayle, but soft,—what
thing comes next?   240

Enter GIOVANNI.

Giovanni! as I would wish; my beleefe is strengthned, 'tis as
firme as Winter and Summer.

GIOVANNI   Where's my Sister?

VASQUES   Troubled with a new sicknes my Lord, she's somewhat ill.

GIOVANNI   Tooke too much of the flesh I beleeve.   245

225–7] *Weber;* You . . . presetly | Come . . . *hagge,* | Gage . . . quickly. *Q;*   225 presently;]
Dodsley; ~, *Q;* ~.— *Dyce*   227] *Wiggins adds* SD [*The* BANDITTI *tie up* PUTANA] *after*
quickly 2; *Massai,* SD [*The Banditti seize Puttana.*] *after* quickly 2.   229 d'ee] *Q;* do you
Dodsley; d'ye *Dyce*   231 bitch!] *Dodsley;* ~; *Q*   231 SD [*He gags* PUTANA.]] *Roper; not*
in Q; [*They gag her.*] *Gifford;* [*Gags Puttana*] *Massai.*   231 Sirs,] *Dodsley;* sirs,
Q   233 d'ee] *Q;* do you *Dodsley;* d'ye *Dyce*   234 SD *Exeunt* [BANDITTI] *with*
PUTANA] *Q,* 'Exit *with* Putana.'; *Dodsley,* 'Exeunt *with* Putana.'; *Gifford places* SD [*Exeunt* BAN.
With PUT.] *between* sure *and* Why 230; *Sherman,* SD '[*Exeunt Ban.*] *with* Putana.' *between* sure
and Why 230.   235 brother?] *Q;* ~! *Reed*   236 age,] *Q;* ~! *Dodsley*   236 Brother,]
Q; ~! *Dodsley* (brother)   237 beginning;] *Dodsley,* ~₄ *Q*   239–40] *Weber,* goes . . . soft—|
what . . . next? *Q*   239 soft,—] *Q;* ~— *Dodsley;* ~! *Dyce;* ~: *Roper*   240.1 SD *Enter*
GIOVANNI.] *Q; Gifford places* SD '*Enter* GIOVANNI' *after* Summer 238; *Wiggins,* SD [*Enter*
GIOVANNI.] *after* tayle 236.   241–2] *Weber, Giovanni!* — strengthned, | 'tis . . . Summer. *Q*

VASQUES   Troth sir and you I thinke have e'en hitt it, but *My vertuous Lady.*

GIOVANNI   Where's shee?

VASQUES   In her chamber; please you visit her; she is alone, your liberality hath doubly made me your servant, and ever shall ever—   250

Exit GIOVANNI.

Enter SORANZO.

Sir, I am made a man, I have plyed my Cue with | cunning and   H4ᵛ success, I beseech you let's be private.

SORANZO   My Ladyes brother's come, now hee'le know all.

VASQUES   Let him know't; I have made some of them fast enough, How have you delt with my Lady?   255

SORANZO   Gently, as thou hast counsail'd; O my soule Runs circular in sorrow for revenge, But *Vasques,* thou shalt know—

VASQUES   Nay, I will know no more; for now comes your turne to know; I would not talke so openly with you: Let my young   260 Maister take time enough, and goe at pleasure; hee is sold to death, and the Devill shall not ransome him, Sir I beseech you, your privacy.

SORANZO   No Conquest can gayne glory of my feare.

Exeunt

5.1   *Enter* ANNABELLA *above.*

ANNABELLA   Pleasures farwell, and all yee thriftlesse minutes, Wherein *False joyes* have spun a weary life,

246–7] *this edn (after Weber);* Troth . . . it, | But . . . Lady. | Q   248] *Weber adds* SD [*Giving him money.*] *at the end of the line; Dyce,* SD [*Giovanni gives him money.*] *between* alone *and* your *245.*   249 her; shee] Q; ~? ~ *Roper* (She)   249 alone, your] Q; ~. ~ *Dodsley* (Your)   250 ever shallₐ] Q (euer shal); shallₐ *Dodsley* ('ever' *omitted*); ~ ~, *Gifford* 250.1 SD 1 Exit GIOVANNI.] *as* 'Exit. Gio.', *set against* 'ever—' 246 *in the margin* Q 250.2 SD 2 *Enter* SORANZO.] *Dodsley; Re-enter* ~. *Dyce; as* 'Enter So-ranzo.' *set against* cunning 251 *in two lines in the margin* | Q.   252 you let's] Q; ~ let us *Dodsley*   254–5] Q; *prose in Weber*   254 know't;] *Weber;* ~, Q; know it, *Dodsley*   264.1 SD Exeunt] *Reed;* Exit.Q   **5.1**] *this edn; Actus Quintus.* Q; SCENE I.—*The Street before* SORANZO'S *House.* | *Weber;* SCENE I. *The street before* SORANZO'S *house.* | *Dyce;* 5[.1] *Massai*   01 SD] Q; *Enter* ANNABELLA *on a Balcony.* | *Weber;* ANNABELLA *appears at a window above.* | *Dyce;* Enter ANNABELA *above,* [*with a letter written in blood*] *Wiggins*   1 farwell,] Q; farwell! *Dodsley* 1 minutes,] Q; ~ₐ *Dodsley*

To these my Fortunes now I take my leave.
Thou *Precious Time*, that swiftly rid'st in poast
Over the world, to finish up the race   5
Of my last fate; here stay thy restlesse course,
And beare to Ages that are yet unborne,
A wretched woefull woemans *Tragedy.*
My Conscience now stands up against my lust
With depositions charectred in guilt,   10

Enter FRYAR [*below*].

And tells mee I am lost: *Now* I confesse,
Beauty that cloathes the out-side of the face,
Is cursèd if it be not cloath'd with grace:
Here like a Turtle (mew'd up in a Cage)
Un-mated, I converse with Ayre and walls,   15
And descant on my vild unhappinesse.
O *Giovanni*, that hast had the spoyle
of thine owne vertues and my modest fame,
Would thou hadst beene lesse subject to those Stars
That luckelesse raign'd at my Nativity: 20
O would the scourge due to my blacke offence
Might passe from thee, that *I alone* might feele
The torment of an uncontrouled flame.

FRYAR   [*Aside*] What's this I heare?

ANNABELLA   That man, that *Blessed Fryar,*
Who joynd in Ceremoniall knot my hand   25
To him whose wife I now am, told mee oft,
I troad the path to death, and shewed mee how.
But they who sleepe in Lethargies of Lust
Hugge their confusion, making Heaven unjust;
And so did I.

FRYAR   [*Aside*]   Here's Musicke to the soule.   30

---

8 *Tragedy.*] *Dodsley* (tragedy); ~, *Q*; ~! *Dyce* (tragedy)   10 depositions] *Dodsley,* dispositions *Q*   10 guilt] *Q*; gilt *Massai*   10.1 SD *Enter* FRYAR [*below*].] *Weber, Q* (corrected); *not in Q* (uncorrected); '*Enter* FRYAR' *set against* guilt 10 *in Q.*   13 cursèd] *Dyce;*
cursed | *Q*   16 vild] *Q*; vile *Dodsley*   20 Nativity:] *Q*; ~! *Dodsley* (nativity)
23 flame.] *Q*; ~! *Dodsley*   24] *Weber,* What's . . . heare? | That . . . *Fryar, Q*   24 SD
[*Aside*]] *Dyce* (aside); *not in Q*; (*apart*) *Weber*   26 am,] *Reed;* ~; *Q*   28–9] *Q*; *roman
in Dodsley*   29 unjust;] *Reed;* ~, *Q*   30] *Weber,* And . . . I. | Here's . . . soul. *Q*
30 SD [*Aside*]] *Dyce* (aside); *not in Q*; *Weber places* SD [*Apart.* | *after* soule.   30 soule.] *Q*;
~! *Weber*

ANNABELLA   Forgive mee my *Good Genius*, and this once
　　Be helpfull to my ends; Let some good man
　　Passe this way, to whose trust I may commit
　　This paper double lin'd with teares and blood:
　　Which being granted; here I sadly vow　　　　　　　　35
　　Repentance, and a leaving of that life
　　I long have dyed in.

FRYAR　　　　　　　　　Lady, Heaven hath heard you,
　　And hath by providence ordain'd, that I
　　Should be his Minister for your behoofe.

ANNABELLA   Ha, what are you?

FRYAR　　　　　　　　Your brothers friend the Fryar;　　40
　　Glad in my soule that I have liv'd to heare
　　This free confession twixt your peace and you;
　　What would you or to whom? feare not to speake.

ANNABELLA   Is Heaven so bountifull? then I have found
　　More favour then I hop'd; here *Holy man*—　　　　45

　　　　　　　　　　　　　　Throwes a letter.

　　Commend mee to my Brother, give him that,
　　That Letter; bid him read it and repent,
　　Tell him that I (imprison'd in my chamber,
　　Barr'd of all company, even of *My Guardian*,
　　Who gives me cause of much suspect) have time　　50　II[v]
　　To blush at what hath past: bidd him be wise,
　　And not beleeve the Friendship of my Lord,
　　I feare much more then I can speake: *Good father*,
　　The place is dangerous, and spyes are busie,
　　I must breake off—you'le doe't?

FRYAR　　　　　　　　　Be sure I will;　　　　　　55
　　And fly with speede—my blessing ever rest
　　With thee my daughter, live to dye more blessed.　　*Exit* FRYAR.

37] *Weber*; I . . . in. | Lady, . . . you, *Q*　　37 dyed] *Q*; liv'd *Dodsley*　　40] *Weber*, Ha, . . .
you? | Your . . . *Fryar*; *Q*　　42 you;] *Reed*; ~, *Q*; ~. *Dyce*　　45.1 SD *Throwes a letter.*] *Q*;
SD [*Throws down a letter.* | *Dyce*; SD '*Throws* [*down the*] *letter*' | *Wiggins*　　49 Barr'd]
Dodsley; Bard *Q*　　50 Who] *Q*; Which *Gifford*　　52 Lord,] *Q*; ~; *Dodsley* (lord); ~: *Dyce*
(lord)　　55] *Weber*; I . . . doe't? | Be . . . will. *Q*　　55 off∧—] *Q*; ~. *Reed*　　55 you'le]
Q; You'le *Reed*　　55 doe't?] *Q*; do it. *Dodsley*　　57 blessed] *Q*; blest *Dodsley*　　57 SD
Exit FRYAR.] *Q* (*Exit Fry*); *Exit.* | *Dyce*

ANNABELLA   Thanks to the heavens, who have prolong'd my
    breath
To this good use: Now I can welcome Death.   *Exit.*

5.2   *Enter* SORANZO *and* VASQUES.

VASQUES   Am I to be beleev'd now? First, marry a strumpet
    that cast her selfe away upon you but to laugh at your
    hornes? to feast on your disgrace, riott in your vexations,
    cuckold you in your bride-bed, waste your estate upon
    Panders and Bawds?   5

SORANZO   No more, I say no more.

VASQUES   *A Cuckold is a goodly tame beast my Lord.*

SORANZO   I am resolv'd; urge not another word,
    My thoughts are great, and all as resolute
    As thunder; in meane time I'le cause our Lady   10
    To decke her selfe in all her bridall Robes,
    Kisse her, and fold her gently in my armes,
    Begone; yet heare you, are the *Banditti* ready
    To waite in Ambush?

VASQUES   Good Sir, trouble not your selfe about other businesse   15
    then your owne resolution; remember that time lost cannot be
    recal'd.

SORANZO   With all the cunning words thou canst, invite
    The States of *Parma* to my Birth-dayes feast,
    Haste to my *Brother rivall* and his Father,   20
    Entreate them gently, bidd them not to fayle,
    Bee speedy and returne.

VASQUES   Let not your pitty betray you, till my comming backe;
    thinke upon *Incest* and *Cuckoldry.*

59 use:] Q; ~! *Reed*   59 SD *Exit.*] Q; [*Exit* ANNABELLA. *Weber,* [*Withdraws from the win-dow.* | *Dyce*   5.2] *this edn; not in* Q; SCENE II. —*An Apartment in the same House.* | *Weber,* SCENE II.—*A Room in* SORANZO'S *House.* | *Dyce;* [5.2] *Massai*   1–4] *after Weber,* Am . . . now? | *followed by prose in* Q   7] Q; A cuckold . . . beast, my lord. *Dodsley (roman)*
8 word,] Q; ~; *Dodsley*   11 Robes,] Q; ~; *Dodsley (robes)*   15 businesse] *Dodsley*
(business); busines, Q   19 feast,] Q; ~; *Dodsley*   21 fayl,] Q; ~; *Dodsley (fail);* ~. *Dyce*
(fail)   23–4] *this edn (after Weber);* Let . . . backe, | Thinke . . . *Cuckoldry.* Q   23 you,]
Q; ~ₐ *Dyce;* ~; *Gibson*   23 backe;] *Reed* (back); ~, Q

SORANZO   Revenge is all the Ambition I aspire,   25
    To that I'le climb or fall; my blood's on fire.   *Exeunt.*   12ʳ

5.3   *Enter* GIOVANNI.

GIOVANNI   *Busie opinion* is an idle Foole,
    That as a Schoole-rod keepes a child in awe,
    Frights the unexperienc't temper of the mind:
    So did it mee; who ere *My precious Sister*
    Was married, thought all tast of love would dye   5
    In such a Contract; but I finde no change
    Of pleasure in this formall law of sports.
    Shee is still one to mee, and every kisse
    As sweet, and as delicious as the first
    I reap't; when yet the priviledge of youth   10
    Intitled her *a Virgine;* O the glory
    Of two united hearts like hers and mine!
    Let *Poaring booke-men* dreame of other worlds,
    My world, and all of happinesse is here,
    And I'de not change it for the best to come,   15
    A life of pleasure is Elyzeum.

Enter FRYAR.

    Father, you enter on the *Jubile*
    Of my retyr'd delights; Now I can tell you,
    The hell you oft have prompted, is nought else
    But slavish and fond superstitious feare;   20
    And I could prove it too—

FRYAR   Thy blindnesse slayes thee,
    Looke there, 'tis writt to thee.   *Gives the Letter.*

GIOVANNI   From whom?

FRYAR   Unrip the seales and see:
    The blood's yet seething hot, that will anon   25

---

26 climb] *Q;* clime *Sherman*   5.3] *this edn; not in Q;* SCENE III.—GIOVANNI'S *Apartment in* FLORIO'S *House.* | *Weber;* SCENE III. *A Room in* FLORIO'S *House.* | *Dyce;* [5.3] *Massai* 3 the unexperienc't] *Q;* th' unexperienc'd *Dodsley;* ~ unexperienced *Dyce*   11 *Virgine;*] *Q;* ~. *Dodsley* (Virgin)   13 worlds,] *Q;* ~; *Dodsley*   15 come,] *Q;* ~. *Dodsley;* ~; *Reed;* ~: *Dyce* 21] *Dyce;* And . . . too— | Thy . . . thee, *Q*   21 thee,] *Q;* ~; *Reed;* ~: *Dyce*   22 SD *Gives the Letter.*] *set against* ll. 21–2 *Q;* [*Gives him the letter.* | *Gifford*   22–4] *Q; verse in Weber*   24 see;] *Q;* ~: *Dyce*   24] *Wiggins places* SD [GIOVANNI *opens and reads the letter*] *after* see.

Be frozen harder then congeal'd Corrall.
Why d'ee change colour sonne?

GIOVANNI   Fore Heaven you make
Some petty Devill factor 'twixt my love
And your relligion-masked sorceries.
Where had you this?

FRYAR   Thy Conscience, youth, is sear'd,   30
Else thou wouldst stoope to warning.

12ᵛ GIOVANNI   'Tis her hand,
I know't; and 'tis all written in her blood.
She writes I know not what; Death? I'le not feare
An armèd thunder-bolt aym'd at my heart.
Shee writes wee are discovered, pox on dreames   35
Of lowe faint-hearted Cowardise; discovered?
The Devill wee are; which way is't possible?
Are wee growne Traytours to our owne delights?
Confusion take such dotage; 'tis but forg'd,
This is your peevish chattering weake old man,   40
Now sir, what newes bring you?   *Enter* VASQUES.

VASQUES My Lord, according to his yearely custome keeping this day a Feast in honour of his Birth-day, by mee invites you thither; your worthy Father with the Popes reverend *Nuntio*, and other Magnifico's of *Parma*, have promis'd 45 their presence, wilt please you to be of the number?

GIOVANNI Yes, tell them I dare come.

VASQUES Dare come?

GIOVANNI So I sayd; and tell him more I will come.

VASQUES These words are strange to mee.   50

27] *Weber*; Why . . . son. | 'Fore . . . make *Q*   27 d'ee] *Q*; d'ye *Dodsley*   30–1] *Weber*, Where . . . this? | Thy . . . sear'd, | Else . . . warning. | 'Tis . . . hand, *Q*   30 Conscience, youth,] *Dodsley* (conscience); ~∧ ~∧ *Q*   34 armèd] *Wiggins*; armed *Q*   35 discovered, pox] *Q*; ~—~ *Reed*; ~: —~ *Dyce* (Pox)   36 Cowardise;] *Q*; ~! *Dodsley* (cowardise) 37 are;] *Q*; ~! *Dodsley*   39 dotage;] *this edn*; ~, *Q*; ~! *Dodsley*   39 forg'd,] *Q*; ~; *Dodsley*; ~: *Dyce* (forged)   40 old man,] *Q*; ~ ~! *Dodsley*   41.1 SD *Enter* VASQUES.] *Q*; *Dyce places after* old man 40.   44 thither; your] *Q*; ~. ~ *Dodsley* (Your)   47 them] *Q*; him *Gifford*

GIOVANNI   Say I will come.

VASQUES   You will not misse?

GIOVANNI   Yet more, I'le come; sir, are you answer'd?

VASQUES   So I'le say—my service to you.   *Exit* VASQUES.

FRYAR   You will not goe I trust.

GIOVANNI   Not goe? for what?   55

FRYAR   O doe not goe, this feast (I'le gage my life)
   Is but a plot to trayne you to your ruine,
   Be rul'd, you sha'not goe.

GIOVANNI   Not goe? stood Death
   Threatning his armies of confounding plagues,
   With hoasts of dangers hot as blazing Starrs,   60
   I would be there; not goe? yes and resolve
   To strike as deepe in slaughter as they all.
   For I will goe.

FRYAR   Goe where thou wilt, I see
   The wildnesse of thy Fate drawes to an end,   13ᵣ
   To a bad fearefull end; I must not stay   65
   To know thy fall, backe to *Bononia* I
   With speed will haste, and shun this comming blowe.
   Parma farwell, would I had never knowne thee,
   Or ought of thine; well *Youngman*, since no prayer
   Can make thee safe, I leave thee to despayre.   *Exit* FRYAR.   70

GIOVANNI   Despaire or tortures of a thousand hells
   All's one to mee; I have set up my rest.
   Now, now, worke serious thoughts on banefull plots,
   Be all a man my soule; let not the Curse
   Of old prescription rent from mee the gall   75
   Of Courage, which inrolls a glorious death.

53 come; sir, are] *Q*; ~. —~, ~ *Weber* (Sir); ~, ~. ~ *Gifford* (Are); ~! ~, ~ *Massai* (Sir)   54 SD
Exit VASQUES.] *Q*; SD [*Exit.* | *Dyce*   55] *Weber*; You . . . trust. | Not . . . what? *Q*
56 goe,] *Q*; ~! *Dodsley* (go); ~: *Dyce* (go)   57 ruine,] *Q*; ~. *Dodsley* (ruin)   58] *Weber*;
Be . . . goe. | Not . . . Death *Q*   63] *Dyce*; For . . . goe. | Goe . . . see *Q*   66 fall,] *Q*
~; *Dodsley*; ~: *Dyce*   66 *Bononia*] *Q*; Bologna *Massai*   68 farwell] *Q*; farewell *Dodsley*
69 thine;] *Q*; ~! *Reed*   70 SD *Exit* FRYAR.] *Q*; [*Exit.* | *Dyce*   71 SP GIOVANNI]
Dodsley (*Gio.*); *not in Q*   71 Despaireₐ] *Q*; ~, *Dodsley* (Despair)   73 plots,] *Q*; ~;
Reed   75 rent] *Q*; rend *Dosdley*

If I must totter like a well-growne Oake,
Some under shrubs shall in my weighty fall
Be crusht to splitts: with me they all shall perish.

Exit.

5.4   *Enter* SORANZO, VASQUES, *and* BANDITTI.

SORANZO.   You will not fayle, or shrinke in the attempt?

VASQUES   I will undertake for their parts; be sure my Maisters
to be bloody enough, and as unmercifull, as if you were
praying upon a rich booty on the very Mountaines of
Liguria; for your pardons trust to my Lord; but for reward   5
you shall trust none but your owne pockets.

BANDITTI   *omnes* Wee'le make a murther.

SORANZO   Here's gold, here's more; want nothing, what you do
Is noble, and an act of brave revenge.
I'le make yee rich *Banditti* and all Free.   10

BANDITTI   *omnes* Liberty, liberty!

VASQUES   Hold, take every man a Vizard; when yee are
withdrawne, keepe as much silence as you can possibly; you
know the watch-word, till which be spoken, move not, but
when you heare *that,* rush in like a stormy-flood; I neede   15
not instruct yee in your owne profession.

BANDITTI   *omnes* No, no, no.

VASQUES   In then, your ends are profit and preferment—away.

Exeunt BANDITTI.

SORANZO The guests will all come *Vasques?*

5.4] *this edn; not in Q;* SCENE IV. —*A Hall in* SORANZO's *House.* | *Weber, Dyce;* [5.4] *Massai*
0.1 SD VASQUES] *Q; ~ with masks* | *Dyce*   0.1 SD BANDITTI] *Reed* (*Banditti*); BANDITTI
| *Q*   2] *Lomax adds* SD [*to Banditti*] *after* parts; *Dyce, a 'long dash'; Massai,* SD [*to the
Banditti*].   7 SP BANDITTI *omnes*] *this edn; Ban. omnes.* | *Q; Bandit. (omnes)* | *Weber,
Banditti.* | *Dyce;* BANDITTI. *Gibson;* ALL [THE BANDITTI] *Wiggins*   8–9] *Q; Here's . . . do* |
Is . . . revenge. *Reed*   8] *Dyce adds* SD [*Gives them money*] *after* gold; *Wiggins,* SD [*Giving
them money*].   11 SP BANDITTI *omnes*] *this edn; Omnes.* | *Q; Bandit* | *Dyce;* BANDITTI
Gibson   11 Liberty, liberty.] *Q; ~! ~!* *Dodsley*   12.1] *Dyce adds* SD [*Gives them masks*]
after Vizard.   17 SP BANDITTI *omnes*] *this edn; Omnes.* | *Q. Bandit.* | *Dyce;* BANDITTI.
Gibson   18.1 SD *Exeunt* BANDITTI.] *Reed; Exit* Banditti. *Q* (*set against* ll. 18–19)

VASQUES   Yes sir, | and now let me a little edge your resolution;   20
    you see nothing is unready to this *Great worke*, but a great   13ᵛ
    mind in you: Call to your remembrance your disgraces,
    your losse of Honour, *Hippolita's* blood; and arme your
    courage in your owne wrongs; so shall you best right those
    wrongs in vengeance which you may truely call *Your owne.*   25

SORANZO   'Tis well; the lesse I speake, the more I burne,
    And blood shall quench that flame.

VASQUES   Now you begin to turne Italian, this beside, when
    my young *Incest-monger* comes, hee wilbe sharpe set on
    his old bitt: give him time enough, let him have your   30
    Chamber and bed at liberty; let my *Hot Hare* have law ere
    he be hunted to his death, that if it be possible, hee may
    poast to Hell in the very Act of his damnation.

                    Enter GIOVANNI.

SORANZO   It shall be so; and see as wee would wish,
    Hee comes himselfe first; welcome my *Much-lov'd brother,*   35
    Now I perceive you honour me; y'are welcome,
    But where's my father?

GIOVANNI   With the other States,
    Attending on the *Nuntio* of the Pope
    To waite upon him hither; how's my sister?

SORANZO   Like a good huswife, scarcely ready yet,   40
    Y'are best walke to her chamber.

GIOVANNI   If you will.

20–5] *prose after Weber*   20 Yes sir, and] *Roper;* ~ ~, | ~ *Q;* ~, ~; ~ *Dodsley;* ~, ~. ~ *Weber*
(And); ~, ~, ~ *Gibson*   20 resolution;] *Dodsley;* ~, *Q;* ~: *Weber;* ~. *Bawcutt*   25 wrongs;]
Reed; ~, *Q*   28 Italian,] *Q;* ~; *Dodsley;* ~: *Reed;* ~. *Weber*   29 wilbe] *Q;* will be *Dodsley*
32 may] *Q, not in Dodsley*   33.1 SD *Enter* GIOVANNI.] *set in left margin opposite* that if it . . .
damnation *in Q; Gifford places after* first 33.   35] *Wiggins adds* SD [*To* GIOVANNI] *before*
welcome; *long dash after* welcome *in Weber*   36 y'are] *Q;* you're *Dodsley*   37] *Weber;*
But . . . father? | With . . . States, *Q*   41] *Dyce;* Y'are . . . Chamber. | If . . . will
Q   41 Y'are] *Q;* You're *Dodsley*

SORANZO   I must expect my honourable Friends,
      Good brother get her forth.

GIOVANNI   You are busie Sir.   *Exit* GIOVANNI.

VASQUES   Even as the great Devill himselfe would have it, let   45
      him goe and glut himselfe in his owne destruction; Harke, the
      Nuncio is at hand; good sir be ready to receive him.   *Florish.*

            Enter CARDINAL, FLORIO, DONADO,
            RICHARDETTO *and* ATTENDANTS.

SORANZO   Most reverend Lord, this grace hath made me proud,
      That you vouchsafe my house; I ever rest
      Your humble servant for this Noble Favour.   50

14ʳ CARDINAL   You are our Friend my Lord, his holinesse
      Shall understand, how zealously you honour
      Saint Peters Vicar in his substitute.
      Our speciall love to you.

SORANZO   Signiors to you
      My welcome, and my ever best of thanks   55
      For this so memorable courtesie,
      Pleaseth your Grace to walke neere?

CARDINAL   My Lord, wee come
      To celebrate your Feast with Civill mirth,
      As ancient custome teacheth: wee will goe.

SORANZO   Attend his grace there, Signior keepe your way.   60
                                          Exeunt.

42 Friends,] *Q*; ~; *Dodsley* (friends)   43–4] *Q*; Good . . . sir. *verse in Dyce*   44 SD
Exit GIOVANNI.] *Q*; [*Exit.* | *Dyce*   47 SD *Florish*] *Dodsley; set in left margin opposite* let him
goe . . . receive him *Q* (uncorrected); *in left margin opposite* Enter . . . Attendants *Q* (corrected);
Gifford places SD *between* destruction 46 *and* Hark 46.   47.1 SD *Enter* . . . ATTENDANTS.]
after Q (corrected); *Flourish. Enter . . . attendants.* | *Dodsley*   47.1 SD RICHARDETTO] *Q* ~
[*disguised as the Doctor*] *Wiggins*   48] *Wiggins adds* SD [*To the* CARDINAL] *before* Most.
51 Lord,] *Q*; ~; *Reed* (lord); ~: *Dyce* (lord)   53 substitute.] *Dodsley;* ~ₐ *Q*; ~: *Dyce*
54] *Weber*, Our . . . you. | Signiors . . . you *Q*   56 courtesie,] *Q* ~. *Dodsley* (courtesy)
57] *Weber*; Pleaseth . . . neere? | My . . . come *Q*   57 Pleaseth] *Q*; Please *Weber*   57 to
walke] *Q*; ₐ walk *Gifford* ('to' omitted)   60] *Massai places* SD [*to Attendants*] *before* Attend.
60 there,] *Q*; ~!— *Dyce*

5.5   *Enter* GIOVANNI *and* ANNABELLA [*in her wedding dress*]
lying on a bed.

GIOVANNI   What chang'd so soone? hath your new sprightly Lord
   Found out a tricke in night-games more then wee
   Could know in our simplicity? ha! is't so?
   Or does the fitt come on you, to prove treacherous
   To your past vowes and oathes?

ANNABELLA   Why should you jeast   5
   At my Calamity, without all sence
   Of the approaching dangers you are in?

GIOVANNI   What danger's halfe so great as thy revolt?
   Thou art a faithlesse sister, else thou know'st,
   Malice, or any treachery beside   10
   Would stoope to my bent-browes; why I hold Fate
   Clasp't in my fist, and could Command the Course
   Of times eternall motion; hadst thou beene
   One thought more steddy then an ebbing Sea.
   And what? you'le now be honest, that's resolv'd?   15

ANNABELLA   Brother, deare brother, know what I have beene,
   And know that now there's but a dyning time
   Twixt us and our Confusion: let's not waste
   These precious houres in vayne and uselesse speech.
   Alas, these gay attyres were not put on   20
   But to some end; this suddaine solemne Feast
   Was not ordayn'd to riot in expence;   14ᵛ
   I that have now beene chambred here alone,
   Barr'd of my Guardian, or of any else,
   Am not for nothing at an instant free'd   25
   To fresh accesse; be not deceiv'd *My Brother*,
   This Banquet is an harbinger of Death
   To you and mee, resolve your selfe it is,
   And be prepar'd to welcome it.

5.5] *this edn; not in Q;* SCENE V.—*A Chamber,* ANNABELLA *discovered lying on a Bed.* | *Weber;*
SCENE V. ANNABELLA'S *Bed-Chamber in the same.* | *Dyce;* [5.5] *Massai*   0.1 SD] *this edn;*
Enter GIOVANNI *and* ANNABELLA. *Q; Enter* GIOVANNI. *Weber;* ANNABELLA *richly dressed and*
GIOVANNI [*discovered*]. *Dyce*   5] *Weber;* To . . . oathes? | Why . . . jeast *Q*   6 sence]
Q; sense *Dodsley*   17 dyning time] *Q* (corrected); dying ~ *Q* (uncorrected); dining-time
Weber   24 Barr'd] *Dodsley* (Bar'd), *Dyce* (Barred); Bard *Q*   28 mee,] *Q;* ~; *Dodsley*
(me)

GIOVANNI   Well then,
The *Schoole-men* teach that all this Globe of earth   30
Shalbe consum'd to ashes in a minute.

ANNABELLA   So I have read too.

GIOVANNI   But 'twere somewhat strange
To see the Waters burne, could I believe
This might be true, I could beleeve aswell
There might be hell or Heaven.

ANNABELLA   That's most certaine.   35

GIOVANNI   A dreame, a dreame; else in this other world
Wee should know one another.

ANNABELLA   So wee shall.

GIOVANNI   Have you heard so?

ANNABELLA   For certaine.

GIOVANNI   But d'ee thinke,
That I shall see you there? you looke on mee:
May wee kisse one another, Prate or laugh,   40
Or doe as wee doe here?

ANNABELLA   I know not that,
But, good, for the present, what d'ee meane
To free your selfe from danger? some way, thinke
How to escape ; I'me sure the guests are come.

GIOVANNI   Looke up, looke here; what see you in my face?   45

ANNABELLA   Distraction and a troubled Countenance.

GIOVANNI   Death and a swift repining wrath—yet looke,
What see you in mine eyes?

ANNABELLA   Methinkes you weepe.

29] *Weber*; And . . . it. | Well then, *Q*   32] *Weber*; So . . . too. | But . . . strange *Q*
33 burne,] *Q*; ~; *Dodsley* (burn); ~: *Dyce* (burn)   35] *Weber*; There . . . Heaven. | That's . . .
certaine. *Q*   37–8] *Weber*; Wee . . . another. | So . . . shall. | Have . . . so? | For certaine |
But . . . thinke, *Q*   38 d'ee] *Q*; do you *Dodsley*; d'ye *Dyce*   39–40] *Reed*; That . . .
there, | You . . . mee, | May . . . another | Prate . . . laugh *Q*   39 mee:] *Reed* (me); ~, *Q*
40 another,] *Q*; ~? *Dodsley*   41] *Weber*; Or . . . here? | I . . . that, *Q*   41 that,] *Q*; ~;
Dodsley; ~. *Dyce*   42 But, good,] *Walley*; ~ˌ ~ˌ *Q*; ~ˌ ~, *Sherman*; ~, ~ brother, *Dodsley*;
~ˌ ~ [brother] *Weber*; But—brother, *Gifford*; But, brother, *Dyce*   42 what] *Q*; how *Dodsley*
42 d'ee] *Q*; do you *Dodsley*; d'ye *Dyce*   46 Countenance] *Q*; conscience *Dodsley*
47 wrathˌ] *Q*; ~, *Reed*; ~: *Dyce*   48] *Weber*; What . . . eyes? | Methinkes . . . weepe. *Q*

GIOVANNI   I doe indeede; these are the funerall teares   Kı^r
   Shed on your grave, these furrowed up my cheeks   50
   When first I lov'd and knew not how to woo.
   Faire *Annabella*, should I here repeate
   The Story of my life, wee might loose time.
   Be record all the spirits of the Ayre,
   And all things else that are; that Day and Night,   55
   Earely and late, the tribute which my heart
   Hath paid to *Annabella's* sacred love,
   Hath beene *these teares*, which are *her mourners now*:
   Never till now did Nature doe her best,
   To shew *a matchlesse beauty* to the world,   60
   Which in an instant, ere it scarce was seene,
   The jealous Destinies required againe.
   Pray *Annabella*, pray; since wee must part,
   Goe thou white in thy soule, to fill a Throne
   Of Innocence and Sanctity in Heaven.   65
   Pray, pray my Sister.

ANNABELLA   Then I see your drift,
   Yee blessed Angels, guard mee.

GIOVANNI   So say I,
   Kisse mee; if ever after times should heare
   Of our fast-knit affections, though perhaps
   The Lawes of *Conscience* and of *Civill use*   70
   May justly blame us, yet when they but know
   Our loves, *That love* will wipe away that rigour,
   Which would in other *Incests* bee abhor'd.
   Give mee your hand; how sweetly Life doth runne
   In these well coloured veines! how constantly   75
   These Palmes doe promise health! but I could chide
   With Nature for this Cunning flattery,
   Kisse mee againe——forgive mee.

---

51 woo] *Q* (corrected); woe *Q* (uncorrected)   62 required] *Q* (corrected); require *Q*
(uncorrected) *followed by Weber*   63 part,] *Q*; ~. *Dodsley*   66–7] *Weber*; Pray, . . .
Sister. | Then . . . drift, | Yee . . . mee. | So . . . I, *Q*   67 mee.] *Q*; ~! *Dodsley* (me)
68] *Wiggins adds* SD [*They kiss.*] *before* if.   76 Palmes] *Q*; pulse *Dodsley*   78–9] *Weber*;
Kisse . . . forgive mee. | With . . . heart. | Farwell. | Will . . . begone? | Be . . . Sunne, *Q*
78 againe∧——] *Q*; ~, *Reed* (again); ~: *Dyce* (again)

ANNABELLA   With my heart.

GIOVANNI   Farwell.

ANNABELLA   Will you begone?

GIOVANNI   Be darke bright Sunne,
   And make this mid-day night, that thy guilt rayes   80
K1^v May not behold a deed, will turne their splendour
   More sooty, then the *Poets* faigne their *Stix*.
   One other kisse my Sister.

ANNABELLA   What meanes this?

GIOVANNI   To save thy fame and kill thee in a kisse.   *Stabs her.*
   Thus dye, and dye by mee, and by my hand,   85
   Revenge is mine; Honour doth love Command.

ANNABELLA   Oh brother by your hand?

GIOVANNI   When thou art dead
   I'le give my reasons for't; for to dispute
   With thy (even in thy death) most lovely beauty,
   Would make mee stagger to performe *this act*   90
   Which I most glory in.

ANNABELLA   Forgive him Heaven—and me my sinnes, farwell.
   Brother unkind, unkind—mercy great Heaven—oh—oh.
                                Dyes.

GIOVANNI   Shee's dead, alas good soule; *The haplesse Fruite*
   That in her wombe receiv'd its life from mee,   95
   Hath had from mee a *Cradle and a Grave.*
   I must not dally, this sad Marriage-bed
   In all her best, bore her alive and dead.
   Soranzo thou hast mist thy ayme in this,
   I have prevented now thy reaching plots,   100
   And kil'd a Love, for whose each drop of blood
   I would have pawn'd my heart; *Fayre Annabella,*

78] *Massai adds* SD [*They kiss.*] *after* againe; *Wiggins,* SD [*They kiss*] *after* heart 78.
79 Farwell] *Q;* Farewell *Dodsley*   82 *Stix.*] *Q;* ~! *Dodsley* (Styx)   83] *Weber;* One . . .
Sister. | What . . . this? *Q*   84 SD *Stabs her.*] *Q;* ~ ~ [*as they kiss*]. *Massai*   86] *Q;*
roman Dodsley   87] *Weber;* Oh . . . hand? | When . . . dead *Q*   87 hand?] *Q;* ~! *Dodsley*
89 thy] *Q;* thee *Weber*   92 sinnes,] *Q;* ~! *Dodsley* (sins)   92 farwell] *Q;* farewell
Dodsley (Farewell)   93 Brother . . . Heaven—oh—oh] *Q;* ~ . . . .~! | O, O. *Dyce*
93 unkind—] *Q;* ~, *Reed*   94 soule;] *Q;* ~! *Dodsley* (soul)   97 dally, this] *Q;* ~; ~
Reed; ~. ~ *Dyce* (This)   102 heart;] *Q;* ~. *Dodsley*

How over-glorious art thou in thy wounds,
Tryumphing over infamy and hate!
Shrinke not Couragious hand, stand up my heart,   105
And boldly act *my last, and greater part.   Exit with the Body.*

> **5.6**   *A Banquet.Enter* CARDINAL, FLORIO, DONADO,
>   SORANZO, RICHARDETTO, VASQUES
>   *and* ATTENDANTS. *They take their places.*

VASQUES   [*Aside*] Remember Sir what you have to do, be wise,
     and resolute.

SORANZO   [*Aside*] Enough—my heart is fix't. [*To the* CARDINAL]
     Pleaseth *Your Grace*
     To taste these Course Confections; though the use
     Of such set enterteynments more consists
     In Custome, then in Cause; yet *Reverend Sir,*   5
     I am still made your servant by your presence.   K2ʳ

CARDINAL   And wee your Friend.

SORANZO   But where's my Brother *Giovanni?*

>   *Enter* GIOVANNI *with a heart upon his Dagger.*

GIOVANNI   Here, here *Soranzo;* trim'd in reeking blood,
     That tryumphs over death; proud in the spoyle   10
     Of *Love* and *Vengeance,* Fate or all the Powers
     That guide the motions of Immortall Soules
     Could not prevent mee.

CARDINAL   What meanes this?

FLORIO   Sonne *Giovanni?*

SORANZO   Shall I be forestall'd?

---

106 SD   *Exit   with   the   Body.*]   *Q;   [The   scene   closes. | Gifford*
5.6] *this edn; not in Q.* SCENE VI. —*The Hall in the same House.* | *Weber;* SCENE VI. *A
banqueting-room in the same.* | *Dyce;* [5.6] *Massai*   0.1 SD *A Banquet.*] *Q; ~ ~ [is set out]
Wiggins,* ~ ~ 'Enter . . . DONADO' *Dodsley*   0.2 SD RICHARDETTO] *Q; ~ [disguised as the
Doctor] Wiggins*   0.3 SD *They take their places.*] *Q; not in Dyce;* ~ ~ ~ ~ [*at the table*]
Wiggins   1 SD [*Aside*]] *Dyce (aside to Sor.); Weber (Apart to Sor.); not in Q*   2 SD1
[*Aside*]] *Dyce (aside to Vas.); not in Q*   2 fix't.] *Reed* (fix'd); ~, *Q*   2 SD2 [*To the*
CARDINAL]] *Roper (To Car.); not in Q;* [*To* CARDINAL] *Wiggins*   2 Pleaseth] *Dyce;*
pleaseth *Q*   3 Course] *Q;* coarse *Dodsley*   3 Confections;] *Q; ~. Dodsley* (confections);
~: *Dyce* (confections); ~? *Walley* (confections)   3 though] *Q;* Though *Dodsley*   4 enter-
teynments] *Q;* entertainments *Dodsley*   7–8] *Q: verse in Weber*   8.1 SD a] *Dodsley, at
| Q*   13–14] *Weber;* Could . . . mee. | What . . . this? | Sonne *Giovanni?* |Shall . . . forestall'd?
Q   14 *Giovanni?*] *Q;* ~! *Weber* (roman)   14] *Gifford adds SD* [*aside before* Shall.

GIOVANNI   Be not amaz'd: If your misgiving hearts   15
   Shrinke at an idle sight; what bloodlesse Feare
   Of Coward passion would have ceaz'd your sences,
   Had you beheld the *Rape of Life and Beauty*
   Which I have acted? my sister, oh my sister!

FLORIO.   Ha! What of her?

GIOVANNI   The Glory of my Deed   20
   Darkned the mid-day Sunne, made Noone as Night.
   You came to feast *My Lords* with dainty fare,
   I came to feast too, but I dig'd for food
   In a much richer Myne then Gold or Stone
   Of any value ballanc't; 'tis *a Heart*,   25
   A Heart my Lords, in which is mine intomb'd,
   Looke well upon't; d'ee know't?

VASQUES   What strange ridle's this?

GIOVANNI   'Tis *Annabella's Heart*, 'tis ; why d'ee startle?
   I vow 'tis hers, this Daggers poynt plow'd up   30
   Her fruitfull wombe, and left to mee the fame
   Of a most glorious executioner.

FLORIO   Why mad-man, art thy selfe?

GIOVANNI   Yes Father, and that times to come may know,
   How as my Fate I honoured my revenge: 35
   List Father, to your eares I will yeeld up
   How much I have deserv'd to bee your sonne.

FLORIO
K2ᵛ   What is't thou say'st?

GIOVANNI   Nine Moones have had their changes,
   Since I first throughly view'd and truely lov'd
   Your Daughter and *my Sister*.

17 sences] *Q*; senses *Dodsley*   20] *Weber*; Ha! . . . her? | The . . . Deed *Q*   22 fare,]
Q ~; *Dodsley*, ~: *Dyce*   26 intomb'd,] *Q*, ~. *Dodsley*, entombed: *Dyce*   27–28] *Q*; *verse*
in Weber   27 d'ee] *Q*; do you *Dodsley*, d'ye *Dyce*   28] *Dyce adds* SD [*aside*] *before*
What.   29 d'ee] *Q*; do you *Dodsley*, d' you *Weber*, d'ye *Dyce*   30 hers, this] *Q*, ~. ~
Dodsley (This); her's. ~ *Weber* (This); ~: ~ *Dyce*   38] *Weber*, What . . . say'st? | Nine . . .
changes, *Q*

FLORIO How! alas, 40
My Lords, hee's a frantick mad-man!

GIOVANNI Father no;
For nine Moneths space, in secret I enjoy'd
Sweete *Annabella's* sheetes; Nine Moneths I liv'd
A happy Monarch of her heart and her.
Soranzo, thou know'st this; thy paler cheeke 45
Beares the Confounding print of thy disgrace,
For her too fruitfull wombe too soone bewray'd
The happy passage of our stolne delights,
And made her Mother to a Child unborne.

CARDINAL Incestuous Villaine.

FLORIO Oh his rage belyes him. 50

GIOVANNI It does not, 'tis the Oracle of truth,
I vow it is so.

SORANZO I shall burst with fury,
Bring the strumpet forth.

VASQUES I shall Sir. *Exit* VASQUES.

GIOVANNI Doe sir, have you all no faith
To credit yet my Triumphs? here I sweare 55
By all that you call sacred, by the love
I bore my *Annabella* whil'st she liv'd,
These hands have from her bosome ript *this heart.*
Is't true or no sir?

Enter VASQUES.

VASQUES 'Tis most strangely true.

FLORIO Cursed man—have I liv'd to— *Dyes.*

40–1] *McIlwraith; Your . . . Sister.* | How! . . . madman! | Father, no: *Q; Your . . . Lords* | Hee's . . .
no. *Weber*   44 her.] *Dodsley;* ~, *Q*   46 disgrace,] *Q;* ~; *Reed*   50] *Weber;*
Incestuous Villaine. | Oh, . . . him. *Q*   50 Villaine.] *Q;* ~! *Dodsley* (villain)   50 him.]
Q; ~! *Dodsley*   51 truth,] *Q;* ~! *Dodsley;* ~; *Dyce*   52] *Weber;* I . . . so. | I . . . fury, *Q*
52 so.] *Q;* ~! *Dodsley*   52 fury,] *Q;* ~! *Dodsley*   53] *Massai adds* SD [*to Vasquez*] *before*
Bring.   53 forth.] *Q;* ~! *Dodsley*   54] *Weber;* I . . . Sir. | Doe . . . faith *Q*   54 Sir.]
Dodsley (sir); ~, *Q*   54 SD *Exit* VASQUES.] *Q; [Exit.* | *Dyce; [Exit Vasquez.] Massai*
59] *Weber;* Is't . . . sir? | 'Tis . . . true. *Q*   59 SD *Enter* VASQUES.] *Q* (*set against* sir?); *Re-*
enter ~. *Dyce, after 'heart'* 58. *Weber places* SD *after 'heart'* 58.

CARDINAL   Hold up *Florio!*   60
Monster of Children, see what thou hast done,
Broake thy old Fathers heart; is none of you
Dares venter on him?

GIOVANNI   Let 'em; oh my Father,
How well his death becomes him in his griefes!
Why this was done with Courage; now survives   65
None of our house but I, guilt in the blood
K3ʳ Of a *Fayre sister* and a *Haplesse Father.*

SORANZO   Inhumane scorne of men, hast thou a thought
T' out live thy murthers?

GIOVANNI   Yes, I tell thee yes;
For in my fists I beare the twists of life,   70
Soranzo, see this heart which was thy wife's;
Thus I exchange it royally for thine,   [*Stabs him.*]
And thus and thus, now brave revenge is mine.

[SORANZO *falls.*]

VASQUES   I cannot hold any longer; you sir, are you growne
insolent in your butcheries? have at you.   *Fight.*   75

GIOVANNI.   Come, I am arm'd to meete thee.

VASQUES   No, will it not be yet? [*Thrusting at him*] If this will
not, another shall. Not yet, I shall fitt you anon—*Vengeance!*

Enter BANDITTI.

60] *Weber;* Cursed . . . to—| Hold . . . *Florio, Q*   60 up] *Q* (vp); ~, *Dodsley*   60 *Florio!*]
this edn; ~; *Q;* ~, *Dodsley,* ~. *Weber*   61] *Wiggins adds* SD [*To* GIOVANNI] *before* Monster.
61 Children,] *Q;* ~! *Dodlsey* (children)   63] *Weber;* Dares . . . him? | Let . . . Father, *Q*
63 venter] *Q;* venture *Dodsley*   66 guilt] *Q;* gilt *Massai*   68 Inhumane] *Dodsley*
(Inhuman); Inhamane *Q*   69] *Weber;* T' . . . murthers? | Yes, . . . yes; *Q*   69 out live]
Q; outlive *Dodsley*   69] *Weber adds* SD [*Draws.* | *after* murthers.   71 wife's;] *Reed;* ~,
Dodsley; wives, *Q*   72 thine,] *Q;* ~. *Sherman*   72 SD [*Stabs him*]] *Sherman; not in Q;*
[*Fight.* | *Weber;* [*They fight.* | *Dyce;* [*Stabbing him.*] *Massai*   73 thus,] *Q;* ~! *Dyce*
73] *Massai adds another* SD [*Stabs him again.*] *after* 'thus,'.   73 SD [SORANZO *falls.*]]
Weber; not in Q; Dyce places SD [SORANZO *falls.* | *after* 'thus,'.   74 longer;] *Q;* ~. *Weber;*
~: *Roper*   74] *Massai adds* SD [*to Giovanni*] *after* longer.   74 youᴧ sir,] *Q;* ~, ~,
Dodsley, Weber (You), *Sherman;* —~, ~, *Bawcutt* (You)   75 SD Fight.] *Q;* [*They*] Fight. |
Bawcutt; Gifford places SD '[*They*] *fight.' after* thee; *Dyce,* SD [*They fight.* | *after* thee;. *Sturgess,*
SD '[*They*] *fight,* [*and* GIOVANNI *is wounded*]' *after* thee; *Wiggins,* SD [VASQUES *and*
GIOVANNI] *fight* | *after* thee.   77–8 No, . . . anon] *this edn; separate lines in Q;* No, . . .
shall.— | Not . . . anon. *Weber*   77] *Massai places* SD [*Stabs Giovanni.*] *before* No.
77 No,] *Q;* ~! *Dodsley*   77 SD [*Thrusting at him*]] *Lomax; not in Q*   77 Not yet,] *Q;*
~ ~? *Dodsley*   78 —*Vengeance!*] *Dyce* (VENGEANCE); —~. *Weber* (Vengeance); — ᴧ ᴧ ~. *Q*
(*printed as if* SD); *Wiggins adds* SD [*Calls off stage*] *before* Vengeance.   78.1 SD *Enter* BANDITTI.]
Q; The Banditti *rush in.* | *Gifford;* ~ ~ [*and fight Giovanni*] *Bawcutt,* ~ ~ [*all masked and armed*]
Wiggins, ~ ~ [*vizarded and armed*] *Massai*

GIOVANNI Welcome, come more of you what e're you be,
I dare your worst!   [*They surround and wound him.*]   80
Oh I can stand no longer, Feeble armes
Have you so soone lost strength?   [*He falls.*]

VASQUES. Now you are welcome Sir; Away my Maisters, all is
done, shift for your selves, your reward is your owne, shift
for your selves.   85

BANDITTI Away, away!   *Exeunt* BANDITTI.

VASQUES How d'ee my Lord? see you this? how is't?

SORANZO Dead; but in death well pleased, that I have liv'd
To see my wrongs reveng'd on the *Blacke Devill.*
O *Vasques,* to thy bosome let mee give   90
My last of breath, let not that Lecher live—oh!   *Dyes.*

VASQUES The Reward of peace and rest be with him, my ever
dearest Lord and Maister.

GIOVANNI Whose hand gave mee this wound?

VASQUES Mine Sir, I was your first man, have you enough?   95

GIOVANNI I thanke thee, thou hast done for me
But what I would have else done on my selfe;
Ar't sure thy Lord is dead?

VASQUES Oh Impudent slave, as sure as I am sure to see thee dye.

80 worst!] *this edn*; ~— *Q*; ~. *Gifford*   80 SD [*They surround and wound him.*]] *Gifford*; *not in* *Q*; [*They surround and stab him.*] *Sherman*; [*They fight; Giovanni is wounded.*] *Massai*   82 strength?] *Reed*; ~. *Q*   82 SD [*He falls.*]] *Gifford (Falls)*; *not in Q*   83–5 Now . . . selves] *after Weber*, Now . . . Sir, | Away . . . done | Shift . . . owne | Shift . . . selues. *Q*   83 Sir;] *Reed* (sir); ~, *Q*; ~! *Dyce* (sir)   83] *Gifford adds* SD [*Aside to Band.* | *after* Sir.   83 Away∧] *Q*; ~, *Dodsley*   84 your selves] *Q*; yourselves. *Dodsley*   84] *Gifford adds* SD [*Aside to* BAND.] *after* your selves.   86 SD *Exeunt* BANDITTI.] *Dyce*; Exeunt Banditti. | *Q*; Exeunt. | *Gifford*   87 d'ee] *Q*; d'ye *Dodsley*   87 Lord?] *Reed* (lord); ~, *Q*   87] *Gifford adds* SD [*pointing to* GIO.] *after* this?.   91 live—oh!] *Dodsley*; ~—~, *Q*; ~ — | Oh!— *Weber, Gifford*; ~— | O! *Dyce*   92–3] *after Weber*, The Reward . . . him, | My . . . Maister. *Q*   92 with him] *Q*; ~ [you] *Gifford*   93 Maister] *Q*; master *Dodsley*   95 man,] *Q*; ~: *Reed*   96–8] *after Reed*; *prose in Q*   96 thee,] *Q*; ~, Vasques, *conj. Dyce*   97 my selfe;] *Dodsley* (myself); ~~, *Q*; ~~. *Dyce* (myself)   98–9] *Q*; Ar't . . . dead? | Oh . . . slave | As sure . . . dye. *Weber*   98 Ar't] *Q* (ar't); Art *Reed*   99 thee *Dodsley*, *Q* the

CARDINAL   Thinke on thy life and end, and call for mercy.   100

GIOVANNI   *Mercy?* why I have found it in this *Justice.*

K3ᵛ CARDINAL   Strive yet to cry to Heaven.

GIOVANNI   Oh I bleed fast,
  Death, thou art a guest long look't for, I embrace
  Thee and thy wounds; oh my last minute comes.
  Where e're I goe, let mee enjoy this grace,   105
  Freely to view *My Annabella's face.*   *Dyes.*

DONADO   Strange Miracle of Justice!

CARDINAL   Rayse up the Citty, wee shall be murdered all!

VASQUES   You neede not feare, you shall not; this strange
  taske being ended, I have paid the Duty to the Sonne,   110
  which I have vowed to the Father.

CARDINAL   Speake wretched Villaine, what incarnate Feind
  Hath led thee on to this?

VASQUES   Honesty, and pitty of my Maisters wrongs; for know *My
  Lord*, I am by birth *a Spaniard*, brought forth my Countrey in   115
  my youth by Lord *Soranzo's* Father; whom whil'st he lived,
  I serv'd faithfully; since whose death I have beene to this man,
  as I was to him; what I have done was duty, and I repent
  nothing, but that the losse of my life had not ransom'd his.

CARDINAL   Say Fellow, know'st thou any yet unnam'd   120
  Of Counsell in this Incest?

VASQUES   Yes, an old woeman, sometimes *Guardian* to this
  murthered Lady.

CARDINAL   And what's become of her?

VASQUES   Within this Roome shee is, whose eyes after her con-   125
  fession I caus'd to be put out, but kept alive, to confirme what
  from *Giovanni's* owne mouth you have heard: now *My Lord*,
  what I have done, you may Judge of, and let your owne
  wisedome bee a Judge in your owne reason.

102] *Weber*; Strive . . . Heaven. | Oh . . . fast, *Q*   103 thou art] *Q*; thou'rt *Weber*
104 wounds; oh] *this edn*; ~, ~ *Q*; ~. ~ *Dodsley* (Oh); ~: ~ *Dyce* (O)   104 comes.] *Q*; ~!
Weber   105 Where e're] *Q*; Where'er *Dodsley*   122 sometimes] *Q*; sometime *Dodsley*
125 is,] *Q*; ~; *Reed*; ~! *Dyce*   127 heard: now ʌ My] *Q*; ~: ~ *Dodsley* (my); ~. ~, ~ *Weber*
(Now) (my)

CARDINAL   Peace; First this woeman chiefe in these effects,   130
My sentence is, that forthwith shee be tane
Out of the Citty, for examples sake,
There to be burnt to ashes.

DONADO   'Tis most just.

CARDINAL   Be it your charge *Donado*, see it done.

DONADO   I shall.   135

VASQUES   What for mee? if death, 'tis welcome, I have beene
honest to the Sonne, as I was to the Father.   K4ʳ

CARDINAL   Fellow, for thee; since what thou did'st, was done
Not for thy selfe, being no Italian,
Wee banish thee for ever, to depart   140
Within three dayes, in this wee doe dispense
With grounds of reason, not of thine offence.

VASQUES   'Tis well; this Conquest is mine, and I reioyce that a
Spaniard out-went an *Italian in revenge.*   *Exit* VASQUES.

CARDINAL   Take up these slaughtered bodies, see them buried,   145
And all the Gold and Jewells, or whatsoever,
Confiscate by the Canons of the Church,
Wee seize upon to the Popes proper use.

RICHARDETTO   [*Discovers himself*] Your graces pardon, thus
long I liv'd disguis'd
To see the effect of *Pride and Lust* at once   150
Brought both to shamefull ends.

CARDINAL   What! *Richardetto* whom wee thoughr for dead?

DONADO   Sir was it you——

RICHARDETTO   Your friend.

CARDINAL   Wee shall have time

---

130 Peace;] *Q;* ~! *Weber*   130 First ʌ] *Q;* ~, *Roper*   131 tane] *Q;* ta'en
Dodsley   133] *Weber;* There . . . ashes. | 'Tis . . . just. *Q*   136 welcome,] *Q;* ~; *Reed;* ~:
Dyce   141 dayes,] *Q;* ~; *Dodsley* (days); ~: *Dyce* (days)   142 reason,] *Dodsley;* ~ʌ
Q   144 SD *Exit* VASQUES.] *Q; Exit.* | *Massai*   148 seize] *Dodsley,* ceaze
Q   149 SD [*Discovers himself*]] *Weber;* not in *Q; Wiggins places* SD [RICHARDETTO *takes
off his disguise*] *after* use 148.   149 pardon,] *Q;* ~; *Reed;* ~: *Dyce*   152 What!] *Reed;* ~,
Dodsley, ~ʌ *Q*   153] *Weber;* Sir, . . . you— | Your friend. | We . . . time *Q*

To talke at large of all, but never yet
Incest and *Murther* have so strangely met.   155
Of one so young, so rich in Natures store,
Who could not say, *'Tis pitty shee's a Whoore ?*   *Exeunt.*

FINIS.

The generall Commendation deserved by the Actors, in their
Presentment of this Tragedy, may easily excuse such few faults, as
are escaped in the Printing: A common charity may allow him the
ability of spelling, whom a secure confidence assures that hee
cannot ignorantly erre in the Application of Sence.   5

157 *'Tis . . . Whore.*] *Q; roman in Gifford*   157 SD *Exeunt.*] *Q; not in Weber;* ~ [*with the
bodies*] *Wiggins*

Commentary to *'Tis Pity She's a Whore*

SETTING

The Sceane *PARMA* City in northern Italy, northwest of Bologna.

ACTORS NAMES

2 BONAVENTURA literally meaning 'good fortune', the name perhaps recalls Saint Bonaventure (1217–74), a leading theologian and revered leader of the Franciscan order (*EB*).

3 Nuntio Nuncio: 'a permanent official representative of the Roman See at a foreign court' (*OED* 1).

4 SORANZO The cast of George Whetstone's *Heptameron of Ciuill Discourses* (1582; reissued in 1593 as *Aurelia*) includes a 'Segnior Soranso, a Gentleman Italion, of wit quick and sharp' (noted by Roper).

5 FLORIO The prominent scholar, translator, and language teacher John Florio (1553–1625) was surely known to Ford. Florio's first manual for teaching Italian, *Firste Fruites* (1578), is quoted at 4.1.73 and 4.3.59, 63, and probably 168–9. Perhaps Ford was thinking of this work when, in his Dedicatory Epistle to the Earl of Peterborough, he described *TPW* itself as '*These First Fruites* of my leasure in the Action' (11–12). Florio was also the author of an Italian dictionary, *A Worlde of Wordes*, 1598 (*ODNB*).

7 GRIMALDI Antonio Grimaldi is the title character in Massinger's *The Renegado* (1624). Like *TPW,* this tragicomedy was performed by Queen Henrietta's Men at the Phoenix Theatre. The extant cast list shows that the outlaw Grimaldi was played by William Allen, a leading actor who was associated with the company until at least 1633 (Moore, pp. 18, 23).

9 BERGETTO Whetstone's *Heptameron* (see note to *Soranzo*) also features a 'Monsier Bargetto' (or Bergetto), 'a Frenchman, amourous and light headed' (sig. C1; Roper).

10 RICHARDETTO As Roper notes, the name *Richardet* occurs in François de Rosset's story, 'Des Amours Incestueses d'un Frère & d'une Soeur' (in *Les Histoires Tragiques de Nostre Temps*, 1615), a likely source for *TPW.*

10 Suppos'd pretended.

12 POGGIO The name, at least, may recall Gian Francesco Poggio Bracciolini, the 15th-century Italian humanist scholar and calligrapher; and appears in

Facetie (humorous sayings or writings) of M. L. Domenichi (Venice, 1581) (cf. note to 2.4.8).

13 BANDITTI bandits. See note to 4.3.223.1.

16 HIPPOLITA The most well-known Hippolyte in classical myth is the Amazon queen whose belt became the object of Heracles' ninth labour. But events at the marriage of Soranzo and Annabella suggest an allusion to another Amazon queen, Antiope, who was also sometimes called Hippolyte. See note to 4.1.35.2.

17 PHILOTIS Greek: 'love, affection'. Philotis was the maidservant who helped her fellow Romans defeat the besieging Latins after the Gauls were driven out by Camillus. In response to the Latins' demands for widows and virgins, Philotis and other maidservants went to the enemy dressed as free women. Inside the enemy camp, she gave the signal to the Romans when it was safe to attack. See Plutarch's *Romulus*, 29. In *TPW*, it is Philotis's uncle, Richardetto, who makes use of disguise to plot against an enemy.

18 PUTANA John Florio's *A Worlde of Wordes*, an Italian dictionary published in 1598, defines *putana* as 'a whore, a harlot, a strumpet, a queane'.

19 (OFFICERS, ATTENDANTS, SERVANTS, *etc.*) this edn.; not in *Q*.

TO MY FRIEND, THE AUTHOR.

The sheet bearing this commendatory poem is found only in the copies of the Quarto at the British Library (BL 1481.bb.18) and the Huntington.

2 admiration Closer at this time to the Latin *admirari*, 'wonder' (*OED* 1). Cf. *LS* 1.1.128: 'rapt in my admiration'.

4 fam'd reported, made famous (*OED n.* 1–3).

6 Graces Minor goddesses personifying beauty, charm, and grace (also favour and gratitude for favour). They were the daughters of Zeus. 'As a group they appear frequently in literature and art in contexts of joy or festivity, as the companions of the Muses, since they were fond of poetry, song and dance, or as attendants upon some god' (March).

7 Pallas Title of uncertain origin given to Athena, one of the twelve great Olympian deities. She was the goddess of war, art, and handicrafts, and was regarded as the personification of wisdom. A patron of Perseus, Bellerophon, and other mortals, she helped in the construction of the Trojan Horse (March). Playing the 'Chamber-maide' to Ford's 'Whore' would indeed be a humbling role for Athena since, in the Judgement of Paris, she had vied with the goddesses Hera and Aphrodite for the title of the fairest.

10 Age The locution seems to require the sense 'time, duration' in general, but *OED* does not record this precise meaning (cf. def. 2: 'The whole duration

of the life or existence of any being or thing'). Perhaps the meaning is 'this age or period' (*OED* 8; cf. 10).

12 **THOMAS ELLICE** 'Nothing is known of this poet; a relative perhaps of "Master Robert Ellice . . . of Gray's Inn", one of the "worthily respected friends" to whom Ford dedicated *The Lover's Melancholy*' (Roper). Both men wrote commendatory poems for D'Avenant's *Albovine* (1629).

[DEDICATORY EPISTLE]

2 **Lord Mordant** John Mordaunt (1599–1643) came from a family of prominent Northamptonshire Roman Catholics. His father, Henry, the fourth Lord Mordaunt, had been linked to the Gunpowder Plot. King James I made John a ward of Archbishop Abbott to ensure that he received a Protestant education. A favourite of James's, he became a knight of the Bath in 1616 and accompanied the king on his Scottish progress in 1617. He married Elizabeth Howard in 1621, converted to Protestantism in 1625, and was raised to the earldom of Peterborough in 1628. He led a regiment for Parliament in the Civil War (*ODNB*, Roper).

5 **Where . . . warrant** Where a person's genuine merit is widely accepted (*OED* warrant *n.*¹ 5 b, 8).

10 **ennobles** confers higher rank, fame, or refinement upon (*OED* ennoble 1–4, Roper).

10 **freedome of Birth** gentle or noble birth (*OED* free *a.* 3).

10–11 **lawfull Interest** legitimate claim.

12 **Noble allowance** 'generous acceptance or approval. "Allow" could mean anything from "praise" to "barely tolerate" ' (Roper; *OED* allow 1–3, allowance 1–4).

12 *First Fruites . . .* **Action** the first profitable results of my work for the theatre. For this reading of *Action*, see *OED* 12 (citing Massinger, *Roman Actor* (1626), 4.2.298 [McIlwraith's ed.], as the earliest instance). The *first fruits* were the choicest first corn, wheat, barley, grapes, figs, pomegranates, olives, honey, etc., which the ancient Hebrews offered to Jehovah. Offerings also included wine, dough, and 'the first of the fleece' (*Catholic Encyclopaedia*; see Leviticus 2:12, 14–15, 23:10114, Numbers 15:201–1, 18:13, Deuteronomy 18:4). In I Corinthians 15:20, the risen Christ is described as 'the first fruits of them that slept'. The phrase also had particular significance in the Catholic Church, where it was used of the annates (Latin, *annatae*), the payments made to the papal treasury upon the appointment of a bishop or other cleric. These payments consisted of a year's income from the ecclesiast's benefice. At the Reformation the right to the annates of English benefices was transferred to the Crown (*OED annates*).

Ford's reference to *TPW* as the '*First Fruites* of my leasure in the Action' suggests to Roper that the play may have been 'the earliest piece of writing Ford was willing in 1633 to acknowledge, and thus the first of his extant independent plays, though other interpretations are possible'. Roper gives good reason to doubt theories that *TPW* was composed shortly before its first publication (see his Introduction, xxiii–xxvi; also, Moore, pp. 2–5).

14 **construction**] interpretation (*OED* 7).

14 **Presentment** Two senses seem most relevant: (1) dramatic performance (continuing the idea of 'Action', l.11; *OED* 4b), and (2) dedication of a book (*OED* 5, quoting *Timon* 1.1.26–7). 'Presentment' also meant 'the act of offering something for acceptance or consideration' (*OED* 5), which in this case might refer to the printed book.

15–16 **particular Ingagement** special obligation (cf. 4.1.55 below). We do not know what this obligation might have been.

17 **leightnesse** frivolity (*OED n.*1 7).

I.1

2 **Schoole-points** topics for debate or instruction, especially by the 'School-men' (university theologians) referred to at 5.5.32 (Roper; *OED* school-point 1). Ford often creates compound words, as at 1.2.48: 'warme-broth', 49: 'spone-meat', 95: 'plaine-sufficient', and many times elsewhere.

2 **nice** Various senses of the word would serve the Friar's critical intention: 'trivial', 'extravagant', 'pampered', 'refined', 'sophisticated'. The oldest meanings include 'foolish' and 'wanton' (*OED* 1b, 2a, c, 3d, 4d, 9b).

4 **admits** allows.

4–8 **wits . . . Atheisme** A possible allusions to Sir Walter Raleigh's 'School of Atheism'.

4 **wits** persons of (or claiming) discernment, wisdom. Roper compares *Christes Bloodie Sweat* 355–60 where scholars are distrusted.

5 **wit** intellect (*OED* 2a). Often denoting a high level of intelligence, or a person of such capacity. Cf. *HT* 636, 644.

6 **Art** scholarship, science (*OED* 3b).

9 **fond** foolish (*OED* 2).

10 **then** variant spelling of 'than', very common in 17th century.

12 **may not** 'cannot'—or 'am not permitted to'.

13 **unclasp't** opened. The expression may refer to books, which were often secured with clasps. Cf. *1 Henry IV* 1.3.188: 'unclasp a secret book', *Twelfth Night* 1.4.13–14: 'I have unclasped | To thee the book even of my secret soul', *LS* 2.3.48–9: 'unclaspe | The book of lust'. The word also appears in a mental

situation: cf. *Cristes Bloodie Sweat* 43: 'Here then unclaspe the burthen of my woes', and *Spanish Gipsy* 1.5.44–5: 'here I unclaspe | The secrets of my heart'.

17 **All what** all that. Vickers comments that 'Ford used this slightly unusual construction eleven times in his plays' (*CWJF* 2, p. 182). See, for example, *LT* 2.1.100: 'All what this paper talks', 2.4.91: 'All what is deerest to me', *The Welsh Ambassador* 5.1.96, and *The Laws of Candy* 1.2.240–1: 'All what my father . . . has discours'd, is true'.

17 **durst** dared.

21 **That beauty** Annabella.

24 **peevish** silly, childish, senseless, spiteful (*OED* 1, 2; see 5.3.40).

25 **A customary . . . man** mere convention shared by human societies, without divine sanction (Roper)

30–1 **Are . . . bound | So . . . nature** A similar phrase occurs in *The Witch of Edmonton* 1.1.199: 'The bonds in which we are to either bound'.

31–2 **links | Of blood** 'affinities of kinship', but 'blood' was also regarded as the seat of passion and sexual appetite (Roper), courage, mettle, and a brave temperament. Cf. Giovanni's 'Neoplatonic' justification of his forbidden love at 1.2.252–4, Hippolita's accusation of Soranzo of his 'rage of blood' at 2.2.28.

34 *All* Q's italic is perhaps for rhetorical purposes. Such 'emphasis italic' is a fairly common feature of Fordian texts and may well be authorial (see Moore, p. 273). For further examples (or possible instances), see 2.5.5, 20, 24, etc.; 2.6.25, 69; 3.8.18; 4.1.46, 103; 4.3.17. See also Ford's dedicatory epistle.

35 **Have done unhappy youth, for thou art lost** in this context perhaps with the sense 'damned'. Elsewhere it means death, as at 1.2.139: 'Lost, I am lost: my fates have doom'd my death'. Similar phrases appear in *The Welsh Ambassador* 5.1.49: 'Thou art lost, for ever lost'; *The Fair Maid of the Inn* 5.1.63–4: 'thou art lost. | Unfortunate young man'.

35 **unhappy** unfortunate, ill-fated, wretched.

38 **change** modulation, interchange (*OED* 8c).

40 **distills** flows (an intransitive use).

41 **Counsell** essence of deliberation or prudence.

42 **ease** relief, alleviation.

42 **extreames** straits, tribulations. Cf. 2.2.1: '*Loves measure is extreame*'; see other occurrences: *GM* title-page 10–11: 'The Noblenesse of perfect | Vertue in extreames', 98: 'perfect vertue in extremitie', 1221: 'Vertue in extreames'; and *CBS* 1521: 'undaunted in extreame'.

43 **Repentance (sonne) and sorrow for this sinne** Cf. *CBS* 775: 'No sin that is not washt in true repentance'.

45 **thy . . . Blasphemy** 'your undisciplined near-blasphemy' (*OED* range *v.*[1] 1c) or 'your almost limitless blasphemy'. The former reading seems more

likely: Giovanni has not spoken impiously about God but about the sacred laws governing relations between the sexes (see *OED* blasphemy 1a, 1b). Sturgess argues that Giovanni's sin 'is, in fact, a double one: the sin of incest, and the sin of blasphemy in his making a religion of his love'. Morris glosses 'un-raungèd' (a tri-syllable) as 'disranged': disordered, deranged (*OED* disranged *ppl. a.*1, citing this passage).

46 Confessor Stressed on the first and third syllables.

47 miracle of Wit Cf. *GM* 312: 'miracles of pittie'; *PW* 5.3.89: 'miracle of Constancie'; 'Wit', intelligence

48 once at one time

49 *Bononia* Latin and early vernacular form of Bologna.

51–2 Cf. Cicero, *De officiis*, 1.5.15, etc., for 'the four cardinal virtues' (Monsarrat, *CWJF* 1, p. 524) as in note to *GM* 806–8: '*Wisdome, Temperance, Valour, Justice*, are the substance and hereditary possessions of a perfectly happy man.'

51 Government self-discipline, moral conduct (Crystal); discretion (*OED* 2b, citing this instance).

53 Tutellage care, guardianship (*OED* 1).

57 Giovanni Pronounced with four syllables throughout the play.

58 Death spiritual death (*OED* 5, Roper, comparing 5.1.36–7). The audience may also note an anticipation of Giovanni's physical death.

59 waites attends on.

64 *Ocean* tri-syllabic

65 floates floods, high tides (*OED* float 2). Ford often associates this word with the surge and abatement of emotion and desire (occasionally with 'ebb'); cf. 5.5.13–14, 'hadst thou beene | One thought more steddy then an ebbing Sea', and *LS* 2.3.88–9: 'Though the float | Of infinite desires swell to a tide'.

65 vowes 'earnest wishes, prayers' (*OED n.* 4; Latin *vota*), 'silent vows of loyalty (to Annabella)' or 'desires' (*OED n.* 4, Roper).

66 flames i.e. the flames of his lust or desire. Cf. 1.2.227 n.

68 voyce of life 'life-giving voice' or 'voice from heaven' (Roper, comparing *LL* 250: 'Oracles of life'). In 4.3.112, 'Life' may mean 'spiritual life' or 'redemption'. Cf. 61 above, 5.1.38–9, and 5.6.51: 'oracle of truth'.

69 Hye hasten.

72 Cry to thy heart appeal to your innermost self, conscience, or desires. Roper compares *King Lear* 2.2.292–4: 'LEAR. O me, my heart! My rising heart! . . . FOOL. Cry to it, nuncle, as the cockney did to the eels when she put 'em i'th' paste alive'. In both passages 'cry' may mean 'call upon, implore' as well as 'weep, cry out in anguish' (*OED* cry *v.* 2, 6–7, heart 5–6, 13). Cf. also *GM* 1059–61, where Monsarrat cites Prov. 16:32: 'He that is slowe unto anger, is better then the mightie man: and he that ruleth his owne minde, is better then he that winneth a citie' (*CWJF* 1, p. 531).

73 teares . . . blood Jeremy Taylor observed that it was 'usuall to call the tears of the greatest sorrows, tears of blood' (*The Great Exemplar*, 1649, pt. 1, p. 127, cited by Roper).

74 leprosie foul infection. In the early modern period some writers associated leprosy with sexual depravity. Cf. 4.3.61: 'Thy lust be-leapred body', *LS* 3.1.1–2: 'leprosy of | my blood', *BH* 4.2.169: 'a leprous soul', and *FCN* 4.1.70–1: 'a leprosie | Of raging lust' (*CWJF* 2, p. 238).

75–6 acknowledge what thou art, |A wretch, a worme, a nothing. Cf. *CBS* 991: 'What is a man but dust'.

83–4 All . . . God A 'rod' is 'an instrument of punishment, either one straight stick or a bundle of twigs bound together' (*OED* 2a). Giovanni's 'rod | Of vengeance' draws on the Christian notion of divine justice or chastisement (cf. 'the rod of heaven', *1 Henry IV* 3.2.10), but the Furies, the merciless goddesses of retribution and vengeance, were also armed with whips of snakes or scorpions. For other references to fate in the play, see 1.2.159 and 235, 3.2.22, 5.5.12, and 5.6.11 and 82.

1.2

1 stand to your tackling literally, 'maintain or hold fast to your weapons'; 'stand and fight' (*OED* tackling 3). Cf. *LS* 5.2.123: 'stand to the hazard of all brunts', and *LT* 2.2.202: 'stand to't', to be brave or firm.

1 *Craven* cowardly (*OED adj.* A2); the only occurrence of this word in Ford.

3 Thou . . . mee the nobleman Grimaldi thinks he would do himself a dishonour to fight with Vasques, a servant. Cf. *BH* 4.4.46–8: 'neither could I | With equal trial of unequal fortune, | By hazard of a duel' (noted by Gibson); *The Welsh Ambassador* 3.2.73: 'any tares sallenge my lord or *Reese* his man vppon duellos, and combats, and battalios and pells mells'.

3 equall i.e. socially equal.

5 Mountibanke in the general sense: 'a charlatan', 'a self-advertising imposter' (*OED* mountebank 1b). Cf. 'shaddow of a Souldier', 12; *FCN* 3.3.28: 'this same Mountbancking new-come foyst', 3.3.28.01 SD '*like a Courtly Mountebank*', *The Fair Maid of the Inn* Persons 10: 'A cheating Mountebank', and *SG* 2.1.14: 'Wee'l entertaine no Mounty-bancking Stroule'.

5–6 a meales meate food ('meat') for one meal.

7 for because of.

7–8 wilt thou to this geere? do you wish to fight? 'Geere' (gear) may mean 'business' of fighting (*OED* gear, *n.* 11 c; cf. *Troilus* 1.1.6) or 'fighting equipment' (*OED* 2, Roper).

9 **slave** a term of contempt: 'wretch, fellow, rascal'.

9 **ballance** counterpoise; give equal weight or value to. *OED*'s earliest example of this sense is dated 1624 (balance *v.* 3; but cf. 2).

10 **Cast-suite** servant or dependent who might wear (or perhaps in this case is wearing) his master's 'cast-suit', i.e. discarded clothing (Morris, Gibson). Roper compares *The Queene* 1.1.275–6: 'the sign lucky to venture the begging of a cast-suit'. Also see *Sun's Darling* 1.1.116: 'waiting-women flant it in Cast-suits'.

10 **Maister** variant spelling of 'Master'.

11 **Cot-queane** Literally, 'the housewife of a cot or labourer's hut'; used opprobriously for a coarse, vulgar, scolding woman (*OED* cotquean 2, cf. def. 1). The term was also applied to a man who meddled in the housewife's province: an 'old woman' (*OED* 3).

12 **shaddow** delusive semblance (*OED* shadow *n.* 6a).

13 **quality** rank and disposition (*OED* 3a, 4a); birth and character (Gibson). Cf. 1.2.38–44.

14 **prate** talk, chat (contemptuously).

18 **these Hilts** the handle of this sword (using the common plural form). The cross-shape of the handle and blade made a suitable object on which to swear. Cf. 2.6.67–78 below.

18 **brave my Lord** perhaps: 'do you dare to challenge (or defy, or provoke) my master?' As T. W. Craik comments (private correspondence), 'Soranzo is a lord and Vasques always calls him so; Grimaldi, though nobly allied, is only "a Roman gentleman" ' ('The Actors Names').

20 **Have at you** a phrase from combat: 'Take care! My aim is you'. Cf. 115, *WoE* 4.1.251–2: 'Gammer Gurton, have at your Needle of Witch-craft', 5.1.39–40: 'When the Devil comes to thee as a Lamb, have at your Throat', and *The Queene* 3.1.126: 'have at ye once more'.

21 **sudden broyles** rash or unexpected quarrels or disturbances, confused fighting (*OED* sudden *adj.* 1a, 2a; broil *n.*1); cf. *BH* 1.2.45–6: 'sudden lightning | Of self-opinion', and *WoE* 2.270–1: 'in your sleep you utter sudden and | Distracted accents'.

23 **spleene** passion, malice, bad temper (*OED n.* 7a, Crystal); bitter passion (Wiggins). Cf. 56: 'unspleened', and 2.2.124: 'your female spleene'. Ford uses this term many times elsewhere: cf. *SD* 1.1.84: 'Contein your float of spleen in seemly bounds'; *LT* 4.3.49–50: 'with all the eagerness of spleen | Of a suspicious rage', *LS* 5.1.65–6: 'the boundless spleen | Of just-consuming wrath', *BH* 3.4.25–6: 'that height | Of arrogance and spleene'.

23 **disordered bloods** 'diseases or passions connected to a surplus of blood in the body' (Massai).

24 **haunted still** constantly bothered or beset.

26 **Is this your love Grimaldi?** Similar phrases occur in *The Laws of Candy* 2.2.174: 'Is this your brother Annophill?', 5.3.156: 'Is this your love?', and *SG* 5.1.58: 'Is this your Husband Lady?'.

26 **naught** worthless (*OED a.* 1).

29 **seconding** encouraging (*OED v.*[1] 1a); stirring up (Roper).

29.1 **SD** *above* On the 'upper stage', where they are able to observe the action below without being noticed. The Jones | Webb collection at Worcester College, Oxford, includes a design for an indoor playhouse by Inigo Jones which has been linked by scholars to the Phoenix Theatre, where, according to the 1633 title-page, *TPW* was performed. The stage façade of Jones's design includes a small window-like opening above the central entrance where Annabella and Putana may have stood.

29 **ground** cause (of the dispute).

30 **resolve** explain (*OED v.* 11c, citing this instance); answer (Gibson).

31 **fame** rumour, report.

32 **else** i.e. by other means than 'fame', 31 (*OED* else 3a).

34 **still preferrs** constantly advances, presents.

34 **to** i.e. resulting in ('my disgrace'), to that effect. Cf. *Cymbeline* 3.2.57–8, and *Othello* 2.3.190: 'I am hurt to danger'.

38 **blood** breeding, gentility.

38 **bewrayes** reveals (*OED* 6)

42 **this** As Lomax notes, *Q*'s 'this' has a more contemptuous edge than the popular emendation 'thy' (see textual notes). Massai adopts Dodsley's 'his', asserting that ll. 41–3 'and on this ground . . . for me' are addressed to Florio.

45 **let . . . gilles** i.e. cut Grimaldi's throat (the 'gills' being the flesh under the jaws and ears; *OED n.* 2b), with a reference to the common therapeutic practice of blood-letting. The phrase 'my Gentleman blood' mocks both Grimaldi's social pretentions and his claims to valour (another sense of 'blood').

46 **worm'd** In 'worming', the 'worm' or lytta was extracted from a dog's tongue as a safeguard against rabies (*OED* worm *v.* 3a, b).

46 **for** 'on account of' or 'to prevent (you)'.

46 **madde** (1) insane; (2) in a furious rage.

48–9 **warme-broth . . . dyet** Cf. *LT* 3.1.57, where 'doe' has the same mocking cadence: 'Brave man-at-arms, go turn pander, do; stalk for a mess of warm broth'. 'Stay your stomack' means 'quiet your appetite' (*OED* stomach *n.* 8), but also 'satisfy your valour, pride, or anger' (Roper).

49 **Innocence** harmless fool.

49 spone-meat i.e. spoon-meat, a soft or liquid food for taking with a spoon, suitable for infants or invalids (*OED*).

53 engag'd pledged.

54 Owing owning (*OED* owe 1a). Perhaps: 'If you own . . .' (Roper).

55 Loosers may talke This proverb (Tilley L458) appears again in *PW* 2.2.95: 'Give losers leave to talk' (Roper).

55 law of any game cf. 'law of sports'; cf. 5.3.7.

57 unspleen'd Dove The gentle character of the dove was popularly believed to derive from its lack of a spleen (the supposed seat of anger or ill temper; see 1.2.23 n); cf. *HT* 566: 'doves without gals'.

61 put up sheathe your sword.

64 *Chardge* Putana is charged with the duty of being the guardian of Annabella, who obediently addresses her as '**Tutresse**' (65).

67 ends probably 'purposes.' Roper glosses as 'matters', comparing *Tempest* 1.2.89, 'I, thus neglecting worldly ends'. This sense is not recorded by *OED*.

69 no marvaile else i.e. there would be no marvel other than that. As Putana goes on to emphasize, she has no intention of leaving Annabella, now or ever. Roper explains 'else' as a colloquial intensive, 'at all, indeed', with the whole phrase meaning 'I don't wonder [that you should ask]!' (cf. *LT* 4.2.6). But this sense of 'else' is not recorded by *OED*.

69 leave . . . leaving presumably, 'do not speak to me of leaving.'

74 well-timbred sturdy.

75 *Mount Ferratto* Montferrat (Italian, *Monferrato*), an area of northwestern Italy now covering most of the province of Alessandria. Since the 1530s it had been ruled by the Gonzaga Dukes of Mantua. Cf. 2.3.35–7.

76 *Millanoys* Milanese.

77 and if it. Cf. 2.6.16.

78 skirmishing To skirmish meant 'to fence, to make flourishes with a weapon' (*OED* 2), but the sense here may be more derisive. A 'skirmish' was 'a petty fight or encounter', or indeed any action, proceeding or display of a slight character (*OED* 1, 3b; cf. *v.* 3); cf. *LT* 5.2.115: 'Skirmish of words'.

79 pryvie (1) secret; (2) in the private parts; hence the bawdy play on 'standing upright'.

79 marres . . . upright makes them impotent.

80 crinkles bends 'shrinkingly or obsequiously with the legs or body'; cringes (*OED* crinkle 2a, citing this instance).

81 serve 'suffice'; but perhaps with a play on the sexual sense: 'to mount, impregnate or satisfy the female' (*OED* n.[1] 52, Roper).

83 Fye . . . prat'st Annabella speaks in prose, as again at 97, 117.

84 **very** 'true, real', and perhaps 'truthful' (*OED a.* 6, Gibson).

89 **wholesome** free from (especially sexual) disease, healthy (*OED* 3, Gibson).

89 **gallant** man of fashion and pleasure; a 'ladies' man', lover (*OED n.* 1, 3, Roper).

90 **liberall** (1) openhearted, frank, humane, gentlemanlike; (2) generous with money (to Putana).

91 **purchast** purchased, i.e. acquired.

91–2 **a good name** 'a favourable reputation' (the usual sense) or 'favour'.

93 **And t'were** if it were.

93 **report** rumour, gossip (Crystal).

94 **'a** colloquial abbreviation of 'he'; cf. 3.9.17.

94 **qualities** accomplishments (*OED n.* 2b).

95 **plaine-sufficient** Roper detects several likely meanings: 'plain but adequate', 'simply (or clearly) sufficient', and 'sufficient for ordinary and obvious needs'. Ford often combined 'plain' with other words: cf *LM* 2.1.86: 'plain, and brief', 2.2.128: 'plain and short', *WoE* 2.2.83–4: 'I am young, | Silly, and plain', and 3.2.113: 'plain and easie'.

97 **mornings Draught** the customary drink of ale, wine, or spirits taken in early or mid-morning

97 **to** variant spelling of 'too'; cf. 3.7.34; *CBS* 69, 185, 1125.

100 **cyphers** literally, 'noughts'; 'nonentities' (*OED* 1a). Cf. *Winter's Tale* 1.2.6–7: 'like a cipher (Yet standing in rich place)'.

100 **fill up the number** add to the list of your suitors, just as 'cyphers' (noughts) augment a number when added to it.

101 **brave** finely dressed (*OED a.* 2).

101 **Ape in a silken Coate** Gibson notes the proverb: 'An ape's an ape, a varlet's a varlet, though they be clad in silk or scarlet' (Tilley A262–3). 'Ape' has the derogatory sense, 'a mere imitator'. Roper compares Tilley D452 and *LM* 2.2.113–14: 'fine apes | In silken coats'.

106 **Coxcomb** (1) simpleton; (2) foolish, conceited, showy person (*OED* 3). The head-dress of the professional fool was in the shape of a cock's crest or comb.

110 **to buy a headfull of wit** Bergetto unintentionally reminds the audience of the proverb: 'Bought wit is dear' (Tilley W545).

110 **wit** intelligence.

111 **sirrah** A common form of address to inferiors (male or female) or to children, 'sirrah' was also used to express reprimand or contempt.

113 **shift socks** change my stockings, slippers, or light shoes (*OED* sock *n.*[1] 1a, 2a).

113 **have at her** begin my amorous assault on her. The fighting phrase 'Have at you' (used at 19) means 'Watch out! My aim is you'.

113 **yfaith** in faith: 'in truth, indeed'.

114 **pace** The absurdly conceited Mauruccio is similarly preoccupied with his 'pace' (manner of walking, gait) in *LS* 2.1.22.

115 **Sir.** This sounds like Poggio's 'reply to Bergetto's command, i.e. "Yes, sir".' He does not openly deride Bergetto' (T. W. Craik, private correspondence).

115–16 **Spanish pavin** A stately 16th- and 17th-century dance in duple time. Though often described as Spanish, it probably originated in Italy and was named after the city of Padua. Popular in England during this period, it was a favourite musical dorm of Byrd, Gibbons, Dowland, and others (*NOCM*).

118 **I, I,** ay, ay (yes, yes).

118 ***Magnifico*** 'A great or noble person (originally as an honorary title applied to any of the magnates of Venice)' (*OED*). The mocking Iago refers to Brabanzio thus in *Othello* 1.2.12.

120 **Cozen** Used of relatives generally; kinsman.

120–1 **golden calfe** 'wealthy simpleton', a calf being a type of stupidity (Dent C16.1). There is also a jocular allusion to the golden calf before which the Israelites 'fell down' (see next line and Exodus 32). An ass laden with gold is another proverbial figure of wealth and folly (Tilley A 356, A 360).

121 **right** true, veritable.

122 **presently** immediately.

123 **a fooles . . . playfellow** According to the proverb, 'Fools and little dogs are ladies' playfellows' (Tilley F 528). Typically, Putana adds a bawdy reference to the bauble, a baton or stick with a carved head carried by the professional fool as an emblem of office. Cf. *R&J* 2.4.91–3 (Roper).

124–5 **cast . . . rate** i.e. reckon on the shortage of suitors or take a gamble (on Bergetto) because of this shortage (*OED* cast *v.* 38b, citing this instance; Morris). 'Flesh' (124) indicates not only suitors but penises (Wiggins). 'At any rate' may modify 'cast': 'make your reckoning at whatever the going rate is', i.e. whatever men are demanding for dowries these days. Or it may modify 'you' (124): 'You, at least . . .' (Roper).

125 **Innocent** simpleton, idiot (*OED n.* 3a). Cf. 'Innocence', 48.

125.1 ***Enter*** i.e. on the main stage.

126 **shape** 'figure' or 'ethereal form' (*OED* 4a, 6b, 6c). In the former sense, the word perhaps emphasizes his physical appeal; in the latter, it suggests a contrast with the rather mundane forms of Annabella's suitors. The theatrical sense—'a character impersonated', 'an assumed appearance' (*OED* 8a, 7)—may also be felt here, as Giovanni makes his entrance 'below' (131) and becomes the subject of the two watchers' commentary. Cf. 129 n.

132 **shaddow** The word denoted an emaciated or feeble person, but also 'a form from which the substance has departed', a spectre or phantom. It was also used of an actor (*OED n.* 6a, b, f, g, 7; cf. 11 above). In *LS* 1.2.273, Fernando describes those oppressed by love as 'bodies' walking 'unsouled'.

135 **pertake** 'learn, be informed of', but also 'partake, share': a potent choice of word. Cf. next note.

137 **partage** share, portion. The term was sometimes used of the division of inherited property (*OED* 1, 2a); cf. 'pertake', 132 above. Ford used 'partage' in *Funerall Elegy* 543–4: 'have partage now, | Of life with mee', *FMI* 3.2.61–2: 'to grant a partage | Of this estate to her who owns it all'.

138.1 *Exeunt* Earlier editors end the scene here, but the action is continuous. Annabella and Putana descend to the main stage as Giovanni begins his speech, his despairing words providing an immediate echo of Annabella's gloomy foreboding at 135.

139 **my fates** The plural form suggests an allusion to the three goddesses of classical mythology (in Greek *moirai*, in Latin *parcae* or *fata*) who controlled human destiny (cf. 3.2.22 and 3.6.82). However, 'my' suggests that he is thinking of his personal fate—even, perhaps, of his own *parcae*. Vickers notes that 'Ford uses the word "fate" over 120 times in his plays' (*CWJF* 2, p. 151).

144 **throughly** thoroughly.

145–6 **O that ... worship it** 'To make our love a God' was 'precisely Adam's sin in Paradise ... Adam sinned deliberately, preferring the love of Eve to the love of God, as St Paul recognizes (1 Timothy 2.14)' (Morris). Cf. *CBS*: 'Love is no god, as some of wicked times | (Led with the dreaming dotage of their folly) | Have set him foorth in their lascivious rimes, | Bewitch'd with errors, and conceits unholy: | It is a raging blood, affections blind, | Which boiles both in the body and the mind' (1081–6; cited by Roper).

147–8 **wearied ... spring of teares** The Friar had advised him to 'weepe, sigh, pray | Three times a day, and three times every night: | For seven dayes space' (1.1.80–2). According to Vickers (*FE* 74n, *CWJF* 1, p. 282), 'spring + of + noun' is a pattern used by Ford six times; the other occurences are *Funerall Elegy* 74: 'his spring of days in sacrid schooles', *LM* 4.3.79: 'the spring of chearefull comfort', *PW* 1.2.105: 'the full spring of youth', 4.5.21: 'the spring of fruitless hopes', *BH* 4.4.71: 'fair spring of manhood', and *LT* 2.4.2: 'the spring of nature'.

149 **Art** medical lore (cf. 2.3.41).

152 **unsteedy youth** unsettled, wavering, fickle.

153 **Or ... or** Either ... or.

153–4 **'tis not I know, | My lust; but 'tis my fate that leads me on** Other Ford characters disclaiming personal responsibility: cf. *WoE* 1.2.182–3: 'But on I must: | Fate leads me'; *PW* 5.1.1: 'It is decreed; and wee must yield to fate';

and *LS* 4.2.125: 'No toyle can shun the violence of Fate'. Cf. also *CWJF* 2, p. 151.

155 **Keepe . . . slaves** Let fear and mean, faint-hearted shame dwell (or keep company) with ignoble wretches (Roper, *OED* keep *v*. 45).

156–7 **though . . . attempt** 'though my attempt should cost my heart' (Massai).

160 **vertue** (1) meritorious quality, moral goodness; (2) strength, power.

162 **how d'ee** A colloquial form of 'how do you', common in Devon.

166 **pryvate** 'confidential', but the sense 'sexually intimate' was already well-established (*OED* private 7a, b).

170 **an office . . . credit** Literally, 'a post of honour', but Putana is thinking of the reward (*credit*) she might receive if she were leaving Annabella alone with other male company. Cf. 4.3.102 below, and *2 Henry IV* 5.1.46 (Morris, Roper).

178 **ist** abbreviation of 'is it'.

179 **franticke** 'affected by wild and ungovernable excitement', or literally mad (*OED* frantic 2a, 1).

183 **Mercy** i.e. 'God's mercy' or 'God in his mercy' (see *OED* mercy *n. and int.* 3c, d).

187 **merry sicknesse** She dismisses his praise of her beauty as jocularity, teasing him by implying that he has a mental disorder.

188 **proves** turns out (i.e. whether his 'sicknesse' will be 'merry').

188 **faigne** 'invent the legend', or simply 'imagine'.

189 *Juno* Juno, Jupiter's sister, who became his mistress and later his wife. Identified with the Greek Hera, she was the Roman queen of heaven, protector of women and goddess of marriage. She was known for her stately bearing (March, Brewer).

192 **Troth** truly, in truth.

192 **pretty** ingenious, clever.

193 *Promethean* **fire** Prometheus, one of the Titans of Greek myth, stole fire from Heaven and used it to animate the human beings he had fashioned from clay. 'Promethean fire' is therefore the vital principle (Brewer). Cf. *LLL* 4.3.298–300: 'From women's eyes this doctrine I derive: | They are the ground, the books, the academes, | From whence doth spring the true Promethean fire', quoted by Wiggins, noting that 'The whole passage plays on the two principle meanings of "glance" [*glaun'st*], to look swiftly and to strike obliquely (here against a stone, producing sparks)'.

194 **gently glaun'st** quickly or lightly glanced at (*OED* gently *adv*. 2, glance *v*.¹ 7).

196–7 **The Lilly . . . change** Ford often used the juxtaposition of these two flowers to describe the conventional red and white of the complexion; cf. *SD* 2.1.28: 'on his smooth cheek such sweet roses set', *LS* 1.1.129: 'Lilies and roses growing in thy cheeks.'

196 **strange** 'contrasting, opposed' or 'wonderful'.

196–7 Giovanni's wooing shifts to rhyme, as again at 231–2.

197 **change** mutual interchange (Roper, comparing *Much Ado* 4.1.185, 'the change of words').

199 ***Anchoret*** variant form of 'anchorite': hermit (*OED* 1).

204 **trime** 'trim', here used ironically: 'handsome, fine' (*OED a.* 3).

205 **here . . . strike home** Ford stages a similar action in *LS* 5.1.158–65. Cf. also Richard Gloucester's wooing of Lady Anne, *Richard III* 1.2.174–83.

206–7 **Rip . . . speake** Giovanni refers to 'Love's Cruelty', a conventional trope of love, according to which true feeling is written on the heart (Neill, 'Strange Riddle', pp. 156–61). Cf. 3.6.2, 4.3.66–7, 5.3.36 below; *The Laws of Candy* 2.1.263, *LS* 2.3.98–101, 2.4.92–5, *SG* 3.3.48–9, and *BH* 3.2.188–9.

206 **there** referring back to 'bosome'; Ford uses this grammatical structure elsewhere; cf. *GM* 468: 'that there he is free', and Monsarrat's note.

207 **writ** written.

208 **stand** hesitate (*OED* 16b).

210 **affliction . . . Death** suffering of mortal intensity (Roper, *OED* heat *n.* 11). 'Heat' also suggests the flames of lust or desire, with an anticipation of the fate awaiting those who succumb to such passions. Cf. the Friar's reference to Giovanni's 'wilfull flames' (1.1.69) and 235 below.

214 **rest** peace (Gibson).

215 **just** well-founded, true. The word may also mean 'honest, honourable'.

218 **hidden flames** Cf. Petrarch, *Rime* 207.66, '*Chiusa fiamma*', 'A hidden flame'. The amorous Fiormonda speaks of her 'hidden flames' in *LS* 4.2.251.

221 **despis'd** attempted to disregard or defy; scorned (*OED* despise *v.* 3b; Roper).

222 **reasons** causes.

223 **smooth'd-cheeke** 'smooth-faced or clean shaven', with a suggestion of inexperience or suave persuasiveness (cf. the 'smooth-fac'd wooers' of *Loves's Labor's Lost* 5.2.828). See *OED* smooth-faced 1–2; cf. *LM* 3.2.34–7: 'a gentleman . . . should be so betrayed | By a young smooth-chinned straggler', *SD* 3.4.56: 'To dote on a smooth face'.

224 **bootelesse** unavailing, useless (*OED a.* 1, 3).

224 **destiny** A key word in Giovanni's wooing: see 143 n. above.

226 **in sadnesse** in earnest.

226 **mischiefe** calamity.

227 **ought** aught: anything.

230 **afford you instance** show you reason.

232–4 **Wise Nature . . . soule** Giovanni resorts to the fashionable notion that 'love results from a congenital affinity of souls which should ideally reveal itself in physical likeness' (Roper). For a similar phrase, see *SG* 1.4.16–17: 'Wise nature meant'.

235–6 **Neerenesse** close blood relatives such as brother and sister should be encouraged to have a '**neerer neerenesse**' in love, that is, a sexual relationship. The rhetorical figure *polyptoton*, which repeats the root of a word while changing its termination, draws attention to this strange argument.

235 **perswade** encourage, recommend (a transitive use; *OED v.* 6b).

240–55 **Must I now live or die? . . . Love me or kill me** Cf. the similar option in *The Laws of Candy* 4.1.101–4: 'Love me, kill me: . . . Say, must I live, or dye?' (*CWJF* 2, pp. 92, 106, 127).

242 **resolv'd** determined, settled (*OED v.* 13d). But as Roper notes, 'the verb is a rich one, with implications not only of firmly deciding and choosing . . . but also of passing from discord into harmony, relaxing, dissolving, and even disintegrating (*OED* 4–5, 21–2)'.

246 **for that** because.

256 **good sooth** 'earnestly' ('sooth' means 'truth', *OED n.* 1a).

256 **troth** truth, faith.

260 **change** exchange.

260 *Elyzium* Elysium: in Greek mythology, the happy domain reserved for those to whom the gods had granted immortality. Here (as often) synonymous with 'heaven', 'paradise'.

261 **doe** The word often had sexual overtones; cf. 4.3.21 n. and 5.5.41. 'What must we next do, sweetheart?' asks the lascivious Ferentes in *LS* 1.2.54–5.

1.3

6 **doubt** fear for.

7 **miscarry** fail (as often in Shakespeare); come to harm (Gibson); die leaving no heir (Wiggins).

8 **Girle** disyllabic, as often in Ford, reproducing the usage in the Devon of his youth; cf. 2.1.89 and *BH* 2.1.69 (Gibson).

11 **I . . . Love** This would be an unusual aspiration for one of his class at this time. The sentiment is rendered darkly ironic by the events of the previous scene.

16 **presently** immediately.

17 **Three thousand** *Florrens* *Florin* was an English name for various continental coins. A substantial sum, since these coins are probably gold (see *OED* florin 3a); 'roughly equivalent to £250; a substantial but not lavish annual income' (Wiggins).

19–20 **meane time . . . suite** 'Florio's decision is mercenary, bearing in mind that he has already pledged his word to Soranzo (1.2.53); alternatively, Florio may be indulging Donado, knowing full well that Annabella will reject Bergetto' (Massai).

23 **wit** sense.

24 **such another** a perfect; cf. Cassio's evaluation of Bianca as 'such another fitchew' at *Othello* 4.1.146 (Massai).

26 **I could have done't** 'I used to be able to do it', as at 2.1.90 (Roper).

26 **yfaith** in faith: 'in truth, indeed'.

27 **in good time** at the right moment.

29 **whether** whither.

30–1 **newes . . . Mynt** Proverbial: 'New out of the Mint' (Tilley M985, *OED* news *n.* 1). Morris compares *Twelfth Night* 3.2.22: 'some excellent jests, fire-new from the mint'.

34 **my Barber** Barber-shops were 'places of great resort, for passing away time in an idle manner' (Robert Nares, ed., *A Glossary; or, Collection of Words, Phrases, Names, and Allusions to Customs, Proverbs, &C. which have been thought to require Illustration, in the Works of English Authors, particularly Shakespeare, and his Contemporaries* (1822)). The relaying of news and gossip was 'a recognized part of the barber's trade' (Roper).

36–7 **to make . . . Sand-bags** evidently a perpetual motion device in which the downward force of the falling sandbags was supposed to keep the wheel in motion. According to the first law of thermodynamics, such a device is impossible because the total energy of a system is always constant. Nevertheless, perpetual motion machines have fascinated inventors for hundreds of years. The physician Robert Fludd claimed to have invented one. Edward Somerset, second Marquis of Worcester, built a gigantic wheel with ascending and descending weights which he exhibited to Charles I in about 1638–9 (see his *Century of Inventions*, 1663, No. 56; *DNB, ODNB, EB*).

37–40 **a strange Horse . . . tayle is** For many years 'The Wonderful Horse, With His Head Where His Tail Ought To Be' was a popular side-show at fairs, where horses had their heads concealed and their tails tied to a manger (Roper).

42 **forsooth** truly.

44 **I** ay: yes.

45 **stil** always.

46 **have more mind of** think more about; have more liking for (*OED* mind *n*.[1] 7, 13 d–e; Roper)

46 **Puppet-play** 'another popular entertainment at fairs; a close counterpart to Bergetto and his penchant for puppet plays is Bartholomew Cokes, *such another dunce* (24), who loses Grace Wellborn to Winwife in Ben Jonson's *Bartholomew Fair*' (Massai).

47 **wu't** colloquial abbreviation for 'wilt'.

48 **May-game** laughing-stock, comic butt (*OED* 3). In his *Survey of London* (1603), John Stow describes how 'the citizens of London of all estates . . . had their severall Mayings, and did fetch in May-poles, with diverse warlike shewes, with good archers, morice-dauncers, and other devices, for pastime all the day long, and towards the evening they had stage-playes and bonefires in the streetes' (quoted by John Brand, *Observations on Popular Antiquities, Chiefly Illustrating the Origin of Our Vulgar Customs, Ceremonies and Superstitions* (London, 1900), 119, who also remarks the custom of 'making fools' on May Day). Morris notes *LM* 1.2.10–1: 'Why should not I, a May-game, scorn the weight | Of my sunk fortunes?'

50 **shu'd** colloquial abbreviation for 'should'.

51 **abroad** here and there.

51 **fashions** the latest styles, what's 'going on' (Roper, Crystal).

52 **hobby-horses** performers dressed as horse-riders—or the framed models of the horses themselves—in morris dances and other entertainments. The type commonly referred to in drama of this period is the Tourney Horse, in which the 'rider' wears a basketware frame suspended by straps, with the likeness of the horse's head and tail (Simpson & Roud). Another childish amusement, like 'Puppet-plays' (46).

54 **uds sa'me** colloquial abbreviation for 'God save me'.

54 **tickled** 'amused' (*OED* tickle *v*. 5), but perhaps with a boastful innuendo: 'sexually aroused or gratified'. Cf. *HT* 708: 'tickling blood' and note. See also *SD* 1.1.81: 'their brides tickle for't', and 3.1.83: 'their wives have tickling humors'.

55 **I . . . belly with laughing** 'belly' the more overt word-play on 'tickled' (54), and at 2.6.63–4 below.

59 **aswell** variant spelling of 'as well' (see *OED* C2).

59 **Parmasent** parmesan cheese (*OED* B 1, citing this instance). A reminder, perhaps, that the play is set in Parma.

60 **wanted** lacked.

72 **wit** 'thought' (Roper)—or perhaps 'sense'

72 **heare on't** hear of it: be told about it, be called to account for it (*OED* hear *v*. 11b).

73 **everlasting glory** perhaps a malapropism for 'shame' (Gibson, Wiggins), or a confused memory of a biblical phrase.

74 **white boy** fair-haired boy; hence, favourite (Roper). For 'white' meaning 'highly prized', 'favourite', see *OED* white, *a.* 9.

74 **guld** gulled: tricked.

75 **fit** (1) 'answer fitly', 'suit the requirements of'; (2) 'deal with', perhaps with a further sexual implication (*OED v.* 4, 7, 8a).

77 **very** perfect, complete (cf. 1.2.86n).

82 **I** ay: yes.

83 **Innocent** simpleton, idiot (as at 1.2.125).

2.1

0.1 *as from their Chamber* i.e. with some indication in their garb or manner to show that they have come from the bed-chamber. See Alan C. Dessen, *Elizabethan Stage Conventions and Modern Interpreters* (Cambridge, 1984), 31. Some commentators suggest they enter to the upper stage area, but that is usually indicated 'above' as in 1.2.29.1, 3.2.17.1, 64.1, and 5.1.0.1.

4 **yeelding** i.e. losing Annabella's virginity.

6 **contents** pleasures, contentment (*OED n.2* 1).

7 **print** imprint; cf. 5.6.46.

10 **toye** trifle (*OED n.* 5).

12 **well for you** 'all right for you' (Roper)

13 **talke** with a teasing implication that he is now able to prate or boast of his conquest.

13–14 **Musicke . . . playing** music 'is composed of the act of hearing as much as it is of the act of performance; but "music" is also a metaphor of love-making' (Gibson).

15 **Tell . . . best** teasingly ironic: 'it would be best for you to tell others about it.'

16 **thus hung** *Jove* **on** *Leda's* **necke** in the Greek myth, Zeus (Jove) in the form of a swan took refuge in Leda's bosom and then seduced her. Morris and others note the aptness (presumably inadvertent on Giovanni's part) of this allusion to an unnatural union between woman and bird.

17 *Ambrosia* the sweet and scented food of the gods, so called because it made those who ate it immortal (from Greek *a-*, 'not', and *brotos*, 'mortal'); cf. *FM* 30: 'Ambrosiack quills', and *The Laws of Candy* 2.1.13–14: '*Ambrosia . . .* Poets' fare'.

22 **Yes, to whome?** in Morris's view, this is playful repartee and it is not until line 32 that Annabella realizes Giovanni's 'serious intent'.

23 **have** 'possess in marriage', and probably 'possess sexually'.

24 **without jesting** seriously. To take this as modifying the following clause 'obscures the sequence of responses and creates tautology, "without jesting . . . in earnest"' (Roper, who punctuates: 'jesting;').

25 **What . . . not** 'What' here is the common exclamation. For Roper, Giovanni's tone is 'half-disbelieving, half-soothing'.

26 **can'st . . . dar'd** will you accept the challenge?

27 **live to mee** devote yourself to me. Roper suggests that this is a demand for 'total loyalty, not just physical "faithfulness"'. He compares 3.6.40: 'live to him'.

32 **keepe . . . heart** cf. 'Love's Cruelty' in the note to 1.2.202–3. Massai compares *Duchess of Malfi* where she woos Antonio: 'Go—go brag | You have left me heartless: mine is in your bosom' (1.2.358–9).

34 **Looke you doe** take care you do.

39 **over** through.

40 **past under** with a bawdy reference, characteristic of Putana. Massai compares *R&J* 1.3.41–3.

41 **commend** praise. The sense, 'to recommend a person to do a thing' (in this instance, to 'feare nothing') is possible, but is not recorded before 1647 (*OED v.* 2d, 3a).

41 **Chardge** ward. Like '*Guardian*' (49, 51), a reminder of Putana's proper duty.

43 **still** 'always' or 'even now'.

44 **fitt** 'impulse, mood'—here sexual, as in 3.1.15 and 5.5.4.

44–5 **let . . . one** cf. *Broken Heart* 2.2.117: 'Brothers and sisters are but flesh and blood'.

47 **for the speech** because of denunciation or gossip.

50 **reach my worke** pass me my needlework.

51.1 *like* disguised as; *Phisicke* physic, i.e. medicine.

54 *Padua* the medical school at the University of Padua was famous.

55 **for that** because.

57 **reverend** cf. 'reverent', a variant spelling of 'reverend' (*see OED* reverent 1): cf. also 2.6.3.

59 **large** full and free (Roper).

60 **perfection** beauty, ripe maturity, surpassing accomplishment, excellence (*OED* 1, 3, 8).

63 **one . . . will** i.e. one who . . . will. The relative pronoun was often omitted (Abbott 244).

64 **parts** accomplishments, gifts (*OED* part *n*.15).

66 **make not strange** 'don't be reserved or unnecessarily formal'; but since 'strange'could also mean 'foreign, unknown, mysterious', the comment may remind the audience of Richardetto's disguise.

67 **Art** (medical) skill.

68 **what I am** ironic, in view of his disguise.

69 **bind . . . you** i.e. by ties of gratitude (Roper).

71 **concernes** the plural form in -s was very common. The subject, 'matters', is 'singular in *thought*' (Abbott 332, 333).

73 **cunning** (musical) skill.

74 **Girle** disyllabic (cf. 1.3.8 above).

75 **touch an Instrument** touch commonly means 'play (a musical instrument)' (*OED* 9), but since 'Instrument' could refer to an organ of the body such as a sexual organ (see *OED n.* 4), Ford's audience may have heard bawdy overtones.

75 **could have don 't** was able to do it (Roper).

76 **waite upon** this courteous phrase has various shades of meaning: attend, accompany, follow, serve.

2.2

1–2 *Loves . . . disdaine* Lines 4–5 and 8 suggest that this may be a quotation from the Italian poet Jacopo Sannazaro, but the text has not been identified.

1 *measure* 'extent, scope, degree, composition or proportion'—perhaps with a suggestion that love is without measure, i.e. immoderate (*vide extreame*). 'Measure' also referred to the treatment meted out to a person (*OED* 2a, 3a, 4a, 4c).

4 **licentious** 'a reference to Sannazaro's reputation as a love poet' (Roper).

5 **Sannazar** the Neapolitan poet Jacopo Sannazaro (1456–1530), author of the popular and influential *Arcadia* (1504), the first pastoral romance. His *Rime* (1540) included lyric poems in the Petrarchan vein.

7 **kist the rod** proverbial (Dent R156).

7 **made the** 'thee' was often spelt 'the' (see *OED*); cf. 5.6.99.

8 **happy Muse** i.e. the presiding spirit behind his creative acts (*OED* muse 2c), called 'happy' as an encouragement to his invention.

9 **envy** 'especially malice shown by calumny and depreciation' (Schmidt).

10 *Loves . . . meane* Love's standard is moderation (or 'the true one'); perhaps glancing at the Golden Mean (*aurea mediocritas*) of Horace's *Odes* II, x (Brewer, Roper). Cf. *CWJF* 1, p. 430.

10 *annoyes* troubles, annoyances, suffering (*OED* annoy *n.*1, 2).

11 *His pleasures life* the lover devotes his life to pleasures.

13 *Encomium* a speech or piece of writing expressing praise; in this case, 'a short Latin poem in praise of Venice, for which the city lavishly rewarded' Sannazaro (Massai).

14 **had** would have.

14 **left** abandoned (Wiggins).

15 **such . . . Gold** see note to 13 above.

16 **one onely looke** but one look.

17 **diviner** most divine, pre-eminently beautiful. A very Fordian superlative; cf. *LS* 2.1.126 and 'chaster', 34 below.

20 **tax't of** blamed or reprimanded for.

26 **perjurd** perjured, having sworn falsely.

27 **distracted** bewildered, agitated, deranged; literally driven hither and thither by conflicting purposes or desires (*OED ppl. a.* 2–5).

28 **sensuall rage of blood** violence of sexual desire (a different type of Fordean superlative, redoubling condemnation). 'Blood', one of the four bodily fluids, was the supposed seat of emotion and sensual appetite (cf. 1.1.32), whence the word also denoted passion and 'the fleshly nature of man' (*OED n.* 5, 6).

29 **scorne** object of contempt.

30 **Be . . . change** 'serve as a dull background to give the zest of contrast to your lust' (Sherman). 'Change' means 'act or fact of changing (his affections)' or 'changefulness, inconstancy' (*OED* 1a, 4a, b).

31 **modest fame** virtuous reputation; for 'fame' = reputation; cf. *LT* 168, and *SG* 5.1.115.

34 **chaster** most chaste.

36 **a heart of steele** proverbial (Dent, H310.1).

39 **urg'd on** partly induced (Wiggins).

40 **woeman-hood** (virtuous) character or reputation considered natural to or appropriate for a woman (*OED* womanhood 2).

42 **distast** dislike, regard with aversion (*OED* distaste *v.* 2).

48 *Madame Merchant* apparently a reference to Annabella's father's trade. Florio refers to his 'worldly fortune' in 1.3.8. Similar derisive phrases occur in *Measure for Measure* 1.2.43, 'Madam Mitigation', and *LS* 2.2.221, 'mistress madam Duchess'.

48–9 **triumph . . . dejection** exult in my abasement, my being cast down (*OED* 1, 2).

48 **triumph** accented on second syllable.

50 **Free** noble, honourable; cf. 'freedome of Birth', i.e. gentle or noble birth, 'Epistle', 9.

51 **violent** fierce, passionate (Schmidt).

51 **double** false, deceitful; leading a double life, the one open or virtuous, the other secret or blameworthy (*OED a. (adv.)* 5).

53 **habit** garb.

53 **weedes** garments.

54 **divorc't** separated.

56 **Widdow . . . widow-hood** a widow twice over, because her 'disgrace' (40) had alienated Richardetto before his apparent death.

57 **thy** the press correction to 'thy' from 'the' (see collation notes) seems right. A similar error may have occurred at 2.5.2.

60 **rules** principles, laws, standards. Roper compares *LT* 5.2.95: 'the rules of friendship as of love'. Cf. also *WoE* 1.1.80: 'All rules of honest duty.'

60 **sence** variant spelling of 'sense' (see *OED* sense *n.*, 5.5.6 and 5.6.17 below).

60 **grace** (1) the favour of God; (b) 'the divine influence which operates within men to regenerate and sanctify and to impart strength to endure trial and resist temptation' (*OED* II, 6a, b).

61 **not . . . reason** beyond the boundaries of reasonable speech and behaviour (Roper). Morris detects careful ambiguity in 'not neere'.

62 **resolution** firmness, unyielding temper (*OED* 15).

63 **unedge** blunt, weaken (Bawcutt).

63 **perplexe** trouble, torment (*OED* 1b).

64 **vent** utterance. The sentiment is all but proverbial; cf. Tilley G447, G449.

65 **freely** readily or without hindrance (*OED adv.* 1a, 3).

66 **frantick** mad, raging, delirious—or one who behaves thus (*OED* frantic *a. & n.*).

66 **the . . . love** the result of your devotion or service. Soranzo seems to be addressing Vasques, 'these' referring to his servant's words of advice.

72 **The Devill in my blood** a similar phrasing occurs in *The Witch of Edmonton* 1.1.78–9: 'the nimble devil | That wanton'd in your blood'.

72 **protests** protestations or declarations (of love) (*OED* 1).

74 **voyage to *Ligorne*** journey to Leghorn (Italian *Livorno*), a coastal city about 80 miles south of the inland town of Parma. 'Voyage' does not necessarily betray geographical confusion, as the word was often used of overland journeys (*OED* 1). Roper notes that the journey would be through dangerous mountain districts; cf. Vasques' allusion to mountain banditry in 5.4.3–4.

76 **unfriended** without a friend or guardian.

79 **deare** (1) incurring a high cost; (2) deeply sad, piteous.

84–6 **The vowes . . . breake them** 'St. Augustine, in *De homo coniugali . . .* argues that breaking a contract made in sin to return to virtue was no sin at all. But this was not everyone's view. See Alan T. Gaylord, "The Promises in the Franklin's Tale", *ELH*, 31 (1964), 331–65' (Morris).

88 **digrest . . . shame** deviated from a respectable sense of shame.

91 **quality, condition** rank, temper.

92 **entertainment** hospitality.

93 **braver** finer.

97 **Coarse** corpse.

100 **scurvily playd** badly acted. The comment, drawing attention to Soranzo's histrionics as well as to the theatrical illusion, seems an appropriate remark to accompany the nobleman's exit, correctly inserted here by Dodsley.

101 **contemnes his Fate** defies or contemptuously disregards his approaching doom; cf. 1.2.235.

102 **that** i.e. her love (responding to Soranzo's reference to her 'lust', 99).

104 **his woe** the woe he has caused.

104.1 SD *offers* prepares, attempts.

110 **mov'd** agitated, angered.

114 **followed** adhered to.

115 **Faith** in faith, indeed.

115 **shrewd** severe, harsh (*OED* 7).

116 **tooke** come upon (often by surprise or when at a disadvantage) (*OED* take *v.* 8b).

118 **waite his leasure** attend upon his pleasure or inclination. Ironic: a phrase of courtesy such as a servant or social inferior might use.

119 **hearty** 'heartfelt' or 'kind-hearted'.

120 **for once** Like 'troth', used for mere emphasis or to express exasperation, annoyance, etc.

124 **spleene** unreasoning passion, ill humour, bitterness, malice; cf. 1.2.22, 56 and *LS* 1.1.89, 'a bold woman's spleen'.

127 **fal out** turn out, prove.

129 **Resolve thy selfe** be assured, convince yourself (*OED3* †22b); cf. 5.5.28: 'resolve your selfe', and *GM* 957: 'resolve himselfe'.

131 **his** i.e. his counsels.

131 **slight acquittance** meagre recompense.

132 **of my selfe** i.e. as her husband.

133 'Vasques's ironic remark suggests that Hippolita has effectively abdicated her aristocratic rank by committing adultery with Soranzo and by promising to bestow herself and her patrimony on a mere servant . . . Similarly in *Lover's Melancholy*, Amethus, suspecting that his sister Thamasta lusts after a low-born page, accuses her of renouncing her aristocratic status: "You have sold your birth | For lust" (4.1.34–5)' (Massai).

135 **daily** (modifies 'see'st').

137 **Beggery and neglect** in *LM*, Thamasta unfairly dismisses 'her maid Kara: "Now poverty and a dishonest fame, | The waiting-woman's wages, be thy payment" (2.1.311–2)' (Massai).

139 **private** intimate, confidential (perhaps with a suggestion of sexual intimacy; *OED* 7b).

139 **protest** declare, promise.

140 **what** that.

140 **dispose** disposal.

141 **Worke** 'practice, operate, labour', probably with implication of deceit, plotting, or insidious persuasion.

141 **old moule** while the phrase perhaps reveals his true opinion of her charms, a 'mole' is also a person who works in secret (*OED n.*³ 3a). Cf. *Hamlet* 1.5.162–3: 'Well said, old mole, canst work i' th' earth so fast? | A worthy pioneer!' and *LM* 2.2.88–91: 'Ye work and work like moles, blind in the paths | That are bored through the crannies of the earth, | To charge your hungry souls with such full surfeits | As being gorged once, make 'ee lean with plenty'.

141–2 **have the wind of you** in nautical terms, to 'have the wind' of another ship was to get to windward of it and so intercept the wind, an advantage in any contest (see *OED* wind *n*. 3b). But Vasques' reference to Hippolita as a 'moule' suggests that he may be imagining himself as a hunter who has gained the advantage over his prey. If so, he is either (a) downwind of his prey and therefore able to observe her without giving away his own presence (*OED* wind *n*. 4), or (b) windward of his prey, allowing her to pick up his scent and drive her into a trap. Cf. *Hamlet* 3.2.334–5, 'recover the wind of me', interpreted by some commentators in the latter sense. Also cf. *Titus* 4.2.132. Roper glosses as 'pick up your scent, guess your intention'.

147 **Give me thy hand** the deliberate echoes of the wedding ceremony emphasize the solemnity of their undertaking. Indeed, a spousal or 'handfasting' ceremony, with exchange of vows before witnesses and followed by cohabitation, was recognized by English common law (Moore, note to a similar episode in *LS* 4.1.167–75, Revels edn.). Cf. 157 n., 158 n., below.

149 **here . . . Heaven** cf. the opening of the marriage ceremony: 'we are gathered together here in the sight of God'.

150 **Lord . . . estate** cf. the marriage ceremony: 'with all my worldly goods I thee endow'.

151 **merry** only joking (Wiggins).

152 **thinke** conceive, imagine, hope for.

154 **good Genii** plural of *genius*: 'In Roman mythology the tutelary spirit that attended a man from cradle to grave, governed his fortunes and determined his character . . . Another belief was that a man had two genii, one good and one evil' (Brewer). Cf. 'Good Angel of my soule' (*LS* 1.1.126).

156 **speciall** leading (Gibson).

160 **bane** poison.

161 **tasted** 'felt, experienced' or 'given a (salt) taste to' (*OED* 3, 11; Gibson).

2.3

4 **act** enact as upon a stage, display, carry out in action, demonstrate (*OED* act *v.* 1–5).

5 **borrowed shape** disguise (as a physician). 'Shape' was a theatrical term for an actor's costume (cf. *LS* 3.4.17.4).

7 **riots** revels, dissoluteness.

8 **secure** complacent; with a false sense of security (Wiggins).

12 **loose** immoral, lecherous.

13 **how the Common voyce allowes** what public opinion thinks or says.

15 **strange** unusual, singular.

16 **Your . . . all** 'Your ignorance of my plans will exonerate you', or perhaps: 'The less you know the better' (Gibson, Morris).

24 **us'd** treated.

32 *Nuntio* Nuncio: 'a permanent official representative of the Roman See at a foreign court' (*OED* 1). Wiggins notes that they had both political and ecclesiastical powers.

33 **by which meanes** i.e. by means of his influential position (Sturgess).

35 **Save you** from 'May God save you'.

36 **through** disyllabic: 'thorough'.

41 **Arts** (medical) studies and skills.

41 **receipts** formulas, prescriptions (in this case for love-potions). Both 'recipe' and 'receipt' derive from Latin *recipere*: 'receive, take (the physician's instruction)'.

42 **move affection** arouse love.

50 *Soranzo* . . . **heart** but cf. 20–2 above.

51 **speed** succeed.

54 **Confusion** ruin, destruction. The word occurs eight times in the play.

61 **Hidra** In classical myth, the Hydra of Lerna, a monstrous serpent proverbial for its many-headedness and invulnerability: whenever one head was destroyed two more would grow in its place.

2.4

1 **Secretary** He wrote the letter mentioned in 1.3.81–2.

3 **worke** produce, bring about.

7 **a fooles head** a foolish head (*OED* fool *n.*¹ & *a.* 7b), perhaps with reference to the court jester's cap, hood, or bauble (a baton often bearing the likeness of a head). Cf. Tilley F519 and *Merry Wives* 1.4.126–7: 'fool's-head of your own'.

8 **wouldst . . . selfe** the *Facetie* (humorous sayings or writings) of M. L. Domenichi (Venice, 1581) include the tale of Marco of Lodi, who 'wrote a letter to a friend at Ferrara, and, as there was no one to carry it for him, he had a fancy to take it himself. He arrived at Ferrara, and, having handed the letter to his friend, without a single word, he immediately departed and returned to Treviso' (*The Facetiae of Poggio and other Medieval Story-tellers*, transl. Edward Storer; noted by Roper).

9 **wut** a variant spelling of would (see *OED* will 8 *past tense*).

13 **indited** written, composed.

16 **hand** handwriting.

20 *fast* deeply, utterly.

21–2 *the . . . beard* a periphrastic reference to his uncle's mature age.

22 *board* 'accost, woo', but perhaps also 'jest, mock' (*OED* bourd, *v* ¹ 1).

23 *occasion* opportunity.

23 *wit* intellect, mental power.

25 *in spight of your teeth* notwithstanding your opposition, in open defiance of you. Cf. the contemporary 'in your face'.

26 *parts* accomplishments, gifts (as at 2.1.77); cf. 2.1.62.

26 **upwards and downewards** perhaps 'from my head to my toes', i.e. entirely; but, like 'parts', 'downewards' may be bawdy.

28 **stuffe** Bergetto claims it as 'good stuff', literary or artistic matter. Donado dismisses it as 'worthless writing, nonsense, rubbish' (*OED* stuff III 7, 8).

33 **wit** intellect, inventive faculty.

36 **yfaith** 'in faith', indeed (often rendered as 'i' faith').

40 **apish** silly, foolish.

41 **motions** puppet-shows. 'In Shakespeare's day a constant succession of these shows could be seen in Fleet Street. Ben Jonson introduces one into *Bartholomew Fair* [5.3–4], with Cokes showing the same unsophisticated pleasure as Bergetto' (Roper). Cf. 1.3.45.

41 **fopperies** follies.

41–2 **you were as good no** an example of meiosis (understatement, often ironic, as here). It would be 'much' better for Bergetto if Donado doesn't hear such reports. Roper cites examples of 'as good no' and 'wert better no' in *Wealth and Health*, ed. Greg, 1907, 658, and *Two Angry Women of Abington*, 1599, 2.1.

43 **shall's** shall us: shall we.

43–4 **Horse . . . tayle** cf. 1.3.39–43.

45 **I** aye.

45 **take . . . whipping** beware of being beaten.

2.5

2 **the** Roper accepts Reed's plausible emendation, 'thy'. The same error occurred at 2.2.57 but was corrected at the press.

4 **one minute deafe, before** struck deaf the moment before.

5–6 **cast-away . . . order** there are two main interpretations: (1) 'cast-away', meaning 'lost, damned' (Roper), refers to Giovanni and is followed by an oath in which the Friar alludes to the pious or holy company (*relligious number*) of his fraternity. (2) The Friar is saying that he himself has been 'cast-away' (rejected) by the more orthodox (*relligious*) members of his society, presumably because of his association with Giovanni. In the latter case, the comma after 'cast-away' should be placed after 'young man' (Gibson, Morris, who points out that the Friar 'chose | Rather to leaue my Bookes' than part with the errant Giovanni, 1.1.56–7).

6 **number** members.

9 **Heaven is angry** cf. *CBS* 1392: 'I see my angry God doth frowne', and *Dr. Faustus* (Revels eds.) XIX 150–1: 'And see where God | Stretcheth out his arme, and bends his irefull browes'.

9 **resolv'd** assured.

10 **remark't . . . mischiefe** marked out for punishment, following on from the Friar's opening judgement: 'thou hast told a tale, whose every word | Threatens eternall slaughter to the soule,' a verdict that he repeats: 'th'art too farre sold to hell' (37). Subsequently the Friar reassures him that 'The Throne of *Mercy* is above your trespasse', and 'time is left you both'—to repent, he would have said—but Giovanni flippantly completes the sentence: 'To

embrace each other' (64–5). There is no need to debate whether Ford was a Calvinist or a Catholic sympathizer.

10 **remark't** marked out, distinguished (*OED* remark $v.^1$ 1a, quoting this instance).

10 **mischiefe** misfortune, calamity (*OED n.* 1b, citing this instance).

15–17 **the Frame . . .** *Body* the theory that the 'temperature'– the mixture of the four elements (hot, cold, wet, dry) that constitute the body—affects that of the mind goes back to Aristotle. It was a fundamental principle in Galenic medicine, becoming diffused throughout the Renaissance. Cf. *Line of Life* 142–3: '*the temperature of the minde followed the temperature of the body*' and *HT* 410, with Monsarrat's note, *CWJF* I, pp. 149–50.

16 **Composition** 'pronounced first with four syllables, then with five' (Roper).

18 **furniture** that with which the body is furnished or adorned. Ford's concept of self-training in virtue appears frequently: *Funerall Elegy* 106–8: 'his furnisht mind | Such harmony of goodnesse did preserve, | A Nature never built in better kind'; *GM* 780: 'The furniture of the minde, is the man himselfe'; *GM* 1074–5: 'O the furniture of the minde . . . indeed the true lasting and onely best Riches!'; *LL* 77–8: 'the furniture of Nature . . . the noble indowments of the mind'; *LL* 98: 'the whole furniture of an inriched soule'.

21 **Quintessence** the most essential part, the highly refined essence; the purest or most perfect form or manifestation (*OED* 2). Monsarrat (commenting on *HT* 251) described it as 'a Fordian word associated with "elixir" in four instances, and in three out of these also with "soul" ': cf. *HT* 653, *FM* 114, *BH* 4.2.24–5, *LM* 2.1.106, *LC* 3.1.39–40.

22 **rarely** extraordinarily.

25 **If** *hers to me* if this is true of her love to me.

31 **By Natures light** on the basis of what nature teaches; empirically.

31–2 **Philosophers Of elder times** pre-Christian philosophers.

32 **instance** provide an instance of (*OED*'s closest definition is 3, with the earliest example dating from 1608).

34 *Nature . . .* **blind** study of nature alone will leave us ignorant of divine teachings. 'Positions' are propositions, affirmations, tenets (chiefly a philosophical term; *OED* position *sb.*1).

42 **variety of lust** 'Marrying another would make Annabella promiscuous, adulterous' (Massai, quoting *BH* 3.2.70). Yet this is what Giovanni advised her to do at 2.1.22–7.

44 **shrive her** impose penance on her, administer absolution and hear her confession (*OED* shrive *v.* 1, quoting this instance).

45 **At your best leasure** 'when it best suits you' (brazenly expressing his equanimity about the Friar's suggestion).

46 Matchlesse without equal.

47–8 what . . . armes cf. *BH* 2.2.99–100: "T had been pity | To sunder hearts so equally consented'.

51–3 For Colour, lips . . . Flowres, cheeks Giovanni uses a blazon, a traditional poetic form celebrating each element of a person's beauty.

54 Throne in *Q*'s reading, Annabella's face is regarded as the throne of her mind, soul or beauty (cf. *OED* 3). There are similar figurative uses in *SD* 3.3.17 and in *LS* 1.2.98–100, where 'beauty and greatness' are said to shine 'like so many stars on several thrones'. Some editors emend to 'form'; see collation notes. Cf. 'The Throne of *Mercy*' (64) below.

55 Sphaeres the nine concentric spheres of Ptolemaic astronomy (i.e. those carrying the Moon, Mercury, Venus, the Sun, Mars, Jupiter, Saturn, the fixed stars, as well as the Crystalline Sphere). According to Pythagoras, they produce harmonious sounds as the heavenly bodies revolve (Brewer). Roper compares *Merchant* 5.1.60–5.

57–8 what . . . un-nam'd the rhyme underscores Giovanni's audacious ribaldry.

60 parts talents, accomplishments.

61 a second Death the damnation which, for some, will follow physical death. Roper cites Revelation 21:8: 'But the fearful, and unbelieving, and the abominable, and murderers, and whoremongers, and sorcerers, and idolaters, and all liars, shall have their part in the lake which burneth with fire and brimstone; which is a second death'.

62 but only.

64 Throne of Mercy i.e. God, or his position of heavenly dominion. (The former sense is a transferred use of 'throne'; *OED* 5.) As Gibson notes, this sounds like a response to Giovanni's blasphemous praise of Annabella at 54.

65 Yet still (Wiggins).

66 time . . . number perhaps in the musical or prosodic sense: 'harmony, rhythm, regularity' (*OED* 14a).

2.6

4–5 I . . . world Sturgess notes the dramatic irony, following the previous scene.

5 another world i.e. heaven.

7 Cozen kinsman.

10 breast . . . heart cf. 'Love's Cruelty' in the note to 1.2.202–3.

13 And if it.

14 first sleepe 'first period of slumber'? (*OED* sleep 3a); Wiggins quotes *Ram-Alley* (1611): 'When maids awak't from their first sleepe, | Deceiu'd with dreames begin to weepe, | And thinke if dreames, such pleasures know, | What sport the substance them would show' (TLN 15814)'.

16 relligiously fervently (*OED adv.* 1b).

17 godamercy an exclamation of applause or thanks, from 'God have mercy', i.e. 'God reward you' (French, *merci*; Latin *merces, merced-*, pay, recompense, revenue; *OED*).

18 prythee '(I) pray thee'; please; **sha'** colloquial abbreviation of 'shall'.

20 *Feeling* understanding, 'with a play on the satisfying tangibility of the evidence' (Roper).

21 mind intentions, desire, disposition.

25 in any case at all events.

26 reade it mee read it immediately; where 'mee' is the dative, meaning 'for me' (*OED* 2b).

35 Ring cf. *BH* 4.1.27–35 where King's daughter, Calantha, casts a ring to Ithocles (a favourite), telling him 'to give it at next morning to a mistress' (28); likewise *FMI* 1.1.115–18, where Cesario gives his younger sister, Clarissa, a ring, on the condition that she gives it back, thus to let him know when she has made her own decision in choosing a husband.

38 send backe that at 1.2.52–3 we heard that Florio had pledged Annabella's 'heart' to Soranzo. As Gifford notes, 'Florio juggles strangely with his daughter's suitors'. Cf. 119–20 below.

40–1 My . . . to Day by wearing this ring Giovanni imagines that he owns Annabella, even if nominally (or lets her know that it could not be given to another man).

43 match marry.

45 What say what do you say?

45 Sir with your leave the exact phrase occurs in *The Welsh Ambassador* 3.3.103: 'Then with your leave'; *PW* 4.3.167: '(Fayre Ladie) with your leave'; and *LT* 3.3.184: 'With your leave'.

48 raise . . . Fortunes improve his prospects (social position or wealth).

58 what doth he make what is he doing (Roper).

63 there . . . yfaith 'The use of dashes in *Q* signals a sexual innuendo . . . as suggested by Poggio's response in the next line' (Massai).

64 tickled tingled, sexually aroused; cf. 1.3.53 above and *HT* 708 n.

65 Sirrah a common form of address to inferiors. It could be used attributively with appellations or proper names (*OED* 1a, b, 2). *Q's* italicization of *Sweet-heart* perhaps indicates a certain silliness.

65 riddle guess (Roper).

69 take . . . me walk nearer to the wall than me. 'Streets were narrow, there was no special paving for pedestrians, and mud and filth drained into a central gutter or "kennel"; so the best and most honourable place to walk was by the wall. To yield this place was a courtesy, to take it by forcing another man towards the kennel was to claim superiority and often led to disputes sometimes to death' (Roper).

70 **thrust me** i.e. pushed me toward the middle of the road.

71 **then so** than to do so.

73 **hilts** handle (the plural form was common; *OED*); cf. 1.2.16.

75 **the like** a comparable.

77 **gull** fool.

79 **a fellow . . . beard** i.e. Richardetto.

85 **la now** a colloquial expression of surprise, irony, etc.; cf. *LS* 1.2.59: 'how shay by that, la?'.

92 **lik't** pleased (*OED v.*¹ 1); cf. *King Lear* 2.2.85: 'His countenance likes me not' (Weber).

97 **simplicity** simpleton (*OED* 2c, citing this instance). Cf. 'innocence', 1.2.48.

99 **given him the lye** accused him of lying (a serious insult).

99 **dry** strictly, 'not drawing blood'; more vaguely, 'hard, severe' (*OED* 11, 12).

109 **halfe a Crowne** according to Antonia Fraser (*The Weaker Vessel*, London, 1984, pp. 410–11), half-a-crown was double the usual price for a prostitute in the 1640s (noted by Lomax). 'Bergetto is probably not speaking from experience' (Wiggins).

112 **recourse** access.

114 **'gainst** i.e. as a present given in anticipation of.

117 **alone** Burton notes that 'too much solitariness' is both a 'cause and symptom' of melancholy (Burton, *Anatomy* I.2.2.6; I, 245).

117 **still, still** always, ever more and more (*OED* 3b).

119 **humour** 'temporary frame of mind' rather than 'disposition'.

120 **match** suitable or advantageous alliance (*OED* II 4).

121 **ment it nothing lesse** i.e. 'there is nothing I intended less'.

122 **the man I onely like** 'the only suitor I like' or 'the suitor I especially like'. For the latter sense of 'onely', see *OED adv.* 3.

129 **jealous** 'suspicious in love' (continuing her teasing jest about the 'lusty youth', Donado), or simply 'suspicious, fearful, doubtful', as often in Shakespeare (e.g. *Caesar* 1.2.162: 'That you do love me I am nothing jealous').

131 **the Evening . . . Day** proverbial (Tilley E190). Roper glosses 'crownes' as meaning 'both "completes" and "rewards", as in *finis coronat opus* and its English derivatives'.

3.1

2 **skonce** literally, 'head', and hence 'wit'. Often jocular.

3 **bobbe you off** deceive you, fob you off (*OED* bob *v.*¹1 b).

3 **an Ape with an apple** Roper compares the proverbial expression 'a toy to mock an ape' (Tilley T456), i.e. a trifle or quaint ploy used to distract or deceive.

4 **Sfoot** oath, from 'God's foot'.

5 **in . . . nose** in spite of his opposition ('maugre his nose' in Middle English; *OED* nose P3a).

6 **Hold . . . Grynd-stone** grind him down, oppress him.

12 **codpeice-point** a lace for fastening the codpiece: 'a bagged appendage to the front of the close-fitting hose or breeches worn by men from the 15th to the 17th c.: often conspicuous and ornamented' (*OED* codpiece 1).

12 **box** pot, or other small container. The word was 'originally applied to a small receptacle of any material for drugs, ointments, or valuable' (*OED n.*² I 1).

12 **Mermalade** marmalade: a fruit preserve of any kind (originally quinces).

13 **chopps** jaws, mouth.

14 **clap up** hastily arrange.

14–15 **in hugger mugger** secretly; cf. *Hamlet* 4.5.83–4: 'we have done but greenly | In hugger-mugger to inter him'.

17 **courage . . . rise** probably with a sexual implication in 'rise'. 'Courage', too, could mean 'sexual vigour and inclination; lust' (*OED n.* 3c).

21 **Constables** officers of the peace, invested with the power of arresting and imprisoning (Schmidt); here 'slow-witted', cf. Dogberry in *Much Ado* and Blurt in *Blurt Master Constable*.

22 **cart . . . charges** exhibit prostitutes in carts drawn through the streets (a familiar punishment), and do so at their own expense.

23 **ere . . . selfe** before I have finished breaking it myself (Roper).

3.2

2 **proffers** proposals, offers.

4 **have** has (referring to 'hope').

5 **Joynctures** (a) unions; (b) provisions for the joint holding of property by husband and wife (see *OED* jointure 4a). Donado makes some such offer in 1.3.15–19.

7 **use** treat.

10 **Agree . . . may** i.e. let them agree as they may.

11 **all woeman** altogether a woman, i.e. weak or inconstant—the stereotypical early modern view of women.

14 **without** outside.

14.1 SD *manent* remain.

15 **should** Roper glosses this as 'may be about to', but the sense is more likely 'ought'. Soranzo, aware of difficulties, is treading warily; and as Abbott notes (323), 'should' is not as imperious as 'shall'.

16 **sweare** i.e. not merely 'say' (17).

17 **poynt of faith** article of faith (requiring you to 'swear' to it).

19 **inferre** bring about (*OED* 1).

20 **regient** regent, ruler. The bold claim is given literal emphasis by his position 'above'.

21 **maide** virgin.

21 **unfit** unsuitable, 'not right'.

22 **but . . . noate** merely a woman's customary 'tune' or characteristic (*OED* note n^2. 3a, c).

25 **winkes** closes her eyes.

30 **strifes** contests.

33 **Have** 'has', an accepted form.

35 *Aqua vitae* brandy or other spirits, taken medicinally (Latin, 'water of life').

37 **nimble** acute, quick-witted (*OED* 4b).

41 **dresse . . . you** 'arrange my speech in your reflection'—or (with a likely jibe about Soranzo's own speech) 'according to your example'.

45 **better tast** sweeter experience, i.e. a more encouraging reception.

47 **spend** expend, wast.

48 **forbeare** dispense with.

49 **I tell you this** since I tell you this (Wiggins).

60 **hereof** of this.

66 **Looke to your daughter** cf. *Othello* 1.1.79: 'Look to your house, your daughter and your bags!'

67 **sounes** swoons.

77 **Byr lady** by our Lady (the Holy Virgin).

78 *Maides sicknesse* chlorosis, a form of anaemia affecting girls at puberty. It was also called green sickness on account of the faintly greenish pallor it causes. Pregnancy was sometimes disguised as green sickness.

79 **over-fluxe of youth** overflow of youthful desire. 'Youth' here stands for 'a quality or condition characteristic of the young', in this instance strong sexual desire or wantonness (see *OED* 3).

79 **present** immediate.

3.3

6 **quicke** 'alive', with a play on another sense: 'pregnant'.

7–8 **'tis . . . us** Wiggins points out an 'element of comic confusion', since 'in orthodox theology, heaven would help people only if they did repent'.

10 **at these yeeres** at my age.

11 **Quames** variant spelling of 'qualm', already obsolete in Ford's time (see *OED* qualm *n.*³).

11–12 **Quames . . . Pukings** fits of fainting or sickness, sudden urges to urinate, changes in the complexion, upset stomachs, and vomiting. All may be symptoms of pregnancy.

12–13 **another thing** probably the fact that Annabella has stopped menstruating.

13 **Credits** reputation's.

16 **water** urine.

17 **case** condition, state (*OED n.*¹ 5a).

18 **Prettily amended** fairly well recovered (*OED* prettily 3).

18 **espi'd** detected.

19 **looke for** expect.

20 **take no care** have no fear or worry.

23 **businesse** concerns, matters, tasks.

24 **discomfort** discourage, make uneasy (Schmidt).

24 **doe** governed by 'newes', plural or singular in this period.

26 **ill dyet** food poisoning.

3.4

1 **Indifferent** reasonably, quite.

4 **Mellownes** Wiggins notes that melons must be eaten when ripe. Richardetto's diagnosis of food poisoning is based only on Annabella's complaints.

5 **young stomacke** Roper finds this 'unintentionally suggestive of pregnancy', comparing phrases such as 'with young' and 'young bones'.

6 easie surfeit water perhaps 'a mild medicine for indigestion' (Lomax). A 'surfeit' is 'an excessive taking of food or drink', or the sickness this causes (*OED* 3, 4); but the word may also suggest other kinds of excessive indulgence.

8 fulnesse . . . blood sexual ripeness (Wiggins). 'Blood' was regarded as the seat of sexual desire.

10 once at some point (*OED* 5).

10 order't arrange it.

11 She . . . married as Roper notes, Florio's prescription is orthodox. Annabella's supposed 'fulnesse' of blood is to be cured by marriage.

11 ere . . . time perhaps 'before she reaches the crucial point of her illness' (Wiggins, suggesting 'a latent secondary meaning, unintended by Florio, referring to pregnancy').

29 ghostly spiritual; here may also be 'used especially with reference to what is rendered by a priest to penitent or one near death' (*OED a.* 1a, c).

35 Fathers . . . impression a loving notion typical of fathers (Wiggins).

40 prosper make happy, cause to flourish.

3.5

2 misse fail to obtain.

4 in termes of in circumstances of, in respect of (*OED* term *n.* 10).

5 Policy sagacity, shrewdness, cunning.

6 am resolv'd have decided.

7 Play . . . hands is not working for both sides (Bawcutt).

9 affied affianced, betrothed.

13 bestow spend.

14 thereabouts referring to the Fryar's cell.

14–15 'tis . . . know all 'you only risk a night: if nothing happens I shall learn the full details tomorrow, and instruct you accordingly' (Morris).

16 Box perhaps a jar or other receptacle (cf. 3.1.12 n.).

18 respect value (*OED v.* 4b).

19 speede despatch, kill (*OED* 7a, b).

22 hitt succeed.

22 hug revenge cherish, delight in (Roper).

26 you . . . bethought 'ee you have reflected, determined.

28 Fashion'd 'adapted'.

30 drift purpose, intention (*OED n.* 4a).

31 **call . . . shrift** call his cousin to a reckoning (literally, 'to penance or confession').

36 **busse** kiss.

37 **There's . . . yet** despite commentators' uncertainty (see collation notes), the line may well belong to Philotis. Roper thinks it is 'a mildly encouraging remark—"He's coming on!" —consistent with [line 41]'.

38 **withdraw a little** Richardetto's lines at 47 and 49–50 seem to suggest that the others do not 'withdraw' until the scene's close.

39 **at large** most likely 'at length, fully' rather than 'as a general body'.

40 **devices** anything fancily devised, like the 'codpeice-point' and the 'box of Marmalade' mentioned in 3.1.11–12 (*OED* device 8; Roper).

42 **You shall enough** with the common ellipsis of the verb.

47 **Phisick** remedy.

3.6

0.1 SD this direction is a good example of Ford's imaginative concern for the 'stage picture', but it is detailed and pragmatic rather than merely impressionistic. Note, for example, the stipulation for 'wax-lights' (wax candles) rather than those made from smokier tallow. Some commentators judge 'in his study' to be a mistake because (a) in 3.4.33 Florio tells the Friar he will conduct him to Annabella's 'chamber', and (b) at line 44 below, Florio says that Soranzo 'stayes [i.e. waits] belowe'. However, in 3.5.8–12, Richardetto says that Soranzo and Annabella are to be affianced 'this very night' in Fryar *Bonauentures* Cell', which may be what is intended by the reference to the Friar's '*study*' here. In general, staging in the Jacobean theatre was fluid and minimal. Cf. *The Fair Maid of the Inn* 4.2.28 SD: '*Enter* FOROBOSCO *as in his Study* [*holding*] *a paper*'. Wiggins and Lowe comment on '*as in his Study*': 'Could refer either to the actor's studious demeanor or to an entrance in the discovery space' (*CWJF* 3, p. 739).

1–5 As Roper notes, 'the Friar's part in this scene has many echoes of the penitential poem *Christes Bloodie Sweat* (1613)'. See now Gilles Monsarrat, 'The Unity of John Ford: *'Tis Pity She's a Whore* and *Christ's Bloody Sweat*', *Studies in Philology*, 77 (1980): 247–70.

2 **unript** 'exposed'. The visceral image, as if her soul has been torn from (or exposed by a ripping open of) her body, emphasizes her spiritual agony. Cf. *LS* 4.1.70–1, 'I would unrip | That womb of bloody mischief'; and 2.3.98–9 'rip | This coffin of my heart'.

2–5 **so foul and guilty, | . . . These teares may doe you good** for 'the idea of guilt as a stain (or "leprosy") to be "washed off" with tears', cf. *SG* 5.2.21–3, and *LS* 5.1.142–4 (*CWJF* 2, p. 194).

6 **reade a Lecture** deliver an admonition or discourse of the nature of a sermon (*OED* lecture *n*. 4b, 6). Roper compares *CBS* 1369–70: 'Guilt reades a lecture of her [the soul's] foule misdeeds, | And bids her looke upon this streame of red'.

8 *a place* i.e. Hell. Italics are used again for 'this place' (21). The Friar's evocation of Hell is most directly indebted to Dante's *Inferno*, which vividly describes the punishments to which the various categories of sinners are assigned. Commentators compare Nashe's description of Hell in *Pierce Pennilesse*: 'A place of horror, stench, and darknesse, where men see meat but can get none, or are ever thirstie, and readie to swellt for drinke, yet have not the power to taste the coole streames that runne hard at their feet . . . he that all his life time was a great fornicator, hath all the diseases of lust continually hanging upon him . . . as so of the rest, as the usurer to swallow moulten gold, the glutton to eate nothing but toades, and the Murtherer to bee still stabd with daggers, but never die' (Nashe I, 218). Ford imitated this in *CBS* 751–74.

9 **List** listen.

11 **horrour** 'horror' derives from Latin *horrēre*, 'stand on end (of hair), tremble, shudder'. Roper may therefore be right that the word suggests 'a surface jagged with flame, or the flame's flickering motion'. 'Horror' also meant 'ruffling of surface' (*OED* 2b).

13 **infeckted** poisoned, filled with corruption (Roper).

24 **stands** remain, are fixed. Gifford's emendation to 'stand' is unnecessary as the use of a singular verb-form before a plural subject was common. 'When the subject is as yet future and, as it were, unsettled, the third person singular might be regarded as the normal inflection' (Abbott 335).

25 **dream't** spent their time in idle reveries, waking dreams.

25 **lawless sheets** Wiggins points out the use of metonymy, in which the name of an attribute or adjunct stands for the thing meant (*OED*). Here, the bed sheets represent unlawful sexual relationships.

28 **a Daggers poynt** anticipating the play's most famous moment (5.6.9.1).

32 **motions** stirrings of the soul; impulses, emotions, desires, inclinations (*OED* motion *n*. 12b). As Roper observes, a closely related sense of 'motion' denotes 'the working of God in the human soul' (see *OED* 12b).

36 **for . . . safety** in Lomax's view, the ranking of her honour before her spiritual welfare 'indicates that the Friar, like the Cardinal, puts worldly matters before spiritual'.

38 **live to him** devote yourself to him (Roper).

39 **baytes** literally, bait: food placed on a hook or in a trap to lure fish or animals. Roper compares *CBS* 534: 'Yet O, tis hard to leave the baites of pleasure'.

41 **what must come** i.e. the afterlife and the possibility of going to Hell.

42 **take the time** seize the opportunity. The phrase is proverbial: 'Take time when time comes' (Tilley T312).

51 **Give mee your hand** As ll. 63–4 and 3.8.1–5 show, these proceedings represent a betrothal, not a marriage. Such undertakings were nevertheless regarded as legally binding if followed by a wedding ceremony (Morris). With its joining of hands and exchange of vows before witnesses, the action here is also strongly reminiscent of the spousal or 'handfasting' ceremony which, if followed by cohabitation, was recognized by English common law (Moore, note to a similar episode in *LS* 4.1.167–75, Revels edn.). Cf. the business between Hippolita and Vasques in 2.2.137ff. In 4.1.46–54, Hippolita herself 'engages' Soranzo and Annabella. Cf. also *PW* 2.3.86–90 and *LS* 5.3.131–8.

51 **for that** 'probably "in exchange for that hand"; but perhaps "in order that", or "since"' (Roper).

54–5 **more . . . Morning-sun** the Friar 'looks forward to a church service in the morning as part of the ceremony or the wedding itself' (Sturgess).

3.7

0.2 SD *Darke-lanthorne* or *dark-lantern*: a lantern with a slide or shutter to conceal the light. *OED*'s earliest instance of 'dark-lantern' is dated 1650.

2–3 **lye | To listen** put my ear to the ground.

3.1 SD *after* after them.

6 **some angry *Justice*** fierce spirit of divine retribution (cf. the Furies of classical myth).

7 **have at you** 'my aim is at you', 'I'll hit you.'

7.1 SD *Strikes* runs him through with the poisoned rapier (Wiggins).

8 **stich fallen** a stitch has burst (*OED* fall *v.* 26c).

9 **Flesh-taylor** surgeon.

14 **next** nearest.

19 **sweat** Bergetto mistakes his bleeding for urine ('piss', 11) or sweat.

20.1 SD *Halberts* or halberds: long-handled weapons combining a spear and a battle-axe, 'the usual weapons of a watch or civic guard' (Roper).

27 **linnen** linen garment(s), often specifically undergarments (*OED* linen *a.* & *n.* 3a).

31 **make much of** treat generously or respectfully, take care of.

31–2 **going . . . way** dying. Cf. 'if he do go the wrong way' (*The Queene* 2.1.86).

35 **to late** variant spelling of 'too'; cf. 1.2.96 n.

3.8

7 **bravely** splendidly, in a becoming manner.

10 **disgrace** most likely referring to the shame brought by her involvement with Soranzo (cf. her next line). Sturgess suggests that she is thinking of 'her social disgrace in marrying a servant'.

14 **resolves** resolutions.

16 **against so hopefull** in comparison to so promising (Lomax).

17 **preferment** advancement.

18 *My youth* 'a contemptuous reference to Soranzo' (Bawcutt; cf. 1.2.88–9).

3.9

1 **bootlesse** useless.

12 **And** if.

14 **Cardinals** i.e. Cardinal's.

17 **'a is** he is.

18 **an't** if it.

27 **present** 'current' or 'urgent, pressing' (*OED adj.* 2, 9a).

29 **sawcy mates** impudent fellows. 'Mates' here is an insulting term, implying that they are of low social status—and perhaps equally so.

30 **nor . . . nor** neither . . . nor.

31 **we** he refers to himself in exalted fashion; cf. the royal 'we'.

31 **hoast** innkeeper, landlord.

34 **fit times** it is still night.

35 **the . . . Common-wealth** not the rulers but the municipal authorities charged with policing the community (Wiggins).

39 **on't** of it.

41 **In . . . Grace** affirming the truthfulness of his declaration (Wiggins).

42 **thought** intention.

46 **else** by other means.

50 **him** Bergetto.

50 **were** for 'was', a common usage. 'Were' was 'often used as the subjunctive where any other verb would not be so used, and indeed where the subjunctive is unnecessary or wrong' (Abbott 301).

57 **Sir** *Florio* The use of this title for a merchant is either flattery or irony.

58 **to meane** too lowly, of low birth.

60 **wit** common sense.

60 **for shame** be ashamed, shame on you!

62–3 *Justice . . .* **heaven** Roper and other commentators see a reference here
to Astraea, the goddess of justice, who lived on earth during the Golden Age
but reluctantly fled to heaven when sin began to prevail during the Iron Age
(Brewer, Roper). Cf. Ovid *Metamorphosis* (l.150), quoted in *Titus Andronicus*
4.3.2–4: '*Terras Astraea reliquit*'.

67 **amisse** wrong.

4.1

0.1 SD ***Banquet*** the word could denote 'a sumptuous entertainment of food
and drink', 'a slight repast', or 'a course of sweetmeats, fruit and wine' (*OED*
banquet *n.*¹ 1, 2, 3). The first sense seems most likely here, given the occasion.
Also witness the 'Hoboyes' and the Friar's anticipation of 'Feast' (2).

0.1 SD **Hoboyes** or Hautboys (from French, *hautbois*), double-reed wood-
wind instruments with a loud, high-pitched sound, the ancestors of the modern oboe. In drama they were conventionally associated with banquets,
weddings and entertainments (as in the openings of *Timon* 1.2, *Henry VIII*
1.4, and the banquet scene in *Titus* 5.3.25.01–04).

1 **take your times** seize your opportunity.

2 **Feast** festivity, celebrations.

3–4 **Saints . . . guests** ' "Saints" probably refers, not just to canonized persons, but to members of the "communion of saints"—a mystical body which
includes the faithful on earth, souls in Purgatory and Heaven, and, according
to St. Thomas Aquinas, the angels . . . . It is consistent with Catholic doctrine
that members of this spiritual family who are not corporeally present may
share in the rejoicing which follows a sacrament of marriage' (Roper, citing
the *Catholic Encyclopaedia*, 1907–12, *s.v.* Communion of Saints).

7 **heard** i.e. in heaven.

7 **the hand of goodnesse** 'Presumably a synonym for the hand of God, and
therefore highly inappropriate in its suggestion that Bergetto's slaughter was
God's means of saving Soranzo' (Sturgess).

10 **this . . . Jewell** i.e. Annabella. Cf. *LS* 4.2.75.

14 **lusty Cups** merry toasts.

15–17 **Oh . . . Confusion** the Quarto's comma after 'undone' (followed by
Roper and others) may suggest that Giovanni's first line modifies the rest of
the speech: 'If the marriage had not yet been formalized, I would dare
"Confusion" (destruction, damnation) rather than endure the sight of
Annabella being "clipt" (embraced) by another.' It is possible, though, that

the first line stands alone and should be punctuated with a full stop or an exclamation mark.

19 wayte 'wait on the guests', 'wait in readiness to receive orders'—and thus with something of the force of 'hold off, be quiet' (*OED* wait $v.^1$ 6a, 9a, b).

23 bowle drinking vessel (*OED* bowl $n.^1$1b).

27 offend displease, vex, upset, cause offence (*OED* 5).

29 noyse besides the more familiar sense, the word also denoted 'a pleasant or melodious sound' (*OED* 3).

32 loves warm good wishes.

32 Masque 'A form of amateur histrionic entertainment, popular at Court and amongst the nobility in England during the latter part of the 16th c. and the first half of the 17th c.; originally consisting of dancing and acting in dumb show, the performers being masked and habited in character' (*OED* masque 2). In a reflection of courtly fashion, many plays feature masques, e.g. *Women Beware Women* 5.2 and *Revenger's Tragedy* 5.1. In *LS* 3.4, the licentious Ferentes is murdered by his jilted lovers during a revenge masque.

34 bound obliged.

35.1 SD *Hoboyes* oboes; see 0.1 SD n above.

35.2 SD *white Roabes* suggesting purity, innocence, and virginity. 'Although there are records of brides wearing white in early times, it was only one of many colours which could be chosen, and it only became an expected bridal colour in the second half of the eighteenth century' (Simpson & Roud, *s.v.* 'Weddings: colours'). Hippolita and her ladies are all likely to be masked.

35.3 SD *Garlands of Willowes* the willow is an emblem of grief for unrequited love, or the loss of a mate. 'A green willow must be my garland,' sings Desdemona shortly before her death (*Othello* 4.3.49).

37 beholding indebted.

37 love act of kindness (*OED* $n.$ I c).

37 this *Q* (corrected); thy *Q* (uncorrected).

40–54 Hippolita uses commercial and legal terms connected with a contract, such as 'defraud' (41), 'claim | Some interest' (47–8), and 'What I have right to do' (49).

40 amaz'd The meaning was stronger than at present: 'bewildered, fearful, greatly astonished'.

42 reckon up go over in detail (*OED* reckon $v.$ 3a).

43 vents utters.

44 report rumour, common talk. Cf. 'RUMOR, *painted full of tongue*' in *2 Henry IV* Induction 6–8: 'Upon my tongues continual slanders ride, | The which in every language I pronounce, | Stuffing the ears of men with false reports.'

46 lend's lend us (i.e. give me).

48 **Lord** husband.

50 **your Noble worth** cf. Hippolita's disdainful remark on Annabella at 2.2.48: 'Madam Merchant'.

52 **Here . . . from me** assuming the role of priest, as the stage-image emphasizes.

53 **joyne** perhaps echoing the marriage service: 'Those whom God hath joined together let no man put asunder'.

54 **allow'd** approved, permitted.

55 **ingag'd us** obliged us, placed us in your debt (Roper). The ironic play on another sense, 'betrothed', points up Soranzo's bitterness, anger, or suspicion—feelings which he may, however, wish to disguise in such a public setting. The word also reminds us that he had 'engaged' (in the sense of 'pledged') himself to Hippolita.

56 **single** 'simple, not duplicitous', perhaps with a glance at her marital status (*OED* 8a, 12a).

56 **charity** benevolence, amiable intentions, Christian love.

57 **interest** concern or stake (in Soranzo). For Hippolita's use of commercial and legal terms, cf. ll. 40–54 above. Cf. *The Laws of Candy* 5.1.385: 'I here disclaim the interest'.

63 **pledge** drink a toast to (*OED* 4).

64 **Union** 'accordance, agreement' (Roper) or, more likely, 'the union between him and Annabella' (Wiggins).

72–4 **like . . . *inganna*** Ford seems to have consulted *Florio his Firste Fruites* (1578), a well-known Italian grammar by the scholar and translator John Florio (d. 1625). As Roper notes, two facing pages in Florio's book (33ᵛ–34ʳ) provide material used here and at 4.3.187–8. The second of these pages in Florio has: 'He is like a brand af [*sic*] fire, kyndeleth others, and burneth hym selfe'. Florio translates *Troppo sperar, inganna* as 'Too much hoping, deceiueth' (33ᵛ; cf. Tilley H 608).

74–5 **thou art but dead** 'you are nothing except dead', i.e. 'you are as good as dead' (with omission of the negative; see Abbott 127). Roper compares *2 Henry VI* 3.2.391: 'If thou be found by me, thou art but dead.'

75 **grace** (a) virtue (considered divine in its origin), sense of propriety; (b) 'the divine influence which operates in men to regenerate and sanctify, to inspire virtuous impulses, and to impart strength to endure trial and resist temptation' (*OED* 11b, e, 13b).

77 **Dye . . . shame** 'shame on you, die in the spirit of Christian love' (cf. 3.9.65).

79 **politique** politic: scheming, crafty.

81 **promis'd her faire** gave her favourable assurances.

81–2 **I knew . . . beene** i.e. I knew she would have broken her promise and let me be blamed for the murder.

83 **disposition** nature.

84 **fitted** prepared, furnished. The word can also mean 'punished, "fixed" '; cf. *LS* 3.2.31, and Moore, p. 270.

84 **payment . . . coyne** proverbial (Dent, C 510).

85 **yet . . . and** *Q*'s dashes highlight a lacuna in the printed text. The manuscript used by the printer may have been incomplete or indecipherable. Perhaps the original reading was something like: 'shee hath yet a moment to live. Repent, and end thy dayes . . .'.

85 **vild** variant spelling of 'vile', common in 17th c. (see *OED* vild *a.*, 4.1.100 and 5.1.16)

89 **minute** appointed time (*OED n.*[1] 6c).

91 **heate . . . hell fire** having drunk poison, Fernando also feels the torment of 'hot flames' (*LS* 5.3.85–97). Stage-poison often had such an effect in this period (see note to *Women Beware Women*, Revels edn., 5.2.139).

98 **Monsters** misshapen births.

103 **forget** neglect, fail to reward or acknowledge.

107 **change** i.e. from marriage celebrations to violent death. Cf. the Abbott's remark after the murder of Ferentes in *LS*: 'Here's fatal sad presages, but 'tis just: | He dies by murder that hath lived in lust' (3.4.62–3).

109 **event** outcome.

4.2

3 **forfeit of her modesty and life** 'forfeit' = offence, transgression. Ford often collocated 'forfeit' 'with ethical terms, especially "shame" ', cf. *SG* 1.3.18: 'Too easy forfeits of their shames', 5.1.42: 'The forfeit of her shame'; *BH* 4.2.149–50: 'the forfeit | Of noble shame'; and *LT* 3.3.75–6: 'and justified the forfeit | Of noble shame' (*CWJF* 2, pp. 195, 237).

4 **hover** 'remain suspended in the air above a particular spot', but also 'hesitate before taking action' (*OED v.*[1] 1a, 3a). The Furies, the classical goddesses of punishment and vengeance, were often depicted as winged (March).

6 **weight** perhaps suggesting the burden of his sins.

8 **further his confusion** facilitate or hasten his destruction.

8–9 **one | Above** God.

10 **Debate** quarrel, dispute.

11 **Thicken . . . head** grow worse and draw to a crisis, like purulent matter coagulating and forming a ripe boil or abscess. *OED*'s earliest instance of

'head' meaning 'the maturated part of a boil, abscess, etc.' is dated 1611 (*n.*¹ 14), but cf. *Richard II* 5.1.58.

12 **Sleightens** slights: disdains, rejects.

12 **abandons** renounces (*OED v.* 7).

16 **flying** fleeing.

17 *Cremona* a city about 30 miles north of Parma, part of the state of Milan; it was notable for its many nunneries (Wiggins).

18 **Votaresse** nun.

19 **extreames** hardships, desperate acts (*OED* extreme *a.*, *adv.* & *n.* 4b, 5).

20 **uneven** 'irregular, rugged, difficult', and perhaps 'unjust' (*OED* 2a, 3, 4).

25 **Hie** make haste.

26 **beades** rosary beads

27 **crowne** adorn as with a crown; fulfil, perfect.

29 **farwell** variant spelling of 'farewell' (see *OED* farewell *int., n, (a) and adv*). Cf. 5.3.68 and 5.5.79.

4.3

0.1 SD **unbrac't** with his doublet or other part of his clothing unfastened or loosened. Ophelia describes how Hamlet came to her chamber 'with his doublet all unbraced' (*Hamlet* 2.1.79; Bawcutt; *OED ppl.a.* 1). Cf. also *JC* 2.1.260–2: 'Is Brutus sick, and is it physical | To walk unbraced and suck up the humours | Of the dank morning?'

1 **famous** infamous.

4 **Confound** destroy.

5 **maintainst** persists in, justifies.

6 **bawd** procurer, pimp.

7 **else but** besides.

8 **plurisie** overabundance, excess (*OED* 2).

9 **heyday** 'excitement of the spirits or passions' (*OED* 1). The word is not recorded in the sense, 'highest pitch of excitement', before 1751 (*OED* 2).

9 **luxury** lechery, lust.

11 **cloake** cover.

11 **close** 'secret, hidden', but perhaps also 'physically close' (Roper).

11 **tricks** 'sexual games' and perhaps 'stratagems, deceptions'. For the first sense, cf. 5.5.2: 'a tricke in night-games'.

12 **belly-sports** cf. *CBS* 1742: 'sensuall sports', *BH* 3.2.135: 'bed-sports'.

13 **gally maufrey** gallimaufry: a confused jumble (*OED* 2).

15 **Shey** there is no need for emendation. As Moore argues (notes to 'how shay by that', *LS* 1.2.59, Revels edn.), this is evidently an idiomatic form, not recorded by *OED* or *EDD*, meaning 'say' or 'say ye'. Moore cites instances of 'shey', 'shay', or 'sha' in *FCN* 2.2.140, *The Welsh Ambassador* 5.1.93, and other plays.

15 **why** an interjection: 'why!'

17 ***Over-loving Lordship*** *Q*'s italic points up her scornful mockery. For further examples of emphasis italic, see 1.2.199 n. and below, 36, 45, 48.

18 **on denyall** at her rejection of him.

19 **case** condition, state.

20 **would . . . doing** had to be 'getting on' with things, couldn't wait (with a coarse play on 'doing': 'copulating'; cf. 1.2.182 n.).

24 **patient** stoical (Wiggins).

25 **Queane** strumpet, prostitute, impudent woman.

28 **'twas . . . bargaine** i.e. to tell you that.

29 **somewhat** something, a little.

29 **stay . . . stomacke** assuage your appetite (for information).

34 **and** if.

35 **A . . . match** a bargain! Agreed! (Bawcutt).

45 ***Father*** pass for or act as father to (cf. 4.1.105).

45 ***Brave*** handsome, excellent.

48 ***a Creature*** a created being, in existence.

48–9 **but for . . . that** 'except for the fact that we have been married, I am scarcely aware of your existence even now'.

53 **ripp up thy heart** cf. 1.2.202–3 n., 3.6.2 n.

55 **prodigious** unnatural, monstrous. The audience may reflect that the word is more apt than Soranzo realizes.

59 ***Che . . . amore*** Italian: 'What death is sweeter than to die for love?' Ford again borrows from John Florio's *First Fruites* (cf. 4.1.81–2 n.). This sentence occurs in a conversation exemplifying 'Amorous talke' (13ᵛ). The next line of Annabella's song is based on the reply given in Florio's text (see 79 n.).

61 **lust be-leapred** corrupted with the moral leprosy of lust. Cf. 1.1.74 'leprosie of Lust'; *The Laws of Candy* 5.1.60–1: 'beleapred with the curse | Of foul ingratitude'.

63 ***Morendo . . . dolore*** 'dying in her favour, I would die without sorrow (or pain)'. In Florio, the reply to the question of l. 58 is: '*Si morendo in gratia, á lei, morirei volentieri, ma altrimenti non voglio*' ('Yea, dying in her fauor, I would dye gladly, but otherwise I wyl not'). Roper suggests that Ford adapted Florio's text to make a rhyme with l. 59.

64 **Triumph** 'exult', with stress on the second syllable (Roper).

65 **redeeme** ransom.

69 *hang-man* executioner (*OED* hangman 1).

71 **I . . . behind** i.e. someone remains who will avenge my murder.

76 **slacke** neglect, delay.

80 **forefend** forbid.

81 **wud** variant spelling of 'would' (*OED*).

82 **hath** for the third-person plural in –*th* see Abbott 334.

84–5 **what . . . not?** cf. *LS* 1.2.38–9: 'a chaste wife or a mother that never slept awry are wonders, wonders in Italy.'

90 **Authors of** persons responsible for. But 'author' also means 'begetter, father' (*OED* author *n*. 1c, 2a). 'The plural may be meant to include accomplices such as Putana, or illogically to insinuate that Annabella has had more lovers than one' (Roper).

90 **warrant 'ee** an asseveration: 'I assure you.'

91 **unconscionable** unreasonable (*OED* 2).

95–6 **I prize my life | As nothing** cf. *Hamlet* 1.4.65: 'I do not set my life at a pin's fee.'

99 **beshrew my heart** literally, 'curse my heart', but the phrase is often used as a mere asseveration.

99 **but** unless.

100 **in any case** by any means (an obsolete use of the phrase; see *OED* case *n*.¹ 13).

103 **were . . . Credit** seemed deserving of any merit or reward.

104 **distractions** mental perturbation.

106 **extremities** hardships.

108–10 **in . . . heart** Roper compares Matthew 6:19–21: 'Lay not up for yourselves treasures upon earth, where moth and rust doth corrupt, and where thieves break through and steal; But lay up for yourselves treasures in heaven . . . For where your treasure is, there will your heart be also.'

112 **Life** 'existence, the fact of being alive', 'eternal life', or perhaps 'spiritual life, redemption' (*OED* life 1, 2, 3).

118 **Follow . . . passion** follow this restraint with (an outburst of) intense feeling. 'Temper' here means 'mental balance or composure, especially under provocation . . . moderation in or command over the emotions, especially anger' (*OED* 3). 'Passion' is a richly suggestive word which may also mean 'sorrow', 'suffering', 'strong affection, desire, love', or an actor's representation of these (*OED* passion 3, 6a, c, 8a).

118 **bee . . . moving** from the time of Horace's *Ars poetica* onwards, dramatic theory adopted from classical rhetoric the three aims of the orator, applied

equally to authors and actors, *docere, delectare, movere*: to instruct, to delight, and to move the passions.

119 **for the purpose** suits the purpose.

122 **superstitiously** idolatrously or extravagantly. *OED* does not give this sense of the adverb, although adjectival usage is recorded as early as 1582 (superstitious 2b).

124 **use** treat.

129 **humourous** fanciful, capricious (*OED* humorous 3a).

137 **above thy strength** beyond your power to resist.

140 **Divinity** cf. Ephesians 5.22–3: 'Wives, submit yourselves unto your own husbands, as unto the Lord. For the husband is the head of the wife, even as Christ is the head of the church.' As Wiggins comments: 'Soranzo will exercise the divine prerogative of forgiveness if Annabella repents.'

141 **remit** pardon.

143 **poynt** instance (*OED* 5).

146 **alteration** change from her present disposition. Roper glosses as 'disturbance', citing *OED* alter *v.* 3: 'To affect mentally, to disturb' (only recorded in the transitive form).

147–8 **'Tis . . . woeman** the sentiment, pointed up by italic in the Quarto, is proverbial: 'Woman is the weaker vessel'. Cf. Peter 1.3.4: 'Giving honour unto the wife, as unto the weaker vessel', and Tilley W655.

150 **to the matter** to the purpose (Roper).

153 **fir'd in** inflamed by the desire for (*OED* fire *v.*[1] 3a; cf. *Caesar* 3.1.36–7).

155 **great** a pun: 'pregnant' and 'high in rank'.

155 **great in the stocke** 'large or thick in the trunk or body' (a 'stocke' is a wooden handle or butt of a musket, pistol, whip, etc.), applied to a pregnant woman.

155–6 **to your hand** the phrase is bitterly ironic or savagely wounding: 'ready for you, without exertion on your own part'(*OED* hand 34c, quoting *Antony* 4.15.28–9: 'What thou wouldst do | Is done unto thy hand'). 'To one's hand' can also mean 'into subjection' (*OED* hand 34b).

157 **haunted** resorted to frequently or habitually (*OED* haunt *v.* 3).

157 **Cunny-berry** rabbit warren (a cunny, or coney, being a rabbit). *OED* does not record 'cunny' in the obscene sense before 1720. Indecent usages of 'cony' and 'coney', however, are recorded in this period (*OED* cony, coney 5b).

157 **cunning** artfulness, cleverness, or an application of this; an ingenious device (*OED* cunning *n.* 3a, b). We might say 'there's the trick'.

160 **sufferance** patient endurance, forbearance (*OED*).

161 **Voluntary** the primary sense appears to be 'spontaneous confession', with an obvious pun on the musical sense: 'a piece or movement added at the will of the performer' (*OED n.* 2a, b), here specified as 'a weeping tune'.

162 **hitt** goes well.

162 **marke** target, aim.

165 **for the nonce** 'for the time being or occasion', or simply 'indeed' (*OED* nonce *n.*[1] 1b, c).

168 **perversnesse** obstinate disposition.

168 **fault-finding** scolding.

169–70 ***Where . . . houses*** Morris compares *Florio his First Fruites* (1578), f. 33ᵛ: 'They are sorry houses, where the Hennes crow, and the cock holdes his peace'. The saying is proverbial (Tilley H778), but a debt to Florio seems likely in view of the other borrowings from his book.

171 ***Cunning*** craft, skilful work in making a dress.

172 **blame** find fault with, complain about (*OED v.* 1).

173 **up** pregnant.

173 **quickly** playing (here or with 'quicke', 173) on another sense: 'pregnant' (*OED adj.* 5b).

174 **policy** stratagem, ploy.

177 **madde** furious, beside himself with anger, deranged (*OED* 4a, 6a).

183–4 **kill . . . unkindnesse** a variation on the proverbial phrase, 'To kill with kindness' (Tilley K51), to cause discomfort to someone by treating him or her in a way that is extremely kind or helpful.

186 **full sore** most grievously.

189 **humour** temperament, frame of mind.

189 **that** as to be able to say that (Wiggins).

190 **streight** straight away.

193–4 **winne . . . force** i.e. make her reveal it by means of violence.

200 **betray . . . affliction** 'wittingly expose her to pain or punishment' (Massai).

202 ***In this*** by telling all.

204 **preferment** advancement, favour.

206 **neere and entire friend** 'intimate and wholly devoted'—or perhaps, in view of Putana's response, 'and perfectly beloved'. 'Neere' can also mean 'loosely related by blood or kinship' (*OED* 1, 8a). 'Entire' may mean 'proper, complete, having all that is desirable', or perhaps (as Roper suggests) 'not castrated' (*OED a., adv. & n.* 2a, 3b, c, 4b).

211 **U'ds pitty** an oath, from 'God's pity'.

211 **what else** of course.

213 **I warrant 'ee** an asseveration usually meaning 'I assure or promise you', here conveying astonishment or incredulity (*OED* warrant *v.* 5a). Cf. the modern 'I declare!'

214 **brave** fine.

219 **to blame** blameworthy (ironic).

220 **a Turke or a Jew** both were used as names of opprobrium in this period (*OED* Turk 2a, Jew 2a); one who cannot be trusted.

221 **belie** tell lies about (*OED v.*² 2).

223.1 SD **Banditti** 'Bandetti', variant of 'banditti': desperate marauders, brigands. The word was often applied to members of the organized gangs in the mountainous districts of Italy and other countries (*OED* bandit 1a). Gifford is understandably sceptical that Vasques would have these bandits ready 'before he had any assurance that they would be needed'. Then again, we have already witnessed Vasques' penchant for violence, murder, and treachery (1.2.1–28, 4.1.70ff), and many in Ford's audience are likely to have heard of the Italian bandits. Massai claims that 'their entrance is a sensational *coup de théâtre* and makes Vaques's power to perpetrate evil seem almost superhuman'.

225 **presently** at once.

225 **take mee** 'take for me': the old dative, as in *Shrew* 1.2.8–12. See Abbott 220.

230–1 **I'le . . . gums** editors often give a stage direction for him to gag her.

231 **Toad-bellied** a term of abuse not recorded by *OED*. Wiggins compares Dekker's *The Noble Spanish Soldier* 4.2.179: 'Sirrah, you Sarsa-Parilla Rascal and Toad-guts'.

231 **bitch** 'applied opprobriously to a woman; strictly, a lewd or sensual woman. Not now in decent use; but formerly common in literature' (*OED n.*¹ 2a).

232 **closely** secretly.

232 **Coale-house** covered storage place for coal.

233 **roares** cries out (see 3.6.17 n).

235 **liberty** freedom, licentiousness.

236 **trayn'd** (a) 'allured, led astray'; (b) 'converted' and 'instructed'.

238 **points** a number of senses seem pertinent: 'details, fine points, aspects'; 'aims, objectives'; and perhaps (continuing the possible mock-scholarly tone of 'tutor', 238) 'propositions, arguments, debating points' (*OED n.*¹ 1a, 10a, b, 13a, 28).

238–9 **how . . . tayle** 'how a smooth-tongued, honest-seeming or insinuating story, speech or falsehood outwits or "gets round" a woman' (Roper). Vasques may be reflecting on how his own 'smooth' words have achieved more than those of Soranzo. Wiggins compares *The Duchess of Malfi* 1.1.339–40: 'What cannot a neat knave with a smooth tale | Make a woman believe?' (*OED* smooth 7a, b, d, 8; tale 5a).

240 **thing** creature.

241–2 **as firme . . . Summer** i.e. as sure as the turn of the seasons.

245 **Tooke too much of the flesh** (a) eaten too much meat; (b) over-indulged in sex.

246 **have . . . it** 'have guessed it exactly'—with the bawdy insinuation (more or less overt) that Giovanni himself has 'taken too much of the flesh' or 'hit the mark' (see *Romeo* 1.1.204, 2.1.33).

250 **liberality** (a) generosity (in tipping him, perhaps); (b) licentiousness (?).

251 **made a man** Roper conjectures that this should be 'a made man', i.e. one whose success is assured. The phrase was long current (see *OED* made 6a), but *Q* is clear enough.

251 **plyed my Cue** applied myself to my part (*OED* cue *n.*² 3). Cf. Vasques' theatrical language in 4.3.116.

254 **fast** secure.

257 **Runs circular** goes in circles.

264 **No . . . feare** either 'There is no conquest whose glory could eclipse my fear', or 'No one who conquers me will have the glory of seeing me show fear'.

5.1

1–43 Annabella's repentance echoes *CBS* 1135–7: 'Never was teare from any heart let fall, | In true repentance, but the Lord of grace, | Hath seene and botled up, and kept it all'. Danielson cites Ps. 56:8: 'Thou hast . . . put my teares into my bottel'.

1 **thriftlesse** unprofitable, wasteful, prodigal. Watt and Vickers describe this as 'a thoroughly Fordian epithet for time wasted in pleasure' in the note to *CBS* 32: 'In the thriftless times (sweete baytes to poyson Youth)'; cf. *FM* 216: 'Not games of thriftles prodigality', and 611: 'Nor thriftless Royott of respec-tles meane'. See also 1.1.12–13.

4–8 **Thou . . . Tragedy** Ford often echoes *Richard II* 5.1.39–45, using 'a lamentable tale of me' (44) for a pattern of a woeful man: *Funeral Elegy* 161–70 (see note), *CBS* 1727–34, *WoE* 4.2.94–8, and *LS* 5.3.105–13.

4 **rid'st in poast** rides in haste, like couriers using post-horses.

5 **race** (1) course, journey; (2) fast ride on horseback (*OED n.*¹ 2b, 4).

6 **stay** 'cease' or perhaps 'restrain'.

7 **yet unborne** another of Ford's favourite words; cf. *The laws of Candy* 5.2.303: 'Children yet unborne', and *Loves Sacrifice* 5.3.110–11: 'Children unborn'. The phrase appears in Shakespeare, *Richard II* 3.3.88: 'children yet unborn and unbegot'.

9 **against** as a witness against.

10 **depositions . . . guilt** *Q*'s reading, 'dispositions', would be actions of disposing: 'bestowal or conveyance by deed or will' (*OED* 4a). Here, the word seems to be used for 'depositions': 'written testimony or allegations used as evidence in court', a usage not recorded by *OED*. In Annabella's metaphor, the depositions are inscribed by (or expressive of) her guilt (with a likely pun on 'gilt lettering', which would display her guilt more prominently; 'guilt' was an established spelling for 'gilt' in this period; *OED* gilt *ppl.a.*). 'Gild' can also mean 'smear with blood' (*OED v.*¹ 1d; also see 'character' *v.* 1). The legal conceit is a reminder that Ford was a member of the Middle Temple. 'This (depositions) seems to fit the legal metaphor better than the reading of *Q*' (Bawcutt).

10.1 SD **Enter Fryar** presumably he enters to the main stage, below Annabella, where his 'invisibility' to her would seem more plausible. When he finally addresses her at l. 43, she seems to have momentary trouble recognizing him.

12–13 **Beauty . . . grace** 'Beauty without goodness is worth nothing' (Tilley B170). Cf. 2.5.18–19 above, and *BH* 2.1.62–3: 'Why to be faire | Should yield presumption of a faulty soule?'

13 **grace** virtue, divine favour (cf. 4.1.75 n).

14 **Turtle** turtle-dove, an emblem of chaste and devoted love (see Tilley T624: 'As true as a turtle to her mate').

14 **mew'd up** confined.

15 **Un-mated** without a mate.

16 **descant** 'comment at large' (Massai).

17–18 **had the spoil | Of** wrecked, ruined.

20 **Nativity** one's birth, especially considered astrologically (*OED* 3a, 4).

21 **scourge** whip, lash; figuratively, 'a thing that is an instrument of divine chastisement (*OED* 2).

23 **an uncontrouled flame** the fire of untamed lust, or the unquenchable flames of hell (cf. *CBS* 762: 'flames of fire, that never shalbe quencht').

25 **Ceremoniall knot** matrimony.

28 **Lethargies of Lust** Roper compares *CBS* 1639–43: 'Inchanting sinne, that with it's cunning charmes | Luls men in death-ful sleepes, and slily makes | Impostum'd ulcers of unsencèd harmes | Rockes them in Lethargies, and never wakes | Reason'.

29 **Hugge their confusion** cherish or cling to their destruction or damnation. Cf. 3.5.24 and *Love's Sacrifice* 2.2.4–5: 'I am sorry | You hug your ruin so'.

29 **making Heaven unjust** 'in their assumption that heaven will not punish them' (Massai).

31 **Good Genius** guardian spirit or good angel.

32 **ends** purposes, aims.

34 **double lin'd** written in blood and tears (Massai).

35 **sadly** solemnly.

36–7 **Repentance, and a leaving of that life | I long have dyed in** cf. *CBS* 1187–8: 'Thus then the promise of al the worlds desire, | Beares life to die, then dies to life intire', and *GM* 212–22 (see note to *CBS* 1187–8).

37 **dyed** died spiritually. Cf. 1.1.58 and 68, where 'death' and 'life' seem to be used in the spiritual sense.

39 **behoofe** benefit, advantage.

42 **peace** calm, tranquility of mind.

49 **Barr'd of** barred from; cf. 5.5.24.

49 *My Guardian* i.e. Putana.

50 **Who** which (see Abbott 264).

50 **suspect** suspicion (*OED n.*₁ 1).

52 **beleeve** trust.

53 **then I can speak** 'than I have time to speak; than I have evidence for, thus suggesting premonition' (Massai).

59 **To** as far as, until.

5.2

2 **but** only.

3 **hornes** cuckolds were popularly said to 'wear the horns'. The notion may be traced to the fact that stags have their mates taken from them by other stags (Brewer; see quotation in 6 n.).

3 **riott in** revel, behave wantonly in the case of (or by means of). The sense, 'to take great delight or pleasure *in* something', is not recorded before 1741 (*OED* riot *v.* 1a, c, 2).

7 *A . . . Lord* cf. D'Avolos in *LS* 2.3.113–15: 'O Acteon! the goodliest-headed beast of the forest amongst wild cattle is a stag, and the goodliest beast among tame fools in a corporation is a cuckold'. In the present scene Vasques bears a strong resemblance to D'Avolos, who is himself a theatrical heir to Iago.

7 *beast* monster; proverbial (Dent, C876.2).

9 **great** various senses seem appropriate: 'full or swollen with anger, sorrow, pride or determination', and perhaps 'pregnant' (*OED* 3a, 4, 15c); cf. 5.4.21.

11 **decke** clothe.

16–17 **time . . . recal'd** proverbial (Tilley, T 332).

19 **States** persons representing the body politic, dignitaries; cf. 5.4.35.

25 **aspire** ardently desire (*OED v.* 4).

5.3

1 **Busie opinion** the meddlesome views of the many. As was common in this period, Ford often uses the term 'opinion' in a pejorative sense; cf. *GM* 350: 'Opinion', where Monsarrat cites Lipsius, stating that the ' "impure commixtion" of body and soul engenders opinion, "*Which is nought els but a vaine image and shadow of reason*: whose seat is the Sences: whose birth is the earth", and "INCONSTANCY is the companion of OPINION" (*Of Constancie*, 1.5 and 6, pp. 12 and 13)'; see also *CBS* 'To such as shall peruse this Booke' 10: '*the doubts of* folly, youth *and* opinion'.

1 **idle** ineffectual, trifling.

2 **Schoole-rod** a switch of twigs. In schools of this period 'the master hung up his rod where all the children could see it' (Campbell & Quinn, *s.v.* 'Education').

6 **In** 'with, on account of' (as again in the next line).

7 **this . . . sports** these merely conventional rules governing sexual relations. Roper compares 1.2.54 and 4.3.12.

8 **one** 'the same', perhaps with a suggestion of their continuing union.

9 **delicious** here Ford connects 'delicious' with sexual pleasure. In the post-classical ethical tradition *virtus* (virtue) was deemed to be antithetical to *voluptas* (pleasure) and its accompaniments, such as *deliciae*. See, e.g., Jonson's masque *Pleasure Reconciled to Virtue* (1618), where 'reconciled' means 'forgiven by', and Milton's *Comus* (1634).

10–11 **when . . . Virgine** when she was still a young virgin. Wiggins notes the quasi-legal language: due to the *priviledge* (legal right or prerogative) of youth, she is granted the title of virgin.

13 **Poaring booke-men** scholars poring over their books. Cf. *FM* 1135: 'pouring scholler'.

16 **Elyzeum** Elysium: in classical myth, 'the dwelling place of a few privileged mortals after death, where through the favour of the gods they lived for ever in blissful ease' (March). But Giovanni perverts it to the place for sexual pleasure.

17 **Jubile** the most immediate sense seems to be 'jubilation, exultant joy', 'occasion of rejoicing or celebration', or perhaps 'time of restitution or release' (*OED* 1b, 4, 5a). But the word has a strong religious resonance which Giovanni, so scornful of 'rellligion-masked sorceries' (31), is all too likely to profane.

18 **retyr'd** secluded, private.

18 **delights** sexual pleasure; cf. 38, 5.6.48.

19 **prompted** reminded me of; suggested, urged (*OED* *v*.1b, 3a).

26 **congeal'd Corrall** some early historians of geology thought that coral had been formed by a process of congelation.

28 **petty** minor; cf. *Perkin Warbeck* 3.4.71: 'a petty burgess of some town'.

28 **factor** agent, intermediary, perpetrator, or author. The word also denotes a mercantile agent, yielding another possible reading: 'pandar', a sense not recorded by *OED*, but see T. J. B. Spencer's note to *Broken Heart*, Revels edn., 2.1.10. Roper takes 'factor' to be a verb: 'act as agent' (*OED v.* 1a; *n.* 1, 4a).

30 **sear'd** dried up, withered away; made incapable of feeling, as by cauterization (*OED v.* 1, 3a, the latter entry quoting this passage). *OED* notes the allusion to 1 Timothy 4:1–2: 'Now the Spirit speaketh expressly, that in the latter times some shall depart from the faith, giving heed to seducing spirits, and doctrines of devils; Speaking lies in hypocrisy; having their conscience seared with a hot iron'.

31 **stoope** bow or humble yourself, yield obedience. In falconry, the hawk is said to 'stoop' or descend to the lure when it is being trained (*OED v.*[1] 1a, 2a, 6a).

31 **hand** handwriting.

34 *armèd* armoured.

35 **pox on** a curse on.

36 **lowe** base, ignoble.

37 **The Devill** expletive expressing astonishment or anger.

39 **Confusion** destruction.

39 **dotage** 'folly' or (in view of next line) 'senile nonsense'.

40 **peevish** senseless, spiteful. Also used as an epithet of mere dislike, hostility, etc.: 'hateful' (*OED* 2a, quoting this passage; 3, 4).

49 **more** further, what is more.

52 **misse** fail.

56 **gage** stake, wager (from 'engage').

57 **trayne** lure, entice.

59 **confounding** ruinous.

60 **blazing Starrs** comets, regarded as both ominous and dangerous in themselves. Cf. *Caesar* 2.2.30–1: 'When beggars die, there are no comets seen, | The heavens themselves blaze forth the death of princes'.

66–7 **backe . . . blowe** Morris compares *BH* 4.1.120ff, where Tecnicus, another wise counsellor, withdraws from the anticipated tragedy.

69 *Youngman* often written as one word (*OED* young man 1b), and 'probably stressed on the first syllable' (Roper).

72 **set up my rest** committed myself, staked all. In the card game Primero or Primiera, players 'set up their rest' when they decide to venture their stakes on the cards in their hand. The game originated in Italy.

73 **banefull** pernicious.

74–5 **Curse . . . prescription** probably referring to the biblical injunction (or 'prescription'): 'Cursed be he that lieth with his sister' (Deuteronomy 27:22; cf. Leviticus 20:17).

75 **rent** rend, tear.

75 **gall** bile, a bitter fluid secreted by the liver and stored in the gall bladder, supposed to produce asperity and rancor (cf. *OED n.*[1] 3a, b). In the following lines the sense shifts to another kind of gall: the abnormal growth produced on the oak (and other trees) by the presence of insect larvae, mites, etc. Oak-galls were commonly used in the making of ink. As Roper suggests, 'gall' may also (by synecdoche) mean 'ink'.

76 **inrolls** records (perhaps in a roll of honour).

77 **well-growne** perhaps 'fully grown' (cf. *OED* well *adv.* 12).

79 **splitts** split pieces, splinters.

5.4

1 Addressed to the banditti.

2 **undertake . . . parts** answer for them, guarantee that they will play their part.

2 **my Maisters** 'my masters': a complimentary title; cf. 'sirs'.

4 **praying** preying.

5 *Liguria* on the mountains of Liguria themselves. This region between Parma and Genoa in northwestern Italy, where the Maritime Alps meet the Appenines, was notorious for its banditry. See 2.2.74 n.

5 **pardons** line 10 suggests that the pardons may be for past crimes as well as for any yet to be committed (Roper).

8 **want** lack.

10 **Free** perhaps 'restored to civil rights and liberties' (*OED* 7, 1; Roper).

12 **Hold** wait!

12 **Vizard** mask.

14 **the watch-word** see 5.6.78.

18 **ends** purposes.

20 **edge** sharpen, whet.

21 **unready to** *OED* records no instance of 'unready' with 'to + noun' (*a.*[1], *Const. for*, †*of*, or *with*), its last quotation being from 1865; *to*: for, in regard to (see Abbott 186).

21–2 **great mind** passionate, noble, firm, or courageous spirit or attitude. Cf. 5.2.8: 'My thoughts are great'. Once again, Vasques' role is rather similar to that of D'Avolos in *LS* 4.1.88–94.

23 *Hippolita's* | **blood** cf. note to 1.1.31–2: 'links of blood', where 'blood' is associated with the seat of passion, courage, mettle, and a brave temperament.

28 **turne Italian** the popular view of Italy, encouraged by works such as Guiccardini's *Storia d'Italia* (1492–1534) and exploited by many English dramatists, was of a nation wedded to violence, intrigue, and revenge. Cf. Vasques' rejoice of superseding Italians in revenge at 5.6.150, Aruia's view of Italian husbands at *LT* 5.2.166–7: 'Italians use not dalliance | But execution'.

29–30 **sharpe . . . bitt** keen to taste his customary (or former) morsel. 'Bit' was also slang for a woman or girl (*OED n.*² 2, 4f; Lomax).

31 *Hot* 'lustful'; referring to the hare's fecundity.

31 **law** a start; 'an allowance in time or distance made to an animal that is to be hunted' (*OED n.*¹ 20).

33 **poast** post: hurry, speed.

33 **poast . . . damnation** similarly, Hamlet contemplates killing Claudius when he is 'about some act | That has no relish of salvation in 't', so that 'his soul may be as damned and black | As hell, whereto it goes' (*Hamlet* 3.3.91–4). Roper compares *White Devil* 5.1.72–4. For other contemporary parallels, see *Hamlet*, ed. Jenkins (2003), Longer Note, pp. 513–14.

37 **father** father-in-law, i.e. Florio.

39 **waite upon** accompany, escort while paying courteous service to.

42 **expect** wait for (*OED v.* 2).

43 **get** bring.

48 **grace** favour, kindness, honour.

49 **vouchsafe** Bawcutt glosses as 'deign to visit', but *OED* does not record this sense. The nearest recorded usage is 'vouchsafe *v.* 3b': 'To receive (a thing) graciously or condescendingly; to deign to accept' (citing *Timon of Athens* 1.1.156: 'Vouchsafe my labour, and long live your lordship!').

53 *Saint Peters Vicar* the Pope.

53 **in** through, in the person of.

53 **substitute** the Cardinal as the Nuncio of the Pope.

57 **neere** probably 'toward (our destination)' (*OED adv.*¹ & *prep.*¹ 1a). Schmidt (*s.v.* 'near', *adj. & adv.*) suggests that phrases such as 'draw near' (*The Tempest* 5.1.322) mean 'come in, enter'.

58 **Civill mirth** civic, communal (and well-mannered) merriment.

60 **keepe your way** continue on in that direction.

5.5

0.1 SD *Enter . . . bed* there is no certainty as to how this was staged in Ford's theatre. Perhaps the bed (with the players already in it) was thrust out onto the main stage, as required by stage directions in *A Chaste Maid in Cheapside* 3.2.0.1 and *A Woman Killed With Kindness* (see Van Fossen's Revels edn. of the latter play, 17.38.1 n). Alternatively, the bed may have been revealed by the opening of doors or curtains.

1 **chang'd** i.e. in her allegiance, but perhaps also referring to her clothing; cf. 'these gay attyres' (line 20 below).

2 **night-games** love-making.

3 **simplicity** innocence.

4 **the fitt** impulse, mood (as in 2.1.43).

6 **Calamity** distress (*OED* 1).

8 **revolt** desertion.

9 **else** otherwise, in other circumstances.

11 **stoope . . . bent-browes** literally, 'bow or yield before my frown'; give way in face of my stern displeasure.

11–13 **I . . . motion** Morris and others compare *1 Tamburlaine* 1.2.173–4: 'I hold the Fates bound fast in iron chains, | And with my hand turn Fortune's wheel about'; cf. 1.2.136 n.

14 **One thought more** a little more.

15 **honest** respectable, chaste.

17 **a dyning time** i.e. a short time, no longer than what it takes to eat dinner.

18 **Confusion** destruction.

19 **vayne** empty, superfluous, unwise.

20 **gay attyres** Soranzo ordered her to 'deck her selfe in her bridal Robes' at 5.2.10.

21 **solemne** reverential, ceremonious, grand.

22 **riott in expence** indulge in unrestrained and expensive revels.

24 **Barr'd of** barred from contact with; cf. 5.1.49.

25–6 **free'd . . . accesse** allowed to receive guests (Massai).

27 **harbinger** forerunner.

28 **resolve your selfe** be sure.

30 *Schoole-men* medieval scholastics—'the succession of writers, from about the 9th to the 14th century, who treat of logic, metaphysics, and theology as taught in the "schools" or universities of Italy, France, Germany, and England'—or those versed in such learning (*OED* schoolman 1, 2).

30–1 **all . . . minute** in God's judgement of the world, as witnessed by St. John, 'whosoever was not found written in the book of life was cast into the lake of fire' (Revelation 20:15).

32–3 **But . . . burne** 'and I saw a new heaven and a new earth,' writes St. John, 'for the first heaven and the first earth were passed away; and there was no more sea' (Revelation 21:1). This passage also puzzled St. Augustine, one of the greatest of the '*Schoole-men*' (30): 'But for that which follows, "There was no more sea," whether it imply that the sea should be dried up by that universal conflagration, or be transformed into a better essence, I cannot easily determine' (*City of God*, 20.16; cit. Roper).

36 **A dreame** cf. 5.3.19–20: 'The hell you oft have prompted, is nought else | But slavish and fond superstitious feare'.

40 **Prate** talk idly, prattle.

42 **good** a vocative: 'good man', 'good brother'. Cf. 'sweet', 'dear', etc.

42 **meane** intend (to do).

47 **repining** discontented.

53 **loose** lose.

54 **record** witness.

54 **spirits . . . Ayre** in his catalogue of incorporeal beings Robert Burton distinguishes between 'fiery spirits', 'water-devils' (or 'water-nymphs'), 'terrestrial devils', and 'aerial spirits or devils', which 'keep quarter most part in the air; cause many tempests, thunder and lightnings, tear oaks, fire steeples, strike men and beasts, make it rain stones, as in Livy's time, wool, frogs, etc . . . . These kind of devils are much delighted in sacrifices . . .' (Burton, *Anatomy* 1.2.1.2, cit. Roper).

62 **Destinies** the Fates of classical mythology. 'My fates have doom'd my death', laments Giovanni in 1.2.136 (see note).

62 **required againe** i.e. in death.

63–7 **Pray . . . Sister** cf. *Othello* 5.2.25–32: 'Have you prayed tonight, Desdemona? . . . | I would not kill thy unprepared spirit, | No, heavens forfend, I would not kill thy soul'.

64–5 **Go . . . Heaven** Neill, 'Strange Riddle', points out that Giovanni is seeking 'to dress the murder in the sainted trappings of a martyrdom' (p. 161).

64 **white in thy soule** 'Ford may have in mind the Neoplatonic doctrine that the soul is immaculate and cannot be defiled by the sins of the body' (Roper, comparing Spenser, *An Hymne in Honour of Beautie*, 159–61). The sentence echoes Winnifride's farewell to Frank in *The Witch of Edmonton* 5.3.93–4: 'now this Repentance makes thee | As white as innocence'.

66 **drift** intention.

70 *Civill use* civilized custom (Roper)

72–3 *That . . .* **abhor'd** the uncertainty here may derive from a shift in the meaning of 'rigour'. At first this seems to mean 'severity' (of the 'Lawes of *Conscience* and of *Civill use*', 70), but l. 73 requires a different sense: 'passionate extremity'. The latter meaning is not recorded by *OED*, though cf. *n.* 4, 'severity of weather, violence of storms', and *LT* 2.4.23: 'The rigour of an uncontrollèd passion' (noted by Roper). In the second reading, 'wipe' would mean 'take away something figured as a stain or defilement' (*OED* wipe *v* 2b, 6a, rigour 4, 5b).

75 constantly assuredly (*OED* 1b).

76–7 chide | With complain aloud against (*OED v.* 2b).

77 Cunning flattery artful and gratifying deception; 'referring to the youthful and healthy appearance of Annabella's hand, which is deceptive in the light of her impending death' (Massai).

79–80 Be . . . night as in an eclipse; cf. 5.6.20–1 n.

80 guilt gilt, golden.

81 will that will.

82 faigne feign: imagine, represent in fable (*OED v.* 3, 4).

82 *Stix* the Styx, the gloomy and pestilential river of the classical Underworld over which the shades of the departed were ferried by Charon.

84 fame (1) reputation; (2) renown.

84 kill thee in a kisse in 3.6.27–8 the Friar warns Annabella that she 'will wish, each kisse your brother gave, | Had beene a Daggers poynt'. Cf. also *Othello* 5.2.358–9: 'I kiss'd thee ere I kill'd thee. No way but this: | Killing myself, to die upon a kiss'.

86 *Revenge is mine* both an echo and an inversion of Paul's counsel: 'avenge not yourselves, but rather give place unto wrath: for it is written, Vengeance is mine; I will repay, saith the Lord' (Romans 12:19); and of Deuteronomy 32:35: 'To me belongth vengeance, and recompence'. As Sturgess notes, Giovanni was by no means the only Elizabethan stage revenger to make this impious declaration; cf. especially Hieronimo in *The Spanish Tragedy* 3.13.1: '*Vindicta mihi*'. Giovanni departs from God's injunction, and then moves to the pagan belief. 'Vengeance' and 'revenge' occur fifteen times in *TPW*. In 5.6.78 we learn that 'Vengeance' is the watchword that brings Giovanni death.

86 *Command* presumably 'rule, control, sway' (*OED n.* 3a).

87–8 When . . . for't cf. *Othello* 5.2.18–19: 'I will kill thee | And love thee after'.

90 stagger begin to doubt or waver (*OED v.* 2a).

90–1 this . . . in cf. 5.6.32: 'most glorious executioner', and 55: 'my triumph'.

93 unkind (1) cruel; (2) unnatural, lacking the kindliness expected of a kinsman (from OE *cynd(e)*, Germanic *kunjam*, 'kin'). Cf. Penthea's complaint to

Calantha in *BH* 3.5.105–6: 'this brother | Hath beene you know unkind, o most unkinde', and Spinella's appeal to Auria in *LT* 5.2.142: '*Auria*, unkind, unkind'.

94 *haplesse* luckless, unfortunate.

98 **In all her best** probably 'at her best, in her best condition'. Massai notes 'the highest point of Annabella's existence is here associated with her *Marriage-bed* (97), which defines her as wife and lover'.

100 **prevented** forestalled, thwarted (*OED* prevent *v*. 8); cf. 5.6.13.

100 **reaching** 'far-reaching': thus perhaps 'formidable', 'insinuating', 'cunning' (cf. *OED ppl.a.* 2a).

102 **pawn'd** 'given', 'forfeited', or 'pledged' (*OED* pawn *v*. 1).

103 **over-glorious** exceedingly beautiful, splendid beyond measure.

5.6

0.1–0.3 SD see 4.1.01 n.

3 **Course Confections** coarse or homely dishes (perhaps mock modesty). A confection was 'a prepared dish or delicacy', often a dessert (*OED n*. 5d).

3–5 **the use . . . in Cause** though the practice of holding such formal, ceremonious or regular entertainments has more to do with custom than any proper (or more pragmatic) purpose (*OED* set *ppl.a.* 2c, 5b; cause *n*. 3b). The distracted Soranzo may verge on incivility in suggesting that such entertainments are merely a matter of custom. In 5.4.56–7 the Cardinal had told him that 'wee come | To celebrate your Feast with Civil mirth, | As ancient custome teacheth'.

7 **wee** the Carinal uses the 'we' of an exalted personage, as at 3.9.31.

8.1 SD [A trope of 'Love's Cruelty' here becomes reality.] the heart on the dagger is the most telling image in the play, a reversal of current Petrarchan tropes of heart and an enacting of the 'Love's Cruelty'. According to Neill, 'the wounded heart' is invested 'with its traditional devotional significance. Carried by a saint, the heart was symbolic of love and piety; when pierced, it stood for "contrition and devotion under . . . extreme trial"' ('Strange Riddle', pp. 161–2). Giovanni intends for Annabella 'to fill a throne | Of innocence and sanctity in heaven' (5.5.64–5), thus trying to depict her as a martyr (e.g. St Teresa; see also Figure 3, in Neill, 'Strange Riddle', p. 153).

9 **trim'd** adorned, decorated.

9 **reeking** steaming.

10 **spoyle** (1) plunder; (2) destruction.

14 **forestall'd** prevented.

15 **amaz'd** 'alarmed, bewildered'.

15 **misgiving** fearful, apprehensive, seized by foreboding.

16 **idle sight** trifling or useless spectacle.

16 **bloodlesse** pale (*OED* 1b). Cf. *Venus and Adonis* 891: 'overcome by doubt and bloodless fear'.

18 *Rape* violent theft, violation.

20–1 **The Glory . . . Night** cf. Giovanni's speech 5.5.79–82, and Othello after he has smothered Desdemona: 'Methinks it should be now a huge eclipse | Of sun and moon, and that th'affrighted globe | Should yawn at alteration' (5.2.108–10).

22 **dainty fare** delicate foods.

24 **Stone** precious stone.

25 **ballanc't** weighed in the opposing scale; valued, estimated (*OED* balance *v.* 1, 2).

26 *A Heart my Lords,* . . . **intomb'd** a trope of 'Love's Cruelty'; cf. note to 1.2.202–3, and 2.6.10.

29 **startle** start, take fright (*OED v.* 3a).

30–1 **Daggers . . . wombe** in Roper's view, the effect of this metaphor 'is to make the murder seem a sadistic version of the sexual act', comparing *Antony and Cleopatra* 2.2.234–5: 'She made great Caesar lay his sword to bed. | He ploughed her, and she cropped'.

34 **times to come** cf. 'Ages that are yet unborn' at 5.1.7.

35 **as . . . revenge** Perhaps: 'I honoured my revenge by regarding it as my fate', where 'honoured' means 'conferred honour upon'.

37 **sonne** Roper points out that 'son' was commonly used for 'son-in-law'.

39 **throughly** thoroughly.

41 **frantick** raging, frenzied.

46 **Confounding** 'shaming, discomfiting' (*OED* confound *v.* 3).

47 **bewray'd** revealed.

48 **passage** interchange, 'exchange of confidences or amorous relations' (*OED* 14, 16).

50 **his . . . him** his madness makes him speak falsely (Roper).

55 **Triumphs** 'Giovanni reassearts the primacy of his claim over Annabella, thus defrauding Soranzo of his wife and of his *reaching plots* (5.5.100)' (Massai).

60 **Hold up** *Florio* addressed to Florio ('Bear up!') or urging others to support him.

62 **Broake . . . heart** cf. the death of Calantha in *BH* 5.3.62ff.

63 **venter** variant spelling of 'venture' (see *OED* venture) often used by Ford.

66 **guilt** 'smeared' but also 'gilded, adorned'. The spelling (common at this time; see *OED* gild *v*.1) points up a further likely meaning; cf. Annabella's 'depositions charectred in guilt', 5.1.10.

67 *Haplesse* luckless, ill-fated.

70 **twists** threads. In classical mythology the three Fates appointed the deaths of mortals. 'Clotho spun the thread of a man's life, Lachesis measured it out to its allotted length, and Atropos cut it off when the time for death was come' (March). Cf. *FM* 480–1, 'fate had weaven | The twist of life', *LS* 5.1.55: 'uncut thy twist of life', *FCN* 4.1.77–8: ''tis in my power to cut off | The twist thy life is spunne by'. Having previously identified himself with Tamburlaine, Giovanni now assumes the role of Atropos.

72 **royally** 'magnificently, as befitting a ruler'.

75 **have at you** 'I shall hit you', 'watch out!'

78 **fitt you anon** deal with or 'fix' you soon.

78 *Vengeance* this is evidently the Banditti's watchword, mentioned at 5.4.13–15.

83 **welcome** perhaps a mocking echo of Giovanni's bold 'Welcome', 79.

84 **shift for your selves** provide for your own interests (or safety).

89 *Blacke Devill* The Devil was proverbially black (Tilley B 217, B 297, D 255).

95 **your first man** i.e. your first opponent (cf. *OED* man *n*.¹ 6: 'a fighting man, a man-at-arms'). Vasques claims to have struck the first blow.

97 **But** only.

98 **Ar't** variant spelling of 'Art' 2nd pers. 'be'.

99 **the** variant spelling of thee (see *OED* and 2.2.7).

102 **cry to** call in supplication to (*OED v*. 2); cf. 1.1.72 n.

103 **look't for** 'hoped for', 'sought', or 'expected'.

106 **Freely** without constraint; readily.

115 *a Spaniard* Spaniards were said to be proud, cunning, and vengeful. Cf. 143–4 below, and *LS* 1.1.46–50.

121 **Of Counsell in** in the secret of (Roper).

122 **sometimes** sometime, formerly.

129 **reason** 'reasoning' or 'reasonableness'; or perhaps 'conclusion' (*OED n*.¹ 14, 17b).

130 **this . . . effects** most commentators take this to refer to Putana: the ensuing dialogue concerns the Cardinal's 'sentence', and that an 'example' is to be made of the woman in question (132–3).

141–2 **dispense . . . reason** probably 'grant a dispensation or relaxation of the strict letter of the law on the grounds of your motive rather than your actual offence'. 'Dispense' may have had doctrinal resonances for some in Ford's audience. Just before the murderous masque in *LS*, the Abbot grants 'an indulgence [favour, pardon] | Both large and general' (3.4.15–6). See *OED* dispense *v.* 4, 5, especially quotations in latter entry.

142 **reason** motive.

145–8 **Take . . . see them buried, | And . . . whatsoever, | Confiscate . . . Church, | Wee . . . proper use** for anti-papal diction, compare *CBS* 1603–4: 'the Anti-christian throne is now | Propt up with scarlet robes and triple crownes'. Descriptions of the Pope as Antichrist were a Protestant commonplace in the 16th and 17th centuries.

147 **Confiscate** appropriated, adjudged forfeited (*OED ppl.a.* 1).

148 **seize upon** seize, take possession of. The Cardinal resorts to legalese, but other meanings of 'seize' may appear relevant: 'clutch', 'fall on', 'take by force', 'take as plunder' (*OED* seize *v.* 2b, 5a, 6, 7a, 9).

148 **proper** personal, exclusive, appropriate (*OED adj.* 3b).

154 **at large** fully, in detail.

155 **strangely** unnaturally.

156 **Natures store** (the gifts of) nature's abundance

157 **'Tis . . . Whoore** Hopkins notes that 'despite the gross inappropriateness [of the Cardinal's] bald judgement on events . . . it is nevertheless his privilege to have not only the last but also the official word on the subject' (*Political*, p. 101), which reduces the shocking and unnatural transgression of incest and murder to a stereotyped verdict on an immoral woman.

K4ʳ

This apology for misprints, perhaps written by Ford, is appended to the text in some copies of the Quarto. Since it does not appear in all copies it must have been added at some point during the print-run. Roper notes that a similarly stilted apology for printing errors was added to *CBS* (1613), 'To such as shall peruse this Booke.'

2 **Presentment** theatrical presentation (*OED n.* 4b).

2–3 **faults, as are escaped** i.e. errors that have been overlooked.

3–5 **A common . . . Sence** we should be charitable enough to grant that a person knows how to spell who can be relied on not to misunderstand the meaning.

3 **charity** a disposition to judge leniently and hopefully; large-heartedness (*OED n.* 3a).

The Lover's Melancholy

Edited by TOM CAIN

DATE

In 1789 Edmond Malone noted that: 'Ford's play was exhibited at the Blackfriars on the 24th of November, 1628, when it was licensed for the stage, as appears from the Office-book of Sir Henry Herbert, Master of the Revels to King Charles the First, a manuscript now before me.'[1] It has been widely accepted that this was *The Lover's Melancholy*, and that Malone's assumption that the performance took place on the same date as the licence was issued was a reasonable one. If the date of August 1628, given under the section 'Burton and Melancholy', for publication of the third edition of the *Anatomy of Melancholy* is correct, then Ford is not likely to have started writing before that month.

CONTEXT AND SOURCES

On balance, the evidence marginally supports the view that this was the first play Ford wrote on his own. It was certainly the first he published as such, as he makes clear in the dedicatory epistle (ll. 16–18). It is possible that such plays as *The Queen*, *The Broken Heart*, *'Tis Pity She's a Whore*, and *Love's Sacrifice* were written earlier and published later,[2] but against this William Singleton's commendatory poem with its optative mood about 'what Ford *may* achieve in the theatre' implies the arrival of a new dramatist,[3] as does Humphrey Howorth's encouragement to 'Write but againe' (*To the Author, Master* John Ford, l. 14).

---

[1] Sir Henry Herbert, Revels Documents to 1642 in N. W. Bawcutt (ed.), *The Control and Censorship of Caroline Drama: The Records of Sir Henry Herbert, Master of the Revels 1623–73* (Oxford, 1996), p. 167. The office book is now lost. For Malone's summary, see *The Plays and Poems of William Shakespeare*, 10 vols. (London, 1790), 1:403.

[2] See e.g. *ODNB*; *JCS*, 3.448–51; Robert Davril, *Le Drame de John Ford* (Paris, 1954), pp. 68–72. Andrew Gurr, agrees that *The Lover''s Melancholy* was 'Ford's first Blackfriars play'; see 'Singing Through the Chatter: Ford and Contemporary Theatrical Fashion' in Neill (ed.), pp. 81–96., esp. p. 90.

[3] Cf. Hill, pp. 2–3.

Ford states in his prologue (as he often did in substance) that 'he doth not owe | To others Fancies, nor hath layne in wait | For any stolne Invention', and this is largely true of the plot of *The Lover's Melancholy*. He does, however, take the highly unusual step of acknowledging his indebtedness to two sources through marginal notes which refer the reader to his imitation of Famiano Strada's neo-Latin poem on a musical duel between a lutenist and a nightingale (1.1.106–9), and his use of Robert Burton's *Anatomy of Melancholy* (3.1.98–100). Of these, the debt to Burton is far the greatest.

Burton and Melancholy

Interest in melancholy had developed throughout the Renaissance period, spurred in part by Aristotle's question 'Why is it that all those men who have become extraordinary in philosophy, politics, poetry, or the arts are obviously melancholic?' (*Problems* XXX.1). The creative, 'genial' aspects of melancholy had been taken up by Ficino, and pictorially in Durer's *Melencolia I*.[4] But it also had a less fertile aspect in the form of mental disturbance shading into madness, and in the form of the deadly sin of despair, sometimes hard to distinguish from a properly remorseful conscience. Such symptoms as could be gathered under this wider heading of melancholy were explored in medical studies, largely from a humoral, Hippocratic, or Galenic approach, towards the end of the sixteenth century, notable publications in England being Timothy Bright's *Treatise of Melancholie* (1586) and the translation of André du Laurens's *Discourse . . . of Melancholike Diseases* (1599). All such studies were to be overshadowed by Robert Burton's great *Anatomy of Melancholy*, the first and shortest edition of which appeared in 1621, and which in its longer 1628 version decisively shaped the treatment of melancholy in Ford's play.

By 1600 the issue flagged in Ford's title, love melancholy, was embedded more in dramatic, poetic, and pictorial discourse than medical, something Burton was to change in his long discussion under the title 'Love-Melancholy' in the 'Third Partition' of the *Anatomy*.[5] In

---

[4] Marsilio Ficino, *De Vita Libri Tres* (1482–9), Book I; Ficino is cited many times by Burton, who also describes Durer's 'Melancholy' as possibly half-mad, 'yet of a deep reach, excellent apprehension, judicious, wise, and witty' (1.3.1.2).

[5] Ford shows no sign of having read Jacques Ferrand's apposite (but still Galenic) *Traicte de l'essence et guerison de l'amour ou de la melancholie erotique* (Toulouse, 1610). He would not have been alerted to it by Burton, who says this 'book came first to my hands after the third [1628] edition' of the *Anatomy*, by which time his pioneering account of love melancholy had been written. Burton's was the 1623 edition of Ferrand (Nicolas K. Kiessling, *The Library of Robert Burton*, Oxford Bibliographical Society (Oxford, 1988), no. 566).

England the tradition went back to Chaucer, who had described the very specific symptoms of hopeless love over two centuries earlier when Arcite 'seen his lady shal he nevere mo':

> His slep, his mete, his drynke, is hym biraft,
> That lene he wex and drye as is a shaft;
> His eyen holwe, and grisly to biholde,
> His hewe falow and pale as asshen colde,
> And solitarie he was and evere allone,
> And waillynge al the nyght, makynge his mone.[6]

Ford's contemporaries would still have recognized this description. So definitive did it remain that Burton quoted these lines under 'Symptoms or signs of Love-Melancholy' (*Anatomy* 3.2.3.1). He also, more confusingly, took over Chaucer's subsequent reference to 'the loveris maladye | Of hereos' (ll. 1373–4), assuming that *hereos* derived from 'hero', when it was in fact a variant spelling of *eros*—in this context, physical desire. This understandably mistaken derivation explains why Burton's category of 'Heroical Melancholy' is anything but heroic, and 'deserves much rather to be called burning lust' (*Anatomy* 3.2.1.2). Following the same tradition, Ford named Palador's father, whose 'burning lust' for Eroclea is the cause of all the problems, 'Agenor'—in Greek, 'heroic', but with connotations of lust and arrogance.[7]

By the 1590s love melancholy, and the more recently arrived melancholy of the malcontent, had become modish forms of adopted identity in England.[8] The malcontent's best known representative is Jacques in *As You Like It*, who 'can suck melancholy out of a song, as a weasel sucks eggs' (2.5.12–13), but who also delights at the prospect of speaking his mind (2.7.47–87). The latter aspect of the type is adopted by the plain-speaking Rhetias, especially in the earlier scenes of *The Lover's Melancholy*, where he defines himself as the 'Anticke' who will 'snarle at the vices | Which rot the Land' (1.2.11–12). This figure emerges in a more extreme form in Meleander's rantings against the world. Corax too, with his rejection of the Court, shows some of the melancholy malcontent's symptoms. The melancholic lover—Palador in the play, and to a lesser extent Menaphon and Amethus—is seen most strikingly

---

[6] Geoffrey Chaucer, *Poetical Works*, ed. F. N. Robinson (Oxford, 1933), 'The Knight's Tale', 1361–6.

[7] For 'hereos/eros' see John Livingstone Lowes, 'The Loveres Maladye of Heroes', *MP* 11 (1914), 491–546, and Roger Boase, *The Origin and Meaning of Courtly Love: A Critical Study of European Scholarship* (Manchester, 1977), pp. 132–3. For '*agenor*' see e.g. Homer, *Odyssey* 1.106, used of the arrogant, lustful suitors.

[8] For the fashionable malcontent see Lawrence Babb, *The Elizabethan Malady: A Study of Melancholia in English Literature from 1580 to 1642* (East Lansing, MI, 1951), pp. 73–101.

in the fine 1590s portrait of Donne with broad hat, dishevelled clothes
and folded arms, with the blasphemous inscription which translates as
'Lighten our darkness O Lady'. This characterization is paralleled in
William Heminges's verbal picture of Ford himself:

> Deepe In a dumpe Jacke forde alone was gott
> Wth folded Armes and Melancholye hatt.[9]

Aspects of both malcontent and lover are commingled—along with
much else—in Hamlet, who has 'something in his soul | O'er which
his melancholy sits on brood' (3.1.164–5), and who accosts Ophelia
with his clothes in disorder (though specifically lacking the near-
obligatory hat) and 'with a look so piteous in purport | As if he had
been loosed out of hell' (2.1.75–80). The Folio stage direction '*Enter
Hamlet, reading on a book*' (2.2.167.1) is echoed by Ford: '*Enter* PALADOR,
the Prince, with a Booke in his hand' (2.1.48.2). Such absorption in
reading, and a concomitant lack of engagement with the world, signifies melancholy. 'Look where sadly the poor wretch comes reading',
says Gertrude, while Corax complains less sympathetically at Palador's
neglect of the regime of exercise he has prescribed (2.1.50–6). Jonson's
Lovell in *The New Inn*, first performed by the King's Men at the
Blackfriars only months after *The Lover's Melancholy*, is another suf-
ferer, who mentions—significantly for *The Lover's Melancholy*, where it
is also an issue—loss of memory as a symptom:

> O my brain
> How art thou turned, and my blood congealed,
> My sinews slackened, and my marrow melted,
> That I remember not where I have been,
> Or what I am? (4.4.256–60)

Chaucer also acknowledged the more generalized condition engendered by the 'humour malencolik' from which Hamlet in particular
suffers. Arcite's is 'Nat oonly lik the loveris maladye . . . but rather lyk
manye, | Engendred of humour malencolik' (ll. 1373–5). Like Meleander,
Pericles, and Lear, Arcite has objective reasons for his condition, but
for the medieval and early modern reader such melancholy was not
simply a depressive interiority, with or without an external cause. The
concept of purely mental illness was a much later one. While melan-

---

[9] *Elegy on Randolph's Finger c.*1630–2, ed. G. C. Moore Smith (Oxford, 1923), p. 24. As has
often been pointed out, this may be no more than an allusion to the recent performance and
publication of *The Lover's Melancholy*. Donne's portrait can be seen at http://www.npg.org.uk/
collections/search/portraitLarge/mw111844/John-Donne (accessed 21 Feb. 2023).

choly could have its origins in emotional disturbance, such as rejected love or grief at the death of loved ones, its manifestation, and frequently its entire origin, was always physical, most often in an imbalance of the humours, specifically a preponderance of black bile (cf. '*To the Author, Master* John Ford', l. 1, and note; note to 1.2.137–8). This could cause depressive emotions and demeanour, including such outlandish behaviour as lycanthropy (3.3.20–5), which might have no external cause. This Hippocratic psychology was as much a physiological one as those which in modern times explain depression by the malfunction of neurotransmitters or the immune system, one crucial difference being that the earlier version was wrong in every respect, leading to a certain amount of self-contradiction among theorists and ineffectiveness among practitioners. Neither Ford nor Shakespeare seem to have been wholly convinced by such orthodox Hippocratic/Galenic explanations. Though they never reject them, they never seriously invoke the humours to explain the psychological state or motivation of disturbed characters. Romeo's 'black and portentous' humour (*Romeo and Juliet* 1.1.141) is more a lover's mood than itself a source of melancholy. Elsewhere Shakespeare mocks the term 'humour' through Nym's mindless use of it in *Henry V* and *Merry Wives*, and he only associates 'sable-coloured melancholy' with 'the black-oppressing humour' in Armado's affected, foolish letter in *Love's Labour's Lost* (1.1.231–3).[10] In *The Lover's Melancholy*, although Corax is praised as one whose 'skill can best discerne the humours | That are predominant' (3.1.97–8), this comes from Aretus, who articulates popular views of melancholy that Corax immediately rejects, specifically invoking the psychological aspects of melancholy: '*Melancholy* | Is not as you conceive, indisposition | Of body, but the mindes disease' (3.1.102–4).

Ford's note acknowledging his source in Burton is placed against this speech, which is derived directly from the *Anatomy*. As it suggests, Burton went beyond many earlier writers in often treating melancholy as in effect a mental illness. Though he accepted the theory of the humours (*Anatomy* 1.1.1.2), and believed that 'the Body workes upon the Mind, by his bad humors, disturbing the Spirits, sending grosse fumes into the Braine; and so *per consequens* disturbing the Soule,' (*Anatomy* 1.2.3.1), he also argued that 'on the other side, the Minde most effectually workes upon the Body, producing by his

---

[10] 'Choler' is for both writers similarly usually synonymous with simple rage or anger rather than a cause of disease, though both Hamlet and Richard II do speak figuratively of purging it (*Hamlet*, 3.2.304–7, *Richard II*, 1.1.153). It is hard to see Hamlet's occasional references to his 'complexion' or 'disposition' as strong evidence for Galenism.

passions and perturbations, miraculous alterations, as Melancholy, Despaire . . .' (ibid.). Melancholy was one of the diseases 'that pertain to the substance of the brain' which 'properly belong to the *Phantasie*, or *Imagination*, or *Reason* it selfe, which [Andreas] *Laurentius* calles the Diseases of the Minde' (*Anatomy* 1.1.1.3). Following Seneca, Burton advocated a form of 'talking cure': 'the best way for ease is to impart our misery to some friend, not to smother it up in our own breast' (2.2.6.1), a view Aurelio puts forward eloquently in *The Lady's Trial*:

> a friend
> Upon whose faith, and confidence, we may
> Vent with security, our griefe becomes
> Oft times the best Physition . . . (1.3)

Such views are intermingled by Burton with more orthodox ones, depending on his sources. His approach is syncretic, and the *Anatomy* is a huge compendium of various views and theories interspersed with Burton's own comments and interpretations, all held together by his compelling voice and intellect. As such Ford was able to take from it whatever pertained to the psychological symptoms and treatment, behaviour and speech, of his central characters. Burton's great book resonates throughout the play, and the unusual step of providing a marginal note indicates that Ford sought to invoke his authority for the psychologies he depicts. His own profound insights are usually based on Burton, and there are over eighty references in the commentary in this edition to passages from the *Anatomy* which shaped Ford's discourse, often in very direct ways. Given the sheer size of Burton's text, it is probable that I have missed many more.[11]

The edition Ford used was the new 1628 one which Burton probably published in August, only three to four months before the play was performed: 'Mense Augusto 1628' is written in his hand on the flyleaf of a copy he presented to his old college, Brasenose, presumably soon after publication.[12] The *Anatomy* had first appeared in 1621, and Burton continued to add and revise substantially through subsequent editions. Of these, the 1628 one contained the most important additions, including the famous engraved title page.[13] Detailed evidence for

---

[11] Herrick also mined the *Anatomy* for ideas, the recent Commentary to *Hesperides* listing 'over one hundred probable or possible echoes'; see *The Complete Poetry of Robert Herrick*, eds. Tom Cain and Ruth Connolly (Oxford, 2013), 2:507.

[12] Now Latham Room: UB/S III 72; the month appears in one of the two 'ex dono' inscriptions in this copy; the other, also in Burton's hand, simply gives the year. See also Kiessling, *Library*, no. 261. The copy in Lincoln College also has an ex dono inscription by Burton dated 1628.

[13] The 1989–2000 Oxford edition edited by Thomas C. Faulkner, Nicolas K. Kiessling, Rhonda L. Blair, J. B. Bamborough, and Martin Dodsworth (6 vols) bases its text on the 1632

Ford's use of this new edition is given in the Commentary notes, but a crucial example is found in Thamasta's speech at 3.2.77–87, which can only have come from the 1628 edition, in which Burton added to the examples of 'Sympathy' between 'animate, & inanimate cretures' the question 'How comes a loadstone to draw iron to it' (3.1.1.2). The close correspondence between several such passages as these and Ford's text (see e.g. all of 3.1.102–112) indicate that this was not a matter of reading and remembering; more likely it was a matter of referring back while he was writing to specific passages in his new copy of the *Anatomy* and incorporating them into his play.[14]

In view of this it is surprising that *The Lover's Melancholy* never reads like a simplistic dramatization of Burton, nor does it seem to have the kind of didactic designs on the audience that Jonson, Shaw, or Brecht sometimes do, even when the latter are less dependent on a single source. Ford does not write as a propagandist for any particular Burtonian approach or ideology, if only because Burton does not have one. When he follows the *Anatomy* closely, as in Thamasta's speech on Sympathy, or the Mask of Melancholy, Ford integrates contemporary theory with the dramatic predicament of his characters or the requirements of his plot. In the case of Corax, whose theory and practice are much better informed than Babb's 'rather hazy Burtonian lore' (p. 115) allowed, he transfers Burton's authority to the doctor, a process underlined by the marginal note. Burton's encyclopaedic variety, his scattered insights and digressions, are transformed into what is at best a focused poetic treatment of melancholy, whether Palador's poignant expression of a memory of lost love (4.3.29–30) or Meleander's angry railing at worldly vanity (2.2.83–97).

Strada

The imitation of Strada's *Sixth Prolusion* is put to very different uses.[15] It is a semi-detached introductory episode which sets the

edition. G. F. Sensabaugh, 'Burton's Influence on Ford's *The Lover's Melancholy*', *SP* 36 (1933), 545–71, Babb, and Ewing Jr., *Burtonian Melancholy in the Plays of John Ford* (Princeton, NJ, 1940). used Shilleto's 1893 edition, which was based on the posthumous one of 1651. Hill used the eccentric Dell and Jordan-Smith edition, also based on 1651. The searchable EEBO text of the *Anatomy* is unhelpfully based on the first, 1621 edition; the searchable Gutenberg one on a Victorian reprint of 1651, and a searchable photographic copy on Google Books is of the 1638 edition.

[14] Cf. Sensabaugh, 'Burton's Influence on Ford's *The Lover's Melancholy*', p. 559: 'all this evidence seems to indicate that Ford had directly before him *The Anatomy of Melancholy* when he wrote *The Lover's Melancholy*.'

[15] It is worth noting that Burton owned a copy of the Cologne 1619 edition of Strada, now in Christ Church College Library, though this poem is not marked (Kiessling, *Library of Robert Burton*, no. 1540). Burton's copy of *The Lover's Melancholy*, unannotated, is now Bodl. 4° T36(6)

emotional tone for the whole play. Menaphon's story is located in the melancholy 'silent Groves, | And solitarie Walkes' of Tempe (1.1.105–6), and Amethus's response, 'Thou hast discourst | A truth of mirth and pitie' (1.1.162–3), underlines how close Menaphon's circumscribed 'discourse' is to Ford's overall tragicomic one. The 'mirth' ('gratification; joy, happiness'; *OED*, †1.a) lies in the emphasis on Eroclea–Parthenophill's beauty, on the harmony and yet discord of the duel itself, and in the discovery in nature of a skill so close to the human. The 'pitie' is not just in the poignant death of the nightingale from a broken heart, but in the 'quaintest sadnesse' Menaphon identifies in Parthenophill's grief. The duel draws attention to the often painful struggle between art and nature (1.1.109–11), and to the relationship of beauty and harmony with the concept of 'Concord in discord, lines of diffring method | Meeting in one full Center of delight' (1.1.142–3) which could almost be taken as a summary of the play's emotional trajectory.[16] Ford shortens Strada's rather prolix poem and integrates it into the play by changing it from a straightforward narrative through Amethus's occasional responses and more importantly by making both Menaphon himself and the woodland birds respond to the contest with strong feeling. The result is a small drama within a drama, in which Menaphon is a participant. The duet he overhears in the 'paradise' of Tempe was 'The sweetest and most ravishing contention, | That Art or Nature ever were at strife in' (1.1.108–9). He tells Amethus how it entranced his soul and he 'stole neerer | Invited by the melody' and saw the 'fairefac'd Youth' (113–15). The same was true of 'the cleare *Quiristers* of the Woods, the Birds' with whom he identifies: 'as they flockt about him, all stood silent, | Wondring at what they heard. I wondred too' (118–20). When the nightingale dies of a broken heart, both Parthenophill and the watching Menaphon respond with grief. The interaction of a witness, the broken heart and the grief, and the idea that this is a contest between Art and Nature are all significant additions by Ford, as are Parthenophill's attempt to break 'his' lute, and Menaphon's hasty intervention.

Art. There is no sign that Ford knew the other popular treatment of the nightingale's duel, from Marino's *Adone*, Canto 7, octaves 32–56 (first published in a musical setting, 1615).

[16] '*Concordia discors*' is Horace's phrase, referring to the paradoxical harmony that comes from the strife between the warring elements (*Epistles* I.12.19).

Other Sources

These are acknowledged 'sources' which Ford may have wanted his audience to recognize in the theatre as much as in the printed quarto, but despite the originality of its plot, there are a number of other texts which bear a contingent relationship to *The Lover's Melancholy*. Of these, Daniel's masque *Hymen's Triumph* is nearest in terms of similarity of plot and characters.[17] It was performed before Queen Anne at Somerset (then Denmark) House in 1615. Whether Ford saw it there, or simply read it, cannot be established, but it is worth noting that he was very probably one of Daniel's circle.[18] In *Hymen's Triumph* Silvia has returned, like Eroclea, from two years' absence from her country and from her lover, Thyrsis, who, like Palador has languished from love melancholy ever since she disappeared, believed dead. He has kept 'holy reliques' of Silvia, rather as Palador keeps Eroclea's miniature, and he sounds very like Palador when he insists the two years have not changed his feelings: 'thinke you any length | Of time can ever have a powre to make | A heart of flesh not mourne, not grieve, not pine?'. Like Palador he is suspicious of any relaxation of his melancholic state: 'Comfort and I have beene | So long time strangers, as that now I feare | To let it in.' Silvia comes back disguised as a young man, Clarindo, and like Eroclea she does not at once make her identity known. This makes possible a scene in which the shepherdess Phillis tries to seduce 'Clarindo' just as Thamasta does 'Parthenophill', an episode witnessed by Phillis's jealous lover Montanus, 'closely busht a pretty distance off', who in this respect parallels Menaphon. Still in the guise of Clarindo, Silvia tells Thyrsis a 'story' which is in fact that of her own abduction on a ship and subsequent escape, just as Rhetias tells Palador a shorter story of the 'pretty accident' which is the truth of Eroclea's ship-born escape and exile.

Although *The Lover's Melancholy* is less static and formal than *Hymen's Triumph*, its obvious indebtedness to Daniel's masque may be one reason why, as Oliver says, it is 'not as dramatic as [Ford's] later works; with its steady succession of set scenes, it retains something of a masque technique and, particularly, tone'.[19] There are other reasons, as will be seen, for the static and set-piece structure, but there is no doubt that

---

[17] Though it is certainly not 'adapted from' or simply 'from' Daniel, as such descriptions as the English Short Title Catalogue or the Library of Congress Catalog say; the similarity was first noticed by S. P. Sherman, *Forde's Contribution to the Decadence of the Drama*, in W. Bang (ed.), *Materialien zur Kunde des älteren Englischen Dramas*, Bd. 23, NS 1, 23 (1908), p. ix.

[18] See Hopkins, *Political*, p. 12.

[19] Oliver, p. 49.

Hymen's Triumph helped shape *The Lover's Melancholy* a good deal more than another play that has been advanced as an influence, Beaumont and Fletcher's *Philaster*, first performed at the Globe in 1609, but still in the King's Mens' repertory in 1630.[20] Arthur C. Kirsch considerably overstated the case when—arguing that in general Ford was heavily reliant on Beaumont and Fletcher—he wrote that 'Many of the resemblances are very specific. Parthenophill-Eroclea, the breeches-part in *The Lover's Melancholy*, frequently acts like Bellario-Euphrasia in *Philaster*, and is placed in comparable predicaments.'[21] Dorothy M. Farr, from a less hostile angle, was still wider of the mark when she claimed that *Philaster* 'provided the framework of the main plot' of *The Lover's Melancholy*. More recently, Michael Shapiro approached the play as a revision of *Philaster*.[22] Except that both plays contain a young woman disguised as a youth, something they have in common with seventy-nine other surviving plays of the period,[23] there is relatively little over-lap. Euphrasia only reveals her identity under duress at the end of the play, whereas Eroclea identifies herself to Thamasta in Act 3, and to a suspicious Palador in Act 4. Well before that, however, Ford has hinted strongly at her identity through Rhetias's story (2.1.191–206). Farr and Davril both state, with surprising incorrectness, that 'like Bellario [Eroclea] is appointed as a page at court': in fact as Parthenophill, she is simply Menaphon's 'friend', and as such is presented at court by Thamasta (2.1.244–6) with no suggestion that 'he' is anything but an interesting and very handsome visitor.[24] Bellario's unwillingness to leave Philaster, her decision to follow him in disguise, her selfless agree-ment to act as a page to the woman he loves, the slander against her by Megra, and her father's relative lack of interest in her two-year absence have no parallels in *The Lover's Melancholy*. Nor does the way in which the other lines of Beaumont's and Fletcher's plot develop with Philaster's jealousy of Bellario and Arethusa, the slightly absurd (if pop-ular) hunting episode in Act 4, and the rebellion which sends the Spanish prince packing. Only one episode in *Philaster* finds a credible echo in *The Lover's Melancholy*: this is Philaster's description of his first

---

[20] Andrew Gurr, *The Shakespeare Company, 1594–1642* (Cambridge, 2004), p. 12.

[21] Kirsch, *Jacobean Dramatic Perspectives* (Charlottesville, VA, 1972), p. 114.

[22] Dorothy M. Farr, *John Ford and the Jacobean Theatre* (New York, 1979), p. 16. Michael Shapiro, 'Revising *Philaster*: Ford's *The Lovers's Melancholy*', in his *Gender in Play on the Shakespearean Stage* (Ann Arbor, 1996), p. 195.

[23] See Shapiro, *Gender in Play*, pp. 8, 221–3.

[24] Farr, *John Ford*, p. 17; Davril, *Le Drame de John Ford*, p. 152. Ewing varies the error by mak-ing Eroclea–Parthenophill 'enter the service of Thamasta' as a page (p. 32). Shapiro (who calls Thamasta 'Thomasta' throughout) also calls Eroclea a page (*Gender in Play*, pp. 195–7).

meeting with 'Bellario', a passage which is very like that in which Menaphon describes his encounter with Parthenophill and which opens in a similar picturesque setting:

> I found him, sitting by a fountaines side,
> Of which he borrowed some to quench his thirst,
> And paid the Nymph again as much in teares;
> A Garland lay by him, made by himselfe,
> Of many severall flowers, bred in the bay,
> Stucke in that misticke order, that the rarenesse
> Delighted me. (1.2.114–20)

Although Ford based his longer account on Strada's poem, the concept of a mood-establishing poem within a play may well have been suggested by this 'mannerist elaboration'.[25]

As this passage shows, *Philaster* has its share of tears wept for love, but melancholy is not an issue central to the play. Elsewhere Fletcher and his collaborators were drawn to melancholy in a way which indicates its currency as a condition to whose manifestations audiences would respond. Their treatment is, however, markedly different from Ford's, in that what are displayed are morbid and extreme states. One sufferer is Memnon in *The Mad Lover* (*c.*1616), an old general who, having managed to avoid women for most of his life, suffers a *coup de foudre* of such enormity that when rejected he proposes to offer his lady his heart, literally. Although this anticipates, and may even have suggested, Giovanni's entrance with his sister's heart in *'Tis Pity She's a Whore*, Memnon is prevented from carrying out his purpose, and all ends well. In *The Nice Valour or The Passionate Madman* (?1615–16), the incomplete subplot shows another extreme case of a 'passionate Lord' who is 'so lost in the wild rage of passion, that he's sensible | Of nought but what torments him' (1.1.48–50). In *A Wife for a Month* (1624) Alphonso suffers a 'sad and silent melancholly, | Laden with griefes and thoughts, no man knows why' (1.2.27–8). Like Pericles, he has not spoken for three months, but he is improbably cured by a failed attempt at poisoning. Both the condition and the cure are extreme, and as in the other plays mentioned, interest is in the contrived dramatic (or melodramatic) potential of madness to arouse the audience, not, as in Ford, in the psychology of the melancholy or the processes of its cure.

---

[25] The phrase is John Greenwood's, *Shifting Perspectives and the Stylish Style* (Toronto, 1988), p. 109; for the full passage, see *Dramatic Works in the Beaumont and Fletcher Canon*, ed. Bowers, I: 414–15 (Cambridge, 1966). Subsequent references are to this edition.

Shakespeare

Though Fletcherian tragedy and tragicomedy had dominated the stage for two decades when Ford came to write *The Lover's Melancholy*, the King's Men's earlier resident dramatist had a much more profound influence on him than Fletcher. *King Lear* and *Pericles* are both strong presences, and the melancholy figure of Prince Hamlet is in evidence behind Prince Palador. But *The Lover's Melancholy* also looks back to *Twelfth Night* (as does *Philaster*). The two princes, Orsino and Palador, are both absorbed by love melancholy, and both enter for the first time to the accompaniment of appropriate music; but a more striking similarity between the two plays lies in the gender confusion which leads to a proud woman, who continues to reject her well-qualified suitor, being humbled by a precipitate infatuation with a hitherto unknown youth who is, in fact, a young woman in disguise. Olivia's words 'Fate, show thy force: ourselves we do not owe; | What is decreed must be; and be this so' (1.5.310–11) anticipate Thamasta's acquiescent ''Tis a Fate | That over-rules our wisdomes; whil'st we strive | To live most free, wee'r caught in our owne toyles' (1.3.94–6) and her later, despairing, 'in all actions, Nature yeelds to Fate' (3.2.93).

Though Eroclea has not, like Viola–Cesario, been sent to plead the rejected lover's case, she ends up doing so with 'a mooving eloquence' (3.2.134) which, like that of Viola, has the unintended consequence of encouraging her hearer's misplaced affections.[26] Viola and Eroclea are alike in that, unlike Portia or Rosalind, they are relatively passive, vulnerable figures, a quality they share with Imogen once she adopts her male disguise as Fidele in *Cymbeline*: though all display moral courage, strength of character, and a willingness to sacrifice themselves to their respective melancholy lovers, none use their disguise to gain power in the masculine world, and none set out to shape the plots within which they function. There is also a minor symmetry, shared with *Pericles*, between the ways in which the disguised girls' identities are established. Sebastian questions his sister: 'What countryman? What name? What parentage?' (5.1.231); Pericles, at greater length, asks for Marina's 'country', 'parentage', and 'name' (*Pericles*, 5.1.102–40). Palador seeks to confirm Eroclea's identity with the same sequence: 'Tell me thy Countrey. . . . thy Father . . . Hast a name? (4.3.103–4).[27] Thamasta's psychologically interesting response when she recognizes,

---

[26] Some of these parallels are noted by Hill, p. 9.

[27] The recognition scene between Bellario and her father in *Philaster* follows the same sequence (5.5.111–12).

but cannot immediately accept, that Eroclea is 'not mankind' is to say that 'I shall a while repute thee still the youth | I lov'd so dearely' (3.2.179–80), and this may have been a development of Orsino's 'Cesario . . . | For so you shall be while you are a man' (5.1.385–6).[28] Finally, there is a different kind of echo of *Twelfth Night* in Grilla's description of Cuculus, 'As rare an old Youth as ever walkt crossegartered' (3.1.2). Hill says, 'Cuculus bears no resemblance to Malvolio', but there can be no mistaking the reference, and both are comic lovers made fools by those around them.[29]

If *Twelfth Night* is a significant presence behind *The Lover's Melancholy*, Shakespeare's late plays involving the restorative return of lost daughters are still more so; but the play to which *The Lover's Melancholy* is most obviously indebted is the slightly earlier *King Lear*. The theme of the redemptive daughter in Shakespeare's late plays grows from Cordelia's role in *Lear*. In *The Lover's Melancholy* that role is divided between Meleander's two daughters. Although the attempted rape of Eroclea and her presumed death have caused Meleander's madness, and her return consolidates his recovery, it is Cleophila who has cared for him in his deranged grief, and it is she who is seen cooperating with Corax to begin his cure, preparing the cup containing a sleeping draught (4.2.166). This not only brings him much-needed rest, but under its influence he is barbered and dressed in clean 'habit and gowne' and brought onstage in a couch, to 'Soft Musicke' (5.1.11–16, 5.2.0.1–2). It was a commonplace that sound sleep was an efficacious treatment for melancholy, 'the chiefest thing in all Physick' (*Anatomy* 2.2.5, 2.5.1.6), but this episode was very probably suggested by that in *King Lear* in which Cordelia asks the doctor 'What can man's wisdom | In the restoring his bereaved sense?' and is told 'There is means, madam | Our foster-nurse of nature is repose, | The which he lacks; that to provoke in him | Are many simples operative, whose power | Will close the eye of anguish' (4.4.8–9, 11–15). Like Meleander, Lear is given such a 'simple', and like him is dressed in 'fresh garments' while asleep (4.7.20–1), and carried onstage 'in a chair' (the Folio stage direction), to the sound of music (4.7.23.1). When Lear awakes he asks 'Where am I? Fair daylight?' (4.7.51), words which announce

[28] Philaster makes a similar remark to Euphrasia–Bellario, probably also derived from *Twelfth Night* (5.5.145–6).

[29] Hill, p. 9; the echo is made all the more likely by the fact that full text EEBO gives only two more uses of 'cross garter' in the period 1473–1629, in Field's *A Woman is a Weather-cocke* (1612), and Thomas Powell's *Wheresoever you see mee, trust unto your selfe* (1623). The point may have been that John Shanks played both Malvolio and Cuculus.

and celebrate his recovery; just so, Meleander asks, 'Where am I? 'Tis day sure' (5.2.11). He, like Lear, has been mired in the dark night of grief. Lear then attempts to kneel to Cordelia, who tells him 'you must not' (4.7.58); in the same way, Meleander starts to kneel, not to his daughter, but to Palador, who says 'Ye shall not' (5.2.208). Lear's 'Pray, do not mock me. | I am a very foolish fond old man' (4.7.58–9) is unmistakeably echoed by Meleander: 'alas, why do you mocke me? | I am a weake old man' (5.2.233–4); and Ford actually quotes Lear's request 'Lend me a looking-glass' word for word, albeit for a different purpose (*Lear* 5.3.262; *Lover's Melancholy* 5.2.203). There is also a jumbled, presumably unconscious, recollection of Gloster's blinding and attempted suicide in the elaborate metaphor Ford employs when Meleander prays to 'keepe me waking till the Cliffes | That over-hang my sight fall off, and leave | These hollow spaces to be cram'd with dust' (5.2.88–90).

These overt echoes now seem much more *hommage* to *Lear* than a challenge to comparison, but the allusions have the inevitable effect of diminishing these episodes in Ford's final acts by contrast to their harrowing equivalents in Shakespeare's play. This is less true of the other play of his that most influenced Ford, *Pericles*. Like *Lear* and *The Lover's Melancholy*, *Pericles* involves the cure of a grief-crazed father by his daughter, this time without the aid of a doctor, the latter's contribution nevertheless made in the resurrection and presentation of Thaisa.[30] Pericles's predicament is closer to Meleander's than to Lear's, in that Lear never believes Cordelia is dead until the very end, when, of course, he is right. His madness comes from betrayal by his other daughters, not from grief at their reputed loss. The cure of that madness brings brief optimism which makes the tragic conclusion all the more terrible, whereas the tragicomic structure of *Pericles* and *The Lover's Melancholy* means that the process of cure is consolidated, as it were, by their plots, as the potentially tragic actions mutate into their comic resolutions.

Pericles shares characteristics of both Meleander and Palador. Like Meleander, he reacts to the news of his daughter's death by swearing 'Never to wash his face, nor cut his hairs' again (4.4.27–8). For three months he does not speak, nor take sustenance (5.1.24–5). When Marina proves her identity, his response is to associate the new life she brings with new clothes: 'Now, blessing on thee! rise; th' art my child. |

---

[30] Babb notes that *Pericles* and *The Lover's Melancholy* are the only two plays he has found in which a cure by the removal of the cause of grief is made 'a matter of some scientific interest' (*Elizabethan Malady*, p. 115).

Give me fresh garments.' As if to underline that he is active in this, whereas Lear and Meleander are freshly dressed while asleep, Pericles impatiently calls again, 'Give me my robes' (5.1.213–14, 222). His therapeutic sleep comes after he has accepted his daughter. As with Lear and Meleander, music accompanies his recovery, though in Pericles's case the 'heavenly music' is only heard by him and (presumably) the audience (5.1.225–32). As with Palador's response to 'Parthenophill', who is 'like to some thing I remember | A great while since' (4.3.29–30), Pericles finds, with a similar plangency, and perhaps a verbal anticipation of Ford, that Marina is 'like something that—'[31]; she reminds him of 'one I lov'd indeed' (5.1.102, 125). Pericles is like Palador too in that he initially rejects Marina, pushing her away. Though his suspicion is less intense than Palador's, both men, like Daniel's Thyrsis, display a fear of being hurt by false hope. But he is willing to believe in her, although—given that he has been shown her tomb—he has more reason for scepticism than Palador. Whereas Pericles is willing to believe Marina because she looks 'Modest as justice' and 'Like one I lov'd indeed' (5.1.121, 125), Palador refuses to accept Eroclea despite her appearance, which he insists is a forgery: ''Tis not the figure stampt upon thy cheekes, | The coozenage of thy beauty, grace, or tongue, | Can draw from me a secret, that hath been | The onely Jewell of my speechlesse thoughts' (4.3.69–72). Finally, the fear that they are being mocked is, as has been said, shared by Meleander and Lear: Pericles twice expresses his anxiety in the same terms. He thinks he is being 'mocked', and Marina is 'by some incensed god sent hither | To make the world to laugh at me' (5.1.142–4; cf. 5.1.161–2).

Romance

Beyond the drama, *The Lover's Melancholy* also, as Lisa Hopkins has noted, 'situates itself squarely within the . . . aesthetic milieu of Sir Philip Sidney',[32] and certainly melancholy, in particular love melancholy, is an ever-present factor in the motivation of Sidney's romance characters. Further, as Hopkins notes, in both old and new versions of the *Arcadia* 'love is consistently constructed as having to be utterly overwhelming and acting in direct opposition to reason before it can

---

[31] The elliptical dash is added by modern editors.
[32] Lisa Hopkins, 'Staging Passion in Ford's *The Lover's Melancholy*', *Studies in English Literature, 1500–1900*, 45 (2005), 443–59, esp. 447.

be counted as worthy of the name of love.'[33] Something similar can be said of the loves of Thamasta and Palador, though less so of Menaphon, and definitely not of Eroclea or Cleophila, whose distinction is precisely not to be overwhelmed by love, however deeply felt. The name Cleophila must have been intended to evoke Sidney to a knowing section of the audience, since in the *Old Arcadia*, which was only circulating in MS in Ford's time, it is taken by Pyrocles in his disguise as an Amazon.[34] That Ford would have known the MS, and was indeed thought to have an excessive admiration for Sidney, is indicated by Shirley's caricature of him as Caperwit in *Love in a Maze*: 'if now and then my brains do sparkle, I cannot help it, raptures will out, my motto is, *Quicquid conabor*—the midwife wrapt my head up in a sheet of Sir *Philip Sidney*, that inspired me.'[35]

These echoes of Sidneian romance point rather bathetically to another possible influence on *The Lover's Melancholy*, the plagiarist John Hynd's justly neglected prose romance, *Eliosto Libidinoso* (1606). This is also set in Cyprus, and has characters with names like Philoclea and Cleodora. Love is certainly experienced by Hynd's protagonists as an utterly overwhelming force, and in the central, quasi-incestuous relationship (between step-mother and son) Ford would have found just the kind of forbidden but irresistible love that he was later to celebrate in *'Tis Pity She's a Whore*. Indeed, it may be significant that in the same year as *Eliosto Libidinoso* Ford published *Fames Memoriall*, which defends another forbidden love, the long extramarital relationship of its subject, Charles Mountjoy, Earl of Devonshire, with Lady Penelope Rich (see *CWJF* I, pp. 21–4, 169–256). Highly suggestive for *The Lover's Melancholy* itself is the plight in *Eliosto Libidinoso* of a woman who, like Eroclea, is forced to disguise herself as a boy and run away to escape a king's lustful advances. Frustrated love consigns all Hynd's lovers to melancholy, even the king who, unable to find the cross-dressed object of desire, falls into 'such a melancholy humour, that his subjects thought him halfe in a frenzie' (p. 65). The unusual Cypriot setting, the libidinous king, and the insidious effects of love melancholy on both individuals and the commonwealth in this third-rate romance may all have remained in Ford's mind in 1628.

---

[33] Ibid., p. 447.

[34] Philip Sidney, *The Countess of Pembroke's Arcadia*, ed. Katherine Duncan-Jones (Oxford, 1994 ed.), pp. 25–49.

[35] *The Dramatic Works and Poems of James Shirley*, ed. William Gifford and Alexander Dyce, 6 vols. (1833), vol. 2, p. 284; '*Quicquid conabor*' is the beginning of an adaptation of Ovid, *Tristia* 4.26 in Sidney's *Apologie for Poetrie*: 'Whatever I tried to say came out in verse'.

THE POLITICAL CONTEXT

Ford's primary interest in *The Lover's Melancholy* is in the psychological effects of passion and sorrow on his main protagonists, and on their cure, issues which did not reflect directly on the contemporary political situation. But unmistakable political allusion materializes in Act 2, which opens with Sophronos saying Palador's is a sick commonwealth in which 'The Commons murmur, and the Nobles grieve' (2.1.4), where his 'subjects mutter strangely, and imagine | More then they dare speake publikely' (2.1.76–7), and where court favourites are accused by 'the unsteady multitude' of 'ingrosse[ing] | (Out of particular Ambition) | Th'affaires of government' (2.1.13–15). Beyond his borders, 'neighb'ring Nations stand at gaze' threatening his realm. Few in the audience could have missed the precision with which these circumstances applied to the England of this time. The years 1626–8 were a tumultuous period in English politics, when a sequence of appalling military failures, resentment of Charles's increasingly arbitrary government, and Buckingham's growing power had indeed caused serious 'murmurs' in the Commons, and grievances both there and in the House of Lords. Charles was, like Palador, often seen as out of touch with his people, and to say that he was 'head-strong | In any passion that misleades [his] Judgement' (2.1.89–90) would have been a good description of his eventually fatal obstinacy. Cuculus's request that Palador should 'by Proclamation' create him overseer of tailors, comic though it is, could not have failed to bring to mind one of the most serious grievances of these years, the widely resisted, deeply unpopular Forced Loan—a tax not authorized by Parliament—which had been ordered by just such a royal proclamation in October 1626. Many gentry refused to pay, and were imprisoned without trial. The threats from 'neighb'ring Nations' (68–75) would have reminded the audience of those from France and Spain (England was currently at war with both countries), and from the victorious Catholic forces in the Thirty Years' War, where many thousands of Scottish and English soldiers were serving. Finally, the assassination of Buckingham in August 1628, about the time Ford began to write the play, had left England with a very melancholy prince indeed, albeit from profound grief rather than love.

Despite these parallels, and despite their mutual 'delight in . . . handsome pictures' (1.1.76–7), Palador is not a covert version of Charles I. Charles was shy, but it is hard to see Palador's 'dull Lethargy' as applicable to a king whom most would have criticized for political

overactivity. Lisa Hopkins has suggested that the way the play celebrates 'the loving reunion of a young and virtuous prince and his
partner after the removal of a powerful blocking figure . . . looks very
like a gratulation on the renewed amity of Charles I and Henrietta
Maria in the wake of the assassination of the Duke of Buckingham'.[36]
This is tempting, but the interpretation must be based on the publication date of 1629. The performance date of the 24th of November
makes it less plausible: Buckingham died on 23rd August, around the
time when Ford started writing, and though the queen's reconciliation
with Charles was relatively quick, it did not happen overnight. If the
action of the play was intended to allude to the improved relations
between king and queen, it might have been more a matter of hope
and anticipation than celebration.[37] Apart from this possible broad
application, political allusion is largely confined to this single scene,
suggesting Ford was less interested in using the play to comment on
English politics than the reverse, using the troubled England of 1628
as a kind of template for the symptoms of a sick commonwealth, even
though the underlying causes may be quite different. The genre of
tragicomedy allows for this serious if limited political discourse, which
would have been inappropriate in a comedy such as *Twelfth Night*,
where the political consequences of the neglect of duty by a similarly
lovelorn prince are never mentioned.

THE PLAY

It is worth examining the flaws in what is probably Ford's first solo
play before exploring its strengths, some of which, as will be seen,
relate to those flaws. Its comic element has often been criticized and,
as Hill says, 'All critics of Ford agree that broad comedy is not his
forte' (p. 19). Nevertheless all critics also miss what was probably one
reason for the inclusion of the comic characters, their role in making
the play a tragicomedy in the original Plautine sense in which the
comic and the tragic are mixed (*commixta*), with gods and kings acting alongside servants (*Amphitruo*, Prologue, l. 59). Ford seems to
have worried about it in this sense of whether the mixture violated
decorum, asking his audience when they 'meet with straines | Of
lighter mixtures, but to cast [their] eye | Rather upon the maine, then

---

[36] Hopkins, 'Staging Passion in Ford's *The Lover's Melancholy*', p. 444.
[37] See Michelle A. White, *Henrietta Maria and the English Civil Wars* (London, 2006),
pp. 13–15.

on the bye' (Prologue, ll. 14–16). Sargeaunt found the 'underplot . . . thin and sometimes unconnected with the main plot' (pp. 74–5), a judgement growing from that desire for 'organic unity' in art that was characteristic of her times, and which failed to recognize the almost detachable quality of the comic 'plot' in early modern drama. Kathleen McLuskie rightly notes how 'the most useful analogy for the construction of Ford's plays is not narrative held together by themes and characters, but the structures of *commedia dell'arte* in which the improvised *lazzi* were held together by the 'turn lines' which moved the action on to the next improvised sequence.'[38] There may indeed have been improvisation by John Shanks, the 'jigging clown' who probably played Cuculus. That role in *The Lover's Melancholy* is scripted, at least as we now have it, but elsewhere Shanks often seems to have ad-libbed, and in this case too he may have added some of his own material.[39] For all this, Ford does integrate Cuculus's role with the 'main' plot, insofar as he is followed and duped by a comic, mirror version of Eroclea, a boy disguised as his 'feminine Page' (1.2.157), a variant of the 'boy bride'. Cuculus is also a comic lover, like Armado or Malvolio, whose letters to his various wished-for mistresses, with their obscene undertones (3.1.1–74) and distinct lack of pathos, provide a comic descant on the idealized if troubled lovers of the main plot. Cuculus, Grilla, and Pelias also give some substance to Ford's presentation, never quite convincingly realized, of the Cypriot court as 'turned antic' and dominated by 'wanton gentry' (2.1.5, 1.2.3), the point being that they are allowed to flourish by Palador's lethargic melancholy, and by the wider, long-term effects of the poisoned legacy of his father. Trollio is a different kind of clown whose role is to lighten the darkness that surrounds Cleophila and Meleander. A distant descendant of the irreverent but usually more intelligent slave of Plautine comedy, Trollio's humour is, like Pelias's, linguistic, but where the latter's vocabulary parodies bombastic mid-Tudor versions of Senecan tragedy, Trollio's is more like Dogberry's. Hill objected to the 'insensitivity' of Trollio's comedy, but in the only modern production, the 2015 Wanamaker Read Not Dead performance (see the section 'Stage History'), he and the other comic characters did not jar, and the 'bye' blended with the 'main' in much the way that Ford must have hoped it would.

---

[38] McLuskie, '"Language and Matter with a Fit of Mirth": Dramatic Construction in the Plays of John Ford', in Neill (ed.), pp. 97–127, esp. 100.

[39] He has no lines at all in *The Wild Goose Chase*, though he is in the cast list. It is, of course, possible that Ford recalled some of his improvisation in the printed text of *Lover's Melancholy*.

Even if the comic roles are not quite such a failure as usually suggested, it must be recognized that the plot of *The Lover's Melancholy* has more anomalies and discrepancies than is usual even in early modern drama. They may in part be attributable to this being Ford's first solo play, but they are also there because his primary interest is not in plot but psychology, in the presentation of disabling grief and love, and their cure. This is the main explanation of the static structure to which Oliver points. The slight, occasionally creaking plot is simply a structure on which to hang these concerns. It provides Ford with a series of scenes within which he explores not *a* lover's melancholy, but three case histories, in which he brings to the fore in successive episodes the disabling, grief-stricken love melancholy of Palador, the equally disabling irrational 'heroic' love of Thamasta, and the paternal grief of Meleander. If the missing apostrophe were to be added to the title of the play, there would be a good case for putting it after, not before the 's': these are lovers' melancholies.

Many of the plot's anomalies stem from Ford's decision to place the crime which precipitates the action, Agenor's attempt to abduct and rape Eroclea, two years before the play opens. This action has something like the consequences for the next generation as Laius's rape of Chrysippus has for Thebes, except that in the world of tragicomedy the cursed legacy can be averted. Here, the consequences of Agenor's 'heroic' lust are Eroclea's escape and exile, and the psychological suffering of Meleander and Palador, who both fear she is dead. Because his concern is with their anguish and the process of recovery, Ford is careless in his handling of the dissembling by Rhetias and Sophronos about Eroclea's fate: the audience learn over the course of the play that they arranged her escape from Agenor, disguised as a 'Saylers Boy', and that Rhetias accompanied her to Athens and stayed with her for two years, during which time she remained dressed as a 'youth', at Sophronos's 'wise command' (5.2.161–74). This caution is not explained, and the audience is entitled to ask, amid all the gratitude to Sophronos in the final act ('A good, good Brother'), why he waited long after Agenor's death to let Palador and his brother, the latter mad with grief, the former rendered a dysfunctional ruler through his melancholy, know Eroclea was alive.

It is a related flaw that Sophronos, the supposed mastermind of all this (his name means 'wise man' in Greek),[40] plays such a minor role

---

[40] For the meanings of the Greek-derived names, see the commentary notes on the Dramatis Personae.

in events following Eroclea's return that the audience could be forgiven for believing him when, asked 'What should this young man bee', he replies "'Tis to me | A mystery, I understand it not' (4.3.2–4). This has to be a lie, but it is not presented or dramatically exploited as such, and is delivered only just before Eroclea abandons her disguise. Here and elsewhere Ford simply ignores Sophronos's privileged knowledge. As far as his part in the play goes (it is one of the smallest), he may as well 'understand it not.' Rhetias, a much more prominent actor in both senses, also knows Eroclea's identity from the outset. He does give hints to Palador (and the audience) over Eroclea's fate at their first private meeting (2.1.161–206), but he is presumably, like her, under Sophronos's instructions—'Directed by the wisdom of my Uncle' (4.3.147)—not to reveal the truth. Eroclea herself lamely explains her silence only at the end of the play ('I was rul'd by councell' (5.2.162)), but this is not really an explanation. In *Hymen's Triumph* Daniel had been careful to give Eroclea's equivalent, Silvia–Clarindo, a good motive for not making herself known to her lover in similar circumstances: she is waiting until the bridegroom her father was forcing on her has married someone else, 'Which shortly as I heare will be.' Ford needs to keep Eroclea's disguise so that he can explore Thamasta's irrational passion, as well as Palador's melancholy and Meleander's grief, but as far as plot goes he gives no good explanation for her delay in revealing her identity.[41]

There is another anomaly, also connected to Agenor's crime, over the inexplicable difficulty Palador's courtiers and physician have in understanding the cause of his melancholy. Babb says, 'Clearly [Corax] knows what is the matter with the Prince. The Cyprian courtiers, however, do not know and are consequently puzzled and anxious' (p.163). And surprisingly, Sophronos, Rhetias, and Aretus are indeed puzzled about Palador, as if the fact that two years earlier his father had attempted to rape his contracted bride, who is now missing, believed by him to be dead, was not a modest clue. Nor does Ford let the audience know whether this case history, or the secret of Eroclea's safe return, has been passed on to the physician Corax until late in the action, an omission which makes Babb's confidence that he 'knows what is the matter with the Prince' misplaced, and renders the doctor's role and motivation in the earlier scenes opaque. It is by no means clear until he discovers it for himself at the end of the masque scene

---

[41] Richard Madelaine suggests that Eroclea delays 'so that she can observe and respond to others' grieving at her absence', but it is hard to discern any such motivation; see Madelaine, ' "Sensationalism" ', pp. 29–53, p.44.

that Corax is sure of the cause of Palador's melancholy, and there is no suggestion before his meeting with Meleander in 4.2, when he recounts the latter's loss of his daughter as if it was his own, that he knows who 'Parthenophill' is. He has prescribed Palador exercises for melancholy (2.1.50–6), but the whole court knows that Palador is broadly melancholic, as Amethus's description in the first scene demonstrates (1.1.69–79), and exercise is a very general remedy 'for such as are . . . troubled in mind' (*Anatomy*, 2.2.4). The issue is about specific causes, since as Rhetias says, only when the cause is known can the disease be cured (4.2.1–2). Rhetias, along with Sophronos, could make a good guess at the cause of Palador's melancholy, and, in the person of Eroclea, both have the means to cure it without the help of a physician. Nevertheless, both Sophronos (3.3.110) and Rhetias (4.2.1–5) joyfully congratulate Corax on discovering that Palador is suffering from love melancholy.

Anomalies over Palador's emotional predicament also relate to his perspective on Agenor's assault, in particular as regards timing. The attempted rape belongs in the not-so-distant past—'almost two yeeres' (2.1.196–7)—but Palador tells Rhetias that 'Parthenophill' reminds him of someone only dimly remembered, 'A great while since, a long, long time agoe' (4.3.30). Earlier he has implied he was too young to be told what his father did, and still remains in the dark: 'in my younger dayes I oft have heard | Agenors name, my Father, more traduc'd, | Then I could then observe' (2.1.148–9). This, and his subsequent urging of Rhetias to provide more information, implies that he is genuinely uncertain about what happened in a distant past, rather than testing Rhetias's honesty. After all, it is Rhetias who has timidly raised the issue of Agenor in the first place (2.1.136), and who has to check whether Palador even remembers Eroclea (2.1.165). Only after he has put Palador straight does the latter say 'th'ast unlockt | A tongue was vow'd to silence' over Eroclea (2.1.214–5), showing him her miniature, and later still telling Eroclea that it was his father's 'tyranny' that 'ravished | The contract of our hearts' (4.3.125–6). There is a discrepancy between Palador's apparently dim memory of events, and the heavy, present burden of his love for his lost bride, and his decision 'for her sake' to advance Sophronos and to restore Meleander (2.1.222–6).

Such anomalies of plot and motive are not related to the inherent instability, the uncertain emotions which Terence Cave describes in his study of recognition plots.[42] Ford takes on three separate recognition

---

[42] Terence Cave, *Recognitions: A Study in Poetics* (Oxford, 1990).

scenes in the play, and handles them convincingly, insofar as such scenes can ever be wholly convincing. In the central one, Palador's strong anxiety that Eroclea may be an impostor reflects an uneasiness that, as Cave points out, is never far from the surface of such scenes for both characters and audience. Eroclea's apparently clinching proof, the miniature she wears round her neck, is on this level not completely reassuring, and is in fact one of the examples Aristotle picks out of the 'the least artistic [devices] and the one used the most from uninventiveness: recognition through tokens . . . such as necklaces' (*Poetics*, 16). The other two recognition scenes in *The Lover's Melancholy* (if that between Thamasta and Eroclea can be so called) are accompanied by less anxiety and uncertainty. Disquiet remains, however, in Thamasta's response that 'It will be | A hard taske for my Reason, to relinquish | The affection which was once devoted thine, | I shall a while repute thee still the youth | I lov'd so dearely' (3.2.176–80), a game which Eroclea is generously willing to play. Later, Meleander's response to Eroclea's question 'Deare Sir, you know me?' is simple and affirmative as far as recognition goes: 'Yes, thou art my Daughter' (5.2.108), but even here, as Rhetias says, 'The good-man rellisheth his comforts strangely' as he looks towards death from a broken heart, and tries to articulate his mixture of emotions (5.2.117–30).

Ford's insightful treatment of the mental and emotional anguish the four main characters undergo in these scenes of *anagnorisis*, and the sometimes violent, sometimes poignantly simple verse through which he articulates their feelings, extends to his handling of them throughout. Eroclea is the common denominator between them, the object of passionate romantic and paternal love, and a symbol of resilient, controlled emotion, though she too suffers, as is seen from her speeches to Palador when she abandons her disguise (4.3.56–118), and in a different way when Thamasta makes love to her. She is a powerful presence in the play: though she has fewer lines than the other leading protagonists, she is onstage more than any other character except Rhetias, who, like her, appears in eight scenes. Ford's handling of her role has far more positives than negatives, once we accept Sophronos's apparent perversity in keeping her identity secret for so long. Ford uncovers that secret deftly and very gradually during the course of the play, so that she is unlike Shakespeare's cross-dressed young women, of whose true identity the audience is always aware, and unlike Bellario in *Philaster*, who is only revealed to cast and audience as Euphrasia in the final scene. There are no obvious hints in Menaphon's description in Act I that Parthenophill is a woman, but there is a suggestive mystery

in 'his' secretiveness, and the sexualized language with which
Menaphon describes it: 'whence he is, | Or who, as I durst modestly
inquire, | So gently hee would woo not to make knowne' (1.1.172–4);
and in retrospect the harmonious blend of beauty and compassion
manifested in the musical duel helps shape the audience's sense of
Eroclea's qualities. She then shows what would have been described as
'feminine' emotion when, as Parthenophill, she first appears onstage,
so that Thamasta asks her, 'Are you well, Sir?'. Eroclea's reply that 'to
see a League | Betweene an humble love, such as my Friends is, | And
a commanding vertue, such as yours is, | Are sure restoratives' (1.3.68–
9) does not address the cause of her disturbance. As often with Ford,
the acting may have clarified matters. There is a similar, more understandable, display of emotion later when, still disguised, she meets her
father and sister:

> CLEOPHILA   This Gentleman is moov'd.
> AMETHUS   Your eyes, *Parthenophill,*
>   Are guilty of some passion.
> MENAPHON   Friend, what ailes thee?
> EROCLEA   All is not well within me, Sir. (2.2.142–4)

This is a strong hint to the audience, but it builds on a still stronger
one in the previous scene, in which Eroclea is mentioned by name for
the first time, when Rhetias asks Palador if he remembers her (2.1.165).
Though Rhetias denies knowledge of her fate, he tells of 'a pretty
accident' which is, in fact, Eroclea's story (2.1.191–8). An audience well
used to disguised heroines, with a 'faire-fac'd' boy actor in front of
them, would have been alerted by this juxtaposition, and their suspicions would have been reinforced by Palador's question, 'In habit of a
man?' Later in the same scene, Eroclea says, with a telling echo of
Rosalind to Phoebe, 'if ever I desire to thrive | In womans favour,
Kala is the first | Whom my ambition shall bend to' (2.1.298–300),
lines helpfully repeated by Thamasta.

Whatever suspicions the audience may have by now that
Parthenophill is a girl are confirmed in the next act when she is forced
to reveal the fact to Thamasta, but her admission that she is 'a maide,
a virgine' is not accompanied by her name. Instead she gives Thamasta
a letter telling her 'unforg'd relation' (3.2.162, 170). She remains
dressed as Parthenophill, with only Thamasta added to those in the
know, until Act 4, when Rhetias ushers her in to Palador '*in womans
attire*' (4.3.42.1.1). Even then Ford delays the revelation of her
name—'A name of misery'—for some time (4.3.104). It is at this point

that Eroclea introduces the issue of her shame, a concept likely to be lost on modern audiences: 'Whil'st I was lost to memory, | *Parthenophill* did shrowd my shame in change | Of sundry rare misfortunes' (111–13). Ford's contemporaries, it seems, would have seen her disguise, however necessary, as a violation of sexual decorum: Bellario's father emphasizes the 'shame' of his daughter's disguise in *Philaster*, and she agrees: 'Would I had died indeed, I wish it too | And so must have done by vow . . . but that there was no means' (5.5.118–21).[43] Some may also have believed that to be the victim of an unsuccessful rape attempt would be experienced as a source of shame, either because of the still familiar suspicion that the victim had unwittingly incited or colluded in the attempt (especially if the rapist was a king), or because the episode had sullied her virgin purity. Even the chaste Lady in *Comus*, stuck to her chair with 'gums of glutinous heat' (916), can only be released from her imprisonment by Sabrina's magic rather than her own virtue.[44] Ford exonerates Eroclea from the need for any such sense of guilt by giving her the alias of Parthenophill, 'lover of virginity'.[45] He was to return to a more complex, but still sympathetic exploration of the issue in *The Broken Heart*, where Penthea sees herself as raped because, in a forced marriage, she was 'a ravish'd wife', her name 'strumpeted' but still 'Of noble shame'. Only at this point is the audience certain who Eroclea is, and only then, following her reunion with Palador, can the crucial meeting with her father take place.

It is Eroclea's interaction with 'great spirited' Thamasta, in Greek the 'glorious one', that dominates her earliest scenes, and it is important to an appreciation of Ford's structuring, and the range of his psychological as well as dramatic interest, that Thamasta's infatuation with 'Parthenophill' should be seen as more than a sideshow. Hers is as much a 'lover's melancholy' as is Palador's, and the part, in terms of lines, is almost exactly the same size as his. In her case it is made very clear that she is suffering what Burton calls 'heroical love' (*Anatomy*, 3.2.1.1). Usually this is love inspired in men by the beauty of women; there is irony then in the apparent reversal of sexes in the beautiful

---

[43] A generation earlier this was not a big problem for Shakespeare's disguised heroines: amongst them, only Jessica is 'much ashamed of [her] exchange' (*Merchant of Venice*, 2.6.35).

[44] See Katherine Maus, 'A Womb of His Own: Male Renaissance Poets in the Female Body', in J. G. Turner (ed.), *Sexuality and Gender in Early Modern Europe: Institutions, Texts, Images* (Cambridge, 1993), pp. 266–88. For a wider discussion of attitudes to rape and attempted rape at this date, see Jocelyn Catty, *Writing Rape, Writing Women in Early Modern England* (Houndmills, Basingstoke, 1999).

[45] Parthenophil was also the name taken by Ford's friend Barnabe Barnes, in his *Parthenophil and Parthenophe. Sonnettes, Madrigals, Elegies and Odes* (1593). Barnes also alludes three times in that collection to the song of the nightingale.

Thamasta's passionate attraction to 'This Youth, this faire-fac'd Youth' (1.1.115). The underlying homoerotic situation is not exploited until later, and then only briefly; at this stage the audience is no more aware of Eroclea's true gender than is Thamasta. But there is further irony in the speed with which her 'great spirit' and aggressive chastity is obliterated by Parthenophill's beauty. In this there is something in her not just of Shakespeare's Olivia, but of Angelo, 'a man whose blood | Is very snow-broth' (*Measure for Measure*, 1.4.57–8), but who becomes another victim of precipitate 'heroic' love when he sets eyes on Isabella. Amethus has said that Thamasta's 'bosome yet | Is intermur'd with Ice' (1.1.61–2), rather as Lucio claims that when Angelo 'makes water his urine is congealed ice' (3.2.110–11). She has not only rejected the faithful Menaphon but refused to court neighbouring kings (1.3.17). There is something in her too of Agenor. As Burton points out, it is 'Noble men, and the most generous spirits [who] are possessed with' heroic love (3.2.1.1), and both Thamasta and those around her are very conscious of her status as 'one who derives her blood from Princes' (1.3.9). Meleander emphasizes the sinister aspect of this heritage: her brother Amethus 'Was sonne to *Doryla, Agenors* Sister. | There's some ill [i.e. bad] blood about him' (2.2.53–4). Amethus, the 'sober one', has escaped this taint, but Thamasta, it seems, has some of her uncle Agenor's temperament. When she first appears she has already fallen: Amethus upbraids her for dressing 'like a Lady of the trim', with 'glittering pompe of ease and wantonnesse' (1.3.2–4). This is not just uncharacteristic vulgarity: Burton has a long, rather overexcited subsection on 'Artificial allurements of Love, Causes and Provocations to Lust; Gestures, Clothes, Dower, &c.' (3.2.2.3), and 'allurement' is evidently what Thamasta has in mind, as is hinted when she claims that she has for Menaphon's

> sake entertain'd *Parthenophill,*
> The handsome Stranger, more familiarly
> Then (I may feare) becomes me; yet for his part,
> I not repent my courtesies. (1.3.36–9)

She responds to Amethus's hope that she will change 'at last' with the ironic comment to herself 'I feare I shall' (1.3.49). She presents herself as a helpless captive of heroic love: she is 'sensible of being traytor | To honour and to shame', she has 'growne base' (1.3.80–2), and has already given way to the 'tyrant' Love. The shame is partly that of a proud woman rendered helpless, but she also recognizes that despite its association with 'Noble men', heroic love, which is a purely physical, sexual attraction, is associated with the animal and vegetable worlds.

Burton describes how 'this tyrant Love . . . rageth with brute beasts and spirits', as well as 'amongst men' (3.2.1.2). Significantly, Thamasta characterizes herself as a 'Lyonesse' (3.2.110). She knows she is going to be 'lost in my new follyes' (1.3.94), but cannot resist the 'tyrant': ''Tis a Fate | That over-rules our wisdomes' (1.3.94–5). This is a distortion of the idea, expressed by Cleophila, Palador, and Meleander, that a 'sacred providence' has watched over them (4.2.207, 4.3.135, 5.2.170). Her sense of helplessness is developed in the scene in which she declares her love to Eroclea (3.2). In a speech based closely on Burton's discussion of the hierarchy of 'natural, sensible, and rational love' (see note to 3.2.77–87), Thamasta makes it clear that her passion belongs only to the first two categories.[46] Her analogies are with the helpless attractions to each other of plants and minerals, the olive and the myrtle, the 'Loadstone, and the Steele'. She knows there is shame in her behaviour, but again claims she cannot resist. Ford uses rhyme for emphasis: 'True love may blush, when shame repents too late, | But in all actions, Nature yeelds to Fate' (3.2.92–3). Eroclea reminds her of the higher, rational love and of how she has lost sight of it:

> If that affection have so oversway'd
> Your Judgement, that it in a manner hath
> Declyn'd your soveraignty of birth and spirit:
> How can yee turne your eyes off from that glasse,
> Wherein you may new Trim, and settle right
> A memorable name? (3.2.118–23)

'Affection' here, as in Burton, means strong, passionate feeling—heroic love. Menaphon is the 'glass' in which Thamasta should see the course of honourable love ruled by 'Judgement'. But for Ford, as for Burton, such orthodox arguments oversimplify by failing to register the overwhelming force of passion, which for post-lapsarian man may indeed be an irresistible 'tyrant'. Before the Fall, appetite was 'well agreeing with reason in us, and there was an excellent consent and harmony betwixt them, but that is now dissolved, they often jarre, Reason is over-borne by Passion. . . . as so many wilde horses runne away with a chariot, and will not be curbed, we know many times what is good, but will not doe it' (*Anatomy*, 1.1.1.13).[47] In *The Broken Heart*,

---

[46] The derivation from Burton answers the criticism that this speech is 'derived from the most hackneyed kind of love poetry'; see Michael Neill, 'The Moral Artifice of *The Lover's Melancholy*', *ELR* 8 (1978), 85–106, p. 97.

[47] This is not, as Ronald Huebert argues, an anticipation of Pascal's 'Le coeur a ses raisons que la raison ne connaît point', which is more about irrational faith than 'appetite'; but he is right to note Burton's sympathetic interest in 'turbulent emotional storms'. See Huebert, p. 59.

Bassanes says with characteristic violence that 'men endow'd with reason . . . | Are verier beasts than beasts' (4.2.22–8). In this context, it is worth noting that not Thamasta, Palador, or Meleander display the kind of stoicism in their suffering, nor the kind of self-fashioning, often associated with Ford. Along with Eroclea, they are acted upon by circumstances, victims of emotional dilemmas which reason cannot help. Only Cleophila, choosing loyalty to her father over her love for Amethus, and troubled by that choice (5.1.26–34), stands out in this respect. Amethus himself is too minor a character for his self-control to register significantly with an audience, while Menaphon, in many ways an exemplar of patient restraint, remains in thrall to Thamasta.[48]

Thamasta then is helpless, but self-deceiving when she pleads that she is a victim of 'The destiny that guides us' (3.2.136). Love is a 'tyrant' whom she cannot resist, and who forces her to abase herself. Her increasingly desperate pleas are only stopped when Eroclea is forced to reveal that she is 'of the selfe same sexe' as her (3.2.162). Since Thamasta's is a strongly sensual love, it must in the circumstances be abandoned, though not through the dutiful application of 'reason' (3.2.177). Ford's handling of her reaction displays acute psychological insight, and a Burtonian—or Montaignesque—flow of responses, characteristics seen later in the rapidly shifting responses of Palador and Meleander. There is instant fear of ridicule and shame ('Pray conceale | The errors of my passions'), followed by an unexpected and poignant desire to retain a fantasy version of the relationship: 'I shall a while repute thee still the youth | I lov'd so dearely' (3.2.179–80). Here for the first time a mildly homoerotic element appears, in which Eroclea colludes. Thamasta insists that 'We must not part yet' and warns her that 'I shall henceforth | Be jealous of thy company with any'. Despite this apparently brief prolongation, what Jonson calls 'tribade [lesbian] lust' is not considered.[49] Thamasta's love melancholy is effectively ended by Eroclea's revelation. Her 'cure' and repentance are signalled by her letter to Cleophila, telling her of Eroclea's safe return, and by her subsequent apology to Cleophila for her arrogance.

Palador's love melancholy is of a very different kind, not a *coup de foudre* but a long-established disabling heartache over a lost love who was his contracted bride. Because he believes Eroclea is dead, that 'No hope lives . . . | Of ever, ever seeing her againe' (2.1.180–1), he is in the

---

[48] Michael Neill argues that emotions are contained 'within linguistic structures or ceremonial gestures' in 'a Stoicism of manners' ('Moral Artifice', p. 102).

[49] *Poems of Ben Jonson*, eds. Tom Cain and Ruth Connolly (London, 2022), *Underwood* 49, 'An Epigram on the Court Pucelle', line 7.

position of the unrequited lover that Burton describes: 'Now if this passion of love can produce such effects, if it be pleasantly intended [directed], what bitter torments shall it breede, when it is with feare and continuall sorrow, suspition, care, agony, as commonly it is, still accompanied, what an intolerable paine must it be?' (3.2.3). Amethus summarizes Palador's symptoms at the outset:

> hee's the same melancholy man,
> He was at's Fathers death, sometimes speakes sence,
> But seldome mirth; will smile, but seldome laugh;
> Will lend an eare to businesse, deale in none;
> Gaze upon Revels, Anticke Fopperies,
> But is not mov'd; will sparingly discourse,
> Heare musicke; but what most he takes delight in,
> Are handsome pictures; one so young, and goodly,
> So sweet in his owne nature, any Story
> Hath seldome mentioned. (1.1.70–9)

Burton describes just such behaviour as symptomatic of melancholics in general: 'They doe not much heed what you say, their minde is on another matter; aske what you will, they doe not attend, or much intend that businesse they are about, but forget themselves what they are saying, doing, or should otherwise say or doe, whither they are going, distracted with their owne melancholy thoughts. One laughs upon a sudden, another smiles to himselfe' (1.3.1.2). This is less dramatic and less specifically connected to love melancholy than the behaviour of Giovanni in *'Tis Pity She's a Whore* who 'with such sad aspect | Walkes careless of him selfe' and who seems 'some woefull thinge | Wrapt up in griefe, some shaddow of a man. | Alas hee beats his brest, and wipes his eyes | Drown'd all in teares: me thinkes I heare him sigh' (1.2.123–4, 128–31). Something like this may, of course, have been conveyed by Taylor's performance as Palador, but although melancholy lovers who have lost hope may, more quietly, 'go smiling to themselves' and 'neglect all ordinary businesse' (*Anatomy* 3.2.3), what the audience hears about Palador from Amethus could apply to any type of melancholy.

Before Palador's first entrance, Sophronos makes his most significant speech, in which he offers a new perspective, relating the prince's melancholy to the sickness of the commonwealth, and declaring that:

> 'tis more then time
> That wee should wake the Head thereof, who sleepes
> In the dull Lethargy of lost security (2.1.1–3).

The security that is lost is that of the stable commonwealth. Palador's condition is such that he is unaware of the threats to his kingdom at home and abroad. His melancholic 'neglect [of] all ordinary business' and general lethargy has inevitably infected the political body of which he is the head, as has Agenor's poisoned legacy. These political consequences are never taken up by Ford, who remains focused on Palador's personal dilemma. Sophronos and Aretus remain puzzled by his 'distemper', but they do know that it is a passion 'of violent'—that is powerful—nature which can only be uncovered, and cured, with patience.[50] Corax is their agent, and he has enlisted Rhetias to their project. Ford uses a brief comic interlude with Cuculus and Grilla to contrast with Palador's Hamlet-like entrance to '*Soft Musicke . . . with a Booke in his hand*' (2.1.48.1–2). The presence of the clowns underlines Palador's desire for solitude: his first speech in the play, before Corax launches into his angry complaint about his exercise regime, is simply to ask 'Why all this Company?' (2.1.49). Corax agrees that Palador's melancholy has blighted the court, infecting even the aggressive doctor himself 'with the sloth | Of sleepe and surfet', and he accuses Palador of a 'wilfull dulnesse' (2.1.58–62), a manifestation of which is the prince's terse reply to Corax: 'I believe it.' Sophronos and Aretus begin their attempt to 'wake' him from his 'dull lethargy' with a series of demands for vital action as head of state, which receive no reply until Corax tells him that his subjects 'talk but odly' of him. This, like Rhetias's subsequent dialogue and the masque, is intended to 'nettle' Palador (2.1.83), and it stirs him to ask his courtiers what they think of him, an opportunity for Ford to enlarge on Palador's symptoms.

Sophronos's analysis points towards a brand of heroic love: Palador is 'head-strong | In any passion that misleades [his] Judgement' ('Judgement' is also invoked by Eroclea in the face of Thamasta's headstrong passion at 3.2.119) and 'too indulgent to such motions, | As spring out of [his] owne affections' (2.1.89–92). 'Headstrong' and 'passion' are put together several times by Burton, as in 'the fury of this head-strong passion' (3.2.5.2), which misleads the lover, whose 'imagination and reason are misaffected' so that 'because of his corrupt judgment, and continuall meditation of that which he desires, hee may truely bee said to be melancholy' (3.2.1.2). Palador's melancholy is introverted, necessarily so in the apparently permanent loss of Eroclea, but nevertheless akin to its more violent manifestation in

---

[50] For the play's demonstration of the need for gradual therapy for 'deeply settled' melancholy, see Hill, p. 20.

Thamasta and Agenor. Whether love is an 'affection' of the heart, liver, blood, or brain, if its motions are indulged, 'misaffection' results, but Palador is too old to be reformed by advice, and 'too young | To take fit councell from [him] selfe' (2.1.93–4).

Aretus is less perceptive. Though he hints at the extent to which Palador, like many melancholics, is self-indulgent about his condition, finding a paradoxical comfort in it, he makes him sound merely lazy. He tells him that 'you doate . . . Too much upon your pleasures, and these pleasures | Are so wrapt up in selfe-love, that you covet | No other change of fortune' (2.2.96–9). This does echo Burton, who has a whole subsection on 'Philautia, or Self-love' (1.2.3.14), but that is about 'Vainglory', which is not Palador's problem. Nor does he seem to have any pleasures on which to dote. Aretus believes Palador wants the title of prince, but is 'loth to toyle | In such affaires of State as breake [his] sleepes' (2.2.100–1). Clearly Palador's lethargy and inattention to 'affaires of State' have deeper causes than this superficial diagnosis suggests.

Corax's contribution is a continuation of the process of 'nettling' on which he has already started. It is deliberately insulting, but in no way a diagnosis. Palador just hasn't grown up. He would like to be taken as a man, but is 'In manners and effect indeed a childe, | A boy, a very boy' (2.1.104–5). Palador doesn't respond, but he does reject the subsequent flattery from Pelias, and Corax takes the initiative in leaving him alone with Rhetias in a crucial dialogue which Rhetias begins by observing that Palador has exchanged his 'happinesse' for 'a misery'. This helps disambiguate his next remark, which again raises the issue of yielding to 'affected passion':

Princes who forget their soveraignty, and yeeld to affected passion, are weary of command. You had a Father, Sir. (2.1.135–6)

Rhetias is provoking Palador by accusing him of abnegating his responsibilities as a ruler. But this first mention of his father in the play is another challenge, another attempt to stir Palador, and it succeeds. The issue becomes one of his confused memory and perception. He questions Rhetias sharply, demanding honesty and at the same time claiming that though he heard his father 'traduced' he was too young to 'observe' why, or to remember Agenor trying to abduct Eroclea, even though he remembers her as 'a lovely beauty' (166). And during the period since Agenor's death, Palador had nobody to tell him: 'I never had a friend, a certaine friend, | That would informe me throughly of such errors, | As oftentimes are incident to Princes' (2.1.151–3).

The audience has to take at face value the proposition that the story Rhetias tells of the attempted rape and rescue is new to Palador. He does not seem to be dissembling in saying he will be 'lost' if Rhetias doesn't complete his account (172), but Rhetias only half-completes it. Eroclea was by 'her father rescude, she convay'd away' (174), but he lies, crucially for the plot, when he says that Eroclea 'never since was heard of'. Palador responds with a poignancy achieved by a piece of simple repetition characteristic of Ford: 'No hope lives then | Of ever, ever seeing her againe' (180–1). This was printed by Weber and all subsequent editors as a question, but in the quarto, as in this edition, it is for him a statement of fact. Rhetias's attempt to mitigate his piece of deception with the tale of a 'young lady' whose story parallels Eroclea's, including her disguise, alerts the audience to what may be happening more than it gives hope to Palador, as is seen soon after when Rhetias says that the portrait in the miniature is '*Erocleas*', and Palador corrects him: 'Hers that was once *Eroclea*' (222).

By telling Palador the story of the rape, and hinting at the possibility of Eroclea's return, Rhetias, in his role as the blunt but truthful malcontent, has stirred Palador to acknowledge his love for Eroclea. Palador shows the miniature he wears secretly in his bosom (as Burton says, 'Her picture [the lover] adores twice a day, and for two hours together will not look off it' (3.2.3)), but anxiously swears Rhetias to secrecy. He is afraid that 'politic lords' will worm the cause of his 'griefs' from him. This mistrust remains even after Eroclea has come to him without disguise, when he still suspects a conspiracy. His secretiveness goes beyond an understandable resentment at the well-meaning attempts to find out why he is melancholy. 'Paranoia' was not in Burton's lexicon, but 'suspicion' is a word that comes up again and again in his account of the melancholic's symptoms: 'Suspition followes Feare and Sorrow at heeles, arising out of the same fountaine, so thinks [Girolamus] Fracastorius, *that Feare is the cause of Suspition, and still they suspect some trechery, or some secret machination to be framed against them*, still they distrust' (1.3.3).[51] Such paranoia lies behind Palador's distracted replies when Menaphon and the disguised

---

[51] Cf. Bright, *Treatise*, p. 105: 'the hart answering with like melancholicke affection, turneth all hope into feare, assurance into distrust and dispaire, joye into discomforte'; Bacon, 'Of Suspicion': '[Suspicions] dispose Kings to Tyranny, Husbands to Jealousie, Wise Men to Irresolution and Melancholy . . . in fearefull Natures, they gaine Ground too fast'. See *The Essayes or Counsels*, XXXI, in *The Oxford Francis Bacon*, ed. Michael Kiernan (Oxford, 1985), vol. 15, p. 102.

Eroclea are presented. 'His wonted melancholy still pursues him', Menaphon observes (2.1.261).

The lover's secretiveness causes problems for the physician, especially since, as Babb says (p. 137), not only is the patient unforthcoming in love melancholy, but he or she usually does not want to be cured except by consummation. There is a tradition of wise physicians curing patients after discovering their secrets by stealth. Burton lists several of them (3.2.3), and Corax joins this line, his next strategy being the 'Maske of Melancholy' (3.3), another and more comprehensive form of 'nettling'. The display of a range of types of melancholy, largely based on Burton (see commentary notes), is a context for the 'empty space' (92), which Corax has left on the plot he has given Palador (for the ruled boxes on such play plots see note to 3.3.91). Undisturbed by the other types of melancholy, Palador confirms Corax's suspicions by reacting violently to his explanation of the empty box, which includes a suggestion that Palador himself may be 'touched home' by Love Melancholy:

CORAX   Love is the Tyrant of the heart, it darkens
            Reason, confounds discretion, deafe to counsell:
            It runnes a headlong course to desperate madnesse.
            O were your Highnes but toucht home, and throughly,
            With this (what shall I call it) Divell—
PRINCE   Hold,
            Let no man henceforth name the word agen! (3.3.103–8)

With a typically deft psychological touch, Ford makes Palador associate Eroclea–Parthenophill with this disturbing diagnosis as he flounces out: 'Wait you my pleasure, Youth; 'tis late, to rest' (109). The next time he is seen, Palador is still 'throughly mov'd' and 'much distemp'red' over both the partially successful attempt to discover the cause of his melancholy, and over the now lost Parthenophill, who has not waited his pleasure. Packed into Palador's angry speech is his continuing suspicion, but also an acceptance that he has been lethargic, and an unknowing testimony to the success of Corax's strategy of nettling him:

            Yee have consented all to worke upon
           The softnesse of my nature; but take heede:
           Though I can sleepe in silence, and looke on
           The mockery yee make of my dull patience;
           Yet'ee shall know, the best of yee, that in mee
           There is a masculin, a stirring spirit;

> Which provokt, shall like a bearded Comet
> Set yee at gaze, and threaten horrour. (4.3.5–12)

Desperate to find Parthenophill, he also still craves solitude, and the brief soliloquy Ford gives him subtly captures his bewilderment, his sense of having seen something in 'the boy' which he cannot understand. He has already called Parthenophill 'this Fantasticke, | This airie apparition' (18–19). Now he reaches in tentative language for this tantalizing vision of something lost:

> Some angry power, cheates with rare delusions,
> My credulous sense: the very soule of Reason
> Is troubled in me—the Physician
> Presented a strange Maske, the view of it
> Puzzl'd my understanding: but the Boy—(22–6)

This hesitant evocation of an elusive memory had been anticipated in a more mundane form when he told Rhetias that he needed a 'a certaine friend' to tell him about Agenor. Now it is developed in the justly celebrated lines in which he says

> *Parthenophill* is lost, and I would see him;
> For he is like to some thing I remember
> A great while since, a long, long time agoe. (4.3.28–30)

The greatness of this lies in the way in which the simple, largely monosyllabic language and the telling repetition apprehend the memory that cannot quite be grasped, the sense of loss that cannot quite be justified. Early modern dramatists usually avoid the issue of recognition of the disguised girl, with consequential strain on the credibility of plots in which lovers and fathers unaccountably fail to recognize their nearest and dearest, but Ford makes this half-recognition pivotal to the development of the play.

Even so, Palador's first reaction on hearing of Eroclea dressed as herself is diametrically opposite to the truth on both counts: 'The young man in disguise upon my life, | To steale out of the Land' (4.3.41–2). Her appearance '*in womans attire*' soon after is thus anticlimactic. Even though Palador has just recognized that his 'heart has been untun'd these many moneths, | Wanting her presence, in whose equall love | True harmony consisted' (52–4), he insists she is just a boy in woman's clothes (which the actor was), a forgery sent to uncover his 'secret':

> 'Tis not the figure stampt upon thy cheekes,
> The coozenage of thy beauty, grace, or tongue,

> Can draw from me a secret, that hath been
> The onely Jewell of my speechlesse thoughts. (4.3.70–3)

The explanation for this apparently churlish response may lie in part in his mistrust of the homoerotic emotions this meeting must involve if he is right, but it depends, again, on the all-pervading mistrust of the lover, 'because feare and love are still linked together. Moreover [lovers] are apt to mistake, amplify, too credulous sometimes, too full of hope and confidence, & then againe very jealous, unapt to beleeve or entertaine any good newes' (*Anatomy* 3.2.3). Palador's cautious 'mistake' is to 'amplify' the negative. But Ford is doing more here than simply applying contemporary psychology. There is also a suggestion, already seen faintly in Thamasta, and manifested more strongly later by Meleander (and seen too in Pericles and Daniel's Thyrsis), of an unwillingness to give up a sustaining fantasy for an uncertain reality, of losing a jewel buried deeper than words. Palador's resistance to accepting Eroclea thus remains angrily firm until she produces the conclusive proof, the miniature which matches his, which has been her 'physicke . . . hourely' (4.3.131–2), to which Palador responds with the fullest reference in the play to an overarching Providential order, an acknowledgement which only underlines his relative passivity, his 'lethargy': 'We are but Fooles | To trifle in disputes, or vainely struggle | With that eternall *mercy* which protects us' (4.3.133–5).

The physic for the future is that most effective treatment, consummation in marriage: 'The last and best Cure of Love-Melancholy, is to let them have their Desire' (*Anatomy* 3.2.5.5). Palador's abrupt welcome of an 'extasie of joyes' in the anticipation of this is correctly but in context rather sanctimoniously tempered by his resolve not to be overcome by passion, not to 'lose that part of man, | Which is reserv'd to intertaine content' (4.3.138–9), or as Burton puts it: 'I may not deny but our passions are violent, and tyrannize over us, yet there be means to curbe them, though they be headstrong, they may be tamed, they may be qualified, if he himselfe or his friends, will but use their honest endeavors' (2.2.6.1). The sentiment is hammered home by Palador's still more sanctimonious concluding couplet, marked as a sententia:

> There is no faith in lust, but baytes of Artes;
> 'Tis vertuous love keepes cleare contracted hearts.

Eroclea by contrast immediately introduces the question of her father, and it is to his cure that the whole of the last act is devoted. Meleander's melancholy is not that of a lover, and yet it is the most desperate in the play, and his is the largest role: he has twenty per cent more words than Corax, the next largest, and over a third more than Palador or Thamasta. Though he dominates Act 5, Meleander is introduced as a study in grief much earlier. His first utterance is a groan, 'able to roote up heart, liver, lungs and all' (2.2.9). His sleep is fitful, his eyes roll, and he has neglected his appearance so much that his servant Trollio considers the possibility of shaving him while 'he sleepes in's naps' (12). He is 'leane | And falne away extremely' (41–2). Uncertain at first who Cleophila and Trollio are, his first thought on waking is of Eroclea's imagined funeral: 'The Raven croakt, and hollow shreeks of Owles | Sung Dirges at her funerall; I laugh'd | The whiles: for 'twas no boot to weepe' (2.2.23–5).[52] Later this mordant laughter is transformed to bitter invective against the vanity of worldly success (2.2.83–97), and grandiose funerals (106–16). In this respect he is like an especially caustic malcontent, a role to which he returns briefly in his confrontation with Corax (4.2.58–75). Believing Eroclea dead, he is suffering from that most devastating cause of melancholy, sorrow, 'The mother and daughter of Melancholy, her Epitome, Symptome, and chiefe cause' which makes sufferers 'weary of their lives, cry out, howle & roare for very anguish of their soules' (*Anatomy*, 1.2.3.4). Later Meleander does indeed roar 'like a Cannon' (4.2.32).

Burton has a long discourse on grief for the 'Death of Friends' (which at this date includes relatives such as daughters) which 'may challenge a first place' as a cause of melancholy. Their temporary absence is bad enough, but if 'absence alone can worke such violent effects, what shall death doe, when they must eternally be seperated, never here to meet againe? This is so grievous a torment for the time, that it takes away all appetite, desire of life, and extinguisheth all delights, it causeth deepe sighes and groanes, teares, exclamations, howling, roaring' (1.2.4.7). Burton adds another cause which also affects Meleander, 'the losse of temporall goods & fortunes, which equally afflicts, and may goe hand in hand with the preceding ['Death of Friends']; losse of time, loss of honour, office, of good name, of labour, frustrate hopes, will much torment; but in my judgment, there is no torture like unto it [i.e. 'Death of Friends'], or that sooner procureth this malady and mischiefe' (1.2.4.7). This is why the subsequent restoration of Meleander's former offices of state, though

---

[52] As Neill suggests, these 'inharmonious dirges' contrast with the harmonies of the nightingale in Menaphon's account ('Moral Artifice', p. 87).

important, takes second place to the restoration of his daughter, the ultimate 'cordial'.[53]

Corax sees this, and this time has no difficulty with his diagnosis. Rhetias describes Meleander's violent symptoms graphically: 'He chafes hugely, fumes like a stew-pot; Is he not monstrously overgone in frenzy?' (4.2.9–10). It is not the madness of frenzy, Corax replies, 'but his sorrow's | Close griping griefe, and anguish of the soule | That torture him: he carries Hell on earth | Within his bosome'. The ultimate cure depends on the cause: since it was 'a Princes tyranny | Caus'd his distraction' so 'a Princes sweetnes | Must qualifie that tempest of his minde' (11–16). It is through Palador's 'sweetnes' that both Eroclea and his offices are restored, as Cleophila makes clear: 'our gracious Prince, | By me presents you (Sir) with this large bounty' (5.2.102–3). As the audience learn later in 4.2, however, considerable preparatory treatment is required before he is in a state to benefit from this final cure. This takes the form of a confrontation between Corax and the angry, deluded Meleander, the winning of his confidence, and finally the drugged 'Cup' (4.2.166) which enables restorative sleep.

The gradual therapy begins with Corax shaking Meleander out of an extreme, potentially violent state of grief. Sorrow, as Burton warns, may cause 'howling, roaring, many bitter pangs' (1.2.4.7). Meleander has been fuming 'like a stew-pot'. His roaring has frightened Cleophila and Trollio, and he enters '*with a poll-axe*' (4.2.49.1), apparently believing himself to be a lion seeking 'the Dog, whose triple throated noyse' has roused him, so he can 'teare the Curre in pieces' (4.2.50–2). Corax's first strategy is an example of driving 'out one passion with another . . . one griefe with another' (*Anatomy* 2.2.6.2).[54] It is remarkably successful: by threatening him wearing a Gorgon mask, Corax reduces him to relative sanity in the space of five and a half lines, then adopts the very different treatment of agreeing with his malcontent view of the world, for friends (and physicians) should humour the patient who cannot 'over-come these heart-eating passions' (*Anatomy* 2.2.6.2). In this case the humouring takes the form of agreeing to let Meleander hang him, the most effective answer to the world's evils (4.2.75), an event Corax postpones effectively by taking on Meleander's own predicament, pleading delay until he can see a daughter who has

---

[53] Sensabaugh, 'Burton's Influence', is surely wrong in suggesting that Meleander's sorrow over loss of office takes precedence over his grief for Eroclea's supposed death (p. 560).

[54] Cf. Bright, *Treatise*, p. 255: 'And if no other perswasion will serve a vehement passion, of another sort is to be kindeled, that may withdrawe that vaine and foolish sorowe into some other extremity'.

been 'Snatcht from me in her youth' (4.2.90). The shock which this
forced confrontation with the pain of his own loss causes to Meleander
introduces one of Ford's most profound passages of psychological
insight, as Meleander recognizes how his frenzied state has shielded
him from the presumed reality of Eroclea's death:

> whilst I am franticke,
> Whilst throngs of rude divisions huddle on,
> And doe disranke my braines from peace, and sleepe;
> So long I am insensible of cares. (96–9)

His 'distemper'd thoughts' find a paradoxical 'rest in their rage' as
long as he is not forced, as now by Corax, to confront his grief:

> Then are my griefes strooke home, when they are reclaym'd,
> To their owne pitty of themselves (105–6)

This moment of insight, and his belief that Corax has like him lost a
daughter, brings Meleander into deeper sympathy with his doctor.
'Like true friends' they can 'Sigh out a lamentable tale of things |
Done long agoe, and ill done' (120–1). He recognizes that his melancholy is not only protective, but that he perversely enjoys it: 'With
what greedinesse | Doe I hug my afflictions?' (126–7). This is a more
self-aware version of Palador's reluctance to let go of his melancholy.
Corax's treatment has induced a calmer, more trusting state, and it is
thus that Meleander feels able to introduce Cleophila to him, mani-
festing an overdue recognition of her virtues, in a tribute which ends
with a brief but now significantly more composed remembrance of
Eroclea: 'I coo'd describe | A pretty piece of goodnesse: let that
passe—| We must be wise somtimes' (4.2.147–8). But if Meleander is
more rational, he is still deeply melancholy, seeing his death as the
only remedy for Cleophila's 'miseries'. He needs the last step in Corax's
preparatory therapy before he is ready for the final 'cordial' of the restoration of Eroclea and of his offices. This is the sleeping draught
which has already been prepared by Cleophila on Corax's instructions,
a 'Nectar' which will indeed be 'divine' for Meleander, as, briefly, it
was for Lear (4.2.175).

The idea that Corax is unsuccessful or 'not necessary to Meleander's
cure' seriously underestimates his careful, Burtonian strategy in this
scene,[55] and his thoughtful regimen continues in the final act, where
Cleophila emphasizes the need to maintain patience and gradualism in

---

[55] Cf. Ewing, p. 45; Babb, *Elizabethan Malady*, p. 116.

her father's treatment, so that when he wakes from his therapeutic sleep 'he may by degrees, digest | The present blessings in a moderate Joy' (5.1.13–14). Ford had already emphasized that both Thamasta and Palador needed time to come to terms with Eroclea's revelation of her true identity. Meleander, further gone in melancholy and with a body 'over spred with severall sorts | Of such diseases as the strength of Youth | Would groane under and sinke' (5.2.30–2), requires more careful preparation.

The fresh garments Meleander wears when he next enters derive, like the couch in which he is carried, from *Lear*. For Lear, Pericles, and Meleander the change in their appearance has a powerful symbolic significance, especially in the visual medium of the theatre. But here too Burton provides common sense therapeutic advice which may explain why Ford goes further than his sources in Shakespeare: 'Let him not be alone or idle . . . but still accompanied with such friends and familiars he most affects, neatly dressed, washed, & combed, according to his ability at least, in cleane sweete linen, spruce, neate, decent, and good apparel, for nothing sooner dejects a man then want, squaler, and nastines, foule, or old clothes out of fashion' (2.5.1.1). Though this comes under the heading of 'Particular Cure of the three several Kinds; of Head Melancholy' it is not in itself a cure, not at least for Meleander. His anger at discovering he has been drugged is vented on Corax when the doctor asks Rhetias to bring another 'Cordiall | Prepar'd for him to take after his sleepe' (5.2.33–4). Assuming this to be another drug, Meleander attacks Corax in a speech which is remarkable in Ford's anticipation of twentieth-century attempts to control mental illness by sedation:

> Foole, the waight
> Of my disease sits on my heart so heavy,
> That all the hands of Art cannot remove
> One graine to ease my griefe. If thou cood'st poyson
> My memory, or wrap my senses up
> Into a dulnesse, hard and cold as Flints!
> If thou cood'st make me walke, speake, eate and laugh
> Without a sense or knowledge of my faculties,
> Why then perhaps at Marts thou might'st make benefit
> Of such an Anticke motion, and get credit
> From credulous gazers, but not profit me. (5.2.37–47)

The dark arts of the chemical cosh, numbing memory, wrapping the 'senses up | Into a dulnesse', and turning the patient into an 'Anticke motion', were not on the horizon in the treatment of mental illness until centuries after this, but the idea of a drug suggests their terrible potential to Ford. For Corax, however, 'Physick' is not the answer.

Instead, the 'cordial' Corax has promised, and arranged with Rhetias and Palador, is purely psychological. Again the process is gradual, and appropriately theatrical, staged first in a series of tableaux, with the restoration and augmentation of various offices of state, and the presentation of the miniature of Eroclea which Palador has been wearing. Despite this care, Meleander is literally shaken—'What Earthquakes | Roule in my flesh?'—and suspicious that these are all 'Inchantments deadly (as the grave)' (5.2.85), but he is now able to look with appreciative resignation at the miniature of Eroclea, his admiration tempered by the wish that the image was alive, that the 'cunning Artsman' might 'have fashen'd | A little hollow space here, and blowne breath | To have made it move, and whisper' (5.2.95–8). Such Pygmalion tropes are common as tributes to great art during this period (see e.g. *Winter's Tale*, 5.3.77–9), but here Meleander's willingness to entertain the idea of a miraculously recreated Eroclea functions as psychological preparation for the subsequent introduction of the real thing, her presentation orchestrated by Corax—''Tis time I see to fetch the Cordiall' (91)—and carried out on Palador's behalf by Cleophila (100–4).

In the reconciliation of Meleander and Eroclea Ford brilliantly exploits the mixed emotions of tragicomedy, emotions encapsulated in Meleander's remark that 'Here in the Legend of thy two yeeres exile, | Rare pity and delight are sweetly mixt' (5.2.171–2). The groundwork for this mixture had been laid in the first scene, in the 'mirth and pitie' of the musical duel. There is an echo of the nightingale's death from a broken heart in Meleander's first reaction to Eroclea's reappearance, thanking her for taking 'so much paines | To live, till I might once more looke upon thee, | Before I broke my heart' (116–18). This is not the response of unalloyed joy that Rhetias, or probably the audience, had been expecting—'The good-man rellisheth his comforts strangely, | The sight doth turne me child' (120–1). Ford's interest is still in a more complex and realistic psychology of the emotions, in which Meleander moves away from the broken heart, to a state in which he can only look at Eroclea and remain confusedly inarticulate:

> Yet let us gaze on one another freely,
> And surfet with our eyes; let me be plaine,
> If I should speake as much as I should speake,
> I should talke of a thousand things at once,
> And all of thee, of thee (my child) of thee' (123–7).

Ford uses double em dashes which here signify confused hesitation as Meleander tries to analyse an appropriate response:

> My teares like ruffling winds lockt up in Caves,
> Doe bustle for a vent—on t'other side,
> To flye out into mirth were not so comely.
> Come hither, let me kisse thee—(5.2.128–31).

Though Eroclea's return brings him 'Strength, courage, and fresh blood' (5.2.132), Meleander's memory of his trauma still remains, like Palador's, very uncertain: 'Let me be thinke me, how we parted first | Puzzles my faint remembrance' (5.2.148–9). Lucidity only returns by stages, as Eroclea and Rhetias tell him what has happened, and as if to symbolize a returning clarity of mind, Meleander belatedly notices his 'fresh rayments' and, looking in a mirror, can pun about being 'in the trim' (204–5). He can also now acknowledge (what some critics cannot) that Corax and Cleophila have managed this recovery: the cordial is 'a rare one' (5.2.219).

It is at this point that Palador begins to organize the conventional closing of the tragicomedy, claiming Eroclea as his bride, and contracting Cleophila to Amethus, Thamasta to Menaphon. But although Meleander does bless his daughters' marriages, Ford ends on a note which does not point to unequivocal resolution. Though Meleander's final words are to thank his brother, he does so brokenly—'Thou art my Brother: I can say no more'—and his powerful penultimate speech returns to his mental and physical frailty in a way that unmistakeably, and presumably intentionally, echoes *King Lear*:

> My braines are dull'd;
> I am intranc'd, and know not what you meane:
> Great, gracious Sir, alas, why do you mocke me?
> I am a weake old man, so poore and feeble,
> That my untoward joynts can scarcely creepe
> Unto the grave, where I must seeke my rest. (5.2.231–6)

The pathos, and indeed darkness, of this leaves the audience with a response in which 'pity and delight' remain mixed, rather as they do for different reasons at the end of *Two Noble Kinsmen*. The arc in which, according to Palador's trite conclusion, 'Sorrowes are chang'd to Bride-songs' has not been fully transacted, and the consequences of melancholy for Meleander, if not for the prince and the other protagonists, have become, as Burton might have said, 'a chronic or continuate disease, a settled humour' (1.1.1.5).

STAGE HISTORY

The quarto's title page indicates that the play was 'acted at the private house in the Blacke Friers, and publikely at the Globe by the Kings Majesties Servants', and Herbert's licence confirms the Blackfriars location, adding the date of 24 November 1628 for the first performance. After the winter of 1628–9, it would have transferred to the Globe in the summer. Ford takes the relatively unusual step of listing 'The names of such as acted', but does not say which parts they took (for suggestions, and the size of the main roles, see the commentary note 'The names of such as acted', 3–14). There is no evidence about the reception of the play, other than Humphrey Howorth's assertion that it 'adorn'd the Stage' ('*To the Author, Master* John Ford', line 8), praise too clichéd to be of any value.

Consideration seems to have been given during the Restoration to abridging *The Lover's Melancholy* for a production by Davenant, but this came to nothing.[56] The next production on 28 April 1747 by Charles Macklin at the Theatre Royal, Drury Lane, was staged as a benefit for his wife, and is memorable because of Macklin's attempt to 'puff' the play through two forged letters. The first, signed 'B.B.', praised the play as being 'after the manner of Shakespeare', not surprisingly according to the letter, since Ford was 'an intimate and professed admirer'. This apparently did not sell enough tickets, so the play was postponed for a week, during which time Macklin claimed to have found (and lost) a pamphlet which claimed 'that *The Lover's Melancholy* was not [Ford's] own, but *purloined from Shakespeare's* papers'. Many years later Malone tried unsuccessfully to persuade the ninety-year-old Macklin, who pleaded senile amnesia, to confess to the forgery; Malone devoted twenty-seven cogent pages to demolishing the claims, but (having been only five at the time) does not describe the production.[57]

Finally, a reading performance was given in the Shakespeare's Globe Wanamaker Playhouse on 7 June 2015, directed by James Wallace as part of the 'Read Not Dead' season. As mentioned earlier, this production went some way to justify the inclusion of the comic 'bye' plot, and it demonstrated that inconsistencies which emerge in critical reading and rereading do not present themselves to an audience watching for the first time. It confirmed the dominance of

---

[56] See Clifford Leech, 'A Projected Restoration Performance of Ford's "The Lover's Melancholy"?', *MLR* 56 (1961), 378–81.

[57] For the extended discussion, 'Shakespeare, Ford, and Jonson', see Malone, *The Plays and Poems of William Shakespeare*, 1:387–414; Malone transcribes the two letters on pp. 202–5.

Meleander, powerfully played by Sam Cox, towards the end of the play. He only appears in three scenes, but his role is not only the largest in terms of words, but in terms of the audience's response to the play as it moves to a conclusion. This scratch performance, with no props or costume, and with the shortest rehearsal time, confirmed that *The Lover's Melancholy* is a play which deserves a fuller outing on the modern stage.

PRINTING HISTORY

'*The lovers Melanchollye* by IOHN FFORD gent' was entered in the Stationer's Register on 2 June 1629 by Henry Seile.[58] The title page records that it was printed in 1629. This gives a possible date between June 1629 and 24 March 1630, but stationers by no means always used old style dating. Indeed, they appear to have preferred that books printed late in the calendar year should be dated to the subsequent one, so it is likely that printing was completed by October–November 1629.[59] The variant imprint surviving in one copy 'printed for *HS* 1629' was probably for copies to be sold by other stationers.

The anonymous printer was Felix Kingston, whose press was in Paternoster Row, on the north side of St. Paul's, between 1599 and 1644.[60] He can be identified by the ornaments on A3ʳ and A4ᵛ, which were used copiously in the same year in Sir John Beaumont's *Bosworth Field: with a Taste of the Variety of Other Poems*, 'printed by Felix Kingston', also for Seile (and entered by him on the same day as *The Lover's Melancholy*). The large capital *T* which begins the dedication of *The Lover's Melancholy* on A2ʳ is also found at the head of the title poem of Beaumont's collection (B1ʳ). The more elaborate device above the dedication is found on a2ʳ and c3ᵛ of Lancelot Andrewes's *Stricturae: or, A briefe answer* (1629) with Kingston's name on the title page. Davenant's *Albovine*, the other play he printed that year, is not acknowledged, but, as in *The Lover's Melancholy*,

---

[58] *A Transcript of the Registers of the Company of Stationers of London; 1554–1640 A.D.*, ed. Edward Arber (Privately Printed, London, 1877), 4.179.

[59] See D. F. McKenzie, *The Cambridge University Press, 1696–1712: A Bibliographical Study* (Cambridge: Cambridge University Press, 1966), 1:145–6; Cain and Connolly, eds., *Complete Poetry of Robert Herrick*, 1:413. For Seile, see *STC*, vol. 3, *Printers' & Publishers' Index, other Indexes & Appendices*, by Katharine F. Pantzer (London, 1991), p. 151; Henry B. Wheatley, 'Signs of Booksellers in St. Paul's Churchyard', *The Library* (1906), *TBS* 9, 67–106, pp. 76–7, 104.

[60] *STC* 3:99. For a study of the printing of Ford's plays, especially their use of emphatic type, see R. J. Fehrenbach, 'Typographical Variation in Ford's Texts: Accidentals or Substantives?', in Anderson, pp. 265–93.

Kingston used the same device above the dedication (A2^r) and at the head of the text on B1^r.

The Lover's Melancholy is a quarto on pot paper with leaves in the largest copies (such as LG, and O5, Burton's own copy) measuring 18.5 × 13.5 cm., giving a sheet size of around 39 × 29 cm. In all the copies whose watermarks I have examined, sig. A is printed on paper with a mark of a quartered coat of arms surmounted by a crown, with a lion passant in each of the bottom quarters, and '1610' below. The top quarters are buried in the gutter, but the mark seems to be Heawood's 576, found by him in the 1629 edition of Hobbes's *Thucydides*, also printed for Seile, but by the Eliot's Court Press. Seile may have supplied the paper to both printers.[61] Kingston also used this paper throughout *Bosworth Field*. Most remaining sheets of the play (sigs. B–M) were printed on paper with a pot watermark with the initials AV (Heawood 3561). Heawood found this paper in Edmondes's *Caesars Commentaries* (1600).[62] Both these papers have chain marks around 20 mm apart. Other paper was used, however: in several copies a single gathering is printed on paper with a pot mark similar to Heawood 3575, but with the letters C (or G) and H. Less often, paper with a pot mark not found in Heawood is used, again for one or two sheets (e.g. L and M of O5). In LVD1 and 2 sheet M is on paper with a mark similar to Heawood 967, used in Amsterdam in 1625. The random, occasional use of these papers may mean they were available from a concurrent job when the 'AV' paper was not ready or, since they are found in sigs. L and M, was running out. The type is English Roman and Italic, body 90, face 80 × 1.9:3.

Kingston had a long career as a printer, from 1597 to 1652, but during this time, in which he printed well over 700 surviving books, only seven English plays or masques produced by him are known: of these, *The Lover's Melancholy* and Davenant's *Albovine* were both printed in 1629.[63] Other plays from his press may be among the many dramas of this period now lost, but even allowing for this, he was

---

[61] Edward Heawood, *Watermarks Mainly of the 17th and 18th Centuries* (Paper Publications Society, Hilversum, 1950), p. 77 and pl. 89.

[62] *Watermarks*, pl. 143 and pl. 481; but see *STC* 7488 for the complex history of the *Commentaries*. The maker may have been Annet Vacherias of Riom, Auvergne: see Raymond Gaudriault avec le concours de Thérèse Gaudriault, *Filigranes et Autres Caractéristiques des Papiers Fabriqués en France aux XVIIe et XVIIIe Siècles* (Paris: CNRS Éditions and J. Telford), p. 273.

[63] Other plays or masques are Anon., *Edward the Fourth* (*STC* 13342, 1600); Beaumont, *Masque of the Inner Temple and Gray's Inn* (*STC* 1663, 1613); Chapman, *Masque of the Middle Temple and Lincoln's Inn* (*STC* 4982, 1614); Fletcher, *The Elder Brother* (*STC* 11066, 1637); and Marmion, *The Antiquary* (Wing, 703, 1641). Kingston also printed editions of Terence (1624 and 1629) and Seneca's tragedies (1634).

clearly not a specialist in this field, which goes some way to explain the frequently eccentric setting of prose as verse (e.g. 1.2.42–7) and vice versa (e.g. 2.1.34–5). There is not enough evidence to identify different compositors with any confidence: Fehrenbach's suggestion that there were two is based mainly on the fact that some pages in sheets H–M and A contain more emphatic pointing and fuller stage directions than B-G.[64] This is, however, because of textual demands, not different compositors' habits: the masque, which needs elaborate italic stage directions and which has songs set in italic was set on both formes of H, while L inner italicizes the long stage direction describing Meleander's entrance 'in a Coach' and the song which follows. Sheets I, K, and L are otherwise indistinguishable from B-G, while M inner appears slightly different because it contains the italic Epilogue. Sheet A inevitably stands out because the introductory material, added by Ford with much emphatic pointing, is set there.

D. F. McKenzie's work on the composition and press-work at Cambridge in the period around 1700 has shown how fallible and unrealistic were traditional twentieth-century attempts to reconstruct printing history.[65] Hill's suggestion that 'seven skeletons were used' (p. 34) for *The Lover's Melancholy* falls into this category. He was identifying skeleton formes by their three-word running titles alone (there are no recurrent rules or ornaments), and it is true that the compositor[s] changed the running title '*The Louers Melancholy*' a number of times, including the mistaken setting which made it '*The Melancholy Louer*' for several leaves. But a running title does not make a skeleton forme, only part of it, and no commercial printer would dismantle and reassemble the furniture of seven skeletons to print the eleven sheets used for the play text of *The Lover's Melancholy* unless he had to. He might, however, find himself forced to correct the running-titles in one or more formes, and this is what happened. In other respects, this was basically a normal two-skeleton job.

As has been said Kingston used different paper for sig. A in all the copies whose watermarks I have been able to examine. This suggests that as usual printing began with sig. B. It was common to start with the inner forme, and in this case it seems that when sheet B was perfected, and the type which had been used for B outer had been distributed, the skeleton was used to set D outer. I make this suggestion because the compositor had to substitute a new running title for the

---

[64] Fehrenbach, 'Typographical Variation', pp. 276–7, 292.
[65] *The Cambridge University Press 1696–1712*, 1:94–146; see also McKenzie, 'Printers of the Mind: Some Notes on Bibliographical Theories and Printing-House Practices', *SB*, 22 (1969), 1–75.

larger half-title and ornament which open the play text on B1^r. On D3^r, which, allowing for rotation, corresponds in the forme to B1^r, a new running title accordingly appears: but instead of *The Louers Melancholy* the compositor absent-mindedly set *The Melancholy Louer*.[66] This error persisted through four formes (D outer, E inner, F inner, and G outer). Worse still, the careless change made to a single heading in D outer had lodged in the compositor's mind, for he now changed all four running titles in E outer to *The Melancholy Louer*, an error that persisted in G inner. F inner follows D outer in having the wrong running title only on one page.

To the extent that they have a completely new set of running titles, E outer and G inner may be said to involve a new skeleton, but in fact they were probably new only in respect of those titles. The compositor's practice was to keep his headlines—running titles and page numbers—as part of the furniture of the skeleton forme, rather than removing them and placing them at the head of new text on the composing stone, and it seems likely that the mis-corrections to the running titles were made in this way. In this respect, D outer and subsequent formes containing the running title *The Melancholy Louer* on one leaf (E and F inner, G outer) were modified versions of skeleton two, while E outer and G inner, even though they contained four incorrect running titles, were still essentially modified versions of skeleton one.

After these errors were noticed, the sequence seems to have continued with F outer, probably a corrected version of skeleton one, and G outer, where the single leaf error had not yet been noticed. H outer was set on the new version of skeleton one, and H inner on a corrected version of skeleton two, so that both skeleton formes now had correct running titles. So much paper had been used up that there was no question of scrapping the four sheets with incorrect running titles; they comprised one-third of the paper budgeted for, and paper was the most expensive item in the printer's costs. From sheet H onwards, Kingston probably continued to alternate the two skeletons as he had first intended. There does not seem much evidence to support Hill's theory that the skeleton used for F outer was not used again until L and M outer. This, again, is based on running titles alone, but any

---

[66] Two surviving copies have a turned *u* in the corresponding running title on C1^r, but this seems unlikely to provide the explanation for the error in D outer. 'Melancholy Louer' was part of the title—though not the running title—of one of the first books Kingston printed, Robert Tofte's *Alba, the Months Minde of a Melancholy Louer* (1598). If Kingston was also the compositor, or somehow influenced him, it may have lurked for over thirty years, to emerge here.

small variations in spacing and type can be accounted for by the need to change page numbers.

If D outer was set before C outer, then clearly the play was cast off for setting by formes, which was common practice at this date. Further evidence for this is the 'wide variation in the spacing of character entries; some are cramped between lines of speech, some are allowed plenty of white space' (Hill, p. 36). This would have allowed the compositor to adjust for any flaws in the casting off. The cramped H3^r, last page to be set in this sheet, is a good example of the problems sometimes caused by casting off: the opening of Act 4, which is on H3^v, had already been printed on H inner, which has generous spacing on all four pages. So on H3^r, at the end of H outer, where Act 3 finishes, the compositor had to squeeze in an extra line, give less space than usual to a stage direction, turn over two long lines, and omit the signature.

COPY

The copy given to Kingston derived directly from the author, or at one remove through a scribe, possibly within the printing house, copying Ford's manuscript. The added dedication, commendatory verses, list of actors, Latin act headings and endings, and the marginal notes all point to a text prepared by Ford for printing. Hill suggests that the Prologue and Epilogue were also added; but the Prologue may well have been spoken in the theatre: it addresses an 'audience' of 'Gentlemen' who could be at home or in the theatre. The Epilogue is less equivocal, in that it distinguishes between 'We', the actors, and 'He', the author, and conventionally, if rather churlishly, asks for applause in a way that would befit an actor on the stage. It, or something like it, was probably spoken at the Blackfriars and the Globe.

Hill is right to point to occasionally elaborate stage directions as necessary authorial additions for a literary text: good examples are those in the masque scene, or the elaborate opening of 5.2: '*Soft Musicke. Enter MELEANDER (in a Coach) his haire and beard trimd, habit and gowne chang'd. RHETIAS and CORAX, and Boy that sings.*' Also authorial is a feature, found as Hill points out in other Ford quartos, of emphatic italic (or roman if appropriate) for words such as 'melancholy' or 'delirium', or for words he wishes to emphasize for other reasons, such as 'the cleare *Quiristers* of the Woods' (1.1.118) who listen to the musical duel. This is said to be the only play printed by Kingston which uses such emphatic typography, confirming that they are Ford's enhancements.[67] Another feature of his text which was probably added for printing, but which harks back to the play as it was acted, is his frequent use of long dashes to indicate such things as *aposiopesis*, asides (e.g. 2.20, 2.1.270), a change of adressee (e.g. 2.2.97 and 102), pauses (e.g. 2.1.220) or hesitation and confusion (e.g. 2.1.289), and possibly stage business of some kind (e.g. 3.1.23–5). This is a device found also in Shirley's quartos, and the reader sometimes must guess at just what was going on. While the dashes could have been in Ford's foul papers, indicating where he wanted such stage business, this seems unlikely. They would have been of no use in the prompt-book, which would have required specific notes, so it seems likely that they were added by Ford from his memory of the play in performance.

COLLATION AND STOP PRESS CORRECTION

Title-Page
See p. 260. CH2 has a variant imprint 'printed for *HS* 1629' in place of '*H. Seile*, and are to be sold at the Ty- | gers head in Saint *Pauls* Church-yard. | 1629.'

Formula
Quarto with leaves measuring approx. 18.5 × 13.5 cm.
RT (A2v) The Epistle Dedicatory;
(B1ᵛ–D2ᵛ, D3ᵛ–D4ᵛ, E3ᵛ–F1ᵛ, F2ᵛ–F4ᵛ, G2ᵛ–G3ʳ, G4ᵛ–M3ᵛ) *The Louers Melancholy*;
(D3ʳ, E1ʳ, E2ʳ–E3ʳ, E4ᵛ, F2ʳ, G1ʳ–G2ʳ, G3ᵛ–G4ʳ) *The Melancholy Louer*.
A–M4 (M4ᵛ blank); H3 not signed. 52 leaves, numbered from B1ʳ to M3ᵛ (irregular pagination in bold): 1–49, **66–7**, 52–3, **70–1**, 56–86.

Technical Notes
Catchwords: B4ʳ Willingly,] *Men.* Willingly.   E3ʳ *Kal.*] *Kala.*   L3ʳ *Ret.*] *Rhet.*

Stop press corrections

Inner C	State 1	State 2
C2ʳ l. 26	matter	matcher

State 1: CH1, EN1, O2.
State 2: CH2, CN, EC, EN2, GU, IU, L1, L2, L3, LG, LVD1, LVD2, MB, MH, NC, NLS, NN, O1, O3, O4, O5, O6, OM, OS, OW, PH, PU, TU1, WF1, WF2, WF3, Y1.

---

[67] See Fehrenbach, 'Typographical Variation', p. 276.

Inner D	State 1	State 2
D1^v l. 23	weary of	weary of.
l. 24	*Sophronos.*	*Aret. Sophronos,*
l. 25	*Aret.* I am	I am
D4^r l. 25	young	Younger

State 1: CN, GU, LVD2, OS, PU, Y1
State 2: CH1, CH2, EC, EN1, EN2, GH, IU, L1, L2, L3, LVD1, MB, MH, NC, NLS, NN, O1, O2, O3, O4, O5, O6, OM, OW, PH, TU1, WF1, WF2, WF3.

Outer H	State 1	State 2	State 3
H1^r l. 31	interpretation	interpretation	interruption
H2^v l. 30	[*indented*]	[*not indented*]	[*not indented*]
H4^v l. 12	equally	equality	equality
l. 13	Lowe	low	Low

State 1: GU
State 2: CH1, EC, EN1, L3, LG, PU, WF1, WF2, WF3.
State 3: CH2, CN, EN 2, IU, L1, L2, LVD1, LVD2, MH, NC, NN, NLS, O1, O2, O3, O4, O5, O6, OM, OS, OW, PH, TU1, Y1.

Outer L	State 1	State 2
L3^r direction	Sig. L3 omitted	L3

State 1: L1, L2, MB, NC, NN, O1, O3, O4, O6.
State 2: CH1, CH2, CN, EC, EN1, EN2, GU, IU, L3, LG, LVD1, LVD2, MH, NLS, O2, O5, OM, OS, OW, PH, PU, TU1, WF1, WF2, WF3, Y1.

CH1	Henry E. Huntington Library, San Marino, Cal., 59795
CH2	Henry E. Huntington Library, 88303
CN	Newberry Library, Chicago, Case Y135 F7566
EC	Eton College, S.178. Plays 51(01)
EN1	National Library of Scotland, Edinburgh, H.28.e.12
EN2	National Library of Scotland, Bute 230
GU	Glasgow University, CO.3.31
IU	University of Illinois, 822 F75L 1629
L1	British Library 644.b.34
L2	British Library C.12.g.3
L3	British Library Ashley 755
LG	Guildhall Library, London, Bay H 4.2, no.11
LVD1	Dyce Collection, Victoria and Albert Museum, London, 3819/25.b.27
LVD2	Dyce Collection, Victoria and Albert Museum, 3819/25.b.28
MB	Boston Public Library, Boston, MA, G.3971.38

MH   Harvard University, Houghton Library, PR2524 .L68 1629[68]
NC   Columbia University, New York, DRAMLIB D823F75 S7
NLS   National Library of Sweden, Stockholm
NN   New York Public Library, Arents Collection, no. 168.
O1   Bodleian Library, Oxford, Mal. 238 (1)
O2   Bodleian Library, Mal. 203 (3)
O3   Bodleian Library, Mal. B 166 (10)
O4   Bodleian Library, 4° S 34 (6) Art
O5   Bodleian Library, 4° T 36 (6) Art
O6   Bodleian Library, Mal. 214 (7)
OM   Magdalen College, Oxford, Arch D 4.3
OS   St John's College, Oxford, HB4/3.a.5.23(1)
OW   Worcester College, Oxford
PH   Haverford College, PA, Phillips Collection, 19
PU   University of Pennsylvania, Philadelphia, PR2524.L6 1629
TU1   University of Texas at Austin, Harry Ransome Center, PFORZ 382 PFZ
WF1   Folger Shakespeare Library, Washington, DC, STC 11163, copy 1
WF2   Folger Shakespeare Library, STC 11163, copy 2
WF3   Folger Shakespeare Library, STC 11163, copy 3
Y1   Yale University, Conn., Beinecke Library, Eliz. 81

Later Editions

The first edition since the quarto was in vol. 1 of Henry Weber's *Dramatic Works of John Ford* (Edinburgh, 1811). This was followed by William Gifford's edition, in vol. 1 of *The Dramatic Works of John Ford* (2 vols., 1827); Gifford's text was re-published with some revisions by Alexander Dyce in the first volume of *The Works of John Ford* (3 vols., 1869). Later significant editions are by Havelock Ellis, *The Best Plays of the Old Dramatists: John Ford* (Mermaid Series, 1888); Willy Bang, *John Fordes dramatische Werke. In Neudruck herausgegeben von W. Bang* (Louvain, 1908), in his *Materialien zur Kunde des älteren englischen Dramas*, Bd. 23. NS, vol. 1; and John Ford, *''Tis Pity She's a Whore' and Other Plays*, ed. Marion Lomax (Oxford, 1995). The only single-volume edition is by R. F. Hill, *The Lover's Melancholy*, Revels Plays (Manchester, 1985). I have made use of Hill's excellent notes, and of MS notes on the text kindly supplied by the late Professor Tom Craik; his conjectures are always perceptive, and whether accepted or not, they are all recorded in the collation.

---

[68] I have not been able to inspect MH and have relied on Carter Hailey's report.

THE
LOVERS
Melancholy.

ACTED
AT THE PRIVATE
HOVSE IN THE BLACKE
Friers, and publikely at the Globe
by the Kings Maiefties Seruants.

LONDON,
Printed for *H. Seile*, and are to be fold at the Ty-
gers head in Saint *Pauls* Church-yard.
1629. *ʃ·m*

2.

Title page of *The Lover's Melancholy* (1629). By permission of the Victoria and
Albert Museum National Art Library

The Lover's Melancholy

The Sceane
Famagosta in Cyprus.

The names of such as acted

JOHN LOWIN	RICHARD SHARPE.
JOSEPH TAYLOR.	THOMAS POLLARD.
ROBERT BENFIELD.	WILLIAM PENN.
JOHN SHANCK.	CURTEISE GRIVILL.
EYLYARDT SWANSTON.	GEORGE VERNON.
ANTHONY SMITH.	RICHARD BAXTER

5

JOHN TOMSON.
JOHN HONYMAN.
JAMES HORNE.
WILLIAM TRIGG.
ALEXANDER GOUGH.

10

TO MY WOR-THILY RESPECTED FRIENDS, NATHANIEL FINCH, JOHN FORD, Esquires; Mr. HENRY BLUNT, Mr. ROBERT ELLICE, and all the rest of the Noble Society of Grayes Inne

5

My Honour'd Friends,

The account of some leisurable houres, is here summ'd up, and offered to examination. Importunity *of Others,* or Opinion *of mine owne, hath not urg'd on any confidence of running the hazard of a censure.*

As plurality hath reference to a Multitude, so, I care not to please
Many: but where there is a Parity of condition, there the freedom of
construction, makes the best musicke. This concord hath equally held 10
betweene YOU THE PATRONES, *and* ME THE PRESENTOR. *I am*
cleer'd of all scruple of dis-respect on your parts; as I am of too slacke
a Merit in my selfe. My presumption of comming in Print in this
kind, hath hitherto been un-reprooveable. This Piece, *being the* first,
A2ᵛ *that ever | courted Reader; and it is very possible, that the like com-* 15
plement with Me, may soone grow out of fashion. A practice of which
that I may avoid now, I commend to the continuance of your Loves,
the memory *of* HIS, *who without the protestation of a service, is*
readily your Friend,
A3ʳ   JOHN FORD

To my Honour'd Friend, Master John
Ford, *on his Lover's Melancholy.*

IF that thou think'st these lines thy worth can raise,
    Thou do'st mistake: *my* liking is no prayse:
Nor can I thinke thy Judgement is so ill,
    To seeke for Bayes from such a barraine Quill:
Let your *true Critick*, that can judge and mend,   5
    Allow thy Sceanes and Stile: I, as a friend
That knowes thy worth, doe onely sticke my Name,
    To shew *my Love*, not to advance *thy Fame*.
                                                George Donne.

To his worthy Friend, the Author,
Master John Ford.

I write not to thy Play: Ile not begin
To throw a censure upon what hath been
By th' *Best* approv'd; *It* can nor feare, nor want
The *Rage*, or *Liking* of the Ignorant.
Nor seeke I Fame for Thee, when thine owne Pen   5
Hath forc'd a praise long since, from knowing Men.
I speake my thoughts, and wish unto the Stage
A glory from thy studies; that the Age
A3ᵛ   May be indebted to Thee, for Reprieve
Of purer language, and that *Spight* may grieve   10
To see *It selfe* out-done. When Thou art read,
The Theater may hope Arts are not dead,

Though long conceal'd; that *Poet-Apes* may feare
To vent their weaknesse, mend, or quite forbeare.
This I dare promise; and keepe this in store;   15
As thou hast done enough, Thou canst doe more.
                    William Singleton.

To the Author, Master John Ford.

BLacke choler, Reasons over-flowing Spring,
Where thirsty Lovers drinke, or any Thing,
Passion, the restlesse current of dull plaints
Affords their thoughts, who deeme lost beauties, Saints:
Here their *best Lectures* read, collect, and see   5
Various conditions of Humanitie
Highly enlighten'd by thy Muses rage;
Yet all so coucht, that they adorn'd the Stage.
Shun *Phocions blushes* thou; for sure to please
It is no sinne, then what is thy disease?   10
Judgements applause? effeminated smiles?
Studie's delight? thy wit mistrust beguiles:
          Establisht Fame will thy Physicion be,
          (Write but againe) to cure thy Jealousie.
                    Hum. Howorth.

Of the Lover's Melancholy.   A4ʳ

'TIS not the Language, nor the fore-plac'd Rimes
Of Friends, that shall commend to after-times
The *Lover's Melancholy:* Its owne worth
Without a borrowed prayse, shall set it forth.
                    Ὁ Φίλος

THE PROLOGUE.

To tell yee (Gentlemen) in what true sense
The Writer, Actors, or the audience
Should mold their Judgements for a Play, might draw
Truth into Rules, but we have no such law.
Our Writer, for himselfe would have yee know,   5
That in his following Sceanes, he doth not owe
To others Fancies, nor hath layne in wait
For any stolne Invention, from whose height
He might commend his owne, more then the right
A Scholer claimes, may warrant for delight.   10
It is Arts scorne, that some of late have made
The Noble use of Poetry a Trade.
For your parts (Gentlemen) to quite his paines,
Yet you will please, that as you meet with straines
Of lighter mixtures, but to cast your eye   15
Rather upon the maine, then on the bye.
His hopes stand firme, and we shall find it true,
The Lover's Melancholy *cur'd by you.*

DRAMATIS PERSONAE

PALADOR, *Prince of Cyprus.*
AMETHUS, *cousin to the prince.*
MELEANDER, *an old lord.*
SOPHRONOS, *brother to Meleander.*
MENAPHON, *son of Sophronos.*   5
ARETUS, *tutor to the prince.*
CORAX, *a physician.*
RHETIAS, *servant to Eroclea.*
PELIAS, *a foolish courtier.*
CUCULUS, *a gull.*   10
TROLLIO, *servant to Meleander.*
GRILLA, *page to Cuculus, in woman's dress.*
THAMASTA, *sister of Amethus, and cousin to the Prince.*
EROCLEA, *daughter to Meleander.*
CLEOPHILA, *daughter to Meleander.*   15
KALA, *waiting-maid to Thamasta.*
PHILOSOPHER, *character in masque.*
SEA-NYMPH, *character in masque.*

Dramatis Personae] *Weber subst.; not in Q.*   17–18 PHILOSOPHER, SEA NYMPH] *this edn.*

I.I   *Enter* MENAPHON *and* PELIAS.

MENAPHON   DAngers? How meane you dangers, that so courtly
  You gratulate my safe returne from dangers?

PELIAS   From Travailes (noble Sir.)

MENAPHON   These are delights,
  If my experience hath not Trewant-like
  Mis-spent the time, which I have strove to use,   5
  For bettering my mind with observation.

PELIAS   As I am modest, I protest 'tis strange:
      But is it possible?

MENAPHON   What?

PELIAS   To bestride
  The frothy fomes of *Neptunes* surging waves,
  When blustring *Boreas* tosseth up the deepe,   10
  And thumps a thunder bounce?

MENAPHON   Sweet Sir, 'tis nothing,
  Straight comes a Dolphin playing neere your ship,
  Heaving his crooked backe up, and presents
  A Feather-bed, to waft'ee to the shoare,
  As easily as if you slept i'th' Court.   15

PELIAS   Indeed, is't true, I pray?

MENAPHON   I will not stretch
  Your Faith upon the Teinters, prethee *Pelias,*
  Where didst thou learne this language?

PELIAS   I this language?
  Alas, Sir, we that study words and formes
  Of complement, must fashion all discourse,   20
  According to the nature of the subject.
  But I am silent, now appeares a Sunne,
  Whose shadow I adore.

      Enter AMETHUS, SOPHRONOS, *and Attendants.*

MENAPHON   My honour'd Father.

I.I] Actus I. Scena I *Q*   23.1 SD] In right margin, ll. 21–3 *Q*

SOPHRONOS   From mine eyes, son, son of my care, my love,
 The joyes that bid thee welcome, doe too much   25
 Speake me a child.

MENAPHON   O Princely Sir, your hand.

AMETHUS   Performe your duties where you owe them first,
 I dare not be so sudden in the pleasures,
 Thy presence hath brought home.

SOPHRONOS   Here thou still findest
 A Friend as noble (*Menaphon*) as when   30
 Thou left'st at thy departure.

MENAPHON   Yes, I know it,
  To him I owe more service—

AMETHUS   [*to Sophronos*] Pray give leave,
 He shall attend your intertainements soone,
 Next day, and next day, for an houre or two,
 I would engrosse him onely.

SOPHRONOS   Noble Lord.   35

AMETHUS   Y'are both dismist.   B2ʳ

PELIAS   Your creature, and your Servant.
   Exeunt all but AMETHUS [*and*] MENAPHON.

AMETHUS   Give me thy hand, I will not say, Th'art welcome,
 That is the common roade of common friends,
 I am glad I have thee here— O, I want words
 To let thee know my heart.

MENAPHON   'Tis peec'd to mine.   40

AMETHUS   Yes, 'tis, as firmely, as that holy thing
 Call'd Friendship can unite it. *Menaphon*,
 My *Menaphon*: now all the goodly blessings,
 That can create a Heaven on earth, dwell with thee.
 Twelve monthes we have been sundred, but henceforth   45
 We never more will part, till that sad houre,
 In which death leaves the one of us behind,
 To see the others funerals perform'd.

---

32 SD] *Hill* (l. 33).

Let's now a while be free. How have thy travailes
Disburth'ned thee abroad of discontents?   50

MENAPHON   Such cure as sicke men find in changing beds,
I found in change of Ayres; the fancy flatter'd
My hopes with ease, as theirs doe, but the griefe
Is still the same.

AMETHUS   Such is my case at home.
Cleophila, thy Kinswoman, that Maide   55
Of sweetnesse and humility, more pities
Her Fathers poore afflictions, then the tide
Of my complaints.

MENAPHON   *Thamasta*, my great Mistris,
Your Princely Sister, hath, I hope ere this,
Confirm'd affection on some worthy choice.   60

AMETHUS   Not any, *Menaphon*. Her bosome yet
Is intermur'd with Ice, though by the truth
Of love, no day hath ever past, wherein
I have not mention'd thy deserts, thy constancy
Thy— Come, in troth I dare not tell thee what,   65
Lest thou mightst thinke I fawnd upon a sinne
Friendship was never guilty of; for flattery
Is monstrous in a true friend.

MENAPHON   Does the Court
Weare the old lookes too?

AMETHUS   If thou mean'st the Prince,
It does, hee's the same melancholy man,   70
He was at's Fathers death, sometimes speakes sence,
But seldome mirth; will smile, but seldome laugh;
Will lend an eare to businesse, deale in none;
Gaze upon Revels, Anticke Fopperies,
But is not mov'd; will sparingly discourse,   75
Heare musicke; but what most he takes delight in,
Are handsome pictures; one so young, and goodly,
So sweet in his owne nature, any Story
Hath seldome mentioned.

MENAPHON   Why should such as I am,
Groane under the light burthens of small sorrowes,   80

B2ᵛ

When as a Prince, so potent, cannot shun
Motions of passion? To be man (my Lord)
Is to be but the exercise of cares
In severall shapes; as miseries doe grow,
They alter as mens formes; but how, none know.   85

AMETHUS   This little Ile of Cyprus sure abounds
In greater wonders, both for change and fortune,
Then any you have seene abroad.

MENAPHON   Then any
I have observ'd abroad: all Countries else
To a free eye and mind yeeld something rare;   90
And I for my part, have brought home one Jewell.
Of admirable value.

AMETHUS   Jewell, *Menaphon?*   B3ʳ

MENAPHON   A Jewell, my *Amethus,* a faire Youth;
A Youth, whom if I were but superstitious,
I should repute an Excellence more high,   95
Then meere creations are; to adde delight.
I'le tell yee how I found him.

AMETHUS   Prethee doe.

MENAPHON   Passing from Italy to Greece, the Tales
Which Poets of an elder time have fain'd
To glorifie their *Tempe,* bred in me   100
Desire of visiting that Paradise.
To Thessaly I came, and living private,
Without acquaintance of more sweet companions,
Then the old In-mates to my love, my thoughts;
I day by day frequented silent Groves,   105
And solitarie Walkes. One morning early
This accident incountred me: I heard
The sweetest and most ravishing contention,
That Art or Nature ever were at strife in.

AMETHUS   I cannot yet conceive, what you inferre   110
By Art and Nature.

96–7 are; . . . delight] are, . . . delight. *Q*   106–9 *Vide Fami. stradam. lib. 2. Prolus. 6.*
Acad. 2. Imitat. Claudian. Q, margin

MENAPHON   I shall soone resolve yee.
   A sound of musicke toucht mine eares, or rather
   Indeed intranc'd my soule: as I stole neerer,
   Invited by the melody, I saw
   This Youth, this faire-fac'd Youth, upon his Lute   115
   With straines of strange variety and harmony,
   Proclaiming (as it seem'd) so bold a challenge
   To the cleare *Quiristers* of the Woods, the Birds,
   That as they flockt about him, all stood silent,
   Wondring at what they heard. I wondred too.   120

AMETHUS   And so doe I, good,— on.

MENAPHON   A Nightingale.
B3ᵛ   Natures best skill'd Musicion undertakes
   The challenge, and for every severall straine
   The wel-shapt Youth could touch, she sung her down;
   He coo'd not run Division with more Art   125
   Upon his quaking Instrument, then she,
   The Nightingale did with her various notes
   Reply too, for a voyce, and for a sound,
   Amethus, 'tis much easier to beleeve
   That such they were, then hope to heare againe.   130

AMETHUS   How did the Rivals part?

MENAPHON   You terme them rightly,
   For they were Rivals, and their Mistris *harmony*.
   Some time thus spent, the young man grew at last
   Into a pretty anger, that a bird
   Whom Art had never taught Cliffs, Moods, or Notes,   135
   Should vie with him for mastery, whose study
   Had busied many houres to perfit practise:
   To end the controversie, in a rapture,
   Upon his Instrument he playes so swiftly,
   So many voluntaries, and so quicke,   140
   That there was curiositie and cunning,
   Concord in discord, lines of diffring method
   Meeting in one full Center of delight.

AMETHUS   Now for the bird.

124 down] *Q*; own *conj. Gifford*

MENATHON   *The bird* ordain'd to be
  Musicks first Martyr, strove to imitate   145
  These severall sounds: which, when her warbling throat
  Fail'd in, for griefe, downe dropt she on his Lute,
  And brake her heart; it was the quaintest sadnesse,
  To see the Conquerour upon her Hearse,
  To weepe a funerall Elegy of teares,   150
  That trust me (my *Amethus*) I coo'd chide
  Mine owne unmanly weakenesse, that made me
  A fellow-mourner with him.   B4ʳ

AMETHUS   I beleeve thee.

MENATHON   He lookes upon the trophies of his Art,
  Then sigh'd, then wip'd his eyes, then sigh'd, and cride,   155
  Alas poore creature: I will soone revenge
  This cruelty upon the Author of it;
  Henceforth this Lute guilty of innocent blood,
  Shall never more betray a harmelesse peace
  To an untimely end: and in that sorrow,   160
  As he was pashing it against a tree,
  I suddenly stept in.

AMETHUS   Thou hast discourst
  A truth of mirth and pitie.

MENATHON   I repriev'd
  Th'intended execution with intreaties,
  And interruption: but (my Princely friend)   165
  It was not strange, the musicke of his hand
  Did over-match *birds*, when his voyce and beauty,
  Youth, carriage and discretion, must, from men
  Indu'd with reason, ravish admiration:
  From me they did.

AMETHUS   But is this miracle   170
  Not to be seene?

MENAPHON   I won him by degrees
  To chuse me his Companion; whence he is,
  Or who, as I durst modestly inquire,
  So gently hee would woo not to make knowne:
  Onely for reasons to himselfe reserv'd,   175
  He told me, that some remnant of his life

Was to be spent in Travaile; for his fortunes,
They were nor meane, nor riotous; his friends
Not publisht to the world, though not obscure:
His Countrey, Athens; and his name, *Parthenophill.*   180

AMETHUS   Came he with you to Cyprus?

MENAPHON   Willingly.
The fame of our young melancholy Prince,
Meleanders rare distractions, the obedience
Of young *Cleophila, Thamasta's* glory,
Your matchlesse friendship, and my desperate love   185
Prevail'd with him, and I have lodg'd him privately
In Famagosta.

AMETHUS   Now th'art doubly welcome:
I will not lose the sight of such a rarity
For one part of my hopes. When d'ee intend
To visit my great-spirited Sister?

MENATHON   May I   190
Without offence?

AMETHUS   Without offence? *Parthenophill*
Shall find a worthy intertainement too.
Thou art not still a coward.

MENATHON   Shee's too excellent,
And I too low in merit.

AMETHUS   Ile prepare
A noble welcome. And (friend) ere we part,   195
Unloade to thee an over-chargèd heart.   *Exeunt.*

1.2   *Enter* RHETIAS *carelesly attyr'd.*

RHETIAS   I will not court the madnesse of the times,
Nor fawne upon the Riots that embalme
Our wanton Gentry, to preserve the dust
Of their affected vanities, in coffins
Of memorable shame; when Common-wealths   5
Totter and reele from that nobilitie
And ancient vertue, which renownes the great,
Who steere the Helme of government, while Mushrooms

Grow up, and make new lawes to licence folly:
Why should not I, a *May-game*, scorne the weight   10
Of my sunke fortunes? snarle at the vices
Which rot the Land, and without feare or wit   C1ʳ
Be mine owne Anticke? 'Tis a sport to live
When life is irkesome, if we will not hug
Prosperity in others, and contemne   15
Affliction in our selves. This Rule is certaine,
"He that pursues his safety from the Schoole
"Of State, must learne to be mad man, or foole.
Ambition, wealth, ease, I renounce the divell
That damns yee here on earth, or I will be—   20
Mine owne mirth, or mine owne tormentor,— So,

Enter PELIAS.

Here comes intelligence, a Buz o'the Court.

PELIAS   *Rhetias*, I sought thee out to tell thee newes,
New, excellent new newes. *Cuculus*, Sirra,
That Gull, that young old Gull, is comming this way.   25

RHETIAS   And thou art his forerunner?

PELIAS   Prethee heare me:
In stead of a fine guarded Page, we have got him
A Boy, trickt up in neat and handsome Fashion;
Perswaded him, that 'tis indeed a Wench;
And he has entertain'd him, he does follow him,   30
Carries his sword and buckler, waits on his trencher,
Filles him his Wine, Tobacco, whets his knife,
Lackeyes his letters, does what service else
He would imploy his man in: being askt,
Why he is so irregular in Courtship?   35
His answer is, that since great Ladies use
Gentlemen Ushers to goe bare before them,
He knowes no reason, but he may reduce
The Courtiers to have women waite on them,

I.2] 21.1 PELIAS] *Pelius Q*   24 *Cuculus*] *Cucolus Q* O1, L1, L2   27–8] *Weber, 4 lines in Q*: In . . . Page | We . . . him | A . . . handsome | Fashion

And he begins the fashion; he is laught at   40
Cr^v   Most complementally. Thou't burst to see him.

RHETIAS   *Agelastus*, so surnamed for his gravity, was a very
wise fellow, kept his countenance all dayes of his life as demurely,
as a Judge that pronounceth sentence of death, on a poore Roague,
for stealing as much bacon, as would serve at a meale with a   45
Calves head. Yet he smil'd once, and never but once: Thou art no
Scholler?

PELIAS   I have read Pamphlets dedicated to me:
Dost call him *Agelastus*? why did he laugh?

RHETIAS   To see an Asse eate Thistles. Puppy, go study to be a   50
singular Coxcomb. *Cuculus* is an ordinary Ape, but thou art an Ape
of an Ape.

Enter CUCULUS *and* GRILLA.

PELIAS   Thou hast a Patent to abuse thy friends:
Looke, looke, he comes, observe him seriously.

CUCULUS   Reach me my sword and buckler.   55

GRILLA   They are here, forsooth.

CUCULUS   How now (*Minkes*) how now? Where is your duty,
your distance? Let me have service methodically tendred; you are
now one of us. Your cursey; [GRILLA *curtsies*] good: remember
that you are to practise Courtship: was thy father a Piper, saist   60
thou?

GRILLA   A sounder of some such wind instrument forsooth.

CUCULUS   Was he so? hold up thy head; be thou musicall to me,
and I will marry thee to a dancer: one that shall ryde on his Foot-
cloth, and maintaine thee in thy Muffe and Hood.   65

GRILLA   That will be fine indeed.

CUCULUS   Thou art yet but simple.

GRILLA   D'ee thinke so?

42–7] *Weber, verse in Q.* . . . gravity, | . . . countenance | . . . that| . . . . Roague | . . . meale | . . . .
once, | Scholler?   59 SD] *Weber*   63–5] *Weber, verse in Q.* . . . musicall | . . . one | . . .
thee | . . . Hood   68 D'ee] *Hill;* Dee *Q*

CUCULUS   I have a braine; I have a head-piece; o' my conscience, if I take paines with thee, I shood | raise thy understanding (Girle)   70   C2ʳ to the height of a nurse, or a Court-midwife at least, I will make thee big in time, wench.

GRILLA   E'en doe your pleasure with me, Sir.

PELIAS   Noble accomplisht *Cuculus.*

RHETIAS   Give me thy fist, Innocent.   75

CUCULUS   Would 'twere in thy belly, there 'tis.

PELIAS   That's well, hee's an honest blade, though he be blunt.

CUCULUS   Who cares? we can be as blunt as he for's life.

RHETIAS   *Cuculus,* there is within a mile or two, a Sow-pig hath suckt a Brach, and now hunts the Deere, the Hare, nay, most   80 unnaturally the wilde Bore, as well as any Hound in Cyprus.

CUCULUS   Monstrous Sow-pig! ist true?

PELIAS   Ile be at charge of a banket on thee for a sight of her.

RHETIAS   Every thing takes after the dam that gave it suck: where hadst thou thy milke?   85

CUCULUS   I? Why, my nurses husband was a most excellent maker of Shittle-cocks.

PELIAS   My nurse was a woman-surgeon.

RHETIAS   And who gave thee pap, Mouse?

GRILLA   I never suckt that I remember.   90

RHETIAS   La now, a Shittle-cock-maker, all thy braines are stucke with corke and feather. *Cuculus,* this learned Courtier takes after the nurse too, a she-surgeon, which is in effect a meere matcher of colours. Goe, learne to paint and dawbe complements, 'tis the next step to run into a new suit; my Lady   95 *Periwinckle* here never suckt; suck thy Master, and bring forth Moonecalves, Fop, doe; This is good Philosophy, Sirs, make use on't.

80–1 nay . . . Cyprus] *Weber; verse in Q*

GRILLA   Blesse us, what a strange Creature this is!

CUCULUS   A Gull, an arrant Gull by Proclamation.   100

C2ᵛ   *Enter* CORAX *passing over.*

PELIAS   *Corax,* the Princes chiefe Physicion; What businesse
speeds his haste— Are all things well, Sir?

CORAX   Yes, yes, yes.

RHETIAS   Phew, you may wheele about, man, wee know y'are
proud of your slovenry and practice, 'tis your vertue; the Princes   105
melancholy fit I presume holds still.

CORAX   So doe thy knavery and desperate beggery.

CUCULUS   Aha: here's one will tickle the ban-dog.

RHETIAS   You must not goe yet.

CORAX   Ile stay in spight of thy teeth. There lyes my gravity: 110
                    Casts off his gowne.
Doe what thou darest, I stand thee.

RHETIAS   Mountebancks, Empricks, Quacksalvers, Mineralists,
Wizards, Alchimists, cast-Apothecaries, old Wives and Barbers, are
all suppositors to the right Worshipfull Doctor, as I take it. Some
of yee are the head of your Art, and the hornes too, but they come   115
by nature; thou livest single for no other end, but that thou fearest
to be a Cuckold.

CORAX   Have at thee; thou affect'st railing onely for thy health,
thy miseries are so thicke and so lasting, that thou hast not one
poore denier to bestow on opening a veine. Wherefore to avoide   120
a Plurisie, thou't be sure to prate thy selfe once a month into a
whipping, and bleed in the breech in stead of the arme.

RHETIAS   Have at thee agen.

CORAX   Come.

CUCULUS   There, there, there; O brave Doctor.   125

C3ʳ PELIAS   Let'em alone.

102] *Weber, verse in Q*: . . .. haste— | . . . Sir?   112 Mountebancks] *Weber,* Mountebanck *Q.*

RHETIAS   Thou art in thy Religion an Atheist, in thy condition
a Curre, in thy dyet an Epicure, in thy lust a Goate, in thy sleepe
a Hogge; thou tak'st upon thee the habit of a grave Phisition,
but art indeed an impostrous Emperike. Physicions are the 130
bodies Coblers, rather the Botchers of mens bodies; as the one
patches our tatterd clothes, so the other solders our diseased
flesh. Come on.

CUCULUS   To't, to't, hold him to't, hold him to't, to't, to't,
to't.   135

CORAX   The best worth in thee, is the corruption of thy minde,
for that onely intitles thee to the dignity of a lowse: a thing bred
out of the filth and superfluity of ill humours: Thou byt'st any
where; and any man who defends not himselfe with the cleane
linnen of secure honesty; him thou darest not come neere. Thou 140
art Fortunes Ideot, Vertues Bankrupt, Times Dunghil,
Manhoods Scandall, and thine owne scourge. Thou wouldst
hang thy selfe, so wretchedly miserable thou art; but that no
man will trust thee with as much money as will buy a halter: and
all thy stocke to be sold, is not worth halfe as much as may 145
procure it.

RHETIAS   Ha, ha, ha; this is flattery, grosse flattery.

CORAX   I have imployment for thee, and for yee all, tut, these are
but good morrowes betweene us.

RHETIAS   Are thy bottles full?   150

CORAX   Of rich wine, lets all sucke together.

RHETIAS   Like so many Swine in a trough.

CORAX   Ile shape yee all for a devise before the Prince, Wee'le
trie how that can move him.

RHETIAS   He shall fret or laugh.   155

CUCULUS   Must I make one?

CORAX   Yes, and your feminine Page too.

GRILLA   Thankes most egregiously.   C3ᵛ

134–5] *Weber*; Tot, tot~tot, ~ toot, tot, tot, tot *Q*   148–9] *Weber*, *verse in Q*: . . . all | . . . us.

PELIAS   I will not slacke my part.

CUCULUS   Wench, take my buckler.   160

CORAX   Come all unto my chamber, the project is cast, the time
onely we must attend.

RHETIAS   The melody must agree well, and yeeld sport,
  When such as these are, Knaves and Fooles consort.   *Exeunt.*

   1.3   *Enter* AMETHUS, THAMASTA, *and* KALA.

AMETHUS   Does this shew well?

THAMASTA   What would you have me doe?

AMETHUS   Not like a Lady of the trim, new crept
  Out of the shell of sluttish sweat and labour,
  Into the glittering pompe of ease and wantonnesse,
  Imbroideries, and all these antike fashions,   5
  That shape a woman monstrous; to transforme
  Your education, and a Noble birth
  Into contempt and laughter. Sister, Sister,
  She who derives her blood from Princes, ought
  To glorifie her greatnesse by humility.   10

THAMASTA   Then you conclude me proud.

AMETHUS   Young *Menaphon,*
  My worthy friend, has lov'd you long, and truly,
  To witnesse his obedience to your scorne,
  Twelve moneths (wrong'd Gentleman) he undertooke
  A voluntary exile. Wherefore (Sister)   15
  In this time of his absence, have you not
  Dispos'd of your affections on some Monarch?
  Or sent Embassadors to some neighbouring King
  With fawning protestations of your graces?
  Your rare perfections, admirable beauty?   20
C4ʳ This had been a new piece of modesty,
  Would have deserv'd a Chronicle!

THAMASTA   You are bitter;
  And brother, by your leave, not kindly wise.
  My freedome is my births, I am not bound
  To fancy your approvements, but my owne.   25

Indeed you are an humble youth, I heare of
Your visits, and your loving commendation
To your hearts Saint, *Cleophila*, a Virgin
Of a rare excellence: what though she want
A portion to maintaine a portly greatnesse? 30
Yet 'tis your gracious sweetnesse to descend
So low, the meeknesse of your pity leades yee.
She is your deare friends Sister, a good soule,
An Innocent.

AMETHUS   *Thamasta.*

THAMASTA   I have given
Your *Menaphon* a welcome home as fits me; 35
For his sake entertain'd *Parthenophill,*
The handsome Stranger, more familiarly
Then (I may feare) becomes me; yet for his part,
I not repent my courtesies, but you—

AMETHUS   No more, no more; be affable to both: 40
Time may reclaime your cruelty.

THAMASTA   I pitty
The youth, and trust me (brother) love his sadnesse:
He talkes the prettiest stories, he delivers
His tales so gracefully, that I coo'd sit
And listen, nay forget my meales and sleepe, 45
To heare his neat discourses. *Menaphon*
Was well advis'd in chusing such a friend,
For pleading his true love.

AMETHUS   Now I commend thee,
Thou't change at last, I hope. C4ᵛ

        Enter MENAPHON *and* EROCLEA *in mans attire.*

THAMASTA [*aside*]   I feare I shall.

AMETHUS   Have ye survaid the Garden?

MENAPHON   'Tis a curious, 50
A pleasantly contriv'd delight.

1.3] 49 *aside*] *Gifford*

THAMASTA   Your eye (Sir)
  Hath in your travailes, often met contents
  Of more variety.

EROCLEA   Not any (Lady.)

MENAPHON   It were impossible, since your faire presence
  Makes every place where it vouchsafes to shine,   55
  More lovely then all other helpes of Art
  Can equall.

THAMASTA   What you meane by helpes of Art,
  You know your selfe best, be they as they are:
  You need none I am sure to set me forth.

MENAPHON   'Twould argue want of manners, more then skill, 60
  Not to praise *praise it selfe.*

THAMASTA   For your reward,
  Henceforth Ile call you Servant.

AMETHUS   Excellent Sister.

MENAPHON   'Tis my first step to honour: May I fall
  Lower then shame, when I neglect all service
  That may confirme this favour.

THAMASTA   Are you well, Sir?   65

EROCLEA   Great Princesse, I am well; to see a League
  Betweene an humble love, such as my Friends is,
  And a commanding vertue, such as yours is,
  Are sure restoratives.

THAMASTA   You speake ingeniously.
  Brother, he pleas'd to shew the Gallery   70
  To this young stranger, use the time a while,
  D1ʳ   And we will altogether to the Court.
  I will present yee (Sir) unto the Prince.

EROCLEA   Y'are all compos'd of fairenesse, and true bounty.

AMETHUS   Come, come, wee'l wait thee, Sister: this beginning 75
  Doth rellish happy processe.

MENAPHON   You have blest me.
                    Exeunt all but THAMASTA *and* KALA.

THAMASTA   *Kala, O Kala,*

KALA   Lady.

THAMASTA   We are private,
Thou art my Closet.

KALA   Locke your secrets close then:
I am not to be forc'd.

THAMASTA   Never till now,
Coo'd I be sensible of being traytor   80
To honour and to shame.

KALA   You are in love.

THAMASTA   I am growne base—— *Parthenophill*—

KALA   Hee's handsome,
Richly indow'd; he hath a lovely face,
A winning tongue.

THAMASTA   If ever I must fall,
In him my greatnesse sinkes. Love is a Tyrant   85
Resisted; whisper in his eare, how gladly
I would steale time, to talke with him one houre;
But doe it honourably; preth'ee *Kala*
Doe not betray me.

KALA   Madame, I will make it
Mine owne case; he shall thinke I am in love with him.   90

THAMASTA   I hope thou art not *Kala.*

KALA   'Tis for your sake:
Ile tell him so; but Faith I am not, Lady.

THAMASTA   Pray use me kindly; let me not too soone
Be lost in my new follyes. 'Tis a Fate
That over-rules our wisdomes, whil'st we strive   95
To live most free, wee'r caught in our owne toyles.   D1ᵛ
Diamonds cut Diamonds: they who will prove
To thrive in cunning, must cure love with love.   *Exeunt.*
          Finis Actus Primi.

98 SD] *Weber; Exit Q*

2.1   *Enter* SOPHRONOS *and* ARETUS.

SOPHRONOS   Our Common-wealth is sick: 'tis more then time
That wee should wake the Head thereof, who sleepes
In the dull Lethargy of lost security.
The Commons murmur, and the Nobles grieve,
The Court is now turn'd Anticke, and growes wilde,   5
Whiles all the neighb'ring Nations stand at gaze,
And watch fit oportunity, to wreake
Their just conceivèd fury, on such injuries,
As the late Prince, our living Masters Father,
Committed against Lawes of truth or honour.   10
Intelligence comes flying in on all sides,
Whilest the unsteady multitude presume,
How that you, *Aretus*, and I, ingrosse
(Out of particular Ambition)
Th'affaires of government, which I for my part,   15
Groane under, and am weary of.

ARETUS   *Sophronos*,
I am as zealous too of shaking of
My gay State-fetters, that I have bethought
Of speedy remedy; and to that end
D2ʳ   As I have told yee, have concluded with   20
Corax, the Princes chiefe Physician.

SOPHRONOS   You should have done this sooner, *Aretus*;
You were his Tutor, and could best discerne
His dispositions to informe them rightly.

ARETUS   Passions of violent nature, by degrees   25
Are easili'st reclaim'd. There's something hid
Of his distemper, which wee'l now find out.

Enter CORAX, RHETIAS, PELIAS, CUCULUS, *and* GRILLA.

You come on just appointment: welcome, Gentlemen,
Have you won *Rhetias (Corax?)*

CORAX   Most sincerely.

CUCULUS   Save yee, Nobilities: doe your Lordships take notice   30
of my Page? 'Tis a fashion of the newest edition, spick and span
new, without example. Doe your honour, Houswife.

GRILLA   There's a cursey for you, and a cursey for you.

SOPHRONOS   'Tis excellent: we must all follow fashion,
        And entertaine Shee-waiters.

ARETUS   'Twill be Courtly.   35

CUCULUS   I thinke so; I hope the Chronicles will reare me one day
for a head-piece—

RHETIAS   Of Woodcocke without braines in't; Barbers shall
weare thee on their Citternes, and Hucksters set thee out in
Ginger-bread.   40

CUCULUS   Devill take thee: I say nothing to thee now; canst let me
be quiet?

GRILLA   Y'are too perstreperous, Sauce-box.

CUCULUS   Good Girle, if we begin to puffe once.

PELIAS   Prethee hold thy tongue, the Lords are in the presence.   45

RHETIAS   Mum, Butterflye.

PELIAS   O the Prince: stand and keepe silence.   D2ᵛ

CUCULUS   O the Prince: Wench, thou shalt see the Prince now.
                                            Soft Musicke.

        Enter PALADOR, *the Prince, with a Booke in his hand.*

SOPHRONOS, ARETUS   Sir; Gracious Sir.

PRINCE   Why all this Company?

CORAX   A Booke! is this the early exercise   50
        I did prescribe? in stead of following health,
        Which all men covet, you pursue your disease.
        Where's your great Horse, your Hounds, your set at Tennis,
        Your Balloone ball, the practice of your dancing,
        Your casting of the sledge, or learning how   55

34–5] *Weber; prose in Q:* 'Tis . . . and | entertain Shee-waiters. | 'Twill . . . Courtly.   48.2 SD]
PALADOR] *PALLADOR Q (also at 4.3.115)*   52 your disease] *Q*, disease *Weber*

To tosse a Pike; all chang'd into a Sonnet?
Pray Sir grant me free liberty to leave
The Court, it do's infect me with the sloth
Of sleepe and surfet: In the University
I have imployments, which to my profession   60
Adde profit and report: Here I am lost,
And in your wilfull dulnesse held a man
Of neither Art nor honesty: you may
Command my head; pray take it, doe; 'twere better
For me to lose it, then to lose my wits,   65
And live in Bedlam: you will force me too't,
I am almost mad already.

PRINCE   I beleeve it.

SOPHRONOS   Letters are come from Creete, which do require
A speedy restitution of such ships,
As by your Father were long since detain'd;   70
If not; defiance threatned.

ARETUS   These neere parts
Of Syria that adjoyne, muster their friends:
And by intelligence we learne for certaine,
The Syrian will pretend an ancient interest
Of tribute intermitted.

SOPHRONOS   Through your Land   75
Your subjects mutter strangely, and imagine
More then they dare speake publikely.

CORAX   And yet
They talke but odly of you.

CUCULUS   Hang 'em Mungrels.

PRINCE   Of me? my subjects talke of me?

CORAX   Yes, scurvily,
And thinke worse (Prince.)

PRINCE   Ile borrow patience   80
A little time to listen to these wrongs,
And from the few of you which are here present,
Conceive the generall voyce.

CORAX   [*aside*]   So, now he is nettled.

PRINCE   By all your loves I charge ye, without feare
Or flattery, to let me know your thoughts,   85
And how I am interpreted: Speake boldly.

SOPHRONOS   For my part (Sir) I will be plaine, and briefe:
I thinke you are of Nature milde and easie,
Not willingly provokt, but withall head-strong
In any passion that misleades your Judgement.   90
I thinke you too indulgent to such motions,
As spring out of your owne affections,
To old to be reform'd, and yet too young
To take fit councell from your selfe, of what
Is most amisse.

PRINCE   So— Tutor, your conceit?   95

ARETUS   I think you doate (with pardon let me speak it)
Too much upon your pleasures, and these pleasures
Are so wrapt up in selfe-love, that you covet
No other change of fortune: would be still
What your birth makes you, but are loth to toyle   100 D3ᵛ
In such affaires of State as breake your sleepes.

CORAX   I thinke you would be by the world, reputed
A man in every point compleat, but are
In manners and effect indeed a childe,
A boy, a very boy.

PELIAS   May it please your Grace,   105
I thinke you doe containe within your selfe
The great *Elixer*, soule and quintessence
Of all divine perfections: are the glory
Of mankind, and the onely strict example
For earthly Monarchies to square out their lives by: 110
Times miracle, Fames pride, in Knowledge, Wit,
Sweetnesse, Discourse, Armes, Arts—

PRINCE   You are a Courtier.

83 SD] *Weber*

CUCULUS But not of the ancient fashion, an't like your
Highnesse. 'Tis I; I, that am the credit of the Court, Noble
Prince: and if thou would'st by Proclamation or Patent, create me   115
Overseer of all the Taylers in thy Dominions; then, then the
golden dayes should appeare againe; bread should be cheaper;
fooles should have more wit; knaves more honesty; and beggers
more money.

GRILLA I thinke now—   120

CUCULUS Peace you Squall.

PRINCE [to Rhetias] You have not spoken yet.

CUCULUS Hang him, hee'l nothing but raile.

GRILLA Most abominable: out upon him.

CORAX Away Cuculus, follow the Lords.   125

CUCULUS Close Page, close.
          They all fall backe, and steale out.
          Manent PRINCE *and* RHETIAS.

PRINCE You are somewhat long a thinking.

D4ʳ RHETIAS I doe not thinke at all.

PRINCE Am I not worthy of your thought?

RHETIAS My pitty you are— But not my reprehension.   130

PRINCE Pitty?

RHETIAS Yes, for I pitty such to whom I owe service, who
exchange their happinesse for a misery.

PRINCE Is it a misery to be a Prince?

RHETIAS Princes who forget their soveraignty, and yeeld to   135
affected passion, are weary of command. You had a Father, Sir.

PRINCE Your Soveraigne whiles he liv'd. But what of him?

RHETIAS Nothing. I onely dar'd to name him; that's all.

122 SD] *Gifford*   126.2 *Manent*] *this edn.* ; *Manet* Q

PRINCE   I charge thee by the duty that thou ow'st us,
    Be plaine in what thou meanest to speake: there's something 140
    That we must know: be free, our eares are open.

RHETIAS   O Sir, I had rather hold a Wolfe by the eares, then
stroake a Lyon, the greatest danger is the last.

PRINCE   This is meere trifling— Ha? are all stollen hence?
    We are alone: Thou hast an honest looke,   145
    Thou hast a tongue, I hope, that is not oyld
    With flattery. Be open, though 'tis true,
    That in my younger dayes I oft have heard
    Agenors name, my Father, more traduc'd,
    Then I could then observe; yet I protest,   150
    I never had a friend, a certaine friend,
    That would informe me throughly of such errors,
    As oftentimes are incident to Princes.

RHETIAS   All this may be. I have seene a man so curious in feeling
of the edge of a keene knife, that he has cut his fingers. My flesh is   155
not of proofe against the metall I | am to handle; the one is tenderer   D4ᵛ
then the other.

PRINCE   I see then I must court thee. Take the word
    Of a just Prince for any thing thou speakest.
    I have more then a Pardon, thankes and love.   160

RHETIAS   I will remember you of an old Tale that somthing
concernes you. *Meleander*, the great (but unfortunate) Statesman,
was by your Father treated with for a Match betweene you and his
eldest daughter, the Lady *Eroclea*. You were both neere of an age.
I presume you remember a Contract, and cannot forget *Her*.   165

PRINCE   She was a lovely beauty: Prethee forward.

RHETIAS   To Court was *Eroclea* brought, was courted by your
Father, not for Prince *Palador*, as it followed, but to be made a
prey to some lesse noble designe— With your favour I have forgot
the rest.   170

PRINCE   Good call it backe agen into thy memory,
    Else losing the remainder, I am lost too.

139–41] *Weber, prose in* Q   148 younger] Q *corr.;* young Q *uncorr.*

RHETIAS   You charme me. In briefe, a Rape, by some bad Agents, was attempted; by the Lord *Meleander* her father rescude, she convay'd away, *Meleander* accus'd of treason, his Land seized, he 175 himselfe distracted and confined to the Castle where he yet lives. What had ensude was doubtfull. But your Father shortly after dyed.

PRINCE   But what became of faire *Eroclea?*

RHETIAS   She never since was heard of.

PRINCE   No hope lives then   180
       Of ever, ever seeing her againe.

RHETIAS   Sir, I feared I should anger yee. There was, as I said, an old Tale: I have now a new one, which may perhaps season the first with a more delightfull rellish.

PRINCE   I am prepar'd to heare, say what you please.   185

RHETIAS   My Lord *Meleander* falling, on whose favour my
E1ʳ fortunes relyde, I furnisht my selfe for travaile, and | bent my course to Athens, where a pretty accident after a while came to my knowledge.

PRINCE   My eare is open to thee.   190

RHETIAS   A young Lady contracted to a noble Gentleman, as the Lady we last mentioned, and your Highnes were, being hindred by their jarring Parents, stole from her home, and was conveyed like a Ship-boy in a Merchant, from the Countrey where she liv'd, into Corinth first, and afterwards to Athens; 195 where in much solitarinesse she liv'd like a Youth almost two yeeres, courted by all for acquaintance, but friend to none by familiaritie.

PRINCE   In habit of a man?

RHETIAS   A handsome young man, till within these three 200 moneths, or lesse, her sweet-heart's Father dying some yeere before, or more, shee had notice of it, and with much joy returned home, and as report voyced it at Athens enjoyed her happinesse:

---

182 feared] *Weber;* fearc *Q*   20 1sweet-heart's] *Gifford;* sweet hearty *Q*   203 it at Athens,] *Gifford;* it, ~ ~*Q*

she was long an exile: For now Noble Sir, if you did love the Lady
Eroclea, why may not such safety and fate direct her, as directed 205
the other: 'tis not impossible.

PRINCE   If I did love her, *Rhetias*: yes I did.
   Give me thy hand: As thou didst serve *Meleander*,
   And art still true to these, henceforth serve me.

RHETIAS   My duty and my obedience are my suretie, but I have 210
been too bold.

PRINCE   Forget the sadder story of my Father,
   And onely *Rhetias*, learne to reade me well,
   For I must ever thanke thee; th'ast unlockt
   A tongue was vow'd to silence, for requitall   215
   Open my bosome, *Rhetias*.

RHETIAS   What's your meaning?

PRINCE   To tye thee to an oath of secrecy—
   Unloose the buttons, man, thou dost it faintly,   E1ᵛ
   What findst thou there?

RHETIAS   A picture in a Tablet.

PRINCE   Looke well upon't.

RHETIAS   I doe— yes— let me observe it— 220
   'Tis hers, the Ladies.

PRINCE   Whose?

RHETIAS   *Erocleas.*

PRINCE   Hers that was once *Eroclea*: for her sake
   Have I advanst *Sophronos* to the Helme
   Of government; for her sake will restore
   Meleanders Honours to him; will for her sake   225
   Beg friendship from thee, *Rhetias*. O be faithfull,
   And let no politicke Lord worke from thy bosome
   My griefes: I know thou wert put on to sift me:
   But be not too secure.

RHETIAS   I am your Creature.

221 Whose?] *Weber subst.*; ~! Q

PRINCE   Continue still thy discontented fashion: 230
   Humour the Lords, as they would humour me;
   Ile not live in thy debt— we are discover'd.

Enter AMETHUS, MENAPHON, THAMASTA, KALA, EROCLEA, *as before.*

AMETHUS   Honour and health still wait upon the Prince.
   Sir, I am bold with favour to present
   Unto your Highnes, *Menaphon* my friend,   235
   Return'd from travaile.

MENAPHON   Humbly on my knees
   I kisse your gracious hand.

PRINCE   It is our duty
   To love the vertuous.

MENAPHON   If my prayers or service
   Hold— any value, they are vow'd yours ever.

RHETIAS   I have a fist for thee too (Strippling) th'art started up 240
prettily since I saw thee. Hast learned any wit abroad? Canst tell
newes, and sweare lyes with a grace like a true Traveller? What new
Owzle's this?

THAMASTA   Your Highnesse shall doe right to your owne
   judgement,
   In taking more then common notice of   245
   This stranger, an Athenian, nam'd *Parthenophill.*
   One, whom (if mine opinion doe not sooth me
   Too grossely) for the fashion of his minde,
   Deserves a deare respect.

PRINCE   Your commendation,
   Sweet Cousin, speakes him Nobly.

EROCLEA   All the powers   250
   That centinell just Thrones, double their guards
   About your sacred Excellence.

PRINCE   What fortune
   Led him to Cyprus?

E2ʳ (margin)

---

232 debt—we] *Hill;* ~. —We *Q*   247 One, whom (if] *this edn.;* One, (~~ *Q*   249 com-
mendation] *this edn.;* commendations *Q*   251 their] *Gifford;* these *Q*   253 Cyprus?]
Weber, ~! *Q*

MENAPHON My perswasions won him.

AMETHUS And if your Highnesse please to heare the entrance
Into their first aquaintance, you will say—   255

THAMASTA It was the newest, sweetest, prettiest accident,
That ere delighted your attention.
I can discourse it, Sir.

PRINCE   Some other time.
How is a cald?

THAMASTA   *Parthenophill.*

PRINCE   *Parthenophill?*
Wee shall sort time to take more notice of him.   260

Exit PRINCE

MENAPHON His wonted melancholy still pursues him.

AMETHUS I told you so.

THAMASTA [*to Eroclea*] You must not wonder at it.

EROCLEA I doe not, Lady.

AMETHUS   Shall we to the Castle?   E2ᵛ

MENAPHON Wee will attend yee both.

RHETIAS All three— [*to Amethus*] Ile goe too. Hark in thine 265
eare, Gallant: Ile keep the old mad man in chat, whilest thou
gabblest to the girle: my thumb's upon my lips, not a word.

AMETHUS [*aside*] I neede not feare thee, *Rhetias.*— Sister, soone
Expect us: this day wee will range the City.

THAMASTA Well, soone I shall expect yee.— [*aside*] *Kala?*

KALA [*aside*]   Trust mee. 270

RHETIAS Troope on— Love, Love, what a wonder thou art!
Exeunt. Kala and Eroclea stay.

KALA May I not be offensive, Sir?

262 SD] *this edn.*   265 SD] *Hill (after* too.)   268 SD] *Hill*   270 SD] *Gifford.*
270 KALA [*aside*] *Hill*   271.1 *stay*] *Hill; stayes* Q

EROCLEA   Your pleasure;
    Yet pray be briefe.

KALA   Then briefly, good, resolve mee:
    Have you a Mistris, or a Wife?

EROCLEA   I have neither.

KALA   Nor did you ever love in earnest any   275
    Faire Lady, whom you wisht to make your owne?

EROCLEA   Not any truly.

KALA   What your friends or meanes are
    I will not be inquisitive to know,
    Nor doe I care to hope for. But admit
    A dowre were throwne downe before your choyce,   280
    Of Beauty, Noble birth, and sincere affection,
    How gladly would you intertaine it? (Young man)
    I doe not tempt you idly.

EROCLEA   I shall thanke you,
    When my unsettled thoughts can make me sensible
    Of what 'tis to be happy: for the present   285
    I am your debtor: and faire Gentlewoman,
    Pray give me leave as yet to study ignorance,
E3ʳ   For my weake braines conceive not what concerns me.
    — [*seeing* THAMASTA *approaching*] Another time— [*she
    begins to leave*]

Enter THAMASTA.

THAMASTA   Doe I breake off your Parley   290
    That you are parting? Sure my woman loves you.
    Can she speake well, *Parthenophill?*

EROCLEA   Yes, Madame:
    Discreetly chaste she can: she hath much won
    On my beliefe, and in few words, but pithy,
    Much moov'd my thankfulnesse. You are her Lady,   295
    Your goodnesse aimes (I know) at her preferment:
    Therefore I may be bold to make confession
    Of truth, if ever I desire to thrive

288 concerns] *Weber,* concerne *Q*   289 *seeing . . . approaching*] *this edn.;*   *begins to leave*]
this edn.

In womans favour, *Kala* is the first
Whom my ambition shall bend to.

THAMASTA   Indeed.   300
But say a Nobler Love should interpose?

EROCLEA   Where reall worth, and constancy first settle
A hearty truth, there greatnesse cannot shake it,
Nor shall it mine: yet I am but an Infant
In that construction, which must give cleare light   305
To *Kala's* merit: riper houres hereafter
Must learne me how to grow rich in deserts.
Madame, my duty waits on you.   *Exit* EROCLEA.

THAMASTA   Come hither.
If ever henceforth I desire to thrive
In womans favours, *Kala* is the first   310
Whom my ambition shall bend to—'twas so.

KALA   These very words he spake.

THAMASTA   These very words
Curse thee, unfaithfull creature, to thy grave:
Thou wood'st him for thy selfe?

KALA   You said I should.   E3ᵛ

THAMASTA   My name was never mentioned?

KALA   Madame, no: 315
We were not come to that.

THAMASTA   Not come to that?
Art thou a Rivall fit to crosse my Fate?
Now poverty and a dishonest fame,
The waiting-womans wages, be thy payment.
False, faithlesse, wanton beast, Ile spoile your carriage;   320
There's not a Page, a Groome, nay, not a Citizen
That shall be cast upon yee. *Kala*,
Ile keepe thee in my service all thy life time,
Without hope of a husband or a suter.

KALA   I have not verily deserv'd this cruelty.   325

THAMASTA   *Parthenophill* shall know, if he respect
My birth, the danger of a fond neglect.   *Exit* THAMASTA

KALA   Are you so quick? Well, I may chance to crosse
Your peevishnesse. Now though I never meant
The young man for my selfe; yet if he love me,   330
Ile have him, or Ile run away with him,
And let her doe her worst then: what, we are all
But flesh and blood; the same thing that will doe
My Lady good, will please her woman too.   *Exit.*

2.2   *Enter* CLEOPHILA *and* TROLLIO.

CLEOPHILA   Tread softly (*Trollio*) my Father sleepes still.

TROLLIO   I forsooth: but he sleepes like a Hare with his eyes
open and that's no good signe.

CLEOPHILA   Sure thou art weary of this sullen living,
But I am not; for I take more content   5
In my obedience here, then all delights
The time presents elsewhere.

E4ʳ   MELEANDER   *Within.*   Oh!

CLEOPHILA   Do'st heare that groane?

TROLLIO   Heare it? I shudder, it was a strong blast, young
Mistris, able to roote up heart, liver, lungs and all.

CLEOPHILA   My much-wrong'd Father: let me view his face.   10
Drawes the Arras, MELEANDER *discovered in a chaire sleeping.*

TROLLIO   Lady Mistris, shall I fetch a Barbour to steale away his
rough beard, whiles he sleepes in's naps? He never lookes in a
glasse, and 'tis high time on conscience for him to bee trimd, 'has
not been under the Shavers hand almost these foure yeeres.

CLEOPHILA   Peace, foole.   15

TROLLIO   I could clip the old Ruffian, there's haire enough to
stuffe all the great Codpieces in Switzerland. A begins to stirre, a
stirres. Blesse us how his eyes rowle. A good yeere keepe your
Lordship in your right wits, I beseech yee.

MELEANDER   *Cleophila?*

2.2] 7 MELEANDER] *Weber,* Menander Q   13 'has] *Weber,* has Q

CLEOPHILA   Sir, I am here, how d'ee Sir?   20

TROLLIO   Sir, is your stomacke up yet? get some warme porredge
in your belly, 'tis a very good settle-braine.

MELEANDER   The Raven croakt, and hollow shreeks of Owles
Sung Dirges at her funerall; I laugh'd
The whiles: for 'twas no boot to weepe. The Girle   25
Was fresh and full of youth: but, O the cunning
Of Tyrants that looke bigge, their very frownes
Doome poore soules guilty, ere their cause be heard.
Good. What art thou, and thou?

CLEOPHILA   I am *Cleophila,*
Your wofull daughter.

TROLLIO   I am *Trollio*   30
Your honest implement.

MELEANDER   I know yee both. 'las, why d'ee use me thus!
Thy Sister, my *Eroclea,* was so gentle,   E4ᵛ
That Turtles in their Downe doe feed more gall,
Then her spleene mixt with: yet when winds and storme   35
Drive dirt and dust on banks of spotlesse snow,
The purest whitenesse is no such defence
Against the sullying foulenesse of that fury.
So rav'd *Agenor,* that great man, mischiefe
Against the Girle— 'twas a politick tricke,   40
We were too old in Honour [*pauses*]— I am leane
And falne away extremely; most assuredly
I have not dyn'd these three dayes.

CLEOPHILA   Will you now, Sir?

TROLLIO   I beseech yee heartily Sir. I feele a horrible puking
my selfe.   45

MELEANDER   Am I starke mad?

TROLLIO   No, no, you are but a little staring— there's difference
betweene staring and starke mad. You are but whymsed, yet
crotchetted, conundroun'd, or so.

30–1] *Gifford subst.; prose in* Q   39 mischiefe Q; in mischiefe *conj. Craik*   41 SD]
this edn.

MELEANDER [*indicating Cleophila*] Here's all my care: and
  I doe often sigh   50
  For thee, *Cleophila*: we are secluded
  From all good people. But take heed, *Amethus*
  Was sonne to *Doryla, Agenors* Sister.
  There's some ill blood about him, if the Surgeon
  Have not been very skilfull to let all out.   55

CLEOPHILA I am (alas) too griev'd to thinke of love,
  That must concerne me least.

MELEANDER   Sirra, be wise, be wise.

Enter AMETHUS, MENAPHON, EROCLEA *(as before) and* RHETIAS.

TROLLIO Who I? I will be monstrous and wise immediately.
Welcome, Gentlemen, the more the merrier, Ile lay the cloth, and
set the stooles in a readinesse, for I see here is some hope of dinner 60
now.   *Exit* TROLLIO.

F1ʳ AMETHUS My Lord *Meleander, Menaphon* your Kinsman
  Newly return'd from travaile, comes to tender
  His duty t'ee: to you his love, faire Mistris.

MENAPHON I would I could as easily remove   65
  Sadnesse from your remembrance, Sir, as study
  To doe you faithfull service— my deare Cousin,
  All best of comforts blesse your sweet obedience.

CLEOPHILA One chiefe of 'em (worthy Cousin) lives
  In you, and your well-doing.

MENAPHON   This young stranger   70
  Will well deserve your knowledge.

AMETHUS   For my friends sake,
  Lady pray give him welcome.

CLEOPHILA   He has met it,
  If sorrowes can looke kindly.

EROCLEA   You much honour me.

RHETIAS [*aside*] How a eyes the company: sure my passion will
betray my weakenesse— [*to Meleander*] O my Master, my Noble 75

50 SD] *this edn.*   74 SD] *Gifford*   75 SD] *Hill*

Master, doe not forget me, I am still the humblest, and the most
faithfull in heart of those that serve you.

MELEANDER   Ha, ha, ha.

RHETIAS   [*aside*] There's wormewood in that laughter, 'tis
    the usher to a violent extremity.   80

MELEANDER   I am a weake old man. All these are come
    To jeere my ripe calamities.

MENAPHON   Good Uncle!

MELEANDER   But Ile out-stare 'ee all, fooles, desperate fooles,
    You are cheated, grossely cheated, range, range on,
    And rowle about the world to gather mosse,   85
    The mosse of honour, gay reports, gay clothes,
    Gay wives, huge empty buildings, whose proud roofes,
    Shall with their pinacles, even reach the starres.
    Ye worke and worke like Moles, blind in the paths,
    That are bor'd through the crannies of the earth,   90
    To charge your hungry soules with such full surfets,
    As being gorg'd once, make 'ee leane with plenty.   F1ᵛ
    And when ye have skimd the vomit of your riots,
    Y'are fat in no felicity but folly,
    Then your last sleepes seize on 'ee. Then the troopes   95
    Of wormes crawle round, and, feast, good cheare, rich fare,
    Dainty delicious— here's *Cleophila*:
    All the poore stocke of my remaining thrift;
    You, you, the Princes Cousin: how d'ee like her?
    (*Amethus*) how d'ee like her?

AMETHUS   My intents   100
    Are just and honourable.

MENAPHON   Sir, beleeve him.

MELEANDER   Take her— we two must part, go to him, doe.

EROCLEA   This sight is full of horror.

RHETIAS   There is sence yet
    In this distraction.

79 SD] *Gifford*   103 There] *Weber*; This Q

MELEANDER   In this Jewell I have given away,   105
   All what I can call mine. When I am dead,
   Save charge; let me be buried in a nooke.
   No guns, no pompous whining: these are fooleries.
   If whiles we live, we stalke about the streets,
   Justled by Carmen, Foot-poasts, and fine Apes,   110
   In silken coates, unminded, and scarce thought on;
   It is not comely to be hal'd to the earth,
   Like high fed Jades upon a Tilting-day,
   In antique trappings: scorne to use-lesse teares.
   Eroclea was not coffind so: she perisht,   115
   And no eye dropt save mine, and I am childish.
   I talke like one that doates; laugh at me, *Rhetias,*
   Or raile at me: they will not give me meate:
   They have starv'd me: but Ile henceforth be mine owne Cook.
   Good morrow: 'tis too early for my cares   120
   To revell. I will breake my heart a little,
   And tell yee more hereafter. Pray be merry.
                                             Exit MELEANDER

RHETIAS   Ile follow him. [*aside*] My Lord *Amethus,* use your
F2ʳ time respectively. Few words to purpose soon'st prevaile: study
   no long Orations; be plaine and short, Ile follow him.   125
                                             Exit RHETIAS.

AMETHUS   *Cleophila,* although these blacker clouds
   Of sadnes, thicken and make darke the sky
   Of thy faire eyes, yet give me leave to follow
   The streame of my affections: they are pure,
   Without all mixture of unnoble thoughts.   130
   Can you be ever mine?

CLEOPHILA   I am so low
   In mine owne fortunes, and my Fathers woes,
   That I want words to tell yee, you deserve
   A worthier choice.

AMETHUS   But give me leave to hope.

MENAPHON   My friend is serious.   135

123 SD] *Hill*

CLEOPHILA   Sir, this for answer: If I ever thrive
    In an earthly happinesse, the next
    To my good Fathers wisht recovery,
    Must be my thankfulnesse to your great merit;
    Which I dare promise for the present time: 140
    You cannot urge more from me.

MELEANDER   [*within*]   Ho, *Cleophila!*

CLEOPHILA   This Gentleman is moov'd.

AMETHUS   Your eyes, *Parthenophill,*
    Are guilty of some passion.

MENAPHON   Friend, what ailes thee?

EROCLEA   All is not well within me, Sir.

MELEANDER   *Within.*   *Cleophila!*

AMETHUS   Sweet Maid, forget me not; we now must part.   145

CLEOPHILA   Still you shall have my prayer.

AMETHUS   Still you my heart.
                                  Exeunt omnes.
                Finis Actus secundi.

3.1   *Enter* CUCULUS *and* GRILLA, CUCULUS
                in a blacke velvet   F2ᵛ
    Cap, and a white Feather, with a paper in his hand.

CUCULUS   Doe not I looke freshly, and like a Youth of the Trim?

GRILLA   As rare an old Youth as ever walkt crosse-gartered.

CUCULUS   Here are my Mistrisses mustred in white and blacke.
[*Reads*] *Kala* the Waiting-woman. I will first begin at the foote:
stand thou for *Kala.*   5

GRILLA   I stand for *Kala,* doe your best and your worst.

CUCULUS   I must looke bigge, and care little or nothing for her,
because shee is a creature that stands at livery. Thus I talke wisely,
and to no purpose. Wench, as it is not fit that thou should'st be

either faire or honest; so considering thy service, thou art as thou 10
art, and so are thy betters, let them bee what they can bee. Thus
in despite and defiance of all thy good parts, if I cannot indure thy
basenesse, 'tis more out of thy courtesie, then my deserving, and
so I expect thy answer.

GRILLA I must confesse—   15

CUCULUS Well said.

GRILLA You are—

CUCULUS That's true too.

GRILLA To speake you right, a very scurvy fellow.—

CUCULUS Away, away, do'st thinke so?   20

F3ʳ GRILLA A very foule-mouth'd, and misshapen Cockscombe.

CUCULUS Ile never beleeve it by this hand.

GRILLA A Magot, most unworthy to creepe into— the least
wrinckle of a Gentlewomans (What d'ee call) good conceit, or so,
or what you will else.— Were you not refin'd by Courtship and   25
education, which in my bleare eyes makes you appeare as sweet as
any nosegay, or savory cod of Muske new fall'n from th'Cat.

CUCULUS This shall serve well enough for the Waiting-woman.
My next Mistris is *Cleophila*, the old mad-mans daughter: I must
come to her in whining tune, sigh, wipe mine eyes, fold my Armes,   30
and blubber out my speech as thus: Even as a Kennell of Hounds
(sweet Lady) cannot catch a Hare, when they are full pauncht on
the Carrion of a dead Horse: so, even so the gorge of my affections
being full cramm'd with the garboyles of your condolements, doth
tickle me with the prick (as it were) about mee, and fellow-feeling   35
of howling outright.

GRILLA This will doo't, if we will heare.

CUCULUS Thou seest I am crying ripe, I am such another tender-
hearted foole.

23–7] *Hill; verse in Q:* . . . in —— | ——To . . . Gentlewomans | . . . what | . . . Courtship | . . .
eyes | . . . nosegay | . . . Cat.

GRILLA   Even as the snuffe of a candle that is burnt in the socket,   40
goes out, and leaves a strong perfume behind it; or as a piece of
toasted cheese next the heart in a morning is a restorative for a
sweet breath: so, even so the odoriferous savour of your love doth
perfume my heart, (Hay ho) with the pure sent of an intolerable
content, and not to be indur'd.   45

CUCULUS   By this hand 'tis excellent. Have at thee last of all: for
the Princesse *Thamasta*, she that is my Mistris | indeed, she is   F3ᵛ
abominably proud. A Lady of a damnable, high, turbulent, and
generous spirit. But I have a loud-mouth'd Cannon of mine owne
to batter her, and a pen'd speech of purpose; observe it.   50

   GRILLA   Thus I walke by, heare and minde you not.

   CUCULUS   [*Reads*] Though haughty as the Divell or his Dam,
      Thou dost appeare, great Mistris: yet I am
      Like to an ugly fire-worke, and can mount
      Above the Region of thy sweet Ac— count.   55
      Wert thou the Moone her selfe, yet having seene thee,
      Behold the man ordain'd to moove within thee.
      — Looke to your selfe, Houswife; answer me in strong
         Lines y'are best.

   GRILLA   Keepe off, poore foole, my beames will strike thee
         blinde: 60
      Else if thou touch me, touch me but behind.
      In Palaces, such as passe in before,
      Must be great Princes; for at the backe dore
      Tatter-demallians waite, who know not how
      To get admittance: such a one— art Thou.   65

CUCULUS   S'foot, this is downe-right roaring.

GRILLA   I know how to present a big Lady in her owne cue. But
pray in earnest, are you in love with all these?

CUCULUS   Pish, I have not a ragge of love about me. 'Tis only a
foolish humour I am possest with, to be surnam'd the Conquerour.   70
I will court any thing; be in love with nothing, nor no— thing.

GRILLA   A rare man you are, I protest.

52 SD] *Gifford*

CUCULUS   Yes, I know I am a rare man, and I ever held my
selfe so.

Enter PELIAS and CORAX.

PELIAS   In amorous contemplation on my life;   75
    Courting his Page by *Helicon*.

F4ʳ   CUCULUS   'Tis false.

GRILLA   A grosse untruth; Ile justifie it, Sir,
    At any time, place, weapon.

CUCULUS   Marry shall she.

CORAX   No quarrels, goody *Whiske*. Lay by your Trumperies,
and fall to your practice. Instructions are ready for you all. *Pelias*   80
is your Leader, follow him. Get credit now or never. Vanish,
Doodles, vanish.

CUCULUS   For the Device?

CORAX   The same, get'ee gone, and make no bawling.
Exeunt [all but CORAX]
    To waste my time thus Droane-like in the Court,   85
    And lose so many houres, as my studies
    Have horded up, is to be like a man
    That creepes both on his hands and knees, to climbe
    A mountaines top, where when he is ascended,
    One carelesse slip downe-tumbles him againe   90
    Into the bottome whence a first began.
    I need no Princes favour: Princes need
    My art. Then *Corax*, be no more a Gull,
    The best of 'em cannot foole thee, nay, they shall not.

Enter SOPHRONOS and ARETUS.

SOPHRONOS   We find him timely now; let's learne the cause.   95

ARETUS   'Tis fit we should— Sir, we approve you learn'd,
    And since your skill can best discerne the humours
    That are predominant, in bodies subject
    To alteration: tell us (pray) what divell

---

79 goody] *Gifford*; good'ee *Q*   84.183 *all . . .* CORAX] *Weber*   90 downe-tumbles
Weber; downe, tumbles *Q*

This *Melancholy* is, which can transforme   100
Men into Monsters.

CORAX   Y'ar your selfe a Scholer,
And quicke of apprehension: *Melancholy*
Is not as you conceive, indisposition
Of body, but the mindes disease. So Extasie,   F4ᵛ
Fantastick Dotage, Madnesse, Phrenzey, Rupture,   105
Of meere imagination differ partly
From *Melancholy*, which is briefly this,
A meere commotion of the minde, o're-charg'd
With feare and sorrow; first begot i'th' braine,
The Seate of Reason, and from thence deriv'd   110
As suddenly into the Heart, the Seate
Of our Affection.

ARETUS   There are sundry kinds
Of this disturbance.

CORAX   Infinite: it were
More easie to conjecture every houre
We have to live, then reckon up the kinds,   115
Or causes of this anguish of the minde.

SOPHRONOS   Thus you conclude, that as the cause is doubtfull,
The cure must be impossible; and then
Our Prince (poore Gentleman) is lost for ever,
As well unto himselfe, as to his subjects.   120

CORAX   My Lord, you are too quick, thus much I dare
Promise, and doe, ere many minutes passe,
I will discover whence his sadnesse is,
Or undergoe the censure of my ignorance.

ARETUS   You are a Noble Scholer.

SOPHRONOS   For reward,   125
You shall make your owne demand.

CORAX   May I be sure?

ARETUS   We both will pledge our truth.

---

103 conceive, indisposition] *Weber*; conceiue. Indisposition *Q*   105 Rupture *Q*; rapture
Dyce   107–9] *Vid. Democrit. Iunior Q, margin.*   113 Infinite: it] *Weber*; ~, ~ *Q*

CORAX   'Tis soone perform'd,
    That I may be discharg'd from my attendance
    At Court, and never more be sent for after:
    Or if I be, may Rats gnaw all my bookes,   130
    If I get home once, and come here againe,
G1ʳ   Though my necke stretch a halter for't, I care not.

SOPHRONOS   Come, come, you shall not feare it.

CORAX   Ile acquaint yee
    With what is to be done, and you shall fashion it.
                                          Exeunt omnes.

    3.2   *Enter* KALA *and* EROCLEA, *as before.*

KALA   My Lady do's expect'ee, thinks all time
    Too slow till you come to her: wherefore young man,
    If you intend to love me, and me onely,
    Before we part, without more circumstance
    Let us betroth our selves.

EROCLEA   I dare not wrong'ee;   5
    You are too violent.

KALA   Wrong me no more
    Then I wrong you: be mine, and I am yours:
    I cannot stand on points.

EROCLEA   Then to resolve
    All further hopes, you never can be mine,
    Must not, (and pardon though I say) you shall not.   10

KALA   [*aside*] The thing is sure a Gelding— [*to her*] Shall not?
    well,
    Y'are best to prate unto my Lady now,
    What proffer I have made.

EROCLEA   Never, I vow.

KALA   Doe, doe, 'tis but a kind heart of mine owne,
    And ill lucke can undoe me— [*aside*] Be refus'd?   15
    O scirvy— [*to her*] Pray walke on, Ile overtake 'ee.
                                          Exit EROCLEA

3.2] 11 *aside*] *Weber*   *To her*] *Hill*   16 SD] *Weber, after l.17 in* Q

What a greene-sicknesse-liver'd Boy is this!
My Maiden-head will shortly grow so stale,
That'twill be mouldy: but Ile marre her market.

Enter MENAPHON.

MENAPHON   *Parthenophill* past this way; prethee *Kala*   20
Direct me to him.   G1ᵛ

KALA   Yes, I can direct'ee:
But you (Sir) must forbeare.

MENAPHON   Forbeare!

KALA   I said so.
Your bounty h'as ingag'd my truth; receive
A secret, that will, as you are a man,
Startle your Reason: 'tis but meere respect   25
Of what I owe to thankfulnesse. (Deare Sir)
The Stranger whom your courtesie received
For Friend, is made your Rivall.

MENAPHON   Rivall, *Kala*.
Take heed, thou art too credulous.

KALA   My Lady
Doates on him: I will place you in a roome,   30
Where, though you cannot heare, yet you shall see
Such passages as will confirme the truth
Of my intelligence.

MENAPHON   'Twill make me mad.

KALA   Yes, yes: it makes me mad too, that a Gentleman
So excellently sweet, so liberall,   35
So kind, so proper, should be so betray'd
By a young smooth-chind straggler: but for loves sake
Beare all with manly courage.— Not a word,
I am undone then.

MENAPHON   That were too much pity:
Honest, most honest *Kala*; tis thy care,   40
Thy serviceable care.

KALA   You have even spoken
  All can be said or thought.

MENAPHON   I will reward thee:
  But as for him, ungentle Boy, Ile whip
  His falshood with a vengeance—

KALA   O speake little.
G2ʳ Walke up these staires, and take this key, it opens   45
  A Chamber doore, where at that window yonder,
  You may see all their courtship.

MENAPHON   I am silent.

KALA   As little noyse as may be, I beseech yee;
  There is a backe-staire to convey yee forth
  Unseene or unsuspected—   *Exit* MENAPHON
                    He that cheates   50
  A Waiting-woman of a free good turne
  She longs for, must expect a shrewd revenge.
  Sheepe-spirited Boy, although he had not married me,
  He might have proferd kindnesse in a corner,
  And ne'er have been the worse for't. They are come;   55
  On goes my set of Faces most demurely.

         Enter THAMASTA *and* EROCLEA.

THAMASTA   Forbeare the roome.

KALA   Yes, Madame.

THAMASTA   Whosoever
  Requires accesse to me, deny him entrance
  Till I call thee, and wait without.

KALA   I shall.
  [*aside*] Sweet *Venus*, turne his courage to a Snow-ball,   60
  I heartily beseech it.   *Exit.*

THAMASTA   I expose
  The Honour of my Birth, my Fame, my Youth,
  To hazard of much hard construction,
  In seeking an adventure of a parley

50 SD] *Weber, after l.47 Q*   57–61 *Weber, prose in Q*   60 SD] *Weber*

So private with a Stranger; if your thoughts   65
Censure me not with mercy, you may soone
Conceive, I have laid by that modesty,
Which should preserve a vertuous name unstain'd.

EROCLEA   Lady, to shorten long excuses; time
And safe experience have so throughly arm'd   70
My apprehension, with a reall taste
Of your most Noble nature, that to question
The least part of your bounties, or that freedome
Which Heaven hath with a plenty made you rich in,   G2ᵛ
Would argue me uncivill, which is more,   75
Base-bred, and which is most of all, unthankefull.

THAMASTA   The constant Loadstone, and the Steele are found
In severall Mines: yet is there such a league
Betweene these *Minerals,* as if one Veine
Of earth had nourisht both. The gentle Mirtle   80
Is not ingraft upon an Olives stocke:
Yet nature hath betweene them lockt a secret
Of Sympathy, that being planted neere,
They will both in their branches, and their rootes
Imbrace each other; twines of Ivie round   85
The well growne Oake; the Vine doth court the Elme;
Yet these are different Plants. *Parthenophill,*
Consider this aright, then these sleight creatures,
Will fortifie the reasons I should frame
For that ungrounded (as thou think'st) affection,   90
Which is submitted to a strangers pitie.
True love may blush, when shame repents too late,
But in all actions, Nature yeelds to Fate.

EROCLEA   Great Lady, 'twere a dulnesse must exceed
The grossest and most sottish kind of ignorance,   95
Not to be sensible of your intents:
I clearely understand them. Yet so much
The difference betweene that height and lownesse,
Which doth distinguish our unequall fortunes,
Disswades me from ambition; that I am   100
Humbler in my desires, then Loves owne power
Can any way raise up.

THAMASTA   I am a Princesse,
And know no law of slavery. To sue,
Yet be denied?

EROCLEA   I am so much a subject
To every law of Noble honesty,   105
That to transgresse the vowes of perfect friendship,
I hold a sacriledge as foule, and curs'd,
As if some holy Temple had bin robd,
And I the thiefe.

THAMASTA   Thou art unwise, young man,
To inrage a Lyonesse.

EROCLEA   It were unjust   110
To falsifie a faith, and ever after
Disroab'd of that faire ornament, live naked,
A scorne to time and truth.

THAMASTA   Remember well
Who I am, and what thou art.

EROCLEA   That remembrance
Prompts me to worthy duty, O great Lady.   115
If some few dayes have tempted your free heart,
To cast away affection on a stranger:
If that affection have so oversway'd
Your Judgement, that it in a manner hath
Declyn'd your soveraignty of birth and spirit: 120
How can yee turne your eyes off from that glasse,
Wherein you may new Trim, and settle right
A memorable name?

THAMASTA   The Youth is idle.

EROCLEA   Dayes, months and yeeres are past, since *Menaphon*
Hath lov'd and serv'd you truly: *Menaphon*;   125
A man of no large distance in his bloud,
From yours; in qualities desertfull, grac't
With Youth, Experience; every happy gift
That can by nature, or by Education
Improve a Gentleman: for him (great Lady)   130

103 slavery. To] *Weber*; ~, to Q

Let me prevaile, that you will yet at last,
Unlocke the bounty, which your love and care
Have wisely treasur'd up, t'inrich his life.

THAMASTA   Thou hast a mooving eloquence; *Parthenophill*,   G3ᵛ
Parthenophill, in vaine we strive to crosse   135
The destiny that guides us. My great heart
Is stoopt so much beneath that wonted pride
That first disguiz'd it, that I now preferre
A miserable life with thee, before
All other earthly comforts.

EROCLEA   *Menaphon*,   140
By me, repeates the selfe-same words to you:
You are too cruell, if you can distrust
His truth, or my report.

THAMASTA   Goe where thou wilt,
Ile be an exile with thee, I will learne
To beare all change of fortunes.

EROCLEA   For my friend,   145
I pleade with grounds of reason.

THAMASTA   For thy love,
Hard-hearted youth, I here renounce all thoughts
Of other hopes, of other intertainements,—

EROCLEA   Stay, as you honour Vertue.

THAMASTA   When the proffers
Of other greatnesse—

EROCLEA   Lady.

THAMASTA   When intreats   150
Of friends—

EROCLEA   Ile ease your griefe.

THAMASTA   Respect of kindred;

EROCLEA   Pray give me hearing.

THAMASTA   Losse of Fame;

140–1 *Weber, prose in Q*   149–53] *Weber, prose in Q*

EROCLEA   I crave
  But some few minutes.

THAMASTA   Shall infringe my vowes,
  Let Heaven—

EROCLEA   My love speaks t'ee; heare, then goe on.

THAMASTA   Thy love, why, 'tis a Charme to stop a vow   155
  In its most violent course.

EROCLEA   *Cupid* has broke
  His Arrowes here; and like a child unarm'd,
  Comes to make sport betweene us with no weapon,
G4ʳ But feathers stolne from his mothers Doves.

THAMASTA   This is meere trifling.

EROCLEA   Lady, take a secret.   160
  I am as you are, in a lower ranke
  Else of the selfe same sexe, a maide, a virgine.
  And now to use your owne words, if your thoughts
  Censure me not with mercy, you may soone
  Conceive, I have laid by that modesty,   165
  Which should preserve a vertuous name unstain'd.

THAMASTA   Are you not mankind then?

EROCLEA   When you shall reade
  The story of my sorrowes, with the change
  Of my misfortunes, in a letter printed
  From my unforg'd relation; I beleeve   170
  You will not thinke the sheading of one teare,
  A prodigality that misbecomes
  Your pitie and my fortune.

THAMASTA   Pray conceale
  The errors of my passions.

EROCLEA   Would I had
  Much more of honour (as for life I value't not)   175
  To venture on your secrecy.

THAMASTA   It will be
A hard taske for my Reason, to relinquish
The affection which was once devoted thine,
I shall a while repute thee still the youth
I lov'd so dearely.

EROCLEA   You shall find mee ever,   180
Your ready faithfull servant.

THAMASTA   O the powers
Who doe direct our hearts, laugh at our follies!
We must not part yet.

EROCLEA   Let not my unworthines
Alter your good opinion.

THAMASTA   I shall henceforth
Be jealous of thy company with any;   185
My feares are strong and many.   G4ᵛ
                         KALA *enters.*

KALA   Did your Ladiship call me?

THAMASTA   For what?

KALA   Your servant *Menaphon*
Desires admittance.

                    Enter MENAPHON.

MENAPHON   With your leave, great Mistris!
I come— [*Seeing* EROCLEA] So private: is this well,
   Parthenophill?

EROCLEA   Sir, Noble Sir.

MENAPHON   You are unkind and treacherous. 190
This 'tis to trust a straggler.

THAMASTA   Prethee servant.

MENAPHON   I dare not question you, you are my Mistris;
My Princes neerest Kinswoman, but he—

THAMASTA   Come, you are angry.

MENAPHON   Henceforth I will bury
Unmanly passion in perpetuall silence.   195

Ile court mine owne distraction, dote on folly,
Creepe to the mirth and madnesse of the age,
Rather then be so slav'd againe to woman,
Which in her best of constancy is steddiest
In change and scorne.

THAMASTA   How dare ye talke to me thus?   200

MENAPHON   Dare? Were you not owne Sister to my friend,
Sister to my *Amethus*; I would hurle ye
As farre off from mine eyes, as from my heart;
For I would never more looke on yee. Take
Your Jewell t'ee. And Youth, keepe under wing,   205
Or— Boy— Boy.

THAMASTA   If commands be of no force,
Let me intreat thee, *Menaphon*.

MENAPHON   'Tis naught,
Fye, fye, *Parthenophill*, have I deserv'd
To be thus us'd?

EROCLEA   I doe protest—

H1ʳ MENAPHON   You shall not,
Henceforth I will be free, and hate my bondage.   210

                Enter AMETHUS.

AMETHUS   Away, away to Court, the Prince is pleas'd
To see a Maske to night, we must attend him:
'Tis neere upon the time.— How thrives your suit?

MENAPHON   The Judge, your Sister, will decide it shortly.

THAMASTA   *Parthenophill*, I will not trust you from me.   215
                                                    [*Exeunt*]

3.3   *Enter* PRINCE, ARETUS, [SOPHRONOS,]
        CORAX (*with a Paper-plot*)
        servants with torches.

CORAX   Lights and attendance, I will shew your highnes,
A trifle of mine owne braine. If you can,

---

199 steddiest] *Weber*; steddist *Q*   206 Boy— Boy] By— By *conj. Craik*   215 SD]
Weber   3.3] 0.1 ARETUS] *Weber*, *Aretas Q*; SOPHRONOS,] *Gifford*;

Imagine you were now in the University,
You'll take it well enough, a Schollers fancy,
A quab. 'Tis nothing else a very quab.   5

PRINCE   We will observe it.

SOPHRONOS   Yes, and grace it too Sir.
For *Corax* else is humorous and testy.

ARETUS   By any meanes, men singular in Art,
Have alwayes some odde whimsey more then usuall.

PRINCE   The name of this conceit?

CORAX   Sir, it is called   10
The Maske of Melancholy.

ARETUS   We must looke for
Nothing but sadnesse, here then.

CORAX   Madnesse rather
In severall changes: *Melancholy* is
The Roote aswell of every Apish Phrensey,
Laughter and mirth, as dulnesse. Pray my Lord   15
Hold and observe the plot, 'tis there exprest
In kind, what shall be now exprest in action.

Enter AMETHUS, MENAPHON, THAMASTA, EROCLEA.

No interruption, take your places quickly.
Nay, nay, leave ceremony: sound to the entrance.   H1v
                    Florish.

Enter RHETIAS, *his face whited, blacke shag haire, long
nailes, a piece of raw meate.*

RHETIAS   Bow, Bow, wow, wow; the Moone's eclipsed, Ile to the   20
Church-yard and sup: Since I turn'd Wolfe, I bark and howle, and
digge up graves, I will never have the Sunne shine againe, 'tis
midnight, deepe darke midnight, get a prey, and fall too, I have
catcht thee now. *Arre.*

CORAX   This kind is called, *Lycanthropia*, Sir,   25
When men conceive themselves Wolves.

10 conceit?] *Weber*; ~. *Q*   18 interruption] *Q corr.*; interpretation *Q uncorr.*   23 get . . .
too] 'gets a prey and falls to' as SD conj. *Craik*

PRINCE   Here I finde it.

Enter PELIAS. *A Crowne of feathers on, Antickly rich.*

PELIAS   I will hang 'em all, and burne my wife: was I not an
Emperour; my hand was kist, and Ladies lay downe before me. In
triumph did I ride with my Nobles about me, till the mad-dog bit
mee, I fell, and I fell, and I fell. It shall be treason by Statute for   30
any man to name water, or wash his hands throughout all my
Dominions; breake all the looking-glasses, I will not see my
hornes; my wife Cuckolds me, she is a whore, a whore, a whore,
a whore.

PRINCE   *Hydrophobia* terme you this?   35

CORAX   And men possess so, shun all sight of water:
Sometimes, if mixt with jealousie, it renders them.
Incurable, and oftentimes brings death.

H2ʳ   *Enter* PHILOSOPHER *in blacke rags, a copper chaine on, an old*
Gowne halfe off, and Booke.

PHILOSOPHER   Philosophers dwel in the Moone. Speculation
and Theory girdle the world about like a wall. Ignorance like an   40
Atheist, must bee damn'd in the pit. I am very, very poore, and
poverty is the phisicke for the soule: my opinions are pure and
perfect. Envy is a monster, and I defie the beast.

CORAX   *Delirium* this is call'd, which is meere dotage,
Sprung from Ambition first, and singularity,   45
Selfe love, and blind opinion of true merit.

PRINCE   I not dislike the course.

Enter GRILLA *in a rich Gowne, great Vardingale, great*
Ruffe, Muffe, Fan, and Coxcombe on her head.

GRILLA   Yes forsooth, and no forsooth, is not this fine, I pray,
your blessing Gaffer, here, here, here did hee give me a shough,
and cut offs taile: busse, busse Nuncle, and ther's a pum for   50
Daddee.

CORAX   You find this noted there, *Phrenitis.*

PRINCE   True.

CORAX   Pride is the ground on't; it raignes most in women.

        Enter CUCULUS *like a Bedlam singing.*

CUCULUS   *They that will learne to drinke a health in Hell,*
    Must learne on earth to take Tobacco well,   55
    To take Tobacco well, to take Tobacco well:
    For in Hell they drink nor Wine, nor Ale, nor Beere,
    But fire, and smoake, and stench, as we do heere.

RHETIAS   Ile soope thee up.   H2ᵛ

PELIAS   Thou'st straight to execution.

GRILLA   Foole, Foole, Foole, catch me and thou canst.   60

PHILOSOPHER   Expell him the house, 'tis a Dunce.
                CUCULUS sings.
    Harke, did yee not heare a rumbling,
    The Gobblings are now a tumbling:
    Ile teare 'em, Ile seare 'em,
    Ile roare 'em, Ile goare 'em: 65
    Now, now, now, my braines are a Jumbling,—
    Bounce, the gun's off.

PRINCE   You name this here, *Hypocondriacall.*

CORAX   Which is a windy flattuous humour stuffing
    The head, and thence deriv'd to th'animall parts   70
    To be too over-curious, losse of goods,
    Or friends, excesse of feare, or sorrowes cause it.

        Enter a SEA-NIMPH *big-bellied, singing and dancing.*

[NYMPH]   *Good your Honours,*
    Pray your Worships,
    Deare your Beauties,   75

CUCULUS   *Hang thee.*
    To lash your sides,
    To tawe your hides,
    To scourge your prides,
    And bang thee.   80

53] *Weber; two lines in Q* 'Pride . . . on't | It . . . women'   64 seare] *Q*; scare *conj. Craik*
73 SH] *Weber subst.*   78 tawe] *Craik; tame Q*

NYMPH   *We're pretty and dainty, and I will begin,*
          See how they doe Jeere me, deride me, and grin:
          Come sport me, come court me, your Topsaile advance,
          And let us conclude our delights in a Dance.

H3ʳ   ALL   A Dance, a Dance, a Dance.   85

CORAX   This is the *Wanton Melancholy*; women
         With child possest with this strange fury often,
         Have danc'd three dayes together without ceasing.

PRINCE   'Tis very strange: but Heav'n is full of miracles.
                         The Dance: —
                Which ended, they all run out in couples.

PRINCE   We are thy debtor (*Corax*) for the gift   90
          Of this invention: but the plot deceives us;
          What meanes this empty space?

CORAX   One kind of Melancholy
         Is onely left untouch'd; 'twas not in Art
         To personate the shadow of that Fancy.
         'Tis nam'd *Love-Melancholy*. As for instance,   95
         Admit this stranger here [*to* EROCLEA] (Young man, stand forth)
         Intangled by the beauty of this Lady,
         The great *Thamasta*, cherisht in his heart
         The waight of hopes and feares: it were impossible,
         To lymne his passions in such lively colours,   100
         As his owne proper sufferance coo'd expresse.

EROCLEA   You are not modest Sir.

THAMASTA   Am I your mirth?

CORAX   Love is the Tyrant of the heart, it darkens
         Reason, confounds discretion, deafe to counsell:
         It runnes a headlong course to desperate madnesse.   105
         O were your Highnes but toucht home, and throughly,
         With this (what shall I call it) Divell—

PRINCE   Hold,
         Let no man henceforth name the word agen!
         Wait you my pleasure, Youth; 'tis late, to rest.   [*Exit*]

---

81 We're] *Weber;* Were Q   92 space?] *Weber;* ~. Q   96 SD] *Weber*   108 agen!]
Weber; ~ [*no punctuation*] Q   109 SD] *Weber*

CORAX   My Lords—

SOPHRONOS   Enough, thou art a perfect Arts-man.   110

CORAX   Panthers may hide their heads, not change the skin:
    And love pent ne're so close yet will be seene.   *Exeunt.*
        Finis Actus Tertii.

        4.1   *Enter* AMETHUS *and* MENAPHON.   H3ᵛ

AMETHUS   Doate on a stranger?

MENAPHON   Court him, plead, and sue to him.

AMETHUS   Affectionately?

MENAPHON   Servilely; and pardon me,
    If I say basely.

AMETHUS   Women in their passions,
    Like false fiers flash, to fright our trembling sences;
    Yet in themselves containe nor light nor heate.   5
    My Sister doe this? Shee, whose pride did scorne
    All thoughts that were not busied on a Crowne?
    To fall so farre beneath her fortunes now?
    You are my friend.

MENAPHON   What I confirme, is truth.

AMETHUS   Truth, *Menaphon?*

MENAPHON   If I conceiv'd you were   10
    Jealous of my sincerity and plainnesse,
    Then Sir—

AMETHUS   What then, Sir?

MENAPHON   I would then resolve,
    You were as changeable in vowes of friendship,
    As is *Thamasta* in her choice of love.
    That sinne is double, running in a blood,   15
    Which justifies another being worse.

AMETHUS   My *Menaphon,* excuse me, I grow wilde,
    And would not willingly beleeve the truth

Of my dishonour: She shall know how much
I am a debtor to thy noble goodnesse,   20
By checking the contempt her poore desires
Have sunke her fame in. Prethee tell me (friend)
How did the Youth receive her?

MENAPHON   With a coldnesse,
As modest and as hopelesse, as the trust
    I did repose in him, coo'd wish, or merit.   25

                    Enter THAMASTA *and* KALA.

AMETHUS   I will esteeme him dearely.

MENAPHON   Sir, your Sister.

THAMASTA   Servant, I have imployment for yee.

AMETHUS   Harke yee:
The maske of your ambition is fallen off,
Your pride hath stoop't to such an abject lownesse,
That you have now discover'd to report   30
Your nakednesse in vertue, honors, shame—

THAMASTA   You are turn'd Satyre.

AMETHUS   All the flatteries
Of greatnesse have expos'd yee to contempt.

THAMASTA   This is meere rayling.

AMETHUS   You have sold your birth,
    For lust.

THAMASTA   Lust?

AMETHUS   Yes, and at a deare expence   35
    Purchast the onely glories of a Wanton.

THAMASTA   A Wanton?

AMETHUS   Let repentance stop your mouth.
    Learne to redeeme your fault.

KALA [*aside to* MENAPHON]   I hope your tongue
    Ha's not betrayd my honesty.

38 SD] *Weber*

MENAPHON   [*aside to* KALA]   Feare nothing.

THAMASTA   If (*Menaphon*) I hitherto have strove;   40
   To keepe a wary guard about my fame;
   If I have used a womans skill to sift
   The constancy of your protested love;   H4ᵛ
   You cannot in the Justice of your judgment,
   Impute that to a Coynesse, or neglect,   45
   Which my discretion and your service aym'd
   For noble purposes.

MENAPHON   Great Mistris, no:
   I rather quarrell with mine owne ambition,
   That durst to soare so high, as to feed hope
   Of any least desert, that might intitle   50
   My duty, to a pension from your favours.

AMETHUS   And therefore Lady (pray observe him well)
   He henceforth covets playne equality;
   Indevouring to rancke his fortunes low,
   With some fit partner, whom without presumption,   55
   Without offence, or danger, he may cherish;
   Yes and command too, as a Wife; a Wife;
   A Wife, my most great Lady.

KALA   [*aside*]   All will out.

THAMASTA   Now I perceive the league of Amitye,
   Which you have long betweene yee, vow'd and kept,   60
   Is sacred and inviolable, secrets
   Of every nature are in common t'ee:
   If I have trespass'd, and I have been faulty:
   Let not too rude a Censure doome me guilty,
   Or judge my errour wilfull without pardon.   65

MENAPHON   Gracious and vertuous Mistris.

AMETHUS   'Tis a tricke,
   There is no trust in female cunning (friend)
   Let her first purge her follies past, and cleere
   The wrongs done to her honor, by some sure
   Apparant testimony of her constancy: 70

39 SD] *Dyce*   40 *Menaphon*] *this edn.*; ~, *Q*   53 equality] *corr. Q*; equally *uncorr. Q*
58 Lady. *Weber*; Lady *Q*   58 SD] *Weber*   63 If I] *Craik*; I *Q*

Or wee will not beleeve these childish plots;
As you respect my friendship, lend no eare
11^r To a reply. Thinke on't.

MENAPHON   [*to* THAMASTA] Pray love your fame.
                              Exeunt MENAPHON [*and*] AMETHUS

THAMASTA   Gon! I am sure awakt. *Kala* I finde,   75
    You have not been so trusty as the duty
    You ow'd, requir'd.

KALA   Not I? I doe protest,
    I have been, Madam.

THAMASTA   Bee no matter what.
    I'me pay'd in mine owne Coyne; something I must,
    And speedily [*pauses*]—so,— seeke out *Cuculus*
    Bid him attend me instantly.

KALA   That Anticke!   80
    The trim old Youth shall wait yee.

THAMASTA   Wounds may be mortall, which are wounds indeed:
    "But no wounds deadly, till our Honors bleed.   *Exeunt.*

        4.2   *Enter* RHETIAS *and* CORAX.

RHETIAS   Thar't an excellent fellow. *Diabolo*! O these lousie
close-stoole Empricks, that will undertake all Cures, yet know not
the causes of any disease. Dog-leaches! By the foure Elements I
honor thee, coo'd finde in my heart to turne knave, and bee thy
flatterer.   5

CORAX   Sirra, 'tis pitty th'ast not been a Scholer;
    Th'art honest, blunt, and rude enough, o' conscience!
    But for thy Lord now, I have put him too't.

RHETIAS   He chafes hugely, fumes like a stew-pot; Is he not
monstrously overgone in frenzy?   10

CORAX   *Rhetias*, 'tis not a madnesse, but his sorrow's
    Close griping griefe, and anguish of the soule
    That torture him: he carries Hell on earth

---

79 SD] *this edn.*   **4.2**] 1 *Diabolo*!] *Weber*; ~. *Q*   1 this] *Q*; these *Weber*   3 Dog-
leaches!] *Weber*; ~. *Q*   6 thou'dst] *Weber*; th'ast *Q*;   7 o'conscience] *Weber*; .
O Conscience *Q*

Within his bosome, 'twas a Princes tyranny
Caus'd his distraction, and a Princes sweetnes   15
Must qualifie that tempest of his minde.

RHETIAS   *Corax*, to prayse thy Art, were to assure
The misbeleeving world, that the Sunne shines,
When 'tis in th'full Meridian of his beauty.   II^v
No cloud of blacke detraction can eclipse   20
The light of thy rare knowledge; henceforth casting
All poore disguises off, that play in rudenesse,
Call me your servant: onely for the present,
I wish a happy blessing to your Labours;
Heaven crowne your undertakings; and beleeve me,   25
Ere many houres can passe, at our next meeting,
The bonds my duty owes, shall be full cancelled.   *Exit.*

CORAX   Farwell— a shrewd-braine Whorson, there's pith
In his untoward plainenesse.—

              Enter TROLLIO *with a Murrion on.*

                    Now, the newes!

TROLLIO   Worshipfull Master Doctor, I have a great deale of   30
I cannot tell what, to say t'ee; My Lord thunders: every word that
comes out of his mouth, roares like a Cannon: the house shooke
once, my young Lady dares not be seene.

CORAX   We will roare with him, *Trollio*, if he roare.

TROLLIO   He has got a great Poll-axe in his hand, and fences it   35
up and downe the house, as if he were to make roome for the
Pageants. I have provided me a Murrion for feare of a clap on the
Coxcombe.

CORAX   No matter for the Murrion, here's my Cap:
Thus I will pull it downe; and thus out-stare him.   40
              [*Puts on a Gorgon mask.*]

TROLLIO   [*aside*] The Physicion is got as mad as my Lord.—
[*to him*] O brave, a man of Worship.

CORAX   Let him come, *Trollio*, I will firke his Trangdido,
And bounce, and bounce in metall, honest *Trollio*.

40.1 SD] *Hill.*   41 SD] *Dyce*   42 SD] *Hill*

TROLLIO   [*aside*] Hee vapours like a Tinker, and struts like a   45
Juggler.

MELEANDER   *within.* So ho, so ho!

TROLLIO   There, there, there; looke to your Right Worshipfull,
    looke to your selfe.

12ʳ   *Enter* MELEANDER *with a poll-axe.*

MELEANDER   Show me the Dog, whose triple throated noyse,   50
    Hath rowzd a Lyon from his uncoth den,
    To teare the Curre in pieces.

CORAX   Stay thy pawes,
    Couragious beast, else lo, the Gorgon's skull,
    That shall transforme thee, to that restlesse stone,
    Which *Sysiphus* roules up against the hill;   55
    Whence tumbling downe againe, it, with his waight
    Shall crush thy bones, and puffe thee into Ayre.

MELEANDER   Hold, hold thy conqu'ring breath, 'tis stronger far
    Then Gun-powder and Garlike. If the Fates
    Have spun my thred, and my spent-clue of life   60
    Be now untwisted, let us part like friends.
    Lay up my weapon, *Trollio*, and be gone.

TROLLIO   Yes Sir, with all my heart—
                    Exit TROLLIO [*with the pole-axe*]

MELEANDER   This friend and I
    Will walke, and gabble wisely.

CORAX   I allow
    The motion: On. [*takes off his mask.*]

MELEANDER   So Polititians thrive,   65
    That with their crabbed faces, and sly tricks
    Legerdemayne, ducks, cringes, formall beards,
    Crisp'd haires, and punctuall cheats, do wriggle in
    Their heads first, like a Foxe, to roomes of State,
    Then the whole body followes.

---

45 SD] *Gifford*   47 MELEANDER] *Weber*, Menander *Q*   47 So ho, so ho!] *Weber*; ~
~. So ~. *Q*   49 yourself Right] *Craik*; your ~ *Q*   53 Gorgon's] *Gifford*; gorgeous *Q*
63 SD *with pole-axe*] *Gifford*   63–5 This . . . thrive] *Hill*; prose in *Q*   65 SD] *Gifford*

CORAX   Then they fill   70
  Lordships, steale womens hearts: with them and their's
  The world runnes round, yet these are square men still.

MELEANDER   There are none poore, but such as ingrosse offices.

CORAX   None wise; but unthrifts, bankrupts, beggers, Rascals.

MELEANDER   The hangman is a rare Phisician.   75

CORAX   [*aside*] Thats not so good. [*To him*] It shalbe granted.

MELEANDER   All the buz of Drugs, and Myneralls and Simples,
  Bloud-lettings, Vomits, Purges, or what else   12ᵛ
  Is conjur'd up by men of Art, to gull
  Liege-people, and reare golden piles, are trash   80
  To a well-strong-wrought halter; there the Goute,
  The stone, yes and the *Melancholy* devill,
  Are cur'd in lesse time then a paire of minutes.
  Build me a Gallows in this very plot,
  And Ile dispatch your businesse.

CORAX   Fix the knot   85
  Right under the left eare.

MELEANDER   Sirra, make ready.

CORAX   Yet doe not be too sudden, grant me leave,
  To give a farewell to a creature long
  Absented from me, 'tis a daughter (Sir)
  Snatcht from me in her youth, a handsome girle,   90
  Shee comes to aske a blessing.

MELEANDER   Pray where is shee?
  I cannot see her yet.

CORAX   Shee makes more haste
  In her quicke prayers then her trembling steppes,
  Which many griefes have weakened.

MELEANDER   Cruell man!
  How canst thou rip a heart, that's cleft already   95
  With injuries of time? whilst I am franticke,

70–2 Then they … still] *Weber; prose in* Q   76 *aside*] *Gifford; To him*] *Hill*   80 Liege-people] *Q; Lewd-people conj. Craik;   81 well-strong-wrought] *Q; strong well-wrought] conj. Gifford*

Whilst throngs of rude divisions huddle on,
And doe disranke my braines from peace, and sleepe;
So long I am insensible of cares.
As balls of wild-fire may be safely toucht,   100
Not violently sundred, and throwne up;
So my distemper'd thoughts rest in their rage,
Not hurryed in the Ayre of repetition,
Or memory of my misfortunes past.
Then are my griefes strooke home, when they are reclaym'd,   105
To their owne pitty of themselves— Proceed;
13ʳ   What of your daughter now?

CORAX   I cannot tell yee,
'Tis now out of my head againe; my braines
Are crazie; I have scarce slept one sound sleepe
These twelve moneths.

MELEANDER   'las poore man; canst thou imagine   110
To prosper in the taske thou tak'st in hand,
By practising a cure upon my weakenesse,
And yet be no Physician for thy selfe?
Goe, goe, turne over all thy bookes once more,
And learne to thrive in modesty; for impudence   115
Does least become a Scholer. Thou art a foole,
A kind of learned foole.

CORAX   I doe confesse it.

MELEANDER   If thou canst wake with me, forget to eate,
Renounce the thought of Greatnesse; tread on Fate;
Sigh out a lamentable tale of things   120
Done long agoe, and ill done; and when sighes
Are wearied, piece up what remaines behind,
With weeping eyes, and hearts that bleed to death:
Thou shalt be a companion fit for me,
And we will sit together like true friends,   125
And never be devided. With what greedinesse
Doe I hug my afflictions? there's no mirth
Which is not truly season'd with some madnesse.
As for example—   *Exit.*

105] *Weber, two lines in Q:* . . . home,| . . . reclaym'd,

CORAX   What new Crochet next?
　　There is so much sence in this wilde distraction,   130
　　That I am almost out of my wits too,
　　To see and heare him: some few houres more
　　Spent here, would turne me Apish, if not frantick.

　　　　　　　　Enter MELEANDER *and* CLEOPHILA.

MELEANDER   In all the volumes thou hast turn'd, thou *Man*
　　Of knowledge, hast thou met with any rarity,   135 13ᵛ
　　Worthy thy contemplation like to this?
　　The modell of the Heavens, the Earth, the Waters,
　　The harmony, and sweet consent of times,
　　Are not of such an excellence, in forme
　　Of their Creation, as the infinite wonder   140
　　That dwelles within the compasse of this face:
　　And yet I tell thee, Scholer, under this
　　Well-ord'red signe, is lodg'd such an obedience,
　　As will hereafter in another age,
　　Strike all comparison into a silence.   145
　　She had a Sister too: but as for her,
　　If I were given to talke, I coo'd describe
　　A pretty piece of goodnesse: let that passe—
　　We must be wise somtimes: What would you with her?

CORAX   I with her? nothing by your leave, Sir, I: 150
　　It is not my profession.

MELEANDER   You are sawcy,
　　And as I take it, scurvy in your sawcinesse,
　　To use no more respect— [*to* CLEOPHILA] good soule, be patient:
　　We are a paire of things the world doth laugh at:
　　Yet be content, *Cleophila*; those clouds   155
　　Which barre the Sunne from shining on our miseries,
　　Will never be chac'd off till I am dead;
　　And then some charitable soule will take thee
　　Into protection. I am hasting on,
　　The time cannot be long.

CLEOPHILA   I doe beseech yee,   160
　　Sir, as you love your health, as you respect
　　My safety, let not passion overrule you.

134 SH] *no SH in* Q   150 her?] *Weber*; her! Q   153 SD] *this edn.*

MELEANDER   It shall not, I am friends with all the world.
Get me some wine, to witnesse that I will be
An absolute good fellow, I will drinke with thee.   165

14ʳ   CORAX   [*aside to* CLEOPHILA] Have you prepar'd his Cup?

CLEOPHILA   [*aside to* CORAX]   'Tis in readinesse.

Enter CUCULUS *and* GRILLA.

CUCULUS   By your leave, Gallants, I come to speake with a young
Lady, as they say, the old *Trojanes* daughter of the house.

MELEANDER   Your businesse with my Lady daughter, Tosse-pot?

GRILLA   Tosse-pot? O base! Tosse-pot?   170

CUCULUS   [*aside to* GRILLA] Peace; do'st not see in what case
he is? [*to* MELEANDER] I would doe my owne commendations to
her; that's all.

MELEANDER   Doe, [*to* CORAX] come my *Genius*, we will
quaffe in wine
Till we grow wise.

CORAX   True Nectar is divine.   175
Exeunt MELEANDER *and* CORAX

CUCULUS   So, I am glad he is gone. Page, walke aside. Sweet
Beauty, I am sent Embassadour from the Mistris of my thoughts,
to you, the Mistris of my desires.

CLEOPHILA   So Sir, I pray be briefe.

CUCULUS   That you may know, I am not as they say, an Animall;   180
which is as they say, a kinde of Cokes, which is as the learned
terme, an Asse, a Puppy, a Widgin, a Dolt, a Noddy, a—

CLEOPHILA   As you please.

CUCULUS   Pardon me for that, it shall be as you please indeed.
Forsooth I love to be courtly, and in fashion.   185

CLEOPHILA   Well, to your Embasie; what, or from whom?

166 SD] *Gifford*   166 *SD*] *Dyce*   171 SD] *Hill*   173 SD] *Hill*   175.1 *Exeunt*]
Weber, Exit Q

CUCULUS   Marry *what* is more then I know? for to know *what's what*, is to know *what's what*, and for *what's what*: but these are foolish figures, and to little purpose.

CLEOPHILA   From whom then are you sent?   190

CUCULUS   There you come to me agen: O, to bee in the favour of great Ladies, is as much to say, as to be great in Ladies favours.

CLEOPHILA   Good time a day t'ee; I can stay no longer.

CUCULUS   By this light but you must, for now I come toot. | The   14ᵛ
most excellent, most wise, most dainty, precious, loving, kinde,   195
sweet, intolerably faire Lady *Thamasta* commends to your little
hands, this letter of importance. By your leave, let me first kisse
and then deliver it in fashion, to your owne proper beauty.

CLEOPHILA   To me from her? 'Tis strange; I dare peruse it.

CUCULUS   Good, [*aside*] O that I had not resolv'd to live a single   200
life! Heer's temptation able to conjure up a spirit with a witnesse.
So so: she has read it.

CLEOPHILA   Is't possible? Heaven, thou art great and bountiful.
  Sir, I much thanke your paines: and to the Princesse,
  Let my love, duty, service, be remembred.   205

CUCULUS   They shall Mad-dame.

CLEOPHILA   When we of hopes, or helpes, are quite bereaven,
  Our humble pray'rs have entrance into heav'n.

CUCULUS   Thats my opinion cleerely and without doubt.

                                              Exeunt.

4.3   *Enter* ARETUS *and* SOPHRONOS.

ARETUS   The Prince is throughly mov'd.

SOPHRONOS   I never saw him
  So much distemp'red.

ARETUS   What should this young man bee,

Or whither can he be convay'd?

SOPHRONOS   'Tis to me
A mystery, I understand it not.

ARETUS   Nor I.

Enter PRINCE AMETHUS *and* PELIAS.

PRINCE   Yee have consented all to worke upon   5
The softnesse of my nature; but take heede:
Though I can sleepe in silence, and looke on
The mockery yee make of my dull patience;
Yet'ee shall know, the best of yee, that in mee
There is a masculin, a stirring spirit;   10
Kiʳ   Which provokt, shall like a bearded Comet
Set yee at gaze, and threaten horrour.

PELIAS   Good Sir.

PRINCE   Good Sir. 'Tis not your active wit or language,
Nor your grave politicke wisdomes (Lords) shall dare
To check-mate and controle my just commands.   15

Enter MENAPHON.

Where is the Youth your friend? is he found yet?

MENAPHON   Not to be heard of.

PRINCE   Flye then to the desart,
Where thou didst first encounter this Fantasticke,
This airie apparition; come no more
In sight: Get yee all from me; he that stayes,   20
Is not my friend.

AMETHUS   'Tis strange.

ARETUS SOPHRONOS   We must obey.
                         Exeunt all but the PRINCE

PRINCE   Some angry power, cheates with rare delusions,
My credulous sense: the very soule of Reason
Is troubled in me— the Physician
Presented a strange Maske, the view of it   25
Puzzl'd my understanding: but the Boy—

Enter RHETIAS.

Rhetias, thou art acquainted with my griefes,
Parthenophill is lost, and I would see him;
For he is like to some thing I remember
A great while since, a long, long time agoe.   30

RHETIAS   I have been diligent (Sir) to pry into every corner for discovery, but cannot meet with him: There is some tricke I am confident.

PRINCE   There is, there is some practice, sleight or plot.

RHETIAS   I have apprehended a faire Wench, in an odde Private   35
lodging in the Citie, as like the Youth in face, as can by possibility
be discern'd.

PRINCE   How *Rhetias*!   K1ᵛ

RHETIAS   If it be not *Parthenophill* in long coates, 'tis a spirit in his
likenesse; answer I can get none from her; you shall see her.   40

PRINCE   The young man in disguise upon my life,
    To steale out of the Land.

RHETIAS   Ile send him t'ee.   *Exit* RHETIAS

Enter EROCLEA *in womans attire, and listens.*

PRINCE   Doe, doe my *Rhetias*. As there is by nature
    In every thing created contrarietie:
    So likewise is there unity and league   45
    Betweene them in their kind; but *Man*, the abstract
    Of all perfection, which the workmanship
    Of Heaven hath model'd, in himselfe containes
    Passions of severall qualitie, the musicke
    Of mans faire composition best accords,   50
    When 'tis in consort, not in single straines.
    My heart has been untun'd these many moneths,
    Wanting her presence, in whose equall love
    True harmony consisted; living here
    We are Heav'ns bounty all, but Fortunes exercise.   55

EROCLEA   Minutes are numbred by the fall of Sands;
    As by an houre-glasse, the span of time
    Doth waste us to our graves, and we looke on it.

35–7] *Weber*; *verse in* Q   56 Sands; *Q*; Sands, *Weber*   57 houre-glasse, *Q*; houre-
glasse; *Weber*

An age of pleasures revel'd out, comes home
At last, and ends in sorrow, but the life   60
Weary of ryot, numbers every Sand,
Wayling in sighes, untill the last drop downe,
So to conclude calamity in rest.

PRINCE   What Eccho yeelds a voyce to my complaints?
Can I be no where private?

EROCLEA   [*coming forward*] Let the substance   65
As suddenly be hurried from your eyes,
As the vaine sound can passe your eare,
If no impression of a troth vow'd yours,   *Kneeles.*
Retaine a constant memory.

PRINCE   Stand up;
'Tis not the figure stampt upon thy cheekes,   70
The coozenage of thy beauty, grace, or tongue,
Can draw from me a secret, that hath been
The onely Jewell of my speechlesse thoughts.

EROCLEA   I am so worne away with feares and sorrowes,
So wintred with the tempests of affliction,   75
That the bright Sunne of your life-quickning presence
Hath scarce one beame of force, to warme againe
That spring of chearefull comfort, which youth once
Apparel'd in fresh lookes.

PRINCE   Cunning Impostor,
Untruth hath made thee subtle in thy trade: 80
If any neighbouring *Greatnesse* hath seduc'd
A free-borne resolution, to attempt
Some bolder act of treachery, by cutting
My weary dayes off. Wherefore (*Cruell-mercy*)
Hast thou assum'd a shape, that would make treason   85
A piety, guilt pardonable, blood-shed
As holy as the sacrifice of peace?

EROCLEA   The Incense of my love-desires, are flam'd
Upon an Altar of more constant proofe.
Sir, O Sir, turne me backe into the world,   90
Command me to forget my name, my birth,

K2ʳ (left margin, at line 67)

65 SD] *Hill*

My Fathers sadnesse, and my death alive,
If all remembrance of my Faith hath found
A buriall, without pitie in your scorne.

PRINCE   My scorne (disdainefull Boy) shall soone unweave   95
The web thy Art hath twisted: cast thy shape off,
Disroabe the mantle of a fainèd Sex,
And so I may be gentle; as thou art,
There's witch-craft in thy language, in thy face,   K2ᵛ
In thy demeanors; turne, turne from me (prethee)   100
For my beliefe is arm'd else. Yet (*faire subtilty*)
Before we part (for part we must) be true,
Tell me thy Countrey.

EROCLEA   *Cyprus.*

PRINCE   Ha: thy Father.

EROCLEA   *Meleander.*

PRINCE   Hast a name?

EROCLEA   A name of misery,
    The unfortunate *Eroclea.*

PRINCE   There is danger   105
In this seducing counterfeit. Great goodnesse!
Hath honesty and vertue left the time?
Are we become so impious, that to tread
The path of impudence, is Law and Justice?
Thou vizard of a beauty ever sacred,   110
Give me thy name.

EROCLEA   Whil'st I was lost to memory,
Parthenophill did shrowd my shame in change
Of sundry rare misfortunes: but since now
I am, before I dye, return'd to claime
A Convoy to my grave, I must not blush   115
To let Prince *Palador* (if I offend,)
Know when he doomes me, that he doomes *Eroclea.*
I am that wofull Maid.

PRINCE   Joyne not too fast
Thy penance, with the story of my suffrings.

106 counterfeit. Great] *Weber*; counterfeit, great *Q*

So dwelt *simplicity* with virgin *truth*;   120
So *Martyrdome* and *holinesse* are twins,
As *innocence* and *sweetnesse* on thy tongue.
But let me by degrees collect my senses,
I may abuse my trust. Tell me, what ayre
Hast thou perfum'd, since Tyranny first ravisht   125
K3^r   The contract of our hearts?

EROCLEA   Deare Sir, in *Athens*
Have I been buried.

PRINCE   Buried! Right, as I
In *Cyprus*.— Come to triall, if thou beest
Eroclea, in my bosome I can finde thee. [*He shows her a tablet*]

EROCLEA   As I, Prince *Palador*, in mine: This gift   130
                    She shewes him a Tablet.
His bounty blest me with, the onely physicke
My solitary cares have hourely tooke,
To keepe me from despaire.

PRINCE   We are but Fooles
To trifle in disputes, or vainely struggle
With that eternall *mercy* which protects us.   135
Come home, home to my heart, thou *banisht-peace*,
My extasie of joyes would speake in passion,
But that I would not lose that part of man,
Which is reserv'd to intertaine content.
Eroclea, I am thine; O let me seize thee   140
As my inheritance. *Hymen* shall now
Set all his Torches burning, to give light
Throughout this Land, new settled in thy welcome.

EROCLEA   You are still gracious. Sir, how I have liv'd,
By what meanes been convey'd, by what preserv'd,   145
By what return'd; *Rhetias*, my trusty servant,
Directed by the wisdome of my Uncle,
The good *Sophronos*, can informe at large.

PRINCE   Enough, in stead of Musicke, every night
To make our sleepes delightfull, thou shalt cloze   150
Our weary eyes with some part of thy story.

129 SD] *this edn.*

EROCLEA   O but my Father!

PRINCE   Feare not: to behold
Eroclea safe, will make him young againe;
It shall be our first taske. Blush sensuall follies,
Which are not guarded with thoughts chastly pure.   155 K3ᵛ
There is no faith in lust, but baytes of Artes;
'Tis vertuous love keepes cleare contracted hearts.   [*Exeunt*]
Finis Actus Quarti

>   **5.1**   *Enter* CORAX *and* CLEOPHILA.

CORAX   'Tis well, 'tis well, the houre is at hand,
Which must conclude the busines, that no Art
Coo'd al this while make ripe for wisht content.
O Lady, in the turmoyles of our lives,
Men are like politike States, or troubled Seas,   5
Tost up and downe with severall stormes and tempests,
Change, and varietie of wracks, and fortunes,
Till labouring to the Havens of our homes,
We struggle for the Calme that crownes our ends.

CLEOPHILA   A happy end Heaven blesse us with.

CORAX   'Tis well said,   10
The old man sleepes still soundly?

CLEOPHILA   May soft dreames
Play in his fancy, that when he awakes,
With comfort, he may by degrees, digest
The present blessings in a moderate Joy.

CORAX   I drencht his cup to purpose; he ne're stir'd   15
At Barber or at Taylor: a will laugh
At his owne Metamorphosis, and wonder.
We must be watchfull. Does the Couch stand ready?

>   *Enter* TROLLIO.

CLEOPHILA   All as you commanded. [*to* TROLLIO] What's
   your haste for?

157 SD] *Weber; SD omitted in Q*   157.1] *Finis Actus Quarti*] *this edn.; omitted in Q*
5.1] *Actus V. Scena I Q*   18 Couch] *Weber, Gifford, Craik (so also at 174);* Coach *Q.*

K4ʳ TROLLIO   A brace of bigge women, usher'd by the young | old   20
Ape, with his shee-clog at his bum, are enterd the Castle; Shall they
come on?

    CORAX   By any meanes, the time is precious now;
       Lady, be quick and carefull. Follow, *Trollio*.

    TROLLIO   I owe all Sir-Reverence to your Right Worshipfulnesse.   25
                 [*Exeunt* CORAX *and* TROLLIO]

    CLEOPHILA   So many feares, so many joyes, encounter
      My doubtfull expectations, that I waver
      Betweene the resolution of my hopes
      And my obedience; 'tis not (O my Fate)
      The apprehension of a timely blessing   30
      In pleasures, shakes my weakenesse; but the danger
      Of a mistaken duty, that confines
      The limits of my reason; let me live,
      Vertue, to thee as chaste, as *Truth* to time.

              Enter THAMASTA.

    THAMASTA   [*speaking to someone without*] Attend me till
      I call.— My sweet *Cleophila*.   35

    CLEOPHILA   Great Princesse—

    THAMASTA   I bring peace, to sue a Pardon
      For my neglect, of all those noble vertues
      Thy minde and duty are apparel'd with.
      I have deserv'd ill from thee, and must say,
      Thou art too gentle, if thou canst forget it.   40

    CLEOPHILA   Alas, you have not wrong'd me; for indeed,
      Acquaintance with my sorrowes, and my fortune,
      Were growne to such familiarity,
      That 'twas an impudence, more then presumption,
      To wish so great a Lady as you are,   45
      Should lose affection on my Uncles Sonne,
      But that your Brother, equall in your blood,
      Should stoope to such a lownesse, as to love
K4ᵛ   A Cast-away, a poore despisèd Maid,

Onely for me to hope was almost sinne, 50
Yet troth I never tempted him.

THAMASTA   Chide not
The grossenes of my trespasse (lovely Sweetnes)
In such an humble language, I have smarted
Already in the wounds, my pride hath made
Upon thy sufferings. Henceforth 'tis in you 55
To worke my happinesse.

CLEOPHILA   Call any service
Of mine a debt, for such it is; the Letter
You lately sent me, in the blest contents
It made me privy to, hath largely quitted
Every suspition of your Grace or goodnesse. 60

THAMASTA   Let me imbrace thee with a Sisters love,
A Sisters love, *Cleophila:* for should
My Brother henceforth study to forget
The vowes that he hath made thee, I would ever
Sollicite thy deserts.

               Enter AMETHUS *and* MENAPHON.

AMETHUS   We must have entrance. 65

THAMASTA   Must? Who are they say, must? you are unmannerly.
Brother is't you, and you too, Sir?

AMETHUS   Your Ladiship
Has had a time of Scolding to your humour:
Does the storme hold still?

CLEOPHILA   Never fell a showre
More seasonably gentle on the barren 70
Parcht thirsty earth, then showres of courtesie
Have from this Princesse been distilled on me,
To make my growth in quiet of my mind
Secure and lasting.

THAMASTA   You may both beleeve
That I was not uncivill.

AMETHUS   Pish, I know 75
Her spirit, and her envy.

L1r CLEOPHILA   Now in troth, Sir,
          Pray credit me, I doe not use to sweare;
          The vertuous Princesse hath in words and carriage
          Been kind, so over-kind, that I doe blush:
          I am not rich enough in thankes sufficient   80
          For her unequall'd bounty.— My good Cousin,
          I have a suite to you.

     MENAPHON   It shall be granted.

     CLEOPHILA   That no time, no perswasion, no respects
          Of Jealousies past, present, or hereafter
          By possibilitie to be conceived,   85
          Draw you from that sincerity and purenesse
          Of love, which you have oftentimes protested
          To this great worthy Lady: she deserves
          A duty more, then what the tyes of Marriage
          Can claime, or warrant: be for ever hers,   90
          As she is yours, and Heaven increase your comforts.

     AMETHUS   *Cleophila* hath play'd the Church-mans part,
          Ile not forbid the Banes.

     MENAPHON   Are you consented?

     THAMASTA   I have one taske in charge first, which concernes me.
          Brother, be not more cruell then this Lady,   95
          She hath forgiven my follies, so may you:
          Her youth, her beauty, innocence, discretion,
          Without additions of estate or birth,
          Are dower for a Prince indeed. You lov'd her;
          For sure you swore you did: else if you did not   100
          Here fixe your heart, and thus resolve, if now
          You misse this Heaven on earth, you cannot find
          In any other choice ought but a hell.

     AMETHUS   The Ladies are turn'd Lawyers, and pleade
               handsomely
          Their Clients cases. I am an easie Judge,   105
          And so shalt thou be *Menaphon*. I give thee
L1v   My Sister for a wife; a good one, friend.

92 *Cleophila*] *Weber;* Clophila *Q*

MENAPHON   Lady, will you confirme the gift?

THAMASTA   The errors
Of my mistaken judgement being lost,
To your remembrance, I shall ever strive   110
In my obedience to deserve your pity.

MENAPHON   My love, my care, my all.

AMETHUS   What rests for me?
I'm still a Batchelor: Sweet Maid, resolve me,
May I yet call you mine?

CLEOPHILA   My Lord *Amethus*,
Blame not my plainenesse, I am young and simple,   115
And have not any power to dispose
Mine owne will without warrant from my father:
That purchast, I am yours.

AMETHUS   It shall suffice me.

Enter CUCULUS, PELIAS, TROLLIO *and* GRILLA *pluckt in by 'em.*

CUCULUS   Revenge, I must have revenge; I will have revenge
bitter and abominable revenge; I will have revenge. This unfashionable 120
Mungrill, this Linsey-woolsey of mortality by this hand, Mistris,
this shee-Roague is drunke, and clapper-clawd me without any
reverence to my person, or good garments, why d'ee not speake,
Gentlemen?

PELIAS   Some certaine blowes have past, and't like your Highnesse. 125

TROLLIO   Some few knocks of Friendship, some love-toyes,
some Cuffes in kindnesse, or so.

GRILLA   Ile turne him away, he shall bee my Master no longer.

MENAPHON   Is this your she-Page, *Cuculus*? 'tis a Boy, sure.

CUCULUS   A Boy, an arrant Boy in long coates.   130

TROLLIO   He has mumbled his nose, that 'tis as big as a | great
Cod peece.   L2ʳ

CUCULUS   Oh thou Cock-vermine of iniquity.

<hr>

124 Gentlemen? *Weber*, ~. Q

THAMASTA   *Pelias*, take hence the wag, and schoole him for't.
  For your part, servant, Ile intreate the Prince   135
  To grant you some fit place about his Wardrobe.

CUCULUS   Ever after a bloody nose do I dreame of good lucke.
I horribly thanke your Ladiship.
  Whil'st I'm in office, the old garbe shall agen
  Grow in request, and Taylors shall be men.   140
  Come *Trollio*, helpe to wash my face, prethee.

TROLLIO   Yes, and to scowre it too—
                  Exit CUCULUS, TROLLIO, PELIAS, GRILLA.

                  Enter RHETIAS, CORAX.

RHETIAS   The Prince and Princesse are at hand, give over
  Your amorous Dialogues. Most honor'd Lady,
  Henceforth forbeare your sadnesse: are you ready   145
  To practise your instructions?

CLEOPHILA   I have studied
  My part with care, and will performe it (*Rhetias*)
  With all the skill I can.

CORAX   Ile passe my word for her.
    Florish. Enter PRINCE, SOPHRONOS, ARETUS, *and* EROCLEA.

PRINCE   Thus Princes should be circled with a guard
  Of truly noble friends, and watchfull subjects.   150
  O *Rhetias*, thou art just; the Youth thou told'st me,
  That liv'd at Athens, is returnd at last
  To her owne fortunes, and contracted Love.

RHETIAS   My knowledge made me sure of my report, Sir.

L2ᵛ   PRINCE   *Eroclea*, cleare thy feares, when the Sun shines,   155
  Clouds must not dare to muster in the skie,
  Nor shal they here— Why do they kneele? Stand up,
  The day and place is priviledg'd.

SOPHRONOS   Your presence,
  Great Sir, makes every roome a Sanctuary.

PRINCE   Wherefore does this young virgin use such circumstance,   160
  In duty to us? Rise.

142.1 GRILLA] *Hill; Grill Q*   143–6] *Weber, prose in Q*   148.1 ARETUS] *Weber,* ARETIUS *Q*

EROCLEA   'Tis I must raise her.
    Forgive me, Sister, I have been too private,
    In hiding from your knowledge any secret
    That should have been in common twixt our soules:
    But I was rul'd by councell.

CLEOPHILA   That I shew   165
    My selfe a Girle (Sister) and bewray
    Joy in too soft a passion 'fore all these,
    I hope you cannot blame me.

PRINCE   We must part
    The sudden meeting of these two faire Rivolets
    With th'Iland of our armes, *Cleophila*,   170
    The custome of thy piety hath built
    Even to thy younger yeeres a Monument
    Of memorable Fame; some great reward
    Must wait on thy desert.

SOPHRONOS   The Prince speakes t'ee, Neece.

CORAX   Chat low, I pray; let's about our businesse.   175
    The good old man awakes: my Lord, with-draw;
    Rhetias, let's settle here the Couch.

PRINCE   Away then.   *Exeunt.*

5.2   *Soft Musicke. Enter* MELEANDER *(in a Couch) his haire
and beard trimd, habit and gowne chang'd.* RHETIAS *and* CORAX,
and Boy that sings.

            The Song.   L3^r
         Fly hence, shadowes, that doe keep
         Watchfull sorrowes, charm'd in sleepe;
         Though the Eyes *be overtaken,*
         Yet the Heart *doth ever waken*
         Thoughts, chain'd up in busie snares   5
         Of continuall woes and cares:
         Love and griefes are so exprest,
         As they rather sigh then rest.
         Fly hence, shadowes, that doe keepe
         Watchfull sorrowes, charm'd in sleepe.   10

168 part] *Gifford*; part: Q   177 SD] *Gifford*; *Exit* Q   **5.2**] 0.1 *in a Couch*] *this edn.*;
in a Coach Q; *on a Couch* Weber, *Gifford*

MELEANDER   [*awakes*] Where am I? Ha? What sounds are these?
    'Tis day, sure.
    Oh, I have slept belike: 'tis but the foolery
    Of some beguiling dreame. So, so, I will not
    Trouble the play of my delighted Fancy
    But dreame my dreame out.

CORAX   Morrow to your Lordship: 15
    You tooke a jolly nap, and slept it soundly.

MELEANDER   Away, beast, let me alone.   *Cease musicke.*

CORAX   O, by your leave, Sir.
    I must be bold to raise yee, else your Phisicke
    Will turne to further sicknes.

MELEANDER   Phisick, Beare-leech?

CORAX   Yes phisick, you are mad.   20

MELEANDER   [*calls*] *Trollio, Cleophila.*

RHETIAS   Sir, I am here.

MELEANDER   I know thee, *Rhetias*, prethee rid the roome
    Of this tormenting noyse. He tells me, sirra,
    I have tooke phisick, *Rhetias*, phisicke, phisicke.

L3ᵛ   RHETIAS   Sir true, you have; and this most learned Scholer   25
    Apply'd t'ee. O you were in dangerous plight
    Before he tooke ye in hand.

MELEANDER   These things are drunke,
    Directly drunke. Where did you get your liquor?

CORAX   I never saw a body in the wane
    Of age, so over-spred with severall sorts   30
    Of such diseases, as the strength of Youth
    Would groane under and sinke.

RHETIAS   The more your glory
    In the miraculous cure.

---

11 SD] *Gifford*   21 SD] *this edn.*   23 sirra,] *Weber subst.*; ~. *Q*   27 in hand] *Weber*;
hand *Q*

CORAX   Bring me the Cordiall
  Prepar'd for him to take after his sleepe,
  'Twill doe him good at heart.

RHETIAS   I hope it will, Sir.   *Exit.*   35

MELEANDER   What do'st think I am, that thou should'st fiddle
  So much upon my patience? Foole, the waight
  Of my disease sits on my heart so heavy,
  That all the hands of Art cannot remove
  One graine to ease my griefe. If thou cood'st poyson   40
  My memory, or wrap my senses up
  Into a dulnesse, hard and cold as Flints!
  If thou cood'st make me walke, speake, eate and laugh
  Without a sense or knowledge of my faculties,
  Why then perhaps at Marts thou might'st make benefit   45
  Of such an Anticke motion, and get credit
  From credulous gazers, but not profit me.
  Study to gull the wise; I am too simple
  To be wrought on.

CORAX   Ile burne my bookes (old man)
  But I will doe thee good, and quickly too.   50

Enter ARETUS *with a Patent.*

ARETUS   Most honor'd Lord *Meleander*, our great Master,
  Prince *Palador* of Cyprus, hath by me   L4^r
  Sent you this Patent, in which is contain'd
  Not onely confirmation of the Honors
  You formerly enjoyed, but the addition   55
  Of the Marshalship of Cyprus, and ere long
  He meanes to visit you. Excuse my haste,
  I must attend the Prince—   *Exit.*

CORAX   There's one Pill workes.

MELEANDER   Do'st know that spirit? 'tis a grave familiar,
  And talkt I know not what.

CORAX   Hee's like, me thinks,   60
  The Prince his Tutor, *Aretus.*

42 Flints!] *this edn.; ~? Q*

MELEANDER   Yes, yes;
  It may be I have seene such a formality;
  No matter where, or when.

                Enter AMETHUS *with a Staffe.*

AMETHUS   The Prince hath sent ye
  (My Lord) this Staffe of Office, and withall
  Salutes you Grand Commander of the Ports   65
  Throughout his Principalities. He shortly
  Will visit you himselfe: I must attend him—   *Exit.*

CORAX   D'ee feele your physick stirring yet?

MELEANDER   A Divell
  Is a rare Juggler, and can cheate the eye,
  But not corrupt the reason in the Throne   70
  Of a pure soule.—

                Enter SOPHRONOS *with a Tablet.*

            Another? I will stand thee,
  Be what thou canst, I care not.

SOPHRONOS   From the Prince,
  Deare Brother, I present you this rich Relique,
  A Jewell he hath long worne in his bosome:
  Henceforth he bade mee say, he does beseech you   75
  To call him sonne, for he will call you Father.
  It is an honor (brother) that a subject
  Cannot but intertaine with thankfull pray'rs.
  Be moderate in your Joyes, he will in person
  Confirme my errand, but commands my service.   *Exit.*   80

CORAX   What hope now of your Cure?

MELEANDER   Stay, stay— What Earthquakes
  Roule in my flesh? here's Prince, and Prince, and Prince;
  Prince upon Prince: the dotage of my sorrowes
  Revells in magick of ambitious scorne,
  Be they Inchantments deadly (as the grave)   85
  Ile looke upon'em: Patent, staffe, and Relick—
  To the last first. [*taking up the miniature*] Round me,
      ye guarding ministers

71 SD] *after* care not *l. 72 Q*   86 Relick—] *this edn.;* ~ Q   87 SD] *Gifford*

And ever keepe me waking till the Cliffes
That over-hang my sight fall off, and leave
These hollow spaces to be cram'd with dust.   90

CORAX   'Tis time I see to fetch the Cordiall. Prethee
Sit downe: Ile instantly be here againe—   *Exit.*

MELEANDER   Good, give me leave, I will sit downe indeed:
Here's Company enough for me to prate to,
Eroclea. 'Tis the same, the cunning Artsman   95
Faultred not in a line. Coo'd he have fashen'd
A little hollow space here, and blowne breath
To have made it move, and whisper, 't had bin excellent.
But faith, 'tis well, 'tis very well as 'tis.
Passing, most passing well.

　　　　　Enter CLEOPHILA, EROCLEA, RHETIAS.

CLEOPHILA   The soveraigne Greatnesse,   100
Who, by Commission from the powers of heaven,
Swayes both this Land and us, our gracious Prince,
By me presents you (Sir) with this large bounty,
A gift more precious to him then his birth-right.   M1^r
Here let your cares take end; now set at liberty   105
Your long imprison'd heart, and welcome home
The solace of your soule, too long kept from you.

EROCLEA   [*kneeling*] Deare Sir, you know me.

MELEANDER   Yes, thou art my Daughter:
My eldest blessing. Know thee? Why *Eroclea*,
I never did forget thee in thy absence.   110
Poore soule, how do'st?

EROCLEA   The best of my well-being
Consists in yours.

MELEANDER   Stand up: the gods who hitherto
Have kept us both alive, preserve thee ever.
Cleophila, I thanke thee and the Prince,
I thanke thee too, *Eroclea*, that thou would'st   115
In pitie of my age, take so much paines
To live, till I might once more looke upon thee,

108 SD] *Gifford*

Before I broke my heart: O 'twas a piece
Of piety and duty unexampled.

RHETIAS   [*aside*] The good-man rellisheth his comforts
　　strangely,   120
The sight doth turne me child.

EROCLEA   I have not words
That can expresse my joyes.

CLEOPHILA   Nor I.

MELEANDER   Nor I:
Yet let us gaze on one another freely,
And surfet with our eyes; let me be plaine,
If I should speake as much as I should speake,   125
I should talke of a thousand things at once,
And all of thee, of thee (my child) of thee:
My teares like ruffling winds lockt up in Caves,
Doe bustle for a vent— on t'other side,
To flye out into mirth were not so comely.   130
Come hither, let me kisse thee— with a pride,
Strength, courage, and fresh blood, which now thy presence
Hath stor'd me with, I kneele before their Altars,
M1ᵛ   Whose soveraignty kept guard about thy safety.
Aske, aske thy Sister (prethee) shee'le tell thee   135
How I have been much mad.

CLEOPHILA   Much discontented,
Shunning all meanes that might procure him comfort.

EROCLEA   Heaven ha's at last been gracious.

MELEANDER   So say I
But wherefore drop thy words in such a sloth;
As if thou wert afraid to mingle truth   140
With thy misfortunes? Understand me throughly,
I would not have thee to report at large
From point to point, a Journall of thy absence:
'Twill take up too much time, I would securely
Ingrosse the little remnant of my life,   145

120 SD] *Gifford*   121–3] *Weber*; I have … joyes | Nor I | Nor I … freely *Q*   144 'Twill]
Weber; T'will *Q*

That thou might'st every day be telling somewhat,
Which might convay me to my rest with comfort.
Let me bethinke me, how we parted first
Puzzles my faint remembrance— But soft,
Cleophila, thou toldst me, that the Prince   150
Sent me this present.

CLEOPHILA   From his own faire hands
I did receive my Sister.

MELEANDER   To requite him,
We will not dig his Fathers grave anew,
Although the mention of him much concernes
The businesse we inquire of— as I said,   155
We parted in a hurry at the Court,
I to this Castle, after made my Jayle.
But whither thou, deare heart?

RHETIAS   Now they fall too't,
I lookt for this.

EROCLEA   I by my Uncles care
(*Sophronos,* my good Uncle) suddenly   160
Was like a Saylers Boy convey'd a shipboord
That very night.

MELEANDER   A policie quicke and strange.

EROCLEA   The ship was bound for Corinth, whither first
Attended onely with your servant *Rhetias,*
And all fit necessaries, we arriv'd: 165   M2ʳ
From thence in habit of a youth we journey'd
To Athens, where till our returne of late,
Have we liv'd safe.

MELEANDER   Oh what a thing is man,
To bandy factions of distemp'red passions,
Against the sacred providence above him!   170
Here in the Legend of thy two yeeres exile,
Rare pity and delight are sweetly mixt.
And still thou wert a Boy?

EROCLEA   So I obey'd
  My Uncles wise command.

MELEANDER   'Twas safely carried,
  I humbly thanke thy Fate.

EROCLEA   If earthly treasures   175
  Are powr'd in plenty downe from Heav'n on mortals;
  They reigne amongst those Oracles, that flow
  In Scholes of sacred knowledge; such is *Athens*:
  Yet *Athens* was to me but a faire prison:
  The thoughts of you, my Sister, Country, Fortunes,   180
  And something of the Prince, barr'd all contents,
  Which else might ravish sence: for had not, *Rhetias*,
  Been alwaies comfortable to me, certainely
  Things had gone worse.

MELEANDER   Speake low *Eroclea*;
  That something of the Prince beares danger in it: 185
  Yet thou hast travayl'd (Wench) for such Indowments,
  As might create a Prince a wife fit for him,
  Had he the World to guide: but touch not there;
  How cam'st thou home?

RHETIAS   Sir, with your Noble favour,
  Kissing your hand first, that point I can answer.   190

MELEANDER   Honest, right honest *Rhetias*.

RHETIAS   Your grave Brother
  Perceiv'd with what a hopelesse love his sonne,
M2ᵛ   Lord *Menaphon*, too eagerly pursu'd
  Thamasta, Cousin to our present Prince;
  And to remove the violence of affection,   195
  Sent him to Athens, where for twelve moneths space
  Your daughter, my young Lady and her Cousin
  Enjoy'd each others griefes, till by his Father
  The Lord *Sophronos* we were all call'd home.

MELEANDER   Enough, enough, the world shall henceforth
      witnesse   200
  My thankfulnes to Heaven, and those people
  Who have been pitifull to me and mine.
  Lend me a Looking-glasse— How now? How came I
  So courtly in fresh rayments?

RHETIAS   Here's the Glasse, Sir.

MELEANDER   [*looking in the mirror*] I'm in the trim too.—
    O *Cleophila*,   205
    This was the goodnesse of thy care and cunning—
                                    Loud Musicke.
    Whence comes this noyse?

RHETIAS   The Prince my Lord in person.

Enter PRINCE, SOPHRONOS, ARETUS, AMETHUS, MENAPHON,
        THAMASTA, CORAX, KALA.

PRINCE   Ye shall not kneele to us; rise all, I charge ye:
    Father, you wrong your age, henceforth my armes
    And heart shall be your guard; we have o're-heard   210
    All passages of your united loves.
    Be young againe, *Meleander*, live to number
    A happy generation, and dye old
    In comforts as in yeeres. The Offices
    And Honours which I late on thee conferr'd,   215
    Are not fantasticke bounties, but thy merit;
    Enjoy them liberally.

MELEANDER   My teares must thanke ye,
    For my tongue cannot.

CORAX   I have kept my promise,
    And given you a sure cordial.

MELEANDER   O, a rare one.   M3ʳ

PRINCE   Good man, wee both have shar'd enough of sadnes: 220
    Though thine ha's tasted deeper of th'extreme;
    Let us forget it henceforth. Where's the picture
    I sent yee? Keepe it, 'tis a counterfeit,
    And in exchange of that, [*Taking* EROCLEA'S *hand*] I ceaze
        on this,
    The reall substance: with this other hand [*Taking*
        CLEOPHILA'S *hand*]   225
    I give away before her Fathers face
    His younger joy, *Cleophila*, to thee
    Cousin *Amethus*: take her, and be to her

205 SD] *Hill*

More then a Father, a deserving husband.
Thus rob'd of both thy children in a minute,   230
Thy cares are taken off.

MELEANDER   My braines are dull'd;
I am intranc'd, and know not what you meane:
Great, gracious Sir, alas, why do you mocke me?
I am a weake old man, so poore and feeble,
That my untoward joynts can scarcely creepe   235
Unto the grave, where I must seeke my rest.

PRINCE   *Eroclea* was you know, contracted mine;
Cleophila, my Cousins by consent
Of both their hearts: *We both* now claime our owne;
It onely rests in you to give a blessing   240
For confirmation.

RHETIAS   Sir, 'tis truth and justice.

MELEANDER   The gods that lent ye to me, blesse your vowes:
O Children, children, pay your prayers to Heaven,
For they have shew'd much mercy. But *Sophronos*,
Thou art my Brother: I can say no more: 245
A good, good Brother.

PRINCE   Leave the rest to time.
Cousin *Thamasta*, I must give you too:
She's thy wife, *Menaphon*. *Rhetias*, for thee
M3ʳ   And *Corax*, I have more then common thanks.
On, to the Temple; there all solemne Rites   250
Perform'd, a generall Feast shall be proclaim'd.
The *Lover's Melancholy* hath found cure;
Sorrowes are chang'd to Bride-songs. So they thrive,
Whom Fate in spite of stormes hath kept alive.
                                   Exeunt omnes.

                    FINIS.

EPILOGUE.

To be too confident, is as unjust
In any Worke, as too much to distrust;
Who from the lawes of study have not swerv'd,
Know, beg'd applauses never were deserv'd.
We *must submit to Censure: so doth* He,   5
Whose houres begot this issue; yet being free
For his part, if He *have not pleas'd you, then*
In this kinde, hee'le not trouble you agen.

FINIS.

Commentary to *The Lover's Melancholy*

SETTING

THE SCEANE *FAMAGOSTA IN CYPRUS* Famagusta, not Nicosia, was commonly called 'the chiefe cittie in Cyprus' (Gascoigne, *Poesies*, 1575, p. xlvi). Cyprus was a location for stories of love because it had been celebrated as the birthplace of Venus and centre of her cult since Homer (*Homeric Hymns* 5 and 10, 'To Aphrodite') and Hesiod (*Theogony*, 192–200); cf. Marston, *Parasitaster*, ed. Blostein 2.568–72: 'I apt for love? . . . I court the Lady? I was not born in Cyprus'. Burton writes, 'Your hot and southern countries are prone to lust, and far more incontinent than those that live in the north' and lists Cyprus among the places where love flourishes (*Anatomy*, 3.2.2.1). See Lisa Hopkins, 'John Ford and Cyprus', *NQ* 44 (March, 1997), 101–2 for the possibility that Ford had read an account of a trip to Jerusalem by his mother's ancestor Sir Harry Stradling, who died at Famagusta in 1453 on his way home.

THE . . . ACTED

Many of these names, along with the parts they played, are found in near-contemporaneous cast lists for Massinger's *The Roman Actor* (1626), *The Picture* (1629), and *Believe as You List* (1631); Carlell's *The Deserving Favorite* (*c.*1629); Clavell's *The Soddered Citizen* (1630); and Wilson's *The Swisser* (1631). Assignment of parts according to the rigid theory that actors played certain specialist 'lines', as proposed by T. W. Baldwin, *The Organization and Personnel of the Shakespearean Company* (Princeton, NJ, 1927; see pp. 367–8 for his casting of *Lover's Melancholy*) is no longer generally accepted, but what is known of these actors, together with the lists in the six contemporaneous plays, makes valid conjecture possible. In terms of words spoken, Meleander is the leading part (2,293 words); Corax has 1,875 words, Rhetias 1,814, Thamasta 1,582, Palador 1,581, Menaphon 1,491, Eroclea 1,390, Cuculus 1,327, Amethus 1,309, and Cleophila 836. Seventeen actors' names are given, but if the Philosopher and Sea-Nymph in the masque are included there are eighteen parts; see note to 3.3.38.1.

4 JOHN LOWIN (1576–1653), with the King's Men from 1603 to 1642, he may have created the parts of Iago, Mammon, and Bosola (Baldwin, *Organization*, p. 366; Gurr, *Shakespeare Company* , pp. 233–4; J. A. Riddell,

'Some Actors in Ben Jonson's Plays', *ShakS*, 5 (1969), 285–98, p. 293). James Wright, *Historia Histrionica* (1699) says that 'before the Wars' he played 'with mighty Applause, *Falstaffe, Morose, Vulpone*, and *Mammon*' (p. 4). Baldwin suggested he played Corax (1,875 words), but the larger, psychologically and histrionically more challenging part of Meleander is more likely, especially in view of Lowin's age and status.

4 **RICHARD SHARPE** (?1602–32), a leading boy actor who had played the Duchess in *Duchess of Malfi*, by 1626 he had graduated to adult roles. He had supporting parts in *The Roman Actor* and *The Picture*, and a prominent supporting role as the king in *The Swisser*, but had the largest role as the lover in *The Deserving Favorite*, and the leading role as the melancholy lover in *The Soddered Citizen*, in which Taylor did not act. These last two roles would have made him suitable for Palador, but the part seems more likely to have been Taylor's, and Sharpe may have played Menaphon.

5 **JOSEPH TAYLOR** (?1586–1652), Burbage's successor as leading actor for the King's Men, he 'Acted *Hamlet* incomparably well, *Iago, Truewit . . . Face*' (Wright, *Historia*, p. 4). With Lowin he was from 1626 co-signatory for court payments (Gurr, *Shakespeare Company*, p. 233). Played Paris in *The Roman Actor*, Mathias in *The Picture*, the title role in *The Deserving Favorite*, Arioldus in *The Swisser*, and Antiochus in *Believe as You List*. These were all leading roles, but fitted a man in his early forties (see *ODNB* for Taylor's probable birth date) better than the young Palador. Taylor's position in the actors' list and seniority in the company, however, both suggest he took the title role.

5 **THOMAS POLLARD** (1597–*c*.1649–55), sharer, 1613–42. He was trained as a boy actor by Shanck (see note 7 for John Schanck), and graduated to playing comic parts. Acted the title role in *The Humorous Lieutenant* (1619), but in general seems to have taken smaller parts: Ubaldo, a 'wild courtier', in *The Picture*, Berecinthius in *Believe as You List*, the cowardly Timentes in *The Swisser*, and doubling as Aelius Lamia and Stephanos in *The Roman Actor*. Pelias or Trollio are likely roles.

6 **ROBERT BENFIELD** (d. 1649), member of King's Men since 1614. Acted the minor part of Rusticus in *The Roman Actor* and the larger supporting roles of Ladislaus in *The Picture*, the King in *The Deserving Favorite*, Antharis in *The Swisser*, Marcellus in *Believe as You List*, and the important part of the doctor in *The Soddered Citizen*. May have played Rhetias or Corax.

6 **WILLIAM PENN** hired man who played Julio Baptista in *The Picture*, the old courtier Clephis in *The Swisser*, and '2nd merchant' in *Believe as You List*. Not in lists for *Roman Actor, Deserving Favorite*, or *The Soddered Citizen*. Likely to have had a small role such as Aretus.

7 **JOHN SHANCK** or Shanks (d. 1636), a 'jigging comedian' who was the King's Men's leading clown; he does not appear in many cast lists (though he was Hilario in *The Picture*) but this may be because he improvised and 'jigged' in others. Very probably played Cuculus.

7 **CURTEISE GRIVILL** or Greville, hired man with King's Men 1626–33; he had minor parts in *The Roman Actor*, *The Swisser*, *The Soddered Citizen*, and *Believe as You List*. He would have had a similarly small part in *Lover's Melancholy*.

8 **EYLYARDT SWANSTON** Eliart or Elliard Swanston (d. 1651), sharer with King's Men 1624–42. He had relatively minor roles in *The Roman Actor*, *The Deserving Favorite*, and *Believe as You List*, somewhat more substantial ones in *The Picture* and *The Swisser*. May have played Rhetias or Corax.

8 **GEORGE VERNON** hired man 1617–30, played first lictor in *The Roman Actor*.

9 **ANTHONY SMITH** hired man 1626–31, minor roles in *The Roman Actor*, *The Deserving Favorite*, *The Soddered Citizen*, and *The Swisser*.

9 **RICHARD BAXTER** (b. 1593), King's Men 1625–42. This and minor parts in *Believe as You List* and a 1630 revival of Fletcher's *Mad Lover* are his only recorded roles.

10 **JOHN TOMSON** (d. 1634), leading boy actor for King's Men from *c.*1620; he played Domitia in *The Roman Actor*, Honoria in *The Picture*, Cleonarda in *The Deserving Favourite*, Miniona in *The Soddered Citizen*, and Panopia in *The Swisser*, all leading female parts, and all regal or dominant women, which would have made him well suited to the role of Thamasta. He had a fine singing voice: see note to 5.2.0.2.

11 **JOHN HONYMAN** (1613–36), Domitilla in *The Roman Actor*, Sophia in *The Picture*, Clarinda in *The Deserving Favourite*; after 1630 he moved to adult roles, beginning with the distinctly unfeminine Sly in *The Soddered Citizen*. Almost certainly played Eroclea.

12 **JAMES HORNE** little is known about him; recorded acting with King's Men occasionally from 1621 (last in cast list of Fletcher's *The Pilgrim*, a woman's part), and second lictor in *The Roman Actor*. His position in the list suggests he played Cleophila, the third largest female part, but see the note for 13, William Trigg.

13 **WILLIAM TRIGG** boy actor who played Julia Titus in *The Roman Actor*, Corisca the waiting woman in *The Picture*, Modestina in *The Soddered Citizen*, and Selina in *The Swisser*. Despite his lower position in the list, these parts make him as likely as Horne to have played Cleophila, or the next largest female part, Kala.

14 **ALEXANDER GOUGH** (b. 1614), played 'Vespasian's concubine' in *The Roman Actor*, and minor female parts in *The Picture* and *The Swisser*. Possibly played the boy Grilla.

[EPISTLE DEDICATORY]

3 **NATHANIEL FINCH** Adm. Gray's Inn, August 1604, later a Serjeant-at-Law, died May 1649; son of the lawyer Sir Henry Finch, and brother of John, Lord Finch, who was Speaker of the House of Commons and a Lord

Chief Justice. In November 1624 Nathaniel signed Dekker's deposition when he was charged over *Keep the Widow Waking*, a lost play on which Ford collaborated (National Archives, STAC 8/31/16).

4 JOHN FORD Ford's cousin, the sole dedicatee of *LS*, author of a commendatory poem to *PW*; Thomas Jordan's *Poeticall Varieties* (1637) was dedicated to him. Adm. Gray's Inn February 1614 'of Hackney, Middlesex, gent.'.

4-5 HENRY BLUNT or Blount, b. 1602, adm. Gray's Inn, June 1620. Aubrey said 'he was pretty wild when young, especially addicted to common wenches' (*ODNB*). Noted as a traveller, first in Spain, France, and Italy, from September 1629, then in 1634-5 journeyed alone in the Middle East, mainly Egypt (*A Voyage into the Levant*, 1636). Knighted 1638. Like Ellice (see note for 5, Robert Ellice) he wrote a commendatory poem to Davenant's *Albovine* (1629).

5 ROBERT ELLICE (b. 1605), son of a merchant tailor; adm. Gray's Inn, August 1627. Elder brother of Thomas, like him and Blount author of commendatory verses to *Albovine* (see Mary Hobbs, 'Robert and Thomas Ellice, Friends of Ford and Davenant', *NQ*, 21 (1974), 292-3). One of this name became a colonel in the Royalist army (*CSPD*, Vol. 80, [195] 7 Dec 1642).

12 plurality . . . Multitude Cf. Thomas Adams, *The Spiritual Navigator* (1615), pp. 26-7: 'to follow a plurality or *multitude*'.

13 Parity... musicke 'where there is equality of station and education, interpretation is informed and harmonious'. The first of several uses of musical metaphor or symbolism; cf. esp. 1.1.112-69, 4.3.47-52, and the healing music that opens 5.2.

15 YOU THE PATRONES Gray's Inn presented many plays and masques during this period, and it is possible *LM* was one of them, but there is no record of a performance there.

15 PRESENTOR Author and organizer; at 4.3.25 Corax is said to have 'Presented a strange Maske'. Appropriate here because (especially spelled thus) it is also a legal term (*OED*, 1†a).

18 un-reprooveable beyond reproach, since this was Ford's first published play. The convention for authors of plays to deprecate having them printed had largely disappeared by Ford's time, partly due to the example set by Jonson's quartos, popular in the Inns of Court, and by 1629 the Jonson (1616) and Shakespeare (1623) folios..

19-20 like complement 'the same courtesy' (of courting the reader).

20-1 practice... avoid 'proceeding (i.e. giving up printing his plays) which, so that I may avoid it'.

[*TO MY HONOUR'D FRIEND*]

3 ill poor, deficient.

4 Bayes laurel wreath which crowns the poet.

4 barraine Quill barren pen.

6 Allow approve of, praise.

8.1 *George Donne* (1605–39), John Donne's third child, a soldier, who, having returned safely from Buckingham's disastrous 1627 expedition to the Ile de Rhé, led in 1629 an expedition to establish a colony on St. Kitts, where a battle with the Spanish began in June, meaning that this poem (and probably the others here) were written early in 1629 or very late in 1628. Later, as Muster Master General of Virginia, Donne wrote *Virginia Reviewed* (1638) and in the same year contributed to *Jonsonus Virbius*.

[*TO HIS WORTHY FRIEND*]

1 to about.

6 long since if, as seems likely, this refers to Ford's early non-dramatic work published between 1606 and 1620, it supports the view that *LM* is his first solo play.

13 *Poet-Apes* Those who ape poets; cf. Jonson, *Epigrams*, 56, 'On Poet-Ape', 'Whose works are e'en the frippery of wit'.

17 *William Singleton* (b. 1578), matric. Oxford 1594, adm. Gray's Inn, August 1601, 'son and heir apparent of William Singleton, of London'.

[*TO THE AUTHOR*]

1 *Blacke choler* translating the Greek μέλαινα χολή ('black bile') produced by the imbalance of the humours which in Hippocratic theory causes melancholy. Cf. *Anatomy*, where 'Old Democritus' is seen in the 1628 frontispiece searching for 'The seat of black choler'. Later, Burton describes '*Melancholy*, cold and dry, thicke, blacke, sowre, begotten of the more faeculent part of nourishment, and purged from the Spleene' (1.1.1.2). Jacques Ferrand agrees: 'there are three kinds of Melancholy: the first is engendred of Black Choler, collected together in the braine. The second is produced, when as this humor is diffused through the veines generally over all the body' (*Erotomania*, trans. Edmund Chilmead, 1640, p. 25).

1–4 obscure; possibly trying to say *Blacke choler* 'affords' (supplies) a flood which overflows reason, and from which unhappy lovers 'drink' sooner than from anything else (for 'or' as equivalent to 'e'er', see *OED*, Or *adv.*[1] 4), producing passion that is expressed in their dull plaints for their lost mistresses.

9 *Phocions blushes* Phocion 'The Good', an Athenian politician who lived austerely, rejecting reward and flattery. Cf. *LL*, ll. 291–3 (*CWJF I*, pp. 584–5).

11 effeminated unmanly, enervated; cf. Donne, *The Juggler*, line 1 'Thou call'st me effeminate, for I love women's joys'.

14.1 *Hum. Howorth* Humphrey, matric. Balliol, Oxford, July 1621, aged 16; adm. Middle Temple, June 1624, 'third son of Epiphanius Howorth, of Whitehouse, Herefords., esq.'.

[*OF THE LOVER'S MELANCHOLY*]

4.1 *Ὁ φίλος* 'The friend'.

THE PROLOGUE

3–4 *might . . . law* the disavowal of 'rules' should be read against the background of attempts to impose neo-Aristotelian laws of unity of time, place, and action during the 16th century; they had been largely ignored by Shakespeare and his contemporaries, and were explicitly challenged by Jonson in the preface to *Sejanus* (ll. 4–17). Nonetheless, *LM* largely fulfils these demands.

6–10 *owe . . . claimes* the denial of plagiarism applies to the 'Invention', i.e. the plot and characters; the defence of the scholar's right to borrow applies to the acknowledged use of Strada (marginal note to 1.1.106–9) and Burton (marginal note to 3.1.107–9). For general influences on Ford's 'Invention', see Introduction, pp. 210–24.

11 *quite* repay, reward.

16 *maine . . . bye* though 'plot' had recently become a literary term (*OED*'s first quotation is from Beaumont, *Knight of the Burning Pestle*, 1613), Ford's distinction between the main plot and the comic 'bye" plot' may be intended to recall the distinction made famous in Raleigh's 1603 treason trial, when Attorney Coke claimed that Raleigh's fellow-accused Lord Cobham had said, 'You are fools, you are on the bye, Raleigh and I are on the main; we mean to take away the king and his cubs' (T. B. Howells, *A Complete Collection of State Trials and Proceedings for High Treason and Other Crimes and Misdemeanors*, 1816, 2.14).

DRAMATIS PERSONAE the mainly Greek-derived names are, as in *BH*, indicative of the characters' defining qualities. No list of *dramatis personae* was printed in 1629, so Ford did not interpret them as he did in the later play.

1 PALADOR in part from 'paladin', as adj. meaning 'knightly, heroic' (*OED*), thus faithful in love, but also playing on Greek πάλαι, 'long ago', hence 'one who dwells on the past', alluding to the fact that he is haunted by the loss of Eroclea (cf. 4.3.28–30).

2 AMETHUS 'sober one', from Greek ἄ- (not) and μέθυ (wine).

3 MELEANDER 'unhappy man', from Greek μέλεος (unhappy) plus ἀνήρ / ἀνδρός man.

4 SOPHRONOS 'wise man' from Greek σώφρων (of sound mind)

5 MENAPHON probably from Greek μένω and φωνή 'steadfast voice', hence a faithful friend and lover. He has no connection to Greene's *Menaphon*, or the character in *Tamburlaine*, or the one mentioned in *Comedy of Errors*, 5.1.360.

6 ARETUS 'virtuous man' from Greek *arete*, latinized.

7 CORAX from κόραξ, Greek for crow or raven and therefore appropriate for a doctor, since they gathered around the dying. A historical Corax (5th century BC) was a Greek teacher of rhetoric.

8 RHETIAS 'a man of words', from *rhetor*, in late Greek and Latin a teacher of rhetoric; his and Corax's names are apt because of their rhetorical 'flyting' in 1.2.

9 PELIAS in Greek mythology the king of Iolcus who sent Jason and the Argonauts on their quest, and who was later cut up and cooked by his daughters in a stew which they mistakenly thought would rejuvenate him. This is described in John Studley's translation of Seneca's *Medea* (1566), a parody of which Ford puts into Pelias's mouth (see 1.1.8–11 and note).

10 CUCULUS Latin for 'cuckoo', used by Plautus for fools (e.g. *Asinaria*, 5.2.73, *Trinummus* 2.1.27).

11 TROLLIO to 'troll' was to talk nimbly and perhaps annoyingly; *OED*, Troll *v.* 4 cites Ford, *FCN*, 3.3.3: 'His tongue troules like a Mill-crack'. *OED* also cites (15b) definitions of canting slang by J. Awdely, *Fraternitye of Vacabondes* (1575): '*Troll with*, is he yᵗ no man shall know the servaunt from yᵉ Maister . . . *Troll hazard of trace* is he that goeth behynde his Maister as far as he may see hym . . . *Troll hazard of tritrace*, is he that goeth gaping after his Master.' All are relevant to the comic servant Trollio.

12 GRILLA Latin *grillus*, a cricket or grasshopper.

13 THAMASTA from Greek θαυμαστός, 'wonderful, marvellous' (cf. 'great-spirited', 1.1.190).

14 EROCLEA Greek, 'one desirous of [keeping her] honour', from ἔρως, 'desire of something', and κλέος, 'fame, reputation'.

15 CLEOPHILA Greek, φίλο κλέος, 'loving honour' or 'good repute'.

16 KALA Greek καλός, 'beautiful'.

1.1

8–11 To . . . bounce Pelias's bombastic, alliterative rhetoric echoes old-fashioned Tudor poets such as George Turberville, in e.g. 'That nothing can cause him to forget his frend, wherein is toucht the hardnes of his travayle', lines 1–2: 'If boystrous blaste of fierce and froward wynde, | If weltring waves, and frothie foming Seas . . .' (*Tragicall Tales*, 1587). It is especially close to Tudor Senecan translations: cf. *Medea*, trans. John Studley (1566): 'Of *Boreas* blustryng out wyth puffed | cheekes hys blastyng breath' (f. 12v). Such drama had been parodied in Jonson's *Poetaster* (1601), 3.4.169–72.

10 **Boreas** short-tempered Greek god of the north wind.

11 **thunder bounce** thunder clap; again echoing Studley (trans.), *Hippolitus* in *Seneca his tenne tragedies, translated into Englysh* (1581), f. 58v: 'The thumping thunder bouncing boltes'.

12–15 the legend of the Greek musician Arion, who was saved from drowning by a music-loving dolphin after being thrown overboard by pirates, was first told by Herodotus (*Persian Wars* 1.24), and retold frequently around this date.

14 **'ee** this unusual form of 'you', abbreviating 'thee' or 'ye', recurs 29 times in *Q*; Sargeaunt (pp. 64–5) was right to suggest it 'probably' reflected Ford's Devon dialect: Peter Trudgill, *The Dialects of English* (Oxford, 1999), locates it in South Devon, where it is still current (pp. 97–8). See also *CWJF* 2, pp. 63–4 for the recurrence of 'd'ee' and 't'ee' in Ford's plays.

17 **Teinters** tenters, wooden frames on which cloth was stretched after milling.

19–21 **we . . . subject** a pretentious appeal to the need to observe literary or rhetorical decorum, that 'which is proper to a personage, place, time, or subject in question, or to the nature, unity, or harmony of the composition' (*OED*, Decorum 1†a).

22–3 **Sunne . . . adore** 'a nonsensical "compliment" since the sun does not make a shadow of itself' (Hill).

24–6 **From . . . child** his tears of joy make him seem like a child; cf. 5.2.121. This passage may have been recalled in a similar situation by Shirley, *The Opportunity* (1640), 1.1: 'My joy of soul, a father's prayers and blessing | Make thee a happy man! my eyes must speak | Part of my joy in, welcome from *Naples*' (Dyce, vol. 3, p. 376).

32 **service—** the long dash indicates that Amethus interrupts Menaphon, who hesitates.

33 **intertainements** acts of welcome.

35 **engrosse** monopolize; cf. 2.1.13–15 below.

36 **creature** instrument, puppet; this is Thamasta's meaning at 2.1.313; cf. also 2.1.229.

40 **peec'd** joined as one.

41–4 echoing *Anatomy*, 3.1.3, where friendship is praised as holy and heavenly: 'Friendship is an holy name and a sacred communion of friends . . . a most divine and heavenly band, take this away and take all pleasure, all joy, comfort, happinesse and true content out of the world, the greatest tye, and as the Poet [Spenser, *Faerie Queene*, 5.9.1–2] decides, is much to be preferred before the rest.' Amethus repeatedly invokes his friendship for Menaphon, in contrast to Palador who 'never had a friend, a certaine friend' (2.1.151). Ford returns to the theme in the friendship between Ithocles and Prophilus in *BH*.

49–50 travailes . . . discontents many writers on love melancholy recommend travel as a cure, but the absence should be at least a year (l. 45) if it is to work (*Anatomy*, 3.2.5.2).

52–3 fancy . . . ease an illusion with no solid grounds had falsely raised his hopes of ease, the latter carrying implications of idleness; cf. *All's Well*, 3.1.17–18: 'the younger of our nature, | That surfeit on their ease'.

57–8 tide . . . complaints cf. 'the restless current of dull plaints' in Humphrey Howorth's commendatory poem l. 3.

59 hope expect, suppose, not implying desire (*OED* †4).

61–2 Her . . . Ice the icy bosom of the cruel mistress was a common trope in Stuart love poetry; see e.g. the 'destructive Ysicles' of Julia's breast in Herrick, *Hesperides*, 115 ('*The frozen Zone, or Julia disdainfull*', ll. 13–14).

62 intermur'd walled in; cf. *FM*, l. 713: 'A bullwarke intermur'd with walls of brasse'.

66–8 Lest . . . friend cf. Cicero, *de Amicitia*, 25.91: 'nothing is to be considered a greater bane of friendship than fawning, cajolery, or flattery'. Hill notes a similarity to *Hamlet*, 3.2.56–62.

73 deale in none Burton stresses 'neglect [of] all ordinary businesse' (*Anatomy*, 3.2.3.1) as a symptom of melancholy several times; see esp. 3.3.2.1, where it is joined to the paranoia Palador displays later.

76–7 Heare . . . pictures Burton praises music and pictures as a cure for melancholy: 'A lover that hath as it were lost himselfe through impotency, impatience, must bee called home as a traveller by musicke, feasting . . . all kinde of sports and merriments, to see some pictures, hangings buildings' (3.2.5.1). 'To read, walke and see Mappes, Pictures, Statues, Jewels, marbles, which some so much magnifie as those that *Phidias* made of old so exquisite and pleasing to be beheld, that as *Chrysostome* thinketh, *if any man be sickly, troubled in mind, or that cannot sleep for griefe, & shall but stand over against one of Phidias images, he will forget all care, or whatsoever else may molest him, in an instant.* There be those as much taken with *Michael Angelos, Raphael de Urbino, Francesco Francias* peices, and many of those Italian and Dutch painters, which were excellent in their ages' (2.2.4, 1628 edn.).

Timothy Bright, *Treatise*, also recommends both: '& here as pleasant pictures, and lively colours delight the melancholicke eye, and in their measure satisfie the heart, so not onely cheerefull musicke in a generalitie, but such of that kinde as most rejoyceth is to be sounded in the melancholicke eare' (p. 247). Hill suggests a reference to Charles I's similar enthusiasm for painting, but it is hard to see how the parallel could hold here without doing so elsewhere, which, except that the subjects of both rulers 'mutter strangely' (2.1.76), it does not (see Introduction, p. 225).

78 Story legend, history.

82 Motions agitations.

82–4 To . . . shapes a Stoical commonplace.

83 exercise 'The object of exercises; "the sport" ', *OED*, exercise, *n.* 8 †f, citing this passage only.

85 formes physical shapes.

88–90 Then . . . rare Menaphon is agreeing that Cyprus is unfortunately abounding in wonders of change and fortune, and that other countries offer something of exceptional merit.

91–3 Jewell . . . Jewell The repetition applied to Eroclea/Parthenophill heralds Palador's description of her memory as 'the only jewel' of his thoughts (4.3.72), and the miniature 'jewel' of her portrait (5.2.74). Menaphon repeats the epithet bitterly at 3.2.205.

94–6 if . . . are if he was superstitious he would believe him to be a supernatural being not a created mortal.

99–100 Poets . . . *Tempe* see esp. Ovid, *Metamorphoses*, 1.568–81. Tempe is a gorge between Mount Olympus, home of the Greek gods, and Mount Ossa. It was the site of Zeus's rape of Io, and a favourite haunt of Apollo. It was commonly used as a *locus amœnus* by later writers: see E. R. Curtius, *European Literature and the Latin Middle Ages*, trans. Willard Trask (London, 1953), pp. 198–200. It is over 200 miles north of Athens, where Ford has Eroclea spending her exile (5.2.166–8).

104 Then than.

104 In-mates to associates of.

105–6 I . . . Walkes the melancholy lover seeks solitude; cf. *Anatomy*, 1.3.1.4: 'it is most pleasant at first . . . a most delightsome humor, to walk alone & meditate, & frame a thousand phantastical Imaginations unto themselves. They are never better pleased then when they are so doing'; cf. du Laurens, *Discourse*, p. 81: 'melancholike men do now and then . . . have no pleasure to bee any where but in solitarie places.'

106–9 One morning early . . . strife in A translation of the Latin marginal note is 'See Famianus Strada, Book 2, Prolusion 6, Academicae 2. Imitation of Claudian'. This poem from the Jesuit Strada's collection of exercises in various styles, the *Prolusiones Academicae, Oratoriae, Historicae, Poeticæ . . . Coloniæ Agrippinæ* (1617), p. 351 was translated or paraphrased by several 17-century writers, including Crashaw, 'Musicks Duell'; Mildmay Fane, 'Philomelæ ac Citharædi Concertatio'; and Herrick, 'Oberons *Feast*', *Hesperides*, 293, ll. 46–7. Of these only Herrick and Ford say the bird died of a broken heart (but see note for 1.1.146–8, 'when . . . heart'). For a free, somewhat lengthened translation of Strada, see *The Poems, English, Latin and Greek of Richard Crashaw*, ed. L. C. Martin, 2nd edn. (1957), pp. 149–53; for a prose version, see Hill, Appendix A, pp. 152–3.

109 **That Art or Nature . . . strife in** perhaps remembering Jonson's poem on Shakespeare's portrait in the 1623 Folio, 'Wherein the graver had a strife | With nature to outdo the life' (ll. 3–4); the theme was a common one in mannerist and baroque art, notably in *Winters Tale* and *Tempest*. Huebert argues that the ultimate victory of art over nature is typically baroque and that 'the musical duel is the closest thing we have to an *ars poetica* from Ford's pen' (*John Ford, Baroque English Dramatist*, pp. 69–70).

111 **resolve yee** make clear to you.

115 **faire-fac'd** the emphasis on Eroclea's beauty (cf. l. 124) is not from Strada; it hints at her gender, but more significantly reflects her virtuous part within a larger cosmic harmony, since as Sir Thomas Browne says: 'there is musicke even in the beauty, and the silent notes which *Cupid* strikes . . . For there is a musicke where-ever there is a harmony, order or proportion; and thus farre we may maintain the musick of the spheares; for those well ordered motions, and regular paces, though they give no sound unto the eare, yet to the understanding they strike a note most full of harmony' (*Religio Medici*, in *Works*, ed. Keynes (London, 1928) 1.84).

115–16 **upon . . . harmony** Eroclea's skill is partly explained by Burton's disapproving comment that it was 'part of a Gentlewomans bringing up, to sing, and dance, and play on the Lute, or some such instrument, before she can say her Pater noster, or ten Commandements' (3.2.2.4), but her exceptional abilities are related to that rare beauty of mind which Meleander later praises in her and her sister (4.2.135–48). See also 1.1.167–9.

116 **straines** tunes.

118–20 **the Birds . . . what they heard** the wondering presence of the silent birds is an addition of Ford's.

123 **severall** separate (see also 146).

124 **down** chorus (*OED*, Down *n.*³ †1), here probably in looser sense of echo.

125 **coo'd** could (see also 151).

125 **run Division** play a rapid, often florid, melodic passage.

127–8 **The Nightingale did . . . Reply too** for the correct belief that the nightingale copied songs of their parents and other birds, see Montaigne, *Essays* trans. Florio (1613), 2.12, 'An Apologie of *Raymond Sebond*', p. 258: 'The yoong-ones wil very sadly [*pensif*] sit recording their lesson, and are often seene labouring how to imitate certain song-notes.' That they copied human musicians has also long been believed. Nevertheless, the bird remains an archetype of the 'natural' rather than 'learnt' musician (133–7).

135 **Cliffs** clefs, characters placed at the beginning of a stave of music to indicate pitch.

135 **Moods** modes; since Ford is stressing the technical, probably either the 'ratio of the duration of a long or a large to that of the next longest note,

which determines rhythm systems' (*OED*, mode, *n.* 1†b), or schemes 'specifying the disposition in a scale of the constituent notes of a melody or harmony' (1c).

137 **busied** occupied his time fully; first use in this sense in *OED*.

137 **to . . . practise** to perfect [his] proficiency.

138 **controversie** contention between parties, strife (*OED*, †1a).

140 **voluntaries** improvisations.

141 **curiositie and cunning** ingenuity and skill (Hill).

142 **Concord in discord** for the most influential formulation of *concordia discors* see Horace, *Epistles*, 1.12.19. See also 4.3.41–9 and notes.

142 **method** design (*OED*, method †7a).

143 **full . . . delight** the figurative centre at which the 'lines' (l. 142) intersect.

146–8 **when . . . heart** cf. *Anatomy*, 1.2.3.6: 'as a Nightingale . . . dies for shame if another bird sing better, [a dishonoured man] languisheth and pineth away for shame and griefe'; and Montaigne, *Essays* (see note for 1.1.127–8): 'to excell one another, [nightingales] will so stoutly contend for the mastery, that many times, such as are vanquished die; their wind and strength sooner failing then their voice.' The idea derives from Pliny, *Natural History*, 10.43.

148–50 **it . . . teares** for the English baroque exploitation of tears mixed with pleasure, cf. Crashaw, *The Weeper*. Donne employs tears across a wide range of emotions and contexts.

148 **quaintest** implying a connoisseurship of sadness; there is a suggestion of art (*OED*, quaint †3b) and refinement (†4a) as well as 'most strange' (*OED*, 8).

159 **peace** absence of noise, quiet.

161 **pashing** breaking.

163 **mirth and pitie** cf. 5.2.172: 'Rare pity and delight are sweetly mixt.' The emotions whose mixture characterizes the play, and Jacobean and Caroline tragicomedy in general, as opposed to the 'pity and fear' of tragedy. Mixture of pleasure and pain is a baroque characteristic, exploited most famously in Bernini's 'Ecstasy of St Teresa' in Santa Maria della Vittoria, Rome.

168 **discretion** perhaps 'tactfulness', but 'courtesy' or 'civility' (*OED*, †7), though not recorded by *OED* until 1752, fits the context better.

169 **Indu'd** endowed.

169 **ravish** forcibly seize.

174 **woo** 'entreat alluringly' (*OED*, *v.* 4). Though it could be used figuratively, as ostensibly here, most definitions in *OED* have some sexual connotation, and the word hints at Eroclea–Parthenophill's true gender.

178 **meane** of low social status.

178 **riotous** extravagant.

179 **Not . . . world** 'not publicly known' (Hill); cf. *TQ* 5: 'Thy cowardice hath publisht thee so base'.

180 *Parthenophill* Greek, 'Loving virginity'. Ford's friend Barnabe Barnes used the name for his sonnet sequence, *Parthenophil and Parthenophe* (1593), and was himself called 'Parthenophil' in William Percy's *Coelia* (1594).

183 **rare distractions** unusual disturbances of mind.

184 *Thamasta's* **glory** for the meaning of Thamasta's name, see note for DRAMATIS PERSONAE, l. 13 Thamasta. Cf. also 'great-spirited', 1.1.90.

185 **desperate** hopeless.

189 **one . . . hopes** 'a sizeable part of what I expect to inherit'; for 'one part' implying a substantial part of a whole, cf. *Lear*, 3.2.72–3: 'Poor Fool and knave, I have one part in my heart | That's sorry yet for thee'.

193 **coward** faint-hearted person.

1.2

1–22 **I will . . . o'er the Court** for this speech as typical of 'the honest and satirical malcontent', see Babb, *Elizabethan Malady*, pp. 95–6. Hill adds, 'The stance of "Be mine own antic" (line 13) is reminiscent of Marston's *Malcontent* and *Antonio* plays, and so are the Stoic sentiments, but the latter reiterate traditional moral ideas in Ford's *LL* and *GM*'. Ford is using the melancholic malcontent type to establish Rhetias's honesty at his first appearance. Later (4.2.21–2) Rhetias casts off the persona.

2–3 **Riots . . . Gentry** see Introduction, p. 225.

5 **Common-wealths** nations, states.

7 **renownes** makes famous.

8 **Mushrooms** upstarts.

10 *May-game* object of ridicule. Cf. *TPW* 1.3.46–7: 'wu't' never have wit, wou't make thyself a May-game to all the world?'

11 **snarle** satirists were characterized as dogs; cf. Marston, *Malcontent*, ed. Hunter, 1.2.10: 'Come down, thou ragged cur, and snarl here.'

12 **wit** prudence.

13 **Anticke** clown, here one licensed to tell the truth.

13 **sport** joke, here one in which life would be meaningless. Cf. *LS* 5.1.25–7: 'for whiles your lips | Are made the book, it is a sport to swear, | And glory to forswear.'

14 **hug** cherish, here for patronage.

17–18 **He that pursues . . . or foole** 'He who does not want to suffer from statecraft must learn to act as a madman or fool', referring to the traditional protection of the court jester from punishment for criticism of those in power. The inverted commas indicate a maxim or *sententia*.

20–1 be— . . . — So the first dash indicates an *aposiopesis* when the actor playing Rhetias led the audience to believe he was about to say 'damned in hell'. The second covers the moment when he turns, realizing he is about to be interrupted by Pelias.

21 Mine . . . tormentor a version of Ford's favoured Stoic self-reliance.

22 intelligence (1) an embodiment of intellect; (2) a source of news.

22 Buz (1) a noisy drone; (2) a source of rumour (cf. 4.2.77). Pelias stresses 'newes' in the next two lines.

25 Gull fool, esp. one easily tricked.

26 forerunner servant who 'runs before' to herald a great person.

27–29 Instead . . . wench reversing the usual device of early modern drama in which the 'wench' is a boy actor playing a young woman disguised as a boy.

27 guarded wearing elaborate livery.

28 trickt up dressed up; cf. *FCN* 3.2.69–70: 'some lewd painted baggage, trick't up gawdily, | Like one of us'.

30 entertain'd retained.

31 sword . . . trencher the sword and buckler (a small round shield) were extremely old fashioned; a trencher was both a platter, and the food served on it; cf. *LT* 2.2.19–20: 'married . . . A trencher-waiter; shrewd preferment!'

33 Lackeyes runs errands for, here specifically by delivering his letters; cf. *BH* 3.2.132: 'I am no clod of trade, to lackey pride'.

35 Courtship behaviour fitting for a courtier; cf. *FCN* 1.1.39–40: 'the young Lord of *Telamon*, her husband, | Was packetted to France, to study courtship'.

37 bare bare-headed.

38 reduce induce, lead (*OED*, †10 c).

41 complementally courteously, inferring the politeness is hypocritical; cf. the '*complimental offers of courtship*' from the women who then stab Ferentes in *LS* 3.4.17.10.

42–50 Agelastus . . . Thistles Agelastus, Greek 'unsmiling'. The source is Cicero, *De Finibus* 5.92: 'Marcus Crassus . . . according to Lucilius laughed but once in his life; that did not prevent his having the name of *agelastos*, as Lucilius says he had.' Jerome, *Letters* 7, quotes this together with the proverb 'like lips, like lettuce', the point here being that, like the ass, Pelias's tastes betray him (Tilley, L326). The introduction of prose here is an aspect of Rhetias being his 'owne Anticke' (1.2.13), 'honest, blunt, and rude' (4.2.7).

50 Puppy conceited and foolish young man.

51 **singular Coxcomb** preeminent fool.

51–2 **Ape of an Ape** mimic of an ape; cf. *Cymbeline*, 2.2.31: 'O sleep, thou ape of death.'

53 **Patent** licence; see 2.1.115 and note, 5.2.50; cf. *FCN* 3.3.213–14: 'You have belike then | A Patent for concealing Virgins'.

57 *Minkes* minx, a pert young woman.

62 **A sounder . . . wind instrument forsooth** 'Grilla's answer is meant to intimate that her father was a sow gelder' (Gifford). They blew a horn to announce their arrival in a village. Burton says seductively dressed women need 'but a crier to goe before them so dressed, to bid us looke out, a trumpet to sound, or for defect a sowgelder to blowe' (3.2.2.3, 1628 edition and later). For Ford's use of the 1628 edition, see Introduction, pp. 214–15.

64 **dancer** professional dancer or dancing master.

64–5 **Foot-cloth** 'a large richly-ornamented cloth laid over the back of a horse and hanging down to the ground on each side' (*OED*, †1).

65 **Muffe and Hood** Linthicum, *Costume*, pp. 274–5, implies hand muffs remained fashionable in 1628–9, but Jonson's satire on the goldsmith's wife Chloe in 1601 (*Poetaster*, 4.1.10) may suggest a degree of vulgarity; certainly the French hood had long been out of fashion at court. In Massinger's near-contemporary *City Madam* (1632), Lady Frugal is distressed at having to wear one; cf. Jonson, *Alchemist* (1610), 2.1.32–3: 'Marry, she's not in fashion yet. She wears | A hood, but 't stands acop.' There is sexual innuendo: Williams, *Dictionary*, p. 920, notes Dekker's use in *Match Me in London* (*c*.1611), 2.1.102, 'where Tormiella's enquiry, "Is the embrodered Muffe perfum'd for the Lady?" is answered: "Yes forsooth, she never put her hand into a sweeter thing".'

70–3 **if I take paines . . . with me, Sir** mild sexual innuendo: 'paines', 'understanding', and 'big' are all *double entendres*, and Grilla's reply continues in the same vein.

71 **nurse . . . Court-midwife** Ford may be thinking of the bawdy, talkative nurse in *R&J*; a Court midwife is synonymous with 'bawd' in Robert Daborne's *The Poor Man's Comfort* (*c*.1617): '*Lucius*. Canst thou be secret Surdo? *Surdo*. As a court Midwife, no Baud like me.'

75 **fist, Innocent** 'hand, Simpleton.' For the fist as an open hand offered for shaking, cf. 2.1.240 below.

77 **blade** fellow (*OED*, blade *n*. 11b, citing this example).

77–8 **blunt . . . blunt** applied to Rhetias, plain spoken, continuing the figurative use of 'blade'; Cuculus's reply unintentionally brings the alternative meaning 'stupid, obtuse' (*OED*, 1) into play.

79–81, 84–5 **a Sow-pig . . . Cyprus . . . thy milke** from *Anatomy*, 1.2.4.1, quoting Giraldus Cambrensis [Gerald of Wales]: 'A sow pigge by chance sucked a Brach, and when she was growne, *would miraculously hunt all manner of Deere, and that as well or rather better then any ordinary hound*. His conclusion is, *that Men and Beast participate of her nature and conditions, by whose milke they are fed*. [Varinus] *Phavorinus* urgeth it farther and demonstrats it more evedently, that if a Nurse be mishapen, unchast, unhonest impudent, drunke, cruell, or the like, the child that sucks upon her breast will be so too.' Burton argues that melancholy may thus be acquired from the cradle through 'a bad [wet] nurse'.

80 **Brach** bitch hound which hunts by scent.

80 **suckt** suckled on.

83 **banket** banquet.

87 **Shittle-cocks** shuttlecocks, often spelled thus: cf. Jonson, *Cynthia's Revels* 2.4.29: 'play at shittle-cock, and that too'.

88 **woman-surgeon** apparently 'a dealer in paints and cosmetics for the ladies' (Gifford), who cites ll. 93–4 in support. This and 'she-surgeon' (l. 87) are the only examples in full text *EEBO*. Neither is in *OED* in this sense.

92 **corke and feather** shuttlecocks were made of a piece of cork with a crown of feathers.

95 **'tis . . . suit** punning on the garment and the grant of a request: 'compliments' may quickly get either.

96 *Periwinckle* Used similarly by Shirley as a term of condescending endearment in *The Brothers* 5.3 (*Works*, I, p. 258), *The Wittie Faire One*, 4.4 (*Works*, I, p. 337), and *Love's Cruelty* 2.1 (*Works*, 2, p. 209)

97 **Moonecalves** congenital idiots, simpletons (*OED*, mooncalf 2c).

97 **Fop** 'fool', not yet the foolish dandy of Restoration drama.

100 **by Proclamation** by public or obvious manifestation (*OED*, †4d).

100.1 SD *passing over* this may have been a modified version of the process proposed by Allardyce Nicoll, who suggested 'passing over' meant the actor[s] moved 'from yard to platform to yard again' ('Passing over the stage', *ShS*, 12 (1959), 47–55). Nicoll was thinking of outdoor theatres, where the press of groundlings might have impeded such movement, but entrances and exits using steps from the pit have become a regular feature of staging at the reconstructed indoor Wanamaker Playhouse at the London Globe. While Corax may similarly have come from the pit at the Blackfriars and walked across the stage in 'haste' (l. 102) as if intending to go down again, he does not 'pass over', but stays until all the characters exit at l. 164.

104 **Phew** at this date expressing disgust or impatience, not relief.

104 **wheele about** turn around (to face them).

105 **slovenry** slovenliness, perhaps here with suggestion of offensive neglect of manners.

105 **practice** scheming.

105 **vertue** special skill.

108 **ban-dog** fierce dog kept on a chain.

110–110.1 **There . . . gowne** Gifford notes the [bathetic] echo of Prospero removing his 'magic garment', *Tempest*,. 1.2.25: 'Lie there my art.'

111–49 **Doe what thou . . . betweene us** the exchange of insults between Rhetias and Corax is a 'flyting' of a type used frequently by Shakespeare, particularly in *Henry IV* parts I and II between the Prince and Falstaff, Falstaff and Doll, and Doll and Pistol. Both draw on the rhetorical training with which their names associate them (see DRAMATIS PERSONAE ll. 7–8, notes)

111 **stand** 'present a firm front . . . await an onset' (*OED*, 10); cf. 5.2.71.

112–13 **Mountebancks . . . Barbers** from *Anatomy*, 1.2.3.15: 'Now for Physitians, there are in every Village so many Mountibanks, Empiricks, Quacsalvers, Paracelsians as they call themselves, Wisards, Alcumists, poore Vicars, cast Apothecaries and Physitians men, Barbers, and Goodwives that professe great skill, that I know not how they [physicians] shal maintaine themselves'.

112 **Mountebancks** travelling quacks who stood on a stall (Italian '*monta in banco*') to sell their usually fake medicine.

112 **Empricks** unqualified doctors who based treatment on experience rather than knowledge of theory; Burton acknowledges that they 'may ease, and sometimes helpe, but not throughly root out' a disease because they cannot know its cause without training in theory (*Anatomy*, 1.2.1.1). This lack probably saved many of their patients.

112 **Quacksalvers** healers who profess to cure with ointments (salves). Burton lumps them together with mountebanks and empirics as making 'this noble & profitable Art [medicine] to be evill spoken of, and contemned, by reason of such base and illiterate artificers' (*Anatomy*, 2.1.4.1).

112 **Mineralists** first example of this word in *OED*, substituted for Burton's more wordy 'Paracelsians as they call themselves'; Paracelsus's highly influential medical theory is often targeted by Burton. In this case it is characterized by his advocacy of 'chemicals' (minerals). Burton says he 'is so stiffe for his Chimicall medicines, that in his cures he will admit almost of no other Physick' (*Anatomy*, 1.2.3.15).

113 **Wizards** men skilled in the occult; Burton believes they can effect cures, but doubts the source of their power is diabolical: 'Nothing so familiar as to heare of such cures, Sorcerers are too common, Cunning men, Wisards, & whitewitches, as they call them, in every village' (*Anatomy*, 2.1.1.1).

113 **Alchimists** forerunners of chemists, at this date still characterized as trying to turn base metals into gold. Burton cites the Swiss Felix Platter

approvingly; he 'is of opinion, all Alcumists are mad, out of their wits' (*Anatomy*, 'Democritus Junior to the Reader'). Later, they 'spend that little which they have to get gold and never find it' (2.3.5). Some, like Simon Forman, gave medical advice.

113 **cast-Apothecaries** cashiered druggists. The Guild of Apothecaries which would have been responsible for their 'casting' out had only been founded in 1617, and its hall was in the same Blackfriar's precinct as the theatre.

113 **Barbers** barbers still performed surgery and dentistry at this period, though more specialist surgeons practised, especially at the London hospitals under physicians. Burton looks down on them: 'an hungry Surgeon often doth prolong & wierdraw [spin out] his cure so long as there is any hope of pay' (*Anatomy*, 2.1.4.1).

114 **suppositors** *OED* defines as 'A person or thing providing support', giving this as first usage; but the context also suggests 'suppositories'; cf. *FCN* 3.1.52–4: 'Evermore phantasticall, | As being the suppositor to laughter: | It hath sav'd charge in physic.' Here the physician's rivals purge him of his practice and fees. For a similar personalization see Jonson, *Alchemist*, 5.5.13 where Mammon calls Doll 'Madam Suppository'.

118 **Have at thee** a formal challenge, sometimes used as here for a verbal duel, as in *Romeo* 4.5.121: 'Then have at you with my wit!' Cf. 1.2.113.

120 **denier** small French coin, the type of an almost worthless sum; cf. *WoE*, 4.1.150–1: 'and being lost, | To pay not a Denier for't?' Rhetias has not even this to pay for opening a vein, i.e. the common medical practice of blood-letting.

121 **Plurisie** used for a variety of stabbing chest pains.

121 **prate** speak foolishly, but significantly for Rhetias's association with a snarling dog (cf. 1.2.11, 1.2.108) it was used for hounds barking or howling (*OED*, 1†b).

122 **bleed in the breech** bleed from the bottom (from being whipped) instead of from a normal blood-letting.

127–9 **Atheist . . . Hogge** cf. *Lear*, 3.4.93–4: 'hog in sloth, fox in stealth, wolf in greediness, dog in madness'.

130 **impostrous** fraudulent, fake.

130–3 **Physicions . . . flesh** from *Anatomy*, 2.4.1.1, in a passage added in the 1624 edition, and retained in 1628: '*Cambyses* in *Xenophon* told *Cyrus*, that to his thinking, Physicians *were like Taylors and Coblers, the one mended our sick bodies, as the other did our cloathes*' (1628, p. 337).

131 **Coblers** to 'cobble' was to mend poorly, to patch up.

131 **Botchers** tailors who patch clothes, usually badly (*OED*, 2b and 3). Cf. *TQ*, 1.169–72: 'I will shred you both so small, that a very botcher shall shred Spanish needles, with every fillet of your itchy flesh.'

137 **dignity** rank.

137 **lowse** louse, someone contemptible.

137–8 **bred . . . humours** corruption of the four bodily humours (black bile, yellow bile, phlegm, and blood) would cause illness, potentially mental, since the humours' psychological counterparts were melancholic, choleric, phlegmatic, and sanguine temperaments. A poor diet was a common diagnosis: see e.g. John Downame, *A Guide to Godlynesse* (1623), p. 644: 'those which are invited to a great feast, doe not, if they have care of their health, eate a little of every dish, or more then their stomackes can well disgest, seeing the superfluities would turne to crudities, and breede ill humours and obstructions in the body.'

140 **secure** safe, assured.

150 **Are . . . full** 'Have you had enough?' Hill suggests a reference to the doctor's urine bottles.

153 **shape . . . devise** prepare you all for a masque.

153–4 **Wee'le . . . him** Corax's plan is to 'move' or 'nettle' Palador to uncover the cause of his melancholy. See 2.1.83.

155 **He shall fret or laugh** Bright, *Treatise*, chapter 28 (pp. 161–6), investigates 'Howe melancholie causeth both weeping and laughing.'

156 **make one** be one of the company; cf. *Love's Labour's Lost* 5.1.153: 'I'll make one in a dance, or so.'

158 **egregiously** invariably used negatively at this date, 'excessively badly', so here a pretentious attempt at courtly language.

161 **cast** devised (*OED*, cast *v.* 43b); the meaning of allotting parts to actors (*OED*, 48) had not yet developed.

162 **attend** wait to be told.

163–4 **The melody . . . consort** 'Rhetias develops a musical metaphor from the suggestion of 'time' in the previous line' (Hill).

1.3

2 **trim** vulgar fashion; cf. its application to Cuculus, 3.1.1, 4.1.81. In *FCN*, 4.1.15–19, Castamela is likewise criticized by her brother as 'a Mistris of the trimme' dressed 'in a hey-de-gay of scurvey Gallantry' and told, as here (l. 10) to appear more humble. Gradually the audience realizes that Thamasta has already met 'Parthenophill' (l. 36), and that her overdressing is a consequence of her passion for him overcoming her judgement (l. 49).

2–3 **new . . . labour** like a parvenu who has just been hatched from the confines of labouring at a trade. *Nouveau riche* tradesmen's wives were a recurrent subject of satire in city comedy.

4 ease and wantonnesse Ovid, *Remedia Amoris*, 135–9, warns that ease is a prerequisite for love ('wantonnesse'); anyone who wants to avoid love should shun *otium* (ease), 'the cause and sustenance of the pleasant evil' of love.

5 antike not clown-like as at 1.2.13, but so over-dressed as to be 'Absurd from fantastic incongruity . . . uncouthly ludicrous' (*OED*, 2c, predating the earliest example).

14–15 undertooke . . . exile cf. *BH* 1.1.76–7: 'from hence, | I undertake a voluntary exile'.

15–22 Wherefore . . . Chronicle earlier Menaphon has expressed 'hope' (1.1.59) that Thamasta has made 'some worthy choice' in his absence, but this speech by Amethus is heavily ironic at the expense of her 'modesty' (here humility rather than chastity). Though there is justice in his criticism, Ford is also interested, as in *BH*, in the potential dangers of brotherly advice.

23 kindly wise wise according to your nature as a brother.

26–34 Indeed . . . Innocent Thamasta points out her brother's inconsistency, but as Hill notes, her heavy sarcasm recoils on her when she descends (l. 31) to Parthenophill.

29 want lack.

30 portly imposing, punning on 'portion'. Cf. *LS* 2.1.116: 'portly grace'; *LoC* 4.1.141 'portly carriage'.

33 Sister a mistake, perhaps because Ford had the brother/sister relationship on his mind: Cleophila is Menaphon's cousin (see 2.2.67, 69).

34 Innocent (1) person free of sin; (2) idiot, simpleton.

37 Stranger (1) foreigner; (2) newcomer. The term is applied to Eroclea throughout; see e.g. 3.2.65, 4.1.1.

39 I not repent for the omission of 'do', cf. Jonson, *Volpone*, 2.4.26–7: 'Nay, then, | I not repent me of my late disguise.'

40 affable courteous, friendly; cf. *Shrew* 2.1.250–1: 'thou with mildness entertain'st thy wooers, | With gentle conference, soft and affable'.

42 sadnesse Hill suggests 'seriousness', but following 'pitty' the common meaning is more likely.

46 neat clear and to the point.

49 Thou't . . . last you will change after a while.

52 contents pleasures; used as singular in *BH* 1.1.108–9: 'to see thee matched | As may become thy choice and our contents.'

56, 57 helpes of Art Burton uses the same phrase in conjunction with 'content', and the combination may have stuck in Ford's mind: '[philosophy] cannot chuse but give some content and comfort. 'Tis true no medicine can cure all diseases, some affections of the mind are altogether incurable, yet these helps of art, Physicke and Phylosophy must not be contemned' (*Anatomy*, 2.3.1.1). Cf. also *FCN* 2.2.44: 'no helpes of art can warrant life'.

62 Servant 'one who is devoted to the service of a lady' (*OED*, 4†b) in the Courtly Love tradition.

65 Are . . . Sir 'Eroclea silently betrays her emotions at Thamasta's acceptance of her cousin's courtship. Cf. her reaction to Cleophila's pledge of love to Amethus [2.2.142–4]' (Hill).

66 League alliance, covenant.

69 ingeniously wisely.

70 Gallery in this context a picture gallery; cf. *LT*, 2.3.1–4: 'In the next gallery you may behold | Such living pictures Lady . . . that you'd think | They breath, and smile upon yee.'

76 processe continuance to an ending.

78 Closet secret repository for papers or valuables.

79 forc'd broken open.

85–6 Love . . . Resisted an abnegation of the reasoned resistance to passion which Ford advocates, although like Burton he is more interested in exploring such irrational responses as this. Cf. Corax on love at 3.3.103–7, and *Anatomy*, 3.2.1.1: 'and therefore Socrates calls Love a tyrant, & brings him triumphing in a Chariot.' See also *Anatomy*, 3.2.1.2, 'How love tyranniseth over men' and 3.2.3: '*For love* (as *Cyrus* in *Xenophon* well observed) *is a mere tyranny, worse then any disease, and they that are troubled with it desire to be free and cannot, but are harder bound then if they were in iron chaines.*'

94–5 'Tis . . . wisdomes proverbial: Tilley, L 517.

97 Diamonds cut Diamonds proverbial: Tilley, D323. First usage in *OED*, here meaning only love can cure love.

97–8 they . . . love meaning her love will be cured if Parthenophill returns it; cf. Nicholas Ling, *Wits Common Wealth* (1598), f. 19v: 'The best Phisition to cure love, is shee that gave the wound.' Cf. Introduction, p. 243.

2.1

1–16 Our . . . of Burton makes the obvious point about a ruler's neglect affecting the commonwealth in his preface, 'Democritus Junior to the Reader': 'where good government is, prudent and wise Princes, there all things thrive and prosper, peace and happinesse is in that land, where it is otherwise, all things are ugly to behold, inculte, barbarous, uncivill, a paradise is turned to a wildernesse.' See also note to 1.1.73.

3 Lethargy . . . security apathy caused by his lost confidence (in Eroclea's love).

4 The Commons murmur . . . grieve for topical applications of this line, see Introduction, p. 225.

5 **Anticke** grotesque; the 2015 staged reading at the Wanamaker Playhouse showed how effectively Cuculus and his fellows, including at times Corax and Rhetias, function to establish that the court is indeed disturbed.

6 **at gaze** in the attitude of gazing in wonder or bewilderment (*OED*, gaze *n.* 3b).

12 **unsteady multitude** cf. *LoC* 3.2.36 'unsteddy multitude', and *GM* 701–3: 'if *Neglect* come from the unsteddinesse of the common people, then it is nothing strange: for as they are wonne in an houre, so are they lost in a minute'.

13 **ingrosse** monopolize; cf. 4.2.73 and note.

14 **particular** personal.

18 **gay State-fetters** brightly coloured livery of state office.

20 **concluded** reached an agreement.

24 **informe** direct.

25–6 **Passions . . . reclaim'd** Burton, discussing cures for melancholy, stresses the need for patience, quoting Montanus who 'injoynes his patient before he take them in hand, perseverance and sufferance, for in such a small time no great matter can be effected' (*Anatomy*, 2.1.4.2).

25 **violent** powerful.

26–7 **There's . . . out** Cf. *Hamlet*, 2.2.157–9: 'I will find | Where truth is hid, though it were hid indeed | Within the centre.'

27 **distemper** disordered state of mind, caused by a lack of balance (temper) between the humours.

28 **on . . . appointment** at exactly the time arranged.

30 **Save yee** shortened form of the greeting 'God save you'.

32 **Doe . . . honour** make a curtsey.

32 **Houswife** hussy, impertinent girl; cf. 3.1.58.

35 **Shee-waiters** a waiter was a person who attended on a superior; usually they were men, but women sometimes played this role; cf. Massinger, *Duke of Milan* (1623), 3.2.38–9: 'There was lately | A fine she waiter in the Court'.

36–7 **reare . . . head-piece** celebrate me as 'A clever or intellectual person' (*OED*, 3c), where the first example given is 1647; cf. Cuculus's slightly different use at 1.2.69.

38 **Woodcocke . . . in't** woodcocks were proverbially foolish because easily trapped; like them, Cuculus has an empty cranium, containing no brains at all.

38–9 **Barbers . . . Citternes** Hill notes, 'The cittern, a stringed instrument sometimes kept in barbers' shops for the use of customers, was often decorated with a grotesquely carved head. Secco, the barber in *FCN*, is abused as "a citterne headed gew-gaw" ' (1.2.39–40).

39–40 **Hucksters . . . Ginger-bread** 'Pedlars will display gingerbread men in the shape of your figure.'

43 **perstreperous** 'noisy', apparently coined by Ford from Latin *perstepere*, 'to make a loud noise'. This is the only example in *OED* or in *EEBO* full text, and is presumably intended to be foolishly pretentious, like the neologisms used by Marston/Crispinus which Jonson mocks in *Poetaster*, 5.3.

43 **Sauce-box** someone addicted to making saucy remarks.

44 **puffe** swagger; perhaps the same meaning in *BH* 3.2.136–7: 'How a' stares, | Struts, puffs, and sweats.'

45 **presence** royal audience chamber.

46 **Mum, Butterflye** 'Silence, fop.'

48.2 ***Enter . . . hand*** cf. *Hamlet*, 2.2.167.1: '*Enter Hamlet, reading on a book*' (Folio SD). See Introduction, p. 212.

50–5 **is this . . . the sledge** Burton, *Anatomy*, 2.2.4 recommends exercise in general as a counter to melancholy, specifying among other forms 'riding at great horse', hunting ('hounds', l. 53), the 'balloon', and 'pitching bars'.

53 **great Horse** the large war horse, used in tournaments. Cf. Massinger, *Bondman*, 1.3.69: 'His singing, dancing, riding of great horses.'

53 **Hounds** hunting with a pack of hounds.

54 **Balloone ball** a kind of hand ball 'played with a large inflated ball of strong double leather, struck to and fro with the arm protected by a wooden bracer' (*OED*, balloon *n*. 1a.)

55 **casting . . . sledge** throwing the hammer, similar to Burton's 'pitching bars'.

56 **tosse a Pike** throw a pike a distance or at a target, perhaps also throw in the air and catch.

56 **Sonnet** the book Palador is reading is a collection of love poems, as expected of the melancholy lover.

58–9 **infect . . . surfet** reinforcing the spread of sickness and 'dull lethargy' which Sophronos speaks of at 2.1.1–3.

63 **wilfull dulnesse** Corax implies Palador's melancholy is self-indulgent. Burton insists similarly on the patient's responsibility not to give way to melancholy. However sick, 'he may choose whether he will give way too farre unto it, he may in some sort correct himselfe . . . Rule thy selfe then with reason, satisfie thy selfe, accustome thy selfe, weane thy selfe from those fond conceipts, vaine feares, strong Imaginations, restlesse thoughts. Thou maist doe it . . . as Plutarch saith, we may frame our selves as we will' (*Anatomy*, 2.2.6.1). Charles I's motto was 'If you would conquer all things, submit your-self to reason' (*ODNB*).

63 **held** (1) regarded as; (2) held captive.

68 **I beleeve it** Palador's terse response is not just to the 'madness' of Corax's dangerous tirade, but points wryly to the 'bedlam' of the court.

72 **defiance** declaration of war.

75–6 **Syrian . . . intermitted** There is no obvious source for this. Diodorus Siculus, *Library of History*, 15.89 says that in 385 BC the Cypriot king Evagoras agreed to 'pay the Persian King a fixed annual tribute'. Or it may have been suggested by knowledge of the 'yeerely tribute, of 8000 Ducats, which the Kings of Cyprus were wont to pay to the Soldans of Aegipt' (Thomas de Fougasses, *The Generall Historie of the Magnificent State of Venice*, 1612, p. 116). In demanding this tribute from Venice when the republic occupied Cyprus, the Ottoman emperor could be said to have 'pretend[ed] an ancient interest'.

75 **pretend** claim, especially falsely; cf. *Cymbeline*, 2.3.112–13: 'For | The contract you pretend with that base wretch.'

76–81 **Through . . . Prince** For the parallels with England in 1628, see Introduction, p. 225.

82–3 **from . . . voyce** by listening to those currently around him at court he will apprehend the opinion of his subjects—a process many in Ford's audience might have cautioned him, and their own prince, against. Cf. *LoC* 1.1.68, 'generall voice'; *LT* 1.3.25–6: 'the generall voice | Sounds him for courtesie'; *WA* 3.3.47: 'The generall voyce proclames you the kings mistris'.

83 **nettled** stirred up; cf. *LS*, 3.3.45–6: 'I knew it would nettle you in the fire of your composition.'

87 **I . . . briefe** cf. the identical phrase in *SG* 1.5.22.

89–90 **Not willingly . . . your Judgement** perhaps recalling *Othello* 5.2.345–6: 'one not easily jealous, but being wrought | Perplex'd in the extreme'.

89–92 **head-strong . . . affections** reiterating Ford's and Burton's emphasis on the desirability of reason and will controlling emotion. Cf. note to 1.3.85–6, and *Anatomy*, 1.1.1.13, 'Of the Will.' Palador is in the position of Burton's Phaedra, whose 'judgement' was also 'mislead' by 'passion': 'We cannot resist, but as Phaedra confessed to her nurse, she [the nurse] said well and true, and she did acknowledge it, but headstrong passion and fury, made her to doe that which was opposite.'

91 **motions** agitations of the mind or feelings.

92 **affections** passions; cf. Corax's use at 3.1.111–12, referencing Burton, who almost always uses 'affection' as 'feeling (as opposed to reason); *spec.* a powerful or controlling emotion, as passion, lust' (*OED*, 1†b).

98 **selfe-love** 'Philautia, or Selfe-love' (*Anatomy*, 1.2.3.14) is a serious vice for Burton; it 'will slily and insensibly pervert' and is 'a most violent batterer of our Soules, and causeth Melancholy and Dotage', but Aretus is wrong in diagnosing it in Palador.

99 **would be** would like to be.

103 **man . . . compleat** perfect, accomplished in all respects; cf. *Troilus* 3.3.181 (Ulysses to Achilles): 'thou great and complete man'.

107–8 **The great *Elixer* . . . perfections** the terms in Pelias's absurdly inflated list are synonymous: see *OED*, elixir 3b: 'The quintessence or soul of a thing.' Cf. *LoC* 3.1.39–40: 'the quintessence, | The soule, and grand elixer of my wit'; *BH* 4.2.24–5: 'The quintessence, | Soul, and elixir of the earth's abundance'.

110 **square out** frame, arrange.

115 **Proclamation** formal order issued by the king which had the force of law without parliamentary approval; Charles I issued hundreds, some of which conferred powers over manufacturers of goods such as Cuculus is seeking. Though they were mostly innocuous, Ford's audience would have been sensitive in particular to the unpopular 'Forced Loan', ordered by proclamation in October 1626, and widely resisted. A group who refused to pay were imprisoned without charge in 1627, and their plea of *habeas corpus* was rejected in November, a year before the play was performed. The Forced Loan festered throughout the parliament of 1628. See Introduction, p. 225.

115 **Patent** letters patent, granted by the king to give the holder authority, in this case over tailors. Cf. 1.2.53 note, 5.2.53.

117 **golden dayes** the myth of the lost Golden Age, first inscribed by Hesiod, *Works and Days*, 106, became still more influential through its celebration in Ovid's *Metamorphoses*, 1: 89–112. Hill suggests Ford may be recalling Gonzalo's ideal commonwealth 'T'excel the golden age' (*Tempest* 2.1.148–69), but Gonzalo is closer to Ovid; Cuculus's is a comically banal version.

121 **Squall** a small person, but when addressed to a woman (as Cuculus believes Grilla to be) the term had sexual connotations; used often by Middleton: see e.g. *Michaelmas Term*, 1.3.4–6: 'Wouldst thou, a pretty beautiful, juicy squall, live in a poore thrummed house i'th' country'.

125 **Away *Cuculus* . . . Lords** 'That Corax should usher everyone out to enable Rhetias to speak his mind privately to the Prince suggests that the two are already conspiring together for his cure' (Hill).

126.2 ***Manent*** 'they remain'; *Q*'s reading '*Manet*' means 'he remains'; Ford uses *Manent* more than most contemporaries (see e.g. *BH* (1), *PW* (3), *LS* (1)), but as in many other plays of the period he (probably not the compositor) is careless about using *manet* when more than one character remains onstage: see e.g. *TPW*, 3.2.14: '*manet Soran. & Anna.*' *Manet* for more than one character recurs numerous times in Shakespeare's quartos and the First Folio. On the rare occasions Jonson uses '*manent*' it is typically always correct. Cf. the more common lack of agreement in use of *Exit* for *Exeunt*.

136 **affected passion** cf. 2.1.89–92 and notes.

142 **hold . . . eares** proverbial for a dilemma in which either choice is dangerous (Tilley, W 603).

143 **stroake a Lyon** deal amicably with a prince. In versions of the fable of Androcles and the lion, the lion which Androcles had earlier helped allows him to stroke it when they meet in the Roman arena.

149 *Agenors* from Greek Ἀγήνωρ 'manly, heroic', but in a bad sense 'arrogant, headstrong', used because of its associations with Burton's category of 'Heroical Melancholy' which 'deserves much rather to be called burning lust', and 'sometimes . . . produceth rapes, incests, murders'. As was the case with Palador's father, it 'subverts kingdoms, overthrows cities, towns, families, mars, corrupts, and makes a massacre of men' (*Anatomy*, 3.2.1.2). For the confusion between 'heroes' and '*hereos*' (erotic love) see Introduction, p. 211. There are various Agenors in Greek mythology, one a king of Tyre, another one of the three sons of Antenor who defended Troy (Homer, *Iliad*, 11.59).

149 **traduc'd** censured.

150 **observe** be conscious of (*OED*, 9a).

152 **throughly** fully, in detail.

164 **neere of an age** this must mean 'nearly the same age'. If it referred to them each being near the minimum age for contracting a marriage in England, which was twelve for girls and fourteen for boys, then Eroclea on her return from 'two years exile' (5.2.171) would only be thirteen or fourteen (close to Juliet), Palador fifteen or sixteen. Though Palador still has a tutor, both behave as if older than this.

165 **Contract** arranged betrothals between teenagers were still common in England among the nobility and wealthy gentry. They had legal force, and as Hill notes, the high public profile of this one makes Agenor's conduct 'particularly reprehensible'. See also note to 3.2.5.

165 *Her* the unusual italicization of the pronoun must have been in the copy, underlined by Ford to represent the actor's emphasis.

173 **Rape . . . Agents** the plural confirms that abduction, with a view to Agenor later raping her in the common modern sense is meant (*OED*, rape, *n.³*).

176 **distracted** driven mad (*OED*, distract *v.* †6).

177 **What . . . doubtfull** what might have happened afterwards was uncertain.

184 **rellish** flavour.

188 **accident** incident.

191–206 **A young Lady . . . not impossible** the first broad hint to the audience as to Eroclea's identity.

193 **jarring** quarrelling, the first usage in this sense in *OED*, antedating the next by 150 years.

194 **conveyed** carried off secretly (cf. 3.2.49, 4.3.145, 5.2.161).

194 **Merchant** merchant ship.

198 **familiaritie** intimacy, close friendship, sometimes with sexual innuendo.

209 **these** hands (Hill).

219 **picture . . . Tablet** miniature portrait in a jewelled case.

220 **— yes— let me observe it—** the dashes indicate Rhetias's pauses while he examines the miniature.

227–8 **let no politicke . . . sift me** Hill suggests that 'Palador's neurotic and groundless fears indicate a mind isolated from the reality of his court', but the audience has just heard Aretus ask Corax if he has 'won Rhetias' over to a scheme to find out what is 'hid | Of his distemper' (2.1.26–9). Du Laurens, *Discourse*, pp. 93–4, notes paranoia as a common symptom of melancholy: 'if he see three or foure talking together, he thinketh that it is of him.' Cf. Introduction, pp. 240–1.

227 **politicke** cunning, crafty; cf. *FCN* 3.1.6–7: 'I shall tred out the toyle of these darke paths | In spight of politique reaches'.

229 **Creature** faithful servant, less pejorative than Pelias's use at 1.1.36.

234 **with favour** with your permission; cf. *BH* 1.2.104–5: 'Sir, with your favour, | I need not a supporter.'

239 **Hold—** the long dash indicates that Menaphon hesitates for some reason.

240 **fist** jocularly for hand, not necessarily clinched; *OED*, 2a, citing this line.

240 **started up** grown up rapidly, normally used of children.

243 **Owzle's** Ousel was an old name for the blackbird; and may be used here (as suggested by *OED*, 1†c) to indicate black hair or complexion, as it is in *Henry IV Part 2*, 3.2.5–8: '*Shallow.* And how doth . . . your fairest daughter and mine, my goddaughter Ellen? *Silence.* Alas, a black woosel' ['Ouzel', Folio]. Eroclea may be wearing a black wig (or the boy playing her may have been dark), but she is so frequently described as 'fair' that, even allowing for the fact that this could just mean 'beautiful', a dark Eroclea is unlikely. Rhetias may be using the word as equivalent to 'little bird'.

247 **sooth me** lie to me.

249–50 **Your . . . him** Palador's language, especially 'Some other time' (l. 258), suggests his melancholy languor prevents him from examining Eroclea, or listening to what she says. This is confirmed by Menaphon's comment (2.1.261).

259 **a** he, possibly from 'ha', a south-western form (*OED*, he ϵ); cf. *Hamlet* 2.1.56.

260 **sort** allot.

264–5 **Wee . . . three** Menaphon and Eroclea will both attend Amethus, hence 'three'.

265–70 **SDs**] Dashes in *Q* indicate asides.

266–7 **mad man . . . girle** Meleander and Cleophila. See 2.2.123–5 for the fulfilment of this strategy.

267 gabblest talk rapidly, often unintelligibly as the implicaton is at 4.2.64; here it is part of Rhetias's 'antic' language, but the stress is on the need to talk quickly to Cleophila. Later (2.2.125) he tells Amethus to 'be plaine and short' with Cleophila.

269 range wander through; Amethus is hiding his visit to Cleophila from Thamasta.

271 Troope on march away.

271 offensive annoying.

272 resolve disclose; cf. 1.1.111 and note.

279–80 admit | A dowre 'suppose a dowry'; for this use of admit, cf. 3.3.96, and *TQ* 2 (ll. 1448–50): 'but admit | I grant it, and you have it; may I then | Lay a light burthen on you.'

282 (Young man) the brackets are for emphasis.

284 sensible capable of an emotional response.

287 give me leave . . . ignorance 'let me pretend for the moment to be unaware.'

288 SD *seeing . . . approaching* *Q*'s dashes indicate Eroclea's confusion at the interruption of what she evidently sees as a compromising exchange.

292–3 won . . . beliefe won over my trust.

296 I may be bold . . . confession cf. *LoC* 1.2.188–9: 'I may be bold | To justifie a truth'

302 hearty heartfelt, deeply held; cf. *PW* 1.2.174: 'hearty love'.

304 construction interpretation; cf. Dedication, line 10; *BH* 3.4.21: 'be not severe in your construction'.

305 riper more experienced.

306 deserts actions that deserve rewards.

313 wood'st didst woo.

319 carriage conduct, actions: she will spoil her prospects; cf 5.1.78.

320 Groome serving man, often used contemptuously; cf. *FCN* 2.1.41: 'sawcy groome, learn manners'.

321 cast upon thrown on, given as master or mistress to.

325 respect values, considers; cf. *TPW* 4.3.100: 'be ruled, as you respect your honour'.

326 fond foolish; cf. *TPW* 1.1.9: 'Such questions, youth, are fond.'

327 crosse thwart, counter; cf. 3.2.135, and *PW* 2.1.8: 'the king must not be crossed.'

332–3 the . . . too Hill notes that this sounds proverbial but is not; it is, however, close to Tilley, J57, 'Joan is as good as my lady (in the dark).'

2.2

2 he . . . open proverbial; Tilley, 153. Melancholics were thought to sleep badly (see e.g. *Anatomy*, 1.2.3.10).

4 sullen melancholy; cf. *SD* 4.1.78–9: 'i'le be melancholly. | Folly. A sullen humor'.

10.1 SD For the probable existence of a 'discovery space' behind an arras in the centre of the tiring house screen in both the Blackfriars and the second Globe, see Gurr, *Shakespearian Stage*, pp. 159–60.

12 sleepes in's naps the only example of this odd plural use in *OED*, emphasizing the uneasiness of Meleander's sleep.

14 foure yeeres Trollio's mangling of time instead of language: Eroclea has only been in exile for about two years (2.1.193–4, 5.2.163–8, 196).

17 great . . . Switzerland the cod-piece was 'a bagged appendage to the front of the close-fitting hose or breeches' (*OED*). They were unfashionable by this time (see Linthicum, *Costume*, pp. 204–5) but were still worn by the Papal Swiss Guard, drawing Montaigne's derision: 'What meant that laughter-mooving, and maids looke-drawing peece our Fathers wore in their breeches, yet extant among the Switzers?' (*Essays*, trans. Florio (1613), 3.5). Stuffing one with hair falsely implied the ownership of a large and firm penis, as Rabelais noted, describing Gargantua's codpiece as not only 'long and capacious' but 'well furnished within and well victualled, having no resemblance to the fraudulent codpieces of so many young gentlemen which contain nothing but wind, to the great disappointment of the female sex' (*Gargantua and Pantagruel*, 1.8).

17–18 A begins . . . a stirres see 2.1.259 note.

18 a good yeere 'what the good year' is normally a casual imprecation to a malign spirit, analogous to 'What the devil' (cf. *Much Ado*, 1.3.1); here Trollio is nonsensically asking such a spirit to protect Meleander.

21 stomacke appetite; cf. *TPW* 1.2.49, 4.3.29.

21–2 porredge . . . settle-braine porridge was a thick broth; in *Every Man Out*, 2.2.138–9, Jonson presents it as dulling the brain: [*Carlo.*] ''Sblood, I think he feeds her with porridge, I; she could ne'er have such a thick brain else.' Trollio confuses this with the mollifying effect he believes it will have on Meleander.

23 The Raven croakt . . . Owles both birds of ill-omen associated with death, often invoked together; see e.g. Thomas May, *The Heir* (1622), Act 3: 'No croking Raven, or ill booding Owle | Make heere their balefull habitation | Frighting thy walkes'.

25 no boot no use.

25 Girle Eroclea.

27 **looke bigge** look threatening; cf. *Winter's Tale*, 4.3.105–6: 'Not a more cowardly rogue in all Bohemia. If you had but look'd big, and spit at him, he'ld have run.'

30 ***Trollio*** Hill notes *Q*'s spelling *Trollia* may be deliberate, 'intended to underline his comic echoing of Cleophila's doleful remark.'

31 **implement** the first use applied to a person recorded in *OED*; the fact that it antedates the next by almost a century may mean that again Trollio is mis-using words, in this case creatively. Cf. Pelias's and Rhetias's use of 'creature' (1.1.36, 2.1.229).

34–5 **Turtles . . . with** 'Unfledged turtle doves still in their downy feathers develop more bile than her spleen engendered.' For the spleen as the source of bile and melancholy see '*To the Author, Master* John Ford', l. 1 and note.

37 **no such** 'no (person or thing) of the kind' (*OED*, such *adj.* 27a).

39 **rav'd . . . mischiefe** *OED* gives no example of this transitive use; the rav-ing confirms Agenor's possession by 'Heroical love'; see Introduction p. 211 and 2.1.149, note.

40 **politick** cunning; cf. *BH* 3.4.32, 'Without our ruin by your politic plots.'

41 **We . . . Honour** either, as Hill suggests, 'too accustomed to honourable dealings to suspect' Agenor, or too long employed by him in a position of honour.

41–2 **I . . . extremely** cf. *Anatomy*, 1.3.1.4: 'Their bodies are lean and dried up, withered, ugly, their looks harsh, very dull, and their souls tormented.'

42 **falne away** gaunt, shrunk.

44 **puking** this is the first instance of the noun given in *OED*, which defines it as 'vomiting; an instance of this'. But Trollio clearly means that he feels sick, not that he is actually vomiting, and the neologism may be another example of his misuse of words.

47–8 **there's . . . mad** Trollio's distinction is nonsensical: the two categories belong together, as in Jonson, *Staple of News*, 5.3.29: 'Stark staring mad, your brother'. For Meleander's 'out-staring' everybody, see 2.2.83; Corax promises to 'out-stare' him (4.2.40).

48–9 **whymsed . . . conundroun'd** Burton puts whimsy and crotchet together to describe 'Symptoms of the Minde', but not until the 1638 edition: 'that crotchet, that whimsy, that fiction' (p. 187). Ford's is the only use of 'conundroun'd' (cited as 'conundrumed') in *OED*, or full text *EEBO*; there were many variant spellings of 'conundrum' at this time, but as Hill suggests this may be another creative malapropism suggesting drowning in madness. In combining it with 'crotchetted' Ford may be recalling Jonson, *Volpone*, 5.11.16–17: 'I must ha' my crotchets! | And my conundrums!' 'B.E.', *New Dictionary of the Canting Crew* (1699) defines 'Conundrums' as 'Whimms, Maggots, and such like'.

49 **crotchetted** made full of confusion; first usage in this sense in *OED*.

58 **monstrous and wise** a confused comic variant of 'monstrous wise', meaning 'exceedingly wise'.

74 **a** he, i.e. Meleander (Hill).

79 **wormewood** bitterness.

80 **usher . . . extremity** precursor to an acute state of his condition.

83 **out-stare** *OED* cites a similar use by Marston, *Antonio's Revenge*, ed. Gair, 3.5.15: 'I will | Outstare the terror of thy grim aspect.'

84–9 **range . . . Moles** for 'range', see note to 2.1.269; here the wandering is morally aimless. Ford combined ranging, pride (l. 87), stars (l. 88), and moles (l. 89) in a very similar way in *FCN* 1.3.30–2: 'A Divell of pride | Ranges in airy thoughts to catch a starre, | Whiles yee graspe mole-hils.'

85–8 adapting the proverb: here the rolling stone does gather moss, but it is worthless.

86–7 **gay . . . gay . . . Gay** often used to suggest empty showiness or promiscuity; cf. *WoE* 4.1.77–9: 'Men in gay clothes, whose backs are laden with Titles and Honours, are within far more crooked than I am.'

87–8 **buildings . . . starres** deriving ultimately from the Tower of Babel, 'whose top may reach unto heaven' (Genesis 11.4) and Martial 8.36.11 in praise of Domitian's palace, 'whose top strikes the constellations'.

92 **make . . . plenty** the more their souls are fed with the 'plenty' of blind worldly ambition, the less true sustenance they have.

93 **skimd . . . riots** taken off (and by implication eaten) the cream from the vomit of your debauchery.

94 **fat . . . felicity** gained no other reward.

97, 102 the dashes indicate actions by Meleander, probably first taking Cleophila by the hand, and then pushing her towards Amethus.

103–4 **There . . . distraction** Hill suggests an echo of *Lear* 4.6.174–5: 'matter and impertinency mixed, | Reason in madness', but the idea of sense or 'method' in madness is a commonplace, as shown by Polonius's use: 'Though this be madness, yet there is a method in't' (*Hamlet*, 2.2.205–6).

103 **This . . . horror** cf. *BH* 4.2.174: 'The sight is full of terror'.

106 **Save charge . . . in a nooke** Save the expense of a funeral by burying me in some obscure corner.

108 **whining** plaintive crying, used contemptuously for mourning; cf. Cuculus's similar false 'whining tune' (3.1.30).

110 **Carmen** carriers, carters.

110 **Foot-poasts** carriers of letters etc. on foot; cf. *LT* 1.1.4–5: 'I am no foot-poast, | No pedlar of Avisos'.

110 **Apes** fools, mimics.

112 **hal'd** dragged in.

113–14 **Like . . . trappings** tilts, largely ceremonial jousts between elaborately armoured riders on richly caparisoned horses, were held in Horse Guards Parade on the Accession Days of Elizabeth and James I. The last had taken place in 1624.

114 **scorne . . . teares** as Hill says, a 'forceful ellipsis' which either refers back to the pomp of funerals which 'make a mockery of tears which are in any case unavailing' or simply means 'I have nothing but scorn for useless tears.'

120–2 **'tis too early . . . more hereafter** The combination of a refusal to weep with heartbreak and madness is strongly reminiscent of *Lear* 2.4.283–6: 'No, I'll not weep. | I have full cause of weeping, but this heart | Shall break into a hundred thousand flaws | Or ere I'll weep. O Fool, I shall go mad!'

121 **revell** Hill suggests 'be freely expressed', but this is a bitter paradox in which Meleander sees his sorrows celebrating by making him break his heart fully, rather than just 'a little'.

124 **respectively** judiciously (*OED*, †2b).

124–5 **Few . . . Orations** proverbial, found in a form close to this in Anthony Munday's versified collection of commonplaces, *Belvedere, or, The Garden of the Muses* (1600), p. 172: 'Few words among the wise have greater grace, | Than long Orations with unskilfulnes.' Cf. the Latin proverb 'vir sapit qui pauca loquitur' and Ecclesiastes 5.2, 'therefore let thy words be few'.

142–3 **Your . . . passion** cf. the similar conceit in Thomas May, trans. *Lucans Pharsalia* (1631), Book 9, p. 127: 'Mine eyes are guilty of a fathers death'.

145–6 **part . . . heart** T. W. Craik's suggestion that Ford's copy read 'heart' to rhyme with 'part' is strongly supported by the fact that not only do all other acts in *LM* end in a rhyme, but so do all those in *BH, PW, SD, TQ,* and *WoE* and all but one in *LS*. A compositor's or copyist's misreading of 'heart' as 'truth', especially in a secretary hand, is possible, if not particularly likely.

146 **Still** on both occasions in this line, the normal 17th-century meaning of 'always' is primary.

3.1

0.1–2 *blacke . . . Feather* Linthicum, *Costume*, p. 221, writes that 'Feathers "peakyng" on top of their heads were desired by both men and women' and a 'hat with a feather, and a sword were named as the requisites of a gallant in *What You Will* (III.1.26).' But here the combination is clearly intended to be risibly outmoded; Shirley, *The Triumph of Peace* (1634), seems to present them as both comic and 'old fashioned' in the costume of the antimasquer

'*Opinion* in an old fashioned doublet of black velvet, and trunk hose, a short cloak of the same with an antique cape, a black velvet cap pinched up, with a white fall' (*Works*, vol. 6, p. 257). 'Fall' here may mean either feather or collar (*OED*, 23a and c), but it seems to be 'with' the cap.

1–2 **Youth . . . Youth** for 'of the Trim' see note to 1.3.2; the designation of the 'Anticke' Cuculus as an 'old youth' is repeated by Kala at 4.1.81.

2 **crosse-gartered** in an earlier period, the costume of a lover and a courtier: see M. C. Linthicum, 'Malvolio's Cross-Gartered Yellow Stockings', *MP* 27 (1925), 87–93, pp. 92–3. By 1628 they would have been very old-fashioned. See also Introduction, p. 221.

7 **looke bigge** see note to 2.2.27.

8 **creature . . . livery** a horse stabled and provided with fodder was so described, but the phrase was also used for servants, 'creature' making it especially demeaning.

23–5 The dashes indicate pauses emphasizing Grilla's sexual innuendo in these lines. There may also have been some physical stage business. There is no evidence of 'conceit' as slang for 'vagina', but cf. Partridge, *Shakespeare's Bawdy* (1968) *s.v.* 'conceive'. Grilla may have lingered suggestively on the first syllable pronounced as 'cun'. The ostensible meaning is 'estimation'.

23 **Magot** (1) a whimsy, 'a maggot in the brain'; (2) the small larva which threatens to 'creepe in . . . To the least wrinckle of a Gentlewomans . . . good conceit'. For the grotesque phallic suggestion of the latter, cf. Marvell, *To His Coy Mistress*, 27–8: 'then worms shall try | That long preserved virginity' (*Poems* ed. Smith, 2003, p. 82).

27 **cod . . . Cat** the sac of sweet-smelling musk taken (in this case) from the anal pouch of the civet-cat, much used in perfumes.

30–1 **whining . . . speech** stereotypical behaviour of the melancholy lover; cf. *Love's Labour's Lost* 3.1.180–2: 'Dan Cupid, | Regent of love-rhymes, lord of folded arms, | Th' anointed sovereign of sighs and groans'; and *Two Gentlemen of Verona*, 2.1.18–26: 'first, you have learn'd, like Sir Proteus, to wreathe your arms, like a malecontent; to relish a love-song, like a robin-redbreast; to walk alone, like one that had the pestilence; to sigh, like a school-boy that had lost his A B C; to weep, like a young wench that had buried her grandam . . . to speak puling, like a beggar at Hallowmas.'

31–6 **Even . . . outright** 'this absurd comparison mocks both Cuculus and the euphuistic style from which it derives' (Hill). Like those of Pelias, Cuculus's literary models are extremely old-fashioned. If he did recall Hynd's *Eliosto Libidinoso* when he wrote *LM* (see Introduction, p. 224), Ford would have remembered many similar speeches there.

33–6 **gorge . . . outright** a nonsensically inflated piece of love rhetoric, meaning something like 'the throat [or stomach] of my affections, being crammed full with the tumults of your sorrowing, tickles me with the goad all over, and [produces] the sympathetic reaction of howling aloud'. 'Prick' already had the meaning 'penis' as well as 'goad'.

37 we Gifford suggests a misprint for 'she', but throughout these exchanges Grilla is taking on the persona of the mistress addressed, so this must be the impersonal 'we' (*OED*, 2b).

40–3 snuffe . . . breath both associated with bad smells; Cade's breath 'stinkes with eating toasted cheese' in *2 Henry VI*, 4.7.12; Nashe, *The Terrors of the Night*, writes of quacks who 'of tosted cheese and candles endes, temper up a fewe oyntments and sirrups' (*Works*, ed. R. B. McKerrow, 5 vols (1904–10), I.364), but does not specify wearing them against the heart.

44 Hay-ho Heigh-ho, commonly used for a sigh of disappointment, often of a melancholy lover; cf. *Much Ado*, 3.4.53–4: 'By my troth, I am exceeding ill. Heigh-ho!'

46 Have at thee a challenge to begin the next impersonation; cf. 1.2.109; *Love's Labour's Lost* 4.3.286: 'Have at you then, affection's men at arms.'

49 loud-mouth'd although *OED* cites this as the first usage, full text *EEBO* gives many examples from 1595 on, including 'lowde mouthed Cannons' (Anon., *The Mariage of Prince Fredericke, and the Kings Daughter*, 1613, sig. A4v). There is again sexual innuendo in the image.

52 Divell . . . Dam the devil or his sexual partner; cf. *Comedy of Errors*, 4.3.50–1: '*S. Ant.* It is the devil. *S. Dro.* Nay, she is worse, she is the devil's dam.'

55 Ac—count The dash indicates a pause as Cuculus throws weight on the obscene pun of the second syllable. As Hill notes, innuendo continues in ll. 56 and 60–4.

58–9 strong Lines a new phrase (*OED*'s first citation is 1627) describing pejoratively the conceits of 'metaphysical' poetry, hence misused here.

63 backe dore Hill notes the obscene sense in Marston, *Insatiate Countess*, ed. Melchiori, 2.2.68–70: '*Thais.* But you mean they shall come in at the back-doors? | *Abig.* Who, our husbands? Nay, and they come not in at the fore-doors, there will be no pleasure in't.'

64 Tatter-demallians persons in tattered clothes; a relatively new term (first *OED* citation 1608).

65 one—art the dash indicates a pause, and perhaps some stage business in the original production.

66 S'foot abbreviation of 'God's foot'.

66 roaring 'noisy, boisterous, or rowdy conduct' (*OED*, roaring *n.* 1†2).

67 big haughty, pompous (*OED*, 10).

67 cue humour, disposition. Hill notes that the 'connection with French "queue" (O.Fr. "cue") suggests . . . the common bawdy pun on tail'.

69 **Pish** expression of contempt, very common in Ford; cf. Amethus's use at 5.1.75.

70 **Conquerour** (1) King William I; (2) continuing the sexual innuendo, 'con-que-ror' (Hill).

71 **no— thing** the vagina.

72 **rare** (1) unusual; (2) undercooked.

76 *Helicon* mountain where in Greek myth the springs of Agannipe and Hippocrene sacred to the Muses were located.

79 **goody** *Whiske* 'goodwife Whipper-snapper' (see *OED*, whisk†6 'A whipper-snapper', citing this as first example). *Q*'s 'good'ee' is the only recorded spelling thus between 1550 and 1650 in *EEBO* fully keyed texts. Ford used 'godee-madam' in *The Fancies*. 'Goody' was the common 16th-century form.

79 **Trumperies** nonsense.

82 **Doodles** foolish people; again, *OED* cites this as the first usage; this is supported by full-text *EEBO*.

83 **Device** masque.

85 **Droane-like** like a drone bee, i.e. idle and unproductive.

90 **downe-tumbles** *OED*, down-tumble *v.* cites this as first and only example.

93 **art** skill as a doctor.

95 **the cause** of Palador's 'distemper' (see 2.1.26–9).

97–101 **humours . . . Monsters** Aretus's question reflects the conventional medical view which saw melancholy as a disease of physiological origin which affected the brain, heart, and other organs, caused by an imbalance of the humours, usually an excess of black bile (see *To the Author*, l. 1 and note).

99 **alteration** disorder; cf. Burton, *Anatomy*, 1.2.2.3: 'strange meats, though pleasant, cause notable alterations and distempers'.

102–12 *Melancholy . . .* **Affection** though his marginal note to Burton as 'Democritus Junior' is placed against ll. 107–9 Ford derived this whole speech from Burton, and must have intended his note to acknowledge this.

102–4 *Melancholy . . .* **disease** for comment on this see Introduction, pp. 213–14.

104–7 **So . . .** *Melancholy* Burton distinguishes most of these categories from melancholy in *Anatomy*, 1.1.1.3 and 1.1.1.4, listing 'such [diseases] as properly belong to the *Phantasie*, or *Imagination*, or *Reason* it selfe . . . which are three or foure in number, *Frensye, Madnes, Melancholy, Dotage*'. In his 'Definition of Melancholy. Name, Difference' (1.1.3.1), he shows how the rest 'differ' (l. 97) from melancholy.

104 **Extasie** in the 1620 and 1624 editions Burton only mentions ecstasy briefly as a temporary state of possession, but he elaborates in 1628 in the passage in *Anatomy*, 1.1.1.4, on which Ford is drawing for other species of

mental illness: 'Of this fury there be divers kindes, *Exstasie*, which is familiar with some persons, as *Cardan* saith of himself, he could be in one when he list; in which the *Indian* priests deliver their oracles, and the witches in Lapland . . . answere all questions in an Exstasis you will aske, what your friendes doe, where they are, how they fare, &c. The other species of this fury are *Enthusiasms, Revelations, & Visions . . .*'.

105 **Fantastick Dotage** for Burton, melancholy involves 'dotage' not in the modern sense of senility but as an abnormal mental condition (reflecting its origins in 'dote'), but without a fever. It occurs when 'some one principal faculty of the mind, as imagination, or reason, is corrupted' (*Anatomy*). Ford may have intended 'Fantastick Dotage' to signify a fevered or otherwise hal- lucinatory variety (*OED*, fantasy, 3a) differing from melancholy.

105 **Madnesse** '*Madnesse* is therefore defined to be a vehement *Dotage*, or raving without a fever, farre more violent then *Melancholy*, full of anger, and clamor, horrible lookes, actions, gestures . . . without all feare and sorrow [the latter subsequently described as "the true Characters, and inseparable companions of *Melancholy*"] with such impetuous force, and boldnesse, that sometimes three or foure men cannot hold them. Differing onely in this from *Frensie*, that it is without a Fever, and their Memory is most part better' (*Anatomy*, 1.1.1.4).

105 **Phrenzey** '*Phrenitis*, [margin "Phrensie"] is a Disease of the Minde, with a continuall Madnesse or Dotage, which hath an acute fever annexed, . . . It differs from *Melancholy* and *Madnesse*, because their Dotage is without an ague: this continuall, with waking, or Memory decayed &c. *Melancholy* is most part silent; this clamorous' (*Anatomy*, 1.1.1.4). Cf. Corax's diagnosis of Meleander as not suffering the 'madnesse' of frenzy but 'sorrow's | Close griping griefe, and anguish of the soule' (4.2.10–13).

105–6 **Rupture . . . imagination** Burton does not use 'rupture', but in the chapter defining melancholy which Ford draws on throughout this speech (1.1.3.1) he writes of the imagination being 'corrupted': 'We properly call that Dotage . . . when some one principall faculty of the minde, as Imagination, or Reason is corrupted.'

108 **meere . . . minde** cf. *Anatomy* 1.1.3.1: '*Haliabbas* simply cals it a commo- tion of the mind.'

108–12 **o're-charg'd . . . Affection** cf. *Anatomy*, 1.1.3.2: 'Feare and Sorrow, which are passions, are seated in the Heart . . . but forasmuch as this malady is caused by precedent Imagination, and the Appetite, to whom Spirits obey, are subject to those principall parts, the Braine must needs be primarily mis- affected, as the seate of Reason, and then the Heart, as the seate of Affection.' For more detailed treatment of sorrow and fear as causes of melancholy see *Anatomy*, 1.2.3.4 and 1.2.3.5; cf. du Laurens, *Discourse*, ch. 5 on 'feare, sadnes, watchings, fearefull dreames, and other Symptomes' (pp. 89–96); Bright, *Treatise*, ch. 17, 'How melancholy procureth feare, sadnes, dispaire, and such other passions' (pp. 101–10). The common emphasis on fear and sorrow is from Hippocrates: 'Fear or depression that is prolonged means melancholia' (*Aphorisms*, 6.23).

113–16 Infinite . . . causes cf. *Anatomy*, 1.1.3.5: '*Savanorola* . . . will have the kinds [of melancholy] to be infinite . . . and so doth *Arculanus* interpret himselfe: Infinite species and symptomes'.

116 anguish of the minde cf. *Anatomy*, 1.1.3.1: 'The *summum genus* [all inclusive characteristic] is *Dotage*, or *Anguish of the Mind*, saith Areteus'. Du Laurens defines melancholy as 'a kinde of dotage without any serue [sorrow = injury], having for his ordinarie companions, feare and sadnes, without any apparant occasion' (pp. 86–7).

117–18 as . . . impossible cf. *Anatomy*, 1.2.1.1: 'those cures must needes be unperfect & lame to no purpose, wherein the causes have not first beene searched . . . Fernelius puts a kinde of necessity in the knowledge of the causes, and without which it is impossible to cure, or to prevent any manner of disease.'

123 discover either 'reveal', suggesting that Corax has already made his tentative diagnosis, and intends to use the masque to confirm it; or 'find out' the cause of Palador's melancholy. Both meanings were current (*OED*, 2a, 6).

3.2

5 betroth our selves Even without a witness, betrothal by a vow taken together would have been a semi-binding legal contract, made irrevocable when sexual intercourse took place. Hence Eroclea's alarmed response. The contract between Eroclea and Palador had been a formal, public one: see note to 2.1.165.

6 violent impassioned, of speech (*OED*, 9a), but the dialogue also suggests a physical advance by Kala which Eroclea rebuffs.

8 stand on points be punctilious about details, here of betrothal; Kala does not want to wait for any ceremony before its sexual consummation. Cf. *Midsummer Night's Dream*, 5.1.118: 'This fellow doth not stand upon points.'

9–10 you . . . not cf. *FCN* 4.1.54–5: 'Trust me, I must not, will not, dare not; | Surely I cannot for my promise past'.

11 Gelding eunuch; still used of persons at this date (*OED*, †1).

12 prate inform, tell tales; cf. *Macbeth*, 2.1.58: 'The very stones prate of my whereabout'.

14–15 a kind heart . . . undoe me The idea of being damaged by having a kind heart is semi-proverbial; see e.g. Nashe, *Christ's Tears* (*Works*, 2.94): 'he is undone by trusting Gentlemen; his kind heart hath made him a begger'.

17 **a greene-sicknesse-liver'd Boy** echoing *Anatomy*, 3.2.3.1, where Burton describes symptoms of love melancholy: 'the Liver doth not performe his part, nor turnes the aliment into blood as it ought, and for that cause the members are weake for want of sustenance, they are leane and pine away, as the hearbs in my garden doe this month of May for want of raine. The greene sicknesse for this cause often happeneth to young women, a Cachexia [malnutrition], or an evil habit to men.' Cf. also *2 Henry IV*, 4.3.91–4: 'thin drink doth so over-cool their blood, and making many fish-meals, that they fall into a kind of male green-sickness; and then, when they marry, they get wenches.' Green sickness was either a form of anaemia or anorexia, usually associated with young women.

18–19 **My . . . mouldy** cf. *All's Well*, 1.1.153–63.

19 **her** Thamasta's.

23 **ingag'd** ensnared; cf. *FCN* 5.1.48–9: 'Those ties of nature . . . How much they doe engage.'

25 **respect** consideration.

32 **passages** parts of a conversation.

33 **intelligence** information.

37 **straggler** tramp or vagabond (*OED*, 1), with the suggestion of an inter-loper (*OED*, †3); Ford uses it again for Eroclea (3.2.191), and for Perkin Warbeck (*PW*, 2.3.35).

40 **Honest . . . honest** *Kala* recalling the epithet of another deceitful servant 'most honest' Iago (*Othello*, 2.3.6), 'honest Iago' (1.3.294, 2.3.177, 5.2.72) and 'honest, honest Iago' (5.2.134).

45–7 **Walke . . . courtship** Menaphon is probably guided through one of the doors in the tiring house screen, and goes up to the gallery from where he watches, but cannot hear (l. 31) the ensuing dialogue between Eroclea and Thamasta. When he returns at l. 188 he is unaware that Eroclea has been pleading his cause, and more importantly gives no sign that he has heard that she is 'not mankind' (l. 167). Ford may be recalling the episode in which Othello is tricked by Iago into misinterpreting the latter's conversation with Cassio, which he watches but cannot hear (*Othello*, 4.1.74–169).

51 **good turne** sexual intercourse: cf. Williams, *Dictionary*, *s.v.* 'turn', Partridge, *Shakespeare's Bawdy*, *s.v.* 'turn i' the bed'.

52 **shrewd** malignant, injurious.

56 **set of Faces** this is the only use of this phrase in full text *EEBO*, but for the idea of 'setting' the face in a mirror in order to dissemble, cf. John Squire, *A plaine exposition upon the first part of the second chapter of Saint Paul his second epistle to the Thessalonians* (1630), p. 632: 'they [Catholics] adde art to their audacious lyes. And as it were set their faces by a glasse, that they may be able to utter such vast lyes.' Cf. also Jonson's character Face in *The Alchemist*, who changes faces according to his role.

60 **turne . . . Snow-ball** make his courage melt away in the heat of love.

63 **hard construction** adverse interpretation.

73 **freedome** magnanimity.

77–87 **The . . . plants** again derived from the 1628 edition of Burton's *Anatomy*, 3.1.1.2: 'How comes a loadstone to draw iron to it, jet, chaff; the ground to covet showres, but for love? No creature, *S. Hierom* concludes, is to be found . . . no stock, no stone, that hath not some feeling of love. 'Tis more eminent in Plants, Hearbes, and is especially observed in vegetals; as betwixt the Vine and Elme a great sympathy; betwixt the Vine and the Cabbage, betwixt the Vine and Olive . . . betwixt the Vine and Bayes, a great Antipathy, the Vine loves not the Bay . . . the Olive and the Myrtle embrace each other, in roots and branches if they grow neere.' The loadstone and iron ('steel' in Ford) did not appear in the editions of 1620 or 1624.

78 **severall** separate.

88–93 **Consider this aright . . . to Fate** the examples of 'inanimate' attraction which Thamasta has just quoted from Burton belong to the lowest of the three essentially Aristotelian categories of love he describes, that of 'Natural love'; above this is 'Sensible love' (i.e. of the senses), the procreative or nurturing drive shared by animals and men, which is in turn lower than the highest 'rational love [which] . . . is proper to men, on which I must insist. This appeares in *God, Angels, Men*.' In aligning her impulses with a natural love dictated by a 'fate' to which she claims she must yield, Thamasta is degrading her love. For an extended discussion of the three divisions of the soul, see *Anatomy*, 1.1.2.5–11.

95 **sottish** stupid; cf. Burton, *Anatomy*, 1.2.3.14: 'Such are many sottish Princes brought into a fool's paradise by their parasites.'

96 **sensible** emotionally aware.

103 **know** recognize.

103 **slavery** ignoble behaviour; cf. *TPW*, 2.2.43–4: 'I have a spirit doth as much distaste | The slavery of fearing thee'.

104–9 **I . . . thiefe** Hill notes of Eroclea's reply: 'that she by contrast does acknowledge the force of vows and laws, is a clever rebuke.'

106 **friendship** with Menaphon.

111 **falsifie a faith** violate a bond (*OED*, falsify *v.* †5).

116 **free** magnanimous; cf. *Othello*, 3.3.199: 'your free and noble nature'.

120 **Declyn'd . . . soveraignty** 'Degraded your pre-eminence' or 'undermined your command'.

121–3 **that . . . name** Menaphon, the mirror in which Thamasta can judge her appearance more honourably and establish her name enduringly.

122 **Trim** dress, restore.

123 **idle** incoherent, foolish.

136 **destiny** harking back to the 'Fate' of l. 93; for a similar claim to be help-less in the hands of destiny, cf. *TPW* 1.2.228–9: ''tis my destiny, | That you must either love, or I must die.' Cf. also Olivia, *Twelfth Night*, 1.5.310–11: 'Fate, show thy force: ourselves we do not owe; | What is decreed must be; and be this so.'

137 **wonted** customary.

145–6 **For . . . reason** Eroclea emphasizes the rational nature of her plea, and thus of Menaphon's love, placing it in the highest of Burton's three cat-egories; see note to 3.2.88–93.

148 **intertainements** (1) supportive relationships, such as marriage; (2) reception in society.

152 **Fame** reputation.

155–6 **Charme . . . course** a spell strong enough to interrupt the vow she is making.

159 **mothers Doves** doves were sacred to Venus, the mother of Cupid.

160 **take** receive; cf. Jonson, *Alchemist*, 4.1.111: 'And take a secret, too'.

163–6 **if . . . unstain'd** quoting Thamasta's words at 3.2.65–8 verbatim.

167 **mankind** masculine; cf. *LT*, 2.2.8–10: 'Sir, consider, | My sex, were I mankinde, my sword should quit | A wounded honour'.

169 **printed** written; cf. *Titus Andronicus*, 4.1.75: 'Heaven guide thy pen to print thy sorrows plain'.

170 **unforg'd relation** genuine story.

176 **venture . . . secrecy** 'to stake it [honour] on that which is your secret'; cf. *BH* 2.3.10–11: 'I'm not inquisitive | Of secresies without an invitation.'

176–80 **It . . . dearly** this is partly a plot device to prevent the knowledge of Eroclea's identity spreading too early, but also an example of the way Ford's interest in the psychology of Thamasta's response eclipses the simpler treat-ment of such revelations in earlier comedy and tragicomedy.

180–1 **You . . . servant** apparently agreeing to play the part of Thamasta's male lover (cf. the epithet used for Menaphon in this role: 1.3.62, 187, 191; 4.1.27), but perhaps simply meaning that she will be at her service.

189 **I come—** the dash indicates his shocked pause; since Menaphon has watched but not heard the encounter between Eroclea and Thamasta (see note to 3.2.45–7) his surprise is contrived.

196 **Ile . . . distraction** seek to lose my senses (Hill).

202–3 **I . . . heart** cf. *LoC* 2.1.251–2 'Out of mine eyes, | As farre as I have throwne thee from my heart'.

205 **Jewell** Menaphon calls Eroclea a 'jewell' at his first mention of her (1.1.91, 93).

205 **under wing** under Thamasta's protection.

206 **Boy— Boy** T. W. Craik makes the plausible suggestion that this should read 'by -- by—': 'Menaphon means to utter an oath, but his anger chokes his speech. After "youth" in the preceding line "boy" is incongruous.' But this does not justify changing *Q*'s defensible reading. Cf. also Aufidius's insulting 'thou boy of tears!' (*Coriolanus*, 5.6.100).

207 **naught** in vain, useless.

3.3

0.1 ***Paper-plot*** Scene by scene outline of a play on one or two sides of paper, giving actors and stagehands brief details of characters, properties, and effects required. For a good example, see https://lostplays.folger.edu/Dead_Man%27s_Fortune,_The (accessed 21 Feb. 2023); for a print version of a plot, see *A Shakespeare Encyclopaedia*, ed. O. J. Campbell, pp. 643–4.

5 **quab** *OED*, quab *n.*² †2 suggests 'a crude or shapeless thing', based entirely on this example, linking it unconvincingly to the name of such small fish as the miller's thumb (quab *n.*² 1); it was also (quab *n.*¹) a marshy area. Gifford, who came from the same area of South Devon as Ford, explained it in the 1820s as an 'unfledged bird, a nestling: metaphorically, any thing in an imperfect, unfinished state. In the first sense, the word is still used in that part of Devonshire where Ford was born'. In this sense it was perhaps a variant of 'squab'; this is supported by 'M.H.', *The Young Cooks Monitor* (1683), p. 41, a recipe for stewing pigeons: 'Take six quab Pidgeons . . .'.

7 **humorous** peevish, easily offended.

11–12 **We . . . then** Aretus again speaks for those who do not fully understand the fine distinctions of Burtonian melancholy: 'The common sort define [melancholy] to be *a kinde of dotage, without any feaver, having for his ordinary companions, feare and sadnesse, without any apparant occasion*' (*Anatomy*, 1.1.3.1).

12 **sadnesse** sorrow or dullness, as suggested by Burton's 'feare and sadnesse', which elsewhere in the *Anatomy* is 'feare and sorrow', and by Corax's statement (l. 15) that 'dulnesse' is not the only symptom of melancholy.

13 **severall changes** a number of different variations. All the forms of melancholy represented in the masque, other than hypochondria (which Burton deals with later), are briefly discussed in *Anatomy*, 1.1.1.3 and 4; see notes to 3.1.95–8.

14 **aswell** commonly spelled as one word at this date.

14 **Apish Phrensey** ape-like irrational behaviour; cf. 4.2.133.

15 **Laughter and mirth** cf. *Anatomy* 1.3.1.3: 'They are much inclined to laughter, witty and merry, concepted in discourse, pleasant, if they bee not farre gone, much given to musicke, dancing, and to bee in womens company.'

17 **In kind** according to their general class; first usage in this sense in *OED*.

19 **sound . . . entrance** in the Blackfriars this might have been played on a cornett, as opposed to the trumpet and/or drum used in the Globe.

19.1 *Anatomy*, 1.1.1.4, describes a lycanthrope: 'a poore Husband-man, that still haunted about graves, and kept in Churchyards, of a pale, blacke, ugly, and fearefull looke.' For lycanthropy on stage, see Webster, *Duchess of Malfi*, 5.2.7–21.

19.1 *shag* shaggy; cf. *LT*, 3.1.51–3: 'Blesse us, a monster . . . a' has chang'd | Haire with a shagge dogge'.

20–3 **Bow . . . midnight** cf. *Anatomy*, 1.1.1.4: 'Woolfe madnesse, when men runne howling about graves and fields in the night, and will not be per-swaded but that they are Wolves . . . They lye hid most part all day, & goe abroad in the night, barking, howling at graves'.

26.1.1 *Crowne of feathers* not mentioned by Burton; it signified a frivolous or empty authority, as suggested by Nathaniel Bacon, *The Continuation of an Historicall Discourse of the Government of England* (1651), p. 137: 'if wee looke upon this title of the Kingdomes Guardianship in its bare lineaments, without lights and shadows, it will appeare little better then a Crown of feathers worne onely for bravery, and in nothing adding to the real ability of the governing part of this Nation.'

26.1 *Antickly* grotesquely; cf. *Much Ado*, 5.1.96: 'Go anticly, show outward hideousness'.

28 **was . . . Emperour** though Burton does not mention grandiose delu-sions in the section on hydrophobia (1.1.1.4), writing on 'The Force of Imagination' (1.2.3.2) he does make the association: 'in Hydrophobia they seeme to see the picture of a Dog, still in their [*sic*] water . . . melancholy men, and sicke men conceave so many phantasticall visions . . . and have so many absurd suppositions, as that they are Kings . . .'. Cf. *Anatomy*, 1.3.1.4: 'If an ambitious man become melancholy, he forthwith thinks he is a King, an Emperour'. He does not mention jealousy (ll. 32–4) as a symptom, but calls hydrophobia 'a kinde of Madnesse . . . which comes by the biting of a mad dogge' (l. 28) and Ford uses these symptoms to illustrate this 'madness'.

30–2 **It . . . looking-glasses** cf. *Anatomy*, 1.1.1.4: 'the parties affected, cannot endure the sight of water . . . they beginne to rave, flye water, and glasses'.

38.1 PHILOSOPHER One actor must have doubled as either the Philosopher or the Sea-Nymph (72.1.1), since they are the seventeenth and eighteenth named parts with a list of only seventeen actors. Hill suggests Kala may have played the nymph, but acknowledges the problem that she appears in the preceding and succeeding scenes; Meleander, Cleophila, and Trollio, however, had not been onstage since 2.2, and do not appear again until 4.2. One of these, probably Cleophila or Trollio, could have doubled in either of these parts, with the seventeenth named actor (probably Baxter or Gough) playing the other part.

38.1 *copper chaine* a cheap substitute for a gold one; thus a sign of poverty.

38.1–2 *old . . . Gowne* Hill suggests this is derived from Ascham's description of a man who, wishing to be like Sir Thomas More, copied him by wearing his gown 'awry upon the one shoulder' (*The Whole Works of Roger Ascham*, ed. Dr. Giles, 4 vols. (1865), 3.252–3). In the 1624 and later editions of the *Anatomy*, Burton writes of the scholar's 'old torne gowne, an ensigne of his infelicity' (1.2.3.15).

39–43 **Philosophers . . . perfect** some aspects of the Philosopher are based on the mythologized life and doctrines of Empedocles. In Lucian's dialogue *Icaromenippus, or The Sky-Man* Empedocles tells Menippus 'now I dwell in the moon' (13); achievement of purification and perfection (cf. ll. 41–43) through reincarnation was central to his philosophy.

39–41 **Speculation . . . pit** in *Icaromenippus* Menippus condemns the 'speculation and theory' of philosophers who were 'so far from ridding me of my old-time ignorance that they plunged me forthwith into even greater perplexities' (5) and who introduce him to atheism (9). Burton also says 'hatred and contempt of Learning proceeds out of Ignorance' (1.2.3.15).

43 **poverty . . . soule** Burton makes a number of similar statements in 2.3.3, 'Against Poverty and Want'.

45–7 *Delirium . . . merit* cf. *Anatomy*, 1.2.3.14: 'Another kinde of mad men there is . . . that are insensibly madde, and knowe not of it, such as contemne all praise and glory, and thinke themselves most free; when as indeed they are most mad: . . . a company of *Cynicks,* such as are Monkes, Hermites, Anachorites, that contemne the world, contemne themselves, contemne all titles, honors, offices: & yet in that contempt, are more proud then any man living whatsoever. They are proud of humility proud in that they are not proud . . . as *Diogenes* . . . they bragge inwardly, & feed themselves fat with a selfe conceit of sanctity.'

47 **1 not dislike** cf. 1.3.39 and note.

47.1 *rich Gowne* splendid, costly dress.

47.1–2 *Vardingale . . . Ruffe* the farthingale was a dress held out over a framework of whalebone hoops, the ruff a frill round the neck; see Linthicum, *Costume*, pp. 161, 182 on both being unfashionable by this date, worn mainly by country women.

47.2 *Coxcombe* a fool's cap, shaped like a cock's comb.

48 **forsooth . . . forsooth** in Jonson's *Poetaster* (1601) the goldsmith's wife Chloe is warned not to use 'your city-mannerly word "forsooth"' at court (4.3.25–6).

49 **Gaffer** a respectful term of address associated with rusticity; significantly it is also used by Roseilli when pretending to be a fool in *LS* 2.2.215: 'a clap cheek for nown sake, gaffer'.

49 **shough** rough haired lapdog; cf. *Macbeth*, 3.1.92–3: 'spaniels, curs, | Shoughs, water-rugs . . .'.

50 **busse** kiss; cf. *TPW* 3.5.36: 'Lass, pretty lass, come buss lass'.

50 **pum** Not in *OED* or full text *EEBO*. Hill plausibly suggests a childish 'lisping pronunciation' of 'plum'.

52 *Phrenitis* see note to 3.1.105 for Burton's definition. He does not associate it with women, or with pride (l. 49).

53.1 *Bedlam* madman. See *OED*, †5: 'An inmate of Bethlehem Hospital, London, or of a lunatic asylum, or one fit for such a place'; cf. *PW* 2.3.31–2: 'Let me be a dotard, | A bedlam, a poor sot'.

54–8 *They . . . heere* perhaps reflecting Burton's mixed feelings about tobacco: '*Tobacco*, divine, rare, superexcellent *Tobacco*, which goes farre beyond all their Panaceas, potable gold, and Philosophers stones, a soveraigne Remedy to all diseases. A good vomit I confesse, a vertuous herbe if it be well qualified, opportunely taken, & medicinally used, but as it is commonly abused by most men, which take it as Tinkars doe ale, 'tis a plague, a mischiefe, a violent purger of goods, lands, health, hellish, divelish and damned *Tobacco*, the ruine & overthrow of Body and Soule' (2.4.2.1). The association with hell was predictably commonplace.

54 *drinke* smoking tobacco was often described as 'drinking' it, as in Dekker, *Shoemakers Holiday*, 3.2.51: 'Mistris, wil you drinke a pipe of Tobacco?'

55 *to . . . well* cf. *Anatomy* 2.3.2: 'take tobacco with a grace'.

59 **soope . . . up** apparently meaning scoop up; not in *OED*, but see John Wilkins, *A Discourse Concerning a New World & Another Planet* (1640) on the '*great Ruck in Madagascar* . . . the feathers in whose wings are twelve foot long, which can soope up a horse and his rider, or an elephant'.

60 **catch . . . canst** 'catch me if you can', a children's game like tag.

61 **house** college.

62 *rumbling* 'rumbling in the guts' is a symptom of 'Hypocondriacall or windy melancholy' (*Anatomy*, 'Synopsis of the First Partition', and 1.3.2.2) because of the flatulence that accompanies hypochondria (l. 65).

63 *Gobblings* goblins and hobgoblins recur in Burton; 'Humorous' melancholics (1628 and subsequent editions) 'sometimes thinke verily they heare and see present before their eyes such phantasmes or goblins, they feare, suspect, or conceave, they still talke with, and follow them' (1.3.1.2). Cf. Bright, *Treatise*, p. 103 on fantasies of 'counterfet goblins'. In this case, the madman thinks they are inside him.

63 *tumbling* accounting for his 'rumbling'. Goblins seem to have been associated with acrobatic tumbling; in an anonymous satire of 1648, *Rombus the Moderator: or, The King Restored*, the army grandees 'shall be called the society of Goblins; you shall practice tumbling' (p. 12). Burton records

hypochondriacs taking a marginally more rational approach to what they believed to be causing their rumblings: 'Trallianus relates a story of a woman that imagined she had swallowed an Eele or a serpent; & Faelix Platerus . . . hath a most memorable example of a country man of his, that in the Spring-time by chance falling into a pit where frogs & frogs-spawn was, & a little of that water swallowed, began to suspect that he had likewise swallowed frog-spawn, and with that conceipt and feare, his phantasy wrought so far, that he verily thought he had yong live frogs in his bellie' (*Anatomy*, 1.3.2.2).

65 *roare* for a similar transitive use see *FCN* 5.1.30–1: 'Fiddle, and play your pranks amongst your neighbours, | That all the towne may roare ye'.

67 **Bounce** 'The loud burst of noise produced by an explosion' (*OED*, bounce, *n.*[1] †2). It may thus have been slang for breaking wind, here as a result of hypochondria; see *Huloets Dictionarie* (1572) [English, Latin, French], '*Cracke, bounce, farte, sounde, or a thumpe*. Crepitus, us. m. g. *Craquement*'.

68 *Hypocondriacall* not related to the modern meaning of imagining or exaggerating illness, but derived from the parts of the abdomen under the ribs, containing the 'hypochondries', including the liver and spleen, sources of melancholy humours.

68–72 *Hypocondriacall* **. . . it** Burton says, 'Hypocondriacall or flatuous melancholy . . . is in my judgement the most grievous and frequent' and that 'most commonly feare, griefe, and some sudden commotion, or perturbation of the minde beginnes it' (*Anatomy*, 1.2.5.4). He does not specify being over-curious or losing goods or friends, but he puts the latter two together in 1.2.4.7: 'Losse of friends, and losse of goods, makes many men melancholy', and in 3.4.2.3, on despair: 'Losse of goods, losse of friends, and those lesser griefes doe sometimes effect it'.

70 **animall parts** responsible for sensation and voluntary movement: 'The Animall Spirits are formed of the Vitall, brought up to the Braine, and dif-fused by the Nerves, to the other Members, give sence and motion to them all' (*Anatomy*, 1.1.1.2).

71 **over-curious** excessively fastidious.

72 **feare, or sorrowes** see 3.1.108–12 note.

72.1 *SEA-NIMPH* For the possibility that this part was taken by the actor play-ing Cleophila or Trollio, see note to 3.3.38.1.

72.1 *big-bellied . . . dancing* see Burton, quoted in note to 3.3.86–8.

78 *tawe . . . hides* soften leather skins by beating; Craik's suggestion of 'tawe' in place of *Q*'s 'tame' fits the context perfectly.

80 *bang* thrash.

83 *sport* OED, *v.* 4†a. 'to play or toy with', often, as here, with a sexual meaning.

83 *Topsaile advance* get under full speed. As Hill notes, the combination of 'big-bellied' and the sail may echo *Midsummer Night's Dream*, 2.1.128–9,

where 'the sails conceive | And grow big-bellied with the wanton wind'.
'Great bellyed' is in Ford's immediate source in Burton (see note to 3.3.86–7).

85 **A Dance . . . a Dance** though headed 'All' it is the masquers who shout
this, and who perform the dance and run out at 3.3.89.1–2.

86–8 **This is the *Wanton Melancholy* . . . ceasing** Burton's description of
this compulsion to dance comes in *Anatomy*, 1.1.1.4 immediately after his
treatment of the other subjects of this masque (except hydrophobia, for
which see notes to 3.3.28). He does not call it 'Wanton Melancholy', but
heads it '*Chorus sancti Viti*, or Saint Vitus dance the lascivious dance
Paracelsus cals it, because they that are taken with it, can doe nothing but
dance till they be dead . . . 'Tis strange to heare how long they will dance, and
in what maner, over stooles, formes, tables, even great bellyed women sometimes (and yet never hurt their childe) will dance so long, that they can stirre
neither hand nor foot, but seeme to be quite dead. One in red clothes they
cannot abide. Musick above all things they love.'

91 **invention** the masque.

91 **deceives** perplexes; not in *OED* in this sense. Palador is still holding the
'paper-plot' (3.3.0.1), which was divided into two columns, with each scene
described briefly in a ruled box. Corax has left one box empty.

94 **shadow . . . Fancy** emphasizing the elusive nature of Love Melancholy:
'shadow' is not a simple image, as Hill suggests, but an insubstantial and
possibly deceptive one, while a 'fancy' is a product of the imagination.

94 *Love-Melancholy* the title of the third of the three 'Partitions' of Burton's
Anatomy, and by far his longest treatment of a specific type of melancholy.

98 **great** cf. Thamasta as 'great-spirited', 1.1.190.

100 **lymne** paint.

101 **proper sufferance** particular suffering.

103–5 **Love . . . madnesse** echoing several passages of the 1628 *Anatomy*,
most relevant are 3.2.1.2: '*How Love tyranniseth over men* . . . You have heard
how this tyrant Love rageth with brute beasts and spirits; now let us consider
what passions it causeth amongst men . . . Love indeed (I may not deny) first
united Provinces, built citties, and by a perpetuall generation makes and preserves mankind, propagates the Church; but if it rage it is no more love, but
burning lust, a disease, Phrensie, Madnesse, Hell . . . either out of their own
weaknesse, a depraved nature, or love's tyranny, which so furiously rageth,
they suffer themselves to bee led like an ox to the slaughter: they goe downe
headlong to their own perdition'; and 3.2.3: 'The major part of lovers are
carried headlong like so many brute beasts, reason counsells one way, thy
friends, fortunes, shame, disgrace, danger, and an Ocean of cares that will
certainely follow; yet this furious lust *precipitates*, counterpoiseth, weighs
down one the other: though it be their utter undoing, perpetuall infamy,
losse, yet they will do it'.

106 **toucht home . . . throughly** deeply affected, overwhelmed throughout; 'touch home' is not in *OED*, but cf. David Blake, *An Exposition Uppon the Thirtie Two* [sic] *Psalme* (1600), p. 6: 'that reverence, that admonitions & rebukes wrought in the Primitive congregations of the Church, when men being touched home, fell upon their faces'.

110 **perfect Arts-man** complete Scholar, but with a suggestion of magician; *OED* cites Gabriel Harvey, *Marginalia*: 'Owr vulgar Astrologers, especially such, as ar commonly termed Cunning men or Artsmen. Sum call them wissards.' Ford uses it to mean a painter at 5.2.95, and in *LS* 2.2.82.

111 **Panthers may hide their heads** derived from Pliny, *Natural History*, 8.23: 'Panthers have small spots like eyes on a light ground. It is said that all four-footed animals are wonderfully attracted by their smell, but frightened by the savage appearance of their head; for which reason they catch them by hiding their head and enticing them to approach by their other attractions.'

112 **pent** narrowly confined.

4.1

6–7 **false fiers . . . heate** Ford seems to be thinking of something like will-o'the-wisps, not as Hill suggests 'blank discharge of firearms'; cf. John Day, *Isle of Gulls* (1633), 2.1: 'our hopes like false fires having brought us within ken, vanish, and leave us out of all comfort.' They derive their light and heat from reflection.

11 **Jealous** mistrustful; cf. *Julius Caesar*, 1.2.162: 'That you do love me, I am nothing jealous'.

15–16 **That sinne is . . . being worse** 'I take Menaphon's sense to be that the sin of broken faith is characteristic of Amethus' family but that his sin is twice that of Thamasta, and worse, in justifying her sin' (Hill).

22 **fame** reputation.

23–5 **With a coldnesse . . . or merit** Menaphon's accurate account of Eroclea's behaviour is inconsistent with his anger with her at 3.2.190–210.

27 **imployment** presumably, as Hill suggests, to take the letter to Cleophila which is later (4.2.167–8) taken by Cuculus.

30 **discover'd to report** exposed to common talk.

31 **nakednesse in** absence of.

32 **Satyre** satirist.

32–3 **flatteries . . . greatnesse** adulation given because of her high position; Ford uses it in the same way as something which turns the head in *BH*, 2.2.44–9: 'consider what the heat | Of an unsteady youth, a giddy brain, | Green indiscretion, flattery of greatness . . . Might lead a boy in years to.'

36 **Wanton** lecherous person; cf. *Othello*, 4.1.71: 'To lip a wanton in a secure couch'.

39 **Ha's** has, commonly spelled thus, for no good reason; cf. esp. *PW, passim*. Ha' was an abbreviated form of have.

45 **Coynesse** reserve signalling rejection.

51 **pension** reward; there is an unromantic suggestion of wages paid, as Hill notes.

53 **playne** complete, perfect (*OED*, †plain, *adj.*¹ 1a).

71 **childish** puerile; cf. *LT* 1.3.38: 'The tricke is childish, base'.

73 **love your fame** cherish your reputation.

78 **pay'd . . . Coyne** (1) treated by Amethus and Menaphon with the same pride and disdain she had previously displayed; (2) rejected by Eroclea as previously she had rejected Menaphon.

79 **—so,—** the dashes indicate a pause as she considers what to do and then decides.

80 **Anticke** someone who played a grotesque or clownish part, here used figuratively.

82–3 **Wounds may be . . . Honors bleed** proverbial, Tilley, W928, 'An ill wound is cured, not an ill name'; Hill notes the first citation is 1640, but it is taken from *Outlandish Proverbs* collected by George Herbert, who died 1633. For the inverted commas marking a *sententia* cf. 1.2.17–18 and note.

4.2

1 *Diabolo* devil (Italian *diavolo*, Latin *diabolus*).

1 **close-stoole Empricks** 'commode quacks'; a close-stool was any enclosed chamber pot, here becoming an adjective for quack doctors who treat diseases without theoretical knowledge of medicine; cf. 1.2.112 and note. The point is that their preferred treatment, as was often the case, was a purgative.

3 **Dog-leaches** strictly a person who treats dogs (cf. *FCN* 4.2.2), but commonly used, as here, to mean a quack doctor (*OED*, †dogleech, *n.* 1).

3 **By . . . Elements** an appropriate oath addressed to a doctor.

8 **thy Lord** subsequent lines indicate this is Meleander.

8 **put him too't** created a challenge for him; cf. *All's Well*, 3.6.1: 'Nay, good my lord, put him to't'.

10–13 **frenzy . . . him** for the distinction, see 3.1.105 and note. For 'Feare and Sorrow' as 'the true Characters, and inseparable companions of Melancholy', see *Anatomy*, 1.1.3.1.

11–12 **sorrow's . . . soule** Cf. *Anatomy*, 1.2.3.10: '[sorrow can] make us howle and roare, and teare our haires . . . and groane for the very anguish of our souls.'

12 **griping** causing physical or mental pain or distress (*OED*, griping *adj.* 2), often used for grief; *OED* cites T. Kendall, tr. Politianus et al. *Flowers of Epigrammes* (1577) sig. Svjv 'Oh grisly gripyng grief.'

16 **qualifie** moderate.

19 **full Meridian** highest point.

21–2 **casting . . . rudenesse** the acting metaphor refers to his 'Anticke' pose (1.2.13) and his flyting attacks on Corax (1.2.103–49), which are now abandoned.

22 **rudeness** uncouthness, aggressiveness.

27 **The bonds my dute owes** referring to the pledge to be Corax's 'servant' (l. 23).

28 **Whorson** literally 'Son of a whore', but here a jocular term of endearment, as in *Romeo*, 4.4.19: 'Mass, and well said; a merry whoreson'.

29 SD *Murrion* 'a kind of brimmed helmet resembling a hat, without a beaver or visor' (*OED*, morion, *n.* 1).

34 **We will roare . . . if he roare** Corax is threatening to cure Meleander by the treatment the doctor advocates in Webster, *Duchess of Malfi* 5.2.23–6: 'I'll goe | A neerer way to worke with him then ever | *Paracelsus* dream'd of: If they'll give me | Leave I'll buffet his madnesse out of him.'

35–7 **He . . . Pageants** 'Meleander is being likened to a whiffler, an armed official employed to clear the way for processions or public spectacles' (Hill). They used a poleaxe, a weapon with an axe blade at one end and a spike at the other.

37–8 **clap . . . Coxcombe** blow on the head.

40.1 *Gorgon mask* in Greek mythology the three Gorgons had a stare which turned those whom they looked at to stone. Cf. 4.2.53–4.

42 **man of Worship** a gentleman of status, below that of a nobleman; cf. *Richard III*, 1.1.66–7: 'that good man of worship, | Anthony Woodvile'.

43 **firke his Trangdido** probably 'whip his arse'. 'Firk' is to beat or whip, and Ford uses it to mean 'whip' in *LT* 2.2.96–7: 'a' has firkt | And mumbl'd the roguie-Turkes'. 'Trangdido' is not in *OED*, and its use in a number of plays does not wholly clarify its meaning, but for Ford 'buttocks', or (since it is clearly impolite slang) 'arse' is the most plausible reading. He uses it again in *FCN*, 4.2. where the enraged barber Secco, thinking he has been cuckolded, says 'nay I will tickle their Trangdidoes'. Secco is carrying a rod and has ordered the page Nitido to 'untruss' so he can beat him, suggesting that he means 'arses'. 'Trangdido' is, however, used as a condescending form of address by 'S.H.', *Sicily and Naples* (1640) 3.3: 'come thou shalt along with us, to a wench, old trangdido, to a wench, and thou shalt so bumfiddle her', and Dekker uses a shorter form similarly in *Satiromastix* 1.4.139: 'my little Trangdo'. It is possible these are equivalent to 'old bum' and 'little bum',

respectively, but this is not totally convincing. It may have the meaning 'arse' in William Haughton's *Englishmen for my Money* (1598) where it is associated with a dildo and dubious un-English sexual practices: 'With Tran-dido, Dil-dido, and I know not what?' (sig. G4v); a sexual meaning is also evident in *Wily Beguiled* (?1606) 'Thou art my Ciperlillie: | And I thy Trangdidowne dilly, | And sing hey ding a ding ding: | And do the tother thing' (p. 71).

44 **bounce, and . . . metal** Hill suggests 'bluster courageously', but see 3.3.63 and note for 'bounce' as an explosion; 'metal' was the barrel of a gun (*OED*, *n*. 5†a), so Corax probably means he will go off like a cannon.

45 **vapours** boasts, brags; 'to swear like a tinker' was a common expression, but this example is the first use of 'vapours' in this sense in *OED*.

45–6 **struts . . . Juggler** like tinkers, jugglers, still often general entertainers, singers, and jesters, were treated with contempt as vagrants.

47 **So ho** hunting cry calling hounds, and hence used generally to call attention to something or somebody. Cf. *SD* 3.4.33–4: '*So ho ho, through the skies | How the proud bird flies*'.

50–2 **Show me the dog . . . pieces** The three headed dog Cerberus guarded the gates of Hades; he was captured (not torn in pieces) by Hercules, who, having agreed not to use metal weapons, used a lion skin as a shield and squeezed the dog's heads until it surrendered. It is the lion skin which makes Meleander personify himself as a lion.

54–7 **stone . . . Ayre** King Sisyphus was punished for his greed, deceit, and general over-cleverness by being condemned to roll a huge stone up a hill, only for it to roll down again, leaving him to repeat the process for eternity. If Meleander is to be turned into this stone (l. 54), it is not clear how it can also crush him (l. 56).

59 **Gun-powder** (1) the sulphur in gunpowder gave it an unpleasant odour; (2) explosive in figurative sense; cf. *Henry IV Part 1*, 5.4.121–2: 'I am afraid of this gunpowder Percy'.

59–61 **Fates . . . untwisted** the three Fates of Greek and Roman mythology, in Greek Clotho, Lachesis, and Atropos, who, respectively, spun, measured, and cut (rather than 'untwisted') the thread of life. Like Tibullus (1.7.1–2) and Herrick (*Hesperides*, 47) Ford has all three sisters working together rather than sticking to their designated roles.

60 **clue** ball of thread.

64–5 **allow . . . motion** parodying the formal legal language in which an application made to a court is accepted by the judge.

67 **Legerdemayne** sleight of hand, deceit; cf. Jonson, *Gypsies*, 130–1: 'It is but a strain | Of true legerdemain'.

67 **ducks** low bows.

67 **formall** over-neat.

68 **Crisp'd** tightly curled.

68 **punctuall** punctilious.

69–70 **Foxe . . . followes** proverbial: 'When the fox has got in his head he will soon make the body follow' (Tilley, F 655).

72 **square** honest, steadfast, contrasted here with 'round'; cf. Daniel Featley, *Clavis Mystica* (1636), p. 782: 'The Pythagorians, who delighted to represent morall truths by mathematicall figures, described a good man by a cube; whence grew the proverb . . . A perfect square man everie way. The reason of this embleme is taken from the uniformitie & stabilitie of this figure, which consisteth of six sides exactly equall, & on which soever it falleth it lies stedfast.'

73 **ingrosse offices** monopolize positions of power, as Sophronos and Aretus say they are unfairly accused of doing (2.1.13–15).

77 **buz** empty talk; Pelias is 'a Buz o'the Court' (1.2.22).

79 **men of Art** physicians; cf. 5.2.39.

80 **Liege-people** loyal, honest subjects; Craik suggests 'Lewd-people' meaning gullible people of low social status; but *Q*'s reading makes better sense.

81 **halter** rope with a noose for hanging people.

82 *Melancholy* **devil** Burton writes of people hanging themselves to be rid of melancholy: 'after many tedious dayes at last, either by drowning, hanging, or some such fearefull end, they precipitate, or make away themselves: many lamentable examples are dayly seene amongst us. 'Tis a common calamity, a fatall end to this disease' (1.4.1.1).

85–6 **Fix . . . eare** tied thus for hanging: cf. Shadwell, *The Libertine* (1676), Act 4: 'I am noos'd already, I feel the knot, methinks, under my left ear'. Perhaps because the 'sinister' left ear was associated with wickedness, misunderstanding and fantasy.

93 **quicke** lively, strong, hence fervent.

97–8 **throngs of rude divisions . . . sleepe** Burton says melancholics 'hot and dry braines make them they cannot sleepe . . . Mighty and often watchings, sometimes waking for a month, a yeare together' (1.3.1.1).

97 **divisions** (1) military units; cf. *PW* 2.2.140: 'The next division we assign to Daubeney'; (2) disturbing feelings and thoughts; cf. *BH* 5.3.9: 'Her own demeanours, passions and divisions.'

97 **huddle on** crowd confusedly along; cf. *BH* 5.3.69: 'one straight news came huddling on another.'

98 **disranke** disorder.

100–1 **balls of wild-fire . . . up** balls of volatile inflammable material fired from a mortar or similarly projected. They are safe until they are 'violently sundred, and throwne up'.

108–10 **my . . . moneths** Corax's shock treatment (see note to 4.2.34) has metamorphosed into one of identification with the patient's mental and physical state, describing Meleander's symptoms as his own, and thus ensuring his 'distemper'd thoughts' can no longer 'rest in their rage' (l. 102). Although Burton includes among his cures a long 'Member' 'Against Sorrow for Death of Friends', including death of children (2.3.5), this strategy is not mentioned.

113 **no . . . selfe** proverbial; cf. Luke 4.23: 'Ye will surely say unto me this proverb, Physician, heal thyself'.

120–1 **things . . . agoe** cf. *LoC* 3.2.100 for the same phrase.

127 **hug** indulge, embrace.

129 **Crochet** crocket, cf. 2.2.48–9 note.

133 **Apish** extremely foolish; cf. 3.3.14 'Apish Phrensey'.

137–45 **The modell . . . into a silence** for the harmony of creation, and its relation to physical beauty, see note to 1.1.115. Cleophila's 'obedience' is an internal, spiritual extension of this beauty and harmony.

137 **modell** 'compass, extent of space' (*OED*, 15b).

138 **harmony . . . times** historical agreement testifying to truth; cf. Matthew Sutcliffe, *A Briefe Replie* (1600), p. 22: 'holy Scriptures, approoved by consent of times'.

143 **signe . . . lodg'd** Hill explains this as a sign of the zodiac, Cleophila being 'thought of as a sign conferring obedience', but 'lodg'd' suggests the sign is simply one outside a house or inn within which Cleophila's obedience dwells.

151 **profession . . . sawcy** Corax has earlier (2.1.60) used 'my profession' to refer to his work as a scholar, but Meleander takes a sexual meaning from his words. Ford gives 'profession' a wide range of meanings: in *TPW* it covers being both a 'cot quean' (1.2.11) and a bandit (5.4.16).

165 **good fellow** often used to suggest a good drinking companion, which subsequent lines show to be Meleander's ironic meaning here.

168 **old *Trojanes*** vague term of approbation, often hinting at a dissolute lifestyle; cf. Jonson, *Every Man In*, 3.5.15–16: 'Oh, the doctor, the honestest old Trojan in all Italy! I do honour the very flea of his dog.'

169 **Tosse-pot** drunkard.

173 ***Genius*** personal tutelary spirit.

175 **True . . . divine** because it is the drink of the gods, a commonplace, one of the earliest formulations is Hesiod, *Theogony*, 640: 'nectar and ambrosia, which the gods themselves eat'; cf. Milton, *Paradise Lost*, 9.838: 'Nectar, drink of Gods'.

177 **Mistris . . . thoughts** a hackneyed formula, recommended in such books of advice on letter writing as Thomas Gainsford's *The Secretaries Studie* (1616), p. 10 (under 'Amorous letters'): 'To the Mistresse of his thoughts',

signed 'Yours dying in constancie'. Exactly the same address and subscription is repeated in Philomusus's *The Academy of Complements* (1640), p. 248. 'Mistress of my/his desires' does not appear.

180–2 **Animall . . . Noddy** theories of animals' intelligence were still based on the Aristotelian view that they lacked the powers of reasoning and consciousness (*De Anima* 2.3); Cuculus's list of alternatives are all terms for the human simple-minded or foolish, seen by him as similarly limited. For 'Cokes' for a simpleton, cf. Jonson, *Bartholomew Fair*.

185 **Forsooth** see note to 3.3.48 for this as the opposite of 'courtly and fashionable'.

187–8 **know . . . what** proverbial (Tilley, K178), here perhaps for sexual 'knowledge'; both vulgar and clichéd, as in Jonson, *Epicene*, 5.1.72: 'but Sir Amorous knows what's what as well.'

187–9 **for to know . . . foolish figures** cf. Polonius, *Hamlet*, 2.2.97–8: 'That he's mad, 'tis true, 'tis true 'tis pity, | And pity 'tis 'tis true—a foolish figure'.

191 **there . . . me** there you have me.

191 **to . . . favour** to be looked on with favour (*OED*, 1c).

192 **to . . . favours** to be given sexual 'favours'; see Williams, *Dictionary, s.v.* 'favour'; Partridge, *Shakespeare's Bawdy, s.v.* 'favours'.

201 **conjure . . . spirit** sexual innuendo, meaning Cleophila's beauty is such as to cause an erection. Cf. *Romeo*, 2.1.24, Jonson, *New Inn*, 3.2.249–50.

201 **with a witnesse** an emphatic expression similar to 'with a vengeance'; cf. *Taming of the Shrew*, 5.1.118–19: 'Here's packing, with a witness, to deceive us all!'

206 **Mad-dame** Hill rightly suggests *Q*'s rare spelling indicates a pun, as William Rowley's *All's Lost by Lust* (1633), sig. E4v, makes clumsily explicit: 'Madam, is the mad dame, and thence mad woman'.

208 **bereaven** poetic form of 'bereaved'. There was a rhyme with 'heav'n' in the next line in contemporary pronunciation.

4.3

1 **The . . . mov'd** Palador's previous line had been to order Eroclea to 'wait his pleasure' (3.3.109).

1 **mov'd** emotionally disturbed.

2 **distemp'red** mentally distressed; cf. 2.1.27, Meleander's 'distempered thoughts' (4.2.102), and *LS* 4.2.80–1: 'The Duke | Is lately much distempered.'

3 **whither . . . convay'd** to where can he have been stolen away.

3–4 **'Tis . . . not** Sophronos is dissembling; like Rhetias, he knows who Eroclea is, as she confirms to Palador later (4.3.146–8).

5 **consented** agreed; cf. 5.1.93.

10 **masculin . . . spirit** cf. *BH* 5.2.95: 'She has a masculine spirit.'

11–12 **bearded . . . horrour** A comet with a 'beard' which seems to precede it was seen as a bad omen; cf. Webster, *White Devil*, 5.3.30–1: 'no rough-bearded Comet, | Stares on thy milde departure'.

12 **Set . . . gaze** make you stare in wonder.

18 **Fantasticke** though Hill notes this could be a noun meaning 'a person given to fanciful ideas or showy dress', Ford usually employs it as an adjective, as he must be doing here, along with 'airie', qualifying 'apparition': Eroclea is an imaginary vision. For a similar use see 5.2.216.

19 **airie apparition** Ford employs this phrase in a strongly pejorative sense in *PW* 1.3.36–7: 'This airy apparition, first discradled | From Tournay into Portugal'. Palador's use here reflects his frustration and bewilderment over Eroclea's disappearance.

22–4 **cheates . . . me** for 'rational love' as 'proper to men' and higher than 'Natural' or 'Sensible' love, see note to 3.2.88–93. Palador's 'sensible' soul is cheated by delusions, and his rational soul troubled. Cf. also *FCN* 3.3: 'I esteem of love | As of a man in some huge place; it puzzles | Reason, distracts the freedom of the soul'.

36 **by possibility** possibly; cf. 5.1.85.

43–6 **As . . . kind** for a similar view of the harmony of Creation depending on the balance of opposing properties, see Jean Bodin, *The Six Bookes of a Common-Weale*, trans. Richard Knolles (1606), p. 496: 'were not the humors of mans bodie much contrarie, a man should quickly perish: the preservation thereof dependeth of the contrarietie of hoat & cold, of moisture and drought, of bitter choller to sweet flegme, of beastly desires to divine reason; as also the preservation of the whole world next unto God dependeth of the contrarietie, which is in the whole and every part thereof.' The repetition of 'after his/their kind' (cf. l. 46) in the opening chapter of Genesis supported such a view. See also 1.1.142 'Concord in discord' and note.

46–51 **but . . . straines** the 'music' to which Palador refers is that 'Humane Musick' eloquently described by John Dowland in his translation of *Ornithoparcus his Micrologus* (1609), C1r: 'the Concordance of divers elements in one compound, by which the spirituall nature is joyned with the body, and the reasonable part is coupled in concord with the unreasonable, which proceedes from the uniting of the body and the soule. For that amitie, by which the body is joyned unto the soule, is not tyed with bodily bands, but vertuall [non-physical], caused by the proportion of humors. For what . . . makes the powers of the soule so sundry and disagreeing to conspire oftentimes each with other? who reconciles the Elements of the body? what other power doth soder and glue that spirituall strength, which is indued with an intellect to a mortall and earthly frame, than that Musicke which every man that descends into himselfe finds in himselfe? For every like is preserved by his like, and by his dislike is disturbed. Hence is it, that we loath and abhorre discords, and are delighted when we heare harmonicall concords, because we know there is in our selves the like concord.'

46–8 **Man . . . model'd** Man's (potential and pre-Fall) perfection depends on the fact that God created him in His own image: see Genesis 1.26–7: 'And God said, Let us make man in our image . . . So God created man in his own image, in the image of God created he him; male and female created he them.'

46 **abstract** ideal form.

49 **severall qualitie** distinct character.

51–2 **When 'tis in consort . . . moneths** For man's ideally harmonious 'composition', cf. the 'Humane Musick' described in note to 4.3.46–51; strains are distinct sections of a piece of music, consort a harmonious blending of them all together.

52–4 **My . . . consisted** cf. *TPW* 1.2.216–8: 'The love of thee, my sister, and the view | Of thy immortal beauty hath untuned | All harmony both of my rest and life.'

53 **Wanting** lacking.

53 **equall** reciprocal and of the same magnitude.

55 **We are Heav'ns bounty . . . exercise** 'We are all the gift of God but subject to the caprice of fortune' (Hill).

56–63 **Minutes are numbred . . . in rest** Weber's change to *Q*'s punctuation, retained by Gifford and Hill (see textual notes), causes Hill to make heavy weather of this. *Q*'s stronger pause after 'Sands' allows the reading 'the span of time wastes us to our graves as if it is measuring it with an hour glass, and we stand by and watch it'. Neill, 'Moral Artifice', p. 101 comments on the distancing effect of the metaphor, in which Eroclea looks at her own suffering 'with melancholy impotence'. The Sun has a very similar speech in *Sun's Darling* 5.1.309–22.

65–9 **substance . . . memory** referring to the 'echo' of l. 64. Eroclea's physical body (the 'substance') can be removed as quickly as the 'vain sound' of the echo if Palador cannot remember her plighted troth.

68 **impression** image on a seal or print; first of a series of allusions to visual representations, true or false, which leads to the exchange of the true images in the miniatures at 4.3.129–30

70 **figure . . . cheekes** 'coinage metaphor' (Hill); like the head of a monarch 'stamped' on a coin (cf. note to 4.3.68 'impression'), she may only be a counterfeit (cf. 4.3.106). Palador's conviction that she is an impostor is partly explained by his unwillingness to give up the idea that she is a boy in disguise (see esp. 4.3.95–7).

71 **coozenage** deception, cheating; a common 17th-century spelling.

72–3 **secret . . . thoughts** although the memory of Eroclea has sustained him, Palador's rejection of her in the subsequent dialogue suggests that keeping her memory locked in his 'speechless thoughts' has been destructive. Ford's psychology may be derived from Burton: '*Seneca* adviseth in such a case, *to get a trusty friend, to whom we may freely and securely poure out our secrets, nothing so delights and easeth the minde, as when we have a prepared bosome, to which our secrets may descend, of whose conscience we are assured as our owne, whose speech may ease our succorlesse estate, counsell relieve, mirth expell our mourning, & whose very sight may be acceptable unto us*' (*Anatomy*, 2.2.6.1; cf. note to 3.1.102–4 Palador has told Rhetias, in a different context, that he 'never had a friend, a certaine friend' (2.1.151) to whom he could talk in this way.

73 **Jewell** as well as its general meaning of something precious, at this date also a miniature portrait in a case, thus continuing the theme of true and false visual representation.

74 **feares and sorrowes** the primary sources of melancholy: cf. 3.1.108–12 and note, 3.3.72.

77 **of force** strong enough; cf. *LS* 2.2.99–101: 'whose very first gaze is of force almost to persuade a substantial love in a settled heart.'

80 **Untruth** lack of honesty.

80 **subtle** deceitful.

81–7 **If any neighbouring . . . peace** Hill says 'precise sense unclear' (of 79–80), and the speech reflects Palador's psychological confusion. He is asking why, if a neighbouring power has seduced her as a willing conspirator to end his 'weary days' in 'some bolder' way, she has come as a 'Cruell-mercy' disguised as Eroclea, her beauty making treason, guilt, and bloodshed seem virtuous.

89 **Altar** for a similar figurative use of 'altar' cf. *BH* 4.4.68–9: 'my last breath, which on the sacred Altar | Of a long-looked-for peace'.

89 **constant proofe** assured constancy.

101 **arm'd** made aggressive.

101 *subtilty* deception.

103–5 **Tell . . . name** for the same sequence of questions in *Twelfth Night* and *Pericles*, see Introduction, p. 220.

107 **time** age.

110 **vizard** mask; for a similar emphasis on moral deception, cf. *Macbeth*, 3.2.34–5: 'make our faces vizards to our hearts, | Disguising what they are.'

112–13 **in . . . Of** in exchange for.

115 **Convoy** funeral cortège.

124 **abuse** be mistaken in.

125 **ravisht** destroyed, corrupted.

129 SD *tablet* see note to 2.1.219.

138–9 **that part . . . content** the rational soul, which moderates 'passion' (l. 135); see notes to 3.2.88–93 and 4.3.22–4.

141–2 **Hymen . . . Torches** Hymen was the Greek god of marriage ceremonies, described as carrying a torch or associated with lights in the wedding procession; cf. Euripides, *Trojan Women*, 308–14.

150, 151 **our** Palador uses the 'royal we'.

156 **baytes of Artes** allurements of cunning.

157 **cleare** pure.

5.1

2–3 **no . . . content** admitting that his medical skill alone could not cure Meleander's melancholy; Corax's plan is to cure him by the simple psychological 'cordial' of the final scene.

11 **sleepes . . . soundly** 'Sleep which so much helps, by like ways . . . *must be procured, by nature or art; inward or outward meanes, & to be protracted longer then ordinary, if it may bee, as being an especiall helpe.* It moistens and fattens the Body, concocts, and helpes digestion, as we see in Dormice' (*Anatomy*, 2.2.5; see also 2.5.1.6 for a list of simples and compounds to induce sleep). For restorative sleeping drugs used to 'close the eye of anguish' cf. *Lear*, 4.4.8–15.

11–12 **May . . . fancy** cf. SD 3.2.6–7: 'Lull me asleep, and when I most am sad, | My sorrows vanish from me in soft dreams.'

15 **drencht** drugged; cf. *Macbeth*, 1.7.67–8: 'in swinish sleep | Their drenched natures lie as in a death'.

18 **Couch** Q reads 'Coach', but as Craik points out 'Coach' is a common mistake for 'Couch', which was also preferred by Weber and Gifford. It would be what Cockeram defines as 'a little bed' (*Dictionary*, 1624, quoted *OED*, 1a). Such couches were often used in the theatre: Dessen and Thomson, *Dictionary of Stage Directions in English Drama 1580–1642* (Cambridge, 1999), p. 58, note several examples, including one used by the King's Men at the Blackfriars in 1626 in Massinger's *Roman Actor*, 5.1.154 (but a 'Triumphant Chariot', perhaps suitable for recycling as a coach also appears at 1.4.13.2). Hill argues that a coach 'is consistent with [Meleander's] final honoured status', but he is asleep, and it is more fitting for him to be brought on in a bed which is put down ('settle[d]' as a coach would not be) at 5.1.174. Lear is carried on in much the same way, also sleeping, in a chair (4.7.23.1). It is

much more fitting, too, for Meleander to play the opening of 5.2 from a couch rather than a coach, even an open one. Against this, *Q* reads 'coach' three times (see 5.1.177, 5.2.1.1), and to substitute 'couch' one has to propose a compositor misreading three times, and the errors not being noticed in proofing. This, however, could be a result of the top of the *u* being almost closed in the copy, something entirely possible in a secretary or italic hand, or indeed a modern one. Once the compositor had misread the copy, he would probably repeat his mistake. In either case Meleander has clearly risen or descended from his couch/coach by 5.2.91–2, where he is asked to 'sit downe' (again a couch is the more likely stage property), to which he agrees.

20 **brace . . . women** Thamasta and Eroclea, 'bigge' because important, of high standing (*OED*, *adj.* 11a). Cf. 2.2.27 and note for 'bigge' as threatening.

21 **Ape . . . shee-clog** pet monkeys (probably not apes) were restrained by a clog, a heavy wooden weight, on a chain. Grilla is the clog to Cuculus's ape.

25 **Sir-Reverence** abbreviated form of 'Save your reverence', but also a euphemism for excrement (*OED*, sir-reverence, *n.* 2); cf. *Romeo*, 1.4.42.

28–9 **resolution . . . obedience** removal of doubt (over her hopes of marriage with Amethus) and the duty she believes she owes Meleander.

30–3 **apprehension . . . reason** it is not grasping with the imagination a well-timed happiness (in marriage to Amethus) that is making her irresolute, but her fear that her sense of obligation to her father may be mistaken, which is restricting her ability to think reasonably and decisively.

39 **ill** hostility, aversion.

43 **Were growne to such familiarity** had become so widely known.

49 **Cast-away** a rejected person, often with the suggestion of a reprobate; cf. *PW* 3.?1: 'A happie Bride, but now a cast away'; *FCN* 3.2.128–30: 'that we should live at distance; | As if I were a Cast-away, and you | For your part take no care on't'.

51 **troth** truly, in truth.

56–7 **Call . . . debt** any service she can do is something she owes to Thamasta.

59 **quitted** cleared.

65 **Sollicite thy deserts** promote what your virtues deserve.

68 **Has had a time . . . humour** she has had enough time to satisfy her desire to scold Cleophila.

77 **I . . . sweare** cf. *WA* 5.1.153: 'nor doe I use to sweare'.

86 **sincerity** freedom from adulteration (*OED*, *n.* †1a) as well as honesty and genuineness of feeling (*OED*, 2).

93 **Banes** banns, proclamations of a forthcoming marriage read out in church to allow for objectors to 'forbid' it.

93 **consented** agreed; cf. 4.3.5.

110–11 **I . . . pity** cf. *LoC* 115 'I will endeavour to deserve your pitty'.

116–17 **dispose . . . father** regulate what I would like to do without my father's permission.

121 **Linsey-woolsey** a cloth woven from a mixture of wool and flax, hence an odd mixture, here of the two sexes.

122 **clapper-clawd** beat, thrashed; cf. *Merry Wives*, 2.3.65–8.

125 **and't like** if it please; cf. *FCN* 5.1.119: 'Yes, an't like your noblenes'.

126 **love-toyes** tokens of love.

131 **mumbled** mauled; cf. *LT* 2.2.97, quoted in note to 4.2.43.

133 **Cock-vermine** chief, leading vermin; first usage in this sense in *OED*.

134 **wag** mischievous joker; cf. *HT* 51: '*To play the wanton wag*'.

134 **schoole** punish.

136 **fit place about** post appropriate to your station and character in.

136 **Wardrobe** department in the royal household concerned with clothing.

139 **garbe** fashion, not necessarily of clothes.

141 **Taylors . . . men** John Day, *Isle of Gulls* (1606), 5.2, alludes to women tailors, one character saying 'your best tailors are arrant botchers to em, you shal have a lady make an end of a sute, a court sute, especially when all the tailors in a countrey know not how to set a stich int.'

142 **scowre** scour had two additional meanings, (1) to wear fetters or sit in the stocks; (2) to stab someone.

143 **Princesse** Eroclea, apparently anticipating her marriage.

145 **forbeare** give up, leave behind.

148 **passe my word** give my word; cf. *Twelfth Night*, 1.5.80–1: 'he will not pass his word for twopence that you are no fool.'

159 **Sanctuary** holy place.

160 **circumstance** formality.

161 **'Tis I must raise her** normally a suppliant would wait for the person of most authority, to whom she kneels, to grant her request. Here Eroclea recognizes that it is her role to ask Cleophila to rise.

166 **bewray** reveal.

168–70 **part . . . armes** Hill notes that the metaphor is 'more pretty than exact'. Ford envisages the sisters as two rivulets which have joined to form a single stream, presumably embodied by an embrace. Palador's arms act like an island in the new stream, separating them again, probably by drawing Eroclea to himself.

174 **Prince . . . Neece** Presumably Cleophila's attention has been drawn to her father who is waking (see l. 173).

177 (and 5.2.0.1) **Couch** see note to 5.1.18.

5.2

0.1 **Soft Musicke** cf. 2.1.44; *BH* 5.3.0.11; *LS* 5.4.0.3. The therapeutic effects of music were widely recognized, and were summarized by Burton: 'Many and sundry are the meanes, which Philosophers & Physitians have prescribed to exhilerate a sorrowfull heart, to divert those fixed and intent cares and meditations, which in this malady so much offend; but in my Judgment none so present, none so powerfull, none so apposite as a cup of strong drinke, mirth, Musick, and merry company . . . [music is] a roaring-meg against Melancholy, to reare and revive the languishing Soule, *affecting not only the eares, but the very arteries, the vitall & animall spirits, it erects the mind, & makes it nimble'* (*Anatomy*, 2.2.6.3, 'Musicke a remedy').

0.3 **Boy that sings** this may have been John Tomson, who probably played Thamasta. He had a fine voice; in Massinger's *The Picture* (acted 1629) he performed a 'song of pleasure' (3.5.25.1) which another character thinks must have been sung by a goddess. He could have left the stage with Cuculus and the rest at 5.1.142; Thamasta does not re-enter until 5.2.207.

0.4 **The Song.** a setting by John Wilson, leading songwriter for the King's Men (*ODNB*) survives; it is reproduced by Hill, Appendix B. Though not published until 1660, Wilson's close connections to the company make it probable that it is essentially the version performed in 1628.

1–10 **Fly hence, shadowes . . . in sleepe** Burton refers often to the troubled sleep of melancholics and the need for 'sweet moistening sleepe': 'To procure this . . . is best to take away the occasions (if it be possible) that hinder it, and then to use such inward or outward remedies, which may cause it. Heat and driness must first be removed: a hot and dry braine never sleepes well, griefe, feares, cares, expectations, anxieties, great businesses . . . and all violent perturbations of the minde, must in some sort be qualified, before wee can hope for any good repose' (*Anatomy*, 2.2.5)

3 **overtaken** overpowered; cf. *SD* 1.1.1–2: 'Let your tunes, you sweet-voic'd sphears, | overtake him'.

11 **Where am I? . . . are these?** For the close parallels with *Lear* 4.7.51 see Introduction, pp. 221–2.

14 **Fancy** fantasy, an illusion furnished by what he thinks is a dream; cf. 5.1.12.

16 **jolly** joyous, gladsome (*OED*, 1).

19 **Beare-leech** bear doctor; cf. 4.2.3 and note.

23 **noyse** Corax. Hill moves the SD '*Cease musicke*' from l. 17 to here, but Meleander has woken with pleasure at the 'beguiling' song, and 'tormenting noyse' is his personification of Corax after their brief skirmish.

24 **phisick** the physic was simply a sleeping draught in wine (5.1.15), rather than the complex mixtures of herbs and minerals in Burton's pharmacopoeia (*Anatomy*, 2.4.1.1–5, 2.4.2.1–3).

26 Apply'd administered (*OED*, 7); cf. *Cor.* 1.6.63–4: 'You were conducted to a gentle bath | And balms applied to you'.

27–8 drunke . . . liquor Meleander assumes he has been given more than a simple sleeping draught. Discussing 'compound' (mixed) medicines which 'are inwardly taken' to cure melancholy, Burton says they can 'be either liquid or solid: liquid, are fluid or consisting [semi-liquid conserves]. Fluid, as wines and syrups. The wines ordinarily used to this disease are wormwood wine, tamarisk, and buglossatum, wine made of borage and bugloss' (*Anatomy*, 2.4.1.5).

28 Directly by a direct process.

28 liquor the liquid 'physic' he assumes has been infused into his 'cup' (4.2.166, 5.1.15).

33–5 Bring . . . heart the 'cordial' that Rhetias is sent to fetch is Eroclea, whom he brings in at 5.2.100, having been given a nudge by Corax (5.2.91). She is the 'sure cordial' (5.2.219) which Meleander finally agrees Corax has provided. The succession of messages which precede her, described by Corax as a 'pill' (5.2.58), 'physick' (5.2.68), and a 'Cure' (5.2.81), are also restorative once they are confirmed by her return.

36 fiddle *OED* cites this passage as a simple figurative use of playing the fiddle or violin (fiddle *v.*¹), which is one meaning, but Ford uses it to mean manipulating someone's mental processes, as probably also here, in *FCN* 5.2.179–80: 'You must fiddle my braines into a jealousie'.

39 hands of Art practitioners of medicine; like Corax (5.1.2–3 and note) he knows conventional treatment like 'physic' can have no effect on his psychological state.

40–4 If . . . faculties a remarkable anticipation by Ford of the control of depression by heavy sedation which did not figure in treatment until relatively recent times.

45 Marts fairs and markets.

45–6 make . . . motion make some money from such a grotesque puppet.

49 burne my bookes cf. *TQ* 1 (ll. 316–18): 'I will burn my books, forsware the liberal sciences, and that is my resolution.' Echoing both the last line spoken by Marlowe's Faustus (both A and B texts), and Caliban's 'Burn but his books' (*Tempest*, 3.2.95).

50.1–71 Enter ARETUS . . . with a Tablet as Hill notes a similar sequence of messengers is used in the denouement of *BH*, 5.2.12ff.

50.1 Patent see note to 2.1.115.

56 Marshalship A prestigious office of state, in England that of Earl Marshal. At the close of *BH* Bassanes is similarly made 'Sparta's marshal' which 'could not | But set a peace to private griefs' (5.3.46–7).

59 grave sober, serious.

59 **familiar** spirit which is controlled by a witch or similar magician; cf. *BH* 3.4.34–5: 'You have a spirit, sir, have ye? A familiar | That posts i' th' air for your intelligence?' In some cases the familiar is the (or a) Devil: in *WoE* one of the characters, 'Dog, a Familiar' claims to be the Devil (2.1.110–11), and Burton describes a melancholic type who 'every black dog or cat he sees, he suspecteth to be a divell' (*Anatomy*, 1.3.1.2).

62 **formality** pompous person; not in *OED* in this sense, but cf. *PW* 5.2.101–2: 'Which of these rebels | Has been the mayor of Cork? *Dau.* This wise formality.'

65 **Grand . . . Ports** the English equivalent was Lord Warden of the Cinque Ports; its prestige is indicated by the fact that in 1628 the holder was the Duke of Buckingham, succeeded after his assassination in August of that year by the Earl of Suffolk.

69 **rare Juggler** excellent trickster; cf. *LS* 1.2.259: 'Here's fine juggling.'

70–1 **reason . . . soule** see notes to 3.1.108–12, 3.2.88–93.

71 SD *Tablet* miniature (so also 'Jewell' l. 74).

71 **stand** confront, withstand; cf. 1.2.111 and note.

72 **canst** are able.

73 **Relique** memento, with the suggestion of something sacred; cf. *FM* 65: 'a rich rellique of memoriall'.

78 **intertaine** receive, accept (*OED*, entertain *v.* †8b).

79 **moderate . . . Joyes** Cleophila expresses exactly this hope for Meleander at 5.1.14.

83–4 **dotage . . . scorne** the madness caused by his grief is taking delight in presenting fantasies of ambition to be mocked. For dotage, see notes to 3.1.104–7, 105.

87 **Round me** gather round me.

88 **Cliffes** eyebrows or eyelids; as Hill says, 'a strained and grotesque metaphor'.

91 **Cordiall** referring to Eroclea's imminent entrance, and Palador's later one, with his confirmation of the 'offices and honours' delivered by the messengers, which Corax refers to as part of the 'sure cordial' (5.2.219).

92 **Sit downe** the first indication that Meleander is not in the couch or coach in which he was brought on at the beginning of this scene; cf. 'I will sit downe' in the next line, and his kneeling to Palador at 5.2.208–9. The couch or coach would presumably still be available for him to sit on.

95 **Artsman** painter; cf. *LS* 2.2.80–3: 'a wondrous sweet picture, if you well observe with what singularity the arts-man hath strove to set forth each limb in exquisitest proportion, not missing a hair.' Ford uses it for sycophantic poets in *FM*, 30.

97 A little hollow . . . blowne breath 'Made room for a soul and infused it with the breath of life.' Cf. *Winter's. Tale,* 5.2.96–9 on Hermione's supposed statue 'by that rare Italian master, Julio Romano, who, had he himself eternity and could put breath into his work, would beguile Nature of her custom'. In Ovid's telling of the Pygmalion myth, the statue comes to life with Pygmalion's kiss (*Metamorphoses,* 10.280–1).

121 turne me child makes me weep; cf. Jonson, *New Inn* 5.5.85–6: 'I am e'en turned child, | And I must weep.'

128 ruffling battling; cf. *PW* 1.2.9–10: 'to wrestle | And ruffle in the world'.

129 bustle for a vent struggle to find a way out.

133 I kneele here (if this is not figurative) and at 5.2.208–9, where he certainly kneels, Meleander's behaviour is reminiscent of Lear kneeling to Cordelia; see *Lear* 4.7.58.

139 in . . . sloth with such slowness.

140–1 mingle . . . misfortunes join the truth to the story of your misfortunes.

143 Journall daily record.

145 Ingrosse completely devote; cf. *BH* 2.2.67: 'engross all duty to your husband'.

146–7 That thou might'st . . . with comfort cf. Palador's sentiments at 4.3.149–51.

154–5 concernes . . . businesse cf. *LoC* 5.1.35 for the same phrase.

155–6 as . . . Court in fact he has just said that how they parted 'puzzles' his memory (ll. 148–9). Ford is showing the gradual return of Meleander's faculties.

158 fall too't begin energetically; cf. 3.1.80, 3.3.23; *BH* 5.2. 'Fall to our dance'.

160 suddenly at once; cf. *BH* 5.2.2–3: 'Use dispatch, my lords. | We'll suddenly prepare our coronation'.

161 Was . . . convey'd cf. 2.1.193–4: 'was conveyed like a Ship-boy'.

162 policie . . . strange prompt and surprising stratagem.

169 bandy (1) throw around (as with tennis balls); (2) band together.

171 Legend narrative.

172 pity and delight cf. the similar tragicomic mixture of 'mirth and pitie' in the musical duel (see 1.1.163 and note).

183 comfortable comforting, reassuring.

186 travayl'd worked, in this case presumably studied in Athens.

186 Indowments special gifts; cf. *Pericles,* 5.1.116: 'And how achieved you these endowments'.

188 touch not there don't approach that subject.

192–9 **Perceiv'd with what . . . call'd home** see note to 1.1.49–50 for a year being the period of absence during which a 'hopelesse love' could be overcome.

198 **Enjoy'd . . . griefes** gained some pleasure or comfort from the sharing of each other's griefs.

205 **in the trim** Meleander is recovered enough to pun on 'trim': not only are '*his haire and beard trimd*' but he has had his '*habit and gowne chang'd*' (5.2.0.1) (see note to 1.3.2 for 'trim' applied to fashion), and he is in good psychological 'trim': see *Henry V*, 4.3.115: 'by the mass, our hearts are in the trim'.

213–14 **dye . . . yeeres** cf. *WA* 3.3.106 'dye in my comforts'.

233–4 **why . . . man** cf. *Lear* 4.7.58–9: 'Pray, do not mock me. | I am a very foolish fond old man'.

235 **untoward** stiff, unwilling.

235–6 **creepe . . . grave** cf. Chettle, *Tragedy of Hoffman* (1602), Act 4: 'alas my poore father, hee'le creepe uppon crutches into his grave'.

237–9 *Eroclea* **. . . hearts** for the contract of marriage between Palador and Eroclea see 2.1.161–2 and note; for the betrothal 'by consent' between Cleophila and Amethus, see note to 3.2.5.

243–4 **Heaven . . . they** Hill notes the same singular 'Heaven' with plural concord in *Richard II* 1.2.6–8: 'Put we our quarrel to the will of heaven, | Who, when they see the hour's ripe on earth, | Will rain hot vengeance on offenders' heads.'

251 **generall Feast** public holiday; cf. Greene, *The Pleasant Historie of Dorastus and Fawnia* (1636), sig. A3v: 'making a generall feast for all his Subjects, which continued by the space of twenty dayes'.

[EPILOGUE]

5 *Censure* critical judgement of the audience, not necessarily anticipating a hostile reception, though Ford sees it as a threat in his Dedication, l. 10: 'running the hazard of a censure'.

6 *free* Hill notes two meanings, (1) that he is free of any obligation to the audience; (2) that he is not obliged to write for a living, unlike those who 'have made | The Noble use of Poetry a Trade' (Prologue, 11–12).

The Broken Heart

Edited by LISA HOPKINS

INTRODUCTION

Date

The Broken Heart was entered in the Stationers' Register on 28 March 1633. Although, as we shall see in the section 'Sources', there are several possible sequences of events which might have inspired the claim in the Prologue that this is a true story, all had happened in Ford's early youth, so there is no *terminus ante quem* it could not have been written, and no obvious means of dating its composition. There are two possible clues. Firstly, *The Broken Heart* and *The Lover's Melancholy* are the only two plays which Ford wrote for the Blackfriars rather than the Phoenix in Drury Lane, so it may be that they belong to the same period and that *The Broken Heart* should thus be seen as close in time to 1628, which is when *The Lover's Melancholy* was published. The other clue would also seem to point in this direction. C. A. Gibson, in 'The Date of "The Broken Heart"', suggests that Christalla's injunction to Hemophil to 'Learne to reel, thrum, or trim a Ladies dog' is indebted to the stage direction '*Vbaldo spinning, Ricardo reeling*' in Massinger's *The Picture*, licensed for performance on 8 June 1629 and published in 1630 and hence suggesting that *The Broken Heart* was written *c.*1630–1.[1] Unless further evidence emerges, *c.*1629–30 may be taken as a reasonable guess, but it is no more than that.

Sources

Several sources have been suggested for *The Broken Heart*. Michael Cameron Andrews, in 'Romei and Ford's *The Broken Heart*', argues that Tecnicus' lines on honour are derived from a passage in Annibal Romei's *Discorsi* (Ferrara, 1586), translated into English in 1598.[2]

---

[1] C. A. Gibson, 'The Date of "The Broken Heart"', *NQ* 216 (1971), 458.
[2] Michael Cameron Andrews, 'Romei and Ford's *The Broken Heart*', *NQ* 27 (1982), 147–8.

Giovanni M. Carsaniga, in '"The Truth in John Ford's *The Broken Heart*', points out that 'On March 17, 1551, in Antwerp, the Lucchese merchant Simone Turchi killed his fellow citizen Jeronimo Deodati by using exactly the same kind of chair described in Ford's tragedy' and that the story appears in one of Matteo Bandelli's *Novelle*.[3] In fact, C. R. Baskervill had already observed this in 'Bandello and *The Broken Heart*', further suggesting that

> Bandello, one of whose novels furnished Ford, possibly directly, with the device of the chair that imprisons Ithocles, has a second novel, the story of Livio and Camilla (I, 33), which may well have furnished suggestions for *The Broken Heart* to a dramatist who adapts with so free a hand as Ford.[4]

The story in question, 'The Long and Loyall Love betwene Lyvyo and Camylla', features two pairs of brothers and sisters and is set during the papacy of Alexander VI. Like Penthea, Cornelia in this narrative interests herself in her brother's love affair, saying to her brother Livio that 'she desiered eftsones, in mery sorte, to knowe the goddesse of his devocions, "to the ende," sayth she, "that I may yelde her honor for youre sake and, seinge you dare not presente her your requeste, I maye enter into the office of an intercessour, and praye for your dely-verye"'.[5] However, Camilla's father, like Crotolon, will not give his consent to their marriage without the approval of his son, and when Claudio returns he objects to the marriage. Ultimately Livio dies during consummation and Camilla of grief at his death. There are some obvious similarities between this narrative and that of *The Broken Heart*, and the name Livio is one which Ford would later use in *The Fancies, Chaste and Noble*. It may also be worth noting that Geoffrey Fenton dedicated his translation of Bandello to Mary Sidney, and that there may, as I shall discuss later, be a connection between *The Broken Heart* and the Sidney family in general.

Also on the subject of Italian literature, Frederick M. Burelbach, Jr, in '"The Truth" in John Ford's "The Broken Heart" Revisited', argues that

> there was one account of an almost exact parallel to the Orgilus–Penthea–Bassanes triangle to be found in a work both available

---

[3] Giovanni M. Carsaniga, '"The Truth in John Ford's *The Broken Heart*', *Comparative Literature* 10 (1958), 344–8 (346).

[4] C. R. Baskervill, 'Bandello and *The Broken Heart*', *MLN* 28 (1913), 51–2 (51).

[5] Matteo Bandello, *Certain Tragical Discourses of Bandello, translated into English by Geffraie Fenton* [1567], introduced by Robert Langton Douglas, 2 vols (London, 1898), Vol. I, Discourse II, p. 96.

and highly congenial to Ford. In Book III of Sir Thomas Hoby's translation of Baldassare Castiglione's *The Book of the Courtier*, Lord Cesar Gonzaga supports his claim that the virtue of continence exists in women as well as men by narrating the plight of a woman he knew. For two years she loved a 'worthie and faire condicioned yong gentleman' and was loved by him in return. When her father tried to force her to marry another she resisted and remained chaste until she died of grief three years later.[6]

Looking further back, R. Jordan, in 'Calantha's Dance in "The Broken Heart" ', argues that the dance owes its origin to Plutarch's account, in his life of Agesilaus, of how the Spartans refused to allows news of the disastrous defeat at the battle of Leuctra to disrupt plans for a dance in the theatre and a banquet.[7]

Many critics have felt that Ford was also indebted to recent and contemporary drama. Robert Davril, in 'John Ford and La Cerda's *Inés de Castro*', argues that La Cerda's play is a source for Ford because of the similarities between the wedding of Ithocles and Calantha and La Cerda's dramatization of

> Inés's unhappy fate: her secret marriage with Don Pedro of Portugal, long before his accession to the throne, and her murder by order of Pedro's father; Pedro's coronation several years after, his immediate cruel revenge upon the murderers, and his decision to have Inés disinterred, dressed in rich garments, and placed on a throne near him with a crown on her head.[8]

G. Fitzgibbon, in 'An Echo of "Volpone" in "The Broken Heart" ', suggests that

> in the earlier part of *The Broken Heart* Ford was consciously or unconsciously identifying Bassanes with Jonson's earlier jealous husband. Such a correspondence is reinforced by the similarities in dramatic situation and by the association of Bassanes with the crude antics of Grausis and Phulas and would seem to imply either a change of intention or boldness of dramatic design on Ford's part in introducing a character so clearly linked with a comic tradition as a central figure in his tragedy.[9]

---

[6] Frederick M. Burelbach, Jr, ' "The Truth" in John Ford's "The Broken Heart" Revisited', *NQ* 14 (1967), 211–12 (212).

[7] R. Jordan, 'Calantha's Dance in "The Broken Heart" ', *NQ* 16 (1969), 294–5.

[8] Robert Davril, 'John Ford and La Cerda's *Inés de Castro*', *MLN* 66 (1951), 464–6 (465).

[9] G. Fitzgibbon, 'An Echo of "Volpone" in "The Broken Heart" ', *NQ* 22 (1975), 248–9 (249).

Shanti Padhi, in '*The Broken Heart* and *The Second Maiden's Tragedy*: Ford's Main Source for the Corpse's Coronation', suggests that the 'marriage' between Calantha and Ithocles is indebted to both *The Second Maiden's Tragedy* and *A Chaste Maid in Cheapside* and that this shows a close link between Ford and Middleton,[10] while it might also be observed that Thomas Heywood's *A Woman Killed with Kindness* shares with *The Broken Heart* the motif of a woman who, either knowing or believing herself to have sinned sexually, starves herself to death.

Another of Heywood's plays, *If You Know Not Me, You Know Nobody*, which dates from 1606, may also have been an influence on *The Broken Heart* (unsurprisingly since Heywood and Ford were clearly members of the same circle).[11] When Sir Thomas Gresham in Heywood's play is waiting for Elizabeth I to arrive, and has heard first of the loss of his pictures of all the rulers of England from Brutus to Elizabeth and secondly that the new King of Barbary has reneged on the sugar deal he had struck with Gresham, the First Lord says

> I feare me this will plague him, a strange crosse,
> How will he take this newes, losse vpon losse.[12]

Sir Thomas, however, announces himself unmoved:

> What 30. thousand pound in sterling money,
> And payd me all in slippes, then Hoboyes play,
> On slippers ile daunce all my care away
>
> (ll. 1500–2)

This seems to come very close to the famous scene at the end of *The Broken Heart* in which Calantha receives three pieces of devastating news but nevertheless continues to dance,[13] and it may conceivably also be worth noting that Gresham refers to himself as 'A London Marchant' (l. 1531), which was listed as a play, apparently lost,[14] in whose authorship Ford was said to have had either a whole or a part share (though it is also the name of the play-within-the-play in

[10] Shanti Padhi, '*The Broken Heart* and *The Second Maiden's Tragedy*: Ford's Main Source for the Corpse's Coronation', *NQ* 31 (1984), 236–7.

[11] See, for instance, Martin Butler, 'The Connection between Donne, Clarendon, and Ford', *NQ* 34 (1987), 309–10 (310).

[12] Thomas Heywood, *If You Know Not Me, You Know Nobody*, Part Two (London, 1606), ll. 1495–6.

[13] Other sources have of course already been noted for this scene; see, for instance, Jordan, 'Calantha's Dance in "The Broken Heart"', who proposes an episode in Plutarch, and Burelbach, '"The Truth" in John Ford's *The Broken Heart* Revisited', who proposes an anecdote from *Il Cortegiano*.

[14] But see Lisa Hopkins, 'Lillo's *The London Merchant*: An Elizabethan Palimpsest?', *English Language Notes* 36 (1998), 4–11.

Beaumont's *The Knight of the Burning Pestle*). A more recent play could also be suggested: in William D'Avenant, *The Tragedy of Albovine, King of the Lombards* (London, 1629), which has commendatory verses from Robert and Thomas Ellice, who were among the dedicatees of Ford's *The Lover's Melancholy* and which also shares with *Love's Sacrifice* the idea of technical infidelity, an imprisoning chair is repeatedly used. Finally in *A Shoemaker, A Gentleman*, having stipulated for her own choice of death, Winifred says,

> Come, tyrants, lance my arm, to death I'll bleed.
> Sweet blood was shed for me, and mine I'll shed.[15]

A Shoemaker, A Gentleman was by William Rowley, Ford's erstwhile collaborator on *The Witch of Edmonton*, where the name Winifred had also been found, so it is perhaps not surprising if Ford remembers it in *The Broken Heart*. There are also two other plays of the period, Chapman's *The Widow's Tears* (in its treatment of Sparta) and Marston's *The Malcontent* (in its representation of Aurelia's dance), which have sometimes been seen as influencing *The Broken Heart*,[16] but I shall return to them later.

The Prologue to *The Broken Heart*, however, declares that

> *What may be here thought a* fiction, *when Times youth*
> *Wanted some riper yeares, was knowne* A Truth
>
> (ll. 15–16)

There has been considerable speculation on what this 'Truth' might have been. Most recently, Michael Neill, in 'New Light on "The Truth" in "The Broken Heart"', recounts the story of the death of Margaret Ratcliffe, a Maid of Honour to Elizabeth, from a broken heart as a source for the death of Penthea, since both starved themselves, and suggests Philip Gawdy's account of the 'strings striped all over her heart' supposedly observed at the subsequent autopsy on her as an influence on 'the rather embarrassing literalness' of Calantha's heart-strings cracking:

> Ther is news besydes of the tragycall death of Mrs Ratcliffe the mayde of honor who ever synce the deathe of Sr Alexander her brother hathe pined in such straunge manner, as voluntarily she

---

[15] William Rowley, *A Shoemaker, A Gentleman*, edited by Trudi L. Darby (London, 2002), 4.3.101–2.

[16] See, for instance, Thelma N. Greenfield, 'John Ford's Tragedy: The Challenge of Re-Engagement', in Anderson, pp. 1–26, who calls Calantha's dance 'a viruous parody of Marston's Aurelia' (p. 20).

hathe gone about to starve her selfe and by the two dayes together hath receyved no sustinaunce, which meeting with extreame griefe hathe made an end of her mayden modest dayes at Richmond uppon Saterdaye last, her Maetie being [present?] who commaunded her body to be opened and founde it all well and sounde, saving certaine stringes striped all over her harte. All the maydes ever synce have gone in blacke. I saw it my selfe at court.

Neill relates this to the deaths of both Calantha and Annabella in *'Tis Pity She's a Whore*,[17] and the story is of particular interest because Margaret Ratcliffe's name had already been coupled with that of a literary character during her lifetime, by the Earl of Essex:

At the end of February 1598 the Earl of Essex wrote to Secretary of State Cecil in France: 'I pray you commend me also to Alexander Ratcliff and tell him for news his sister is married to Sir John Falstaff' . . . the allusion to Shakespeare's character is part of an in-joke about Lord Cobham (now nicknamed 'Falstaff' for his family's opposition to Shakespeare's use of the name Oldcastle) playing the marital field, pursuing Ratcliff's beautiful sister Margaret.[18]

In *The Broken Heart*, Margaret Ratcliffe's story might perhaps be touching for a second time on literary history.

Alternatively, some details of *The Broken Heart* seem to be derived from Sir Kenelm Digby's *Private Memoirs. Loose Fantasies*, which tells the stories of himself and his wife, Venetia Stanley, fictionalized as Theagenes and Stelliana. This work, which Digby wrote in 1628, is intertextually linked with that of Sir Philip Sidney, whose story was, as we shall see, also a possible source for *The Broken Heart*—Vittorio Gabrieli notes that 'Stelliana probably stems from a contamination of Sidney's Stella with the maiden family name of Lady Digby, and Henry Rich, son of Sidney's Stella, is represented as the Earl of Arcadia'.[19] Digby's work seems to have been known to Ford, despite the fact that it was not published: Gabrieli suggests an echo of it in *The Lover's Melancholy*, and it certainly foreshadows the plot of *The Broken Heart*, since Stelliana initially refuses Theagenes on the grounds that she had agreed to marry Mardontius and 'she would never suffer that one man

---

[17] Michael Neill, 'New Light on "The Truth" in "The Broken Heart"', *NQ* 22 (1975), 249–50 (250). See also Michael Neill, '"What Strange Riddle's This?": Deciphering *'Tis Pity She's a Whore*', in Neill (ed.), pp. 153–80 (156).

[18] James Shapiro, *1599: A Year in the Life of William Shakespeare* (London: Faber and Faber, 2005), p. 21.

[19] Kenelm Digby, *Private Memoirs: Loose Fantasies*, ed. Vittorio Gabrieli (Rome, 1968), p. 101.

should possess her, and another such a gage of a former, though half-constrained, affection', just as Penthea says she will never marry Orgilus even if Bassanes should die.[20] Moreover, Stelliana's father is called Nearchus, Theagenes' mother Arete sends him to Athens to separate him from Stelliana just as Orgilus ostensibly travels there to forget Penthea, and Theagenes leaves Athens because of plague just as Orgilus says he has had to do. Sir Kenelm also visited the oracle at Delphi,[21] which is mentioned in the play. Ford had family connections with Sir Kenelm Digby through his mother's relatives, the Stradlings of South Wales: Matthew Steggle notes that in 1629 Richard Holford sold parts of the same plot of land to Sir Edward Stradling and Sir Kenelm Digby and in 1630 they jointly petitioned the king for permission to develop it,[22] and on Digby's Mediterranean voyage his vice-admiral was Sir Edward Stradling,[23] whom his most recent biographer describes as 'an old friend'.[24] Henry A. Bright also notes that 'Sir Kenelm Digby's second son, John Digby . . . was married first to a daughter of the Earl of Arundel',[25] who had been an early dedicatee of Ford's. It is perhaps also worth observing that Ford himself actually refers to Sir Kenelm Digby's ancestor, Sir John Digby, in *Perkin Warbeck*, where we hear of 'Digby, the Lieutenant of the Tower',[26] and that John Mordaunt, earl of Peterborough, dedicatee of *'Tis Pity She's a Whore*, had once been the lover of Digby's wife and may be the person represented by Digby as Mardontius.

There may also be other connections between Digby and *'Tis Pity*. It is intriguing that a copy of 'L'Arcadie de Messire Jacques Sannazar' is included in the list of books which George Digby, earl of Bristol, inherited from Sir Kenelm Digby,[27] and that Sannazaro is mentioned by name in *'Tis Pity She's a Whore* (II.ii.5), in a passage in which, although Sannazaro was associated almost entirely with Naples, Ford

---

[20] Ibid., pp. 10, n. 101, 186–7, n., and 121.

[21] E. W. Bligh, *Sir Kenelm Digby and his Venetia* (London, 1932), p. 150.

[22] Matthew Steggle, *Richard Brome: Place and Politics on the Caroline Stage* (Manchester, 2004), p. 39.

[23] R. T. Petersson, *Sir Kenelm Digby, The Ornament of England, 1603–1665* (London, 1956), p. 92.

[24] Roy Digby Thomas, *Digby: The Gunpowder Plotter's Legacy* (London, 2001), p. 81.

[25] Henry A. Bright, *Poems from Sir Kenelm Digby's Papers in the Possession of Henry A. Bright* (London, 1877), p. i.

[26] John Ford, *Perkin Warbeck*, in Lomax, V.ii.119.

[27] *Bibliotheca Digbeiana, sive, Catalogus librorum in variis linguis editorium quos post Kenelmum Digbeium eruditss. virum possedit illustrissimus Georgius Comes Bristol nuper defunctus . . .* (London, 1680). It should, of course, be noted that Digby was not the only man in London known to possess a volume of Sannazaro. The author was also listed among the books mentioned in the will of John Florio: see Lukas Erne, *Beyond the Spanish Tragedy: A Study of the Works of Thomas Kyd* (Manchester, 2001), p. 194.

links him to Venice. We do not know when Sir Kenelm acquired it, but *DNB* notes that 'Late in 1632 his Oxford friend Thomas Allen died and left him a huge collection of manuscripts . . . and all the printed books he fancied, apart from special bequests'. When his wife, the beautiful Venetia Stanley, died suddenly in her sleep on 1 May 1633, Kenelm Digby wrote an elegy for her which explicitly compared her to the city of Venice:

> What Trauelers of machles VENICE say,
> Is true of thee Admyr'd VENECIA.[28]

Digby noted that Venetia acquired her unusual name because she was born on St Venetia's Day,[29] but for him it also clearly associates her with the city of Venice. *'Tis Pity She's a Whore* was published in 1633, though because it has no Stationers' Register entry it is impossible to know whether it belongs early or late in the year (and it might, of course, have been written much earlier), and there are some suggestive similarities between Ford's play and Digby's life. *DNB* notes that according to his own account, when Marie de' Medici fell in love with him 'Digby gave out that he was dead and fled south, taking ship to Leghorn', like Richardetto in *'Tis Pity* (and like Richardetto he also dabbled in medicine). Like Ford's Giovanni, Digby was interested in the interiors of bodies: he dissected snakes, paying particular attention to their hearts, and also took detailed notes on the post-mortem examination on Venetia, and his interest in embryos was such that *DNB* observes that 'he has been called the father of modern embryology'. He was also, like Giovanni, interested in what was contained within the heart, writing in one of his poems,

> Look in my heart wherin as in a shrine
> The liuelie picture of thy beautie lyes
> Or if thy harmles modestie think shame
> To look upon the horrours of my heart
> Look on these lines and looking sie in them
> The trophie of thy beautie and my smart.[30]

When Venetia died, he did, in fact, look upon the the horrors of her heart, noting that 'When she was opened, her heart was founde perfect and sounde, a fitt seate for such a courage as she had when she

---

[28] 'An Elegie in remembrance of the Lady VENECIA DIGBY', in Bright, *Poems from Sir Kenelm Digby's Papers*, p. 17.

[29] Vittorio Gabrieli, 'A New Digby Letter-Book: "In Praise of Venetia"', *The National Library of Wales Journal* 9 (Winter 1955), 113–48 (135).

[30] Bright, *Poems from Sir Kenelm Digby's Papers*, p. 13.

liued; wch surely was beyond all that euer I knew: it neuer stooped to a lowe or meane action or thought'[31] and later speculating that 'her heart that was the seate of goodnesse, truth and vertue, hath now nothing in it but peraduenture some presumptuous worme feeding on the middle of it'.[32] Digby also sounds like Giovanni when he speculates at great length on 'the content we should haue in one an other in the other world'.[33] The story of Sir Kenelm and Venetia might, then, have been of interest to Ford, and might conceivably be the 'truth' behind *The Broken Heart*.

Another idea, however, has found more general support. In 1909 Stuart Sherman suggested that behind the fictional love story of Penthea and Orgilus lay the real-life love story of Sir Philip Sidney and Penelope Devereux, the sister of the Earl of Essex, who had been forced by her family to marry Robert, Lord Rich, whom she detested, but who never succumbed to Sidney's pleadings, immortalized in his 'Astrophil and Stella' sonnet sequence; amongst the various other pieces of evidence he adduced, he pointed out that that in his elegy for Sidney, *Astrophel*, Spenser imagined the two lovers as transformed into one flower, whose name is Starlight, Astrophel, or Penthia.[34] By 1943, this view had become orthodoxy: Thomas Marc Parrott and Robert Hamilton Ball in *A Short View of Elizabethan Drama* baldly asserted that 'The "truth" to which Ford alludes is the well known story of Philip Sidney's passion for Penelope Devereux'.[35] Similarly Cyril Falls, in 'Penelope Rich and the Poets: Philip Sidney to John Ford', simply accepted the similarity of the events of *The Broken Heart* to the story of Penelope and Sidney and further noted the fact that John Stradling, who was a cousin of Ford's, wrote a Latin eulogy on what Penelope's second husband Lord Mountjoy had achieved in Ireland.[36] It may therefore be worth observing that Stephen O'Neill has recently drawn attention to the violent connotations of the word 'broached' as applied apparently to Essex (and if not then certainly to Mountjoy) in the chorus which opens the fifth act of *Henry V*,[37] and that that word is also applied by Orgilus to the quarrel between Crotolon and Thrasus:

[31] Gabrieli, 'A New Digby Letter-Book', p. 134.
[32] Ibid., p. 145.
[33] Ibid., p. 139.
[34] Stuart P. Sherman, 'Stella and *The Broken Heart*', *PMLA* 24 (1909), 274–85 (285).
[35] Thomas Marc Parrott and Robert Hamilton Ball, *A Short View of Elizabethan Drama* (New York, 1943), p. 242.
[36] Cyril Falls, 'Penelope Rich and the Poets: Philip Sidney to John Ford', *Essays by Divers Hands* 28 (1956), 123–37 (130).
[37] Stephen O'Neill, *Staging Ireland: Representations in Shakespeare and Renaissance Drama* (Dublin, 2007), p. 166.

> After so many quarrels, as dissention,
> Fury, and Rage had brauch't in blood
>
> (1.1.17–18)

This is, of course, only a tiny detail, but in the context it may be significant. Finally, Lesel Dawson suggests that *The Queen*, which is almost certainly by Ford, may have been directly influenced by the story of the Essex rebellion.[38]

Verna Ann Foster and Stephen Foster offer a slightly modified version of this equation when they suggest that Penthea and Orgilus can be perceived as Penelope and Sidney / Mountjoy only because Ithocles is readily identifiable as Essex, and declare that 'Ford dedicated *The Broken Heart* to the only English soldier who could possibly have claimed Essex's mantle in that decade, William, Lord Craven'; pointing to the mention of the Essex ring story in *The Devil's Law-Case* and in John Manningham's diary and the fact that Naunton's *Fragmenta Regalia* was circulating privately in the 1630s, they argue that

> the future relations between Sparta and Argos can hardly have failed to remind a Caroline audience of those already existing between England and Scotland, ruled by one king but separately governed. Like James VI and I, Nearchus is to leave his first kingdom to take up residence in his second and more important one. The third realm Calantha bequeaths, the recently conquered Messene, suggests Ireland, which had been effectively subdued for the first time in the reign of Elizabeth.[39]

There certainly seems to be a strong suggestion that *The Broken Heart* could be perceived by contemporary audiences as interesting itself in questions pertaining to the succession in a 1640 play called *Sicily and Naples, or, The Fatall Vnion* written by Samuel Harding, who like Ford had attended Exeter College Oxford (though Harding was some thirty years younger than Ford). This play, which is preceded by a commendatory verse by Nicholas Downey comparing the play to Shakespeare and Jonson and others by Robert Stapylton, Richard Doddridge, who invokes Thomas Randolph as Jonson's heir, A. Short, Ed.[mund?] Hall, who tells us that the play was 'Printed though not acted', and J. and S. Hall, has, like *The Broken Heart*, a heroine called Calantha. Harding's Calantha, though, is the princess

---

[38] Lesel Dawson, 'Dangerous Misogyny: John Ford's *The Queen* and the Earl of Essex's 1601 Uprising', *Explorations in Renaissance Culture* 33 (2007), 64–82.

[39] Verna Ann Foster and Stephen Foster, 'Structure and History in *The Broken Heart*: Sparta, England, and the "Truth"', *ELR* 18 (1988), 305–28 (315, 312, 318–19, 313, and 305).

not of Sparta but of Sicily (though the reference to Messina echoes that to Messene in *The Broken Heart*), which she unites with Naples by marrying its king, Ferrando, who has just killed her father; the play opens immediately after the conquest, in an atmosphere of suspicion about the state of mind of the conquered Sicilians and fear about the behaviour of the returning Neapolitan army. Already tormented with guilt because of that and at one stage running mad with it, a condition exacerbated, like the madness of Penthea, by not eating or sleeping, Calantha is falsely persuaded to believe that Ferrando has seduced another woman, which leads to a mass slaughter. Ferrando's niece Charintha succeeds in Naples, though it is not explicit what will happen to Sicily. Harding does, then, seem to be associating Ford's play with the idea of succession and changes of rule.

Sparta

Someone encountering *The Broken Heart* for the first time may perhaps feel at a loss, because the play itself seems at first glance to be entirely devoid of feeling. Ford is often compared to Webster, but *The Duchess of Malfi* seethes with emotion: love, hatred, jealousy, the fierce devotion of motherhood. In *The Broken Heart*, however, the attraction between Calantha and Ithocles may well feel understated, and Orgilus' polite dispatching of Ithocles is a far cry from the lycanthropy of Ferdinand. But to value *The Broken Heart* we need to understand and respond to what it is, not what it is not, and the first thing to understand is that for all its ethos of restraint, this too is a play that seethes with emotion. Perhaps the finest of all comments on Ford's art is Havelock Ellis's

> It is the grief deeper than language that he strives to express . . .
> He is a master of the brief mysterious words, so calm in seeming,
> which well up from the depths of despair. He concentrates the
> revelation of a soul's agony into a sob or a sigh. The surface seems
> calm; we scarcely suspect that there is anything beneath; one gasp
> bubbles up from the drowning heart below, and all is silence.[40]

[40] Ellis, introduction, pp. xiv–xv. Robert Davril ('Shakespeare and Ford', *Shakespeare Jahrbuch* 94 (1958), 121–31 (129)) similarly comments on the importance of silence in Ford, particularly where female characters are concerned. Silence was, of course, the most prized of all female qualities: see, for instance, Christina Hole, *The English Housewife in the Seventeenth Century* (London, 1953), p. 136; Wallace Notestein, 'The English Woman, 1580–1650', in J. H. Plumb (ed.), *Studies in Social History: A Tribute to G. M. Trevelyan* (London, 1955), p. 77; and Lisa Jardine, *Still Harping on Daughters: Women and Drama in the Age of Shakespeare* (London, 1983), pp. 37–62.

These characters do have hearts which feel, and indeed break; they just don't talk about it. This might seem to be a problem for drama, but Ford's genius lies in making us feel the force of their emotions without using language.

One reason for the characters' reticence is the play's setting, Sparta. As discussed in the section 'Sources', the story of Orgilus and Penthea has elements in common with that of Sidney and his Stella, while the names of Ford's characters may well seem to echo those of Argalus and Parthenia, who feature in one of the numerous subplots of the new *Arcadia*. Ford's borrowings from Sidney are certainly extensive and sustained. In both *The Broken Heart* and the *Arcadia*, events unfold against the backdrop of a riddling oracle which has foretold the fall from power of the present royal family. In Sidney, too, the King of Laconia is called Amiclas, matching Ford's Amyclas; Parthenia when deformed refuses to marry Argalus, just as Penthea refuses Orgilus, though Parthenia later, in disguise, tries to trick Argalus into marrying her with a ring, rather as Calantha asserts her wedding to Ithocles.

The difference, however, is that while the *Arcadia* is (of course) set in Arcadia, *The Broken Heart* is set in Sparta. Rowland Wymer terms Sparta 'a state which resembled Rome in the range of connotations it possessed for the Renaissance',[41] and T. J. B. Spencer suggests that Sparta might have meant three main things to Ford:

> powers of endurance and self-restraint (Lamb rightly reminded us, in his note to the play, of 'the fortitude of the Spartan boy who let a beast gnaw out his bowels till he died without expressing a groan'; . . . brevity and conciseness of speech ('laconism'); . . . the chastity and moral strength of their women.[42]

Laconism is certainly there; foxes are remembered when Grausis is termed a 'bitch-foxe' at 2.1.120, and implicitly also when Bassanes' desire to stop the windows so clearly recalls what is done to Celia in *Volpone*, whose subtitle is *The Fox*; and the chastity and moral strength of both Calantha and Penthea are beyond dispute. But Sparta also seems to mean some other things to Ford. For Sidney, Arcadia had been a playland in which he could discuss political systems and dangerous political issues in an atmosphere of comparative safety and pastoral playfulness. Ford's Sparta is directly contrasted with that Arcadian

---

[41] Wymer, p. 108. He goes on to consider some of these (pp. 108–9).

[42] Spencer, Introduction, p. 21. Elizabeth Rawson, in *The Spartan Tradition in European Thought* (Oxford, 1990), also suggests that Ford chose Sparta because he 'felt it to be a suitable setting for his heroine's constancy' and points out that 'the later ancient sources do paint Spartan women as models of conjugal chastity' (pp. 208, 209).

world when Penthea and Ithocles join in antiphonal lament for their plight:

> PENTHEA   The handmaid to the wages
> Of Country toyle drinkes the untroubled streames
> With leaping kids, and with the bleating lambes;
> And so allayes her thirst secure, whiles I
> Quench my hot sighes with fleetings of my teares.

> ITHOCLES   The labouror doth eat his coursest bread,
> Earn'd with his sweat, and lyes him downe to sleepe;
> Which every bit I touch turnes in disgestion
> To gall, as bitter as Penthea's curse.
> Put me to any pennance for my tyranny,
> And I will call thee mercifull.

(III.ii.54–64)

Briefly, the tragic pair imagine the pastoral; but they have been irretrievably alienated from it by tyranny, forced marriage, and suffering. Perhaps most sadly, the characters in Sidney's *Arcadia* talk about how they feel in a variety of ways including songs, but this is as close as Penthea and Ithocles ever really come to expressing their emotions.

One reason why the Sparta of *The Broken Heart* is such a bleak place may be found in a play which seems to be very obviously a source for part of the plot of *The Broken Heart*, Chapman's *The Widow's Tears*. Set in Cyprus, home of the goddess of love and location of Ford's *The Lover's Melancholy*, Chapman's comedy makes ongoing fun of its party of visiting Spartans, who are insistently characterized as Scots. Since Chapman was writing shortly after the accession of James I,[43] the satirical intent is quite obvious, and makes for an interesting sidelight on Verna Ann Foster's and Stephen Foster's argument that *The Broken Heart*, too, remembers the events surrounding James I's accession when Nearchus, the 'new prince' from a neighbouring country, succeeds Calantha, last of her line (in Michael Boyd's 1994 RSC production Nearchus had a pronounced Scottish accent, while Calantha was costumed in such a way as to vaguely recall portraits of Elizabeth I).[44] Arcadia was an important concept for the Stuart court: in Chelsea, Sir John Danvers, relative of Ford's dedicatees the Earls of Arundel

---

[43] For the date, see George Chapman, *The Widow's Tears*, ed. Ethel M. Smeak (Lincoln, NE, 1966), introduction, pp. xi–xii. All quotations from the play will be taken from this edition and references will be given in the text.

[44] See Kristin Crouch, 'The Silent Griefs Which Cut the Heart Strings', in Edward J. Esche and Dennis Kennedy (eds.), *Shakespeare and his Contemporaries in Performance* (Aldershot, 2000), pp. 61–74.

and Pembroke, was creating a garden specifically designed as an Arcadia, and court masques for Henrietta Maria evoked a similar mood.[45] Ford, though, connects the Stuart monarchy with a society which is ideologically and emotionally repressive, and underscores that by moving a story once set in Arcadia to Sparta.

Hearts

The titles of all Ford's single-authored plays represent a conundrum. *'Tis Pity She's a Whore*, the flippant summing-up of the Cardinal, is a formulation which raises as many questions as it answers: is that really all that need be said about Annabella? And what are we to make of the fact that there is another character in the play, Putana, whose name actually means 'whore', and who enthusiastically encourages Annabella's actions? *The Chronicle History of Perkin Warbeck* is equally ambiguous, for nowhere in the play is it ever actually made clear that the title character *is*, in fact, Perkin Warbeck and not, as he claims, Richard, Duke of York. *The Lady's Trial* and *The Lover's Melancholy* both arouse uncertainties about the very punctuation of their titles: is there only one lady who is on trial, and only one lover who is melancholy, or are there in each case two or more? Perhaps even more puzzlingly, are the Fancies chaste and noble really chaste and noble, and who or what is love's sacrifice?

The Broken Heart, although often the most admired of Ford's plays, is no exception to this general trend. Indeed, the poet Richard Crashaw directly compared it to the ambiguities of *Love's Sacrifice* in his couplet

> Thou cheat'st us, Ford; mak'st one seem two by art;
> What is Love's Sacrifice but the Broken Heart?[46]

Crashaw seems to be assuming or implying a religious meaning to both terms, but even that is not clear. Tecnicus' prophecy appears to make clear that it is Calantha who is the broken heart, united with Ithocles in death to fulfil the prediction that 'the lifeless trunk shall wed the broken heart'. But Penthea and Orgilus also suffer from broken hearts, as presumably do Ithocles when he realizes that he is about to die and be parted from Calantha, Euphranea when she has to watch her brother bleed to death, and Bassanes when he learns that Penthea is dead. Once again, then, Ford has chosen a title for his play which

---

[45] Roy Strong, *The Renaissance Garden in England* (London, 1979), p. 179.
[46] Richard Crashaw, *The Complete Works of Richard Crashaw*, ed. William B. Turnbull (London, 1858), p. 109.

poses a puzzle rather than providing a solution, for which of these are we to regard as the central character?

For many critics, the main focus of interest has been Penthea. Penthea, whose name means sorrow, has a good claim to be the saddest character in a sad play, and although she owes something to Shakespeare,[47] she is a wholly original creation. What makes her so extraordinary is not only her combination of absolute purity with self-identified corruption, but her troubling liminality as virgin wife. It is from this anomalous position which she has constructed for herself that the apparently oppressed Penthea dictates a terrifying and absolute law: Orgilus may never have her even if she is widowed, and she herself must starve to death. In fact, the play suggests that Penthea does not need to do this. Her argument for dismissing Orgilus forever is that

> The Virgin dowry which my birth bestow'd
> Is ravish'd by another: my true love
> Abhorres to thinke, that Orgilus deserv'd
> No better favours than a second bed.
>
> (2.3.99–102)

Bassanes himself, however, laments, 'O that I could preserve thee in fruition | As in devotion!' (3.2.165–6), and his fury when Grausis suggests that Penthea might be pregnant would seem to confirm this clear suggestion that he is in fact impotent.[48] And Penthea's attitude to Bassanes is also far from the dutiful submission it appears to be, as we see when she neatly sidesteps the issue of whether she supports him during his dispute with Ithocles:

> ITHOCLES   Well Sir,
> I dare not trust her to your fury.
> BASSANES   But
> Penthea sayes not so.
> PENTHEA   She needs no tongue
> To plead excuse, who never purpos'd wrong.
>
> (3.2.190–3)

---

[47] In her madness she resembles Ophelia, and Roberta Barker points out that 'Penthea's use of the word "livery" [2.1.101] echoes Angelo's speech in *Measure for Measure*, when the deputy bids Isabella prove her womanhood by "putting on the destined livery" (*Measure* 2.4.138)'. See Barker, *Early Modern Tragedy, Gender and Performance, 1984–2000: The Destined Livery* (Basingstoke, 2007), p. 146.

[48] For the argument that Bassanes is impotent, see, for instance, Sensabaugh, pp. 60–1.

This, one might well conclude, is passive aggression; painting herself as a helpless victim and a pawn in affairs, Penthea is, in fact, coldly, furiously manipulating them.

In a play where characters' names openly draw attention to their association with emotional states and issues, it is also clear that Penthea alerts us to an image pattern which is extremely important in the play, identified by Sharon Hamilton as 'images . . . related to nurture: metaphors of health, and nourishment, and growth'.[49] Orgilus tells his father that

> From this time sprouted up that poysonous stalke
> Of Aconite, whose ripened fruit hath ravisht
> All health, all comfort of a happy life:
> For Ithocles her brother, proud of youth,
> And prouder in his power, nourisht closely
> The memory of former discontents.
>
> (1.2.36–41)

Normally, ripened fruit would be associated with fulfilment and pleasure, as in the Latin tag *carpe diem* (literally 'pluck the fruit of the day') poetry; here, it destroys, and the only things 'nourished' are 'discontents'. Nursing of other kinds is also associated with destruction and unhappiness when Orgilus goes on to tell Crotolon that

> Bassanes
> The man that calls her wife, considers truly
> What Heaven of perfections he is Lord of,
> By thinking faire Penthea his: this thought
> Begets a kinde of Monster-Love, which Love
> Is nurse unto a feare so strong, and servile,
> As brands all dotage with a Jealousie.
>
> (1.2.57–63)

Crotolon himself speaks of 'the painted meat of smooth perswasion' (2.2.22), and Penthea again links with ripeness with pain and sorrow when she tells Orgilus that what he has said 'Ripens a knowledge in me of afflictions, | Above all suffrance' (2.3.44–5).

The most sustained example of this association between pain and what would normally nourish is the dialogue between Penthea and Ithocles about the bitterness of what they eat and drink (3.2.54–62), but throughout the play things that are eaten or drunk are persistently

---

[49] Sharon Hamilton, '*The Broken Heart*: Language Suited to a Divided Mind', in Anderson, pp. 171–93 (181).

imaged as harmful. Bassanes assumes that Ithocles' indisposition is
caused by 'Some surfeit or disorder' (2.3.142), while Ithocles says to
Bassanes

> But that I may conceive the spirit of wine
> Has tooke possession of your soberer custome,
> I'de say you were unmannerly.
>
> (3.2.138–40)

Later, imagery of food consumption comes naturally to Bassanes when
he wants to talk about suffering: he tells Armostes 'Make me the patterne of digesting evils' (5.2.58), and says of Orgilus' blood that 'It
sparkles like a lusty wine new broacht' (5.2.125). One of the characters
is even named Hemophil, 'eater of blood', and quite unusually in a
Renaissance tragedy, for which the bloody banquet is such a staple
device (as in *'Tis Pity She's a Whore*), there is no eating, not even at the
wedding.

No wonder, then, that Penthea refuses to eat. What, though, does
that mean? For a modern audience, such a refusal proved easy to
decode. Roberta Barker points to the number of reviews of Boyd's
production which identified Penthea as anorexic.[50] However the idea
of self-starvation might well be susceptible of a less transhistorical
analysis. Penthea herself, speaking of herself in the third person, says

> But since her blood was season'd by the forfeit
> Of noble shame, with mixtures of pollution,
> Her blood ('tis just) be henceforth never heightned
> With tast of sustenance. Starve; let that fulnesse
> Whose plurisie hath fever'd faith and modesty—
> Forgive me; o, I faint.
>
> (4.2.149–54)

As Cynthia Marshall points out, 'The link she draws between blood
and sustenance seems remote to modern readers, but seventeenth-
century audiences would understand the humoral physiology Penthea
appeals to here: blood, according to the standard models, was produced from food, in a three-step process'.[51] If, as I have suggested
elsewhere,[52] Ford was a Catholic, imagery of starvation could also
indicate a sense of the loss caused by the substitution of Protestant
idea of consubstantiation for the Catholic idea of transubstantiation.

---

[50] Barker, *Early Modern Tragedy*, p. 154.
[51] Cynthia Marshall, *The Shattering of the Self: Violence, Subjectivity and Early Modern Texts*
(Baltimore, MD, 2002), p. 148.
[52] See Hopkins, *Political*.

Alternatively, to see Calantha as the focus rather than Penthea would shift our attention to another pattern which is also crucially important in the play. Almost as insistent as the references to food are the references to dance. We find these in frivolous vein, as in the exchange between Phulas and Bassanes:

PHULAS   Yes truly, and 'tis talkt about the streete,
         That since Lord Ithocles came home, the Lyons
         Never left roaring, at which noyse the Beares
         Have danc'd their very hearts out.
BASSANES   Dance out thine too.
                                            (2.1.49–52)

The idea of dancing is also stated more seriously, in the precept of Ithocles:

                    Morality appli'd
         To timely practice, keeps the soule in tune,
         At whose sweet musicke all our actions dance;
                    (2.2.8–10)

Most tellingly, dance and what it means are evoked by the disguised Orgilus when talking to Penthea:

         Speake on, faire nimph, our soules
         Can dance as well to musicke of the Spheares
         As any's who have feasted with the gods.
                    (2.3.18–20)

The literal culmination of this imagistic pattern, Calantha's dance, has attracted more attention and more criticism, favourable and unfavourable, than any other aspect of the play: Lamb thought it reminiscent of Calvary; Hazlitt thought it ridiculous and contemptible. What it certainly is, though, is a visual expression of the principles of order, proportion, and harmony, and when Calantha, whose name means flower of beauty, engages in that performance of order, we come close to the expression of a platonic ideal.

The association of names with states is, however, emblematized perhaps most strongly in the character of Ithocles, who also has a claim to be the centre of attention. What Ithocles stands for is not so much the abstract quality which is his name connotes ('Honour of loveliness') but for the essence of abstraction itself, particularly in its capacity of forcing speech apart from experience. He is first mentioned to Calantha in a speech remarkable for its preponderance of abstract nouns:

> Excellent Princesse,
> Your owne faire eyes may soone report a truth
> Unto your judgement, with what moderation,
> Calmenesse of nature, measure, bounds and limits
> Of thankfulnesse, and joy, 'a doth digest
> Such amplitude of his successe, as would
> In others, moulded of a spirit lesse cleare,
> Advance 'em to comparison with heaven.
>
> (1.2.33–40)

Ithocles also uses abstraction as part of an attempt to dissociate himself from the potentially compromising revelation of his own love for Calantha:

> 'twas a fault,
> A Capitall fault, for then I could not dive
> Into the secrets of commanding Love:
> Since when, experience by the extremities (in others)
> Hath forc'd me to collect.
>
> (2.2.49–53)

He himself says of war 'Judgement commands, | But Resolution executes' (1.2.87–8), and in a play where a song asks the rhetorical question '*Can you paint a thought?*' (3.2.1), and in which we are treated to a lengthy definition of honour in entirely abstract terms (3.1.30 ff), Ithocles draws our attention to the way in which *The Broken Heart* can at times sound almost like a morality play. Harriett Hawkins observes that one possible reading of the play is 'as a critical indictment of an abstract idealism so at odds with human nature as to demand that living men and women sacrifice and "real, visible, material happiness" ';[53] Ithocles is arguably the character who does most to support that reading. As a successful soldier, he is presumably a man of blood, but the impression he creates in the play is ironically one of bloodlessness.

Orgilus too has a claim to centrality, and he too is linked with an important image pattern. Ford's almost obsessive interest in the words 'blood' and 'heart', presumably fuelled by the publication of Harvey's *De motu cordis* (Leiden, 1628), has often been remarked,[54] and at times he seems to figure the blood and heart as operating almost independently

---

[53] Harriett Hawkins, 'Mortality, Morality, and Modernity in *The Broken Heart*: Some Dramatic and Critical Counter-arguments', in Neill (ed.), pp. 129–52 (131).

[54] See, for instance, Marshall, *The Shattering of the Self*, pp. 144–5, and Colin Gibson, ' "The Stage of My Mortality": Ford's Poetry of Death', in Neill (ed.), pp. 55–80 (68).

of the rest of the body, as when Euphranea says 'thus our hearts may talke when our tongues cannot' (1.3.152). Nancy A. Gutierrez suggests that Ford models the scene of Ithocles's death on the anatomy theatre, where the anatomist's apparent control is, in fact, subverted by the corpse, as on the frontispiece of Andreas Vesalius's 1543 *De Humani Corporis Fabrica* where

> The cadaver—lying on its back, slightly raised, with the middle part of its torso cut open—is the passive object of the audience's gaze, and thus has a feminized position within the scene, as it is subjected to the controlling and curious gaze of the spectators.[55]

The Broken Heart does indeed make suggestive use of the language of anatomy: Bassanes exclaims 'Rip my bosome up' (3.2.188), we hear of 'the opening of this Riddle' (4.3.24), and Orgilus chaffs Ithocles that 'Calantha's brest is open'd' (4.3.113) by Cupid's arrows. In all these instances, the emphasis is on the idea of human bodies invaded and the secrets of their interiors laid disturbingly, shockingly bare, so that we see the broken heart inside.

In one sense, though, the heart can be mended. 'Our scene is Sparta' not only evokes the connotations of Sparta itself but also activates another set of associations, since such an announcement at the beginning of a prologue might well seem to recall Shakespeare's *Romeo and Juliet*, where the Prologue opens with the words 'In fair Verona, where we lay our scene'. Again, this is a dramatic strategy that Ford had either already used or was about to do so, for *'Tis Pity She's a Whore*, with its young lovers, its nurse, its friar, and its death of an innocent halfway through, is obviously modelled on the structure of Shakespeare's tragedy, accentuating the startling fact that here the lovers' family backgrounds are not too far apart but too close together. In *The Broken Heart*, too, the similarity seems to be evoked only in order to emphasize a difference, because Ford's Prologue is not in the form of a sonnet but of eighteen lines of rhyming couplets. That this is a deliberate deviation from an expected norm is made clear by the Prologue's sustained literary self-consciousness, and seems to suggest that, despite its title, this is a play which does not confine itself to the matters of the heart which are traditionally the province of the sonnet, but ranges further afield. This appears to be confirmed by the fact that the Epilogue of the

---

[55] Nancy A. Gutierrez, 'Trafficking in John Ford's *The Broken Heart*', in Corinne S. Abate (ed.), *Privacy, Domesticity, and Women in Early Modern England* (Aldershot: Ashgate, 2003), pp. 65–81 (75–7). See also Christian Billing, 'Modelling the Anatomy Theatre and the Indoor Hall Theatre: Dissection on the Stages of Early Modern London', *Early Modern Literary Studies* Special Issue 13 (April, 2004), http://extra.shu.ac.uk/emls/si-13/billing/index.htm.

play *is* only fourteen lines, thus at least gesturing towards the shape of the sonnet, and, despite the fact that all the principal characters are dead, the Epilogue ends with the suggestion that 'by th'allowance of this strain, | *The Broken Heart* may be pieced up again'. This not only recalls the Prologue—'*HE whose best of Art* | *Hath drawne* this Peece, *cals it the* Broken Heart' (Prologue 1–2)—but also makes it clear that the play is interested not only in the story which it tells but also in the mode of telling it, and that, even if the material of the play is tragedy and loss, success may nevertheless have been achieved in its form. Art, then, is the only and ultimate answer to problems of the heart.

Theatre History

The Broken Heart has not been much produced. The Elizabethan Stage Society, directed by William Poel, performed it at St George's Hall, London, 11 June 1898.[56] The Mermaid Society, directed by Philip Carr, acted it at the Royalty Theatre, London, for one week from 21 November 1904, and the Dramatic Society of Queen's University, Belfast, directed by Derek Bailey, in 1959.[57] There was a celebrated production directed by Laurence Olivier (who also played Bassanes) at the Chichester Festival from 9 July 1962 with Keith Michell as Ithocles, Rosemary Harris as Penthea, and Joan Greenwood as Calantha, although A.M. in *The Stage and Television Today* (12 July 1962) called the play 'a dreary museum-piece' which failed to involve its audience.[58] In 1967 there was a French television production directed by Jean de Beer, and radio versions appeared in 1956 and 1970. There was also an excellent production directed by Simon Usher at the Leicester Haymarket in 1988. This was well-omened from the start, since Usher had given an interview in *The Guardian* (4 October 1988) which indicated a strong sensitivity to the formal, ritualistic, life-denying quality of the play, and this was admirably brought out in the production. The solemn, static acting style pointed up the importance in the play of

---

[56] The production is discussed by William Archer in *Study and Stage* (London, 1899), pp. 238–9, and by Robert Speaight, *William Poel and the Elizabethan Revival* (London, 1954), pp. 128–30.

[57] This was reviewed by Ray Rosenfield in *Plays and Players* (August 1959), p. 32 and Phyllis Hartnoll in *Theatre Arts* (December 1959), pp. 9–83.

[58] See http://www.picks.plus.com/howard/broken.htm. Other reviews included J. C. Trewin in *The Birmingham Post*, 10 July 1962, Kenneth Tynan in *The Observer*, 15 July 1962, and in *The Times* on 11 July 1962. See also Roger Warren, 'Ford in Performance', in Neill (ed.), pp. 11–27 (19–21).

codified gesture—not only did Orgilus and Penthea kneel to each other, but characters bowed and clasped their hands together in submission, and held them above their heads whenever one of the frequent invocations to Apollo was uttered. Duckings of the knee emphasized the importance of rank in this play. When not involved in one of these formalized gestures the main characters moved little, standing for the most part still and stiff, as they needed to in order to point up the contrast with the occasions on which characters are so forcibly made to sit down (something underlined by the ingenious touch of having Penthea make her first entrance in a wheelchair). In keeping with their Spartan code, both Calantha and Orgilus died standing, and Dhobi Oparei's admirable Orgilus further added to the sense of constraint by managing to introduce into his voice both a sense of breathless passion fighting to be let out and, superimposed on it, a relentless control which appeared at every word to be trying to fight back expression. Unfortunately, a cast of only seven players meant that in the final scene there were simply not enough people to provide both the dancers and the bringers of bad news, and Anthony Douse had to come on as Armostes and Bassanes in quick succession. David Gant doubled Crotolon, Tecnicus, Amelus, Amyclas, and Phulas, while Frank Stirling as Ithocles also had to play his own best friend Prophilus, and in fact created the difference between the two with an extraordinary degree of success. Veronica Smart's unbending, anorexic Penthea was the only character not to be doubled; even Calantha also appeared as Grausis and Christalla. The austerity of the casting policy was matched by the simplicity of the set, a small polygon with a screen round the back sides punctuated by doorways, one of which was used as the discovery space. For certain scenes the doorways were closed off with white curtains when the feeling of a more enclosed space was wanted. Apart from chairs when needed, the set was bare; even bloodbags were mere token gestures. The power of the language was left to do its own work, and in this it succeeded admirably.

Most notably, *The Broken Heart* was directed by Michael Boyd at the Swan in 1994, with some spectacular effects. The production opened with music, as Iain Glen's Orgilus slowly sang his Act III epithalamion to his own accompaniment on a lute, and the play was underscored throughout by a haunting courtly accompaniment on harp, harmonium, strings, percussion, and wind. The play proper opened on a backdrop of heavy turquoise curtains and a ghostly presence: as well as Orgilus and Tony Britton's massively dignified Crotolon, Emma Fielding's Penthea stalked the scene. Veiled and wearing her bridal garland, she circled the stage, half a phantom ever present to Orgilus' mind, half a sorrowful warning to the audience of what was to come. When the setting moved to the court, the curtains were swung back to reveal thinner, more ethereal drapes of a deeper green, spangled with snowflake flowers lit variously as white or green. The production pivoted mainly around these curtained spaces, but in the scene when Armostes visited Tecnicus a corrugated metal backdrop slowly descended, bringing with it a new atmosphere of menace. The grille was used repeatedly thereafter, but not always to entirely satisfactory effect: it was slow-moving, and creaks—a technical difficulty echoed when in at least one performance at Calantha's cry of 'Crack, crack!' the turquoise curtains clattered to the ground in a way that may or may not have been intended.

Costuming for this production was lavish. Taken from Ford's own period rather than the historical Sparta of his setting, it was markedly Caroline, but was, appropriately enough, subdivided into two distinct styles of dress, roughly approximating to Cavalier and Puritan. There were rich lace collars and pearl ropes for Calantha and her ladies, but stark, high-necked white for Penthea, accentuating the pallor of her make-up as strident, unpitying, she tormented Bassanes with her silence, Orgilus and Ithocles with her words, and herself with self-starvation in ways which made this seventeenth-century character instantly recognizable to modern theories of the psychology of anorexia. Her mad scene was played out against the background of Prophilus' and Euphranea's wedding feast, with the bride and groom themselves still seated at the table and occasionally giggling to one another, while, in a nice verbal correlative for the play's persistent verbal imagery of untasted banquets, all the other characters ignored the laden tables. The centrepiece of the meal was a magnificent lifesize swan, in full plumage, and neatly alluding to both the Swan Theatre itself and to the idea of the swansong as well as serving as a powerful emblem for the sacrificed purity of Penthea herself. When Orgilus and Ithocles found Penthea dead, she was seated in front of the now despoiled dinner table: the swan was still there, but now hanged by its neck, suspended above the table, and with its breast partially gutted. As Kristin Crouch puts it, at the wedding feast 'crowning the centrepiece of the table is the delicate figure of a swan. Later in the performance, the shutters are again raised to reveal the same banquet, but with a crucial difference—the food is rotting and decaying, the sound of buzzing flies fills the air, and the swan is hung by the neck, dripping blood from its disembowelled body onto the wasted scene'.[59] As Penthea sat slumped beneath it, the precise quality of her suffering was both brilliantly and brutally conveyed by the stage picture.

After her tête-à-tête with Penthea, Olivia Williams' Calantha too took on something of Penthea's terrifying starkness. Initially little more than a very stately and gracious princess, she developed into increasing isolation and hauteur; her voice became imperious, her gestures impatient, her glance directed at something that others did not see. Her famous dance was, with almost certain accuracy, performed as a brawl, or ring dance; but, in an interesting variation, when Orgilus arrived with the news of Ithocles' death he took Calantha's place in the circle and she danced for a little while completely alone in the centre. The symbolic significance of the dance was bolstered in this production not only by Ithocles' speech about morality but by several other dances. Penthea's circling movements in the opening and during her mad scene resembled Calantha's, while Groneas and Hemophil performed their courtship of Christalla and Philema as a dance, punctuated by an exhibition of some splendid swordplay by Groneas which Hemophil rather lamely tried to imitate, only to find Groneas knocking his sword down. This got a laugh, as did various other elements of the production, in particular the line 'Hold your chops, nightmare!' from Philip Voss's excellent Bassanes, who moved from a character initially resembling a pantomime dame into one who struggled for stoicism, his transformation signalled by his adoption of a starkly Puritan style of dress which made him the masculine correlative of his wife. For Roberta Barker, Bassanes was a pivotal character for how in Boyd's production 'Ford's "stage of mortality" became the stage on which a profoundly conflicted discourse of gender was exposed as a death-trap'; she argues that Penthea's apparent obedience to Bassanes is really a form of passive aggression, particularly in Boyd's production, where Bassanes'

> whole identity had visibly come to revolve around his precarious possession of, and strenuous efforts to win over, his beautiful young wife. But Penthea's perfect façade refused to allow him any access to her inner life; he was blocked off from exchange with her, and her submission folded him in the cloud of unknowing that gave rise to his brutal jealousy. Their interaction provided a frightening spectacle of a powerful discursive system undermining itself from within.[60]

[59] Crouch, ' "The Silent Griefs Which Cut the Heart Strings" ', p. 261. It was also reviewed by Peter Holland in the *TLS*, 28 October 1994.
[60] Barker, *Early Modern Tragedy*, pp. 137 and 147.

Certainly Boyd's production revealed Bassanes as far more than a plot device, and rather as a character whose heart was as broken as anyone else's.

Not all the male characters were as impressive as Bassanes. Iain Glen's Orgilus was fiery and splendid; one particularly effective aspect was his disguise, a long green robe and a huge, floppy green hat which—so rare in a disguise—actually did render him unrecognizable. Tecnicus was made blind, a justified addition to a play with a direct reference to Oedipus; Armostes was coldly impressive. Robert Bowman's Ithocles, though, seemed an odd choice for the lordly general, being, physically, rather unimpressive—indeed his shortness allowed for another piece of comedy when David Beames' Nearchus towered above him to say with considerable point, 'Sirrah, low mushrooms never rival cedars'. Nearchus himself, splendidly dressed in white and gold doublet and hose, was given a strong Scottish accent, to underline the parallels pointed out in the programme between the triads of Elizabeth I/Essex/James I and Calantha/Ithocles/Nearchus. Special mention should go to William Houston's Prophilus: raw-boned, red-haired, Irish-accented, and perpetually on the alert, his was a performance which provided strong support to every scene in which it featured, even if the nature of the friendship which linked him to Ithocles was made by this prominence to seem even more sketchily developed than usual. Such a performance provided a measure of the production's excellence in that it pleased in its detail, too, as well as in its grand design, and also helped testify conclusively that this was a play which could still work to magnificent effect on the modern stage.

Most recently, there has been a reading of the play in 2005 at the Red Bull Theatre in New York and a production in 2006 at the White Bear Theatre in London, which updated the play to the 1940s to convey the sense of a society coming to terms with the end of a war.[61] The production that was at the Sam Wanamaker Playhouse from 12 March to 18 April 2015 was unfortunately hampered by two things, the director not knowing what kind of play it was and several of the cast (at least at the beginning of the run) not knowing their lines (Amyclas, in particular, stumbled repeatedly). The director Caroline Steinbeis, who had never before directed anything other than modern work, cheerfully

---

[61] The only record of this appears to be a theatre review by Natalie Bennett posted at http://blogcritics.org/archives/2006/01/15/143213.php, which puzzlingly declares that that one of the best lines in the play is 'It is a villainous world for one who can't hold his own in it' and, even more worryingly, commends 'the use of the wheelbarrow as a playful toy in the courtship scene between Euphranea and her paramour Prophilus'.

opined in the programme that 'Ultimately we are dealing with a Caroline soap opera', and everything possible was played for laughs, with Nearchus channelling Lord Flashheart ('Hello Sparta! Ding-dong!'), the second half opening with Penthea, Calantha, and Euphranea coming out of three doors like a demented cuckoo clock, and Bassanes inadvertently sitting in the trick chair and having to be rescued from it by a solicitous Orgilus. The audience even laughed as Orgilus bled to death, possibly because of the noise the blood made as it splashed into the metal basins placed to catch it. Perhaps the business was intended to compensate for what was clearly felt to be the insuperable difficulty of the language, because the production was dogged from the outset by a sense that no one could possibly be expected to follow it. It opened with the backstory of how Penthea and Orgilus came to be parted, with a snatch of invented dialogue, and this freedom with Ford's words extended to other aspects of the production too: there was no Christalla, Philema, Groneas, or Hemophil—their parts were either excised entirely or given to Grausis and Prophilus respectively— and in another simplification Penthea (who appeared to be simply very cross rather than pathologically self-sabotaging) had only one thing to leave, Ithocles. Despite the fact that everyone else's costume was ancient Greek, she also wore a Tudor headdress, presumably in the hope that it would offer an audience likely to have been recently watching *Wolf Hall* some way of latching onto events.

The audience were certainly likely to be in need of all the guidance they could get, because several moments were potentially baffling. The fact that Orgilus and Crotolon were both Scots but Nearchus was not made it difficult to recognize the parallel with James I; the fact that the dead Ithocles was standing up made it hard to read him *as* dead (Calantha also died standing); the fact that the dance was not a round but similar to the closing jig made it difficult to see any potential parallel to the Dance of Death. Sarah MacRae's Calantha was excellent, and the terrifying golden carapace into which she had to be strapped in order to be crowned was visually very strong, but ultimately this was a production which offered no serious insight into the play and failed to do justice to its austere beauty.

The production directed by Iqbal Khan at RADA from 10 to 19 March 2016 was better. This was a slimmed-down version of the play with no Phulas, Christalla, Philema, Hemophil, or Groneas (some speeches were reassigned to compensate), and there was a similar spareness to the staging: the set consisted of tall pillar-like blocks not unlike the sarsens of Stonehenge, which could be moved into various positions and configurations. Sections of these pillars could be pulled out to form rudimentary seats, and this was particularly effective in the final scene, in which the dead Ithocles was placed by attendants on one. This worked much better than the production at the Sam Wanamaker Playhouse, in which the corpse was ludicrously and incomprehensibly standing, and it was also a nice touch that the dying Calantha sank onto the seat of another pillar, marking her separation from him. What did not work so well, however, was having the dead body of Penthea standing in a glass case (opaque at first but mysteriously made transparent by Orgilus). Possibly the intention was to make her appear like a Snow White who fails to wake, but overall the effect was simply odd, and there were other oddities too. Calantha (Evlyne Oyedokun) seemed to have her own story arc, and appeared to be simply cross at the successive interruptions to the dance. Ithocles (Thomas Martin) didn't bat an eyelid when Penthea informed the entire assembled company that 'his heart | Is crept into the cabinet of the princess' (4.2.117–18), as if he didn't understand the implications. There was some very heavy endstopping of the verse which at times threatened to undermine sense, and the ensemble rendering of the songs seemed designed to showcase the performers' musical skills rather than to be guided by the text. It also became unusually apparent that this is a play structured by intergenerational conflict, and also has some characters who are supposed to be very ugly, and is therefore not best suited to performance by a cast of impossibly beautiful twenty-somethings. Nevertheless there were compelling performances from Ithocles, Orgilus (Matt Gavan), and a Penthea (Polly Misch) whose black dress and plain headscarf gave her something of an Amish appearance, and the production did capture something of the strange spare beauty of the play and its atmosphere of a calm which kills.

The Text

Hugh Beeston entered *The Broken Heart* in the Stationers' Register on 28 March 1633 and it appeared at an unknown date the same year, as testified by the title page. The entry in the Stationers' Register reads 'Entred for his Copy under the hands of Sir Henry Herbert and master Aspley Warden a Tragedy called *The broken heart* by John fford'. The play was not reprinted until the nineteenth century, when Ford attracted renewed interest. T. J. B. Spencer's edition of the play for the Revels series provides a full account of his printing, but since then,

R. J. Fehrenbach has also addressed the question in in his illuminating study of the use of different fonts in the quartos of Ford's plays, observing that although 'The evidence . . . suggests that Ford did have . . . some interest in conveying verbal emphasis with a typographical variation of italics and roman and upper and lower cases',

> The text of *The Broken Heart* . . . contains only a few instances of emphatic typography, though all the extratextual material—a dedication, a prologue and an epilogue—are characteristically of mixed type. The Bridal Song in the text is, however, heavily marked with italicized words.

He therefore suggests that 'one might reasonably conclude with Spencer that the printer's copy of *The Broken Heart* was not in mixed hands or copy-edited for italics', for which 'One explanation is that *The Broken Heart* was brought to be printed only after it had been some time on the boards'.[62] I also append the results of Carter Hailey's optical collation of the surviving texts, undertaken for this volume.

APPENDIX A

Carter Hailey, Optical Collation of Surviving Quarto Texts

The quarto volume collates A–K4 with the first leaf blank and leaf A3 missigned as A2. A4^r presents 'The Speakers names, fitted to their | Qualities', with the Prologue printed on the verso of this leaf. In several copies this leaf is reversed. There are only a handful of substantive stop-press corrections in the text, and several of these occur early in the run: the error 'She' for 'We' at D2^v, l. 37 occurs in only a single copy as does the missing stage direction '*Enter Org.*' at G4^v, l. 29. This may indicate that the text had been carefully proofread before sheets were printed off, perhaps by Ford himself.

The most interesting feature of the text bibliographically is forme outer H which, late in the press run, evidently suffered some sort of accident which 'pied' the type, necessitating a hasty resetting of much of the forme. The result, found only in the St. John's Cambridge copy (coincidentally the base copy for collation), is a sloppy forme with a number of turned, foul-case and

---

[62] R. J. Fehrenbach, 'Typographical Variants in Ford's Texts: Accidentals or Substantives', in Anderson, pp. 265–94 (272, 279, 280).

wrong-font letters. There are additionally numerous variants in spelling, punctuation, and capitalization; most are probably without authority, but it is just possible that some are authentic, for example in H2^v, l. 21 where the sense seems to call for a question mark following 'wild' which is supplied in the resetting.

I have preferred to designate variant states 'State 1, State 2, etc.' rather than 'uncorrected' and 'corrected' because a later state of a forme may result from damage or deterioration as well as from active correction as is the case with outer H. It is not in every case possible to certainly determine the priority of variant states. For example, on I1^v, l. 20 the line-end 'friendship' is missing the 'p' in just over half the copies. The word could have been mis-set originally, not noted in the initial proofing, and later corrected. But the greater likelihood is that the 'p' was pulled from the forme by the inkball during the machining of the sheet (a not uncommon occurrece). In such cases I have used my best judgment as to the priority of the variant states.

Copies

The following 20 copies *The Broken Heart* have been collated using digital images from the Yamada microfilms. Where individual institutions hold multiple copies, call numbers have been supplied:

L$_{(1)}$ [644.b.35.], L$_{(2)}$ [C.12.g.3(2)], L^{18}$_{(1)}$ [3820/25.b.29], L^{18}$_{(2)}$ [3820/25.b.30], O$_{(1)}$ [Mal.205(6)], O$_{(2)}$ [Mal.238(2)], O^6, C^5, SH, E$_{(1)}$ [H.28.c.12], E$_{(2)}$ [Bute 232], G^2; F, HN, BO, PN, TEX$_{(1)}$ [Wh/F753/633b], TEX$_{(2)}$ [Ah/F753/633b], Y^2; HAGUE

Outer A	State 1	State 2
A4^v, 23	GRANSIS	GRAVSIS

State 1: L$_{(2)}$, L^{18}$_{(1)}$, O$_{(2)}$, O^6, SH, E$_{(2)}$; HN, BO, PN, TEX$_{(2)}$
State 2: L$_{(1)}$, L^{18}$_{(2)}$, O$_{(1)}$, C^5, E$_{(1)}$, G^2; F, TEX$_{(1)}$, Y^2; HAGUE
Note: Yamada incorrectly lists C^5 as State 1.

Inner B	State 1	State 2
B1^v, 15	vnion	holy vnion

State 1: L$_{(2)}$, L^{18}$_{(1)}$, O$_{(2)}$, O^6, C^5, G^2; TEX$_{(1)}$
State 2: L$_{(1)}$, L^{18}$_{(2)}$, O$_{(1)}$, SH, E$_{(1)}$, E$_{(2)}$; F, HN, BO, PN, TEX$_{(2)}$, Y^2; HAGUE

Outer D	State 1	State 2
D2^v, 37	She	We

State 1: TEX$_{(1)}$
State 2: L$_{(1)}$, L$_{(2)}$, L^{18}$_{(1)}$, L^{18}$_{(2)}$, O$_{(1)}$, O$_{(2)}$, O^6, C^5, SH, E$_{(1)}$, E$_{(2)}$, G^2; F, HN, BO, PN, TEX$_{(2)}$, Y^2; HAGUE

G Outer	State 1	State 2
G4^v, margin	{omit}	Exit Org.

State 1: O$_{(2)}$
State 2: L$_{(1)}$, L$_{(2)}$, L$^{18}_{(1)}$, L$^{18}_{(2)}$, O$_{(1)}$, O^6, C^5, SH, E$_{(1)}$, E$_{(2)}$, G^2; F, HN, BO, PN, TEX$_{(1)}$, TEX$_{(2)}$, Y^2; HAGUE

H Outer	State 1	State 2
H1^r, 2	Betake'ee	Betake you
5	reformation,	reformation
	More	More
6	employment	imployment
	Gran.	*Gran.* [swash cap.]
	man	wan [turned 'm']
10	Moile	Moyle
	ancient	ancient [turned 'a']
11	Beasts	Beasta
12	and ease with	with ease and
26	leuel't	level't
33	*Enter Orgilus.*	*Enter Orgilus.* [shifted to the right]
H2^v, 8	He (2nd)	he (2nd)
11	checks	checkes
16	Amethist,	Amethist
19	madnesse	wrdnesse [turned 'm' foul-case 'r']
21	wild.	wild?
28	liu'd,	liu'd
29	must	wust [turned 'm']
33	marriage	mareiage
37	iust	iuh [foul case for 'st' ligature]
H3^r, 5	daughter, monster	daughter monster
7	be	Be
19	*Exeunt*	*Exeunt* [swash cap.]
26	clogge	clog
29	Thunder	thunder
33	disorder;	disorder
36	not yet shook	not shook

H4^v, 4	carkasse	Carkasse
6	cares	Carer
10	*Hemophil*	*Lemophil*
	Groneas	*Groneas* [swash cap.]
11	Master?	master!
21	Which with	Which, with
	leaue you	leaue, you
29	*Euph.*	*Euphr.* [swash cap.]
37	foe	For

State 1: L$_{(1)}$, L$_{(2)}$, L^{18}$_{(1)}$, L^{18}$_{(2)}$, O$_{(1)}$, O$_{(2)}$, O^6, SH, E$_{(1)}$, E$_{(2)}$, G^2; F, HN, BO, PN, TEX$_{(1)}$, TEX$_{(2)}$, Y^2; HAGUE
State 2: C^5

Inner I	State 1	State 2
I1^v, 20	friendship	friendship

State 1: L$_{(1)}$, C^5, SH, G^2; HN, BO, PN, Y^2; HAGUE
State 2: L$_{(2)}$, L^{18}$_{(1)}$, L^{18}$_{(2)}$, O$_{(1)}$, O$_{(2)}$, O^6, E$_{(1)}$, E$_{(2)}$; F, TEX$_{(1)}$, TEX$_{(2)}$

	State 1	State 2
I4^r, 34	you with	you

State 1: G^2; BO
State 2: L$_{(1)}$, L$_{(2)}$, L^{18}$_{(1)}$, L^{18}$_{(2)}$, O$_{(1)}$, O$_{(2)}$, O^6, C^5, SH, E$_{(1)}$, E$_{(2)}$; F, HN, PN, TEX$_{(1)}$, TEX$_{(2)}$, Y^2; HAGUE

THE
BROKEN
HEART.

A Tragedy.

ACTED
By the KING'S Majesties Seruants
at the priuate Houſe in the
BLACK-FRIERS.

Fide Honor.

LONDON:
Printed by I. B. for HVGH BEESTON, and are to
be ſold at his Shop, neere the Caſtle in
Corne-hill. 1633.

Title page of *The Broken Heart* (1633). By permission of the British Library Board

The Brokenheart.
A Tragedy.

DEDICATION TO THE MOST WOR-
THY DESERVER OF THE
noblest Titles in Honour,
WILLIAM, LORD CRAVEN,
Baron of HAMSTEED-MARSHALL.

MY LORD:

THE glory of a great name, acquired by a greater glory of Action, hath in all ages liv'd the truest chronicle to his owne Memory. In the practise of which Argument, your grouth to perfection (even in youth) hath appear'd so sincere, so un-flattering a Penne-man; that Posterity cannot with more delight read the merit of Noble endeavours, than noble endeavours merit thankes from Posterity to be read with delight. Many Nations, many eyes, have beene witnesses of your Deserts, and lov'd Them. Be pleas'd then, with the freedome of your owne Nature, to admit ONE amongst All, particularly into the list of such as honour a faire Example of | Nobilitie. There is a kinde of humble Ambition, not un-commendable, when the silence of study breakes forth into Discourse, coveting rather encouragement than Applause; yet herein Censure commonly is too severe an Auditor, without the moderation of an able Patronage. I have ever beene slow in courtship of great-nesse, not ignorant of such defects as are frequent to Opinion: but the Justice of your Inclination to Industry, emboldens my weaknesse, of confidence, to rellish an experience of your Mercy, as many brave Dangers have tasted of your Courage. Your Lordship strove to be knowne to the world (when the world knew you least) by voluntary but excellent Attempts: like Allowance I plead of being knowne to your Lordship (in this low presumption) by tendring to a favourable entertaiment, a Devotion offred from a heart, that can be as truely sensible of any least respect, as ever professe the owner in my best, my readiest services, A Lover of your naturall Love to Vertue,

JOHN FORD.

The Sceane,
Sparta.

The Speakers names, fitted to their Qualities.

AMYCLAS, *Common to the Kings of Laconia.*
ITHOCLES, *Honour of lovelinesse*, A favourite.
ORGILUS, *Angry*, Sonne to Crotolon.
BASSANES, *Vexation*, A jealous Nobleman.
ARMOSTES, *An appeasor*, A Counsellor of State.
CROTOLON, *Noyse*, Another Counsellor.
PROPHILUS, *Deare*, Friend to Ithocles.
NEARCHUS, *Young Prince*, Prince of Argos.
TECNICUS, *Artist*, A Philosopher.
HEMOPHIL, *Glutton*, A Courtier.
GRONEAS, *Tavernhaunter*, A Courtier.
AMELUS, *Trusty*, Friend to Nearchus.
PHULAS, *Watchfull*, Servant to Bassanes.
CALANTHA, *Flower of beauty*, The Kings daughter.
PENTHEA, *Complaint*, Sister to Ithocles.
EUPHRANEA, *Joy*, A Maid of Honor.
CHRISTALLA, *Christall,*
PHILEMA, *A Kisse*, Maids of Honour.
GRAUSIS *Old Beldam.* Overseer of Penthea.

Persons included.

THRASUS, *Fiercenesse*, Father of Ithocles.
APLOTES, *Simplicity*, Orgilus so disguis'd.

THE PROLOGUE.

OUr Scaene is Sparta. *HE whose best of Art*
Hath drawne this Peece, *cals it the* Broken Heart.
The Title lends no expectation here
Of apish laughter, or of some lame Jeere
At place or persons; no pretended clause   5
Of jests fit for a brothell Courts applause
From vulgar admiration: such low songs,
Tun'd to unchast eares, suit not modest tongues.
The Virgine Sisters then deserv'd fresh bayes
When Innocence *and* Sweetnesse *crown'd their layes.*   10
Then vices gasp'd for breath, whose whole Commerce
Was whip'd to Exile by unblushing verse.
This law we keepe in our Presentment now,
Not to take freedome more than we allow;
What may be here thought a fiction, *when Times youth*   15
Wanted some riper yeares, was knowne A Truth:
In which, if words have cloath'd the subject right,
A3   *You may pertake, a Pitty, with Delight.*

Prologue jests] *Weber;* jest's *Q.*

I.I *Enter* CROTOLON *and* ORGILUS

CROTOLON   Dally not further, I will know the reason
  That speeds thee to this journey.

ORGILUS   Reason? Good Sir,
  I can yeeld many.

CROTOLON   Give me one, a good one;
  Such I expect, and e're we part must have:
  Athens? Pray why to Athens? You intend not   5
  To kicke against the world, turne Cynicke, Stoicke,
  Or read the Logicke Lecture, or become
  An Areopagite, and Judge in causes
  Touching the Common-wealth? For as I take it,
  The budding of your chin cannot prognosticate   10
  So grave an honour.

ORGILUS   All this I acknowledge.

CROTOLON   You doe: then (Son) if books and love of knowledge
  Enflame you to this travell, here in Sparta
  You may as freely study.

ORGILUS   'Tis not that Sir.

CROTOLON   Not that Sir? As a father I command thee   15
  To acquaint me with the truth.

ORGILUS   Thus I obey 'ee: B
  After so many quarrels, as dissention,
  Fury, and Rage had brauch't in blood, and sometimes
  With death to such confederates, as sided
  With now dead Thrasus, and your selfe my Lord,   20
  Our present King Amyclas reconcil'd
  Your eager swords, and Seal'd a gentle peace:
  Friends you profest your selves, which to confirme,
  A resolution for a lasting league
  Betwixt your Families was entertain'd,   25
  By joyning in a Hymenean bond,
  Me, and the faire Penthea, onely daughter
  To Thrasus.

CROTOLON   What of this?

ORGILUS   Much, much (deere sir).
    A freedome of converse, an enterchange
    Of holy, and chast love, so fixt our soules   30
    In a firme grouth of union, that no Time
    Can eat into the pledge; we had enjoy'd
    The sweets our vowes expected, had not cruelty
    Prevented all those triumphs we prepar'd for,
    By Thrasus his untimely death.

CROTOLON   Most certaine.   35

ORGILUS   From this time sprouted up that poysonous stalke
    Of Aconite, whose ripened fruit hath ravisht
    All health, all comfort of a happy life:
    For Ithocles her brother, proud of youth,
    And prouder in his power, nourisht closely   40
    The memory of former discontents.
    To glory in revenge, by cunning partly,
    Partly by threats, 'a wooes at once, and forces
    His virtuous sister to admit a marriage
    With Bassanes, a Noble-man, in honour   45
    And riches, I confesse beyond my fortunes.

CROTOLON   All this is no sound reason to importune
    My leave for thy departure.

ORGILUS   Now it followes:
    Beauteous Penthea wedded to this torture
    By an insulting brother, being secretly   50
    Compeld to yeeld her virgine freedome up
    To him, who never can usurpe her heart
    Before contracted mine, is now so yoak'd
    To a most barbarous thraldome, misery,
    Affliction, that he savors not humanity   55
    Whose sorrow melts not into more than pitty,
    In hearing but her name.

CROTOLON   As how pray?

ORGILUS   Bassanes
    The man that calls her wife, considers truly
    What Heaven of perfections he is Lord of,

I.I] 31 union] *Q corr.*; holy union *Q uncorr.*   36 sprouted] *Weber*; splouted *Q.*

By thinking faire Penthea his: this thought   60
Begets a kinde of Monster-Love, which Love
Is nurse unto a feare so strong, and servile,
As brands all dotage with a Jealousie.
All eyes who gaze upon that shrine of beauty,
He doth resolve, doe homage to the miracle;   65
Some one, he is assur'd, may now or then
(If opportunity but sort) prevaile:
So much out of a selfe-unworthinesse
His feares transport him, not that he findes cause
In her obedience, but his owne distrust.   70

CROTOLON   You spin out your discourse.

ORGILUS   My griefs are violent;
    For knowing how the Maid was heretofore
    Courted by me, his jealousies grow wild
    That I should steale againe into her favours,
    And undermine her vertues: which the gods   75
    Know I nor dare, nor dreame of: hence, from hence,
    I undertake a voluntary exile.
    First, by my absence to take off the cares
    Of Jealous Bassanes, but chiefly (Sir)
    To free Penthea from a hell on earth: 80
    Lastly, to lose the memory of something,
    Her presence makes to live in me afresh.

CROTOLON   Enough (my Orgilus) enough: to Athens
    I give a full consent. Alas good Lady –
    Wee shall heare from thee often?

ORGILUS   Often.

CROTOLON   See   85
    Thy Sister comes to give a farewell.

                    Enter EUPHRANEA.

EUPHRANEA   Brother.

ORGILUS   Euphranea, thus upon thy cheekes I print
    A brother's kisse, more carefull of thine honour,   B2
    Thy health, and thy well-doing, than my life.
    Before we part, in presence of our father,   90
    I must preferre a suit to 'ee.

EUPHRANEA   You may stile it,
  My brother, a command.

ORGILUS   That you will promise
  To passe never to any man, how ever worthy,
  Your faith, till with our Fathers leave
  I give a free consent.

CROTOLON   An easie motion;   95
  I'le promise for her, Orgilus.

ORGILUS   Your pardon;
  Euphranea's oath must yeeld me satisfaction.

EUPHRANEA   By Vesta's sacred fires I sweare.

CROTOLON   And I
  By great Apollo's beames joyne in the vow;
  Not without thy allowance, to bestow her   100
  On any living.

ORGILUS   Deere Euphranea
  Mistake me not; farre, farre 'tis from my thought,
  As farre from any wish of mine, to hinder
  Preferment to an honourable bed,
  Or fitting Fortune: thou art young, and handsome;   105
  And 'twere injustice, more, a tyrannie
  Not to advance thy merit. Trust me Sister,
  It shall be my first care to see thee match'd
  As may become thy choyce, and our contents:
  I have your oath.

EUPHRANEA   You have: but meane you brother   110
  To leave us as you say?

CROTOLON   Aye, aye, Euphranea:
  He has just grounds direct him: I will prove
  A father and a brother to thee.

EUPHRANEA   Heaven
  Does looke into the secrets of all hearts:
  Gods you have mercy with 'ee, else—

CROTOLON   Doubt nothing: 115
  Thy brother will returne in safety to us.

ORGILUS   Soules sunke in sorrowes, never are without 'em;
   They change fresh ayres, but beare their griefes about 'em.
                        Exeunt omnes. Flourish.

    1.2   *Enter* AMYCLAS *the King,* ARMOSTES, PROPHILUS,
                  and attendants.

AMYCLAS   The Spartane gods are gracious; our humility
   Shall bend before their Altars, and perfume
   Their Temples with abundant sacrifice.
   See Lords, Amyclas your old King is entring
   Into his youth againe. I shall shake off   5
   This silver badge of age, and change this snow
   For haires as gay as are Apollo's lockes;
   Our heart leaps in new vigour.

ARMOSTES   May old time
   Run backe to double your long life (great Sir).

AMYCLAS   It will, it must Armostes; thy bold Nephew,   10
   Death-braving Ithocles, brings to our gates
   Triumphs and peace upon his conquering sword.
   Laconia is a monarchy at length;
   Hath in this latter warre trod underfoot
   Messenes pride; Messene bowes her necke   15
   To Lacedemons royalty: o 'twas
   A glorious victory, and doth deserve
   More than a Chronicle; a Temple Lords,
   A Temple, to the name of Ithocles.
   Where didst thou leave him Prophilus?

PROPHILUS   At Pephon   20
   Most gracious Soveraigne; twenty of the noblest
   Of the Messenians, there attend your pleasure
   For such conditions as you shall propose,
   In setling peace, and liberty of life.

AMYCLAS   When comes your friend the General?

PROPHILUS   He promis'd   25
   To follow with all speed convenient.

        Enter CROTOLON, CALANTHA, CHRISTALLA,
            PHILEMA *and* EUPHRANEA.

AMYCLAS   Our daughter—deere Calantha, the happy newes,
The conquest of Messene, hath already
Enrich'd thy knowledge.

CALANTHA   With the circumstance
And manner of the fight, related faithfully   30
By Prophilus himselfe; but pray Sir, tell me,
How doth the youthfull Generall demeane
His actions in these fortunes?

PROPHILUS   Excellent Princesse,
Your owne faire eyes may soone report a truth
Unto your judgement, with what moderation,   35
Calmenesse of nature, measure, bounds and limits
B3   Of thankfulnesse, and joy, 'a doth digest
Such amplitude of his successe, as would
In others, moulded of a spirit lesse cleare,
Advance 'em to comparison with heaven.   40
But Ithocles—

CALANTHA   Your friend—

PROPHILUS   He is so Madam,
In which the period of my Fate consists:
He in this Firmament of honour, stands
Like a Starre fixt, not mov'd with any thunder
Of popular applause, or sudden lightning   45
Of selfe-opinion: he hath serv'd his Country,
And thinks 'twas but his duty.

CROTOLON   You describe
A miracle of man.

AMYCLAS   Such Crotolon,
On forfeit of a Kings word thou wilt finde him:
Harke, warning of his comming, all attend him.   50
            Flourish.

        Enter ITHOCLES, HEMOPHIL, *and* GRONEAS: *the rest of the*
            Lords ushering him in.

AMYCLAS   Returne into these armes, thy home, thy sanctuary,
Delight of Sparta, treasure of my bosome,
Mine owne, owne Ithocles.

ITHOCLES   Your humblest subject.

ARMOSTES   Proud of the blood I claime an Interest in,
As brother to thy mother, I embrace thee   55
Right noble Nephew.

ITHOCLES   Sir, your love's too partiall.

CROTOLON   Our Country speakes by me, who by thy valour,
Wisdome and service, shares in this great action;
Returning thee, in part of thy due merits,
A generall welcom.

ITHOCLES   You exceed in bounty.   60

CALANTHA   Christalla, Philema, the Chaplet. Ithocles
Upon the wings of Fame, the singular
And chosen fortune of an high attempt
Is borne so past the view of common sight,
That I my selfe, with mine owne hands, have wrought   65
To crowne thy Temples, this provinciall garland;
Accept, weare, and enjoy it, as our gift
Deserv'd, not purchas'd.

ITHOCLES   Y'are a royall mayd.

AMYCLAS   Shee is in all our daughter.

ITHOCLES   Let me blush,
Acknowledging how poorely I have serv'd,   70
What nothings I have done, compar'd with th' honours
Heap'd on the issue of a willing minde;
In that lay mine ability, that onely.
For who is he so sluggish from his birth,
So little worthy of a name, or country,   75
That owes not out of gratitude for life,
A debt of Service, in what kinde soever
Safety or Counsaile of the Common-wealth
Requires for payment?

CALANTHA   'A speaks truth.

ITHOCLES   Whom heaven
Is pleas'd to stile victorious, there, to such,   80
Applause runs madding, like the drunken priests

1.2] 61 Philema] *Weber*; Philena *Q*.

In Bacchus sacrifices without Reason,
Voycing the Leader-on a Demi-god:
When as indeed, each common souldiers blood
Drops downe as current coyne in that hard purchase,   85
As his, whose much more delicate condition
Hath suckt the milke of ease. Judgement commands,
But Resolution executes; I use not
Before this royall presence, these fit sleights,
As in contempt of such as can direct: 90
My speech hath other end; not to attribute
All praise to one mans fortune, which is strengthed
By many hands. For instance, here is Prophilus
A Gentleman (I cannot flatter truth)
Of much desert; and, though in other ranke,   95
Both Hemophil and Groneas were not missing
To wish their Countries peace; for in a word,
All there did strive their best, and 'twas our duty.

AMYCLAS   Courtiers turne souldiers? We vouchsafe our hand.
  Observe your great example.

HEMOPHIL   With all diligence.   100

GRONEAS   Obsequiously and hourely.

AMYCLAS   Some repose
  After these toyles are needfull; we must thinke on
  Conditions for the Conquered; they expect 'em.
  On; come my Ithocles.

EUPHRANEA   Sir with your favour,
  I need not a supporter.

PROPHILUS   Fate instructs me.   105
          Exeunt. Manent HEMOPHIL, GRONEAS, CHRISTALLA
                et PHILEMA. HEMOPHIL *stayes* CHRISTALLA,
  B4   GRONEAS, PHILEMA.

CHRISTALLA   With me?

PHILEMA   Indeed I dare not stay.

HEMOPHIL   Sweet Lady
  Souldiers are blunt. Your lip.

CHRISTALLA   Fye, this is rudenesse;

You went not hence such creatures.

GRONEAS   Spirit of valour
  Is of a mounting nature.

PHILEMA   It appeares so;
  Pray in earnest, how many men apiece   110
  Have you two beene the death of?

GRONEAS   Faith not many;
  We were compos'd of mercy.

HEMOPHIL   For our daring
  You heard the Generals approbation
  Before the King.

CHRISTALLA   You 'wish'd your Countries peace':
  That shew'd your charity; where are your spoyles,   115
  Such as the Souldier fights for?

PHILEMA   They are comming.

CHRISTALLA   By the next Carrier, are they not?

GRONEAS   Sweet Philema,
  When I was in the thickest of mine enemies,
  Slashing off one mans head, anothers nose,
  Anothers armes and legs—

PHILEMA   And altogether.   120

GRONEAS   Then would I with a sigh remember thee;
  And cry 'Deare Philema, 'tis for thy sake
  I doe these deeds of wonder'. Dost not love me
  With all thy heart now?

PHILEMA   Now as heretofore.
  I have not put my love to use, the principall   125
  Will hardly yeeld an Interest.

GRONEAS   By Mars
  I'le marry thee.

PHILEMA   By Vulcan y'are forsworne,
  Except my mind doe alter strangely.

111 you] *Weber*, yon *Q*.   117 Philema] *Weber*, Philena *Q*.   122 Philema] *Weber*,
Philena *Q*.

GRONEAS   One word.

CHRISTALLA   You lye beyond all modesty. Forbeare me.

HEMOPHIL   I'le make thee mistresse of a City, 'tis   130
  Mine owne by conquest.

CHRISTALLA   By petition; sue for't
  In *Forma pauperis.* City? Kennell. Gallants
  Off with your Feathers, put on aprons, Gallants;
  Learne to reele, thrum, or trim a Ladies dog,
  And be good quiet soules of peace, Hobgoblins.   135

HEMOPHIL   Christalla?

CHRISTALLA   Practise to drill hogs, in hope
  To share in the Acorns. Souldiers? Corn-cutters;
  But not so valiant: they oft-times draw blood,
  Which you durst neuer doe. When you have practis'd
  More wit, or more civility, wee'll ranke 'ee   140
  I'th list of men: till then, brave things at armes
  Dare not to speake to us. Most potent Groneas.

PHILEMA   And Hemophil the hardy, at your services.

GRONEAS   They scorne us as they did before we went.

HEMOPHIL   Hang 'em, let us scorne them, and be reveng'd.   145
                        Exeunt CHRISTALLA *et* PHILEMA.

GRONEAS   Shall we?
HEMOPHIL   We will; and when we sleight them thus,
  Instead of following them, they'll follow us.
  It is a womans nature.

GRONEAS   'Tis a scurvy one.   *Exeunt omnes.*

       1.3   *Enter* TECNICUS *a Philosopher, and* ORGILUS
                  disguised like a Scholler of his.

TECNICUS   Tempt not the Stars (young man) thou canst not play
  With the severity of Fate: this change
  Of habit, and disguise in outward view,
  Hides not the secrets of thy soule within thee,

133 Feathers] *Weber*; Fathers *Q.*

From their quicke-piercing eyes, which dive at all times   5
Downe to thy thoughts: in thy aspect I note
A consequence of danger.

ORGILUS   Give me leave
(Grave Tecnicus) without fore-dooming destiny,
Under thy roofe to ease my silent griefes,
By applying to my hidden wounds, the balme   10
Of thy Oraculous Lectures: if my fortune
Run such a crooked by-way, as to wrest
My steps to ruine, yet thy learned precepts
Shall call me backe, and set my footings streight:
I will not court the world.

TECNICUS   Ah Orgilus,   15
Neglects in young men of delights, and life,
Run often to extremities; they care not
For harmes to others, who contemne their owne.

ORGILUS   But I (most learned Artist) am not so much
At ods with Nature, that I grutch the thrift   20
Of any true deserver: nor doth malice
Of present hopes, so checke them with despaire,
As that I yeeld to thought of more affliction   C
Than what is incident to frailty: wherefore
Impute not this retired course of living   25
Some little time, to any other cause
Then what I justly render: the information
Of an unsetled minde, as the effect
Must clearely witnesse.

TECNICUS   Spirit of truth inspire thee.
On these conditions I conceale thy change,   30
And willingly admit thee for an Auditor.
I'le to my study.   *Exit*

ORGILUS   I to contemplations
In these delightfull walkes. Thus metamorphiz'd,
I may without suspition hearken after
Pentheas usage, and Euphraneas faith.   35
Love! thou art full of mystery: the Deities

1.3] 32.0 *Exit*] *this edn.; not in Q.*

Themselves are not secure, in searching out
The secrets of those flames, which hidden waste
A breast made tributary to the Lawes
Of beauty; Physicke yet hath never found   40
A remedy, to cure a Lovers wound.
Ha? who are those that crosse yon private walke
Into the shadowing grove, in amorous foldings?

> PROPHILUS *passeth over, supporting*
> EUPHRANEA, *and whispering.*

My Sister; o my Sister? 'Tis Euphranea
With Prophilus, supported too; I would   45
It were an Apparition; Prophilus
Is Ithocles his friend: it strangely pusles me:
Againe? Helpe me my booke; this Scholler's habit
Must stand my privilege: my mind is busie,

Mine eyes, and eares are open.   *walke by reading.*

> *Enter againe* PROPHILUS *and* EUPHRANEA.

PROPHILUS   Doe not waste   50
The span of this stolne time (lent by the gods
For precious use) in nicenesse! Bright Euphranea,
Should I repeat old vowes, or study new,
For purchase of beleefe to my desires—

ORGILUS (*Aside*)   Desires?
PROPHILUS   My service, my integrity—   55

ORGILUS (*Aside*)   That's better.

PROPHILUS   I should but repeat a lesson
Oft conn'd without a prompter but thine eyes;
My Love is honourable.

ORGILUS   So was mine
To my Penthea: chastly honourable.

PROPHILUS   Nor wants there more addition to my wish   60
Of happinesse, than having thee a wife,
Already sure of Ithocles, a friend
Firme, and un-alterable.

38 waste] *Weber*; wast *Q.*   50 waste] *Weber*; wast *Q.*

ORGILUS (*Aside*)   But a brother
  More cruell than the grave.

EUPHRANEA   What can you looke for
  In answer to your noble protestations,   65
  From an unskilfull mayd, but language suited
  To a divided minde?

ORGILUS (*Aside*)   Hold out Euphranea.

EUPHRANEA   Know Prophilus, I never under-valued
  (From the first time you mentioned worthy love)
  Your merit, meanes, or person. It had beene   70
  A fault of judgement in me, and a dulnesse
  In my affections, not to weigh and thanke
  My better Starres, that offered me the grace
  Of so much blisfulnesse. For to speake truth,
  The law of my desires kept equall pace   75
  With yours, nor have I left that resolution;
  But onely in a word, what-ever choyce
  Lives nearest in my heart, must first procure
  Consent, both from my father, and my brother,
  E're he can owne me his.

ORGILUS (*Aside*)   She is forsworne else.   80

PROPHILUS   Leave me that taske.

EUPHRANEA   My brother e're he parted
  To Athens, had my oath.

ORGILUS (*Aside*)   Yes, yes, 'a had sure.

PROPHILUS   I doubt not with the meanes the Court supplies,
  But to prevaile at pleasure.

ORGILUS (*Aside*)   Very likely.

PROPHILUS   Meane time, best, dearest, I may build my hopes   85
  On the foundation of thy constant suffrance
  In any opposition.

EUPHRANEA   Death shall sooner
  Divorce life, and the joyes I have in living,
  Than my chast vowes from truth.

PROPHILUS   On thy faire hand
  I seale the like.

ORGILUS   There is no faith in woman –   90
  Passion, o, be contained: my very heart-strings
  Are on the Tenters.

EUPHRANEA   Sir, we are over-heard;
C2 Cupid protect us: 'twas a stirring (Sir)
  Of some one neare.

PROPHILUS   Your feares are needlesse, Lady;
  None have accesse into these private pleasures,   95
  Except some neere in Court, or bosome Student
  From Tecnicus his Oratory; granted
  By speciall favour lately from the King
  Unto the grave Philosopher.

EUPHRANEA   Me thinkes
  I heare one talking to himselfe: I see him.   100

PROPHILUS   'Tis a poore Scholler, as I told you Lady.

ORGILUS   I am discovered. Say it: is it possible
  With a smooth tongue, a leering countenance,
  Flattery, or force of reason (I come t'ee Sir)
  To turne, or to appease the raging Sea?   105
  Answer to that. Your Art? What Art to catch
  And hold fast in a net the Sunnes small Atomes?
  No, no; they'll out, they'll out; ye may as easily
  Outrun a Cloud, driven by a Northerne blast,
  As fiddle faddle so. Peace, or speake sense.   110

EUPHRANEA   Call you this thing a Scholler? 'Las hee's lunaticke.

PROPHILUS   Observe him (sweet); 'tis but his recreation.

ORGILUS   But will you heare a little! you are so teatchy,
  You keepe no rule in argument; philosophy
  Workes not upon impossibilities,   115
  But naturall conclusions. Mew! Absurd;
  The metaphisicks are but speculations
  Of the celestiall bodies, or such accidents
  As not mixt perfectly, in the Ayre ingendred,
  Appeare to us unnaturall; that's all.   120

Prove it. Yet with a reverence to your gravity,
I'le baulke illiterate sawcinesse, submitting
My sole opinion to the touch of writers.

PROPHILUS   Now let us fall in with him.

ORGILUS   Ha ha ha.
These Apish boyes, when they but tast the Grammates,   125
And principals of Theory, imagine
They can oppose their teachers. Confidence
Leads many into errors.

PROPHILUS   By your leave Sir.

EUPHRANEA   Are you a Scholler (friend?)

ORGILUS   I am (gay creature)
With pardon of your Deities, a mushrome   130
On whom the dew of heaven drops now and then:
The Sunne shines on me too, I thanke his beames,
Sometime I feele their warmth; and eat, and sleepe.

PROPHILUS   Does Tecnicus read to thee?

ORGILUS   Yes forsooth,
He is my master surely, yonder dore   135
Opens upon his Study.

PROPHILUS   Happy creatures;
Such people toyle not (sweet) in heats of State,
Nor sinke in thawes of greatnesse: their affections
Keepe order with the limits of their modesty:
Their love is love of vertue. What's thy name?   140

ORGILUS   Aplotes (sumptuous master) a poore wretch.

EUPHRANEA   Dost thou want any thing?

ORGILUS   Books (Venus) books.

PROPHILUS   Lady, a new conceit comes in my thought,
And most availeable for both our comforts.

EUPHRANEA   My Lord—

PROPHILUS   Whiles I endevour to deserve   145
Your fathers blessing to our loves, this Scholler
May daily at some certaine houres attend,

What notice I can write of my successe,
Here in this grove, and give it to your hands:
The like from you to me; so can we never,   150
Barr'd of our mutuall speech, want sure intelligence;
And thus our hearts may talke when our tongues cannot.

EUPHRANEA   Occasion is most favourable, use it.

PROPHILUS   Aplotes, wilt thou wait us twice a day,
At nine i'th morning, and at foure at night,   155
Here in this Bower, to convey such letters
As each shall send to other? Doe it willingly,
Safely, and secretly, and I will furnish
Thy Study, or what else thou canst desire.

ORGILUS   Jove make me thankfull, thankfull, I beseech thee   160
Propitious Jove, I will prove sure and trusty.
You will not faile me bookes.

PROPHILUS   Nor ought besides
Thy heart can wish. This Ladies name's Euphranea,
Mine Prophilus.

ORGILUS   I have a pretty memory,
It must prove my best friend. I will not misse   165
One minute of the houres appointed.

PROPHILUS   Write
C3   The bookes thou wouldst have bought thee in a note,
Or take thy selfe some money.

ORGILUS   No, no money:
Money to Schollers is a spirit invisible,
We dare not finger it; or bookes, or nothing.   170

PROPHILUS   Bookes of what sort thou wilt: doe not forget
Our names.

ORGILUS   I warrant 'ee, I warrant 'ee.

PROPHILUS   Smile Hymen on the grouth of our desires,
Wee'll feed thy torches with eternall fires.
                                        Exeunt. Manet ORGILUS.

ORGILUS   Put out thy Torches Hymen, or their light   175
Shall meet a darkenesse of eternall night.

Inspire me Mercury with swift deceits;
Ingenious Fate has lept into mine armes,
Beyond the compasse of my braine. Mortality
Creeps on the dung of earth, and cannot reach   180
The riddles, which are purpos'd by the gods.
Great Arts best write themselves in their owne stories;
They dye too basely, who out-live their glories.   *Exit.*

2.1   *Enter* BASSANES *and* PHULAS.

BASSANES   I'le have that window next the street dam'd up;
It gives too full a prospect to temptation,
And courts a Gazers glances: there's a lust
Committed by the eye, that sweats, and travels,
Plots, wakes, contrives, till the deformed bear-whelpe   5
Adultery be lick'd into the act,
The very act; that light shall be dam'd up;
D'ee heare Sir?

PHULAS   I doe heare my Lord; a Mason
Shall be provided suddenly.

BASSANES   Some Rogue,
Some Rogue of your confederacy, (factor   10
For slaves and strumpets) to convey close packets
From this spruce springall, and the tother youngster;
That gawdy Eare-wig, or my Lord, your Patron,
Whose pensioner you are. I'le teare thy throat out
Sonne of a Cat, ill-looking Hounds-head; rip up   15
Thy ulcerous maw, if I but scent a paper,
A scroll, but halfe as big as what can cover
A wart upon thy nose, a spot, a pimple,
Directed to my Lady: it may prove
A mysticall preparative to lewdnesse.   20

PHULAS   Care shall be had. I will turne every thread
About me to an eye. Here's a sweet life.

BASSANES   The City houswives, cunning in the traffique
Of Chamber-merchandise, set all at price

---

182 Great Arts] *Q*; 'Great Acts' *Spencer conj.*   **2.1**] 13 Eare-wig] *Weber* (*subst.*); Eare-wrig *Q.*
16 ulcerous] *Weber*; ulterous *Q.*

By whole-sale, yet they wipe their mouthes, and simper,   25
Cull, kisse, and cry Sweet-hart, and stroake the head
Which they have branch'd, and all is well againe:
Dull clods of dirt, who dare not feele the rubs
Stucke on the fore-heads!

PHULAS   'Tis a villanous world,
One cannot hold his owne in't.

BASSANES   Dames at Court   30
Who flaunt in riots, runne another byas:
Their pleasure heaves the patient Asse that suffers
Up on the stilts of Office, titles, Incomes;
Promotion justifies the shame, and sues for't:
Poore Honour! Thou art stab'd, and bleed'st to death   35
By such unlawfull hire. The Country mistresse
Is yet more wary, and in blushes hides
What ever trespasse drawes her troth to guilt;
But all are false. On this truth I am bold,
No woman but can fall, and doth, or would.   40
Now for the newest newes about the Citie;
What blab the voyces sirrha?

PHULAS   O my Lord,
The rarest, quaintest, strangest, tickling newes
That ever—

BASSANES   Hey da, up and ride me Rascall,
What is't?

PHULAS   Forsooth (they say) the King has mew'd   45
All his gray beard, in stead of which is budded
Another of a pure Carnation colour,
Speckled with Greene and Russet.

BASSANES   Ignorant blocke.

PHULAS   Yes truly, and 'tis talkt about the streete,
That since Lord Ithocles came home, the Lyons   50
C4   Never left roaring, at which noyse the Beares
Have danc'd their very hearts out.

BASSANES   Dance out thine too.

PHULAS   Besides, Lord Orgilus is fled to Athens
    Upon a fiery Dragon, and 'tis thought
    A' never can returne.

BASSANES   Grant it Apollo.   55

PHULAS   Moreover, please your Lordship, 'tis reported
    For certaine, that who ever is found jealous
    Without apparent proofe that's wife is wanton,
    Shall be divorc'd: but this is but she-newes,
    I had it from a midwife. I have more yet.   60

BASSANES   Anticke, no more; Ideots and stupid fooles
    Grate my calamities. Why to be faire
    Should yeeld presumption of a faulty soule.
    Looke to the doores.

PHULAS (*Aside*)   The horne of plenty crest him.
                         Exit PHULAS.

BASSANES   Swormes of confusion huddle in my thoughts   65
    In rare distemper. Beauty? O it is
    An unmatcht blessing, or a horrid curse.

        Enter PENTHEA, *and* GRAUSIS *an old Lady.*

Shee comes, she comes, so shoots the morning forth,
Spangled with pearles of transparent dew;
The way to poverty is to be rich;   70
As I in her am wealthy, but for her
In all contents a Bankrupt. Lov'd Penthea,
How fares my hearts best joy?

GRAUSIS   In sooth not well,
    She is so over-sad.

BASSANES   Leave chattering Mag-pie.
    Thy brother is return'd (sweet) safe, and honour'd   75
    With a Triumphant victory: thou shalt visit him;
    We will to Court, where, if it be thy pleasure,
    Thou shalt appeare in such a ravishing lustre

67 An] *Weber*, And *Q.*   67.0 Grausis] *Weber*; Gransis *Q.*

Of Jewels above value, that the Dames
Who brave it there, in rage to be out-shin'd,   80
Shall hide them in their Closets, and unseene
Fret in their teares; whiles every wondering eye
Shall crave none other brightnesse but thy presence.
Choose thine owne recreations, be a Queene
Of what delights thou fanciest best, what company,   85
What place, what times, doe any thing, doe all things
Youth can command; so thou will chase these clouds
From the pure firmament of thy faire lookes.

GRAUSIS   Now 'tis well said my Lord; what Lady? Laugh,
Be merry, time is precious.

BASSANES   Furies whip thee.   90

PENTHEA   Alas my Lord, this language to your Hand-maid
Sounds as would musicke to the deafe: I need
No braveries nor cost of Art, to draw
The whitenesse of my name into offence;
Let such (if any such there are) who covet   95
A curiosity of admiration,
By laying out their plenty to full view,
Appeare in gawdy out-sides; my attires
Shall suit the inward fashion of my minde;
From which, if your opinion nobly plac'd,   100
Change not the Livory your words bestow,
My Fortunes with my hopes are at the highest.

BASSANES   This house me thinkes stands somewhat too much
inward;
It is too melancholy, wee'll remove
Nearer the Court; or what thinks my Penthea   105
Of the delightfull Island we command?
Rule me as thou canst wish.

PENTHEA   I am no Mistresse;
Whither you please, I must attend; all wayes
Are alike pleasant to me.

GRAUSIS   Island? Prison!
A prison is as gaysome: wee'll no Islands: 110
Marry out upon 'em, whom shall we see there?
Sea-guls, and Porpiseis, and water-rats,

And Crabs, and Mewes, and Dogfish? Goodly geere
For a young Ladies dealing, or an old ones.
On no termes Islands, I'le be stew'd first.

BASSANES   Grausis,   115
You are a Jugling Bawd. This sadnesse (sweetest)
Becomes not youthfull blood (I'le have you pounded).
For my sake put on a more chearefull mirth,
Thou't marre thy cheekes, and make me old in griefes.
(Damnable Bitch-foxe.)

GRAUSIS   I am thicke of hearing   120
Still when the wind blowes Southerly. What thinke 'ee,
If your fresh Lady breed young bones (my Lord?)
Wood not a chopping boy d'ee good at heart?   D
But as you said.

BASSANES   I'le spit thee on a stake,
Or chop thee into collops.

GRAUSIS   Pray speake louder.   125
Sure, sure, the wind blowes South still.

PENTHEA   Thou prat'st madly.

BASSANES   'Tis very hot; I sweat extreamely.—Now.

                        Enter PHULAS.

PHULAS   A heard of Lords, Sir.

BASSANES   Ha?

PHULAS   A flock of Ladies.

BASSANES   Where?

PHULAS   Shoalds of horses.

BASSANES   Peasant, how?

PHULAS   Caroches
In drifts—th'one enter, th'other stand without, sir.   130
And now I vanish.   *Exit* PHULAS.

---

115 Grausis] *Weber*, Gransis *Q*.   129 horses] *Weber*, hores *Q*.

Enter PROPHILUS, HEMOPHIL, GRONEAS,
CHRISTALLA *and* PHILEMA.

PROPHILUS   Noble Bassanes.

BASSANES   Most welcome, Prophilus, Ladies, Gentlemen,
    To all, my heart is open, you all honour me.
    (A tympany swels in my head already)
    Honour me bountifully. (How they flutter,   135
    Wagtailes and Jayes together!)

PROPHILUS   From your brother,
    By virtue of your love to him, I require
    Your instant presence, fairest.

PENTHEA   He is well Sir?

PROPHILUS   The gods preserve him ever: yet (deare beauty)
    I finde some alteration in him lately,   140
    Since his returne to Sparta. My good Lord,
    I pray use no delay.

BASSANES   We had not needed
    An invitation, if his sisters health
    Had not fallen into question. Haste Penthea,
    Slacke not a minute: lead the way good Prophilus,   145
    I'le follow step by step.

PROPHILUS   Your arme faire Madam.
           Exeunt omnes sed BASSANES *&* GRAUSIS.

BASSANES   One word with your old Bawdship: th' hadst bin better
    Raild at the sinnes thou worshipst, than have thwarted
    My will. I'le use thee cursedly.

GRAUSIS   You dote,
    You are beside your selfe. A Politician   150
    In jealousie? No, y'are too grosse, too vulgar.
    Pish, teach not me my trade, I know my cue:
    My crossing you sinks me into her trust,
    By which I shall know all: my trade's a sure one.

BASSANES   Forgive me, Grausis, 'twas consideration   155
    I rellisht not, but have a care now.

144 Haste] *Weber*, Hast *Q.*   155 Grausis] *Weber*, Gransis *Q.*

GRAUSIS   Feare not,
  I am no new-come-too't.

BASSANES   Thy life's upon it,
  And so is mine. My Agonies are infinite.   *Exeunt omnes.*

2.2   *Enter* ITHOCLES *alone.*

ITHOCLES   Ambition? 'Tis of vipers breed, it knawes
  A passage through the wombe that gave it motion.
  Ambition? Like a seeled Dove, mounts upward,
  Higher and higher still to pearch on clouds,
  But tumbles headlong downe with heavier ruine.   5
  So squibs and crackers flye into the ayre,
  Then onely breaking with a noyse, they vanish
  In stench and smoke. Morality appli'd
  To timely practice, keeps the soule in tune,
  At whose sweet musicke all our actions dance;   10
  But this is forme of books, and schoole-tradition,
  It physicks not the sicknesse of a minde
  Broken with griefes: strong Feavers are not eas'd
  With counsell, but with best receipts, and meanes:
  Meanes, speedy meanes, and certaine; that's the cure.   15

Enter ARMOSTES *and* CROTOLON.

ARMOSTES   You sticke (Lord Crotolon) upon a point
  Too nice, and too unnecessary. Prophilus
  Is every way desertfull. I am confident
  Your wisdome is too ripe to need instruction
  From your sonnes tutillage.

CROTOLON   Yet not so ripe   20
  (My Lord Armostes) that it dares to dote
  Upon the painted meat of smooth perswasion,
  Which tempts me to a breach of faith.
ITHOCLES   Not yet
  Resolv'd (my Lord?) Why if your sonnes consent
  Be so availeable, wee'll write to Athens   25
  For his repaire to Sparta. The Kings hand
  Will joyne with our desires, he has beene mov'd too't.

2.2] 15.0 Armostes] *Weber*; Armoster *Q.*

ARMOSTES   Yes, and the King himselfe importun'd Crotolon
    For a dispatch.

D2 CROTOLON   Kings may command, their wils
    Are Lawes not to be questioned.

ITHOCLES   By this marriage   30
    You knit an union so devout, so hearty,
    Betweene your loves to me, and mine to yours,
    As if mine owne blood had an interest in it;
    For Prophilus is mine, and I am his.

CROTOLON
    My Lord, my Lord.

ITHOCLES   What, good Sir? Speak your thought.   35

CROTOLON   Had this sincerity beene reall once,
    My Orgilus had not beene now un-wiv'd,
    Nor your lost Sister buried in a Bride-bed.
    Your Unckle here, Armostes knows this truth,
    For had your father Thrasus liv'd—but peace   40
    Dwell in his grave: I have done.

ARMOSTES   Y'are bold and bitter.

ITHOCLES   'A presses home the injury, it smarts;
    No reprehensions Uncle, I deserve 'em.
    Yet gentle Sir, consider what the heat
    Of an unsteady youth, a giddy braine,   45
    Greene indiscretion, flattery of greatnesse,
    Rawnesse of judgement, wilfulnesse in folly,
    Thoughts vagrant as the wind, and as uncertaine,
    Might lead a boy in yeeres to; 'twas a fault,
    A Capitall fault, for then I could not dive   50
    Into the secrets of commanding Love:
    Since when, experience by the extremities (in others)
    Hath forc'd me to collect. And trust me Crotolon,
    I will redeeme those wrongs with any service
    Your satisfaction can require for currant.   55

ARMOSTES   Thy acknowledgement is satisfaction.
    What would you more?

CROTOLON   I'me conquer'd: if Euphranea
    Her selfe admit the motion, let it be so.
    I doubt not my sonnes liking.

ITHOCLES   Use my fortunes,
Life, power, sword, and heart, all are your owne.   60

    Enter BASSANES, PROPHILUS, CALANTHA, PENTHEA,
    EUPHRANEA, CHRISTALLA, PHILEMA, *and* GRAUSIS.

ARMOSTES   The Princesse with your sister.

CALANTHA   I present 'ee
A stranger here in Court (my Lord,) for did not
Desire of seeing you, draw her abroad,
We had not beene made happy in her company.

ITHOCLES   You are a gracious Princesse. Sister, wedlocke   65
Holds too severe a passion in your nature,
Which can engrosse all duty to your husband,
Without attendance on so deare a mistresse.
'Tis not my brothers pleasure, I presume,
T'immure her in a chamber.

BASSANES   'Tis her will,   70
Shee governes her owne houres; (noble Ithocles)
We thanke the gods for your successe, and welfare.
Our Lady has of late beene indispose'd,
Else we had waited on you with the first.

ITHOCLES   How does Penthea now?

PENTHEA   You best know brother,   75
From whom my health and comforts are deriv'd.

BASSANES   I like the answer well; 'tis sad, and modest;
There may be tricks, yet, tricks. Have an eye Grausis.

CALANTHA   Now Crotolon, the suit we joyn'd in must not
Fall by too long demurre.

CROTOLON   'Tis granted, Princesse,   80
For my part.

ARMOSTES   With condition, that his sonne
Favour the Contract.

CALANTHA   Such delay is easie.
The joyes of marriage make thee, Prophilus,

62.0 Grausis] *Weber*; Gransis *Q.*   78 Grausis] *Weber*; Gransis *Q.*

A proud deserver of Euphranea's love,
And her of thy desert.

PROPHILUS   Most sweetly gracious.   85

BASSANES   The joyes of marriage are heaven on earth,
Life's paradise (great Princesse), the soules quiet,
Sinewes of concord, earthly immortality,
Eternity of pleasures; no restoratives
Like to a constant woman. [*Aside*] (But where is she?   90
'Twould puzzle all the gods, but to create
Such a new monster.) I can speake by proofe,
For I rest in Elizium, 'tis my happinesse.

CROTOLON   Euphranea how are you resolv'd, (speake freely)
In your affections to this Gentleman?   95

EUPHRANEA   Nor more, nor lesse than as his love assures me,
Which (if your liking with my brothers warrants)
I cannot but approve in all points worthy.

CROTOLON   So, so, I know your answer.

ITHOCLES   'T had bin pitty
D3   To sunder hearts so equally consented.   100

Enter HEMOPHIL.

HEMOPHIL   The King (Lord Ithocles) commands your presence;
And (fairest Princesse) yours.

CALANTHA   We will attend him.

Enter GRONEAS.

GRONEAS   Where are the Lords? All must unto the King
Without delay: the Prince of Argos—

CALANTHA   Well Sir.

GRONEAS   Is comming to the Court, sweet Lady.

CALANTHA   How!   105
The Prince of Argos?

GRONEAS   'Twas my fortune, Madam,
T'enjoy the honour of these happy tidings.

ITHOCLES   Penthea!

PENTHEA   Brother!

ITHOCLES   Let me an howre hence
Meet you alone, within the Palace grove,
I have some secret with you. Prethee friend   110
Conduct her thither, and have speciall care
The Walks be clear'd of any to disturbe us.

PROPHILUS   I shall.

BASSANES   How's that?

ITHOCLES   Alone, pray be alone.
I am your creature, princesse. On, my Lords.   *Exeunt.*
          Manet BASSANES.

BASSANES   Alone, alone? What meanes that word alone?   115
Why might not I be there? Hum! Hee's her brother;
Brothers and sisters are but flesh and blood,
And this same whorson Court-ease is temptation
To a rebellion in the veines. Besides,
His fine friend Prophilus must be her guardian.   120
Why may not he dispatch a businesse nimbley
Before the other come? Or—pandring, pandring,
For one another? Bee't to sister, mother,
Wife, Couzen, any thing, 'mongst youths of mettall,
Is in request; it is so. Stubborne Fate!   125
But if I be a Cuckold, and can know it,
I will be fell, and fell.

                    Enter GRONEAS.

GRONEAS   My Lord, y'are call'd for.

BASSANES   Most hartily I thanke ye; where's my wife pray?

GRONEAS   Retir'd amongst the Ladies.

BASSANES   Still I thanke 'ee:
There's an old waiter with her, saw you her too?   130

GRONEAS   She sits i'th presence Lobby fast asleepe Sir.

BASSANES   Asleepe? Sleepe Sir!

GRONEAS   Is your Lordship troubled?
You will not to the King?

BASSANES   Your humblest Vassaile.

GRONEAS   Your servant my good Lord.

BASSANES   I wait your footsteps.

                                                     Exeunt.

2.3   PROPHILUS, PENTHEA.

PROPHILUS   In this walke (Lady) will your brother find you:
　　And with your favour, give me leave a little
　　To worke a preparation. In his fashion
　　I have observ'd of late, some kind of slacknesse
　　To such alacrity as Nature   5
　　And custome tooke delight in. Sadnesse growes
　　Upon his recreations, which he hoards
　　In such a willing silence, that to question
　　The grounds will argue little skill in friendship,
　　And lesse good manners.

PENTHEA   Sir, I'me not inquisitive   10
　　Of secrecies without an invitation.

PROPHILUS   With pardon, Lady, not a sillable
　　Of mine implyes so rude a sense; the drift—

                          Enter ORGILUS.

PROPHILUS   Doe thy best
　　To make this Lady merry for an houre.   *Exit.*   15

ORGILUS   Your will shall be a law, Sir.

PENTHEA   Prethe leave me,
　　I have some private thoughts I would account with;
　　Use thou thine owne.

ORGILUS   Speake on, faire nimph, our soules
　　Can dance as well to musicke of the Spheares
　　As any's who have feasted with the gods.   20

PENTHEA   Your Schoole terms are too troublesome.

2.3]　9 little skill] *Weber;* skill *Q.*　　11 an] *Weber;* and *Q.*

ORGILUS   What heaven
  Refines mortality from drosse of earth,
  But such as uncompounded beauty hallowes
  With glorified perfection?

PENTHEA   Set thy wits
  In a lesse wild proportion.

ORGILUS   Time can never   25
  On the white table of unguilty faith
  Write counterfeit dishonour; turne those eyes
  (The arrowes of pure love) upon that fire
  Which once rose to a flame, perfum'd with vowes
  As sweetly scented as the Incense smoking   30
  On Vesta's Altars; Virgin teares (like   D4
  The holiest odours) sprinkled dewes to feed 'em,
  And to increase their fervour.

PENTHEA   Be not franticke.

ORGILUS.   All pleasures are but meere imagination,
  Feeding the hungry appetite with steame,   35
  And sight of banquet, whilst the body pines,
  Not relishing the reall tast of food;
  Such is the leannesse of a heart divided
  From entercourse of troth-contracted loves;
  No horror should deface that precious figure   40
  Seal'd with the lively stampe of equall soules.

PENTHEA   Away, some fury hath bewitch'd thy tongue:
  The breath of ignorance that flyes from thence
  Ripens a knowledge in me of afflictions,
  Above all suffrance. Thing of talke, be gone,   45
  Be gone without reply.

ORGILUS   Be just, Penthea,
  In thy commands: when thou send'st forth a doome
  Of banishment, know first on whom it lights;
  Thus I take off the shrowd, in which my cares
  Are folded up from view of common eyes;   50
  What is thy sentence next?

31 Altars] *Weber*; Artars *Q.*   31–2 On Vesta's Altars; Virgin teares (like / The holiest
odours)] *Gifford conj.*; The holiest Altars; Virgin teares (like / On Vesta's odours *Q.*

PENTHEA   Rash man, thou layest
   A blemish on mine honour with the hazard
   Of thy too desperate life: yet I professe,
   By all the Lawes of ceremonious wedlocke,
   I have not given admittance to one thought   55
   Of female change, since cruelty enforc'd
   Divorce betwixt my body and my heart:
   Why would you fall from goodnesse thus?

ORGILUS   O rather
   Examine me how I could live to say
   I have bin much, much wrong'd; 'tis for thy sake   60
   I put on this Imposter; deare Penthea,
   If thy soft bosome be not turn'd to marble,
   Thou't pitty our calamities; my Interest
   Confirmes me thou art mine still.

PENTHEA   Lend your hand;
   With both of mine I claspe it thus, thus kisse it,   65
   Thus kneele before ye.

ORGILUS   You instruct my duty.

PENTHEA   We may stand up. Have you ought else to urge
   Of new demand? As for the old forget it,
   'Tis buried in an everlasting silence,
   And shall be, shall be ever; what more would ye?   70

ORGILUS   I would possesse my wife, the equity
   Of very reason bids me.

PENTHEA   Is that all?

ORGILUS   Why 'tis the all of me, my selfe.

PENTHEA   Remove
   Your steps some distance from me; at this space
   A few words I dare change; but first put on   75
   Your borrowed shape.

ORGILUS   You are obey'd, 'tis done.

PENTHEA   How (Orgilus) by promise I was thine,
   The heavens doe witnesse; they can witnesse too
   A rape done on my truth: how I doe love thee
   Yet, Orgilus, and yet, must best appeare   80

In tendering thy freedome; for I find
The constant preservation of thy merit
By thy not daring to attempt my fame
With injury of any loose conceit,
Which might give deeper wounds to discontents: 85
Continue this faire race; then though I cannot
Adde to thy comfort, yet I shall more often
Remember from what fortune I am fallen,
And pitty mine owne ruine. Live, live happy,
Happy in thy next choyce, that thou maist people   90
This barren age with vertues in thy issue:
And o, when thou art married, thinke on me
With mercy, not contempt. I hope thy wife,
Hearing my story, will not scorne my fall:
Now let us part.

ORGILUS   Part! Yet advise thee better: 95
Penthea is the wife to Orgilus,
And ever shall be.

PENTHEA   Never shall nor will.

ORGILUS   How!

PENTHEA   Heare me, in a word I'le tell thee why:
The Virgin dowry which my birth bestow'd
Is ravish'd by another: my true love   100
Abhorres to thinke, that Orgilus deserv'd
No better favours than a second bed.

ORGILUS   I must not take this reason.

PENTHEA   To confirme it,
Should I outlive my bondage, let me meet
Another worse than this, and lesse desir'd,   105   E
If of all the men alive thou shouldst but touch
My lip, or hand againe.

ORGILUS   Penthea, now
I tell 'ee you grow wanton in my sufferance;
Come sweet, th'art mine.

PENTHEA   Uncivill Sir, forbeare,
Or I can turne affection into vengeance;   110
Your reputation (if you value any)

Lyes bleeding at my feet. Unworthy man,
If ever henceforth thou appeare in language,
Message, or letter to betray my frailty,
I'le call thy former protestations lust,   115
And curse my Starres for forfeit of my iudgement.
Goe thou, fit onely for disguise and walkes,
To hide thy shame: this once I spare thy life;
I laugh at mine owne confidence; my sorrowes
By thee are made inferiour to my fortunes.   120
If ever thou didst harbour worthy love,
Dare not to answer. My good Genius guide me,
That I may never see thee more. Goe from me.

ORGILUS   I'le teare my vaile of politicke French off,
And stand up like a man resolv'd to doe.   125
Action, not words, shall shew me. O Penthea.

Exit ORGILUS.

PENTHEA   'A sigh'd my name sure as he parted from me;
I feare I was too rough. Alas poore Gentleman,
'A look'd not like the ruines of his youth,
But like the ruines of those ruines. Honour,   130
How much we fight with weaknesse to preserve thee.

Enter BASSANES *and* GRAUSIS.

BASSANES   Fye on thee, damb thee, rotten magot, damb thee,
Sleepe? Sleepe at Court? And now? Aches, convulsions,
Impostumes, rhemes, gouts, palsies clog thy bones
A dozen yeeres more yet.

GRAUSIS   Now y'are in humors.   135

BASSANES   Shee's by her selfe, there's hope of that; shee's sad too,
Shee's in strong contemplation: yes, and fixt,
The signes are wholesome.

GRAUSIS   Very wholesome truly.

BASSANES   Hold your chops night mare. Lady, come: your brother
Is carried to his closet; you must thither.   140

124 I'le] *Modern British Drama*; I'e *Q*; I *Weber*.   124 French] *Q*; frenzy *Brooke and
Paradise conj.*   131.0 Grausis] *Weber*; Gransis *Q*.

PENTHEA   Not well, my Lord?

BASSANES   A sudden fit, 'twill off;
   Some surfeit or disorder. How doest deerest?

PENTHEA   Your newes is none o'th best.

                    Enter PROPHILUS.

PROPHILUS   The chiefe of men,
   The excellentest Ithocles, desires
   Your presence Madam.

BASSANES   We are hasting to him.   145

PENTHEA   In vaine we labour in this course of life
   To piece our journey out at length, or crave
   Respite of breath; our home is in the grave.

BASSANES   Perfect Philosophy: then let us care
   To live so that our reckonings may fall even   150
   When w'are to make account.

PROPHILUS   He cannot feare
   Who builds on noble grounds: sicknesse or paine
   Is the deservers exercise, and such
   Your vertuous brother to the world is knowne.
   Speake comfort to him Lady, be all gentle;   155
   Starres fall but in the grossenesse of our sight,
   A good man dying, th'Earth doth lose a light. *Exeunt omnes.*

     3.1   *Enter* TECNICUS, *and* ORGILUS *in his owne shape.*

TECNICUS   BE well advis'd, let not a resolution
   Of giddy rashnesse choake the breath of reason.

ORGILUS   It shall not, most sage Master.

TECNICUS   I am jealous:
   For if the borrowed shape so late put on
   Inferr'd a consequence, we must conclude   5
   Some violent designe of sudden nature
   Hath shooke that shadow off, to flye upon
   A new-hatch'd execution; Orgilus,

Take heed thou hast not (under our integrity)
Shrowded unlawfull plots: our mortall eyes   10
Pierce not the secrets of your hearts, the gods
Are onely privie to them.

E2 ORGILUS   Learned Tecnicus,
    Such doubts are causelesse, and to cleere the truth
    From misconceit, the present State commands me.
    The Prince of Argos comes himselfe in person   15
    In quest of great Calantha for his Bride,
    Our kingdomes heire; besides, mine onely sister
    Euphranea is dispos'd to Prophilus.
    Lastly, the King is sending letters for me
    To Athens, for my quicke repaire to Court.   20
    Please to accept these Reasons.

TECNICUS   Just ones, Orgilus,
    Not to be contradicted: yet beware
    Of an unsure foundation; no faire colours
    Can fortifie a building faintly joynted.
    I have observ'd a growth in thy aspect   25
    Of dangerous extent, sudden, and (looke too't)
    I might adde certaine—

ORGILUS   My aspect? Could Art
    Runne through mine inmost thoughts, it should not sift
    An inclination there, more than what suited
    With justice of mine honour.

TECNICUS   I beleeve it.   30
    But know then Orgilus what honour is:
    Honour consists not in a bare opinion
    By doing any act that feeds content;
    Brave in appearance, 'cause we thinke it brave:
    Such honour comes by accident, not nature,   35
    Proceeding from the vices of our passion
    Which makes our reason drunke. But reall Honour
    Is the reward of vertue, and acquir'd
    By Justice or by valour, which for Bases
    Hath Justice to uphold it. He then failes   40
    In honour, who for lucre or Revenge

3.1] 41 lucre or Revenge] *Gifford*; lucre of revenge *Q*.

Commits thefts, murthers, Treasons and Adulteries,
With such like, by intrenching on just Lawes,
Whose sov'raignty is best preserv'd by Justice.
Thus as you see how honour must be grounded   45
On knowledge, not opinion: for opinion
Relyes on probability and Accident,
But knowledge on Necessity and Truth:
I leave thee to the fit consideration
Of what becomes the grace of reall Honour,   50
Wishing successe to all thy vertuous meanings.

ORGILUS   The gods increase thy wisdome (reverend Oracle)
And in thy precepts make me ever thrifty.   *Exit* ORGILUS.

TECNICUS   I thanke thy wish. Much mystery of Fate
Lyes hid in that man's fortunes. Curiosity   55
May lead his actions into rare attempts;
But let the gods be moderators still,
No humane power can prevent their will.

                    Enter ARMOSTES.

From whence come 'ee?

ARMOSTES   From King Amyclas; (pardon
My interruption of your Studies). Here   60
In this seal'd box he sends a treasure deare
To him as his Crowne: 'a prayes your gravity
You would examine, ponder, sift and bolt
The pith and circumstance of every tittle
The scroll within containes.

TECNICUS   What is't Armostes?   65

ARMOSTES   It is the health of Sparta, the Kings life,
Sinewes and safety of the Common-wealth,
The summe of what the Oracle deliver'd,
When last he visited the propheticke Temple
At Delphos; what his reasons are for which   70
After so long a silence he requires
Your counsaile now (grave man) his majesty
Will soone himselfe acquaint you with.

70 Delphos] *Weber*; Delphes *Q.*   72 Your] *Weber*; you *Q.*

TECNICUS   Apollo
   Inspire my Intellect. The Prince of Argos
   Is entertain'd.

ARMOSTES   He is, and has demanded   75
   Our Princesse for his wife; which I conceive
   One speciall cause the King importunes you
   For resolution of the Oracle.

TECNICUS   My duty to the King, good peace to Sparta,
   And faire day to Armostes.
E3 ARMOSTES   Like to Tecnicus.   80

Exeunt.

3.2   *Soft Musicke. A Song.*

Can you paint a thought? Or number
Every fancy in a slumber?
Can you count soft minutes roving
From a dyals point by moving?
Can you graspe a sigh? Or lastly,   5
Rob a Virgins honour chastly?
  No, o no; yet you may
     Sooner doe both that and this,
     This and that, and never misse,
  Than by any praise display   10
     Beauties beauty, such a glory
     As beyond all Fate, all Story,
       All armes, all arts,
       All loves, all hearts,
     Greater than those, or they,   15
     Doe, shall, and must obey.

During which time, enters PROPHILUS, BASSANES, PENTHEA,
GRAUSIS, *passing over the Stage;* BASSANES *and* GRAUSIS *enter
againe softly, stealing to severall stands, and listen.*

BASSANES   All silent, calme, secure. Grausis, no creaking?
   No noyse; dost heare nothing?

GRAUSIS   Not a mouse,
   Or whisper of the winde.

3.2] 16.0 Grausis] *Weber*, Gransis *Q.*   17 Grausis] *Weber*, Gransis *Q.*

BASSANES   The floore is matted,
  The bed-posts sure are steele or marble. Souldiers   20
  Should not affect (me thinkes) straines so effeminate;
  Sounds of such delicacy are but fawnings
  Upon the sloth of Luxury: they heighten
  Cinders of covert lust up to a flame.

GRAUSIS   What doe you meane (my Lord)? Speak low;
    that gabling   25
  Of yours will but undoe us.

BASSANES   Chamber-combats
  Are felt, not heard.

PROPHILUS (*Within*)   'A wakes.

BASSANES   What's that?

ITHOCLES (*Within*)   Who's there?
  Sister? All quit the roome else.

BASSANES   'Tis consented.

          Enter PROPHILUS.

PROPHILUS   Lord Bassanes, your brother would be private,
  We must forbeare; his sleepe hath newly left him.   30
  Please 'ee withdraw?

BASSANES   By any meanes, 'tis fit.

PROPHILUS   Pray Gentlewoman walke too.

GRAUSIS   Yes, I will Sir.
                    Exeunt omnes.
      ITHOCLES *discovered in a Chayre, and* PENTHEA.

ITHOCLES   Sit nearer sister to me, nearer yet;
  We had one Father, in one wombe tooke life,
  Were brought up twins together, yet have liv'd   35
  At distance like two strangers. I could wish
  That the first pillow whereon I was cradell'd
  Had prov'd to me a grave.

---

27 felt not heard] *Weber*; felt not hard *Q*.

PENTHEA   You had beene happy:
  Then had you never knowne that sinne of life
  Which blots all following glories with a vengeance,   40
  For forfeiting the last will of the dead,
  From whom you had your being.

ITHOCLES   Sad Penthea,
  Thou canst not be too cruell; my rash spleene
  Hath with a violent hand pluck'd from thy bosome
  A lover-blest heart, to grind it into dust,   45
  For which mine's now a breaking.

PENTHEA   Not yet, heaven,
  I doe beseech thee: first let some wild fires
  Scorch, not consume it; may the heat be cherisht
  With desires infinite, but hopes impossible.

ITHOCLES
  Wrong'd soule, thy prayers are heard.

PENTHEA   Here lo I breathe   50
  A miserable creature led to ruine
  By an unnaturall brother.

ITHOCLES   I consume
  In languishing affections for that trespasse,
  Yet cannot dye.

PENTHEA   The handmaid to the wages
  Of Country toyle drinkes the untroubled streames   55
  With leaping kids, and with the bleating lambes,
  And so allayes her thirst secure, whiles I
  Quench my hot sighes with fleetings of my teares.

ITHOCLES   The labourer doth eat his coursest bread,
  Earn'd with his sweat, and lyes him downe to sleepe;   60
  While every bit I touch turnes in disgestion
E4   To gall, as bitter as Penthea's curse.
  Put me to any pennance for my tyranny,
  And I will call thee mercifull.

54–5 The handmaid to the wages, / Of Country toyle drinkes the untroubled streames] *Mitford*;
The handmaid to the wages, / The vntroubled of Country toyle, drinkes streames
Q.   61 While] *Gifford*; Which *Q*; Whilst *Weber*.

PENTHEA   Pray kill me,
  Rid me from living with a jealous husband,   65
  Then we will joyne in friendship, be againe
  Brother and sister. Kill me pray: nay, will 'ee?

ITHOCLES   How does thy Lord esteeme thee?

PENTHEA   Such an one
  As onely you have made me; a faith-breaker,
  A spotted whore. Forgive me; I am one   70
  In art, not in desires, the gods must witnesse.

ITHOCLES   Thou dost belye thy friend.

PENTHEA   I doe not Ithocles;
  For she that's wife to Orgilus, and lives
  In knowne Adultery with Bassanes,
  Is at the best a whore. Wilt kill me now?   75
  The ashes of our parents will assume
  Some dreadfull figure, and appeare to charge
  Thy bloody gilt, that hast betray'd their name
  To infamy, in this reproachfull match.

ITHOCLES   After my victories abroad, at home   80
  I meet despaire; ingratitude of nature
  Hath made my actions monstrous. Thou shalt stand
  A Deity (my sister) and be worship'd,
  For thy resolved martyrdome: wrong'd maids
  And married wives shall to thy hallowed shrine   85
  Offer their orisons, and sacrifice
  Pure Turtles crown'd with mirtle, if thy pitty
  Unto a yeelding brothers pressure lend
  One finger but to ease it.

PENTHEA   O no more.

ITHOCLES   Death waits to waft me to the Stygian bankes,   90
  And free me from this Chaos of my bondage,
  And till thou wilt forgive, I must indure.

PENTHEA   Who is the Saint you serve?

71 art] *Q*; act *Spencer conj.*

ITHOCLES   Friendship, or nearness
Of birth to any but my sister, durst not
Have mov'd that question; 'tis a secret, Sister,   95
I dare not murmure to my selfe.

PENTHEA   Let me,
By your new protestations I conjure 'ee,
Partake her name.

ITHOCLES   Her name,—'tis,—'tis—I dare not.

PENTHEA   All your respects are forg'd.

ITHOCLES   They are not. Peace.
Calantha is the Princesse, the King's daughter,   100
Sole heire of Sparta. Me most miserable,
Doe I now love thee? For my injuries
Revenge thy selfe with bravery, and gossip
My treasons to the King's eares. Doe; Calantha
Knowes it not yet, nor Prophilus, my nearest.   105

PENTHEA   Suppose you were contracted to her, would it not
Split even your very soule to see her father
Snatch her out of your armes against her will,
And force her on the Prince of Argos?

ITHOCLES   Trouble not
The fountaines of mine eyes with thine owne story,   110
I sweat in blood for't.

PENTHEA   We are reconcil'd:
Alas, Sir, being children, but two branches
Of one stocke, 'tis not fit we should divide:
Have comfort, you may find it.

ITHOCLES   Yes in thee:
Onely in thee Penthea mine.

PENTHEA   If sorrowes   115
Have not too much dull'd my infected braine,
I'le cheere invention for an active straine.

93 Friendship, or nearness] *Lamb*; Friendship, or *Q*; Friendship or [nearness] *Weber*.
95 question; 'tis a secret] *Dyce*; question as a secret *Q*.

ITHOCLES   Mad man! why have I wrong'd a maid so excellent?

Enter BASSANES *with a poynard,* PROPHILUS, GRONEAS,
HEMOPHIL *and* GRAUSIS.

BASSANES   I can forbeare no longer: more, I will not:
Keepe off your hands, or fall upon my point: 120
Patience is tyr'd, for like a slow-pac'd Asse
Ye ride my easie nature, and proclaime
My sloth to vengeance, a reproach and property.

ITHOCLES   The meaning of this rudenesse?

PROPHILUS   Hee's distracted.

PENTHEA
O my griev'd Lord.

GRAUSIS   Sweet Lady come not neere him;   125
He holds his perilous weapon in his hand
To pricke 'a cares not whom, nor where. See, see, see.

BASSANES   My birth is noble, though the popular blast
Of vanity, as giddy as thy youth,
Hath rear'd thy name up to bestride a cloud,   130
Or progresse in the Chariot of the Sunne;
I am no clod of trade, to lackey pride,
Nor like your slave of expectation wait
The baudy hinges of your dores, or whistle   F
For mysticall conveyance to your bed-sports.   135

GRONEAS   Fine humors, they become him.

HEMOPHIL   How 'a stares,
Struts, puffes, and sweats: most admirable lunacy!

ITHOCLES   But that I may conceive the spirit of wine
Has tooke possession of your soberer custome,
I'de say you were unmannerly.

PENTHEA   Deare brother.   140

BASSANES   Unmannerly? Mew Kitling. Smooth formality
Is usher to the ranknesse of the blood,
But Impudence beares up the traine. Indeed, sir,
Your fiery mettall, or your springall blaze

118.0 Grausis] *Weber*; Gransis *Q.*

Of huge renowne, is no sufficient Royalty   145
To print upon my forehead the scorne Cuckold.

ITHOCLES   His Jealousie has rob'd him of his wits,
'A talkes 'a knowes not what.

BASSANES   Yes, and 'a knows
To whom 'a talkes; to one that franks his lust
In Swine-security of bestiall incest.   150

ITHOCLES   Hah, devill!

BASSANES   I will hallo't, though I blush more
To name the filthinesse, than thou to act it.

ITHOCLES   Monster!

PROPHILUS   Sir, by our friendship.

PENTHEA   By our bloods,
Will you quite both undoe us, Brother?

GRAUSIS   Out on him,
These are his megrims, firks and melancholies.   155

HEMOPHIL   Well said, old Touch-hole.

GRONEAS   Kick him out at dores.

PENTHEA   With favour, let me speake. My Lord? What slacknesse
In my obedience hath deserv'd this rage?
Except humility and silent duty
Have drawne on your unquiet, my simplicity   160
Ne're studied your vexation.

BASSANES   Light of beauty,
Deale not ungently with a desperate wound!
No breach of reason dares make warre with her
Whose lookes are soveraignty, whose breath is balme:
O that I could preserve thee in fruition   165
As in devotion!

PENTHEA   Sir, may every evill
Lock'd in Pandora's box, showre (in your presence)
On my unhappy head, if since you made me

159 silent] *Weber*, sinlent *Q*.

A partner in your bed, I have beene faulty
In one unseemely thought against your honour.   170

ITHOCLES   Purge not his griefes, Penthea.

BASSANES   Yes, say on,
Excellent creature. Good, be not a hinderance
To peace, and praise of vertue. O my senses
Are charm'd with sounds caelestiall. On, deare, on;
I never gave you one ill word; say, did I?   175
Indeed I did not.

PENTHEA   Nor, by Juno's forehead,
Was I e're guilty of a wanton error.

BASSANES   A goddesse! Let me kneele.

GRAUSIS   Alas kind Animall.

ITHOCLES   No, but for pennance.

BASSANES   Noble sir, what is it?
With gladnesse I embrace it; yet pray let not   180
My rashnesse teach you to be too unmercifull.

ITHOCLES   When you shall shew good proofe that manly wisdome,
Not over-sway'd by passion, or opinion,
Knowes how to lead judgement, then this Lady
Your wife, my sister, shall returne in safety   185
Home to be guided by you; but till first
I can, out of cleare evidence, approve it,
Shee shall be my care.

BASSANES   Rip my bosome up,
I'le stand the execution with a constancy:
This torture is unsufferable.

ITHOCLES   Well Sir,   190
I dare not trust her to your fury.

BASSANES   But
Penthea sayes not so.

PENTHEA   She needs no tongue
To plead excuse, who never purpos'd wrong.

HEMOPHIL   Virgin of reverence and antiquity
Stay you behind.

GRONEAS   The Court wants not your diligence.   195
     Exeunt omnes, sed BASSANES *&* GRAUSIS.

GRAUSIS   What will you doe my Lord? My Lady's gone,
 I am deny'd to follow.

BASSANES   I may see her,
 Or speake to her once more.

GRAUSIS   And feele her too, man.
 Be of good cheare, she's your owne flesh and bone.

BASSANES   Diseases desperate must find cures alike: 200
 She swore she has beene true.

GRAUSIS   True, on my modesty.

BASSANES   Let him want truth who credits not her vowes;
 Much wrong I did her, but her brother infinite;
 Rumor will voyce me the contempt of manhood,
 Should I run on thus. Some way I must try   205
F2 To out-doe Art, and cry a Jealousie.   *Exeunt omnes.*

  3.3   *Flourish. Enter* AMYCLAS, NEARCHUS *leading* CALANTHA,
  ARMOSTES, CROTOLON, EUPHRANEA, CHRISTALLA,
    PHILEMA, *and* AMELUS.

AMYCLAS   Cozen of Argos, what the heavens have pleas'd
 In their unchanging Counsels to conclude
 For both our kingdomes weale, we must submit to:
 Nor can we be unthankfull to their bounties,
 Who when we were even creeping to our graves,   5
 Sent us a daughter; in whose birth, our hope
 Continues of succession. As you are
 In title next, being grandchilde to our Aunt,
 So we in heart desire you may sit nearest
 Calantha's love; since we have ever vow'd   10
 Not to inforce affection by our will,
 But by her owne choyce to confirme it gladly.

NEARCHUS   You speake the nature of a right just father.
 I come not hither roughly to demand

195.0 *Bassanes & Grausis*] *Weber (subst.)* Bass. & Grans. *Q.*   206 cry a Jealousie] *Q*
(subst.); try a jealousy *Weber*; jealousy decry *Gifford*; tie up jealousy *Brooke and Paradise*; cry 'a
jealousy *Harrier.*

My Cozens thraldome, but to free mine owne: 15
Report of great Calantha's beauty, vertue,
Sweetnesse, and singular perfections, courted
All eares to credit what I finde was publish'd
By constant truth: from which if any service
Of my desert can purchase faire construction,   20
This Lady must command it.

CALANTHA   Princely Sir,
So well you know how to professe observance
That you instruct your hearers to become
Practioners in duty; of which number
I'le study to be chiefe.

NEARCHUS   Chiefe, glorious Virgine,   25
In my devotions, as in all mens wonder.

AMYCLAS   Excellent Cozen, we deny no libertie;
Use thine owne opportunities. Armostes,
We must consult with the Philosophers;
The businesse is of weight.

ARMOSTES   Sir, at your pleasure.   30

AMYCLAS   You told me, Crotolon, your sonne's return'd
From Athens? Wherefore comes 'a not to Court
As we commanded?

CROTOLON   He shall soone attend
Your royall will, great Sir.

AMYCLAS   The marriage
Betweene young Prophilus and Euphranea   35
Tasts of too much delay.

CROTOLON   My Lord.

AMYCLAS   Some pleasures
At celebration of it would give life
To th'entertainment of the Prince our kinsman:
Our Court weares gravity more than we rellish.

ARMOSTES   Yet the heavens smile on all your high attempts,   40
Without a Cloud.

CROTOLON   So may the gods protect us.

CALANTHA   A Prince, a subject?

NEARCHUS   Yes, to beauties scepter:
As all hearts kneele, so mine.

CALANTHA   You are too Courtly.
                    To them,
        ITHOCLES, ORGILUS, PROPHILUS

ITHOCLES   Your safe returne to Sparta is most welcome;
I joy to meet you here, and as occasion   45
Shall grant us privacy, will yeeld you reasons
Why I should covet to deserve the title
Of your repected friend: for without Complement
Beleeve it, Orgilus, 'tis my ambition.

ORGILUS   Your Lordship may command me your poore servant.   50

ITHOCLES (*Aside*) So amorously close? So soone? My heart!

PROPHILUS   What sudden change is next?

ITHOCLES   Life to the King,
To whom I here present this Noble gentleman,
New come from Athens; royall Sir, vouchsafe
Your gracious hand in favour of his merit.   55

CROTOLON   My sonne preferr'd by Ithocles!

AMYCLAS   Our bounties
Shall open to thee, Orgilus; for instance,
Harke in thine eare; if out of those inventions
Which flow in Athens, thou hast there ingrost
Some rarity of wit to grace the Nuptials   60
Of thy faire sister, and renowne our Court
In th' eyes of this young Prince, we shall be debtor
To thy conceit; thinke on't.

ORGILUS   Your Highnesse honors me.

NEARCHUS   My tongue and heart are twins.

CALANTHA   A noble birth
Becomming such a father. Worthy Orgilus,   65
You are a guest most wish'd for.

3.3] 51 so amorously close] *Gifford*; so amorously close, close *Q.*

ORGILUS   May my duty
  Still rise in your opinion, sacred Princesse.   F3

ITHOCLES   Euphranea's brother, sir, a Gentleman
  Well worty of your knowledge.

NEARCHUS   We embrace him,
  Proud of so deare acquaintance.

AMYCLAS   All prepare   70
  For Revels and disport; the joyes of Hymen,
  Like Phoebus in his lustre, puts to flight
  All mists of dulnesse. Crowne the houres with gladnesse:
  No sounds but musicke, no discourse but mirth.

CALANTHA   Thine arme I prethe Ithocles. Nay, good   75
  My Lord, keepe on your way, I am provided.

NEARCHUS   I dare not disobey.

ITHOCLES   Most heavenly Lady. *Exeunt.*

      3.4   *Enter* CROTOLON, ORGILUS.

CROTOLON   The King hath spoke his mind.

ORGILUS   His will he hath:
  But were it lawfull to hold plea against
  The power of greatnesse, not the reason, haply
  Such under-shrubs as subjects sometimes might
  Borrow of Nature Justice, to informe   5
  That licence soveraignty holds without checke
  Over a meeke obedience.

CROTOLON   How resolve you
  Touching your sisters marriage? Prophilus
  Is a deserving, and a hopefull youth.

ORGILUS   I envy not his merit, but applaud it: 10
  Could wish him thrift in all his best desires,
  And with a willingnesse inleague our blood
  With his, for purchase of full growth in friendship.
  He never touch'd on any wrong that malic'd
  The honour of our house, nor stirr'd our peace;   15

3.4]   11 wish] *Weber*, with *Q.*

Yet, with your favour, let me not forget
Under whose wing he gathers warmth and comfort,
Whose creature he is bound, made, and must live so.

CROTOLON   Sonne, sonne, I find in thee a harsh condition;
No curtesie can winne it; 'tis too ranckorous.   20

ORGILUS   Good Sir, be not severe in your construction;
I am no stranger to such easie calmes
As sit in tender bosomes. Lordly Ithocles
Hath grac'd my entertainment in abundance;
Too humbly hath descended from that height   25
Of arrogance and spleene which wrought the rape
On griev'd Penthea's purity; his scorne
Of my untoward fortunes is reclaim'd
Unto a Courtship, almost to a fawning:
I'le kisse his foot, since you will have it so.   30

CROTOLON   Since I will have it so? Friend, I will have it so,
Without our ruine by your politicke plots,
Or Wolfe of hatred snarling in your breast;
You have a spirit, Sir, have ye? A familiar
That poasts i'th ayre for your intelligence?   35
Some such Hobgoblin hurried you from Athens,
For yet you come unsent for.

ORGILUS   If unwelcome,
I might have found a grave there.

CROTOLON   Sure your businesse
Was soone dispatch'd, or your mind alter'd quickly.

ORGILUS   'Twas care, Sir, of my health, cut short my journey;   40
For there, a generall infection
Threatens a desolation.

CROTOLON   And I feare
Thou hast brought backe a worse infection with thee,
Infection of thy mind; which, as thou sayst,
Threatens the desolation of our family.   45

ORGILUS   Forbid it our deare Genius! I will rather
Be made a Sacrifice on Thrasus monument,

Or kneele to Ithocles his sonne in dust,
Than wooe a fathers curse. My sisters marriage
With Prophilus, is from my heart confirm'd: 50
May I live hated, may I dye despis'd,
If I omit to further it in all
That can concerne me.

CROTOLON   I have beene too rough,
My duty to my King made me so earnest;
Excuse it Orgilus.

ORGILUS   Deare Sir.

Enter to them,
PROPHILUS, EUPHRANEA, ITHOCLES, GRONEAS, HEMOPHIL.

CROTOLON   Here comes   55
Euphranea, with Prophilus and Ithocles.

ORGILUS   Most honored, ever famous.

ITHOCLES   Your true friend,
On earth not any truer. With smooth eyes
Looke on this worthy couple; your consent
Can onely make them one.

ORGILUS   They have it. Sister,   60   F4
Thou pawn'dst to me an oath, of which ingagement
I never will release thee, if thou aym'st
At any other choyce than this.

EUPHRANEA   Deare brother,
At him or none.

CROTOLON   To which my blessing's added.

ORGILUS   Which till a greater ceremony perfect,   65
Euphranea, lend thy hand; here take her, Prophilus,
Live long a happy man and wife; and further,
That these in presence may conclude an omen,
Thus for a Bridall song I close my wishes:
    Comforts lasting, Loves increasing,   70
    Like soft houres never ceasing;
    Plenties pleasure, peace complying
    Without jarres, or tongues envying;
    Hearts by holy Union wedded

More than theirs, by custome bedded;   75
Fruitfull issues; life so graced,
Not by age to be defaced;
Budding, as the yeare ensu'th,
Every spring another youth:
All what thought can adde beside,   80
Crowne this Bridegroome and this Bride.

PROPHILUS   You have seal'd joy close to my soule: Euphranea,
   Now I may call thee mine.

ITHOCLES   I but exchange
   One good friend for another.

ORGILUS   If these Gallants
   Will please to grace a poore invention,   85
   By joyning with me in some slight devise,
   I'le venture on a straine my younger dayes
   Have studied for delight.

HEMOPHIL   With thankfull willingnesse
   I offer my attendance.

GRONEAS   No endevour
   Of mine shall faile to shew it selfe.

ITHOCLES   We will   90
   All joyne to wait on thy directions, Orgilus.

ORGILUS   O my good Lord, your favours flow towards
   A too unworthy worme; but as you please,
   I am what you will shape me.

ITHOCLES   A fast friend.

CROTOLON   I thanke thee sonne for this acknowledgement,   95
   It is a sight of gladnesse.
ORGILUS   But my duty.   *Exeunt omnes.*

   3.5   *Enter* CALANTHA, PENTHEA, CHRISTALLA, PHILEMA.

CALANTHA   Who e're would speake with us, deny his entrance;
   Be carefull of our charge.

CHRISTALLA   We shall madam.

CALANTHA   Except the King himselfe, give none admittance,
  Not any.

PHILEMA   Madam it shall be our care.
                        Exeunt PHILEMA *and* CHRISTALLA.

CALANTHA   Being alone, Penthea, you have granted   5
  The opportunity you sought, and might
  At all times have commanded.

PENTHEA   'Tis a benefit
  Which I shall owe your goodnesse even in death for.
  My glasse of life (sweet Princesse) hath few minutes
  Remaining to runne downe; the sands are spent;   10
  For by an inward messenger I feele
  The summons of departure short and certaine.

CALANTHA   You feed too much your melancholly.

PENTHEA   Glories
  Of humane greatnesse are but pleasing dreames,
  And shadowes soone decaying: on the stage   15
  Of my mortality, my youth hath acted
  Some scenes of vanity, drawne out at length
  By varied pleasures, sweetned in the mixture,
  But Tragicall in issue; Beauty, pompe,
  With every sensuality our giddinesse   20
  Doth frame an Idoll, are unconstant friends
  When any troubled passion makes assault
  On the unguarded Castle of the mind.

CALANTHA   Contemne not your condition, for the proofe
  Of bare opinion onely: to what end   25
  Reach all these Morall texts?

PENTHEA   To place before 'ee
  A perfect mirror, wherein you may see
  How weary I am of a lingring life,
  Who count the best a misery.

CALANTHA   Indeed
  You have no little cause; yet none so great   30
  As to distrust a remedy.

PENTHEA   That remedy
  Must be a winding sheet, a fold of lead,
  And some untrod-on corner in the earth.
  Not to detaine your expectation, Princesse,
  I have an humble suit.

G CALANTHA   Speake, I enjoin it.   35

PENTHEA   Vouchsafe then to be my *Executrix*,
  And take that trouble on 'ee, to dispose
  Such Legacies, as I bequeath impartially:
  I have not much to give, the paines are easie,
  Heaven will reward your piety, and thanke it   40
  When I am dead; for sure I must not live,
  I hope I cannot.

CALANTHA   Now beshrew thy sadnesse;
  Thou turn'st me too much woman.

PENTHEA   Her faire eyes
  Melt into passion; then I have assurance
  Encouraging my boldnesse. In this paper   45
  My Will was Character'd; which you, with pardon,
  Shall now know from mine owne mouth.

CALANTHA   Talke on, prethe:
  It is a pretty earnest.

PENTHEA   I have left me
  But three poore Jewels to bequeath. The first is
  My youth; for though I am much old in griefes,   50
  In yeares I am a child.

CALANTHA   To whom that?

PENTHEA   To Virgin wives, such as abuse not wedlocke
  By freedome of desires, but covet chiefly
  The pledges of chast beds, for tyes of love,
  Rather than ranging of their blood; and next   55
  To married maids, such as preferre the number
  Of honorable issue in their vertues,
  Before the flattery of delights by marriage;
  May those be ever young.

CALANTHA   A second Jewell
  You meane to part with?

35 Speake, I enjoin it] *Dyce conj.*; enioy it *Q*; Speak and enjoy it *Lamb*.

PENTHEA   'Tis my Fame, I trust   60
  By scandall yet untouch'd; this I bequeath
  To memory, and Times old daughter Truth:
  If ever my unhappy name find mention
  When I am falne to dust, may it deserve
  Beseeming charity without dishonour.   65

CALANTHA   How handsomely thou playst with harmlesse sport
  Of meere imagination; speake the last,
  I strangely like thy will.

PENTHEA   This Jewell, Madam,
  Is dearely precious to me; you must use
  The best of your discretion to imploy   70
  This gift as I entend it.

CALANTHA   Doe not doubt me.

PENTHEA   'Tis long agone since first I lost my heart,
  Long I have liv'd without it, else for certaine
  I should have given that too; but in stead
  Of it, to great Calantha, Sparta's heire,   75
  By service bound, and by affection vow'd,
  I doe bequeath in holiest rites of love
  Mine onely brother Ithocles.

CALANTHA   What saydst thou?

PENTHEA   Impute not, heaven-blest Lady, to ambition,
  A faith as humbly perfect as the prayers   80
  Of devoted suppliant can indow it:
  Looke on him, Princesse, with an eye of pitty;
  How like the ghost of what he late appear'd,
  'A moves before you.

CALANTHA   Shall I answer here,
  Or lend my eare too grossely?

PENTHEA   First, his heart   85
  Shall fall in Cynders, scorch'd by your disdaine,
  E're he will dare, poore man, to ope an eye
  On these divine lookes, but with low-bent thoughts
  Accusing such presumption; as for words,
  A' dares not utter any but of service: 90
  Yet this lost creature loves 'ee. Be a Princesse

In sweetnesse as in blood; give him his doome,
Or raise him up to comfort.

CALANTHA   What new change
Appeares in my behaviour, that thou dar'st
Tempt my displeasure?

PENTHEA   I must leave the world   95
To revell in Elizium, and 'tis just
To wish my brother some advantage here:
Yet by my best hopes, Ithocles is ignorant
Of this pursuit. But if you please to kill him,
Lend him one angry looke, or one harsh word,   100
And you shall soone conclude how strong a power
Your absolute authority holds over
His life and end.

CALANTHA   You have forgot, Penthea,
How still I have a father.

PENTHEA   But remember
I am a sister, though to me this brother   105
Hath beene you know unkinde, o most unkinde.

CALANTHA   Christalla, Philema, where are 'ee? Lady,
Your checke lyes in my silence.

G2   *Enter* CHRISTALLA *and* PHILEMA.

BOTH   Madam, here.

CALANTHA   I thinke 'ee sleep, 'ee drones; wait on Penthea
Unto her lodging. (*Aside*) Ithocles? Wrong'd Lady!   110

PENTHEA   My reckonings are made even; Death or Fate
Can now nor strike too soone, nor force too late.   *Exeunt.*

4.1   *Enter* ITHOCLES *and* ARMOSTES.

ITHOCLES   Forbeare your Inquisition; curiosity
Is of too subtill, and too searching nature:
In feares of love too quicke; too slow of credit;
I am not what you doubt me.

ARMOSTES   Nephew, be then
As I would wish; all is not right. Good heaven   5

96 revell in *Elizium*] *Lamb;* reuell *Elizium Q;* rest me in Elysium *Spencer conj.*

Confirme your Resolutions for dependance
On worthy ends which may advance your quiet.

ITHOCLES   I did the Noble Orgilus much injury,
But griev'd Penthea more; I now repent it;
Now, Uncle, now; this Now, is now too late: 10
So provident is folly in sad issue,
That after-wit, like Bankrupts debts, stand tallyed
Without all possibilities of payment.
Sure he's an honest, very honest Gentleman,
A man of single meaning.

ARMOSTES   I beleeve it: 15
Yet Nephew, 'tis the tongue informes our eares;
Our eyes can never pierce into the thoughts,
For they are lodg'd too inward: but I question
No truth in Orgilus. The Princesse (Sir).

ITHOCLES   The Princesse? Ha?

ARMOSTES   With her the Prince of Argos.   20

            Enter NEARCHUS *leading* CALANTHA, AMELUS,
                    CHRISTALLA, PHILEMA.

NEARCHUS   Great (faire one) grace my hopes with any instance
Of Livery, from the allowance of your favour—
This little sparke.

CALANTHA   A Toy.

NEARCHUS   Love feasts on Toyes,
For Cupid is a child. Vouchsafe this bounty:
It cannot be deny'd.

CALANTHA   You shall not value   25
(Sweet Cozen) at a price what I count cheape,
So cheape, that let him take it who dares stoope for't,
And give it at next meeting to a Mistresse;
Shee'le thanke him for't, perhaps.   *Casts it to* ITHOCLES.

AMELUS   The Ring, Sir, is
The Princesses; I could have tooke it up.   30

4.1] 25 It cannot be deny'd] *Weber;* it cannot beny'd *Q.*

ITHOCLES   Learne manners, prethe. To the blessed owner
   Upon my knees.

NEARCHUS   Y'are sawcy.

CALANTHA   This is pretty:
   I am, belike, a Mistresse. Wondrous pretty!
   Let the man keepe his fortune, since he found it;
   He's worthy on't. On Cozen.

ITHOCLES   Follow Spaniell,   35
   I'le force 'ee to a fawning else.

AMELUS   You dare not.
              Exeunt. Manent ITHOCLES *&* ARMOSTES.

ARMOSTES   My Lord, you were too forward.

ITHOCLES   Looke 'ee Uncle:
   Some such there are whose liberall contents
   Swarme without care in every sort of plenty;
   Who, after full repasts, can lay them downe   40
   To sleepe; and they sleepe, Uncle: in which silence
   Their very dreames present 'em choyce of pleasures:
   Pleasures (observe me Uncle) of rare object:
   Here heaps of gold, there Increments of honors;
   Now change of garments, then the votes of people;   45
   Anon varieties of beauties, courting
   In flatteries of the night, exchange of dalliance,
   Yet these are still but dreames. Give me felicity
   Of which my senses waking are partakers;
   A reall, visible, materiall happinesse,   50
   And then too, when I stagger in expectance
   Of the least comfort that can cherish life.
   I saw it (Sir) I saw it; for it came
   From her owne hand.

ARMOSTES   The Princesse threw it t'ee.

ITHOCLES   True, and she said—well I remember what.   55
   Her Cozen Prince would beg it.

ARMOSTES   Yes, and parted
   In anger at your taking on't.

ITHOCLES   Penthea!
  Oh thou hast pleaded with a powerfull language!   G3
  I want a fee to gratifie thy myrit.
  But I will doe—

ARMOSTES   What is't you say?

ITHOCLES   In anger,   60
  In anger let him part; for could his breath,
  Like whirlewinds, tosse such servile slaves as licke
  The dust his footsteps print, into a vapour,
  It durst not stirre a haire of mine; it should not,
  I'de rend it up by th' roots first. To be any thing   65
  Calantha smiles on, is to be a blessing
  More sacred than a petty-Prince of Argos
  Can wish to equall, or in worth or Title.

ARMOSTES   Containe your selfe, my Lord; Ixion ayming
  To embrace Juno, bosom'd but a cloud,   70
  And begat Centaures: 'tis an usefull morall.
  Ambition, hatch'd in clouds of meere opinion,
  Proves but in birth a prodigie.

ITHOCLES   I thanke 'ee;
  Yet, with your Licence, I should seeme uncharitable
  To gentler Fate, if rellishing the dainties   75
  Of a soules setled peace, I were so feeble
  Not to digest it.

ARMOSTES   He deserves small trust
  Who is not privy Counsellor to himselfe.

           Enter NEARCHUS, ORGILUS, *and* AMELUS.

NEARCHUS   Brave me?

ORGILUS   Your Excellence mistakes his temper,
  For Ithocles in fashion of his mind   80
  Is beautifull, soft, gentle, the cleare mirror
  Of absolute perfection.

AMELUS   Was't your modesty
  Term'd any of the Prince his servants Spaniell?
  Your Nurse sure taught you other language.

ITHOCLES   Language?

NEARCHUS   A gallant Man at armes is here: a Doctor   85
  In feats of Chivalry; blunt, and rough spoken,
  Vouchsafing not the fustian of civility,
  Which rash spirits stile good manners.

ITHOCLES   Manners!

ORGILUS   No more (Illustrious Sir), 'tis matchlesse Ithocles.

NEARCHUS   You might have understood who I am.

ITHOCLES   Yes,   90
  I did—else—but the presence calm'd th' affront;
  Y' are Cozen to the Princesse.

NEARCHUS   To the King too;
  A certaine Instrument that lent supportance
  To your Collossicke greatnesse; to that King too
  You might have added.

ITHOCLES   There is more divinity   95
  In beauty than in Majesty.

ARMOSTES   O fie, fie.

NEARCHUS   This odde youths pride turnes hereticke
     in loyalty.
  Sirrah! Low Mushroms never rivall Cedars.
                          Exeunt NEARCHUS *and* AMELUS.

ITHOCLES   Come backe: what pittifull dull thing am I
  So to be tamely scoulded at? Come backe;   100
  Let him come backe and eccho once againe
  That scornefull sound of Mushrome; painted colts,
  Like Heralds coats, guilt o're with Crownes and Scepters,
  May bait a musled Lion.

ARMOSTES   Cozen, Cozen,
  Thy tongue is not thy friend.

ORGILUS   In point of honour   105
  Discretion knowes no bounds. Amelus told me
  'Twas all about a little Ring.

ITHOCLES   A Ring
   The Princesse threw away, and I tooke up:
   Admit she threw't to me; what arme of brasse
   Can snatch it hence? No, could a' grind the hoope   110
   To power, a' might sooner reach my heart
   Than steale and weare one dust on't. Orgilus,
   I am extreamely wrong'd.

ORGILUS   A Ladies favour
   Is not to be so slighted.

ITHOCLES   Slighted?

ARMOSTES   Quiet
   These vaine unruly passions, which will render ye   115
   Into a madnesse.

ORGILUS   Griefes will have their vent.

                  Enter TECNICUS.

ARMOSTES   Welcome; thou com'st in season (reverend man)
   To powre the balsome of a supplying patience
   Into the festering wound of ill-spent fury.

ORGILUS   What makes he here?

TECNICUS   The hurts are yet but mortall,   120
   Which shortly will prove deadly. To the King,
   Armostes, see in safety thou deliver
   This seal'd up counsaile; bid him with a constancy
   Peruse the secrets of the gods. O Sparta,
   O Lacedemon! Double nam'd, but one   125
   In fate: when Kingdomes reele (marke well my saw)
   Their heads must needs be giddy. Tell the King
   That henceforth he no more must enquire after
   My aged head: Apollo wils it so;   G4
   I am for Delphos.

ARMOSTES   Not without some conference   130
   With our great master.

TECNICUS   Never more to see him;
   A greater Prince commands me. Ithocles,
   When youth is ripe, and Age from time doth part,
   The livelesse Trunke shall wed the Broken Heart.

ITHOCLES   What's this, if understood?

TECNICUS   List Orgilus,   135
   Remember what I told thee long before;
   These teares shall be my witnesse.

ARMOSTES   'Las good man.

TECNICUS   Let craft with curtesie a while conferre,
   Revenge proves its owne Executioner.

ORGILUS   Darke sentences are for Apollo's Priests: 140
   I am not Oedipus.

TECNICUS   My howre is come;
   Cheare up the King: farewell to all. O Sparta,
   O Lacedemon.

ARMOSTES   If propheticke fire   *Exit* TECNICUS.
   Have warm'd this old mans bosome, we might construe
   His words to fatall sense.

ITHOCLES   Leave to the powers   145
   Above us, the effects of their decrees;
   My burthen lyes within me. Servile feares
   Prevent no great effects. Divine Calantha.

ARMOSTES   The gods be still propitious.
                                   Exeunt, manet ORGILUS.
ORGILUS   Something oddly

   The booke-man prated; yet a' talk'd it weeping: 150
   '*Let craft with curtesie a while conferre,*
   Revenge proves its own executioner.'
   Conne it againe; for what? It shall not puzzle me;
   'Tis dotage of a withered braine. Penthea
   Forbad me not her presence; I may see her,   155
   And gaze my fill: why see her then I may;
   When if I faint to speake, I must be silent.   *Exit* ORGILUS.

   4.2   *Enter* BASSANES, GRAUSIS, *and* PHULAS.

BASSANES   Pray use your Recreations. All the service
   I will expect, is quietnesse amongst 'ee:

4.2] o Grausis] *Weber;* Gransis *Q.*

Take liberty at home, abroad, at all times,
And in your charities appease the gods
Whom I with my distractions have offended.   5

GRAUSIS   Faire blessings on thy heart.

PHULAS   Here's a rare change:
My Lord, to cure the itch, is surely gelded;
The Cuckold, in conceit, hath cast his hornes.

BASSANES   Betake 'ee to your severall occasions,
And wherein I have heretofore beene faulty,   10
Let your constructions mildly passe it over;
Henceforth I'le study reformation—more
I have not for employment.

GRAUSIS   O sweet man!
Thou art the very hony-combe of honesty.

PHULAS   The garland of good-will.—Old Lady, hold up   15
Thy reverend snout, and trot behind me softly,
As it becomes a Moile of ancient carriage.
                              Exeunt, manet BASSANES.

BASSANES   Beasts, onely capable of sense, enjoy
The benefit of food and ease with thankfulnesse;
Such silly creatures, with a grudging, kicke not   20
Against the portion Nature hath bestow'd;
But men endow'd with reason, and the use
Of reason, to distinguish from the chaffe
Of abject scarscity, the Quintescence,
Soule, and Elixar of the Earthes abundance,   25
The treasures of the Sea, the Ayre, nay heaven,
Repining at these glories of creation,
Are verier beasts than beasts; and of those beasts
The worst am I; I, who was made a Monarch
Of what a heart could wish for, a chast wife,   30
Endevour'd what in me lay, to pull downe
That Temple built for adoration onely,
And level't in the dust of causelesse scandall;
But to redeeme a sacrilege so impious,

30 wish for] *Gifford*; wish, for *Q*.

Humility shall powre before the deities   35
I have incenst a largenesse of more patience
Then their displeased Altars can require:
No tempests of commotion shall disquiet
The calmes of my composure.

Enter ORGILUS.

ORGILUS   I have found thee,
Thou patron of more horrors than the bulke   40
Of manhood, hoop'd about with ribs of Iron,
H   Can cramb within thy brest. Penthea (Bassanes)
Curst by thy Jealousies—more, by thy dotage—
Is left a prey to words.

BASSANES   Exercise
Your trials for addition to my pennance,   45
I am resolv'd.

ORGILUS   Play not with misery
Past cure: some angry Minister of Fate hath
Depos'd the Empresse of her soule, her reason,
From its most proper Throne; but what's the miracle
More new, I, I have seene it, and yet live.   50

BASSANES   You may delude my senses, not my judgement:
'Tis anchor'd into a firme resolution;
Dalliance of Mirth or Wit can ne're unfixe it.
Practise yet further.

ORGILUS   May thy death of love to her
Damne all thy comforts to a lasting fast   55
From every joy of life! Thou barren rocke,
By thee we have bee split in ken of harbour.

Enter ITHOCLES, PENTHEA *her haire about her eares,*
PHILEMA, CHRISTALLA, [*and* ARMOSTES].

ITHOCLES   Sister looke up, your Ithocles, your brother
Speakes t'ee: why doe you weepe? Deere, turne not from me:
Here is a killing sight: lo, Bassanes,   60
A lamentable obiect.

ORGILUS   Man, dost see't?
Sports are more gamesome; am I yet in merriment?
Why dost not laugh?

BASSANES   Divine and best of Ladies,
   Please to forget my out-rage. Mercy ever
   Cannot but lodge under a roof so excellent: 65
   I have cast off that cruelty of frenzy
   Which once appear'd, Impostors, and then jugled
   To cheat my sleeps of rest.

ORGILUS   Was I in earnest?

PENTHEA   Sure if we were all Sirens, we should sing pittifully:
   And 'twere a comely musicke, when in parts   70
   One sung anothers knell: the Turtle sighes
   When he hath lost his mate; and yet some say
   A' must be dead first. 'Tis a fine deceit
   To passe away in a dreame; indeed I've slept
   With mine eyes open a great while. No falsehood   75
   Equals a broken faith; there's not a haire
   Sticks on my head but like a leaden Plummet
   It sinkes me to the grave: I must creepe thither.
   The journy is not long.

ITHOCLES   But thou, Penthea,
   Hast many yeeres, I hope, to number yet   80
   Ere thou canst travell that way.

BASSANES   Let the Sun first
   Be wrap'd up in an everlasting darknesse,
   Before the light of nature, chiefly form'd
   For the whole worlds delight, feele an Ecclipse
   So universall.

ORGILUS   Wisdome (looke 'ee)   85
   Begins to rave; art thou mad too, antiquity?

PENTHEA   Since I was first a wife, I might have beene
   Mother to many pretty pratling Babes:
   They would have smil'd when I smil'd; and, for certaine,
   I should have cry'd when they cry'd;—truly brother,   90
   My father would have pick'd me out a husband,
   And then my little ones had beene no bastards:
   But 'tis too late for me to marry now,
   I am past child-bearing; 'tis not my fault.

---

65 roof] *Weber*; root *Q*.   81 Sun] *Weber*; Swan *Q*.

BASSANES   Fall on me, if there be a burning Etna,   95
    And bury me in flames; sweats hot as sulphure,
    Boyle through my pores; affliction hath in store
    No torture like to this.

ORGILUS   Behold a patience!
    Lay by thy whyning gray dissimulation,
    Doe something worth a Chronicle; shew Justice   100
    Upon the Author of this mischiefe; dig out
    The Jealousies that hatch'd this thraldome first
    With thine owne poynard. Every anticke rapture
    Can roare as thine does.

ITHOCLES   Orgilus, forbeare.

BASSANES   Disturbe him not, it is a talking motion   105
    Provided for my torment: what a foole am I
    To bawdy passion? E're I'le speake a word
    I will looke on and burst.

PENTHEA   I lov'd you once.

ORGILUS   Thou did'st, wrong'd creature, in despite of malice;
    For it I love thee ever.

PENTHEA   Spare your hand,   110
    Beleeve me, I'le not hurt it.

ORGILUS   Paine my heart to.

PENTHEA   Complaine not though I wring it hard: I'le kisse it;
    O 'tis a fine soft palme. Harke in thine eare:
H2   Like whom doe I looke, prethe? Nay, no whispering.
    Goodnesse! We had beene happy; too much happinesse   115
    Will make folke proud, they say—but that is he;
                     points at ITHOCLES.
    And yet he paid for't home; alas, his heart
    Is crept into the cabinet of the Princesse;
    We shall have points and bridelaces. Remember
    When we last gather'd Roses in the garden   120
    I found my wits, but truly you lost yours:
    That's He, and still 'tis He.

---

107 To bawdy passion] *Q*; To bandy passion *Dyce, Spencer.*   107 bandy] *Dyce*; bawdy *Q.*
112 PENTHEA] *Weber, no speech prefix in Q.*

ITHOCLES   Poore soule, how idely
  Her fancies guide her tongue.

BASSANES   Keepe in vexation,
  And breake not into clamour.

ORGILUS   She has tutor'd me:
  Some powerfull inspiration checks my lazinesse.   125
  Now let me kisse your hand, griev'd beauty.

PENTHEA   Kisse it.
  Alacke, alacke, his lips be wondrous cold;
  Deare soule, h'as lost his colour. Have 'ee seene
  A straying heart? All crannies, every drop
  Of blood is turn'd to an Amethist,   130
  Which married Bachelours hang in their eares.

ORGILUS   Peace usher her into Elizium.
  If this be madnesse, madnesse is an Oracle.   *Exit* ORGILUS.

ITHOCLES   Christalla, Philema, when slept my sister,
  Her ravings are so wild?

CHRISTALLA   Sir, not these ten dayes.   135

PHILEMA   We watch by her continually; besides,
  We cannot any way pray her to eat.

BASSANES   Oh, misery of miseries!

PENTHEA   Take comfort;
  You may live well, and dye a good old man:
  By yea and nay, an oath not to be broken,   140
  If you had joyn'd our hands once in the Temple—
  'Twas since my father dy'd, for had he liv'd
  He would have don't—I must have call'd you father.
  Oh my wrack'd honour ruin'd by those Tyrants,
  A cruell brother, and a desperate dotage!   145
  There is no peace left for a ravish'd wife
  Widdow'd by lawlesse marriage; to all memory,
  Penthea's, poore Penthea's name is strumpeted:
  But since her blood was season'd by the forfeit
  Of noble shame, with mixtures of pollution,   150
  Her blood ('tis just) be henceforth never heightned
  With tast of sustenance. Starve; let that fulnesse

Whose plurisie hath fever'd faith and modesty—
Forgive me; o, I faint.

ARMOSTES   Be not so wilfull,
Sweet Neece, to worke thine owne destruction.

ITHOCLES   Nature   155
Will call her daughter monster. What? Not eat?
Refuse the onely ordinary meanes
Which are ordain'd for life? Be not, my sister,
A murthresse to thy selfe. Hear'st thou this, Bassanes?

BASSANES   Fo, I am busie; for I have not thoughts   160
Enow to thinke. All shall be well anon;
'Tis tumbling in my head: there is a mastery
In Art to fatten and keepe smooth the outside;
Yes, and to comfort up the vitall spirits
Without the helpe of food. Fumes or perfumes,   165
Perfumes or fumes; let her alone, I'le search out
The tricke on't.

PENTHEA   Lead me gently; heavens reward ye.
Griefes are sure friends; they leave (without controule)
Nor cure nor comforts for a leprous soule.
                    Exeunt, the maids supporting PENTHEA.

BASSANES   I grant t'ee; and will put in practice instantly   170
What you shall still admire: 'tis wonderfull,
'Tis super singular, not to be match'd.
Yet when I've don't, I've don't; ye shall all thanke mee.
                    Exit BASSANES.

ARMOSTES   The sight is full of terror.

ITHOCLES   On my soule
Lyes such a infinite clogge of massie dulnesse,   175
As that I have not sense enough to feele it.
See, Uncle, th'angry thing returnes againe;
Shall's welcome him with Thunder? We are haunted,
And must use exorcisme to conjure downe
This spirit of malevolence.

161 thinke. All] *Weber*, thinke all *Q.*   177 th'angry thing] *Weber*, th'augury *Q.*

ARMOSTES   Mildly, Nephew.   180

        Enter NEARCHUS *and* AMELUS.

NEARCHUS   I come not, sir, to chide your late disorder,
   Admitting that th'inurement to a roughnesse
   In Souldiers of your yeares and fortunes, chiefly
   So lately prosperous, hath not yet shooke off   H3
   The custome of the warre in houres of leisure;   185
   Nor shall you need excuse, since y'are to render
   Account to that faire Excellence, the Princesse,
   Who in her private Gallery expects it
   From your owne mouth alone. I am a messenger
   But to her pleasure.

ITHOCLES   Excellent Nearchus,   190
   Be Prince still of my services, and conquer,
   Without the combat of dispute; I honour 'ee.

NEARCHUS   The King is on a sudden indispos'd;
   Physicians are call'd for; 'twere fit, Armostes,
   You should be neere him.

ARMOSTES   Sir, I kisse your hands. *Exeunt.*   195
         Manent NEARCHUS *&* AMELUS.

NEARCHUS   Amelus, I perceive Calantha's bosome
   Is warm'd with other fires than such as can
   Take strength from any fuell of the love
   I might addresse to her: young Ithocles,
   Or ever I mistake, is Lord ascendant   200
   Of her devotions; one, to speake him truly,
   In every disposition nobly fashioned.

AMELUS   But can your Highnesse brooke to be so rival'd,
   Considering th'inequality of the persons?

NEARCHUS   I can, Amelus; for affections injur'd   205
   By tyrannie, or rigour of compulsion,
   Like Tempest-threatned Trees unfirmely rooted,
   Ne're spring to timely growth: observe, for instance,
   Life-spent Penthea, and unhappy Orgilus.

AMELUS   How does your grace determine?

NEARCHUS   To be jealous   210
  In publike, of what privately I'le further;
  And though they shall not know, yet they shall finde it.
                                        Exeunt omnes.

  4.3   *Enter* HEMOPHIL *and* GRONEAS *leading* AMYCLAS,
  and placing him in a Chayre, followed by ARMOSTES, CROTOLON,
                     and PROPHILUS.

AMYCLAS   Our daughter is not neere?

ARMOSTES   She is retired, Sir,
  Into her gallery.

AMYCLAS   Where's the Prince our Cozen?

PROPHILUS   New walk'd into the Grove (my Lord.)

AMYCLAS   All leave us
  Except Armostes, and you, Crotolon;
  We would be private.

PROPHILUS   Health unto your Majesty.   5
                Exeunt PROPHILUS, HEMOPHIL, *and* GRONEAS.

AMYCLAS   What, Tecnicus is gone?

ARMOSTES   He is to Delphos;
  And to your Royall hands presents this box.

AMYCLAS   Unseale it, good Armostes, therein lyes
  The secrets of the Oracle; out with it;
  Apollo live our patron: read, Armostes.   10

ARMOSTES   *The plot in which the Vine takes root,*
  Begins to dry, from head to foot,
  The stocke soone withering, want of sap
  Doth cause to quaile the budding grape:
  But from the neighboring Elme, a dew   15
  Shall drop and feed the Plot anew.

AMYCLAS   That is the Oracle; what exposition
  Makes the Philosopher?

ARMOSTES   This briefe one, onely:
  The plot is Sparta, the dry'd Vine the King;
  The quailing grape his daughter; but the thing   20

Of most importance, not to be reveal'd,
Is a neere Prince, the Elme; the rest conceal'd.
                    Tecnicus.

AMYCLAS   Enough; although the opening of this Riddle
    Be but it selfe a Riddle, yet we construe   25
    How neere our lab'ring age drawes to a rest:
    But must Calantha quaile too, that young grape
    Untimely budded! I could mourne for her;
    Her tendernesse hath yet deserv'd no rigor
    So to be crost by Fate.

ARMOSTES   You misapply, Sir –   30
    With favour let me speake it—what Apollo
    Hath clouded in hid sense: I here conjecture
    Her marriage with some neighb'ring Prince, the dew
    Of which befriending Elme shall ever strengthen
    Your Subjects with a Soveraignty of power.   35

CROTOLON   Besides, most gracious Lord, the pith of Oracles
    Is to be then digested, when th'events
    Expound their truth, not brought as soone to light
    As utter'd; Truth is Child of Time, and herein
    I finde no scruple, rather cause of comfort,   40   H4
    With unity of kingdomes.

AMYCLAS   May it prove so
    For weale of this deare Nation. Where is Ithocles?
    Armostes, Crotolon: when this wither'd Vine
    Of my fraile carkasse, on the funerall Pile,
    Is fir'd into its ashes, let that young man   45
    Be hedg'd about still with your cares and loves;
    Much owe I to his worth, much to his service.
    Let such as wait come in now.

ARMOSTES   All attend here.

    Enter ITHOCLES, CALANTHA, PROPHILUS, ORGILUS,
        EUPHRANEA, HEMOPHIL, *and* GRONEAS.

CALANTHA   Deare Sir, King, Father!

4.3] 25 Be but it selfe] *Q;* 'Is but' *Spencer.*   27 quaile too, that] *Merivale;* quaile to that *Q.*

ITHOCLES   O my royall Master!

AMYCLAS   Cleave not my heart (sweet Twins of my life's solace)   50
   With your fore-judging feares: there is no Physicke
   So cunningly restorative to cherish
   The fall of Age, or call backe youth and vigor,
   As your consents in duty; I will shake off
   This languishing disease of time, to quicken   55
   Fresh pleasures in these drooping houres of sadnesse;
   Is faire Euphranea married yet to Prophilus?

CROTOLON   This morning, gracious Lord.

ORGILUS   This very morning;
   Which with your Highnesse leave you may observe too.
   Our sister lookes (me thinks) mirthfull and sprightly,   60
   As if her chaster fancy could already
   Expound the riddle of her gaine in losing
   A trifle Maids know onely that they know not:
   Pish, prethe blush not; 'tis but honest change
   Of fashion in the garment, loose for streight,   65
   And so the modest maid is made a wife;
   Shrewd businesse, is't not, sister?

EUPHRANEA   You are pleasant.

AMYCLAS   We thanke thee, Orgilus, this mirth becomes thee;
   But wherefore sits the Court in such a silence?
   A wedding without Revels is not seemely.   70

CALANTHA   Your late indisposition, Sir, forbade it.

AMYCLAS   Be it thy charge, Calantha, to set forward
   The bridall sports, to which I will be present;
   If not, at least consenting. Mine owne Ithocles,
   I have done little for thee yet.

ITHOCLES   Y'have built me   75
   To the full height I stand in.

CALANTHA   Now or never—
   May I propose a suit?

AMYCLAS   Demand and have it.

CALANTHA   Pray, Sir, give me this young man, and no further
   Account him yours, than he deserves in all things

To be thought worthy mine; I will esteeme him   80
According to his merit.

AMYCLAS   Still th'art my daughter,
Still grow'st upon my heart. Give me thine hand;
Calantha, take thine owne; in noble actions
Thou'lt find him firme and absolute. I would not
Have parted with thee, Ithocles, to any   85
But to a mistresse who is all what I am.

ITHOCLES   A change (great King) most wisht for, cause the same.

CALANTHA   Th'art mine. Have I now kept my word?

ITHOCLES   Divinely.

ORGILUS   Rich fortunes guard to favour of a Princesse,
Rocke thee (brave man) in ever crowned plenty;   90
Y'are minion of the time, be thankfull for it:
[*Aside*] Ho, here's a swinge in Destiny. Apparent,
The youth is up on tiptoe, yet may stumble.

AMYCLAS   On to your recreations; now convey me
Unto my bed-chamber. None on his forehead   95
Weare a distempered looke.

OMNES   The gods preserve 'ee.

CALANTHA   Sweet, be not from my sight.

ITHOCLES   My whole felicity.
    Exeunt carrying out of the King, ORGILUS *stayes* ITHOCLES.

ORGILUS   Shall I be bold, my Lord?

ITHOCLES   Thou canst not, Orgilus;
Call me thine owne, for Prophilus must henceforth
Be all thy sisters; friendship, though it cease not   100
In marriage, yet is oft at lesse command
Than when a single freedome can dispose it.

ORGILUS   Most right, my most good Lord, my most great Lord,
My gracious Princely Lord, I might adde royall.

ITHOCLES   Royall, a Subiect royall?

---

96 weare] *Weber (subst.)*; were *Q.*

ORGILUS   Why not, pray Sir?   105
  The Soveraignty of Kingdomes in their nonage
  Stoop'd to desert, not birth; there's as much merit
  In clearenesse of affection, as in puddle
  Of generation. You have conquer'd Love
  Even in the loveliest; if I greatly erre not,   110
I The sonne of Venus hath bequeath'd his quiver
  To Ithocles his manage, by whose arrowes
  Calantha's brest is open'd.

ITHOCLES   Can't be possible?

ORGILUS   I was my selfe a peece of suitor once,
  And forward in preferment too; so forward,   115
  That speaking truth, I may without offence (Sir)
  Presume to whisper, that my hopes, and (harke 'ee)
  My certainty of marriage stood assured
  With as firme footing (by your leave) as any's
  Now at this very instant—but—

ITHOCLES   'Tis granted: 120
  And for a league of privacy between us,
  Read o'er my bosome, and pertake a secret;
  The Princesse is contracted mine.

ORGILUS   Still: why not?
  I now applaud her wisdome; when your kingdome
  Stands seated in your will secure, and setled,   125
  I dare pronounce you will be a just Monarch:
  Greece must admire, and tremble.

ITHOCLES   Then the sweetnesse
  Of so imparadis'd a comfort, Orgilus,
  It is to banquet with the gods.

ORGILUS   The glory
  Of numerous children, potency of Nobles,   130
  Bent knees, hearts pav'd to tread on!

ITHOCLES   With a friendship
  So deare, so fast as thine.

ORGILUS   I am unfitting
  For Office, but for service.

ITHOCLES　　　　　　　　　Wee'll distinguish
Our fortunes meerely in the Title; partners
In all respects else but the bed.

ORGILUS　　　　　　　　　　The bed?　　　　　　　　135
Forefend it Joves owne Jealousie, till lastly
We slip downe in the common earth together;
And there our beds are equall, save some Monument
To shew this was the King, and this the Subject.
List, what sad sounds are these? Extremely sad ones.　　140

ITHOCLES　Sure from Penthea's lodgings.

ORGILUS　　　　　　　　　　　　　Harke, a voyce too.
　　　　　　Soft sad musicke.　A Song.

　　Oh no more, no more, too late
　　Sighes are spent; the burning Tapers
　　Of a life as chast as Fate,
　　Pure as are unwritten papers,　　　　　　　145
　　　Are burnt out: no heat, no light
　　　Now remaines, 'tis ever night.
　　Love is dead, let lovers eyes,
　　　Lock'd in endlesse dreames,
　　　Th' extremes of all extremes,　　　　　　150
　　Ope no more, for now Love dyes,
　　　Now Love dyes, implying
　　Loves Martyrs must be ever, ever dying.

ITHOCLES　Oh my misgiving heart!

ORGILUS　　　　　　　　　　A horrid stilnesse
Succeeds this deathfull ayre; let's know the reason.　　155
Tread softly, there is mystery in mourning.　　　*Exeunt*

4.4　*Enter* CHRISTALLA *and* PHILEMA, *bringing in* PENTHEA
in a chaire vaild: two other servants placing two chaires, one on the one
side, and the other with an Engine on the other; the maids sit downe at her
feet mourning, the servants goe out; meet them ITHOCLES *and* ORGILUS.

SERVANT (*To Orgilus*)　'Tis done, that on her right hand.

ORGILUS (*Aside*)　　　　　　　　　　　Good, begone.

136 forefend] *Weber;* foresend *Q.*

ITHOCLES   Soft peace inrich this roome.

ORGILUS   How fares the Lady?

PHILEMA   Dead.

CHRISTALLA   Dead!

PHILEMA   Starv'd.

CHRISTALLA   Starv'd!

ITHOCLES   Me miserable!

ORGILUS   Tell us,
How parted she from life?

PHILEMA   She called for musicke,
And begg'd some gentle voyce to tune a farewell   5
To life and griefes; Christalla touch'd the Lute,
I wept the funerall song.

CHRISTALLA   Which scarce was ended,
But her last breath seal'd up these hollow sounds,
'O cruell Ithocles, and injur'd Orgilus!'
So downe she drew her vaile, so dy'd.

ITHOCLES   So dy'd.   10

ORGILUS   Up; you are messengers of death, goe from us;
12   Here's woe enough to court without a prompter.
Away; and harke ye, till you see us next,
No sillable that she is dead. Away;
              Exeunt PHILEMA *and* CHRISTALLA.
Keepe a smooth brow. My Lord.

ITHOCLES   Mine onely sister,   15
Another is not left me.

ORGILUS   Take that chayre,
I'le seat me here in this. Betweene us sits
The object of our sorrowes. Some few teares
Wee'll part among us; I perhaps can mixe
One lamentable story to prepare 'em.   20
There, there, sit there, my Lord.

ITHOCLES   Yes, as you please.
              ITHOCLES *sits downe, and is catcht in the Engine.*
What meanes this treachery?

ORGILUS   Caught, you are caught,
  Young master: 'tis thy throne of Coronation,
  Thou foole of greatnesse! See, I take this vaile off;
  Survey a beauty wither'd by the flames   25
  Of an insulting Phaeton, her brother.

ITHOCLES   Thou mean'st to kill me basely.

ORGILUS   I foreknew
  The last act of her life, and train'd thee hither
  To sacrifice a Tyrant to a Turtle.
  You dream't of kingdomes, did 'ee? How to bosome   30
  The delicacies of a youngling Princesse,
  How with this nod to grace that subtill Courtier,
  How with that frowne to make this Noble tremble,
  And so forth; whiles Penthea's grones, and tortures,
  Her agonies, her miseries, afflictions,   35
  Ne're toucht upon your thought; as for my injuries,
  Alas they were beneath your royall pitty,
  But yet they liv'd, thou proud man, to confound thee.
  Behold thy fate, this steele.

ITHOCLES   Strike home; a courage
  As keene as thy revenge shall give it welcome: 40
  But prethe faint not; if the wound close up,
  Tent it with double force, and search it deeply.
  Thou look'st that I should whine, and beg compassion,
  As loath to leave the vainnesse of my glories;
  A statelier resolution armes my confidence,   45
  To cozen thee of honour; neither could I
  Wish equall tryall of unequall fortune,
  By hazard of a duell; 'twere a bravery
  Too mighty for a slave intending murther.
  On to the Execution, and inherit   50
  A conflict with thy horrors.

ORGILUS   By Apollo,
  Thou talk'st a goodly language; for requitall,
  I will report thee to thy mistresse richly.
  And take this peace along: some few short minutes
  Determin'd, my resolves shall quickly follow   55
  Thy wrathfull ghost; then if we tug for mastery,

4.4] 47 Wish] *this edn.*; With Q.

Pentheas sacred eyes shall lend new courage.
Give me thy hand, be healthfull in thy parting
From lost mortality: thus, thus, I free it.   *kils him.*

ITHOCLES   Yet, yet, I scorne to shrinke.

ORGILUS.   Keepe up thy spirit: 60
I will be gentle even in blood; to linger
Paine, which I strive to cure, were to be cruell.

ITHOCLES   Nimble in vengeance, I forgive thee; follow
Safety, with best successe—o may it prosper!
Penthea, by thy side thy brother bleeds,   65
The earnest of his wrongs to thy forc'd faith;
Thoughts of ambition, or delitious banquet,
With beauty, youth, and love, together perish
In my last breath, which on the sacred Altar
Of a long look'd for peace—now—moves—to heaven. *moritur.*   70

ORGILUS   Farewell, faire spring of manhood; henceforth
    welcome
Best expectation of a noble suffrance!
I'le locke the bodies safe, till what must follow
Shall be approv'd. Sweet Twins shine stars for ever.
In vaine they build their hopes whose life is shame;   75
No monument lasts but a happy Name.   *Exit* ORGILUS.

5.1   *Enter* BASSANES *alone.*

BASSANES   Athens, to Athens I have sent, the Nursery
I₃   Of Greece for learning, and the Fount of knowledge;
For here in Sparta there's not left amongst us
One wise man to direct; we're all turn'd madcaps.
'Tis said, Apollo is the god of herbs;   5
Then certainly he knowes the vertue of 'em.
To Delphos I have sent to; if there can be
A help for nature, we are sure yet.

Enter ORGILUS.

ORGILUS   Honour
Attend thy counsels ever.

BASSANES   I beseech thee
With all my heart, let me goe from thee quietly;   10

I will not ought to doe with thee of all men.
The doublers of a Hare, or, in a morning,
Salutes from a splay-footed witch, to drop
Three drops of blood at th' nose just, and no more,
Croaking of Ravens, or the screech of Owles,   15
Are not so boading mischiefe as thy crossing
My private meditations. Shun me, prethe;
And if I cannot love thee hartily,
I'le love thee as well as I can.

ORGILUS   Noble Bassanes,
  Mistake me not.

BASSANES   Phew, then we shall be troubled;   20
  Thou wert ordain'd my plague. Heaven make me thankfull,
  And give me patience too, heaven I beseech thee.

ORGILUS   Accept a league of amity, for henceforth,
  I vow by my best Genius, in a sillable,
  Never to speake vexation. I will study   25
  Service and friendship with a zealous sorrow
  For my past incivility towards 'ee.

BASSANES   Heyday! Good words, good words, I must beleeve 'em,
  And be a Coxcombe for my labor.

ORGILUS   Use not
  So hard a Language; your misdoubt is causelesse.   30
  For instance: if you promise to put on
  A constancy of patience, such a patience
  As Chronicle, or history ne're mentioned,
  As followes not example, but shall stand
  A wonder, and a Theame for imitation,   35
  The first, the Index pointing to a second,
  I will acquaint 'ee with an unmatch'd secret,
  Whose knowledge to your griefes shall set a period.

BASSANES   Thou canst not (Orgilus), 'tis in the power
  Of the gods onely; yet for satisfaction,   40
  Because I note an earnest in thine utterance,
  Unforc'd, and naturally free, be resolute
  The Virgin Bayes shall not withstand the lightning

5.1] 12 doubles] *Q*; doublers *Gifford, Spencer.*

With a more carelesse danger, than my constancy
The full of thy relation: could it move   45
Distraction in a senselesse marble statue,
It should finde me a rocke. I doe expect now
Some truth of unheard moment.

ORGILUS   To your patience
You must adde privacie, as strong in silence
As mysteries lock'd up in Joves owne bosome.   50

BASSANES   A skull hid in the earth a treble age
Shall sooner prate.

ORGILUS   Lastly, to such direction
As the severity of a glorious Action
Deserves to lead your wisdome and your iudgement,
You ought to yeeld obedience.

BASSANES   With assurance   55
Of will and thankfulnesse.

ORGILUS   With manly courage
Please then to follow me.

BASSANES   Where e're, I feare not.

                                                            Exeunt omnes.

   5.2   *Enter* GRONEAS *and* HEMOPHIL *leading* EUPHRANEA,
   CHRISTALLA *and* PHILEMA *leading* PROPHILUS, NEARCHUS
   supporting CALANTHA; CROTOLON, *and* AMELUS; *cease loud
                   Musicke, all make a stand.*

CALANTHA   We misse our servant Ithocles and Orgilus;
   On whom attend they?

CROTOLON   My sonne, gracious Princesse,
   Whisper'd some new device, to which these Revels
   Should be but usher, wherein I conceive
   Lord Ithocles and he himselfe are Actors.   5

CALANTHA   A faire excuse for absence; as for Bassanes,
   Delights to him are troublesome: Armostes
   Is with the King.

CROTOLON   He is.

CALANTHA On to the dance:
Deare Cozen, hand you the Bride, the Bridegroome must be
Instructed to my Courtship. Be not jealous, 10 14
Euphranea, I shall scarcely prove a temptresse;
Fall to our dance.
Musicke.
NEARCHUS *dance with* EUPHRANEA, PROPHILUS *with*
CALANTHA,
CHRISTALLA *with* HEMOPHIL, PHILEMA *with* GRONEAS.
Dance the first change; during which, enter ARMOSTES.

ARMOSTES The King your father's dead. [*in* CALANTHA*'s
eare*].

CALANTHA To the other change.

ARMOSTES Is't possible?
Dance againe. Enter BASSANES.

BASSANES O Madam!
Penthea, poore Penthea's starv'd.

CALANTHA Beshrew thee!
Lead to the next.

BASSANES Amazement duls my senses. 15
Dance againe. Enter ORGILUS.

ORGILUS Brave Ithocles is murther'd, murther'd cruelly.

CALANTHA How dull this musicke sounds! Strike up more
sprightly;
Our footings are not active like our heart,
Which treads the nimbler measure.

ORGILUS I am thunder-strooke.
Last change. Cease musicke.

CALANTHA So, let us breath a while; hath not this motion 20
Rais'd fresher colour on your cheeks?

NEARCHUS Sweet Princesse,
A perfect purity of blood enamels
The beauty of your white.

5.2] 9 Deare Cozen] Q; Cozen *Gifford conj.*

CALANTHA   We all looke cheerfully;
And Cozen, 'tis, me thinks, a rare presumption
In any, who prefers our lawfull pleasures   25
Before their owne sowre censure, to interrupt
The custome of this Ceremony bluntly.

NEARCHUS   None dares, Lady.

CALANTHA   Yes, yes; some hollow voyce deliver'd to me
How that the King was dead.

ARMOSTES   The King is dead;   30
That fatall newes was mine; for in mine armes
He breath'd his last, and with his Crowne bequeath'd 'ee
Your mothers wedding Ring, which here I tender.

CROTOLON
Most strange!

CALANTHA   Peace crown his ashes; we are queen then.

NEARCHUS   Long live Calantha, Sparta's Soveraigne Queene.   35

OMNES   Long live the Queene.

CALANTHA   What whispered Bassanes?

BASSANES   That my Penthea, miserable soule,
Was starv'd to death.

CALANTHA   Shee's happy; she hath finish'd
A long and painefull progresse. A third murmure
Pierc'd mine unwilling eares.

ORGILUS   That Ithocles   40
Was murther'd; rather butcher'd, had not bravery
Of an undaunted spirit, conquering terror,
Proclaim'd his last Act triumph over ruine.

ARMOSTES
How? Murther'd?

CALANTHA   By whose hand?

ORGILUS   By mine; this weapon
Was instrument to my revenge. The reasons   45
Are just and knowne; quit him of these, and then
Never liv'd Gentleman of greater merit,
Hope, or abiliment to steere a kingdome.

CROTOLON   Fye Orgilus.

EUPHRANEA   Fye brother.

CALANTHA   You have done it.

BASSANES   How it was done let him report, the forfeit   50
 Of whose alleageance to our lawes doth covet
 Rigour of Justice; but that done it is,
 Mine eyes have beene an evidence of credit
 Too sure to be convinc'd. Armostes, rent not
 Thine Arteries with hearing the bare circumstances   55
 Of these calamities. Thou'st lost a Nephew,
 A Neece, and I a wife; continue man still,
 Make me the patterne of digesting evils,
 Who can out-live my mighty ones, not shrinking
 At such a pressure as would sinke a soule   60
 Into what's most of death, the worst of horrors:
 But I have seal'd a covenant with sadnesse,
 And enter'd into bonds without condition
 To stand these tempests calmly; marke me, Nobles,
 I doe not shed a teare, not for Penthea: 65
 Excellent misery!

CALANTHA   We begin our reigne
 With a first act of Justice: thy confession,
 Unhappy Orgilus, doomes thee a sentence;
 But yet thy fathers, or thy sisters presence
   Shall be excus'd. Give, Crotolon, a blessing   70
   To thy lost sonne; Euphranea, take a farewell,
 And both be gone.

CROTOLON   Confirme thee, noble sorrow,
 In worthy resolution.

EUPHRANEA   Could my teares speake,
 My griefes were sleight.

ORGILUS   All goodesse dwell amongst yee.
 Enjoy my sister, Prophilus; my vengeance   75 K
 Aym'd never at thy prejudice.

CALANTHA   Now withdraw.
       Exeunt CROTOLON, PROPHILUS, *and* EUPHRANEA.
 Bloody relator of thy staines in blood,
 For that thou hast reported him whose fortunes

And life by thee are both at once snatch'd from him,
With honourable mention, make thy choyce   80
Of what death likes thee best; there's all our bounty.
But to excuse delayes, let me (deare Cozen)
Intreat you and these Lords see execution
Instant before 'ee part.

NEARCHUS   Your will commands us.

ORGILUS   One suit, just Queene, my last; vouchsafe your
    clemency   85
That by no common hand I be divided
From this my humble frailty.

CALANTHA   To their wisdomes
Who are to be spectators of thine end,
I make the reference. Those that are dead,
Are dead; had they not now dy'd, of necessity   90
They must have payd the debt they ow'd to nature
One time or other. Use dispatch, my Lords;
Wee'll suddenly prepare our Coronation.
                    Exeunt CALANTHA, PHILEMA, CHRISTALLA.

ARMOSTES   'Tis strange, these Tragedies should never touch on
    Her female pitty.

BASSANES   She has a masculine spirit: 95
And wherefore should I pule, and like a girle,
Put finger in the eye. Let's be all toughnesse,
Without distinction betwixt sex and sex.

NEARCHUS   Now, Orgilus, thy choyce?

ORGILUS   To bleed to death.

ARMOSTES   The Executioner?

ORGILUS.   My selfe, no Surgeon.   100
I am well skill'd in letting blood. Bind fast
This arme, that so the pipes may from their conduits
Convey a full streame. Here's skilfull Instrument:
Onely I am a beggar to some charity
To speed me in this Execution,   105
By lending th'other pricke to th' tother arme,
When this is bubling life out.

BASSANES   I am for 'ee.
  It most concernes my art, my care, my credit;
  Quicke, fillet both his armes.

ORGILUS.   Gramercy friendship;
  Such curtesies are reall, which flow cheerefully   110
  Without an expection of requitall.
  Reach me a staffe in this hand. If a pronenesse,
  Or custome in my nature, from my cradle,
  Had beene inclin'd to fierce and eager bloodshed,
  A coward guilt, hid in a coward quaking,   115
  Would have betray'd fame to ignoble flight,
  And vagabond pursuit of dreadfull safety:
  But looke upon my steddinesse, and scorne not
  The sicknesse of my fortune, which since Bassanes
  Was husband to Penthea, had laine bed-rid.   120
  We trifle time in words; thus I shew cunning
  In opening of a veine too full, too lively.

ARMOSTES   Desperate courage.

ORGILUS   Honourable infamy.

HEMOPHIL   I tremble at the sight.

GRONEAS   Would I were loose.

BASSANES   It sparkles like a lusty wine new broacht;   125
  The vessell must be sound from which it issues.
  Graspe hard this other sticke; I'le be as nimble.
  But prethe looke not pale; have at 'ee, stretch out
  Thine arme with vigor, and unshooke vertue.
  Good; o I envy not a Rivall fitted   130
  To conquer in extremities. This pastime
  Appeares majesticall: some high tun'd poem
  Hereafter shall deliver to posterity
  The writers glory, and his subjects triumph.
  How is't man, droope not yet.

ORGILUS   I feele no palsies.   135
  On a paire royall doe I wait in death,
  My Soveraigne, as his Liegeman; on my Mistresse,

109 his] Weber; this Q.   123 ARMOSTES] Q; NEARCHUS Gifford conj.

As a devoted servant; and on Ithocles,
As if no brave, yet no unworthy enemy.
Nor did I use an engine to intrap   140
His life out of a slavish feare to combate
Youth, strength, or cunning, but for that I durst not
Ingage the goodnesse of a cause on fortune,
By which his name might have out-fac'd my vengeance.
Ah Tecnicus, inspir'd with Phoebus fire,   145
I call to mind thy Augury, 'twas perfect:
'Revenge proves its owne Executioner.'
When feeble man is bending to his mother,
The dust 'a was first fram'd on, thus he totters.

BASSANES   Life's fountaine is dry'd up.

ORGILUS   So falls the Standards   150
Of my prerogative in being a creature.
A mist hangs o're mine eyes; the Sun's bright splendor
Is clouded in an everlasting shadow.
Welcome thou yce that sit'st about my heart,
No heat can ever thaw thee.

NEARCHUS   Speech hath left him.   *Dyes.*   155

BASSANES   'A has shooke hands with time. His funerall urne
Shall be my charge. Remove the bloodlesse bodie.
The Coronation must require attendance;
That past, my few dayes can be but one mourning.   *Exeunt.*

5.3   *An Altar covered with white. Two lights of Virgin wax, during which
musicke of Recorders, enter foure bearing* ITHOCLES *on a hearse, or in a
chaire, in a rich robe, and a Crowne on his head; place him on one side of the
Altar, after him enter* CALANTHA *in a white robe, and crown'd;*
EUPHRANEA; PHILEMA, CHRISTALLA *in white,* NEARCHUS,
ARMOSTES, CROTOLON, PTOPHILUS, AMELUS, BASSANES, LEMOPHIL,
and GRONEAS. CALANTHA *goes and kneeles before the Altar, the rest
stand off, the women kneeling behind; cease Recorders during her devotions.
Soft musicke.* CALANTHA *and the rest rise doing obeysance to the Altar.*

CALANTHA   Our Orisons are heard, the gods are mercifull.
Now tell me, you whose loyalties payes tribute
To us your lawfull Soueraigne, how unskilfull

5.3] o *crown'd; Euphranea*] Weber; *crown'd Euphranea* Q.

Your duties or obedience is to render
Subjection to the Scepter of a Virgin,   5
Who have beene ever fortunate in Princes
Of masculine and stirring composition?
A woman has enough to governe wisely
Her owne demeanours, passions, and divisions.
A Nation warlike and inur'd to practice   10
Of policy and labour, cannot brooke
A feminate authority; we therefore
Command your counsaile, how you may advise us
In choosing of a husband whose abilities
Can better guide this kingdome.

NEARCHUS   Royall Lady,   15
Your law is in your will.

ARMOSTES   We have seene tokens
Of constancy too lately to mistrust it.

CROTOLON   Yet if your highnesse settle on a choice
By your owne iudgement both allow'd and lik't of,
Sparta may grow in power, and proceed   20
To an increasing height.

CALANTHA   Hold you the same minde?

BASSANES   Alas great mistris, reason is so clouded
With the thicke darkenesse of my infinite woes
That I forecast, nor dangers, hopes, or safety.
Give me some corner of the world to weare out   25
The remnant of the minutes I must number,
Where I may heare no sounds, but sad complaints
Of Virgins who have lost contracted partners;
Of husbands howling that their wives were ravisht
By some untimely fate; of friends divided   30
By churlish opposition, or of fathers
Weeping upon their childrens slaughtered carcasses;
Or daughters groaning o're their fathers hearses,
And I can dwell there, and with these keepe consort
As musicall as theirs. What can you looke for   35
From an old foolish peevish doting man,
But crasinesse of age?

23 infinite] *Weber*; infinites *Q*.

CALANTHA Cozen of Argos.

NEARCHUS Madam.

CALANTHA   Were I presently
To choose you for my Lord, Ile open freely
What articles I would propose to treat on   40
Before our marriage.

NEARCHUS   Name them, vertuous Lady.

CALANTHA   I would presume you would retaine the royalty
Of Sparta in her owne bounds: then in Argos
Armostes might be Viceroy; in Messene
Might Crotolon beare sway, and Bassanes—   45

BASSANES   I, Queene? Alas! what I?

CALANTHA   Be Sparta's Marshall.
The multitudes of high imployments could not
But set a peace to private griefes. These Gentlemen,
Groneas and Hemophil, with worthy pensions
Should wait upon your person in your Chamber;   50
K3   I would bestow Christalla on Amelus,
Shee'll prove a constant wife, and Philema
Should into Vesta's Temple.

BASSANES   This is a Testament;
It sounds not like conditions on a marriage.

NEARCHUS   All this should be perform'd.

CALANTHA   Lastly, for Prophilus,   55
He should be (Cozen) solemnly invested
In all those honors, titles, and preferments
Which his deare friend, and my neglected husband
Too short a time enjoy'd.

PROPHILUS   I am unworthy
To live in your remembrance.

EUPHRANEA   Excellent Lady!   60

NEARCHUS   Madam, what meanes that word 'neglected husband'?

CALANTHA   Forgive me: now I turne to thee, thou shadow
Of my contacted Lord: beare witnesse all,

I put my mothers wedding Ring upon
His finger, 'twas my fathers last bequest.   65
Thus I new marry him whose wife I am;
Death shall not separate us. O my Lords,
I but deceiv'd your eyes with Anticke gesture,
When one newes straight came hudling on another,
Of death, and death, and death, still I danc'd forward,   70
But it strooke home, and here, and in an instant,
Be such meere women, who with shreeks and out-cries
Can vow a present end to all their sorrowes,   .
Yet live to vow new pleasures, and out-live them;
They are the silent griefes which cut the hart-string;   75
Let me dye smiling.

NEARCHUS   'Tis a truth too ominous.

CALANTHA   One kisse on these cold lips, my last; cracke, cracke.
Argos now's Sparta's King. Command the voices
Which wait at th' Altar, now to sing the song
I fitted for my end.

NEARCHUS   Sirs, the song.   80
            A Song.

ALL   *Glories, pleasures, pomps, delights, and ease,*
              Can but please
         Outward senses, when the mind
     Is not untroubled, or by peace refin'd.

1.   *Crownes may flourish and decay,*   85
       Beauties shine, but fade away,

2.   *Youth may revell, yet it must*
       Lye downe in a bed of dust:

3.   *Earthly honors flow and waste,*
       Time alone doth change and last.   90

ALL.   *Sorrowes mingled with contents, prepare*
              Rest for care;
         Love onely reignes in death: though Art
         Can find no comfort for a broken heart.

64 mother's] *Lamb*; mother *Q*.   73 vow] *Q*; court *Gifford conj.*   83 Outward
senses] *Q (indented)*; The outward senses *Spencer conj.*   89 waste] *Weber*; wast *Q*.

ARMOSTES   Looke to the Queene.

BASSANES   Her heart is broke indeed: 95
O royall maid, would thou hadst mist this part;
Yet 'twas a brave one: I must weepe to see
Her smile in death.

ARMOSTES   Wise Tecnicus, thus said he,
'*When youth is ripe, and age from time doth part,*
The livelesse Trunke shall wed the broken heart.'   100
'Tis here fulfill'd.

NEARCHUS   I am your King.

OMNES   Long live
Nearchus, King of Sparta.

NEARCHUS   Her last will
Shall never be digrest from; wait in order
Upon these faithfull lovers as becomes us.
The Counsels of the gods are never knowne,   105
Till men can call th' effects of them their owne.

FINIS.

THE EPILOGUE.

WHere Noble Judgements, and cleare eyes are fix'd
To grace Endevour, there sits Truth not mix'd
With Ignorance; those censures may command
Beleefe, which talke *not, till they* understand.
Let some say This was flat; *Some here* the Sceane   5
Fell from its height; *Another that the Meane*
Was ill observ'd, *in such a growing passion*
As it transcended either state or fashion:
Some few may cry 'twas pretty, well *or* so,
But,—*and there shrugge in silence; yet we know*   10
Our writer's ayme, was in the whole addrest
Well to deserve of All; *but please the* Best.
Which granted, by th' allowance of this straine,
The Broken Heart *may be piec't up againe.*

FINIS.

Commentary to *The Broken Heart*

TITLE PAGE

The text is based on the copy held in the British Library: C.12.g.3 (2).

FIDE HONOUR 'Fide Honour' or 'Fide Honor', which means 'Honour Through Faith' in Latin and is an anagram of 'Iohn Forde', appears on the title-pages of several Ford works. The faith referred to is probably synonymous with 'integrity' but could conceivably be read as an indication of Catholicism on Ford's part.

Hugh Beeston Also published *Love's Sacrifice* (1633) and *Perkin Warbeck* (1634).

DEDICATION

William, Lord Craven William Craven matriculated at Trinity on 11 July 1623, when he was 13, and the following year entered the Inner Temple. He was of good but not great family (his parents had been a Lord Mayor of London and an alderman's daughter). He came to prominence in the early 1620s on account of his distinguished service with the Dutch troops who were fighting the Spanish. In 1627 he was knighted by Charles I; in 1631 he commanded English troops fighting for Gustavus Adolphus and was raised to the peerage; and from 1632 onwards he was famous principally for his whole-hearted devotion to Charles I's sister, the widowed Elizabeth of Bohemia, to whom he was rumoured (without much probability) to be secretly married, and whom he assisted out of his enormous fortune. Hamstead Marshall is in Berkshire, not far from Littlecote, where Ford's great-uncle Lord Chief Justice Popham lived.

DRAMATIS PERSONAE

Hemophil This character is listed initially as Lemophil, but more often occurs as Hemophil in Q, though this translates as 'eater of blood' rather than 'glutton'.

PROLOGUE

5–6 **no pretended clause / Of jests** no supposedly comic phrases. To use 'clause' in this sense seems forced, but suits the rhyme scheme. I am unconvinced by Spencer's suggestion that 'clause' means 'close' and refers to scenes which end with comic business by clowns. Morris glosses the phrase as 'group of stories offered', but that does not really mean much.

6 **brothell Courts applause** on the first reading of this line, there is a suggestive syntactical ambiguity about 'court', which, though ultimately revealed as a verb, could initially appear to be a noun qualified by 'brothel', especially given that *Q* gives the word 'courts' a capital letter. Weber prints 'brothel court's', implying that 'brothel' describes 'court'.

9 **The Virgine Sisters** the nine Muses.

13 **Presentment** presentation, performance. Foster and Foster observe that 'The lines, "This law we keep in our presentment now, / Not to take freedom more than we allow," look very like a pun, for if "presentment" means theatrical presentation, its earlier signification, known certainly to Ford and the large contingent of lawyers in the Blackfriars audience and probably to most of the rest, is that of "a statement on oath by a jury of a fact within their own knowledge" that is, their own personal knowledge' (309).

16 **was knowne A Truth** see the section 'Sources' in the Introduction for some possible explanations of the 'truth' behind *The Broken Heart*.

I.I

6 **Cynicke** the Cynics were a philosophical school founded by Antisthenes (*c*.445–365 BC), a follower of Socrates. Cynics despised wordly success and emphasized the necessity of leading a virtuous life, which they saw as the foundation of happiness.

6 **Stoicke** Stoic philosophers cultivated indifference to emotion and to external events. The name came from the *stoa*, or porch, of the Agora (marketplace) at Athens. Ford's cousin Sir John Stradling translated into English the *De Constantia* (*Of Constancy*) of the famous Low Countries stoic Justus Lipsius.

7 **read the Logicke Lecture** study logic.

8 **Areopagite** member of the Council of the Areopagus, the hill in Athens on which the law court sat.

13 **Sparta** in fact ancient Sparta was famous predominantly for military activity rather than learning. Crotolon's words might well strike the audience as more patriotic than accurate.

18 **brauch't** broached, i.e. drew liquid from a container (in this case blood from the bodies of those who supported Thrasus and Crotolon).

18–20 **and sometimes . . . my Lord** Orgilus notes almost in passing that the 'quarrels' were so bad that some of those who took the side of Thrasus died, and so too did some of those who took the side of Crotolon. 'Confederates' refers equally to sympathizers of both lords.

20 **Thrasus** Thrasus, now dead, was the father of Ithocles and Penthea. His quarrel with Crotolon, which Ithocles renewed after Thrasus' death, has produced a Romeo-and-Juliet-like situation for the lovers Orgilus and Penthea.

26 **Hymenean** marital. From the Greek Hymen, god of marriage.

37 **Aconite** a poisonous shrub, also known as monkshood. Margaret Willes argues that in *Romeo and Juliet* the drug Romeo uses to commit suicide is aconite, because Shakespeare compares it to gunpowder and in *Henry IV* 2 he explicitly connects aconite to gunpowder (Margaret Willes, *A Shakespearean Botanical* (Oxford: Bodleian Library, 2015), p. 83.

50 **insulting** abusive.

67 **If opportunity but sort** if events works out in a particular way, so as to give the prospective lover a decent chance.

93–4 line 93 has thirteen syllables and l. 94 eight. Spencer followed Gifford in moving 'worthy' to the beginning of l. 94, giving one line of eleven syllables and one of ten. However, 'Worthy, your faith' is not metrically felicitous, and the irregularity of the line lengths would give point to the social irregularity of Orgilus' request (which is particularly odd coming from a man who has just been complaining of how a brother's attitude blighted his own hopes).

98 **Vesta** Roman goddess of the hearth and of virginity, in which capacity she was patron of the Vestal Virgins. There will be two further references to Vesta in the play.

99 **Apollo** Greek and Roman god of archery and the sun. The oracle at Delphi was dedicated to him, which is ironic in view of the fact that Orgilus will later disclaim the identity of Oedipus, whose fate was predicted by the oracle. This is the first of ten references to Apollo in the play, and the name of Orgilus' disguise, Aplotes, may also evoke that of the god.

117 **without 'em** free from those sorrows.

1.2

13 **Laconia** alternative name for Sparta (whence the term 'laconic').

15 **Messene** city in southern Greece. It was conquered by Sparta in the eighth century BC and the majority of its population were made Helots, the Spartan term for slaves.

16 **Lacedemon** alternative name for Sparta.

20 **Pephon** Probably a mistake for Pephnos or Pephnon, which Pausanias names as the boundary between Sparta and Messene.

42 **period of my Fate** end point of my destiny.

59 **in part of** in part payment of (Spencer).

63 **chosen** select, exemplary.

66 **provinciall garland** Gifford is surely right to suggest that Ford thought there was a special triumphal wreath for those who had added a province to the empire (though see Spencer's note explaining that there wasn't).

71 **What nothings I have done** Coriolanus similarly calls his achievements 'nothings'.

72 **the issue of a willing minde** the results of an eager disposition. As Ithocles explains in the next line, he presents a readiness to have a go as his only virtue.

74–9 The syntax is difficult here. Ithocles asks what kind of man could be so sluggish, so undeserving of his name and country, that he would not feel sufficient gratitude (for the gift of having been born) to acknowledge that he has an obligation to serve the commonwealth in whatever way considerations of its safety and best interests call for. Spencer observes that the idea is 'ultimately Socratic'.

82 **Bacchus** god of wine.

109 **Is of a mounting nature** with sexual pun.

125 **not put my love to use** not invested my love, with the result that it has not grown.

126 **Mars** Roman god of war.

127 **Vulcan** Roman god of smithery, who was cuckolded when Mars slept with his wife Venus.

131 **By petition** Hemophil says he has acquired a city by right of conquest; Christalla scoffs that if he wants a city he will have to plead for one, and mockingly uses a legal term ('In *Forma pauperis*', in the character of a pauper) which implies that Hemophil is little better than a beggar.

132 **Kennell** Hemophil claims to be master of a city, but Christalla declares that he owns nothing better than a kennel.

133 **Feathers** all subsequent editors have adopted Weber's suggestion that *Q*'s 'Fathers' should be 'Feathers', the ornaments of soldiers.

134 **thrum** adorn with ends of thread.

1.3

8 **fore-dooming destiny** prophesying a momentous consequence.

20 **thrift** prosperity, well being. Tecnicus explains that he does not grudge that anyone should thrive who deserves to do so.

49 **stand my privilege** supply me with authorization.

92 **Tenters** wooden frames for stretching cloth, which had tenterhooks set into them.

93 **Cupid** son of Venus and god of love.

116–23 A parody of scholarly debate. Orgilus adopts different personae who argue amongst themselves.

125 **Apish** in a way that mimics. The boys imitate without understanding, in the way that apes do.

125 **Grammates** *OED* gives the meaning as 'rudiments', but cites no other instance of the word.

130 **mushrome** humble creature. Because they shoot up overnight, mushrooms become a proverbial way of describing an upstart or parvenu.

141 **sumptuous** finely dressed.

177 **Mercury** messenger and herald of the gods in Roman mythology, and hence metaphorically associated with quick-wittedness and rapidity of communication.

2.1

1 cf. Ben Jonson, *Volpone*, 2.5.59ff, where Corvino similarly resolves to have Celia's window blocked.

4 **travels** travails, labours.

5–6 **till the deformed . . . the act** this alludes to the Renaissance belief that bear cubs were born shapeless and were literally licked into shape by their mothers.

10 **factor** agent who does business for someone else.

12 **springall** young man.

13 **Eare-wig** flatterer (Spencer); someone who insinuates themself into a person's confidence.

16 **maw** stomach.

26 **Cull** embrace (variant of 'coll').

28–9 **rubs | Stucke on the foreheads** horns which supposedly grow on cuckolds amd which get in the way. Spencer sees it exclusively as a bowling metaphor, but there is also surely a suggestion of wanting to rub one's forehead.

32–4 **Their pleasure . . . sues for't** a wife's pleasure (sex with a lover) causes her husband ('the patient Asse who suffers') to be raised to office, title, and wealth; this promotion of the husband makes the wife's shame acceptable, and indeed makes some husbands actively encourage their wives' adultery ('sues for't').

45 **mew'd** shed, moulted.

54 **fiery Dragon** Spencer suggests 'a burlesque allusion to Medea's escape to Athens in a chariot drawn by winged dragons' (Ovid, *Metamorphoses* vii.398, Euripides, *Medea* 1318).

69 **pearles** almost certainly pronounced as two syllables ('purruls') by the Devon-born Ford.

76 **Triumphant victory** a ceremonial procession named a triumph was awarded to victorious Romans.

113 **Mewes** seamews (gulls).

115 **stew'd** ostensibly cooked by being boiled, and so killed. But 'stews' can also mean a brothel, so Grausis could be hinting that she will go and work in one, a suggestion not calculated to appease Bassanes.

2.2

1 **'Tis of vipers breed** it is the offspring of vipers. Young vipers were thought to eat their way out of their mother, killing her.

3 **seeled Dove** dove that has had its eyelids sewn up, on the grounds that it will then fly high. Spencer suggests an allusion to one of Sidney's *Certain Sonnets* here.

25 **availeable** able to make things happen.

134 **wait** wait on, follow.

2.3

0 the absence of the word 'Enter' and the nature of the scene make it likely that Prophilus and Penthea are in the 'discovery space', a recess at the back of the stage which could be screened from view when not being used.

14 **Doe thy best** the fact that this is a line fragment may perhaps imply that some business occurs, such as Prophilus gesturing to Penthea.

21 **Schoole terms** terms drawn from the tradition of scholastic philosophy.

63 **Thou't** thou wouldst.

86 **race** career, course of behaviour.

124 **French** Brooke and Paradise suggested emending to 'frenzy'. Craik suggested that it should, in fact read, 'politic study', on the grounds that the metre calls for a two-syllable word and that a long s at the beginning of the word and a tailed y at the end could have plausibly given rise to the misreading. However, 'French' is used in *Perkin Warbeck* as a term which appears to connote deception and there seems no compelling reason to adopt an emendation which is at best conjectural.

134 **Impostumes** cysts or abscesses.

150 **may fall even** may balance properly.

153 **the deservers exercise** something sent (implicitly by the gods) to test the deserving.

3.1

3 **jealous** mistrustful.

18 **dispos'd to** engaged to.

29–30 **more than . . . mine honour** more than was consistent with what my sense of honour thinks right.

53 **in thy precepts make me ever thrifty** make me always able to profit from your advice.

55 **Curiosity** this could mean a simple desire to know or to probe, or it could imply that Tecnicus thinks Orgilus is taking an undue interest in Penthea's situation

63 **bolt** sieve.

70 **Delphos** alternatively 'Delphi', this was the seat of the oracle of Apollo.

3.2

16 sd *severall stands* different places to listen and watch. A stand could mean the place where hunters wait concealed to kill animals (*OED*, n1 13).

41 **the dead** Thrasus, the father of Penthea and Ithocles, who had wanted her to marry Orgilus.

58 **fleetings** skimmings from whey or curds.

64–6 cf. the scene in *'Tis Pity She's a Whore* where Giovanni and Annabella both kneel.

71 **In art, not in desires** many editors emend to 'act', but Penthea means that she has been manipulated into behaviour that she categorizes as whorish, rather than having chosen to act so. 'Art' is consistently opposed to 'heart' in the play.

87–9 **if thy pitty . . . ease it** if your pity for the weight lying heavy on a repentant (yielding) brother will just lend a finger to relieve the pressure.

117 **I'le cheere . . . straine** I'll cudgel my brains for something positive I can do.

118 **maid** Ithocles' reference to Penthea as a 'maid'—i.e. a virgin—is one of the text's many hints that the relationship between Bassanes and Penthea has not been consummated.

123 **property** personality trait, (shameful) characteristic (of mine).

133 **slave of expectation** person whose livelihood depends on keeping a lookout, as in a brothel.

135 **mysticall conveyance** unseen assistance.

141 **Mew Kitling** cf. Romeo referring to the similarly combative Tybalt as 'more than king o'cats'.

144 **springall** youthful.

149 **franks his lust** feeds his desire like an animal.

155 **megrims, firks** headaches, caprices.

156 **Touch-hole** an insult presumably implying in some way that Grausis is a bawd. See also *The Fancies Chaste and Noble*, 2.2.132, where Morosa, whose role initially appears to be that of a bawd, is called a touch-hole.

161 **studied your vexation** aimed to achieve annoyance in you.

165–6 **O that . . . devotion** if only I were able to keep you in a real sense (in fruition) as well as intending to do so (in devotion). This seems to be another sign that, despite the excuse Penthea gives to Orgilus, Bassanes cannot consummate the marriage.

206 **cry a Jealousie** although the precise logic of the phrase is unclear, its general meaning is obviously that Bassanes will seek to renounce jealousy. Perhaps it is like 'cry off from', which seems to be the sense in which Falstaff is said in *Henry V* to have 'cried out of sack' (2.3.26); it might be supposed that he cried *for* it, but that seems not to be the case because he cried out of women too, and went on to say that 'they were devils incarnate' (30).

3.3

8 **grandchilde to our Aunt** this closely mimics the relationship of James VI and I to Elizabeth I. 'James was great-grandchild to Elizabeth's aunt, Henry VII's daughter Margaret, whose marriage to James IV of Scotland Ford celebrates in *Perkin Warbeck*' (Foster and Foster 306).

19–21 **from which . . . construction** having heard what is said about Calantha, if there is anything I can do which will show my merit and secure a favourable interpretation, she has only to name it.

72 **Phoebus** Apollo.

3.4

35 **poasts** travels by post, i.e. at maximum speed.

46 **our deare Genius** the good spirit who protects our family.

47 **Thrasus monument** the tomb of Thrasus, father of Penthea and Ithocles.

87 **straine** entertainment.

3.5

5 **you have granted** you have had granted to you.

24–5 **for the proofe . . . onely** just in order to make an abstract point.

35 **Speake, I enjoin it** Q prints 'enjoy', but it seems clear that Calantha is commanding Penthea to express her thoughts.

48 **earnest** token (of the bequests still to come).

108 **checke** rebuke.

4.1

5 **As I would wish** the way I would like you to be.

22 **Livery** clothing or jewellery denoting allegiance. Nearchus wants something of Calantha's which will show that he belongs to her, though it will, of course, also imply that she belongs to him.

87 **fustian** elaborate speech. Ithocles will not descend to the circumlocutions of politeness.

91 **the presence calm'd th' affront** the fact that Calantha was there prevented Ithocles from challenging Nearchus on the spot, since it was forbidden to draw a sword in the presence of the monarch. Since Calantha is not yet the monarch, Ithocles is displaying a pointed degree of reverence for her.

94 **Collossicke** massive. The Colossus of Rhodes was a byword for size.

98 **low Mushroms never rivall Cedars** upstarts cannot compete with those who are long-established. For mushrooms as a metaphor for upstarts, see 1.3.130; the cedar, as the tallest tree in the forest, is conversely an emblem of kingship, and especially favoured as such by James VI and I.

107 **'Twas all about a little Ring** legend had it that Robert Devereux, 2nd Earl of Essex, was given a ring by Elizabeth I which he tried to send to her before his execution as a plea for mercy, only for it to be intercepted by his enemy, the Countess of Nottingham. For Webster in *The Devil's Law Case* (3.3.270–5), it was grief at her eventual discovery of this that prompted the queen to starve herself to death. Essex was the brother of Penelope Devereux, sometimes seen as the original of Penthea.

126 **saw** proverb or proverb-like utterance.

129 **My aged head** it is common in the classical languages for the word 'head' to stand as synecdoche for the whole person.

141 **I am not Oedipus** in Greek mythology, Oedipus solved the riddle of the sphinx. He also inadvertently committed incest with his mother Jocasta, and incest is what Bassanes suspects Penthea and Ithocles of.

147–8 **Servile feares . . . effects** basely fearing things doesn't stop them happening.

4.2

8 **in conceit** in (his own) imagination.

15 **The garland of good-will** the name of a popular song-book.

17 **Moile** hornless cow (*OED*, moil 3).

44 **a prey to words** Penthea no longer knows what she is saying, but this evocative phrase suggests that language has power over all of us. It perhaps also encodes a recollection of Queen Elizabeth in *Richard III* calling the dead Princes in the Tower 'the prey for worms' (4.4.46).

57.0 [*and Armostes*]] Q does not list Armostes amongst those who enter, but he speaks later in the scene.

67 **Impostors** Spencer amends to 'imposturous', a word found in *The Lover's Melancholy* (1.2.119) and the plural form is certainly problematic. However, meaning can be derived from it: Bassanes' frenzy did not really represent his true nature, and he has now rid himself of it.

86 **antiquity** old person.

107 **bawdy** some editors emend to bandy, but bawdy yields sense.

112–22 Q has this as a continuation of Orgilus' speech, but it must belong to Penthea.

122–3 Ithocles is trying to distract attention from what Penthea has revealed about his love for Calantha.

125 **lazinesse** reluctance to act.

129 **crannies** nooks and corners (of Penthea's heart, which she imagines herself as having lost literally as well as metaphorically).

130 **Amethist** amethyst, whose name derives from the Greek for 'not drunk', was proverbially reputed to prevent intoxication, but the force of its mention here is unclear.

153 **plurisie** literally a chest abscess, but often used figuratively to mean an excess.

181 **disorder** disorderly behaviour.

190 **Excellent Nearchus** Ithocles' dramatically changed attitude towards the prince is presumably caused by his weariness of spirit in the wake of the interview with Penthea.

4.3

24 **opening** explanation, exegesis.

40 **scruple** doubt.

65 **streight** strait, narrow.

87 **cause** because.

89 **Rich fortunes guard to favour of a Princesse** This is a difficult line. *Q*'s 'fortuness' is clearly wrong. Spencer inserts a comma after fortunes; so did Gifford, but he also changed 'to' to 'the'. Weber printed 'fortune's'. I am unconvinced by any of these and have left it alone because the line yields some sense if we silently supply 'you': 'Rich fortunes guard [you] to [the] favour of a princess [and] rock thee'.

98 **Thou canst not** it is impossible for anything you may do to count as (over) boldness.

102 **dispose it** allocate time to it (i.e. to friendship).

106 **nonage** period before the attainment of the legal age of majority.

108 **puddle** confusion (*OED* 2b). Cf. Dalyell in *Perkin Warbeck* disclaiming the importance of a semi-royal ancestor because it was a long time ago (1.2.34–5).

111 **The sonne of Venus** Cupid.

134–5 **partners In all respects else but the bed** sharers in everything except Calantha.

156. **mystery** something which should stay secret and private.

4.4

0 *Engine* trick chair in which Ithocles is trapped as soon as he sits down.

20 This is wrongly lineated in the Revels edition, where the line number marker is positioned after 'lord' rather than 'please', leading to mislineation throughout the rest of the scene.

26 **Phaeton** son of Apollo who pleaded to be allowed to drive his father's chariot of the sun, but proved unable to control the horses and was killed.

42 **Tent** probe with a surgical instrument.

63–4 **follow | Safety, with best successe** do whatever you can to avoid punishment.

72 **suffrance** bearing pain or misfortune well.

5.1

12 **doublers** criss-cross movements supposed characteristic of the hare and considered unlucky (Tilley H150).

35–6 **A wonder . . . a second** the fact that this is a wonder (the first term applied to it) will make it act as a signpost exhorting people to imitate it ('a Theame for imitation' being the second quality claimed).

43–4 **The Virgin Bayes . . . danger** Spencer notes that according to Pliny laurel trees (bays) were never struck by lightning. They are therefore impervious to its apparent danger.

53 **the severity of a glorious Action** rigour required by behaviour which will lead to glory.

5.2

76 **thy prejudice** harm to you.

136 **a paire royall** three cards of a kind.

156 **'A has shooke hands with time** he has died. Perhaps a reference to a common trope of ancient Greek funerary statuary of the dead person shaking hands with a friend or relative; bloodless, Orgilus becomes like a statue.

5.3

5 **Subjection to the Scepter of a Virgin** as Foster and Foster observe, this would clearly remind the audience of the rule of Elizabeth I.

37–8 Cramping on the page makes it difficult to deduce what lineation is intended in Q here. 'Madam' may originally have belonged to l. 37 rather than 38, but either way there is metrical irregularity.

72–4 **Be such . . . out-live them** let the classification 'mere women' be applied to those who can swear, with shrieks and cries, that they will instantly end all their sorrows (by dying), but go on to live for new pleasures, and live even longer than those.

The Queen

Edited by ELEANOR LOWE and MARTIN WIGGINS

INTRODUCTION

A Reading of the Play

The focus of *The Queen* involves the treatment of a king's condition. In the introduction to his 1963 edition of the play, Douglas Sedge states that: 'The main action centres on the cure of Alphonso's misogyny.'[1] There is some disagreement about its diagnosis, both in the play and by critics. S. Blaine Ewing identifies that 'The principle action of *The Queen* deals with the cure of a king's distraction' which he further pinpoints as a form of melancholy.[2] The play voices troubling questions regarding sexism, especially in its implied links with mental health.

This isn't immediately clear when seeing or reading the play for the first time; however, there are clues which Ford includes in the dialogue so that this doesn't come entirely as a shock revelation. Here is the explicit evidence of Alphonso's misogyny:

> ALPHONSO: I hate your sex in general, not you
> As y'are a Queen, but as y'are a woman: (1.1.224–5)

In this statement Alphonso voices his general sexism, but in Act 2 his words specifically focus on the Queen:

> From this time forth
> I hate thy sex; of all thy sex, thee worst. (2.2.172–3)

It is Muretto, the King's friend, who 'undertakes cure of the melancholy'.[3] Ewing identifies that 'Alphonso is the only melancholic of *The Queen*. His affliction is not explained in the customary lengthy initial

---

[1] Douglas Sedge, 'An Edition of *The Queen, or The Excellency of Her Sex*' (University of Birmingham, MA thesis, 1963), p. xliii.
[2] S. Blaine Ewing, *Burtonian Melancholy and the Plays of John Ford* (Princeton: Princeton University Press, 1940), p. 80.
[3] Ibid.

description, but is commented upon by many characters'.[4] Again, some confusion about how to name his condition is present in these examples: Petruchi, an important young lord of the court, finds the King 'distracted' (1.1.150); Almada, a young counsellor, 'drown'd | In melancholy and sowre discontent' (l. 260); the Queen says he looks 'sadly' (2.2.135). Pynto, the court astronomer who 'scientifically' predicts every major turn of events in the play, gives us the key to the cause of Alphonso's melancholy: 'Here's a high Saturnal spirit', he exclaims as the King goes to execution captious and stubborn. Alphonso is melancholy, then, as a result of the maleficent influence of the stars. Muretto, the King's truest friend, states that he suffers from a 'distraction' caused by his 'discontents'.[5]

Moretto's speech in Act 5 details how he approaches curing Alphonso's misogyny. Critic Ralph Kaufmann terms this cure 'homeopathic': it 'is effected by the skilful ministrations of Muretto, whose silent diagnosis and methods of treatment are delineated in his speech of revelation in the last scene':[6]

MURETTO: Wonder not, my Lords, but lend mee your attentions. I saw with what violence he pursude his resolutions not more in detestation of the Queen in particular, then of all her sex in generall. That I may not weary your patience: I bent all my Studies to devise which way I might do service to my country by reclayming the distraction of his discontents. And having felt his disposition in every pulse, I found him most addicted to this pestilence of jealosy with a strong persuasion of which, I from time to time ever fed him by degrees, till I brought the Queen and the noble Petruchi into the dangers they yet stand in. But with all (and herin I appeale to your Majesties own approbation) I season'd my words with such an intermixing the praises of the Queens bewty, that from jealosy I drew the King into a serious examination of her perfections . . . At length having found him indeed surely affected, I perceav'd that nothing but the suppos'd blemish of her dishonour could work a second divorce between them. (5.2.155–68)

The speech begins with an implicit stage direction: 'Wonder not, my lords, but lend me your attention', indicating that the lords have reacted with great surprise; perhaps they are staring at each other in astonishment and/or talking amongst themselves. Muretto emphasizes that his

---

[4] Ibid., p. 81.
[5] Ibid., p. 81.
[6] Ralph Kaufmann, 'Ford's Tragic Perspective', in *Elizabethan Drama: Modern Essays in Criticism* (New York: Oxford University Press, 1961), pp. 356–72; p. 360.

cure results from 'studies' of Alphonso's behaviour and knowledge of how he might reclaim 'the distraction of his discontents'. He points to the use of jealousy as a tool to draw the King away from his melancholy and misogyny towards love for the Queen. This differs from the physiological treatment of melancholy, which, according to humoural theory, is a cold, dry humour in the body, caused by an excess of black bile, which could either be balanced with hot, wet foods or by purgation.

Sedge comments that 'Muretto has observed from the baseless accusation of his Queen's infidelity, Alphonso's "addiction to this pestilence of jealousy"—the weakness that he will play upon in order to drive out Alphonso's misogyny.'[7] Sedge further notes that 'Muretto has already begun feeding Alphonso with strong suspicions of the Queen's adultery'[8] and quotes the following as proof:

> ALPHONSO: You have prevail'd, yet e're you came (my Lord)
> *Muretto*, here this right, right, honest man
> Confirm'd me thoroughly (3.1.1–3)

Ewing notes that Muretto's description of his cure for Alphonso is a 'strikingly literal application of Burton's statement of the offices of friendship in the cure of melancholy'[9] and uses this quotation to identify 'Alphonso's Saturnine traits and Muretto's scheme of treatment and cure'.[10] The first trait is Alphonso's hatred of all womankind and of the Queen in particular. As Act 3 opens, Muretto has already begun his treatment: 'I season'd my words' by praising the Queen's beauty with such success that Alphonso is willing to acknowledge his gratitude to, and love for, the Queen. He calls her virtuous and asks to be commended to her. Although Muretto thinks he has the King's confidence, he doesn't realize he is being duped, for in one of the King's soliloquies he confides to his audience:

> So, so, far reaching pollicy, I adore thee . . .
> Henceforth my Stratagem's of scorn and hatred
> Shall kill in smiles. I will not strike and frown,
> But laugh and murther. (3.1.28, 31–3)

The tendency to dissemble is a characteristic of Saturnine melancholy.

Ewing points out that the 'whole difference between this play as comedy and as tragedy lies in the friendship of Muretto and his benevolent

---

[7] Sedge, 'An Edition of *The Queen*', p. xliv.
[8] Ibid.
[9] Ewing, *Burtonian Melancholy*, p. 82.
[10] Ibid.

ministrations'.[11] H. J. Oliver predominantly notes the play's focus on policy and political behaviour. Quoting the lines above, Oliver comments that 'Alphonso sees himself . . . as a skilful "politician" '.[12] Salassa is described by Lodovico as 'as pestilent a piece of policy, as ever made an ass of love' (4.3.3–4). Sedge identifies that, perhaps because of the play's focus on public politics, Alphonso and the Queen 'never have a private interview together where Alphonso might begin to discover his love for her'.[13]

Language, Tongues, Power, and Politics

In this play about politics, 'good language' (1.1.16) is identified early on as being essential to its machinations. The function of language is carefully demonstrated by Muretto's plot both to convince Alphonso of his wife's infidelity and to cause him to see her with new eyes as a beautiful woman. Ford dexterously demonstrates the shifts between different registers of language in the first scene: the formal pardoning of Alphonso's rabble in verse gives way to less reverent prose once Petruchi (the pardoner) has exited. Muretto advises: 'Now, mark, what good language and fair words will do, Gentlemen' (1.1.15–16), a point proved once his plot has been revealed at the end of the play. Pynto the astrologer rejects Muretto's praise for speech, dismissing it instead as 'Cankred breath; the poyson of a flatterers tongue' (1.1.18–19), stating that this is 'a thousand times more deadly, then the twinges of a rope' (1.1.19–20). Pynto's vocabulary reflects his occupation in a traditional way, making reference to oil of serpents, mermaids, crocodiles, and planets. Muretto vents his anger at Pynto's shoddy self-publicized learning, providing important exposition to the audience who learn that the rebellion mounted by Alphonso was based on 'prognosticating ignorance' (1.1.72). The gang's language changes again after the entrance of Velasco and Lodovico at l. 109: there is a contrast in Muretto, Bufo, and Pynto's rough language towards each other and that used towards their superiors.

The first scene's sudden changes in language are also reflected in its tone: the play opens with freedom, forgiveness, and reconciliation of the rebels, in direct contrast with Alphonso's procession to his execution. It contains several examples of strong visual and dramatic use of stage space, movement, and height in both its stage directions and dialogue. This visual clarity augments the structural clarity of the plot, which exam-

---

[11] Ibid., p. 88.
[12] Oliver, p. 73.
[13] Sedge, 'An Edition of *The Queen*', p. li.

ines the rise and fall of both Alphonso and the Queen, the subplot of Velasco's complex relationship with Salassa, and the impact of Bufo, Muretto et al. on both. This simplicity is necessary to make way for the extraordinary revelation of Muretto's scheme at the play's climax, which is only vaguely hinted at in the text (although there is a possibility that it might be made clearer in performance). In this, it bears similarities with Richard Brome's play *The Love-Sick Court* (which also makes a surprising revelation towards the end, causing the plot to untangle effortlessly).

Lisa Hopkins usefully discusses issues of language and power in *John Ford's Political Theatre*. She identifies that Ford alerts his audience to a 'hierarchy of speech, which means that the utterances of some characters are privileged over those of others'.[14] Hopkins selects Alphonso's lines from 2.2 as evidence that to 'talk like a king is, it seems, to threaten and to silence'.[15]

> As I am King, the tongue
> Forfeits his head that speaks another word.
> *Muretto*, Talk we not now like a King? (2.2.98–100)

The number and variety of tongues which appear in the text are interesting to note: characters are accused of having lying tongues (4.2.171) and unruly tongues (1.1.208), and according to Pynto, Muretto has 'the poyson of a flatterers tongue' (1.1.19). Velasco uses his tongue as evidence of his fidelity to Salassa: 'Mock you? Most fair Salassa, if e're truth | Dwelt in a tongue, my words and thoughts are twins' (2.3.31–2). Tongues are also gendered: Lodovico criticizes Salassa's 'squawling tongue' (2.1.87) while Alphonso, displaying his trademark misogyny comments to the Queen that a 'woman's tongue | Is sharper than a pointed steel' (1.1.233–4). Tongues can be used to celebrate women's good qualities: Muretto remarks to Alphonso that the Queen's 'perfections busied all tongues' (4.2.27). Women's tongues are loud and discordant or sharp weapons; their features can be praised or gossiped about (removing agency from them and objectifying them). This language helps to contribute to the misogynist elements of the cultural context of *The Queen*.

Elevation: Themes and Theatricality

The Queen revisits and recycles common dramatic topics of power, gender, and politics. As part of this, the play looks to past traditions:

---

[14] Hopkins, *Political*, p. 114.
[15] Ibid., p. 115.

the archaic combat in arms nearly fought by Alphonso against Velasco for a woman's favour, the *de casibus* rise and fall of men in the plot, and Ford's referencing of older plays from the late sixteenth century: there are strong suggestions of echoes from *Romeo and Juliet*, *Friar Bacon and Friar Bungay*, and *Titus Andronicus*, thematically or through almost direct quotation. In 4.2, Muretto says to Alphonso: 'You are set upon the high stage for action' (l. 1). This section will explore the metaphorical ways in which characters are elevated, before considering the literal ways in which Ford's stagecraft gives them height. The basis of the action lies in Alphonso's recent rebellion against the Queen, his capture, and near execution. His success was erroneously predicted by Pynto the astrologer. Muretto accuses Pynto of (falsely) raising Alphonso up: 'your divination hath fairly mounted him' (1.1.70–1). Both the Queen and Alphonso (when King) are referred to as 'Highness' in the dialogue.

The play's title foregrounds the character of the Queen, but we never learn her name: she is 'the Queen' in name and function, of her country and her gender; as the subtitle states, 'the Excellency of her sex'. Although this textual naming (in speech prefixes and stage directions) serves the purpose of locating power in her character, it is at the same time distancing; however, consider also that Alphonso is known throughout by his name—his speech prefixes do not change to 'King' once he has been crowned. Alphonso has an ordinary name to signal his base origins; his title (and life) is in the Queen's gift. She is the only source and vessel of royal blood in the play. In contrast, Alphonso is cast by Petruchi's first description of him as 'the vein that swell'd with such a frenzy | Of dangerous blood against your Queen and Country' (1.1.137–8); i.e. he has an excess of impassioned blood which needs letting to re-balance the nation's humours. Petruchi uses the metaphor of doctor's physic to describe how to remedy the situation; Muretto also subscribes to humoural theory, but instead works on Alphonso's melancholy temperament and tendency towards jealousy in order to effect a cure.

Dorothy Farr comments that the play:

> abounds in opportunities for the kind of spectacle a popular audience would appreciate. The presentation of a public execution with the added excitement of a last-minute reprieve was likely to please and the dramatist is not niggardly! There are three such scenes, following the same visual pattern.[16]

---

[16] Dorothy Farr, *John Ford and the Caroline Theatre* (London, New York: Macmillan, 1979), p. 164.

Richard Madelaine has identified that these moments 'are something of a motif in Ford's plays, for good thematic reasons: execution requires "resolution" and it can manifest earthly justice'.[17] He further identifies that *The Queen* is the only play in Ford's repertory in which he resorts to a pseudo-execution.[18] There are two in the play: of Alphonso (1.1) and of Salassa (5.1); additionally the Queen's own execution is threatened. The first of these occurs in the opening moments of Act 1 and perhaps best exemplifies the employment of *de casibus* tragedy: Alphonso's men are freed moments before Alphonso himself is lead onstage for his supposed execution. Later in Act 4, Velasco describes this dramatic pattern clearly when he says:

> Thus when men are blown up
> At the highest level of conceit, then they fall down
> Even by the peevish follies of their frailties. (4.3.27–9)

The Queen self-consciously dramatizes a series of elevations and falls, physically, theatrically, morally, and politically, in a self-conscious fashion. A full reversal of fortune for both the Queen and the King has been achieved by 3.3.70ff. when Alphonso declares his 'lenient' sentence on the Queen for her fabricated adultery: he will be the judge and she will lose her head if found guilty. The circumstance is created entirely by Alphonso and culminates in the final scene, in what Alphonso calls 'the wide theater of blood and shame' (5.2.35) before the Queen's impending execution.

Madelaine is interested in the effect of the executions: are they excessively repetitive? Or does each have its own meaning and weight within the play? Is dramatic tension in the final proposed execution (for the Queen) heightened because the audience by now expects it to be cancelled but is anxious to find out how? Alphonso's execution is stopped at the last minute by the Queen and gives opportunity for him to express his misogyny by resenting that she can't let him die in peace. It comes directly after the liberation of Alphonso's men as the first action of the play, so that it is bookended by liberty and reconciliation. Velasco waits until the very last moment before stopping Salassa's executioner. He orders the executioner to strike and the subsequent stage direction reads: '*As he is about to strike, VELASCO steps out*' (5.1.84 SD). According to Madelaine, he 'has been waiting to make sure that Salassa has most of the experience and misses none of

---

[17] Madelaine, ' "Sensationalism" ', pp. 29–53; p. 32.
[18] Ibid., p. 42.

the meaning'.[19] There is no mention of a scaffold in the stage directions for Alphonso's near-execution, whereas it is the first item named
in Act 5. Salassa enters with her hair loose and is instructed to go 'merrily up the stayers' by Lodovico (5.1.69–70); the subsequent stage
direction confirms that she *goes up the Scaffold* (l. 72). The overall
effect is of making an example of Salassa as a sinful woman. In her
speech, standing on the scaffold, she entreats other women:

> O women, in my fall,
> Remember that your beauties, youth and pride
> Are but gay tempters . . . let me ever
> Be an example to all fickle dames . . . . (5.1.76–8, 79–80)

The contradiction between her heightened position and her 'fall' on
stage serves to augment the extent to which she is being made an
example. Once the execution has been stopped (cruelly, at the absolute last minute) and Velasco has ordered her to 'come down' (l. 89),
he compounds her lowered physical status with his words:

> Base woman, take thy life, thy cursed life,
> I set thee free, and for it pawn a soul:
> But that I know heaven hath more store of mercy,
> Then thou and all thy sex of sin and falsehood. (5.1.93–6)

Salassa serves to represent all fallen women guilty of original sin and
the dramatization of this moment emphasizes the fall theatrically.
Women need to be made an example of by being elevated for all to
see, to increase the visual impact of the physical and moral fall.

Later, Salassa enters again with her hair loose, this time most explicitly
as a sign of her penitence, '*a white rod in her hand*' (5.2.276.1 SD):

> I'll take my leave,
> And like a penitentiary walk
> Many miles hence to a religious shrine
> Of some chast sainted Nun, and wash my sin off
> In tears of penance, to my last of breath. (5.2.287–91)

This speech prompts Alphonso to intercede (along with his wife) on
her behalf to Velasco, urging her to take Salassa's hand. Velasco concludes that 'He hath enough who hath a virtuous wife' (5.2.323).

There is no mention of a scaffold in 5.2 when the Queen walks out
to meet her fate, as decreed by her husband; however, it would be very
convenient for the scaffold noted in 5.1 (for Salassa's near execution) to

---

[19] Ibid., p. 43.

remain present onstage. Alphonso orders 'Place her on yonder throne' (5.2.62) so that he might draw strength from her beauty. Perhaps the scaffold has become a dais supporting the throne for this scene [a scaffold is just a platform and has much more a multifunctional usage than perhaps the word signifies today]. The theatrical association of the scaffold as platform for execution and for the throne neatly combines the play's key themes of fortune, monarchy, and punishment. It is ironic that the Queen who pardoned Alphonso at his own execution is now awaiting the same treatment at his hands. Alphonso, being a somewhat melodramatic melancholic, cannot let the moment pass without incorporating the archaic theatrics of a battle by combat, as if the helmeted champions were fighting for the Queen's love, rather than for her life. As with Salassa, the Queen is elevated on the platform, as an example for Alphonso of extreme beauty, but also to make her example of women (for which the title has prepared us). The stage direction '*Place the QUEEN*' suggests physical manhandling to position her correctly.

As an augmentation of the play's focus on elevation and debasement, the female characters are frequently discussed using the language of cleanliness and dirt; Alphonso is particularly prone to it.[20] Act 4 scene 2 marks a stark change in his misogynist attitude towards the Queen. He describes her using the traditional poetic language of female beauty, comparing her cheeks with lilies and roses (which she surpasses), and claiming her to be 'superlative . . . Rich, bright' (4.2.39, 41). Alphonso is torn because the moment he realized her beauty and value is also the point at which he has said she must die for adultery (unless a champion can defend her honour). He falls into a trance in her presence (see l. 103) and echoes *Romeo and Juliet*: 'May I presume with my irreverent lips | To touch your sacred hand' (4.2.107–8). Alphonso admits that he is culpable: he has 'soyl'd a beauty | As glorious, as sits yonder on her front' (4.2.133–4). Petruchi (falsely accused of adultery with the Queen) compounds Alphonso's imagery by offering to 'defend | Her spotless vertue' (ll. 141–2), at the same time discrediting the King's power, saying he will have no respect for 'an host of Kings' which he likens to 'a poor stingless swarm of buzzing flies' (l. 144). This image further elevates the Queen who in contrast is pure and clean. Later in the scene, Alphonso begs his wife to state she is 'honest' so that he can believe her to be 'white and chast' (l. 163)

---

[20] Perhaps this is in keeping with the plot's theme of sickness and health, as commented on by Sensabaugh, p. 81.

even if she is 'as fowl | As sin can black your purity' (ll. 161–2). But the King's temperament is very changeable and he dismisses both the Queen and Petruchi in his confusion over what course to take. Alphonso's melancholy temperament infects his vision of his wife. In Act 5 scene 2, he again uses unclean language to categorise his wife:

> But when a beauty
> So most incomparable as yours, is blemish'd
> With the dishonourable stamp of whoredom:
> When your black tainted name, which should have been
> (Had you preserv'd it nobly) your best Chronicle,
> Wherein you might have liv'd, when this is stain'd,
> And justly too, then death doth but heap
> Affliction on the dying. (5.2.3–10)

In Alphonso's mind, both the Queen's physical beauty and her reputation are irreparably disfigured; he blames her for allowing this to happen. But these blemishes arise from Alphonso's own infected mind: he has been the one holding the stamp and calling her whore; he has stained and tainted her reputation. The result is a manifestation of the impurity of his own mind (whether ill or base because not truly royal). Knowing it is his own fault, he blames her purity and goodness for perverting him (and this is also explored through the staging, as discussed earlier). When he arrives to defend the Queen, Velasco uncomplicatedly acknowledges her as 'A Queen as free from stain of your disgrace, | As you are fowle in urging it' (5.2.80–1), thus confirming her goodness and Alphonso's own blighted personality. But the Queen takes her marital duty seriously (perhaps more than she should, given Alphonso's imperfections and misogyny): when Velasco insists on defending her honour against the King she implores him not to strike her husband, as 'every blow thou givest the King, | Wounds mee' (5.2.108–9). The thought of Alphonso being struck causes her to swoon, to fall down from the throne and scaffold (though Alphonso calls it 'dissimulation' at l. 116).

The impossible situation is saved by a sudden revelation from Muretto: that this was all a cunning plot designed to make Alphonso fall in love with the Queen. Alphonso believes his counsellor Muretto and asks for confirmation of his wife's chastity from Petruchi (her alleged lover). Only at this point, despite her own protestations of her innocence, does he accept that she is clear of misdoing: 'Let's kneel to this (what shall I call her?) Woman? | No, she's an Angel' (5.2.191–2). At this point, 'All kneel', so that instead of the Queen being aloft on a platform to make an example of her, she is the example, 'the excellency of her sex', which they all venerate. The Queen continues to illustrate her submissive female perfection by admonishing her husband for being 'so low . . . in your own thoughts' and in his physical position on the stage (5.2.198) and offering to kneel with him. She raises him up (as implied by his command 'Let's rise' at l. 205) with her, both physically and morally. Perhaps the act of kneeling and rising serves to re-enact and re-state their marriage vows; they have fallen to a kneeling position but their union is reborn as they rise. The multifunctional scaffold has transformed from a site of execution to a place when both the dual monarchy and marriage are resurgent.

Alphonso ends the play: 'Thus after storms a calm | Is ever welcomest' (5.2.326–7).[21] In this ending Alphonso confirms his desire to play Prospero, to orchestrate the action using false means (when it is, of course, Muretto who fulfils this role). Although Salassa is asked by Velasco 'Why do you play the Tyrant thus?' (2.3.104), it is Alphonso who enjoys playing this role most explicitly, as Columello acknowledges at 3.3.99. His role-playing is most evident in Act 4 scene 2 (when he brings the Queen and Petruchi onstage to interview them) and finally in Act 5 scene 2 when he strides into his own constructed 'wide theater of blood and shame' (5.2.35) and 'places' both the Queen and Salassa on the scaffold as examples to be looked on.[22] He has referred to the superficial trappings of monarchy in 3.3 when he describes the music as 'the seeming forms of State' (3.3.8).

The section of the scene in which Petruchi and the Queen are brought before the King has an otherworldly feel (like that of a dumbshow), as if a manifestation of the torment occurring in the King's ill, melancholic mind. Although it is not clearly stated that he is seated on a dais, the positioning of the other two characters suggests a formal hearing of some kind as the implicit and explicit action is dramatized. That the King might be seated on a throne upon a dais is partially suggested by Muretto's line 'Sir, you are set high upon the stage for action' (4.2.1). The stage directions specifically state: '*Enter at one door PETRUCHI, and [at] the other MURETTO and the QUEEN, they stand at several ends of the Stage*' awaiting the King's instructions (4.2.81 SD). Ewing also notes the way Ford dramatizes Alphonso's cure, his being torn in two different directions:

---

[21] This is also an echo of Heywood's summary of comedy and tragedy in his *Apology for Actors* (1612).

[22] Alphonso also 'seats' the Queen at 3.3.13.

The Queen and Petruchi are made to sit at opposite sides of the stage where the king (standing between them) can see but one at a time. They symbolize the two passions which distract his mind: the Queen, love; Petruchi, jealousy—or as Alphonso names them: the Queen, his 'comforts'; Petruchi, his 'shame'. As he looks from one to the other, his disposition is swayed back and forth.[23]

Sedge comments that the staging is crucial to Muretto's plan, so that 'Alphonso should be paralized by this dilemma into a state of inaction in order to avert tragedy which might otherwise result from Alphonso's desire for revenge'.[24]

Alphonso calls for both to be seated (though on different seats, perhaps to differentiate between their status): 'Reach yond fair sight a chair, | That man a stool' (ll. 82–3). Seating them could be a gracious act but it is also a way of controlling their movement in his presence, by fixing their positions both in relation to him and to each other. If he is seated on a dais, his physical position is elevated all the more; if not (and his troubled words suggest an agitation which might be reflected in the character's movements), he can exert power over them on foot via his proximity and distance. Both of them appear to undermine his attempt to be both magnanimous and authoritative by offering to kneel instead (see ll. 86 and 90), physically signifying a respectful plea (though Petruchi perhaps unwisely kneels to the Queen rather than the King). The King's power is reclaimed through Muretto who entreats them both to sit, which they do (as is confirmed by the stage direction at l. 95). At the end of the scene, both exit '*contrary waies*' (4.2.175 SD) as they came in, compounding the sense that this scene is staged and controlled by the King.

There is no mention of a scaffold onstage for Alphonso's execution; this appears to be reserved for the women. By the time the Queen enters at the last minute, Alphonso appears to be kneeling (to meditate, as requested) for Columello instructs him to rise at l. 195. Despite a last-minute stay of execution, Alphonso is annoyed at being interrupted and pardoned, claiming 'my thoughts | Were fixt upon an upper Region now' (1.1.196–7). So although his physical body was in the lowest place onstage, his mind was above all the other characters and their realm. He continually forgets that his status is entirely dependent on the Queen's grace. In 2.2 Columello has to remind him: 'remember what you are' (l. 89), i.e. a king made by the Queen, ele-

---

[23] Ewing, *Burtonian Melancholy*, pp. 86–7.
[24] Sedge, 'An Edition of *The Queen*', p. xlv.

vated by her, 'who hath rais'd you to this height' (l. 89). Madelaine
concludes of Ford that 'the symbolic associations of his stage images
are, in his best writing, unforced, and play an important part in the
dramatization of themes'.[25]

The Origins of the Play

Like much of the pre-1642 drama that was first printed during and
after the Interregnum, *The Queen, or The Excellency of Her Sex* is a play
almost without a history. It appears in none of the early seventeenth-
century repertory lists, nor the surviving fragments of the office-book
of the Master of the Revels, nor the records of the plays that were
performed at court, nor the miscellaneous other documents that have
come down to us. Had it not been published in 1653, when the London
theatres had been officially closed for eleven years, we should never
have known that such a play had ever existed.

The Quarto (Wing Q155), a book of 24 leaves collating A–F⁴, was
printed by Thomas Newcombe for Thomas Heath, and was on sale by
mid-August; the London bookseller and collector George Thomason,
who usually acquired publications on or soon after the date of publication, wrote the date 13 August on his copy, now in the British
Library.[26] Newcombe (d. 1681/2) was an established tradesman who
was briefly imprisoned in 1649 for printing an oppositional tract by
John Lilburne, but who subsequently managed to stay on the right
side of both the Commonweath and the restored monarchy; in the
1650s he printed pro-government publications (including one by
Milton) and from the 1660s held a one-sixth share in the King's
Printing House.[27] At the time of *The Queen*, his experience with
drama was limited to the first edition of *The Changeling* (Wing
M1980), which he printed during the winter of 1652–3, but he was
later responsible for a number of significant dramatic publications,
including Robert Cox's *Actaeon and Diana* (1655; Wing C6710),
Massinger's *Three New Plays* (1655; Wing M1050), Middleton's *Two
New Plays* (1657; Wing M1989), the first section of Davenant's *Works*

---

[25] Madelaine, '"Sensationalism"', pp. 48–9.

[26] G. K. Fortescue, *Catalogue of the Pamphlets, Books, Newspaper, and Manuscripts Relating to the Civil War, the Commonwealth, and Restoration, Collected by George Thomason, 1640–1661* (London, 1908), ii. 33.

[27] Henry R. Plomer, *A Dictionary of the Booksellers and Printers who were at Work in England, Scotland and Ireland from 1641 to 1647* (London, 1907), pp. 136–7.

(1763; Wing D320), and the second section of the second Beaumont and Fletcher Folio (1679; Wing B1582). His client for the edition of *The Queen*, the London bookseller Thomas Heath, was trading only during the first half of the 1650s, and in the summer of 1653 seems to have been developing his portfolio in the direction of plays: that August, he also published *The Ghost* (Wing G641), and the following year, apparently his last in business, saw him issue *The Extravagant Shepherd* (Wing C6323), T. R.'s translation of Corneille's *Le Berger extravagant*.[28]

The book is as uncommunicative about the play as were the earlier records. It bears no author's name on its title page and makes no mention of the acting company or playhouse for which the play was written. Its every indication of textual ownership relates instead to the play's immediate provenance. Though the project was underwritten by Heath, it is Alexander Gough whom the book names as 'the publisher', not in the modern sense but signifying rather the person who procured or commissioned the publication. Gough is treated as effectively a surrogate author, with his name prominently displayed on the title page; it was also he who wrote the dedication and he who is addressed by the complimentary poems such as were customarily prefixed to literary publications in the period. It is a publication that attests to an absence of authorship or institutional origin; but the central involvement of Gough gives us lines to read between.

Alexander Gough (b. 1614) was a diminutive man who was then nearing the end of his 40s, and who had a long-standing association with one particular theatrical institution. In the mid-1650s, he wrote the epistle not only for *The Queen* but also for Middleton's *The Widow* (1652; Wing J1015) and Lodowick Carlell's *The Passionate Lovers* (1655; Wing C581), both of which had belonged to the King's Men. Around the same time, or perhaps during the preceding decade, he was instrumental in facilitating illicit private performances for 'Persons of Quality': he 'used to be the Jackal and give notice of Time and Place'.[29] Before that, he was an actor: he is one of eight members of the King's Men named in a pass issued by the Lord Chamberlain's Office on 17 May 1636, five days after plague closed the London theatres, to allow

[28] Ibid., p. 95.

[29] James Wright, *Historia Histrionica* (London, 1699), p. 9. Wright says that these performances were given 'in *Oliver*'s time' (i.e. 1653–8) by a troupe made up of surviving personnel from various pre-War companies, but Leslie Hotson (*The Commonwealth and Restoration Stage* (Cambridge, MA, 1928), pp. 23–4) associates them instead with attempts by the rump of the King's Men to resume playing after the end of the Civil War in 1647.

them to travel around the country and perform without molestation or opposition by local communities.[30] And before that, he had served the company as an apprentice actor, with known roles spanning six years from *The Roman Actor* (1626) to the 1632 revival of *The Wild-Goose Chase*, in which he played Lilia Bianca; he was also in the cast of *The Lover's Melancholy*.[31] Since James Wright's *Historia Histrionica* (1699) describes him as 'the Woman Actor at *Blackfriars*', it is possible that he continued to play female parts after the formal end of his apprenticeship; roles from his late teens, including not only Lilia Bianca but also Fewtricks in *The Soldered Citizen* (1630) and Eurinia in *The Switzer* (1631) attest to his slightness of stature.[32] Even before he was indentured to them, the King's Men were part of his life: his father, Robert Gough (d. 1624), had been a company apprentice in the 1590s and continued to act with them until at least 1619, notably playing Peregrine in *Volpone*. The family lived in St Saviour's parish, close to the Globe playhouse. In short, Alexander Gough was a King's Man through and through.

However, there is no deep history of the play to be inferred here, for at the time of publication the script had not been in Gough's possession for very long. He acquired it after it had been, as the title page puts it, 'Found out by a Person of Honour'—a polite, vague, genderless phrase that tantalizingly hints at a prior provenance even as it contrives to say as little as possible. But, even so, it says somewhat more than nothing, if only by indirection. We have no way of knowing who in particular the 'person of honour' was, though the phrase was often used in Interregnum publications as a coded reference to some defeated cavalier.[33] But we can deduce how that person came to own a copy of *The Queen*, and why he should have handed it over to Gough; and out of that deduction will emerge the play's elusive earlier history.

When the first collected edition of Beaumont and Fletcher was published in 1647 (Wing B1581), it failed to include *The Wild-Goose Chase*, one of Fletcher's most popular late comedies. The publisher, Humphrey Moseley, apologetically explained that the play 'hath beene long lost, and I feare irrecoverable; for a *Person of Quality* borrowed it from the *Actours* many yeares since, and (by the negligence of a

---

[30] E. K. Chambers (ed.), 'Dramatic Records: The Lord Chamberlain's Office', Malone Society *Collections* 2.3 (Oxford, 1931), pp. 378–9.
[31] *JCS*, ii.446–7.
[32] Wright, *Historia Histrionica*, 9.
[33] For instance, *The Country Captain* and *The Variety*, written in 1641 by the Duke of Newcastle, subsequently a royalist general, were printed in 1649 (Wing N877) as the work of a nameless 'person of honour'.

Servant) it was never return'd', and he asked anyone who had a copy 'please to send it home'.[34] Five years later, in 1652, home it came, and Moseley published it (Wing B1616) with a title page averring that it had been 'Retriv'd for the publick delight of all the Ingenious . . . By a Person of Honour'. This was not necessarily the *same* person of honour, but the analogy with *The Queen* is exact.

During the 1630s, a minor sideline of the King's Men was to supply well-off enthusiasts with copies of its plays, specially transcribed by its bookkeeper, Edward Knight; some of these manuscripts are still in existence today.[35] The practice seems to have been unique to the King's Men; at least, no comparable 'favour manuscripts' survive for plays belonging to any other company. That is the principal means by which a seventeenth-century commercial play could have been in the private ownership of a 'person of honour'; and when the request went out for the King's Men's plays to be given back for publication, it is plausible to infer that someone remembered he had a copy of *The Queen* in his collection.

Attribution scholarship, presented at length elsewhere in this edition, establishes that everything about the play—its language, its tone, its verbal tropes—corresponds with the literary fingerprints of John Ford. Collocated with the institutional attribution to the King's Men, this enables us to establish the play's date of origin with some precision. After half a decade of collaboration with more experienced dramatists, and some script-doctoring for the King's Men on *The Fair Maid of the Inn* (1626) and perhaps others, Ford began writing plays unaided in the late 1620s. During this period he wrote *The Lover's Melancholy* (November 1628), *The Broken Heart* (1629), and *Beauty in a Trance* (1630), after which he stopped working for the King's Men, who seem to have had a concatenation of difficulties with disgruntled scriptwriters in 1629–30. If the spread of these plays indicates his work rate, or his contractual obligations, then he is likely to have written *The Queen* in 1627, making it his earliest surviving solo-written play.

At that time, the King's Men were in the artistic doldrums. They had a strong back catalogue of plays by dead stalwarts like Shakespeare and Fletcher, but needed to supplement it with new work, and to that

---

[34] Francis Beaumont and John Fletcher, *Comedies and Tragedies* (London, 1647), sig. A4ʳ.

[35] For example, the MSS of *Bonduca* (London: British Library, Add. MS 36758), *Beggars' Bush* (Washington: Folger, MS J. b. 5, fos. 158–204), and *The Elder Brother* (London: British Library, MS Egerton 1994, fos. 2–29). The company practice may date back to the 1610s, when Sir Henry Neville (1588–1629) was in possession of a MS transcript of *A King and No King*, which served as copy for the first edition of 1619 (*STC* 1670).

end were bringing forward new writers, among them William Davenant as well as Ford. (The more established and experienced Philip Massinger was not under exclusive contract: he wrote *The Great Duke of Florence* for Queen Henrietta's Men in July 1627.) However, they were not being asked to write anything radically innovative; *The Queen*, a quirky political tragicomedy in the mode of late Fletcher, is just the sort of thing that would be commissioned by a company that was following a conservative literary policy, and looking to refresh its repertory with 'more of the same'. Perhaps there is significance in the fact that Ford did not choose to offer it for publication, as he did the slightly later plays in which he began to find his own original mode, *The Lover's Melancholy* (published in 1629) and *The Broken Heart* (in 1633).

With seventeen speaking parts, four of them female, the play comfortably matches the casting parameters of most surviving King's Men plays of the late 1620s; the company seems to have routinely used four or five apprentices and an indeterminable number of younger boys. We learn from the cast list of *The Roman Actor* that in October 1626 the apprentices were John Thompson, John Honyman, William Trigg, and Alexander Gough, all of whom continued to play women until at least 1629. In all likelihood, they would also have played the four apprentices' roles in *The Queen* the following year: the Queen herself, Salassa, Chaperon, and Herophil. Perhaps, a generation later, that unknown 'person of honour', who must have liked the play enough to acquire a copy, knew exactly what he was doing when he gave his manuscript to the same Alexander Gough with a view to its publication. *The Queen* had come full circle.

THE
QUEEN,
OR THE
EXCELLENCY
OF HER
SEX.

An Excellent old Play.

Found out by a Perſon of Honour, and given to the Publiſher,
ALEXANDER GOUGHE.

Ἀυϑις ἔτ᾽ ἀλλο τέταρτον ἐπὶ χϑονὶ πѫλυϐοτείρη,
Ζdὺς Κρονίdης ποίησε δικαιότερον, ϗ ἄρειον
Ἡρωιναων ϑεῖον γίν⊙-, αἵ καλέονται
Ἡμίϑεαι.   Heſiod: lib: 1.

——— *Cedat jam Graia vetuſtas*
Peltatas mirata Nurus, jam Volſca Camillas
Cedat, & Aſſyrias quæ fœmina flectit habenas
Fama tace, Majore cano ———

LONDON,
Printed by *T. N.* for *Thomas Heath*, in *Ruſſel* Street, Neer
the *Piazza* of Covent-Garden, 1653.

Title page of *The Queen* (1653). By permission of the British Library
Board

The Queen,
or The Excellency of her Sex

THE PERSONS OF THE PLAY

Lord PETRUCHI, a young nobleman and knight
BUFO, a captain, Alphonso's follower, later his groom
Signor PYNTO, an astrologer, Alphonso's follower; later Shaparoon's
    husband
Signor MURETTO, Alphonso's follower
Lord VELASCO, a soldier
LODOVICO, Shaparoon's kinsman
An Executioner
Lord ALPHONSO, the rebels' young leader; later the Queen's husband and
    King of Aragon
OFFICERS at the executions
The QUEEN of Aragon; later Alphonso's wife
COLUMELLO, a lord of the Council
Lord ALMADA, a lord of the Council
HEROPHIL, the Queen's lady in ordinary
Attendants on the Queen
A MESSENGER
A Guard of soldiers
Madam SHAPAROON, an old country gentlewoman, widow, and bawd,
    Lodovico's kinswoman; later Pynto's wife
MOPAS, Velasco's gentleman usher
Madam SALASSA, a lady widow
Attendants on Alphonso
An Attendant, who serves wine
A GROOM
Three Heralds at the trial by combat
Attendants on Almada and Columello
Attendants on Velasco
Two or three Attendants carrying money

B1ʳ   **I.I**   *Enter* PETRUCHI *with* BUFO, PYNTO *and* MURETTO,
                        in poor habits

PETRUCHI   All free, and all forgiven.

BUFO, PYNTO, and MURETTO   Bless her Majesty.

PETRUCHI   Henceforth (my friends) take heed how you so hazard
Your lives and fortunes on the peevish motion
Of every discontent; you will not finde
Mercy so rife at all times.

MURETTO   Gratious Sir!   5
Your counsel is more like an Oracle,
Then mans advice; for my part I dare speak
For one, I rather will be rackt asunder
Then e're again offend so wise a Majesty.

PETRUCHI   'Tis well, your lives are once more made your own;   10
I must attend the execution
Of your hot General, each shift now for your selves.
                                            Exit PETRUCHI

BUFO   Is he gone, ha, ha, ha! We have the common Canopy of
the cleer heavens once more o're our heads, Sirs.

MURETTO   We are at liberty out of the Hangmans clutches; Now,   15
mark, what good language and fair words will do, Gentlemen.

PYNTO   Good language! O, let me go back and be hang'd, rather
then live within the rotten infection of thy Cankred breath; the
poyson of a flatterers tongue is a thousand times more deadly,
then the twinges of a rope; Thou birth of an unlucky Planet: 20
I abhor thee.

MURETTO   Fy, fy! Can you rail on your friends thus?

PYNTO   Friends, my friend! Captain, come from that slippery
Ele, Captain. His very cradle was in dirt and mud; his milk the oyl
of serpents; his mother a mangy Mermaid, and a male Crocodile
begat him.   25

MURETTO   This needs not, sweet Signior Pynto.

Bang is a type facsimile of *Q*; his readings are therefore not incorporated into the text he prints.
I.I] 4 discontent;] *Sedge*; discontent, *Q*   7 advice;] *Sedge*; advice, *Q*   13 Canopy]
Sedge; Capony *Q*   15 clutches;] clutches, *Q*   22 thus?] *Sedge*; thus. *Q*   26 not,
sweet] *Sedge*; not sweet, *Q*

PYNTO   Sweet Signior? Sweet Cog a foyst, go hang thy self,   Bɪᵛ
thou'dst jeer the very rags I wear off my back with thy fustians of
sweet, precious, unmatchable, rare, wise, juditious, hey do! Pox on
thee; Sirrah, Sirrah, Hast not thou many a time and often devoured   30
a whole table of mine, garnisht with plenty, nay, variety of good
wholesome fare, under the colour of telling news with a roguy
complement?

MURETTO   Good fare of thine!

BUFO   Nay, dear Gentlemen.   35

PYNTO   Mine! I mine, Sycophant, I (dost mark me) to supply thy
totters, paun'd a whole study of Ephimerides, so rich, that they
might have set up a Corporation of Almanack makers; and what
had I in return? But protestations, (hearest thou this maunderer)
that I was, for learning, the soundest; for bounty, the royallest; for   40
discourse, the sententioust; for behavour, the absolutest; for all
endowments of minde and body, the most accomplisht that nature
ever call'd her workmanship: but thou dog, thou scoundrel, my
beggery was the fruits of thy flattery. Stand off, Rascal, off.

BUFO   This is excellent 'faith.   45

MURETTO   How, how! I flatter ye? What thee, thee? A poor
lousy uncloakt imposter, a deceitful, couzening, cheating, dull
decoying fortune teller! Thou pawn books? Thou, patcht out of
an old shepheards Calender, that discoursest in time of the change
of the weather. And whose were thy Ephemerides? Why,   50
Impudence, wert thou ever worth *Erra Pater*'s Prognostication?
Thou learned! In what? By filching, stealing, borrowing, eating,
collecting, and counting with as weather-wise Ideots as thy self;
once in twelve moneths thou wert indeed delivered, (like a big
bellied wife) of a two penny Almanack, at Easter. A Hospital boy   55
in a blew coat shall transcribe as much in six hours to serve all the
year. Thou a table of meat, yes, Astronomers fare, air; or at a feast
upon high holy dayes, three red Sprats in a dish; that was held
glutony too. I flatter thee? Thou learned?

PYNTO   Rascal, Cannibal that feedest upon mans flesh.   60

31 nay,] *Sedge*; nay; *Q*   32 roguy] *Sedge*; roughy *Q*   45 'faith.] *Sedge*; faith; *Q*
48 teller! . . . books?] *Sedge*; teller; . . . books; *Q*   59 glutony] *Sedge*; gultony *Q*

BUFO   Nay, pray, pray heartily Gentlemen; in good earnest, and as I live, and by this hand now—

MURETTO   Right thou put'st me in minde what I should call thee; Who was't the cause of all the late insurrection for which we were all like to be hang'd, and our brave General *Alphonso* is this day to suf-   65 fer for; who but thou, forsooth; the influences of the Stars, the conjunction of the Planets, the prediction of the celestial bodies were peremptory, that if a' would but attempt a civil commotion, a' should (I marry should a') be strait crown'd present King of *Arragon*. Now your Gipsonly man i'th moon, your divination hath fairly mounted   70 him; poor Gentleman, he's sure to leave his head in pawn for giving credit to thy prognosticating ignorance.

PYNTO   I scorn thee, Parasite.

MURETTO   You are a stinking starv'd-gut star-gazer. Is that flattery or no?   75

BUFO   'S foot, What do you mean, Signior *Pynto*, Signior *Muretto*?

PYNTO   I will be reveng'd, and watch my time, Sirrah.

MURETTO   Do.

BUFO   This is strange my Masters, to be so neer the place of exe-   80 cution and prattle so loud; Come, Signior *Pynto*, indeed la you shall shake hands.

PYNTO   Let me alone, y'are a foolish Captain. *Muretto*, I will display thee for a—

MURETTO   Hang thy self, I care not for thee, this.   85

BUFO   Foolish Captain, foolish Captain, heark ye, *Pynto*, there's no such good meaning in that word.

PYNTO   A Parrat can eccho, talk to Schollers so.

MURETTO   A proper Scholler, stitcht up of waste paper.

BUFO   Sneaks, if I be a fool, I'll bang out the wits of some of your   90 nodles, or dry bastinado your sides. Ye *Dogrel*, maungy scabbed B2ʳ owlaglasses, | I'll mawle yee, so I will.

70 man] may *Q*   75 no?] *Sedge*; no. *Q*   85 thee,] thee *Q*

MURETTO   Captain, sweet Captain, nay, look, now will you put
your discretion to coxcombs?

BUFO   Yes, the proudest coxcombs of 'em all, if I be provok'd;   95
foolish, flesh and blood cannot eudur't.

MURETTO   [*to* PYNTO] So, goodman sky walker, you have made
a trim hand on't, to chafe your self into a throat cutting.

BUFO   I will shred you both so small, that a very botcher shall
thred Spanish needles, with every fillet of your itchy flesh; call me   100
foolish, ye whelps-moyles; my father was a Corn-cutter, and my
mother a muscle woman, 'tis known what I am, and I'll make you
know what I am, If my choler be raised but one inch higher.

PYNTO   Well, I see *Mars* and *Saturn*, were thy Planets. Thou art
a valiant souldier, and there's no dealing with ye. For the Captains   105
sake, I will abate my indignation, *Muretto*. But—

BUFO   But i'thy face, I'll have no buts, S' bores, the black guard
is more honorably suted then any of us three. Foolish, foolish, will
never out of my head whilst I live.

Enter VELASCO *and* LODOVICO

MURETTO   Long life, eternal prosperity, the blessing o'th heav-   110
ens, and honors of the Earth, crown the glorious merits of the
incomparable, Captain Don *Velasco*.

PYNTO   The Chime goes again, Captain.

VELASCO   Who are these poor Creatures, *Lodovico*?

LODOVICO   My Lord, I know them now, they are some of the   115
late mutineers, whom you (when you took *Alphonso* prisoner)
presented to the rigor of the Law, but since they are by the Queen's
pardon set at liberty.

VELASCO   I should know yonder fellow. Your name is *Bufo*, if
I mistake not.   120

BUFO   My name is my own name, Sir, and *Bufo* is my name, Sir; if
any man shall deny't, I dare challenge him in defence of my God-
fathers that gave me that name, Sir; and what say you to that, Sir?

100 thred Spanish] *Sedge*; shred Spanish *Q*   114 *Lodovico?*] *Sedge*; *Lodovico*. *Q*   116 when
you] *Sedge*; when you, *Q*

MURETTO   A shallow, unbrain'd, weak, foolish fellow, and so
forth: Your lordship understands me; But for our parts my good   125
Lord—

VELASCO   Well, Gentlemen, I cannot tell you now,
That any poor endeavours of mine own
Can work *Alphonso*'s peace, yet I have spoke
And kneell'd and sued for his reprieve. The Queen   130
Hath heard, but will not grant; This is the day,
And this the time, and place, where he must render
The forfeit of his life unto the Law.
I onely can be sorry.

> Enter PETRUCHI, *after the hangman bearing the axe before*
> ALPHONSO, *with Officers*

PETRUCHI   *Alphonso*, here's the place, and this the hour;   135
Your doom is past, and now the sword of Law
Must cut the vein that swell'd with such a frensy
Of dangerous blood against your Queen and Country.
Prepare yourself, 'tis now too late to hope.

ALPHONSO   *Petruchi*, what is done I did, my ground   140
Was pitty of my country, not malice to't.
I sought to free wrack'd *Arragon* from ruin,
Which a fond womans government must bring.
O had you and the nobles of this land,
A touch but of the miseries her weakness   145
Must force ye of necessity to feel,
You would with me have bent your naked swords
Against this female Mistriss of the Crown,
And not have been such children to have fawn'd
B2ᵛ   Upon a girles nodd.

PETRUCHI   You are distracted;   150
She is our lawful Soveraign, we her Subjects.

ALPHONSO   Subjects, *Petruchi*, abjects, and so live;
I come to die: on to the execution.

PYNTO   Here's a high Saturnal spirit, Captain.

---

145 miseries] *Sedge*; miseries, Q   146 necessity] *Sedge*; neceessity Q   153 die:] die, Q

BUFO   Pox o' spirits when they mount a man to the Hangmans 155
mercy, I do not like such spirits, let me rather be a moon calf.

VELASCO   I come to bid farewel, and in farewel,
    To excuse my much ill fortune, for beleeve, Sir,
    I hold my victory an overthrow.
    To tell you how incessantly I ply'd   160
    Her Grace, for your remission, were as useless
    As was my suit, I'me sorry for your youth.
    Let's part yet reconcil'd.

ALPHONSO   With all my heart;
    It is my glory, that I was reduc'd
    By the best man at arms, that ever knighthood   165
    Hath stil'd a Souldier—Alas! What souls are those?
    Now, now, in seeing them I die too late.

BUFO   O brave General, O noble General, we are still the rags of
the old Regiment. The truth on't is, we were loth to leave thee, till
thy head and shoulders parted companies. But sweet good dear 170
General take courage, what, we are all mortal men, and must every
one pass this way, as simple as we stand here.

ALPHONSO   Give me thy hand, farewel; the Queen is merciful in
    sparing you;
    I have not ought to give thee but my last thanks.

BUFO   Blirt o' giving, our clothes are paid for, and a day will 175
come shall quit us all.

ALPHONSO   [*to* MURETTO *and* PYNTO]
    Art thou, and thou there too; well, leave thy art,
    And do not trust the fixions of the stars,
    They spoke no truth by me: My Lord *Velasco*,
    That creature, there, *Muretto*, is a man   180
    Of honest heart, for my sake take him to you:
    And now soft, peace to all.

PYNTO   I will burn my books, forsware the liberal sciences, and
that is my resolution.

BUFO   Go thy way for the arrantest General, that ever led crew of 185
brave Skeldrers.

PETRUCHI   Will you make ready, Sir.

ALPHONSO   *Petruchi*, yes,
  I have a debt to pay, 'tis natures due.
            [*To the* HANGMAN] Fellow before thou ask my
                                    pardon, take it;
  Be sure and speedy in thy fatal blow.   190

HANGMAN   Never fear clean shaving, Sir.

ALPHONSO   May I have leave to meditate?

PETRUCHI   You may.

LODOVICO   A gallant resolution, even in death.

       Enter QUEEN, COLLUMMELLO, ALMADA, HEROPHIL,
                    and attendants

COLUMELLO   Stay execution 'tis her Highnes pleasure;
  Alphonso rise ye, and behold the Queen.   195

ALPHONSO   Beshrew the voice of Majesty, my thoughts
  Were fixt upon an upper Region now,
  And traffick not with Earth; alas great woman,
  What newer tyranny, what doom, what torments
  Are borrowed from the conclave of that hell,   200
  Where legions of worse Devils, then are in hell
  Keep revels, a proud womans heart. What plagues
  Are broacht from thence to kill me?

PYNTO   *(Aside)* The moon is now Lady of the ascendant, and
  the man will dye raving.   205

ALMADA   Fy, *Alphonso*,
  Will you commit another strange commotion
  With your unruly tongue. And what you cannot
  Perform in act, attempt to do in words?
  A dying man be so uncharitable.   210

ALPHONSO   Cry mercy, she is Queen of *Arragon*,
B3ʳ   And would with her own eyes (insteed of maskes
  And courtly sports) behold an act of death.
  Queen, welcom, Queen, here quaff my blood like wine;
  And live a brave she tyrant.

QUEEN   Alas, poor man.   215

ALPHONSO   Poor man: that looks on me, delighted to destroy me.

BUFO   Good boy i'faith, by this hand a' speaks just as I would do,
for all that he is so near being made puddings meat.

QUEEN   You are sorry
For your late desperate rudeness, Are you not?   220

ALPHONSO   By all my miseries these taunts are cruelty
Worse then the Hangmans ax, I am not sorry,
Nay more, will not be sorry, know from me
I hate your sex in general, not you
As y'are a Queen, but as y'are a woman: 225
Had I a term of life could last for ever,
And you could grant it, yes, and would, yet all
Or more should never reconcile my heart
To any she alive—are ye resolved?

QUEEN   [*aside*]   His spirit flies out in his daring language.   230
[*Aloud*]   *Alphonso* though the law require thy head,
Yet I have mercy where I see just cause:
You'l be a new man?

ALPHONSO   Oh! A womans tongue
Is sharper then a pointed steel; Tender Madam,
I kiss your Royal hand, and call you fair,   235
Assure this noble, this uncovered presence,
That richest vertue is your bosoms tenant,
That you are absolutely great and good;
I'll flatter all the vices of your sex,
Protesting men are monsters, women Angels,   240
No light ones, but full weighty, natures best,
I'll proclaim lust a pitty, pride a handsomness,
Deceit ripness of wit, bold scandalous scolding
A bravery of spirit, bloody cruelty
Masculine justice; more, I will maintain   245

216 man:] man, *Q*   221 cruelty] *Sedge*; cruelty. *Q*   234 Tender] *Sedge*; Tender, *Q*
242 handsomness] handsomness. *Q*   243 scolding] scolding, *Q*   244 spirit, . . . cru-
elty] spirit; . . . cruelty, *Q*   245 more,] *Sedge*; more *Q*

That Queens are chief for rule, you chief of Queens,
If you'l but give me leave to die in peace.
Pray give me leave to die. Pray good now do,
What think ye, 'tis a Royal grant; henceforth
Heaven be the rest you chose, but never come at.   250
A kinde farewel to all.

COLUMELLO   Can you endure
To let a Rebel prate? Off with his head,
And let him then dispute.

PETRUCHI   I should have us'd
The priviledge of time, had I known this. You must not talk
    so loud.

QUEEN   My Lords, a word: What if we pardoned him,   255
I think the neerness of his arrival to the stroke of death,
Will ever be a warning to his Loyalty.

ALMADA   How pardon him! What means your Majesty?
What can you hope from one so wholly drown'd
In melancholy and sowre discontent;   260
That should he share the Crown, a' would imploy t
On none but Apes and Flatterers.

VELASCO   Spare, my Lord
Such liberal censure, rather reyn the fury
Of Justice, then so spur it on. Great Mistris,
I will not plead my services, but urge   265
The glories you may challenge by your mercy.
It will be a most sweet becoming act
To set you in the Chronicles of memory.

QUEEN   *Velasco,* thou art not more brave in arms
To conquer with thy valour, then thy courtesie.   270
Alphonso, take thy life, who took thee prisoner,
Is now become thy spokesman.

B3ᵛ ALPHONSO   Phew, mock not
Calamity so grosly.

VELASCO   You are too desperate: The Queen hath freely
    pardoned you.

QUEEN   And more to purchase kinde opinion of thy Sex,   275
Our self will lend our help. Lords, all your hands.

LODOVICO   But is the Queen in earnest?

VELASCO   It becomes her,
  Mercy is God like.

QUEEN   Officers be gone.
                              Exit Officers [and HANGMAN]
  Such objects for a Royal presence are
  Unfit; here kiss our hand, we dare conceive   280
  That 'twas thy hight of youth, not hate of us
  Drew thee to those attempts, and both we pardon.

MURETTO   Do not the stars run a wrong byas now, Signior *Pynto?*

PYNTO   *Venus* is Lady of the Ascendant, man. I knew if once he
pass the fatal hour, the influence would work another way.   285

MURETTO   Very likely, your reasons are infallible.

QUEEN   What can our favours challenge.

ALPHONSO   More true service,
  True faith, true Love, then I have words to utter.

QUEEN   Which we accept; lead on, here ends this strife,
  When Law craves justice, mercy should grant life.   290
                          Exit all but PYNTO *and his fellows*

PYNTO   Go thy waies for a sure sound brain'd piece whilst thou
livest; *Pynto,* say I, now, now, now, am I an ass, now my Masters,
hang your selves, 'S foot, I'll stand to't; that man whoever he be,
(better or worse, all's one) who is not star wise, is natures fool;
your Astonomer hath the heavens, the whole globe of the earth, 295
and the vast gulf of the Sea it self, for his proper kingdom, his fee-
simple, his own inheritance, who looks any higher then the top of
a steeple, or a may-pool, is worthy to die in a ditch. But to know
the conjunctions of the Planets, the influences of the celestial
body, the harmony of the spheares, frost and snow, hail and tem- 300
pests, rain and sun-shine, nay, life and death; here's cunning, to be
deep in speculation, to be groping the secrets of nature.

MURETTO   O, Sir, there, there, there.

280 Unfit;] Unfit, *Q*   289 accept;] accept, *Q*

PYNTO   Let me alone, I say it my self, I know I am a rare fellow;
why, look, look ye, we are all made, or let me be stew'd in Star-   305
shut; pish, I am confident, and we shall all mount, beleeve it.

BUFO   Shall we, nay, then I am resolv'd.

MURETTO   Frier *Bacon* was but a brazen head, in comparison of
him.

BUFO   But why should you not have said so much before, good-   310
man Jolthead?

MURETTO   Nay, look ye, Captain, there's a time for all things.

BUFO   For all this, what will become of us; is the sign lucky to
venture the begging of a cast sute? Let me be resolved of that
once.   315

MURETTO   'Twas wisely urg'd, Captain.

PYNTO   Mans richest ornament is his nakedness, Gentlemen,
variety of clothing is the surquedry of fools; wise men have their
proper solace in the linings of their mindes; as for fashions, 'tis a
disease for a horse.   320

MURETTO   Never richer stuff came from man.

BUFO   'Zookes, 'tis a scurvy, a pocky, and a naked answer; a
plague of all your sentences, whilst I am like to starve with hunger
and cold.

Enter Messenger

MESSENGER   By your leave, Gentlemen, the Lord *Alphonso* hath   325
sent you this purse of gold, commands ye to put your selves into
costly sutes, and repair to Court.

[BUFO, PYNTO, *and* MURETTO]   How! To Court!

MESSENGER   Where you may happily see him Crowned King, for
that's the common report; I was charg'd to urge you to be very   330
speedy: farewel, Gentlemen.
                                                                Exit

PYNTO   What think ye now, my hearts of gold?

---

323 sentences,] sentences; *Q*   324 cold.] *Sedge*; cold, *Q*   327 Court.] *Sedge*; Court; *Q*

MURETTO   Hearts of gold indeed now, Signior.

PYNTO   Pish, I am a coxcomb, I; Oh, the divinity of—   B4ʳ

BUFO   Bawll no more the weather's cold, I must have utensicles,   335
follow your leader, ho.

Exit all

I.2   *Enter* VELASCO *and* LODOVICO

VELASCO   Prethee perswade me not.

LODOVICO   You'l loose your honor.

VELASCO   Ide rather loose my honor then my faith:
O, *Lodovico*, thou art witness with me,
That I have sworn, and pledg'd my heart, my truth
To her deserving memory, whose beauty,   5
Is through the world unfellowed.

LODOVICO   Here the wisdom of sword men, they deal all
by strength not policy. What excuse shall be fain'd, let me
know that?

VELASCO   Excuse, why, *Lodovico*, I am sick,   10
And I am sick indeed, sick to the soul.

LODOVICO   For a decay'd tilter, or a known Coward, this were
tollerable now: But to the business; I have solicited your
widow.

VELASCO   Will she not speak with me?   15

LODOVICO   Young widows, and grave old Ones too, by your
leave, care not so much for talking if you come once to them, you
must do, and do, and do again, Again, and again, all's too little,
you'l finde it.

VELASCO   Come, friend, you mock my miseries.   20

LODOVICO   It's a fine laughing matter when the best and most
approved souldier of the world, should be so heart-sick for love of a
placket: Well I have sent your wise servant (for fools are best to be

I.2] 3–6 prose in *Q*   7 excuse] *Sedge*; exercise *Q*   15 not] *Sedge*; nor *Q*
16 and 18 too] *Sedge*; two *Q*   17 leave,] *Sedge*; leave *Q*   17 talking] *Sedge*; talking; *Q*
17 them,] them *Q*

trusted in womens things) to my couzen *Shaparoon*, and by him
your second letter, you shall shortly hear what news: My couzen is   25
excellently traded in these mortal businesses of flesh and blood,
and will hardly come of with two denials.

VELASCO   If she prevail, *Lodovico*—

LODOVICO   What then? Ply your occupation when you come
to't, 'tis a fit season of the year; women are hony-moon if a man   30
could jump with them at the instant, and prick 'em in the right
vain; else this Queen would never have sav'd a Traytor from the
block, and suddenly made him her King and Husband. But no
more of that, there's danger in't; Y'are sick you say?

VELASCO   Pierc't through with fiery darts, much worse then death.   35

LODOVICO   Why your onely present remedy is, then as soon as
you can, to quench those fires in the watry Channels of qualification: soft, no more words, behold a prodegy.
                              Florish.

Enter COLUMELLO, ALMADA *bare,* ALPHONSO *and the*
QUEEN *Crowned,* HEROPHIL, PETRUCHI *with a Guard,*
the King and QUEEN *take their States.*

ALL   Long live *Alphonso* King of *Arragon.*

ALPHONSO   Then we are Soveraign.

QUEEN   As free, as I by birth: 40
    I yeeld to you (my Lord) my Crown, my Heart,
    My People, my Obedience; In exchange
    What I demand is Love.

ALPHONSO   You cannot miss it,
    There is but one thing that all humane power
    Or malice of the Devil could set a broach,   45
    To work on for a breach 'twixt you and me.

QUEEN   One thing! Why, is there one thing then, my Lord?

ALPHONSO   Yes, and 'tis onely this; y'are still a woman.

30 year;] year, *Q*

QUEEN   A woman! Said you so, sir?

ALPHONSO   I confess
You have deserv'd more service, more regard   50
From me, in my particular, then life
Can thank you for; and that you may conceive
My fair acknowledgment; although 'tis true,
I might command; yet I will make a suit,
An earnest suit t'ee.

QUEEN   It must then be granted.   55 B4ᵛ

ALPHONSO   That, to redeem a while some serious thoughts
Which have misdeem'd your sex, you'l be content
I be a married Batchelor one sennight.
You cannot but conceive.

COLUMELLO   How's this?

PETRUCHI   Fine work.

QUEEN   Alas my Lord, this needs no publick mention.   60

ALPHONSO   Nay, Madam, hear me—That our Courts be kept
Under a several roof; that you and I
May not for such a short time, come together.

QUEEN   I understand you not.

ALPHONSO   Your patience, Madam,
You interrupt me—That no message pass   65
Of commendation, questioning our healths,
Our sleeps, our actions, or what else belongs
To common curtesie, 'twixt friend, and friend.
You must be pleas'd to grant it, I'll have it so.

QUEEN   No message of commends!

ALPHONSO   Phew, you demur,   70
It argues your distrust.

QUEEN   I am content
The King should be obeyed. Pray heaven all be well. [Exit]

---

49 sir?] *Sedge*; sir. Q   56–7 That, . . . sex,] *Sedge*; That . . . sex. Q   61 me—. . . our]
Sedge; me, . . . our our Q   65 me—] *Sedge*; me, Q

ALPHONSO   *Velasco*, thou wer't he didst conquer me,
Didst take me prisoner! wer't in that the means
To raise me up thus high. I thank thee for't;   75
I thought to honour thee in a defence
Of the Queens beauty; but wee'l now deferr't.
Yet hand your mistris, lead her to the Court,
We and our Lords will follow, there wee'l part;
A seven dayes absence cannot seem but short.   80

Exeunt all

2.I   *Enter* SHAPAROON *and* MOPAS

SHAPAROON   And as I said (nay pray my friend be covered) the
business hath been soundly followed on my part. Yet again, in
good sooth, I cannot abide you should stand bare before me to so
little purpose.

MOPAS   Manners is a Jewel (Madam) and as for standing bare,   5
I know there is som difference, the putting down of a mans
cap, and the putting down of his breeches before a reverend
gentlewoman.

SHAPAROON   You speak very properly, there is a great deal of
difference indeed. But to come to the point; Fy, what a stir I had   10
to make her to receive the letter, and when she had received it, to
open it, and then to read it; nay, to read it again and again; that as
I am a very woman, a man might have wrong my smock dropping
wet, with the pure sweat that came from my body. Friend, I took
such pains with her. Oh my conscience, to bear a child at those   15
years would not trouble me half so much as the delivery of that
letter did.

MOPAS   A man-child of my age perhaps, Madam, would not.

SHAPAROON   Yet that were a sore burthen for one that is not
us'd to't, I may tell you. O these coy girles are such wild cattel to   20
have dealing with.

MOPAS   What ancient Madams cannot do one way, let them do
another; she's a rank Jade that being past the breeder, cannot kick
up her heels, wince, and cry wee-hee: good examples cannot chuse

74 prisoner!] prisoner? *Q*

from ones elders, but work much to the purpose, being well ply'd, and in season. 25

SHAPAROON   In season? True, that's a chief thing; yes, I'll assure you my friend, I am but entring into eight and twenty.

MOPAS   Wants somwhat of that too, I take it; I warrant ye your mark ap|pears yet to be | seen for proof of your age, as plain as 30 Cr^r when you were but fifteen.

SHAPAROON   Truly, if it were well searcht, I think it does. Your name is *Mopas*, you told me?

MOPAS   *Mopas* my name is, and yours Madam *Shaparoon* I was told.

SHAPAROON   A right Madam born I can assure ye. 35

MOPAS   Your Ancestors will speak that, for the *Shaparoons* have ever took place of the best French-hoods in the parish, ever since the first addition.

SHAPAROON   All this with a great deal of modesty I must confess. Ud's Pittikins, stand by, aside a little: see where the lady coms; 40 do not appear before you are call'd, in any case: but mark how I will work her like wax.

Enter SALASSA *reading a letter*

SALASSA   'Your servant in all commands, *Velasco*.' So, and I am resolved to put ye to the test, servant, for your free fools heart, e're I give you the slip, I warrant ye. 45

SHAPAROON   Your ladyship hath considered the premises e're this time, at full, I hope.

SALASSA   O, *Shaparoon*, you keep true sentinel, what? I must give certain answer; must I not?

SHAPAROON   Nay, Madam, you may chuse, 'tis all in your 50 Ladiships discreet consideration. The sum of all is, that if you shew him not some favour, he is no long lived man.

SALASSA   Very well; how long have you been a factress for such Merchants, *Shaparoon*.

2.1] 37 parish,] *Sedge*; parish; *Q*   43 'Your . . . commands, *Velasco*.'] *Sedge*; Your . . . commands *Velasco*. *Q*   52 lived] *Sedge*; lives *Q*

SHAPAROON   O my Religion! I a factress? I am even well enough   55
serv'd for my good will; and this is my requital. Factress, quoth
you?

SALASSA   Come, your intercession shall prevail, which is his letter
carrier?

MOPAS   At your ladiships service.   60

SALASSA   Your Lord *Velasco* sent you?

MOPAS   Most true, sweet madam.

SALASSA   What place hold you about him?

MOPAS   I am his Drugster, Madam.

SALASSA   What Sir?   65

MOPAS   Being hard bound with melancholy, I give him a purge,
with two or three soluble stools of laughter.

SALASSA   Belike you are his fool, or his jester.

MOPAS   Jester if you please, but not fool, Madam; for bables
belong to fools, and they are then onely fit for ladies secresies, not   70
for Lords.

SALASSA   But is he indeed sick of late?

SHAPAROON   Alas good heart, I suffer for him.

Enter LODOVICO

LODOVICO   By your leave lady, without ceremony, you know
me, and may guess my errand.   75

SALASSA   Yet more trouble, nay, then I shall be hail-shot.

LODOVICO   To be brief. By the honors of a good name, you are
a dry-skinn'd widow, and did not my hast concern the life of the
noblest Gentleman in *Europe*, I would as much scorn imployments of this nature to you, as I do a proud woman of your   80
condition.

MOPAS   I marry here's one will thunder her widow-head into
flitters: stand to't, Signior, I am your second.

SALASSA   Sir y'are uncivil to exclaim against a lady in her own
house.   85

LODOVICO   A lady, yet a paraquitto, popingjay, your whole worth lies in your gay out side, and your squawling tongue. A Wagtail is a glorious fowl in respect of many of ye. Though most of ye are in nature as very fowl as wagtayles.

SALASSA   Are such as you the Lord *Velasco's* agents in his hot   90 affection?

SHAPAROON   Sweet cousen, *Lodovico*, pray now, the lady is most vertuously resolved.

MOPAS   Heark ye middle-ag'd countess, do not take anothers tale into your mouth, I have occasion to use you in private, and   95 can finde you work enough my self; a word in your ear.

SALASSA   I protest, I meant more noble | answer for his satisfac-   Cıᵛ tion, then ever your railing language shall force from me.

LODOVICO   Were I the man that doated on you, I would take a shorter course with you, then to come humbly whining to   100 your sweet—pox of all such ridiculous foppery—I would—

SALASSA   Weep your self to death, and be chronicled among the regiment of kinde tender hearted souls.

LODOVICO   Indeed, forsooth, I would not; what, for a widdow, one that hath jumpt the old moyles trot, so oft, that the   105 sciatica founders her yet in both her thighs.

SALASSA   You abuse me grosly.

LODOVICO   One that hath been so often drunk with satiety of pleasure, that fourteen husbands are but as half a draught to quench her thurst in an afternoon.   110

SALASSA   I will no longer endure ye.

LODOVICO   For you, you? That are neither noble, wise, rich, fair, nor wel-favoured. For you?

MOPAS   You are all these, if you can keep your own counsel and let no body know, Mistris Madam.   115

SHAPAROON   Nay I am so perswaded, and assure your self no body shall know.

96 self;] self, *Q*   104 widdow,] widdow *Q*

LODOVICO   Yet forsooth, must you be the onely precious piece
the Lord *Velasco* must adore, must dye for. But I vow, if he do
miscarry, (as I fear he cannot recover)—   120

SALASSA   Goodness forbid, Alas! Is he sick, sir?

LODOVICO   Excellent dissimulation! Yes sure, he is sick, and an
everlasting silence strike you dumb that are the cause on't. But, as
I said, if he do go the wrong way, as I love vertue, your ladiship
shall be ballated through all Christendom, and sung to scurvy   125
tunes, and your picture drawn over every ballad, sucking of rotten
eggs among wheasels.

SALASSA   Pray give me leave; Is Lord *Velasco* sick? And lies there
ought in me to comfort, or recover him?

LODOVICO   Marry does there, the more Infidel he: And what   130
of all this now?

SALASSA   What would you have me do?

LODOVICO   'Wonders, either go and visit him, or admit him
to visit you; these are mighty favours are they not?

SALASSA   Why, good Sir, I will grant the later willingly; he shall   135
be kindly welcom.

LODOVICO   And laught at while he is here: shall a not?

SALASSA   What would you have me say? My best entertainment
shall be open to him; I will discourse to him freely, if he requires it
privately: I will be all what in honour I should.   140

LODOVICO   Certifie him so much by letter.

SALASSA   That cannot stand with my modesty, my word and
truth shall be my gage.

LODOVICO   Enough, do this, and by this hand I'll ask you
pardon for my rudeness, and ever heartily honour you.   145

MOPAS   I shall hear from you when my leasures serves.

SHAPAROON   Most assuredly. Good destines speed your journey.

---

120 recover)—] *Sedge*; recover.) *Q*   125 scurvy] *Sedge*; sciroy *Q*   133 visit him] *Sedge*;
visi him *Q*

MOPAS   All happiness ride ever before you, your disgraces behinde you, and full pleasure in the midst of ye.

Exeunt

2.2   *Enter* BUFO *in fresh apparel, ushering* HEROPHIL

HEROPHIL   My over kinde Captain, what would you say?

BUFO   Why, Mistris, I would say, as a man might say forsooth, indeed I would say—

HEROPHIL   What, Captain?

BUFO   Even whatsoever you would have me to say, forsooth.   5

HEROPHIL   If that be all, pray say nothing.

BUFO   Why look ye, Mistris, all what I say if you mark it well, is just nothing; As for example, To tell you that you are fair, is nothing, for you know it your self; to say you were honest, were an indignity to your beauty, and upon the matter nothing, for honesty   10 in a fair woman is as good as nothing.

HEROPHIL   That is somwhat strange to be proved.

BUFO   To a good wit, dear Mistris, nothing's impossible.

HEROPHIL   Sure the Court and your new clothes have infected   C2ʳ you: Would I were a purse of gold, for your sake, Captain, to   15 reward your wit.

BUFO   I would you were, mistris, so you were not counterfeit metal; I should soon try you on the too true touchstone of my affections, indeed forsooth.

HEROPHIL   Well, witty Captain, for your love I must pass away in   20 debt, but will not fail to think on't. But now I am in hast.

BUFO   If you would but grant me but one poor request, before you go, I should soon dispatch and part.

HEROPHIL   Name it, Captain.

BUFO   Truly, and as I live, 'tis a very small triffle for your part, all   25 things considered.

HEROPHIL   But cannot you tell what it is?

BUFO   That were a fine jest indeed, why, I would desire, intreat, and beseech you.

HEROPHIL   What to do?   30

BUFO   There you have it, and thank you too.

HEROPHIL   I understand you not.

BUFO   Why, To do with you, forsooth, to do with you.

HEROPHIL   To do what?

BUFO   In plain words, I would commit with you, or as the   35
more learned phrase it, if you be pleased to consent, I would
ravish you.

HEROPHIL   Fy, fy, Captain, so uncivil, you made me blush.

BUFO   Do I say; why, I am glad I have it for you: Souldiers are
hot upon service, mistris, and a wise mans bolt is soon shot; as the   40
proverb says:

HEROPHIL   Good Captain, keep up your bolt till I am at leasure
to stand fair for your mark. If the Court Stalions prove all so rank,
I will vow all to ride henceforth upon an ass; so, Captain, I must
leave you.   45

Exit HEROPHIL

BUFO   Fare-wel heartily to you forsooth. Go thy waies for as true
a Mistris as ever fowled clean Napary. This same whorson Court
diet, cost, lodging, change of clothes, and ease, have addicted me
villanously to the itch of concupiscence.

Enter ALPHONSO; PYNTO *and* MURETTO
complementing on either side of him

ALPHONSO   They all shall not intreat me.   50

MURETTO   Your Majesty were no King, if your own will were
not your own law.

PYNTO   Always, my Lord, observing the domination of the
Planets: As if *Mars* and *Venus* being in conjunction, and their
influence working upon your frailty; then in any case you must not   55
resist the motion of the celestial bodies.

MURETTO   All which (most gracious Soverain) this most famous
Scoller will at a minute foretel.

BUFO   All hail to the King himself, my very good Liege, Lord,
and most gratious benefactor.   60

ALPHONSO   What need I other counsellors then these.
   Shall I be forc't to be a womans slave?
   That may live free, and hate their fickle sex.

MURETTO   O 'tis a glorious vertue in so magnificent a Prince to
abstain from the sensual surfets of fleshly and wanton appetites.   65

ALPHONSO   I finde the inclination of such follies.
   Why, what are women?

BUFO   Very pleasant pretty necessary toys, an't please your Majesty;
I my self could pass the time with them, as occasion might serve,
eight and forty hours out right, one to one alwaies provided.   70

PYNTO   Yet of all the seven planets, there are but two women
among them, and one of them two is chast, which is as good as if
shee were a boy.

MURETTO   That is not to be questioned; the best of women are
but troubles and vexations, 'tis man that retains all true perfection,   75
and of all men your Majesty.

              Enter ALMADA *and* COLLUMMELLO

ALPHONSO   Ye are to rude to enter on our privacies,   C2ᵛ
   Without our license; speak, your business Lords.

ALMADA   We came from your most vertuous Queen.

ALPHONSO   No more.

COLUMELLO   A month is well nigh past, and yet you slack   80
   Your love to her: What mean you, sir, so strangely
   To slight a wife whose griefs grow now too high,
   For womanhood to suffer.

ALMADA   Is't your pleasure
   To admit her to your bosom?

---

69 might] *Sedge*; migh *Q*   78 license;] license, *Q*

ALPHONSO   Y'are too sawcy.
Return, and quickly too, and tell her thus;   85
If she intend to keep her in our favour,
Let us not see her.

COLUMELLO   Say you so, Great Sir;
You speak it but for tryal.
ALL [except COLUMELLO] Ha, ha, ha.

COLUMELLO   O, Sir, remember what you are, and let not
The insinuations of these servile creatures,   90
Made onely men by you, sooth and traduce
Your safety to a known and willful danger.
Fix in your thoughts the ruine you have scap't;
Who freed you; who hath rais'd you to this height,
And you will then awake your judgments eye: 95
The Commons murmur, and the streets are fill'd
With busie whispers: Yet in time recal
Your violence.

ALPHONSO   As I am King, the tongue
Forfeits his head that speaks another word.
Muretto, Talk we not now like a King?   100

MURETTO   Like one that hath the whole World for his proper
Monarchy, and it becomes you Royally.

          Enter QUEEN, PETRUCHI, *and* HEROPHIL

BUFO   The Queen, and my Mistris; O brave, we shall have some
doings hard to hand now, I hope.

ALPHONSO   What means the woman? Ha! Is this the duty   105
Of a good wife, we sent not for you, did we?

QUEEN   The more my duty that I came unsent for;
Wherein my gratious Lord have I offended?
Wherein have I transgrest against thy laws
O sacred Marriage? To be sequestred   110
In the first spring and *April* of my joys
From you, much dearer to me, then my life?
By all the honour of a spotless bed,

---

88 tryal.] *Sedge*; tryal *Q*

Shew me my fault and I will turn away,
And be my own swift executioner.   115

ALPHONSO   I take that word. Know then you married me
Against my will, and that's your fault.

QUEEN   Alas!
Against your will? I dare not contradict
What you are pleased to urge. But by the love
I bare the King of *Arragon*, (an oath   120
As great as I can swear by) I conceiv'd
Your words to be true speakers of your heart,
And I am sure they were; you swore they were.
How should I but beleeve, that lov'd so dearly?

ALPHONSO   Come then you are a trifler, for by this   125
I know you love me not.

QUEEN   Is that your fear?
Why la now, Lords, I told you that the King
Made our division but a proof of faith.
Kinde husband, now I'm bold to call you so;
Was this your cunning to be jealous of me   130
So soon? We women are fine fools
To search mens pretty subtilties.

MURETTO   (*aside*) You'l scarce finde it so.

ALPHONSO
She would perswade mee strangely.

QUEEN   Prethee, Sweet heart,
Force not thy self to look so sadly; troth   135
It sutes not with thy love, 'tis well. Was this
Your sennights respite? Yet, as I am a Queen,   C3ʳ
I fear'd you had been in earnest.

ALPHONSO   Earnest: Hence
Monstrous enchantress, by the death I owe
To Nature, thou appear'st to me in this   140
More impudent then impudence, the tyde
Of thy luxurious blood is at the full;
And cause thy raging plurisie of lust

117 fault.] *Sedge*; fault Q

Cannot be sated by our royal warmth,
Thou tri'st all cunning petulent charms to raise   145
A wanton devill up in our chast brest.
But we are Canon-proof against the shot
Of all thy arts.

QUEEN   Was't you spoke that, my Lord?

PYNTO   [*aside*] *Phaeton* is just over the orb of the moon, his
horses are got loose, and the heavens begin to grow into a   150
combustion.

ALPHONSO   I'll sooner dig a dungeon in a mole-hill,
And hide my crown there, that both fools and children
May trample o're my Royalty, then ever
Lay it beneath an antick womans feet.   155
Couldst thou transhape thy self into a man,
And with it be more excellent then man
Can be; yet since thou wer't a woman once,
I would renounce thee.

PETRUCHI   Let the King remember
It is the Queen he speaks too.

ALPHONSO   Pish, I know   160
She would be well contented but to live
Within my presence; not for love to me,
But that she might with safety of her honour,
Mix with some hot vein'd letcher, whose prone lust
Should feed the rank impostume of desires,   165
And get a race of bastards, to whose birth
I should be thought the Dad. But thou, thou woman,
E're I will be the cloak to thy false play,
I'll couple with a witch, a hag; for if
Thou canst live chast, live by thy self like me.   170
Or if thou wouldst perswade me that thou lov'st me,
See me no more, never. From this time forth
I hate thy sex; of all thy sex, thee worst.
                              Exit ALPHONSO, BUFO, PYNTO

ALMADA   Madam, dear Madam, yet take comfort, time
Will work all for the best.

170 self] *Sedge*; sel *Q*   174 best.] *Sedge*; best *Q*

QUEEN   Where must I go?   175

COLUMELLO Y'are in your own Kingdom, 'tis your birth-right,
We all your Subjects; not a man of us,
But to the utmost of his life, will right
Your wrongs against this most unthankful King.

QUEEN Away, ye are all Traytors to profane His sacred merits
 with your bitter terms.   180
Why, am I not his Wife? A wife must bear
Withal what likes her Lord t'upbraid her with,
And yet 'tis no injustice. What was't he said?
That I no more should see him, never, never.
There I am quite divorst from all my joys,   185
From all my paradice of life. Not see him?
'Twas too unkinde a task. But he commanded
I cannot but obey. Where's *Herophil*?

HEROPHIL Here Madam.

QUEEN Go hang my Chamber all with mourning black; 190
Seal up my windows, let no light survey
The subtle tapers that must eye my griefs.
Get from me Lords, I will defie ye all,
Y'are men, and men (O me) are all unkinde.
Come hither *Herophil*, spread all my robes,   195
My jewels and apparel on the floor,
And for a Crown get me a Willow wreath:
No, no, that's not my colour, buy me a veil
Ingrayn'd in tawny. Alas, I am forsaken,   C3ᵛ
And none can pitty me.

PETRUCHI   By all the faith   200
I ow to you my soveraign, if you please
To enjoyn me any service, I will prove
Most ready and most true.

QUEEN   Why should the King
Despise me? I did never cross his will,
Never gainsaid his yea; yet sure I fear   205
He hath some ground for his displeasure.

---

191 survey] *Sedge*; survey, Q   202 enjoyn] *Sedge*; enjoy Q   203 true.] *Sedge*; true, Q
205 his] *Sedge*; his, Q

HEROPHIL   None,
  Unless because you sav'd him from the block.

QUEEN   Art thou a pratler too? Peace, *Herophil,*
  Tempt not a desperate woman. No man here
  Dares do my last commends to him.   210

MURETTO   If your excellent Majesty please to repose confidence
in me, I will not onely deliver him your commendations, but think
my self highly dishonored, if he return not his back to you by
letter.

PETRUCHI   Off beast, made all of baseness, do not grieve   215
  Calamity, or as I am a knight,
  I'll cut thy tongue out.

MURETTO   Sweet Signior, I protest—

                                          Exit MURETTO

PETRUCHI   Madam, beleeve him not, he is a Parasite;
  Yet one the King doth dote on.

QUEEN   Then beshrew ye,   220
  You had not us'd him gently; had I known't,
  I would have kneell'd before him, and have sent
  A handful of my tears unto the King.
  Away, my Lords, here is no place to revel
  In our discomfits. *Herophil,* let's hast,   225
  That thou and I may heartily like widows
  Bewail my bridal mockt Virginity.

                              [*Exit* QUEEN *and* HEROPHIL]

COLUMELLO   Let's follow her my lords; I fear to late
  The King will yet repent these rude divisions.

                                          Exeunt

              2.3   *Enter* VELASCO, LODOVICO, MOPAS

LODOVICO   Complement? 'Tis for Barbors shops; know your
own worth, you speak to a frail commodity; and barter't away
roundly, my Lord.

VELASCO   She promis'd free discourse?

---

212 me,] *Sedge*; me; *Q*   221 gently;] gently, *Q*

LODOVICO   She did: Are ye answer'd?   5

Enter SALASSA, SHAPAROON

SHAPAROON   Madam, my Lord *Velasco* is come, use him nobly
and kindly, or—I say no more.

SALASSA   To a poor widow's house my Lord is welcom. Your
lordship honours me in this favor; in what thankful entertainment
I can, I shall strive to deserve it.   10

SHAPAROON   Your sweet lordship is most heartily welcom, as
I may say.

MOPAS   Instead of a letter, Madam goodface, on my Lord's
behalf, I am bold to salute you.

LODOVICO   Madam *Salassa*, not distrusting the liberty you   15
granted, now you and my Lord are in your own house, we will
attend yee in the next room; Away, Couzen; follow, sirrah.

SHAPAROON   It is a womans part to come behinde.

MOPAS   But for two men to pass in before one woman, 'tis too
much a conscience; on reverend antiquity.   20

Exit LODOVICO, SHAPAROON, MOPAS

SALASSA   What is your lordships pleasure?

VELASCO   To rip up
A story of my fate. When by the Queen
I was imploy'd against the late Commotioners,
(Of whom the now King was chief Leader) then
In my return you pleas'd to entertain me   25
Here in your house.

SALASSA   Much good may it do your lordship.

VELASCO   But then, what conquest gain'd I by that conquest,
When here mine eyes, and your commanding beauty
Made me a prisoner to the truest love,   30
That ever warm'd a heart.

SALASSA   Who might that be?

2.3] 16 you] *Sedge*; your *Q*   18 womans] *Sedge*; woman *Q*   21 lordships] *Sedge*; lor-
ships *Q*

VELASCO   You, Lady, are the deity I adore,
C4ʳ   Have kneell'd too in my heart, have vow'd my soul to,
      In such a debt of service, that my life
      Is tenant to your pleasure.

SALASSA   Phew, my Lord;   35
      It is not nobly done to mock me thus.

VELASCO   Mock you? Most fair *Salassa*, if e're truth
      Dwelt in a tongue, my words and thoughts are twins.

SALASSA   You wrong your honor in so mean a choise.
      Can it be though, that that brave man, *Valasco*,   40
      Sole Champion of the world, should look on me?
      On me, a poor lone Widow? 'Tis impossible.

VELASCO   I am poorer
      In my performance now, then ever; so poor,
      That vows and protestations want fit credit   45
      With me to vow the least part of a service
      That might deserve your favour.

SALASSA   You are serious?

VELASCO   Lady, I wish that for a present tryal,
      Against the custome of so sweet a nature,
      You would be somwhat cruel in commands.   50
      You dare not sift the honor of my faith
      By any strange injunction, which the speed
      Of my glad undertaking should not cheerfully
      Attempt, or perish in the sufferance of it.

SALASSA   You promise Lordly.

VELASCO   You too much distrust   55
      The constancy of truth.

SALASSA   It were unnoble,
      On your part to demand a gift of bounty,
      More then the freedom of a fair allowance,
      Confirm'd by modesty and reason's warrant
      Might without blushing yeeld unto.

VELASCO   Oh, fear not,   60
      For my affections aim at chast contents;
      Not at unruly passions of desire.

I onely claim the title of your servant,
The flight of my ambitions soars no higher,
Then living in your grace, and for incouragement   65
To quicken my attendance now and then
A kinde unravisht kiss.

SALASSA   That's but a fee,
Due to a fair deserver: but admit
I grant it, and you have it; may I then
Lay a light burthen on you.

VELASCO   What is possible   70
For me to venture on, by how much more
It carries danger in't; by so much more
My glorie's in the atchievement.

SALASSA   I must trust ye.

VELASCO   By all the vertues of a Souldiers name,
I vow and sware.

SALASSA   Enough, I take that oath: 75
And thus my self first do confirm your warrant.

VELASCO   I feel new life within me.

SALASSA   Now be Steward,
For your own store, my lord, and take possession
Of what you have purchased freely.

VELASCO   With a joy
As willing as my wishes can arrive at.   80

                                        kisses her

SALASSA   So, I may claim your oath now.

VELASCO   I attend it.

SALASSA   *Velasco*, I do love thee, and am jealous
Of thy spirit, which is hourly apt
To catch at actions; if I must be Mistris
Of thee and my own will, thou must be subject   85
To my improvements.

VELASCO   'Tis my souls delight.

79 joy] *Sedge*; joy. Q

SALASSA   Y'are fam'd the onely fighting Sir alive;
    But what's this if you be not safe to me?

VELASCO   By all—

SALASSA   You shall not sware, take heed of perjury.   90
    So much I fear your safety, that I command,
C4ᵛ   For two years space, you shall not wear a sword,
    A dagger, or stelletto; shall not fight
    On any quarrel be it neer so just.

VELASCO   Lady!

SALASSA   Hear more yet; if you be baffled,   95
    Rail'd at, scorn'd, mock'd, struck, baffl'd, kick'd,

VELASCO   (O Lady!)

SALASSA   Spit on, revil'd, challeng'd, provok'd by fools,
    Boyes, anticks, cowards,

VELASCO   ('Tis intollerable.)

SALASSA   I charge you (by your oath) not to reply.
    In word, deed, look: and lastly, I conjure ye   100
    Never to shew the cause to any living
    By circumstance or by equivocation;
    Nor till two years expire to motion love.

VELASCO   Why do you play the Tyrant thus?

SALASSA   'Tis common
    T' observe how love hath made a Coward valiant;   105
    But that a man as daring as *Velasco*,
    Should to express his duty to a Mistris,
    Kneel to his own disgraces, and turn Coward,
    Belongs to me and to my glories onely;
    I'm Empress of this miracle. Your oath   110
    Is past, if you will lose your self you may.
    How d'ee, Sir?

VELASCO   Woman thou art vain and cruel.

88 this . . . me?] *Sedge*; this; . . . me. *Q*   96 mock'd,] *Sedge*; mock'd *Q*   98 cowards,]
cowards. *Q*   99 reply] *Sedge*; reply. *Q*

SALASSA   Wilt please your lordship tast a cup of wine,
Or stay and sup, and take a hard bed here?
Your friends think we have done strange things this while.   115
Come let us walk like Lovers: I am pittiful,
I love no quarrels.

VELASCO   Triumph in my ruins.
There is no act of folly but is common
In use and practise to a scornful woman.

Exeunt

3.1   *Enter* ALPHONSO, ALMADA, MURETTO, BUFO, PYNTO,
and attendants

ALPHONSO   You have prevail'd, yet e're you came (my Lord)
Muretto, here this right, right, honest man
Confirm'd me throughly; now to witness further
With what a gratitude I love the Queen,
Reach me a bowle of wine.   5

ALMADA   Your Majesty more honors me, in making me the
Messenger of this most happy concord, then addition of greatness
can express.

MURETTO   I ever told you how you would find his Grace inclin'd
at last.   10

PYNTO   The very *Jove* of benignity, by whose gentle aspect the whole
sphere of this Court and Kingdom are (like the lesser orbes)
moved round in the harmony of affability.

Enter one with wine

ALPHONSO   My Lord *Almada*, health unto your Mistris,
A hearty health, a deep one.   *Drinks*

ALMADA   Upon my knee   15
My duty gladly answers.

ALPHONSO   [*to Attendant*]   Give him wine.
There's not a man whoever in our Court
(Greater or meaner) but shall pledge this health,

3.1] 3 throughly;] throughly, *Q*   4 Queen,] *Sedge*; Queen. *Q*   9 you . . . inclin'd]
Sedge; you, . . . inclin'd, *Q*   would find] *Sedge*; would *Q*   10 last.] *Sedge*; last *Q*   14 *Almada*]
Almado Q   15 s.d. after line 14a in *Q*   16 answers.] *Sedge*; answers *Q*

In honor of our Queen, our vertuous Queen.
Commend us, and report us as you finde.   20

ALMADA   Great Sir, I shall with joy.   [ALMADA *drinks*]

ALPHONSO   *Bufo* and *Pynto,*
All in, and drink, drink deep, let none be spar'd,
Comers or goers, none.
    [*The cup is passed round to* BUFO *and* PYNTO, *who each*
    drink in turn]

BUFO   Away, my hearts.

PYNTO   Wee'll tickle it till the welkin | bussle again, and all the   25
Dʳ fixt Stars dance the old measures.

MURETTO   I shall attend to wait upon your lordship to the Caraoch.
                              Exeunt. Manet ALPHONSO

ALPHONSO   So, so, far reaching pollicy, I adore thee,
    Will hug thee as my dearling. Shallow fools
    Dive not into the pitch of regular Statists.   30
    Henceforth my Stratagem's of scorn and hatred
    Shall kill in smiles. I will not strike and frown,
    But laugh and murther.

                    Enter MURETTO

                Welcom, are we safe?

MURETTO   Most free from interruption: The Lord *Velasco*
is newly entred the Court; I have given the watch word that they   35
ply him mainly; the conclusion (I know) cannot but break off in
hurleburly.

ALPHONSO   Good, good, I hate him mortally. 'Twas he
    Slaved me to th' hangmans ax: But now go on;
    Petruchi is the man, you say, must stand
    The Champion of her lust.   40

MURETTO   There may be yet vertuous intention even in bad
actions, in lewd words, I urge no further then likelyhoods may
inform.

ALPHONSO   Phew, that's thy nobleness: But now *Muretto*,
The eye of luxury speaks loud in silence.   45

MURETTO   Why look ye, Sir, I must confess I observ'd some odd
amorous glances, some sweet familiar courteous toying smiles;
a kinde of officious boldness in him, Princelike and Queenlike
allowance of that boldness in him again; sometimes I might warily
overhear her whispers. But what of all this? There might be no   50
harm meant.

ALPHONSO   Fy, no, the grafting of my forehead, nothing else.
Grafting, grafting, *Muretto*. A most Gentleman-like exercise; a
very mystery belongs to't. And now and then they walk thus, arm
in arm, twist fingers: ha. Would they not *Muretto*?   55

MURETTO   'Tis wondrous fit a great Queen should be supported, Sir; and for the best lady of 'em all, to discourse familiarly
with her supporter, is courtly and passing innocent.

ALPHONSO   She and *Petruchi* did so?

MURETTO   And at her passing to her private lodgings, attended 60
onely with her lady in ordinary. *Petruchi* alone went in before her.

ALPHONSO   Is't true? Went in before her! Canst prove that?

MURETTO   Your Majesty is too quick, too apprehensive of the
worst: I meant he perform'd the office of an Usher.

ALPHONSO   Guilty apparently: Monstrous woman! Beast!   65
Were these the fruits of her dissembling tears!
Her puling, and her heart sighs. But, *Muretto*,
I will be swift, *Muretto*, swift and terrible.

MURETTO   I am such another Coxcomb o' my side too. Yet
faith, let me perswade ye; I hope your wife is vertuous.   70

ALPHONSO   Vertuous? The Devil she is, 'tis most impossible.
What kiss and toy, wink, prate, yet be vertuous?

MURETTO   Why not Sir? I think now a woman may lie four or
five nights together with a man, and yet be chast; though that be
very hard, yet so long as 'tis possible, such a thing may be.   75

---

53 *Muretto.*] *Muretto,* Q   62 true?] *Sedge*; true! Q   67–8 *Muretto, . . .* swift,] *Sedge*;
Muretto. . . . swift Q   69 Coxcomb o'] *Sedge*; Coxcomb; O Q

ALPHONSO   I have it, wee'll confer; let's stand aside.

Enter BUFO *and another* GROOM *with wine, both drunk;*
BUFO *handing* VELASCO *by the shoulders*

BUFO   Not drink more? By this hand you shall drink eleven
whole healths, if your cap be wooll or beaver; and that's my
resolution.

GROOM   'Sfoot, eleven score, without dishonor be it spoken to   80
any mans person out of this place.

Di^v VELASCO   Prethee, I can no more, 'tis a profession
I dare not practice, nay, I will not.

BUFO   How will not? Not her Queenships health?
Hark ye, thy stincking and unwholesom words—   85
Will not—You will not—You say you will not?

VELASCO   I say so, pray be answer'd.

GROOM   Pox of all flinchers; if a' say a will not,
Let him chuse, like an arrant dry lord as he is.

BUFO   Give me the bowl, I must be valiant.   90
[*To* VELASCO] You, Sirrah, man at arms; Here's a carouse
To the King, the Queen, and my self.

GROOM   Let't come, I'll have that i'faith,
Sweet, sweet, sweet, Captain.

BUFO   Hold, give the lord first, drink it up, lord, do, ump.   95

VELASCO   Away I say, I am not in the tune.

BUFO   Tune, tune? 'Sblood, d'ee take us for fiddlers, scrapers,
rime canters by tune? By this light, I'll scourge ye like a town top:
Look ye, I am urg'd—Ump—And there's a side blow for ye, like a
sober thing as ye are.   100

GROOM   Well done i'faith, precious Captain.

VELASCO   Dar'st thou do this to me knowing who I am?

BUFO   Yes, in the way of daring, I dare kick you thus, thus, Sir,
up and down. There's a jolt on the bum too: How d'ee like it?

95 up,] *Sedge*; up Q   97 scrapers] *Sedge*; scrappers Q   103 Sir,] *Sedge*; Sir Q

VELASCO   'Tis well! You use the priviledge of the place.   105
There was a time the best of all this Court
Durst not have lift a hand against me then.
But I must bear it now.

ALPHONSO   Is not this strange *Muretto*?

MURETTO   I can scantly credit mine own eyes: The Captain   110
follows his instructions perfectly.

BUFO   Not drink? Mahound, Infidel. I will fillip thy nose, spit in
thy face, Mungrel; brave, a Commander, ha?

VELASCO   O woman—woman—woman.

BUFO   That's a lie, a stark one, 'tis known I nere was a woman in   115
my life. I am weary beating of him, and can stand no longer.
Groom, kick him thou up and down in my behalf; or by this flesh
I'll swinge you, sirrah.

GROOM   Come aloft, Jackanapes: come aloft, sirrah.

                                        kicks, beates him

ALPHONSO   Why sure *Velasco* dares not fight.   120

MURETTO   It must be some or other hath bewitched him.

                    Enter PYNTO

PYNTO   Avant, I saw twelve dozen of Cuckolds in the middle
region of the air, galloping on a black Jack, Eastward ho. It is certain that every dozen went for a company, and they are now
become a corporation. *Aries* and *Taurus*, the Bull and the Ram,   125
two head signs, shall be henceforth their recognizances, set up in
the grand hall of their politick convocations—whirr, whirr, there,
there, just under the rainbow ambles *Mercury*, the thin bearded
thief that stole away the Drapers wife, while the good man was
made drunk at the Stillyard, at a beaver of Dutch bread and Renish   130
wine, and lay all night in pure holland in's stocking and shoes.
Pish, Talke not to me, I will maintain against the Universities of
both the *Indies*, that one Aldermans horse is more right worshipful, then any six Constables, brown bills and all. Now, now, now,
my brains burn in Sulphur, and thus will I stalk about, and swim   135

129 Drapers] *Sedge*; Drappers *Q*

through a whole Element of dainty, neat, brisk, rich claret, canary, or maligo. Am not I *Pynto*, have not I hiren here? What art thou, a full moon, or a moon calf?

BUFO   No, no, 'tis a dry Stock-fish, that must be beaten tender.

VELASCO   Was ever man so much a slave as I?   140

PYNTO   Does *Saturn* wince? Down with him, let *Charles* his wayn run over his North pole; it shall be justified too.

GROOM   Now, Sir, having taken a little breath, have at ye once D2ʳ more, and I have done.

Enter MOPAS *and* LODOVICO

MOPAS   Clubs, clubs, I have been the death of two Brewers   145 horses, and two catch-poles, my self, and now be try'd by two fools and ten knaves: O monstrous base, horrible; is my lord past recovery?

VELASCO   Hold, prethee, fellow hold, I have no sword,
   Or if I had, I dare not strike again.   150

BUFO   U'ds bones, were ye an invincible Armado, Ide pound ye all like brown paper rags.

LODOVICO   Let me be strucken blind! The shame of fate;
   Velasco, baffled, and not dare to strike!
   Dogs, drunken dogs, I'll whip ye to your kennels.   155

VELASCO   Nay good, forbear.

MOPAS   Bilbo come forth and shew thy foxes tayl. Nay, nay, give me liquor, and I'll fight like a rorer.

PYNTO   Keep standing, ho; the Almanack says plainly 'tis no season to be let blood, the sign is mortal. Hold!   160

ALPHONSO   Yes, I command. Uncivil ill bred beasts,
   How dares ye turn our pallace to a booth?
   How dare the proudest of ye all lift up
   A hand against the meanest of those creatures

159 standing,] *Sedge*; standing *Q*   161 Yes, . . . beasts,] *Sedge*; Yes . . . beasts. *Q*

Whom we do own for ours? Now, now you spit   165
The ancient rancor of your bitter galls
Wherewith you strove to wound us heretofore.

LODOVICO   We are abus'd, My Lord.

ALPHONSO   Fellow, Thou lyest.
Our Royal eyes beheld the pride and malice
Of thee *Velasco*; who in hate to us   170
Deny'st to honour our remembrance, though
But in a pledg'd health.

VELASCO   Therein I was wrong'd.

ALPHONSO   No, therein all thy cunning could not hide
The rage of thy malitious heart to us;
Yet know, for tryal of thy love we caus'd   175
This onset. We will justifie the hight
Of thy disgraces; what they did was ours.
Hence, Coward, baffled, kickt, despis'd and spurn'd.

BUFO   Hang thy self; a pox on thee.
        Exit ALPHONSO, MURETTO, PYNTO, BUFO, GROOM

LODOVICO   O y'are undon: What Devil, Hag, or Witch   180
Hath stoln your heart away?

VELASCO   I cannot tell.

LODOVICO   Not fight! 'Tis enough to shame us all.

VELASCO   Happy was I, that living liv'd alone,
Velasco was a man then, now is none.
        Exeunt [LODOVICO *and* VELASCO]

MOPAS   Is't even so, no man now; then I smell how things stand: 185
I'll lay my life, his lady sweet heart hath given him the Gleek, and
he in return hath gelded himself, and so both lost his courage and
his wits together.
        Exit

166 your] *Sedge*; you *Q*   176 onset.] *Sedge*; onset, *Q*   178 Hence,] *Sedge*; Hence *Q*
182 fight!] *Sedge*; fight *Q*

3.2   *Enter* QUEEN, ALMADA, COLLUMMELLO, PETRUCHI
      and HEROPHIL

QUEEN   Speak o're the words again; and good my lord
  Be sure you speak the same, the very words;
  Our Queen, our vertuous Queen; Was't so?

ALMADA   Just so;
  And was withal in carriage so most kinde,
  So Princely, that I must do wrong to gratitude,   5
  In wanting action to express his love.

QUEEN   I am the happiest she that lives. *Petruchi*,
  Was I mistook or no? Why, good my lords,
  Observe it well. There is a holy league
  Confirm'd and ratify'd 'twixt Love and Fate.   10
  This sacred Matrimonial tye of hearts,
  Call'd marriage, has Divinity within't.
  Prethee, *Almada*, tell me, smil'd the King
  When he commended to me?

ALMADA   Madam, yes;
  And affably concluded all in this;   15
  Commend us, and report us as you find.

QUEEN   For loves sakes, no man prattle of distrust.
D2ᵛ   It shall be treason whosoever says
  The King's unkinde. My thinks I am all air,
  My soul has wings.

PETRUCHI   And we are all o'rejoy'd   20
  In this sweet reconciliation.

QUEEN   Wee'll visit him (my Lords) in some rich mask
  Of rare device, as thus; Pish, now I think on't,
  The world yeelds not variety enough
  Of cost, that's worthy of his Royal eyes.   25
  Why, *Herophil?*

HEROPHIL   Here, Madam.

QUEEN   Now beshrew me
  But I could weep for anger—If 'twere possible

3.2] o s.d. *Almada*] *Almado* Q   3 vertuous] vetuous Q   8 Why,] *Sedge*; Why Q
13 *Almada*] *Almado* Q   25 eyes.] *Sedge*; eyes, Q   26 Why,] *Sedge*; Why Q

To get a chariot cut out of a rock,
Made all of one whole Diamond, drawn all on Pavements
Of pearls and amber, by four Ivory steeds   30
Of perfect Christal, this were worth presenting.
Or some bright cloud of Saphirs—Fy you are all
So dull, you do not love me.

COLUMELLO   Y'are transported
To strange impossibilities: our service
Shall wait upon your happiness.

QUEEN   Nay, nay,   35
I know you laugh at me, and well you may;
I talk I know not what. I would 'twere fit
To ask one queston of ye.

ALL   Madam, any thing.

QUEEN   You'l swear that I am Idle, yet you know
'Tis not my custom; Look upon me well;   40
Am I as fair as *Herophil*?

PETRUCHI   Yes, Madam,
Or any other creature else alive.

QUEEN   You make me blush in troth. O would the King
Could see me with your eyes. Or would I were
Much courser then I am to all the world;   45
So I might onely seem more fair to him.

                    Enter VELASCO *and* LODOVICO

See here come more. *Velasco*, thou art welcom.
Welcom, kinde *Lodovico*. You I know
Bring fresh supplies of comfort; do not cloud
Your news with circumstance: Say, doth the King   50
Expect me? Yes, good man, I know he does.
Speak briefly, good my Lord, and truly.

VELASCO   Madam, Take all at once, he is the King;
And Kings may do their pleasures.

QUEEN   True, *Velasco*.
But I have from my heart forgot remembrance   55

31 Christal,] *Sedge*; Christal; *Q*   48 Welcom,] *Sedge*; Welcom *Q*

Of former passages; the world is chang'd:
Is a' not justly royal?

LODOVICO Would a' were, I wish it for your sake, Madam,
but my wishes and his inclinations are quite opposite.

PETRUCHI What said you, *Lodovico?*   60

LODOVICO Thus *Petruchi.* *Velasco* hath been by the King
disgrac'd, by his minions abused, baffled, they justified by the
King in't. In a word; *Alphonso* is, and will be the scourge of
Arragon.

QUEEN I'll stop my ears, they shannot let in poyson,   65
Rank treacherous searching poyson.

ALMADA   'Tis impossible.

QUEEN Yes, 'tis impossible; but now I see
Y'are all agreed to curse me in the hight
Of my prosperities. O that at once
I could have leave to dye and shun the times.   70

               Enter MURETTO

MURETTO His excellent Majesty by me commends to your
Royal hands this letter, Madam.

QUEEN [*receiving the letter*] Why thus I kiss,
And kiss again; Welcom, what e'er it speaks.

MURETTO That you may all conceive (my Lords) the Kings   75
hearty zeal to unity and goodness, he by me intreats your attendance
on the Queen to him: To you, Signior *Petruchi*, he sends this
Diamond from his own finger.

PETRUCHI You strike me into wonder.

D3ʳ MURETTO I should excuse his highness | violence to you, my   80
lord *Velasco*; but he says, that your own indiscretion deserv'd your
late reproof: And futher, (pardon me that I mince not the sum of
his injunction) he says your cowardice is now so vulgarly palpable,
that it cannot stand with his honour to countenance so degenerat-
ing a spirit.   85

---

56 passages;] *Sedge*; passages, Q   58 sake,] *Sedge*; sake Q   77 you, Signior] *Sedge*; you
Signior, Q

VELASCO   I thank him; yet, if you remember well,
Both he and you prov'd me another man.

QUEEN   The sweetest letter that ever was writ:
Come we must to the King—How! 'Tis my ring,
The first ring that I ever gave the King.   90
Petruchi, I must have it.

PETRUCHI   'Twas the King sent it:
I mean to yeeld it back again.

QUEEN   No, I will.
And in exchange take that of equal value;
But not with me, 'cause it comes from my husband.
Let's slack no time, this day shall crown our peace.   95
               Exit all but VELASCO *and* LODOVICO

LODOVICO   You see, my Lord, how the world goes.
What your next course?

VELASCO   Would I could leave my self, I am unfit
For company of men: Art thou my friend?

LODOVICO   I cannot tell what I am, your patient humor indeed   100
perswades me I am nothing. Ladies little puppy dogs shortly
will break your shins with milke-sops, and you dare not cry,
come out, cur. Faith tell me for our wonted frindships sake;
hath not this Madam sweet heart of yours a share in your
Metamorphosis?   105

VELASCO   You are unkinde, as much as in a thought,
To wrong her vertue. *Lodovico*, no;
I have resolv'd never to fight again.

LODOVICO   'Tis a very safe resolution: but have you resolv'd
never to be beaten again?   110

VELASCO   That goodly sound of gallant valiant man
Is but a breath, and dyes as soon as utter'd.
I'll seek my fame henceforward in the praise
Of sufferance and patience, for rash man-hood
Adds onely life to cruelty, yet by cruelty   115

Takes life away, and leaves upon our souls
Nothing but guilt, while patience if it be
Settl'd, doth even in bondage keep us free.

LODOVICO   Excellent morality; but, good my Lord, without
more circumstance, the cause, let me know the ground and   120
cause on't.

VELASCO   My will, or if you please, my cowardice;
    More ask not, more, I vow, you shall not know.

Enter MOPAS

MOPAS   O Fy, fy, I were better be the Hangmans deputy, then my
Lord *Velasco*'s Gentleman usher; all the streets as I pass whoot at me,   125
and ask me if I be so valiant as my master the coward; they swear
their children carry woodden daggers to play a prize with him, and
there's no talk but of the arrant coward *Velasco*.

VELASCO   I care not, let 'em talk.

MOPAS   Care not? By these hilts, I had rather then a hundred   130
ducates, I had but as much spirit as to have drawn upon a couple
of men in Ginger-bread, which a hucsters crook't legged whorson
ape held up, and swore they were two taller fellows then you are.

LODOVICO   Your readiest way were to get you into a cloyster; for
there's no going to Court.   135

MOPAS   Yes, to have our brains rubb'd out with the heel of a
brown manchet.

VELASCO   As y'are my friend forbear to come more neer me.

                                                    Exit VELASCO

LODOVICO   Gone so quickly? *Mopas*, I'll finde out this mystery,
and thou shalt be the instrument.   140

D3ᵛ MOPAS   Shall I? Why agreed, let me | alone for an instrument, be
it a winde or string'd instrument, I'll sound at one end or other I'll
warrant ye.

                                                    Exeunt

119 but,] *Sedge*; but Q   122 please,] please Q   cowardice;] cowardice, Q   131 spirit]
Sedge; spirit: Q   135 Court.] *Sedge*; Court: Q   138 As] *Sedge*; As, Q   139 *Mopas*,]
Sedge; Mopas Q

3.3   *Enter* ALPHONSO, PYNTO, BUFO

ALPHONSO   Are all things ready as we gave charge?

PYNTO   Yes all, and the face of the heavens are passing favourable.

ALPHONSO   *Bufo*, Be it thy care, the watch word given,
To seize *Petruchi* suddenly.

BUFO   If the Devil be not in him, I'll make him fast enough.   5

ALPHONSO   Mean time wee'll take our place, they are at hand.
Some sound our choisest musick t'entertain
This QUEEN with all the seeming forms of State.

Loud Musick. Enter QUEEN *supported by* PETRUCHI, HEROPHIL,
COLLUMELLO, ALMADA, *and* MURETTO

ALL   All joy to *Aragons* great King.

ALPHONSO   You strive to act in words (my lords) but we our self   10
Indeavor rather how to speak in act.
Now is a time of peace, of amity.
The Queen is present; Lady, seat you here,
As neer, as if we plac'd you in our heart,
Where you are deep in thron'd.

QUEEN   As you in mine,   15
So may I ever live in yours, my Lord.

ALPHONSO   How so? You are too charitable now,
That covet but equality in love;
A cold, a frozen love; for I must think
The streams of your affections are dry'd up,   20
Or running from their wonted channels, range
In lawless paths of secresie and stealth;
Which makes us love you more.

QUEEN   I would your words
Dissented not from your resolved thoughts
For then (if I mistake not) you would feel   25
Extremity of passion, which indeed
Is noble jealousie.

3.3]   12 peace,] *Sedge*; peace Q

ALPHONSO   Are you so plain?
I thank you, Madam; lend me your fair hand.
What's here? O my presages! Whence got you this ring?

QUEEN   This ring, my lord?

ALPHONSO   This ring, my lord!   30
By honours reverend crest 'tis time to wake.
Art thou not pale, *Petruchi*?

PETRUCHI   Gratious Sir,
This is the ring you sent me by *Muretto*,
Which 'cause it came from you, the Queen would needs
Exchange it for another of her own.   35

ALPHONSO   True, 'cause it came from me, I take it so,
And grant ye, know the word: *'Tis won and lost.*

> *Enter a Guard,* BUFO *with them seize* PETRUCHI;
> PYNTO *the* QUEEN

PETRUCHI   What mean ye, Helhounds? Slaves, let go my sword.

BUFO   Keep in your chaps, and leave scolding, my small friend,
'tis now no time to wrangle or to rore.   40

QUEEN   Nay, nay, with what you please I am content.

COLUMELLO   What means your Highness?

ALMADA   Wronge not Majesty
With such unnoble rigour.

ALPHONSO   O, my lords,
The weight of all this shame falls heaviest here
In my afflicted bosome. Madman like   45
I would not credit what mine ears had heard
From time to time of that adulterous woman.
For this have I liv'd widowed from her bed,
Was deaf to proofs, to oaths, and ever thought
That whoredom could not suit her self so trimly   50
On vertues outside. But *Petruchi* there
Hath a loud speaking conscience, can proclaim
Her lust, and my dishonour.

---

28 you,] *Sedge*; you *Q*   hand.] hand, *Q*   32 Gratious Sir,] *Sedge*; Gratious, Sir. *Q*
37 word:] *Sedge*; word. *Q*   46 credit . . . heard] *Sedge*; credit, . . . heard, *Q*   53 dishonour.] *Sedge*; dishonour *Q*

PETRUCHI   Grant me hearing.   D4ʳ

ALPHONSO   Away with him to prison, make him fast On pain of
all your lives.   55

BUFO   Come, Sir, there is no playing fast and loose, which for a
ducat now.

          Exit BUFO [*and Guard?*] *with* PETRUCHI

COLUMELLO   But what now for the Queen?

ALPHONSO   As she deserves.

ALMADA   Our law requires a clear and open proof,
   And a juditial trial.

ALPHONSO   Yes to subjects   60
   It does, but who among you dares speak justice
   Against your natural Soveraign? Not one.

PYNTO   Your Majesty hath most wisely considered that point.

MURETTO   I have stood silent all this while, and cannot but with
astonishment and unutterable grief bear a share of sadness in these   65
disasters. But, Madam, be not altogether dejected on your part:
there is more mercy in this soveraign Prince, then that you should
any way distrust.

QUEEN   Nay, even proceed and question me no more.

ALPHONSO   I will be gentle to you, and the course   70
   That I will take shall merit your best thanks.
   If in a moneth a Champion shall appear,
   In single opposition to maintain
   Your honor, I will be the man my self
   In person to avouch this accusation: 75
   And which of us prevails, shall end this strife.
   But if none come, then you shall lose your head.
   Mean time your usage shall be like a Queen.

MURETTO   Now by the life of honour, 'tis a most Princely tryal,
and will be worth you eternal memory.   80

QUEEN   Where must I then be led!

---

56 for] *Sedge*; fit *Q*   74 honor,] *Sedge*; honor; *Q*

ALPHONSO   No where but here
  In our own palace; and as I am King,
  None worse then I shall be her Guardian.

ALMADA   Madam, Heaven is the Guardian of the just;
  You cannot miss a Champion.

QUEEN   E're I go,   85
  May I entreat a word?

ALPHONSO   O yes, you may.

QUEEN   *Collumello* and *Almada*, hear me,
  I speak to you, and to your felow Peers,
  Remember both by oaths and by allegiance
  You are my subjects.

COLUMELLO *and* ALMADA   Madam, true, we are.   90

QUEEN   Then as you ever bore respect or truth
  To me as to your Soveraign, I conjure ye
  Never to levy arms against the King,
  Singly or openly, and never else
  To justifie my right or wronge in this.   95
  For if you do, here I proclaim ye all
  Traytors to loyalty and me: for surety,
  I crave your oaths a new.

COLUMELLO and ALMADA   Since you enforce us,
  We sware: and heaven protect you.

QUEEN   Let me be gone.

ALPHONSO   Well as they please for that: 100
  Muretto, follow.
                        Exit all but ALMADA *and* COLLUMMELLO

ALMADA   Here is fine work, my lord. What's to be done?

COLUMELLO   Stand still while this proud Tyrant cuts our throats.

ALMADA   She's wrong'd, and this is onely but a plot.
  Velasco now might binde his Country to him;   105

But he is grown so cowardly and base,
That boys and children beat him as they list.

COLUMELLO   I have be thought me: we, with th' other Peers,
Will set a proclamation out, assuring
What worthy Knight soever undertakes,   110
By such a day, as Champion for the Queen,
Shall have a hundred thousand ducats paid,
Withal, what honors else he shall demand.

ALMADA   This must be speeded, or 'twill come to late.

COLUMELLO   It shall be suddain: Here our hope must stand;   115
Kings command Subjects; Heav'n doth Kings command.

                                      Exeunt   D4ᵛ

      4.1   *Enter* SALASSA *and* SHAPAROON

SALASSA   A coward? 'Tis impossible; *Velasco* a coward? The brave
man? The wonder of the time? Sure, *Shaparoon*, 'tis a meer scandal
rais'd by an enemy.

SHAPAROON   'Tis most certain, most apparent; Taylors,
Prentizes, nay, Bakers and Weavers (things that drink cannot put   5
spirit into, they are such mighty bread-eaters), they, as I am an
honest woman, fling old shoes at him, and he dares not turn back
to give an angry word.

SALASSA   I had been sweetly promoted to such a tame Champion.

SHAPAROON   Gallants! Out upon 'em, 'tis your tough clown is   10
your only raiser up of man or woman.

SALASSA   A Proclimation is sent out for certain?

SHAPAROON   Most assuredly.

SALASSA   The sum proposed, a hundred thousand ducats.

SHAPAROON   Present payment, without attendance.   15

SALASSA   'Tis a glorious reward—speak low, and observe.

        Enter MOPAS *reading a Proclamation*

108 me:] *Sedge*; me, *Q*   111 Queen,] *Sedge*; Queen. *Q*   **4.1**] 5 Weavers] Weavers; *Q*
6 bread-eaters),] bread-eaters) *Q*   they,] *Sedge*; they *Q*

MOPAS 'Whosoever, man or woman, can, or will procure any
such foresaid defendant, against the said day; let them, him,
or she repair to the said lords of the Councel, and give in such
sufficient assurance for such defence, and they or any of them shall   20
receive a hundred thousand ducats in ready cash; with what honors may give them, him, or her content or satisfaction.' O that
I durst be valiant: A hundred thousand. A hundred thousand; how
it rumbles in my chops.

SALASSA   Prethee, a word, my friend.   25

MOPAS   Sweet Lady, all fair weather upon ye. As for you, Madam,
time was, I recommend to your ancient remembrance, time is
past: with my service forwards and backwards, when 'tis time present, resting yours in the whole, *Mopas.*

SHAPAROON   Very courtly and pithy.   30

SALASSA   Pray let me view your paper.

MOPAS   'Tis your ladiships.

SHAPAROON   Some proclamation as I take it.

MOPAS   Madam Reverence, you have taken it in the right cue.

SALASSA   I am o'rejoy'd; there's gold for thy news. Friend, I will   35
make thee the happiest and most welcom messenger to thy lord,
that ever received thanks from him; without delay, wait on me for
instructions.

MOPAS   I am at your ladiships beck.

Exeunt

4.2   *Enter* ALPHONSO, *and* MURETTO

MURETTO   True, true, Sir, you are set high upon the stage for
action. O the top of my ambition, my hearts Idol! What a perplex-
ity are you twin'd into? And justly; so justly, that it is hard to judge,
whether your happiness were greater in the possession of an
unmatchable beauty, or your present misery, by inforcing that   5
beauty to expose her honor to so apparent a contempt: This is not
the least, that might have been in time prevented.

17–22 'Whosoever, . . . satisfaction.'] *Sedge;* no quotation marks in *Q.*   29 whole,] *Sedge;*
whole *Q*   35 Friend,] Friend. *Q*

ALPHONSO   O I am lost *Muretto*, my sunke eyes
  Are buried in their hollows: busie thoughts
  Press on like legions of infernal hags   10
  To menace my destruction: Yet my judgment
  Still prompts my senses that my Queen is fair.

MURETTO   Fair! Unspeakable workmanship of Heavens bounty.
Were all the skilfullest Painters that ever discern'd colours moulded
into one, to perfect an Artist, yet that Artist should sooner want   15
fansie or imagination, for personating a curious medal, then ever
to patern a counterfeit so exquisitely excellent, as is the QUEEN by
nature.

ALPHONSO   I have surveyed the wonder of her cheeks,
  Compar'd them with the lillies and the rose   20
  And by my life, *Muretto*, Roses are   E1ʳ
  Adulterate to her blush, and lilies pale,
  Examin'd with her white; yet, blear eyed fool,
  I could not see those rarities before me.

MURETTO   Every man is blind (my lord) in his own happiness,   25
there's the curse of our mortality. She was the very tale of the
world: Her perfections busied all tongues. She was the onely wish
of *Europes* chiefest Monarchs, whose full fruition you (and 'twas
your capital sin) most inhumanly abandoned.

ALPHONSO   Villain, *Petruchi*, let me for ever curse him: 30
  Had he not been the man; who else had durst
  To hazard a denyal from her scorns?

MURETTO   See now herein you are monstrous discourteous,
above excuse; why, Sir, what hath *Petruchi* done? Which (from any
King to a Vassal) al men would not eagerly have persued. Alas, my   35
lord, his nobleness is eternal, by this means, in attempting, and his
felicity unmatchable in injoying, the glory of his time, a beauty so
conquering, so unparalell'd.

ALPHONSO   She is superlative.

MURETTO   Divine.   40

4.2] 12 senses] *Sedge*; senses, Q   14–15 colours . . . an Artist,] *Sedge*; colours, . . . an Artist.
Q   20 with] *Sedge*; wth Q   28 Monarchs,] *Sedge*; Monarchs. Q   36–7 attempting,
. . . unmatchable] *Sedge*; attempting . . . unmatchable, Q   37 injoying,] injoying
Q   beauty] *Sedge*; beau Q

ALPHONSO   Rich, bright.

MURETTO   Immortal.

ALPHONSO   Too too worthy for a man.

MURETTO   The Gods might enjoy her.

ALPHONSO   Nature ne're fram'd so sweet a creature.   45

MURETTO   She is self Nature's Nature.

ALPHONSO   Let me for ever curse the frail condition
Of our deluded faculties, *Muretto*;
Yet being all, as she is all, her best
Is worst considering that she is a wanton.   50

MURETTO   Build you a Palace, arch it with Diamonds, roof it
with Carbuncles, pave it with Emraulds, daub it with Gold, furnish
it with all what cost can lay on, and then seal up the doors, and at
best 'tis but a solitary nest for Owles and Daws. Beauty was not
meerly created for wonder, but for use: 'Tis you were in the fault;   55
'tis you perswaded her, urg'd, compell'd, inforc'd her: I know it,
my truth and plainness trumpets it out to ye: Besides, women (my
lord) are all creatures, not Gods nor Angels.

ALPHONSO   I must confess 'tis true, yet by my Crown
She dyes, if none defend her, I'm resolv'd.   60

MURETTO   'Tis a heroical disposition, and with your honour she
cannot, must not live. Here's the point; If she live and you receive
her to favour, you will be a noted Cuckold; which is a recognizance dishonorable to all, but to a King fearfully infamous. On the
other side, if you prevail, and she be put to death, you do as it were 65
deprive the Firmanent of the Sun, and your self of the treasure of
the whole earth.

ALPHONSO   Right, right, *Muretto*, there thou strik'st the wound
Too deeply to be cur'd, yet I must do't.
I would fain see her now.   70

MURETTO   Pray do, Sir; and let *Petruchi* come face to face to
her; observe them both, but be very mild to both: use extremity
to neither.

48 faculties, *Muretto*,] faculties: *Muretto*, Q

ALPHONSO   Well counsell'd; call them hither, but none with them:
Wee'll strive with grief.   [*Exit* MURETTO]
                         Heaven! I am plung'd at full.   75
Never henceforward shall I slumber out
One peaceful hour; my enraged blood
Turns coward to mine honour. I could wish
My Queen might live now though I did but look
And gaze upon her cheeks, her ravishing cheeks.   80
But, oh, to be a Cuckold; 'sdeath, she dyes.

> *Enter at one door* PETRUCHI, *and the other* MURETTO *and the*
> QUEEN, *they stand at several ends of the Stage*

MURETTO   My gratious Lord.

ALPHONSO   Reach yond fair sight a chair,
That man a stool; sit both, wee'll have it so.

MURETTO   'Tis Kingly done; in any case | (my lord) curb now a   E1ᵛ
while the violence of your passion, and be temperate.   85

QUEEN   Sir, 'tis my part to kneel, for on your brow
I read sad sentence of a troubled wrath,
And that is argument enough to prove
My guilt, not being worthy of your favour.

PETRUCHI   Let me kneel too, though not for pardon, yet   90
In duty to this presence: else I stand
As far from falsehood, as is that from truth.

MURETTO   Nay, Madam, this is not the promise on your part.
It is his pleasure you should sit.

QUEEN   His pleasure is my law.

ALPHONSO   Let him sit too, the man.
                                      Both sit

PETRUCHI   Sir, you are obey'd.   95

ALPHONSO   Between my comforts and my shame I stand
In equal distance; this way let me turn
To thee, thou woman. Let me dull mine eyes

---

74 grief.] *Sedge*; grief, *Q*   83 stool;] stool, *Q*   92 truth.] *Sedge*; truth *Q*   93 this
is] *Sedge*; this *Q*   94 man.] *Sedge*; man, *Q*   98 thee,] *Sedge*; thee *Q*

With surfeit on thy beauty. What art thou,
Great dazeling splendor? Let me ever look   100
And dwell upon this presence.

MURETTO   Now it works.

ALPHONSO   I am distract. Say? What! Do not, do not—

MURETTO   My lord the King—Why, Sir?—He is in a trance, or
else metamorphis'd to some some pillar of marble: How fixedly a'
stands. D'ee hear, Sir? What d'ee dream on? My lord, this is your 105
Queen; speak to her.

ALPHONSO   May I presume with my irreverent lips
To touch your sacred hand.

QUEEN   I am too wretched
To be thought but the subject of your mirth.

ALPHONSO   Why she can speak, *Muretto*! [*To the* QUEEN] O tell
me pray,   110
And make me ever, ever fortunate;
Are you a mortal creature? Are ye indeed
Moulded of flesh and blood like other women?
Can you be pittiful? Can ye vouchsafe
To entertain fair parley? Can you love,   115
Or grant me leave to love you; can you, say?

QUEEN   You know too well, my lord, instead of granting,
I ow a duty, and must sue to you,
If I may not displease.

ALPHONSO   Now I am great,
You are my Queen, and I have wrong'd a merit,   120
More then my service in the humblest lowness
Can ever recompence. I'll rather wish
To meet whole hosts of dangers, and encounter
The fabled whips of steel, then ever part
From those sweet eyes: not time shall sue divorce   125
'Twixt me and this great miracle of Nature.
Muretto?

MURETTO   Soveraign Sir.

99 thou,] *Sedge*; thou *Q*   106 Queen;] *Sedge*; Queen *Q*   110 *Muretto!*] *Sedge*;
Muretto? Q   124 fabled] *Sedge*; flabled *Q*

ALPHONSO   I'll turn away,
And mourn my former errors.—Worse then death!
Look where a Basilisk with murthering flames
Of poyson, strikes me Blinde. [*To* PETRUCHI] Insatiate tempter, 130
Patern of lust, 'tis thou alone hast sundred
Our lawful bride bed, planted on my crest
The horned Satyrs badge; hast soyl'd a beauty
As glorious, as sits yonder on her front.
Kill him, *Muretto*, why should he receive   135
The benefit of the law, that us'd no law
In my dishonours?

PETRUCHI   Were you more a King
Then Royalty can make you, though opprest
By your commanding powers, yea, and curb'd
In bonds most falsely, yet, give me a sword   140
And strip me to my shirt, I will defend
Her spotless vertue, and no more esteem,
In such a noble cause, an host of Kings,   E2ʳ
Then a poor stingless swarm of buzzing flies.

QUEEN   *Petruchi*, in those words thou dost condemn   145
Thy loyalty to me; I shall disclaim
All good opinion of thy worth or truth,
If thou persevere to affront my lord.

PETRUCHI   Then I have done. Here's misery unspeakable;
Rather to yeeld me guilty wrongfully,   150
Then contradict my wrongs.

ALPHONSO   High impudence.
Could she be ten times fairer then she is,
Yet I would be reveng'd. You sweet, I would
Again—Her beams quite blast me.

MURETTO   If you will be an Eaglet of the right aery, you must 155
endure the Sun. Can you chuse but love her?

ALPHONSO   No by the Stars. [*To the* QUEEN] Why would not
you be honest; and know how I do dote?

QUEEN   May I be bold
To say I am, and not offend?

128 errors. . . . death!] errors . . . death *Q*   146 me;] me, *Q*

ALPHONSO   Yes, yes,   160
Say so for heavens love, though you be as fowl
As sin can black your purity. Yet tell me
That you are white and chast, that while you live
The span of your few dayes, I may rejoyce
In my deluded follies; least I dye   165
Through anguish, e're I have reveng'd my injury,
And so leave you behind me for another;
That were intollerable.

QUEEN   Heaven knows, I ne're abus'd my self or you.

PETRUCHI   As much sware I, and truly.

ALPHONSO   Thou proud Devil,   170
Thou hast a lying tongue; They are consented
In mischief. Get ye hence, seducing horrors.
I'll stop mine eyes and ears till you are gone.
As you would be more merciful, away,
Or as you would finde mercy.   175
                    Exeunt QUEEN, PETRUCHI *contrary waies*

MURETTO   Sir, they are gone.

ALPHONSO   And she too; then let me be seen no more.
I am distracted, both waies I feel my blame;
To leave her death, to live with her is shame.   *Exit*

MURETTO   Fare ye well, King. This is admirable; I will be chron- 180
icled, all my business ripens to my wishes. And if honest intentions
thrive so successfully; I will henceforth build upon this assurance,
that there can hardly be a greater Hell or Damnation, then in
being a Villane upon earth.

                                                         Exit

        4.3   *Enter* LODOVICO, SALASSA, SHAPAROON

LODOVICO   I am wonder stricken—And were you i'faith the she,
indeed, that turn'd my Lords heart so handsomly, so cunningly?
O how I reverence wit. Well, lady, you are as pestilent a piece of
policy, as ever made an ass of love.

SALASSA   But, *Lodovico,* I'll salve all again quickly.   5

163 chast,] *Sedge;* chast; *Q*   172 hence,] *Sedge;* hence *Q*   177 too;] too *Q*
180 well, King.] *Sedge;* well King, *Q*   admirable;] admirable, *Q*   **4.3**] 1 she,] she *Q*

SHAPAROON   Yes indeed forsooth, she has the trick on't.

LODOVICO   You have undertaken with the lords already, you say.

SALASSA   I have, and my life is at stake, but I fear not that.

LODOVICO   Pish, you have no need; one smile or kinde simper
from you does all; I warrant ye the sight of so much gold, as you   10
are to receive, hath quickned your love infinitely.

SALASSA   Why, Sir, I was not worthy of my lords love before;
I was too poor: but now two hundred thousand ducats is a dower
fit for a lord.

LODOVICO   Marry is't. I applaud your consideration. 'Twas neatly   15
thought on.

Enter COLLUMELLO *and* ALMADA

COLUMELLO   Have you prevail'd yet, lady; time runs on,
You must not dally.

SALASSA   Good my lords, fear nothing:
Were it but two hours to't, I should be ready.   E2ᵛ

Enter VELASCO *very sad*

LODOVICO   He comes himself; 'tis fit we stood unseen.   20
Ply him soundly, lady.

ALMADA   Let us withdraw then.
Exeunt [*all but* VELASCO *and* SALASSA]

VELASCO   I cannot be alone, still I am hunted
With my confounding thoughts: Too late I finde,
How passions at their best are but sly traytors
To ruin honour. That which we call love,   25
Was by the wisest power above forethought
To check our pride. Thus when men are blown up
At the highest of conceit, then they fall down
Even by the peevish follies of their frailties.

SALASSA   The best of my lord *Velasco*'s wishes ever   30
Crown him with all true content.

VELASCO   Cry ye mercy, Lady.

9 smile] *Sedge*; smile, *Q*   13 ducats] *Sedge*; ducats, *Q*   17 lady;] lady, *Q*   20 himself;] *Sedge*; himself, *Q*   30 ever] *Sedge*; ever. *Q*

SALASSA   I come to chide you, my Lord; can it be possible that ever any man could so sincerely profess such a mightiness of affection, as you have done to me, and forget it all so soon, and so unkindely?   35

VELASCO   Are you a true, very lover, or are you bound
    For pennance to walk to some holy shrine
    In visitation? I have seen that face.

SALASSA   Have you so? O you are a hot lover; a woman is in fine case to weep out her eyes for so uncertain a friend, as your protes- 40
tations urg'd me to conceive you: But come I know what you'll say aforehand, I know you are angry.

VELASCO   Pray give me leave to be my own tormentor.

SALASSA   Very angry, extreamly angry; But as I respect perfection, tis more then I deserve. Little know you the misery I have 45
endured, and all about a hasty word of nothing, and I'll have it prove nothing e're we part.

VELASCO   Her pride hath made her lunatick, alas!
    She hath quite lost her wits; those are the fruits
    Of scorns and mockeries.   50

SALASSA   To witness how indearedly I prefer your merits, and love your person, in a word, my lord, I absolve you, and set you free from the injunction I bound you in; as I desire to thrive, I meant all but for a tryal in jest.

VELASCO   These are no words of madness; whither tends 55
    The extremity of your invention, Lady?
    I'll swear no more.

SALASSA   I was too blame, but one fault (me thinks) is to be pardoned, when I am yours and you firmly mine: I'll bear with many in you.   60

VELASCO   So, if you be in earnest; What's the matter?

SALASSA   The sum of all is, that I know it suits not with the bravery of the lord *Velasco*'s spirit, to suffer his Queen and soveraign

32 you,] *Sedge*; you *Q*   35 unkindely?] *Sedge*; unkindely. *Q*   36 true,] *Sedge*; true *Q*
49 wits;] wits, *Q*   52 person,] person; *Q*

stand wrongfully accused of dishonour, and dye shamefully for a
fault never committed.   65

VELASCO   Why 'tis no fault of mine.

SALASSA   Nor shall it be of mine: Go be a famous subject; be a
ransomer of thy Queen from dangers, be registred thy Countries
patron: Fight in defence of the fairest and innocentest princess
alive: I with my heart release you. First conquer; that done, enjoy   70
me ever for thy wife: Velasco, I am thine.

VELASCO   Pish, you release me! All their cunning strains
    Of policy that set you now a work,
    To treble ruin me, in life, fame, soul,
    Are foolish and unable to draw down   75
    A greater wrath upon my head; in troth
    You take a wrong course, lady.

SALASSA   Very good, Sir, 'tis prettily put off, and wondrous modestly, I protest; no man hath enjoyn'd me to this task; 'tis onely to
do service to the State, and honour to you.   80

VELASCO   No man enjoyn'd you but your self?

SALASSA   None else, as I ever had truth in me.

VELASCO   Know then from me, you are a wicked woman,   E3ʳ
    And avarice, not love to me, hath forc'd ye
    To practice on my weakness. I could raile,   85
    Be most uncivil; But take all in short:
    I know you not.

SALASSA   Better and better, the man will triumph anon sure.
Prethee, good, dissemble no longer; I say you shall fight, I'll have
it so: I command you fight, by this kiss you shall.   90

VELASCO   Forbear, let me in peace bid you forbear;
    I will be henceforth still a stranger to you,
    Ever a stranger; look, look up; up there
    My oath is bookt; no humane power can free me.

72 me!] *Sedge*; me, *Q*   77 course,] *Sedge*; course *Q*   79 task;] *Sedge*; task *Q*
88 sure.] sure; *Q*   89 good,] *Sedge*; good *Q*   93 stranger;] stranger, *Q*   up; up] *Sedge*;
up, up *Q*   94 bookt;] *Sedge*; bookt, *Q*

SALASSA   I grant you none but I.

VELASCO   Be not deceived, I have   95
Forgot your scorns: you are lost to me.
Witness the Genius of this place, how e're
You tempt my constancy, I dare not fight.

SALASSA   Not dare to fight, what, not for me?

VELASCO   No, Lady.
I durst not, must not, cannot, will not fight.   100

SALASSA   O me undone.

VELASCO   What ayles you?

SALASSA   Now my life
Hath run it's last for I have pawn'd it, Sir,
To bring you forth as champion for the Queen.

VELASCO   And so should have the promis'd Gold.

SALASSA   I, I.

VELASCO   You have reveng'd my wrongs upon your selfe.   105
I cannot helpe you, nay, alas, you know
It lay not in me.

SALASSA   O take pitty on mee,
Look heer, I hold my hands up, bend my knees,
Heaven can require no more.

VELASCO   Then kneel to heaven:
I am no God, I cannot do you good.   110

SALASSA   Shall not my tears prevayle? Hard-hearted Man.
Dissembler, loves dishonour, bloody butcher
Of a poor Lady, be assured my Ghost
Shall haunt thy soule when I am dead.

VELASCO   Your curse
Is falne upon your own head; herein show   115
A noble piety, to beare your death

96 scorns:] scorns; *Q*   me.] *Sedge*; me, *Q*   99 what,] what *Q*   100 No,] *Sedge*; No *Q*
102 it, Sir,] *Sedge*; it Sir *Q*   106 nay, alas,] *Sedge*; nay alas *Q*   109 heaven:] heaven *Q*
115 your] *Sedge*; youur *Q*   head;] head, *Q*

With resolution, and for finall answer,
Lady, I will not fight to gain the world.

Exit

SALASSA   Gone! I have found at length my just reward,
And henceforth must prepare to welcom Death.   120
Velasco, I begin to love thee now.
Now I perceave thou art a noble man,
Compos'd of Goodnes; what a foole was I?
It grieves me more to loose him then to die.

Enter ALMADA, COLUMELLO, LODOVICO, SHAPROON

COLUMELLO   Lady, we have heard all that now hath past.   125
You have deceav'd your selfe and us; the time
We should have spent in seeking other means
Is lost, of which you are the cause.

ALMADA   And for it
The senats strickt decree craves execution.
What can you say?   130

SALASSA   My Lords, I can no more but yeild me to the law.

SHAPAROON   O that ever you were born! You have made a sweet
hand on't, have you not?

LODOVICO   Here is the right recompence of a vain confidence,
Mistresse: But I will not torture you, being so neer your end;   135
lady, say your prayers and die in Charity; that's all the pitty I can
take on ye.

Exit LODOVICO

COLUMELLO   Ten times the gold you should have had now, Lady,
cannot release you.

ALMADA   You alone are shee   140
Ruins your country. Heres the price of sin:
Ill thrift. All loose in seeking all to win.

Exeunt all but SHAPROON   E3ᵛ

117–18 answer, | Lady,] *Sedge*; answer | Lady *Q*   121 *Velasco*,] *Sedge*; *Velasco Q*
123 Goodnes;] Goodnes, *Q*   125 Lady, . . . past.] *Sedge*; Lady . . . past, *Q*   126 us;]
us, *Q*   127 means] *Sedge*; means. *Q*   129 execution.] *Sedge*; execution, *Q*
131 Lords,] *Sedge*; Lords *Q*   132 born! . . . not?] *Sedge*; born, . . . not. *Q*   135 you,]
you *Q*   135–6 end; . . . Charity;] end, . . . Charity, *Q*   136–7 lady, . . . ye.] *Sedge*; lady . . .
ye. *Q*   138 had now, Lady,] *Sedge*; had, now Lady *Q*   141 sin:] *Sedge*; sin,
Q   142 thrift.] thrift, *Q*

SHAPAROON   Nay, even go thy ways; 'tis an old proverbe that leachery and covetousnes go together, and 'tis a true one too. But I'le shift for one. If some proper squire or lustly yeoman have a 145 mind to any thing I have about me, 'a shall soon know what to trust too for I see the times are very troublesome.

Enter PYNTO

PYNTO   Now is the prosperous season when the whole round of the planets are coupling together. Let birds and beasts observe valentines day; I am a man and all times are with me in season. 150 This same Court ease hath sett my blood on tiptoe: I am Madder then a march hare.

SHAPAROON   Blessing on your fair face, your handsome hand, your clean foot, sir. Are you a Courtier, sir?

PYNTO   Good starrs direct me, sweet woman, I am a Courtier; if 155 you have any suit, what is't, what is't? Be short.

SHAPAROON   [*Aside*] Lord, what a Courteous proper man 'a is; trust me, 'a hath a most eloquent beard. [*To* PYNTO] Suit, Sir? Yes, Sir; I am a countrey gentlewoman by father and Mothers side, one that comes to see fashions and learne newes. And How I pray, sir 160 (if I may be so bold to aske) stand things at Court, Sir, now a dayes?

PYNTO   A very modest, necessary and discreet Question. Indeed, Mistris Countrey-Gentlewoman, things at Court stand as they were ever wont, some stiffe and some slacke, every thing accord- 165 ing to the imployment it hath.

SHAPAROON   Mary, the more pitty sir, that they have not all good doing a like, methinkes; they should be all and at all times ready heer.

PYNTO   You speake by a figure, by your leave, in that. But 170 because you are a stranger, I will a little more amply informe you. Heer at our Court of *Arragon*, Schollars for the most part

---

143 Nay, . . . ways;] Nay . . . ways, Q   144 too.] *Sedge*; too, Q   150 day; . . . season.] *Sedge*; day, . . . season, Q   151 tiptoe:] tiptoe, Q   154 foot, sir.] foot sir, Q   Courtier,] *Sedge*; Courtier Q   155 Courtier] Courtier, Q   157 Lord,] *Sedge*; Lord Q   is;] is, Q 158–9 Suit, Sir? Yes, Sir;] *Sedge*; Suit Sir, Yes Sir, Q   160 pray,] *Sedge*; pray Q   161 Court, Sir,] *Sedge*; Court Sir Q   163 modest, . . . Indeed,] *Sedge*; modest . . . Indeed Q 168 methinkes;] methinkes, Q   171 little] *Sedge*; litte Q

are the veriest fooles for that they are allways beggerly and prowd. And foolish citizens the wisest schollars for that they never run at charges for greater learning to cast up their reck'nings, then their Horn-book. Here every old lady is cheaper then a proctor, and will as finely convey an open act, without any danger of a consistory. Love and money sweepes all before them, be they cut or longtayle. Do not I deserve a kisse for this discovery, Mistris.

SHAPAROON A kisse! O my dear chastity, yes indeed forsooth, and I pray please your selfe.

PYNTO Good wench by Venus, but are you any thing rich?

SHAPAROON Rich enough to serve my turn.

PYNTO I see you are reasonable fair.

SHAPAROON I ever thought my selfe so.

PYNTO Will you survey my lodgings?

SHAPAROON At your pleasure, sir, being under your gard as I am.

Enter MOPAS *and* BUFO

BUFO Sirrha *Mopas*, If my mistresse say but the word, thou shalt see what an exployt I will doe.

MOPAS You'le undertake it, you say? Though your throat be cut in your own defence, 'tis but manslaughter: you can never be hang'd for it.

BUFO Nay, I am resolute in that point. Heer's my hand: let him shrinke that list, I'le not flinch a hayres breadth, *Mopas*.

MOPAS What, old huddle and twang so close at it, and the dog dayes so neer! [*To* PYNTO] H+ark ye, your lady is going the way of all flesh. [*To* SHAPAROON] And so is that schollar with you, methinkes, though not in the same cue, is 'a not?

173 allways] *Sedge*; allways, *Q*   180 discovery,] *Sedge*; discovery *Q*   181 kisse!] kisse, *Q*   188 pleasure, sir,] *Sedge*; pleasure sir *Q*   190 exployt] *Sedge*; exployt, *Q* 191 it, . . . say?] *Sedge*; it . . . say, *Q*   192 manslaughter:] manslaughter, *Q*   194 Nay, . . . point. . . . shrinke] *Sedge*; Nay . . . point, . . . shrinke, *Q*   hand:] hand, *Q*   195 breadth,] *Sedge*; breadth *Q*   197 neer!] *Sedge*; neer, *Q*   198 you,] *Sedge*; you *Q*

SHAPAROON   'A has promist to tell me my fortune at his cham- 200
ber, and do me some other good for my ladies safety.

PYNTO   I have spoken, the planets shall be rul'd by me, Captain,
you know they shall.

BUFO   Let the planets hang themselves in the elements, what
care I; I have other matters to trouble my braines.   205

MOPAS   Signior *Pynto*, take her to you, as true a mettall'd blade
as ever was turn'd into a dudgion; hearke in your eare.

Enter LODOVICO *and* HEROPHILL

LODOVICO   I know not how to trust you, you ar all so fickle, so
E4ʳ unconstant.

HEROPHIL   If I faile, let me be mark't a Strumpet.   210

LODOVICO   I apprehend you use him kindly still,
    See where 'a is. Captain, you are well mett;
    Her'es one whose heart you have.

HEROPHIL   He knowes he has.

BUFO   Why, by my troth, I thanke you forsooth; 'tis more of your 215
curtesie then my deserving, but I shall study to deserve it.

HEROPHIL   I hope so, and doubt it not.

LODOVICO   Madam, Cosen *Shaproon.*

SHAPAROON   You are welcom, sir.

PYNTO   Cosen, Nay then I smell she is a gentlewoman indeed.   220

MOPAS   Yes, and as antiently descended as Flesh and blood can
derive her.

PYNTO   I am a made man and I will have her.

HEROPHIL   You'le walke with me, sir?

BUFO   Even through fire and water, sweet Mistres.   225

205 I; I] I, I Q   206 *Pynto,*] *Sedge*; *Pynto Q*   207 dudgion;] dudgion, Q
208 fickle,] *Sedge*; fickle Q   212 is. Captain, . . . mett;] *Sedge*; is, Captain . . . mett, Q
215 Why, . . . troth,] *Sedge*; Why . . . troth Q   forsooth;] forsooth, Q   218 Madam,]
Sedge; Madam Q   219 welcom,] *Sedge*; welcom, Q   224 me,] *Sedge*; me Q
225 water,] *Sedge*; water. Q

LODOVICO   Let's every one to what concerns us most,
For now's the time all must be sav'd or lost.

Exeunt all

5.1   *A Scaffold Enter* VELASCO *and* LODOVICO

VELASCO   This is not kindly done, nor like a friend.

LODOVICO   Keep your chamber then, what should owles and
batts do abroad by day light? Why, you are become so notoriously
ridiculous, that a Craven is reputed of nobler spirit amongst birds,
then *Velasco* among men.   5

VELASCO   Why, *Lodovico*, dost thou tempt my wrongs?
O friend, 'tis not an honor or a fame
Can be a gain to me, though I should dare
To entertain this Combatt; say my fate
Did crown mine arm with conquest of the King,   10
Put case the cause add glory to the justice
Of my prevaling sword, what can I win?
Saving a pair of lives I lose a soule,
My rich soule, *Lodovico*. Does not yet
The heart even shrill within thee? All thy spirits   15
Melt into Passions, All thy manhood stagger
Like mine? Nay canst thou chuse but now confess
That this word Coward is a name of Dignity?

LODOVICO   Faint hearts and strong toungs are the tokens of many
a tall prattling Ghossipe. Yet the truth is you have halfe convinced   20
me. But to what end will you be a looker on the Tragedy of this shee
Beast? It will but breed your greater vexation.

VELASCO   I hope not so, I looke for Comfort in't.

LODOVICO   Mass: that may be too, it cannot but make your
melancholy a little merry, to see the woodcockes neck caught in a   25
worse noose, then shee had set for you.

VELASCO   That's but a poor revenge, I'de rather weep
On her behalfe, but that I hope her courage
Will triumph over Death.

5.1] o *Scaffold*] *Sedge*; Scassold *Q*   6 Why, *Lodovico*,] *Sedge*; Why *Lodovico* *Q*
9 Combatt;] *Sedge*; Combatt, *Q*   12 sword,] *Sedge*; sword? *Q*   14 soule, *Lodovico*.]
Sedge; soule *Lodovico*, *Q*   21 me.] *Sedge*; me, *Q*

LODOVICO   My Lord, they come.

VELASCO   Let me stand back unseen. Good Angells guard her.   30
                    VELASCO *Muffles himselfe*

Enter executioner before SALASSA, *her Hayre loose, after her,*
ALMADA, COLLUMELLO *and officers*

ALMADA   Tis a sad welcom
    To bid you welcome to the stroak of Death,
    Yet you are come too't, Lady.

COLUMELLO   And a curse
    Throughout the land will be your generall knell,
    For having bin the wilfull overthrow,   35
    First of your Countreys Champion, next your Queen,
E4ᵛ   Your Lawfull Soveraign, who this very day
    Must act a part which you must act before,
    But with less guilt.

ALMADA   Use no long speeches, lady,
    The danger of the time calls us away,   40
    We cannot listen to your farewells now.

SALASSA   I have few words to say: my heart is lodg'd
    In yon same upper Parliament, yet now
    If ere I part, and shall be seen no more,
    Some man of mercy could but truly speake   45
    One word of pardon from the Lord *Velasco*,
    My peace were made in earth, and I should fly
    With wings of speed to Heaven.

ALMADA   Pish, here's not any.

SALASSA   Not any? On then, why should I prolong
    A minute more of life, that live so late,   50
    Where most I strive for love to purchace hate?
    Beare witnes, Lords, I wish not to call back
    My younger dayes in promise that I would
    Redeem my fault and do in *Velasco* right,

29 Lord,] *Sedge*; Lord *Q*   30 unseen.] *Sedge*; unseen, *Q*   31 welcom] *Sedge*; welcom. *Q*
32 Death,] *Sedge*; Death. *Q*   33 too't,] *Sedge*; too't *Q*   37 day] *Sedge*; day. *Q*
39 speeches,] *Sedge*; speeches *Q*   40 time] *Sedge*; time, *Q*   42 say:] say,
Q   48 Pish,] *Sedge*; Pish *Q*   51 hate?] *Sedge*; hate , *Q*   52 witnes, Lords,] *Sedge*;
witnes Lords *Q*

But could I but reverse the doom of time,   55
I would with humblest suit make prayers to heaven
For his long florishing welfare.

COLUMELLO   Dispatch, dispatch;
You should have thought on this before, pray now
For your own health, for you have need to pray.

LODOVICO   Madam *Salassa*, I am bold to take leave of ye before   60
your long journey: All the comfort that I can give you is, that the
weather is like to hold very fair, you need not take much care for
either hood or cloke for the matter.

SALASSA   Are you come? Worthy Sir, then I may hope
Your noble friend hath sent one gentle sigh   65
To grace my funeral: For vertues sake
Give me a life in death; tell me, O tell me,
If he but seal my pardon, all is well.

LODOVICO   Say ye so? Why then in a word, go merrily up the
stayers; my lord *Velasco* desires Heaven may as heartily forgive   70
him, as he does you.

SALASSA   Enough, I thank his bounty, on I go
                    Goes up the Scaffold
To smile on horror: so, so, I'm up,
Great in my lowness, and to witness further
My humbleness, here let me kneel and breath   75
My penitence: O women, in my fall,
Remember that your beauties, youth and pride
Are but gay tempters, 'less you wisely shun
The errors of your frailties: let me ever
Be an example to all fickle dames,   80
That folly is no shrine for vertuous names.
Heaven pardon all my vanities, and free
The lord *Velasco*, what e're come of me.
Bless, bless, the lord *Velasco*.—[*To the executioner*] Strike.
                    As he is about to strike, VELASCO *steps out*

VELASCO   Villain, hold, hold! Or thou dyest, Slave.   85

ALMADA   What means that countermand?

73 up,] *Sedge*; up. Q   76 women,] *Sedge*; women Q

LODOVICO   Hey, do! More news yet; you will not be valiant
when 'tis too late, I trust?

VELASCO   Woman, come down: Who lends me now a sword?

LODOVICO   Marry, that do I, Sir, I am your first man; Here,   90
here, here, take heed you do not hurt your fingers; 'twill cut
plaguely: and what will you do with it?

VELASCO   Base woman, take thy life, thy cursed life,
    I set thee free, and for it pawn a soul:
    But that I know heaven hath more store of mercy,   95
    Then thou and all thy sex of sin and falsehood.
    My Lords, I now stand Champion for the Queen:
    Doth that discharge her?

COLUMELLO   Bravest man, it doth:
    Lady, y'are safe; now, Officers away.
    This is a blessed hour!   *Exeunt Officers*

Fiʳ ALMADA   You shall for ever   100
    Bind us your servants.

LODOVICO   Aha: Why then, however things happen, let them
fall, as they fall. God a' mercy, my lord, at last.
                              Shout within

COLUMELLO   Hark how the people ring a peal of joy,
    For this good news. My lord, time steals away;   105
    We may not linger now.

SALASSA   You give me life;
    Take it not, Sir, away again. I see
    Upon your troubled eyes such discontent
    As frights my trembling heart; Dear Sir—

VELASCO   The Gold
    You hazarded your life for, is your own,   110
    You may receive it at your pleasure.

ALMADA   Yes,
    'Tis ready for you, lady.

SALASSA   Gold? Let gold,
    And all the treasures of the earth besides

87 yet;] yet, Q   104 a peal] *Sedge*; apeal Q

Perish like trash; I value nothing, Sir,
But your assured love.

VELASCO   My love! Vain woman,   115
Henceforth thus turn I from thee, never look
For Apish dotage, for a smile, a how d'ee,
A fare ye well, a thought from me: let Snakes
Live in my bosom, and with murderous stinges
Infect the vital warmth, that lends them life,   120
If ever I remember thee or thine.
If I prevail, my services shall crave
But one reward, which shall be, if that ever
Thou come but in my sight, the State wil please
To banish thee the land; or else I vow,   125
My self to leave it.

SALASSA   My ill purchast life!

VELASCO   Ill purchast life, indeed, whose ransom craves
A sadder price, then price of bloodshed saves.
Go, learn, bad woman, what it is, how foul,   130
By gaining of a life, to lose a soul.
The price of one soul doth exceed as far
A life here, as the Sun in light a Star.
Here though we live some threescore years, or more,
Yet we must dye at last, and quit the score
We ow to nature. But the soul once dying,   135
Dyes ever, ever; no repurifying;
No earnest sighs or grones; no intercession;
No tears; no pennance; no too late confession
Can move the ear of justice, if it doom
A soul past cure to an infernal tomb.   140
Make use of this, *Salassa.*

LODOVICO   Think upon that now, and take heed, you look
my lord no more in the face.

SALASSA   Goodness protect him! now my life so late
I strove to save, which being sav'd I hate.   145

Exeunt all

---

119 murderous] *Sedge*; muderous *Q*   130 learn,] *Sedge*; learn *Q*   131 soul] *Sedge*; oul
Q   141 this,] *Sedge*; this *Q*

5.2   *Enter* ALPHONSO *armed all save the head, leading the* QUEEN,
        a Herauld going before, MURETTO, HEROPHIL, *a Guard*

ALPHONSO   Are you resolv'd to dye?

QUEEN   When life is irksom
        Death is a happiness.

ALPHONSO   Yes, if the cause
        Make it not infamous: But when a beauty
        So most incomparable as yours, is blemish'd
        With the dishonorable stamp of whoredom: 5
        When your black tainted name, which should have been
        (Had you preserv'd it nobly) your best Chronicle,
        Wherein you might have liv'd, when this is stain'd,
        And justly too, then death doth but heap
        Affliction on the dying. Yet you see   10
        With what a sympathie of equal grief
        I mourn your ruine.

QUEEN   Would you could as clearly
        Perceive mine innocence, as I can clearly
        Protest it.

F1ᵛ ALPHONSO   Fy, to justify a sin
        Is worse then to commit it; now y'are faulty.   15

MURETTO   What a royall pair of excellent creatures are heer both
upon the castaway. It were a saint like mercy in you (my Lord) to
remitt the memory of a past errour. And in you, Madam (if you be
guilty of the supposed crime) to submitt your selfe to the King.
I dare promise, his love to you is so unfayned, that it will relent in   20
your humility. Pray do, good Madam, do.

QUEEN   But how if I be free?

MURETTO   By any means, for your honors cause do not yeeld
then one jot. Let not the faint feare of Death deject you before the
royalty of an erected heart. D'ee heare this, my Lord? 'Tis a doubt-   25
full case, almost impossible to be decided. Look upon her well: as
I hope to prosper, shee hath a most vertuous, a most innocent

5.2] 9 too,] *Sedge*, too; *Q*   14 Fy,] *Sedge*, from *Q* catchword; Fy *Q*   15 it;] *Sedge*;
it, *Q*   18 you, Madam] *Sedge*; you Madam *Q*   21 Madam,] *Sedge*; Madam *Q*
25 this, my Lord?] *Sedge*; this my Lord, *Q*   26 decided.] *Sedge*; decided, *Q*   well:] well, *Q*

countenance. Never heed it. I know, my Lord, your jealousy and
your affections wrestle together within you for the mastery. Mark
her beauty throughly. Now by all the power of Love, tis pitty Shee   30
should not be as fair within as without.

ALPHONSO   Could that be prov'd, I'de give my kingdom straight
And live a slave to her, and her perfections.

Enter ALMADA, COLUMELLO, *Attendants*

Lords, welcome, see thus arm in arm we pace
To the wide theater of blood and shame,   35
My QUEEN and I—my Queen? Had shee bin still
As shee was, mine, we might have liv'd too happ'ly
For eithers comfort. Heer on this sweet modell,
This plott of wonder, this fair face, stands fixt
My whole felicity on earth. In witnes   40
Whereof, behold (my Lords) those manly tears
Which her unkindnes and my cruell fate
Force from their quiet springs. They speak alowd
To all this open ayre, their publick eyes,
That whither I kill or dy in this attempt   45
I shall in both be vanquisht.

ALMADA   'Tis strange, my Lord,
Your love should seem so mighty in your hatred.

ALPHONSO   *Muretto*, go, and guard *Petruchy* safe.
                                        Exit MURETTO
We must be stout now, and give over whineing.
IIc shall confesse strange things (my Lords) I warrant ye.   50
Comes not a champion yet?

QUEEN   None dares, I hope.

COLUMELLO   The Queen, you know, hath bound us all by Oath:
We must not undertake to combat you
Although the cause should prove apparent for her.

28 know, my Lord,] *Sedge*; know my Lord *Q*   29 the mastery] *Sedge*; them astery *Q*
34 Lords,] *Sedge*; Lords *Q*   35 shame,] shame *Q*   36 I–] *Sedge*; I, *Q*   37 happ'ly]
Sedge; happ'ly, *Q*   43 springs.] *Sedge*; springs, *Q*   46 strange, my Lord,] *Sedge*;
strange my Lord *Q*   48 *Muretto*,] *Sedge*; *Muretto Q*   50 ye.] *Sedge*; ye,
Q   51 dares,] *Sedge*; dares *Q*   52 Queen,] *Sedge*; Queen *Q*   Oath:] *Sedge*; Oath, *Q*

ALPHONSO   Must not? why then y'are cowards all, all base,   55
And fall off from your duties; but you know
Her follies are notorious; none dares stand
To justify a sin they see so playnely.

COLUMELLO   You are too hard a censurer.

ALPHONSO   Give me your hand. Farewell; thus from my joys   60
I part, I ever part. Yet, good my Lords,
Place her on yonder throne, where shee may sit
Just in mine eye, that so if strength should fail,
I might fetch double strength from her sweet beauty.
I'le heare no answers.

QUEEN   Heaven be always guard   65
To Noble actions.

                                    Place the QUEEN

COLUMELLO   Heer's a medley love
That kills in Curtesie.

ALPHONSO   Herauld, sound a warning to all defendants—
                                    Trumpet sounds
What, comes no one forth?
How like you this, my Lords?   70
Sirrah, sound again.
                            Second sound

        A Trumpet within. Enter herauld sounding, after him
    VELASCO *arm'd all save the head,* LODOVICO *and attendants*

VELASCO?   Ha? Art thou the man? Although
F2ʳ   Thy cowardice hath publisht thee so base,
As that it is an injury to honour
To fight with one that hath been baffl'd, scorn'd,   75
Yet I will bid thee welcom.

VELASCO   Nobly spoken.
Past times can tell you, sir, I was no coward,
And now the justice of a gallant quarrell

---

56 duties;] duties, *Q*   57 notorious; . . . dares] *Sedge*; notorious . . . dare's *Q*   58 sin]
Sedge; sin, *Q*   60 hand. . . . joys] *Sedge*; hand, . . . joy's *Q*   Farewell;] Farewell, *Q*
61 part. Yet,] *Sedge*; part, Yet *Q*   66 actions.] *Sedge*; actions *Q*   68 Herauld,]
Herauld *Q*   69 What, . . . forth?] *Sedge*; What . . . forth: *Q*   70 this,] *Sedge*; this *Q*
71 Sirrah,] *Sedge*; Sirrah *Q*   75 baffl'd,] *Sedge*; baffl'd *Q*   77 you,] *Sedge*; you *Q*

Shall new revive my dulnes. Yonder sits
A Queen as free from stain of your disgrace,   80
As you are fowle in urging it.

ALPHONSO   Thou talk'st couragiously, I love thee for it,
And, if thou canst make good what thou avouchest,
I'le kneel to thee, as to another nature.

VELASCO   We come not heer to chide. My sword shall thunder   85
The right for which I strike.

QUEEN   Traytor to loyalty,
Rash and unknown fool, what desperate lunacy
Hath led thee on to draw thy treacherous sword
Against thy King, upon a ground so giddy
That thou art but a stranger in the cause   90
Thou wouldst defend? By all my royall blood
If thou prevailst, thy head shal answer it.

COLUMELLO   Madam, you wrong his truth, and your own fame.

ALMADA   You violate the liberty of armes.

ALPHONSO   Pish, listen not to her, 'tis I'me your man.   95

QUEEN   Why, foolish Lords, unsensible and false,
Can any drop of blood be drawn from him
My Lord, your King, which is not drawn from me?
Velasco, by the duty that thou ow'st me
I charge thee to lay by thy armes.

VELASCO   I must not,   100
Unles this man whom you call king, confess
That he hath wrong'd your honor.

QUEEN   Wilt thou fight then
When I command the contrary?

VELASCO   I will.

QUEEN   *Velasco*, heare me once more, thou were wont
To be as pittifull as thou wert valiant;   105

79 dulnes.] *Sedge*; dulnes, *Q*   80 stain] *Sedge*; stain, *Q*   84 nature.] *Sedge*; nature *Q*
85 chide.] *Sedge*; chide, *Q*   91 defend?] *Sedge*; defend, *Q*   93 Madam,] *Sedge*;
Madam *Q*   96 Why,] *Sedge*; Why *Q*   99 *Velasco*,] *Sedge*; *Velasco Q*   104 *Velasco*,]
Sedge; *Velasco. Q*   105 valiant;] valiant, *Q*

I will entreat thee, gentle kind *Velasco*,
A weeping Queen sues to thee: Doe not fight,
Velasco, every blow thou givest the King,
Wounds mee. Didst ever love? *Velasco*, hear me.

ALPHONSO   Shee must not be endur'd.

VELASCO   Nor can shee win me.   110
Blush you, my Lord, at this?

QUEEN   O let me dy
Rather then see my Lord affronted thus.
                            QUEEN *falls into a sound*

VELASCO
Hold up the *Queen*, she swouns.

ALMADA   Madam, Deare Madam.

COLUMELLO   Can you see her and not be toucht, my Lord?
Was ever woman false that lov'd so truly?   115

ALPHONSO   'Tis all dissimulation.

VELASCO   You dishonour her;
To prove it I'le fight both quarrels now.

        Enter a herauld sounding a trumpett, after him PETRUCHI
        arm'd head and all

LODOVICO   *Heydo*? Here comes more work for mettall men.

ALMADA   Another! Who should he be?

ALPHONSO   Speake; what art thou?

PETRUCHI   One that am summon'd from the power above   120
To guard the innocence of that fair *Queen*
Not more against the man that would accuse her
Then all the world besides. Th' art welcome too.

VELASCO   You come too late, friend; I am he alone
Stand ready to defend that gracious beauty.   125
You may return.

106 thee,] thee *Q*   107 thee:] thee, *Q*   109 mee. . . . *Velasco*,] *Sedge*; mee, . . . *Velasco*
Q   110 me.] *Sedge*; me, *Q*   111 you, my Lord, . . . this?] *Sedge*; you my Lord . . . this.
Q   112 thus.] *Sedge*; thus *Q*   113 Madam,] *Sedge*; Madam *Q*   114 toucht,]
Sedge; toucht *Q*   115 truly?] *Sedge*; truly *Q*   116 her;] her, *Q*   119 Another!]
Sedge; Another *Q*   Speake;] Speake *Q*   124 late, friend;] *Sedge*; late friend, *Q*

PETRUCHI   Ther's not a man alive
Hath interest in this quarrel but my selfe;
I out of mine own knowledg can avouch
Her accusation to be meerly false,
As hel it selfe.

QUEEN   What mortall man is he,   130   F2ᵛ
So wilfull in his confidence, can sweare
More then he knowes?

PETRUCHI   I swear but what I know.

ALPHONSO   Hast thou a name?

PETRUCHI   Yes, helpe my beaver down.
                    LODOVICO *discovers him*
D'ee know me now?

ALPHONSO   Petruchi! Death of manhood,
I am plainly bought and sold. Why, wher's *Muretto*?   135

                Enter MURETTO *with a sword drawn*

MURETTO   Here as ready to stand in defence of that Miracle of
chast women, as any man in this presence.

ALPHONSO   Are all conspir'd against me? What, thou too?
Now by my fathers ashes, by my life
Thou art a villain, a grosse rank'rous villain,   140
Did'st not thou only first inforce my thoughts
To jealousy?

MURETTO   'Tis true I did.

ALPHONSO   Nay more,
Didst not thou feed those thoughts with fresh supplies,
Nam'd every circumstance?

MURETTO   All this I grant.

ALPHONSO   Dost grant it, Dog, slave, Helhound?   145

MURETTO   Will you hear me?

---

126 selfe;] *Sedge*; selfe, Q   132 knowes?] *Sedge*; knowes. Q   133 down.] *Sedge*; down,
Q   135 and sold. Why,] *Sedge*; & sold, why Q   138 What,] *Sedge*; what Q
143 supplies,] *Sedge*; supplies Q

COLUMELLO   Heare him, good my Lord, let us perswade ye.

ALPHONSO   What canst thou say, Impostor? Speake and choake.

MURETTO   I have not deserv'd this, my Lord, and you shall find
it. 'Tis true, I must confesse, that I was the only instrument to   150
incense you to this distemperature and I am prowd to say it,
and say it again before this noble presence, that I was my selfe the
only man.

ALPHONSO   Insufferable Devil!

ALMADA   Pray, my Lord.

MURETTO   Wonder not, my Lords, but lend mee your atten-   155
tions. I saw with what violence he pursude his resolutions not
more in detestation of the Queen in particular, then of all her sex
in generall. That I may not weary your patience: I bent all my
Studies to devise which way I might do service to my country by
reclayming the distraction of his discontents. And having felt his   160
disposition in every pulse, I found him most addicted to this pestilence of jealosy with a strong persuasion of which, I from time to
time ever fed him by degrees, till I brought the Queen and the
noble Petruchi into the dangers they yet stand in. But with all
(and herin I appeale to your Majesties own approbation) I sea-   165
son'd my words with such an intermixing the praises of the Queens
bewty, that from jealosy I drew the King into a serious examination of her perfections.

ALPHONSO   Thus farr I must acknowledg, he speaks truth.

MURETTO   At length having found him indeed surely affected,   170
I perceav'd that nothing but the suppos'd blemish of her dishonour could work a second divorce between them.

ALPHONSO   True, truly fates own truth.

MURETTO   Now, my Lords, to cleer that imputation, I knew
how easie it would be by the apparent certainty it selfe; In all   175

147 him, . . . ye] *Sedge*; him . . . ye, *Q*   148 say,] *Sedge*; say *Q*   149–50 this, . . . it.] *Sedge*;
this . . . it, *Q*   154 Pray,] *Sedge*; Pray *Q*   155 not, . . . attentions.] *Sedge*; not . . . attentions, *Q*   159 devise] *Sedge*; devise, *Q*   country] *Sedge*; country, *Q*
162 which, . . . to time] *Sedge*; which; . . . to time, *Q*   171 perceav'd] *Sedge*; perceav'd,
Q   171 dishonour] *Sedge*; dishonour, *Q*   174–5 Now, . . . be] *Sedge*; Now . . . be, *Q*
175 selfe;] selfe, *Q*

which, if I have erred, it is the error of a loyall service. Only I must ever acknowledg how justly I have deserved a punishment, in drawing so vertuous a princesses honor into publick question; and humbly referr my selfe to her gracious clemency, and your noble constructions.   180

ALPHONSO   But can, can this be so?

MURETTO   Let me ever else be the subject of your rage in the sufferance of any torture.

ALPHONSO   And is shee chast, *Petruchi*?

PETRUCHI   Chast by vertue,
    As is the new born virgin, for ought I know.   185

MURETTO   I ever whisperd so much in your ears, my Lord, and told you that it was impossible such singular endowments by nature should yeild to the corruption so much as of an unworthy thought. Did I not tell you so from time to time?

ALPHONSO   Lay by your arms, my lords, and joyn with me.   190 F3ʳ
    Let's kneel to this (what shall I call her?) Woman?
    No, she's an Angel.
                        All kneel
                    Glory of Creation,
    Can you forget my wickedness? Your Peers,
    Your Senators, your bravest men, make
    suit on my behalf. Why speak ye not, my lords?   195
    I am I know too vile to be remitted,
    But she is merciful.
    ALL [*except the* QUEEN *and* ALPHONSO] Great Soveraign Lady—

QUEEN   Be not so low, my lord, in your own thoughts:
    You are, as you were, Soveraign of my heart;
    And I must kneel to you.

ALPHONSO   But will you love me?   200

QUEEN   'Tis my part to ask that: will you love me?

ALPHONSO   Ever, yours ever; let this kiss new marry us.
    What say?

182 else . . . rage] *Sedge*; else, . . . rage, *Q*   184 chast,] *Sedge*; chast *Q*   186 ears, . . . you] *Sedge*; ears . . . you, *Q*   188 nature . . . much] *Sedge*; nature, . . . much, *Q*   189 to time?] *Sedge*; to time, *Q*

QUEEN   It does; and heaven it self can tell
I never did, nor will wrong our first loves.

ALPHONSO   Speak it no more. Let's rise, now I am King   205
Of two rich Kingdoms, as the world affords:
The Kingdom of thy beauty, and this land.
But what rests for *Muretto*?

QUEEN   I account my worthiest thanks his debt.

ALMADA   And he deserves all honor, all respect.   210

COLUMELLO   Thus my imbraces
Can witness how I truly am his friend.

VELASCO   And I whilst I have life.

LODOVICO   Nay, when I am dead I will appear again, clap thee
on the shoulder and cry, God a' mercy, old Suresby.   215

PETRUCHI   I must ask pardon of him; still I thought
His plot had aim'd all at his own behoof,
But I am sorry for that misconceit.

MURETTO   My lords, What I have been heretofore, I cannot
altogether excuse; but I am sure my desires were alwaies honest,   220
however my low fortune kept me down: But now I finde 'tis your
honest man is your honest man still, howere the world go.

ALPHONSO   *Muretto*, Whilst I live thou shalt be neer me,
As thou deservest: And noble Gentlemen,
I am in all your debts: henceforth beleeve me,   225
I'll strive to be a servant to the State.
ALL [*except the* QUEEN *and* ALPHONSO] Long live happy both.

ALPHONSO   But where are now my brace of new-made Courtiers,
My Scholler and my Captain?

LODOVICO   I cry guilty, there is a large story depends upon their   230
exploits, my Lord; for both they, thinking in such perilous times to
be shifting every man for one, have took a passing provident
course to live without help hereafter. The man in the moon,

214–15 Nay, . . . I will . . . a'mercy,] *Sedge*; Nay . . . I, will . . . a'mercy *Q*   216 him;] *Sedge*;
him, *Q*   224 Gentlemen,] *Sedge*; Gentlemen *Q*   231 they,] they *Q*

Signior *Pynto*, for the raising of his fortune a Planet higher, is by
this time married to a kinde of loose-bodied widow, called by   235
Sirname a Bawde; one that, if he follow wholesom instructions,
will maintain him, there's no question on't. The captain, for his
part, is somwhat more delicately resolv'd for as adventurous
(though not as frail) a piece of service. For he, in hope to marry
this lady attending on the Queen, granted *Petruchi* his liberty, and   240
by this time hath received a sufficient *quietus est*.

ALPHONSO   Are these my trusty servants? What a blindness was
I led into!

LODOVICO   If your Highnesses both will in these daies of mirth
crown the Comedy; first let me from the Queens royal gift be bold   245
to receive *Herophil* for my wife; She and I are resolv'd of the business already.

QUEEN   With all my heart, I think her well bestow'd,
    If she her self consents.

HEROPHIL   My duty, Madam,
    Shall ever speak my thankfulness; in this   250
    I reckon all my services rewarded.   F3ᵛ

VELASCO   Much comfort to you, friend.

ALL   All joy and peace.

LODOVICO   My duty to my Soveraigns, to all the rest at once, my
heartiest heartiest thanks. Now, lady, you are mine; why so, here's
short work to begin with. If in the end we make long work, and   255
beget a race of mad-caps, we shall but do as our fathers and mothers did, and they must be cared for.

Enter PYNTO, BUFO, MOPAS *with a tire upon his head,*
and SHAPAROON

PYNTO   Follow me not, bawde; my lord the King;
    My Jove, justice, justice!

---

236 that,] that *Q*   237 on't. . . . captain,] *Sedge*; on't, . . . captain *Q*   239–40 he, . . . lady]
Sedge; he . . . lady, *Q*   250 thankfulness;] *Sedge*; thankfulness, *Q*   252 you,] *Sedge*;
you *Q*   253 the rest] *Sedge*; therest *Q*   258 not,] *Sedge*; not *Q*   259 justice!]
Sedge; justice. *Q*

BUFO   Justice to me, I was like to have been married to these 260
black muschatoes insteed of that lady.

PYNTO   I to this ugly bawde.

PYNTO *and* BUFO   Justice!

ALPHONSO   Hence, you ridiculous fools, I banish you
    For ever from my presence: Sirrah, to thee   265
    I give the charge, that they be forthwith stript,
    And put into such rags they came to Court in;
    And so turn'd off.

PYNTO   Dost hear me, King?

BUFO   King, hear me, I'me the wiser man.   270

ALPHONSO   No more, I say.

MOPAS   Come away, come away for shame; you see what 'tis to
be given to the flesh: the itch of letchery must be cured with the
whip of correction. Away, away.

                 Exeunt BUFO, PYNTO, MOPAS *and* SHAPAROON

ALPHONSO   What else remains   275
    But to conclude this day in *Hymen*'s Feasts?

        Enter SALASSA *her hair loose, a white rod in her hand, two or*
                    three with bags of money

    To whom? For what?
    Your meaning, name, and errand?

SALASSA   At those feet
    Lay down those sums of gold, the price of guilt,
    Of shame, of horror.

QUEEN   What new riddle's this?   280
                 MURETTO *whispers* [*to*] *the King*, COLUMELLO
                                     [*to*] *the* QUEEN

MURETTO   My Gratious lord.

COLUMELLO   I shall inform your Highness.

---

263 Justice!] *Sedge*; Justice. Q   264 Hence,] *Sedge*; Hence Q   269 me,] *Sedge*; me Q
270 King,] *Sedge*; King Q   271 more,] *Sedge*; more Q   277 whom? . . . what?] *Sedge*;
whom; . . . what; Q

VELASCO   Woman of impudence.

SALASSA   Your looks proclaim
My sentence banishment, or if you think
The word of banishment too hard to utter,   285
But turn away, my lord, and without accent
I'll understand my doom, I'll take my leave,
And like a penitentiary walk
Many miles hence to a religious shrine
Of some chast sainted Nun, and wash my sin off   290
In tears of penance, to my last of breath.

VELASCO   You come to new torment me.

SALASSA   (*Going out*) I am gone, my lord; I go for ever.

LODOVICO   Faith, be merciful; the woman will prove a wife
    worth the having, I'll Pass my word.

ALPHONSO   E'ne so; stay, lady, I command you, stay.   295
Velasco, here's occasion proffer'd now
For me to purchase some deserving favour
From woman; honour me in my first suit;
Remit and love that lady.

VELASCO   Good my lord.

ALPHONSO   Nay, nay, I must not be deny'd; my Queen   300
Shall joyn with me to mediate for her.

QUEEN   Yes, I dare undertake, she that presents
Her pennance in such sorrow, hearty sorrow,
Will know how to redeem the time with duty,
With love, obedience.   305

LODOVICO   D'ee hear, my lord; all the ladies in *Arragon*, and my
wife among the rest, will bait ye like so many wild cats, | if you
should triumph over a poor yeelding creature, that does in a manner lye down to ye of her own accord. Come, I know you love her
with all the very vaines of your heart.   310   F4ʳ

MURETTO   There's more hope of one woman reclaim'd (my
lord) then of many conceited of their own innocence, which
indeed they never have but in conceit.

285 utter,] utter. *Q*   290 sin] *Sedge*; fin *Q*   294 Faith, . . . merciful;] *Sedge*; Faith . . .
merciful, *Q*   296 *Velasco*,] *Sedge*; *Velasco Q*   300 deny'd;] deny'd, *Q*

VELASCO   To strive against the ordinance of fate,
  I finde is all in vain. Lady, your hand: 315
  I must confess I love you, and I hope
  Our faults shall be redeem'd in being henceforth
  True votaries to vertue, and the faith
  Our mutual vows shal to each other ow.
  Say, are you mine, resolv'd?

LODOVICO   Why that's well said.   320

SALASSA   Yours, as you please to have me.

VELASCO   Here then ends
  All memory of any former strife:
  He hath enough who hath a vertuous wife.

ALL   [*except* VELASCO *and* SALASSA]
  Long joy to both.

ALPHONSO   The money we return
  Where it is due; and for *Velasco*'s merits   325
  Will double it. Thus after storms a calm
  Is ever welcomest: Now we have past
  The worst, and all I hope is well at last.

                                    Exeunt

315 vain. . . . hand:] *Sedge*; vain: . . . hand, *Q*   328 last.] *Sedge*; last *Q*

Paratexts of The 1653 Edition

TITLE PAGE

[facsimile]

DEDICATION

TO THE VER-
TUOUSLY NOBLE
AND TRULY HONORABLE LADY,
The Lady
CATHERINE MOHUN,
Wife to the Lord WARWICK MOHUN, Baron of
Okehampton , my highly honored LORD.

May it please your Ladiship,

Madam, Imbolden'd by your accustomed candor and unmerited favours to things of the like nature, though disproportion'd worth: (Because this Excellency seems to contract those perfections her Sex hath been invested with, which are as essential to your Ladiship, as light to the Sun) I presumed to secure this innocent Orphan from the Thunder-shocks of the present blasting age, under the safe protecting wreath of your name; which (I am confident) the vertues of none can more justly challenge, then those of your Ladiship; who alone may seem to quicken the lifeless Scene, and to demonstrate its possibility; reducing Fables into Practicks; by making as great honour visible in the mirror of your dayly practise. Your pardon, Madam, for daring to offer such adulterate Metals, to so pure a Mine; for making the Shadow a present to the Substance; the thoughts of which was an offence, but A2ᵛ

Appendix **Dedication**] Polititian] Politian *Q*

the performance, a crime beyond the hopes of pardon. When my Fate had cast me on the first, I esteemed my self unsafe (with the Polititian) should I not attempt the latter, securing one error by soaring at a greater: but my duller eyes endured not the proof of so glorious a Test, and the waxed juncture of my ill contrived feathers melt me into the fear of a fall: Therefore (with the most desperate offenders) I cast my self on the mercy of the Bench; and since I have so clement a Judge as your self, do not wholly despair of absolution, by reason my Penetential acknowledgement attones part of the offence; and your remission of the whole will eternally oblige,

MADAM,

The humblest of your

Ladiships Servants,

ALEXANDER GOUGHE.

A3ʳ COMMENDATORY VERSES

To Mr. *Alexander Goughe* upon his publishing
The excellent Play call'd the QUEEN;
or the Excellencie of her Sex.

If Playes be looking glasses of our lives
Where dead examples quickning art revives:
By which the players dresse themselves, and we
By them may forme a living Imagry
To let those sullied, lie in age in dust   5
Or break them with pretense, of fit and just,
Is a rude cruelty, as if you can
Put on the christian, and put off the man.
But must all morall handsomnes undoe
And may not be divine and civill too?   10
What though we dare not say the Poets art
Can save while it delights, please and convert;
Or that blackfriers we heare which in this age
Fell when it was a church, not when a stage,
Or that the Presbiters that once dwelt there,   15
Prayed and thriv'd though the playhouse were so near.
Yet this we dare affirme: there is more gain

Commendatory verse] R.C. 6 just,] just. *Q*   10 too?] *Sedge*; too. *Q*   17 affirme:]
Sedge; affirme *Q*

In seeing men act vice then vertue fain;
And he less tempts a danger that delights
In profest players then close Hypocrites.   20
Can there no favour to the scæne be shown
Because Jack Fletcher was a Bishops son,
Or since that order is condemn'd doe you
Think poets therefore Antichristian too?
Is it unlawfull since the stage is down   25
To make the press act? where no ladies swoune
At the red coates intrusion: none are strip't;
No Hystriomastix has the copy whip't
No man d' on Womens cloth's: the guiltles presse
Weares its own innocent garments: its own dresse,   30
Such as free nature made it: Let it come
Forth Midwife Goughe, securely; and if some
Like not the make or beautie of the play
Bear witnes to 't and confiden tly say
Such a relict as once the stage did own,   35
Ingenuous Reader, merits to be known.

                     R. C.   A3ᵛ

For Plays.

Do you not Hawke? Why mayn't we have a Play?
Both are but recreations. You'll say
Diseases which have made Physitians dumb,
By healthful excercise are overcome.
And Crimes escap'd all other laws, have been   5
Found out, and punish'd by the curious Scene.
Are Stages hurtful for the ill they teach,
And needless for the good? Which Pulpits preach:
Then sports are hurtful, for the time they lose,
And needless to the good, which labour does.   10
Permit 'm both; or if you will allow
The minde no Hawke, leave yours, and go to Plough.
               EDMOND ROOKWOOD.

20 Hypocrites.] *Sedge*; Hypocrites, *Q*   24 too?] *Sedge*; too; *Q*   26 act?] act: *Q*

To Mr. *Goughe* , upon the publication of the Play, call'd, *The* QUEEN, *or the Excellency of her* SEX.

GOUGHE, In this little Present you create
Your self a Trophee, may become a State;
For you that preserve wit, may equally
Be ranck'd with those defend our Liberty;
And though in this ill treated Scene of sense,   5
The general learning is but in pretence;
Or else infus'd like th' Eastern Prophet's Dove,
To whisper us, Religion, Honour, Love;

A4ʳ
Yet the more Generous race of men revives
This Lamp of Knowledge, and like Primitives   10
In Caves, fearless of Martyrdom, rehearse
The almost breathless, now, Dramatick verse.
How in the next age will our Youth lament
The loss of wit, condem'd to banishment.
Wit that the duller rout despise, 'cause they   15
Miss it in what their Zealous Priests display;
For Priests in melancholy Zeal admit
Onely a grave formality for wit;
And would have those that govern us comply
And cherish their fallacious tyranny.   20
But wherein States can no advantage gain,
They harmless mirth improperly restrain;
Since men cannot be naturally call'd free,
If Rulers claim more then securitie.
How happens then this rigour o're the Stage   25
In this restor'd, free, and licentious age?
For Plays are Images of life, and cheat
Men into vertue, and in jest repeat
What they most seriously think; nor may
We fear lest Manners suffer: every day   30
Does higher, cunninger, more sin invent
Then any Stage did ever represent.
It may indeed shew evil, and affright,
As we prize day by th' ugliness of night.
But in the Theatre men are easier caught,   35
Then by what is in clamorous pulpits taught.

T. C.

T.C. 16 display;] *Sedge*; display *Q*

Original Persons of the Play List

Persons of the PLAY.

QUEEN *of* Arragon.
PETRUCHI, *a Young Lord.*
BUFO, *a Captain.*
PYNTO, *an Astronomer.* } *Kings Party:*
MURETTO.
VELASCO, QUEENs *General.*
LODOVICO, *his friend.*
ALPHONSO, *afterwards King.*
COLLUMELLO,
ALMADO, } *Counsellors to the* QUEEN.
HEROPHIL, *her Woman.*
SALASSA, *widow, Mistriss to* VELASCO.
SHAPAROON, *her friend.*
MOPAS, VELASCO's *man.*
Hangman.
Messenger.
GROOM.
Officers.

Commentary to *The Queen*

1.1

3 motion both a mental impulse (*OED*, 12a) and political unrest (*OED*, 1a).

12 shift . . . selves 'every man for himself'; also used by Ford in *'Tis Pity* 5.6.85.

20 birth . . . Planet child born at a time when a malign astrological influence is in the ascendant, and therefore dominant.

22–5 slippery . . . begat him Muretto is associated with both noxious reptiles and conventional types of hypocrisy. Eels were a byword for something insecure, fickle, or shifty (as in *The Lady's Trial*, 3.1, where the possession of money is said to be like holding a slippery eel by the tail). Eels, snakes, and crocodiles were thought to be born from mud and slime. Oil was usually reckoned to be a healthful opposite of poison (compare Juvenal, *Satire* 5, 86–91, where the only advantage of the nasty oil being served at the feast is that it bestows immunity to snake-bite), but the two had recently been collocated in the title of Francis Rous's Puritan tract, *Oil of Scorpions* (1623); in James Mabbe's *The Spanish Bawd* (translated by 1598, but unpublished until 1631), the witch Celestina has a bottle of 'oil of serpents' among the nasty ingredients in her lair (ed. H. Warner Allen, Library of Early Novelists (London and New York, 1908), 60, 85). Crocodiles, notorious for the insincerity of their tears, were conventionally gendered as female (as in *The White Devil*, 4.2), hence the specifying adjective 'male' here.

27 Cog a foyst a nonce name derived from terms for deceit and cheating; compare *The Sun's Darling* (1624), 1.1.151–3: 'Drinkeing, Whoring, Singing, Dancing, Dicing, Swearing, Roring, Foisting, Lying, Cogging, Canting, & *cetero*'.

28 fustians bombastic, meaningless jargon; but, coming after 'rags', perhaps also alluding to the coarse cloth of the same name.

29 hey do probably an unrecorded variant of the jubilant expression, 'Heyday!' (Also at 5.1.82, 5.2.113).

32–3 roguy complement compare *The Fancies*, 5.2: 'roguy bargaine'.

37 totters tatters.

37 Ephimerides almanacs.

39 maunderer professional beggar (*OED*, n^1), though *OED* cites this passage as the first usage of the word in the sense 'grumbler' (n^2), not recorded again until 1755.

41 **behavour** a recorded early spelling of 'behaviour', but old-fashioned by the seventeenth century.

49 **shepheards Calender** a rustic almanac. There is no need to infer an allusion to Edmund Spenser's 1579 poem of the same title.

51 *Erra Pater*'s **Prognostication** a popular book of 'learned' predictions first published in *c.*1536, and reprinted at least ten times up to 1609 (and twice more in the 1630s).

53 **weather-wise** adjective used of a seventeenth-century weather forecaster; used as a proper name for an almanac-obsessed gull in Thomas Middleton's *No Wit, No Help Like a Woman's* (1611).

55 **Hospital . . . coat** schoolboy at Christ's Hospital in London, whose pupils wore a distinctive blue uniform.

58 **red Sprats** smoked sprats: mean, unappetizing fare (but more festive than a dish of air).

70 **Gipsonly** gypsy-like, 'Egyptian'. (The gypsies were thought to have originated in Egypt.)

85 **this** probably accompanied by an abusive gesture.

87 **word** phrase (i.e. 'Foolish captain').

90 **Sneaks** an oath, but a deliberately inoffensive one ('God's neaks', or 'nigs', being meaningless); compare W. R., *A Match at Midnight* (1622), sc.1: 'wee sweare nothing but niggers noggers'.

92 **owlaglasses** buffoons; from the English form of Till Eulenspiegel, a German clown.

93–4 **put . . . coxcombs** waste your wisdom on fools.

96 **foolish** Pynto's insult of line 66 continues to rankle.

97 **goodman** a polite form of address, equivalent to 'Mr', accorded someone below the rank of gentleman; here, therefore, a sly social put-down.

101–2 **my father . . . woman** imagined abusive claims, rather than the truth, about his parents' lowly station in life: chiropodists were considered a lowly rank of the surgical profession, and selling seafood, such as mussels, was a plebeian and unladylike occupation; compare Dekker and Massinger, *The Virgin Martyr* (1620), 3.3.102–3: 'the noyse of a scolding oyster wench'.

104 *Mars . . . Saturn* not only planets but also gods, one martial and the other full of irascible discontent; compare *The Pedlar's Prophecy* (1561), TLN 122 (Malone Society Reprint): 'Saturne was angry and verie fearse'.

107 **S' bores** an oath, listed by *OED* as both 'euphemistic' (*'sbores n*) and 'profane' (*bore n*¹), both illustrated by the same passage of Brome's *The Sparagus Garden*. 'Bores' may imply the wounds of the crucified Christ, but Bufo's previous oath was of the 'polite' variety.

107 *black guard* kitchen scullions.

113 **The . . . again** 'here he goes, flattering again'.

134 SD *hangman* generic term for any type of executioner, such as, here, a headsman.

136 **doom** sentence of death.

137 **cut the vein** to draw off blood to relieve swelling or other disorder, either physical or mental; a commonplace medical procedure.

175 **Blirt** a derisive sound made with the tongue, comparable with the modern raspberry.

178 **fixions** (a) illusory retinal after-image caused by spending too long looking at a light source (such as the stars); (b) fictions.

186 **Skeldrers** beggarly former soldiers.

266 **challenge** claim.

272 **Phew** a derisive exclamation; compare the modern 'Pooh!'

276 **Our . . . hands** if Alphonso is restrained for execution, the Queen may release him herself, and call on the lords to help her. 'Your hands' could alternatively be an order to applaud the reprieve.

283 **run . . . byas** swerve the wrong way; a term from bowls.

305–6 **Star-shut** i.e. 'star-shot', a gelatinous substance, also called nostoc, supposed to be a stellar secretion (but actually a bacterial colony).

308 **Frier . . . head** the Oxford scholar Roger Bacon (*c.*1214–92) was thought to have manufactured a brazen head which uttered prophecies; the story was dramatized in Robert Greene's *Friar Bacon and Friar Bungay* (1589).

311 **Jolthead** blockhead.

312 **there's . . . things** biblical (Ecclesiastes 3.1).

314 **cast sute** discarded clothing. The reprieved rebels are dressed in rags and need new outfits.

318 **surquedry** haughty excess.

319 **fashions** punning on 'farcin', an obsolete form of farcy, a horse disease similar to glanders.

322 **'Zookes** an abbreviation of 'Gadzooks'; another 'inoffensive' oath from Bufo.

335 **utensicles** not in *OED*; probably an error for 'utensils', but whether by Bufo or the compositor cannot be said.

I.2

12 **tilter** someone whose sole experience of fighting is in staged jousts, rather than genuine combat.

18 **do** implying that widows have a rapacious sexual appetite.

23 **placket** woman's underskirt, worn near the genitals and therefore a common metonymy for a woman as a sexual object.

37 **qualification** amendment, amelioration. In *Wine, Beer, Ale, and Tobacco* (1625), Water offers to quench the fire of contention between the other liquors: 'I will vndertake your reconcilement and qualification' (ed. James Holly Hanford, *SP* 12 (1915), p. 33, line 367). Lodovico seems to mean that Velasco should seek out 'reconcilement' with another 'placket' in order to quench his own ardour for the time being.

59 **conceive** understand (*OED*, 9d); but a possible emendation might be *concede*.

68 **'twixt friend, and friend** compare *Love's Sacrifice*: 'the sacred vows of faith 'twixt friend and friend' (5.1.126).

78 **hand** take by the hand.

2.1

15–16 **at those years** at Salassa's age. Sedge emends to 'these years', making the phrase refer to Shaparoon herself; but she is pretending to be a youngish woman of 28, and is contrasting herself with the widow.

30 **mark** a depression in a horse's incisor tooth, which gradually wears away as the horse ages (*OED*, *v*¹ 20).

37 **French-hoods** a particular style of pleated hood, round at the front, worn over the back of the head to frame the face; associated with citizen wives, rather than elite wearers, by the start of the seventeenth century.

37–8 **since . . . addition** since they began to acquire their present status ('addition' meaning an indication of rank, *OED*, 4). Sedge emends to 'edition', quoting *The Lover's Melancholy*, 'a fashion of the newest edition' (2.1.31); but whichever word Ford wrote, the other could be present as a subtext of the line as spoken.

40 **Ud's Pittikins** a 'genteel' oath, minced from 'God's pity'.

43 **servant** Velasco, her suitor (addressed through the letter he sent her).

53 **factress** female agent or go-between.

69 **bables** fool's stick, sometimes with a caricatured head on it; a common metaphor for a penis, which is why it is fitting only for a lady's 'secresies'.

82–3 **thunder . . . flitters** rage so much that she will be struck by her own metaphorical lightning and smashed to smithereens; for the imagery, compare *'Tis Pity She's a Whore*, 'crusht to splitts' (5.3.79).

83 **stand to't** adopt an aggressive posture, as if about to fight a duel (for which he will need a second).

88 **Wagtail** an especially small species of bird; but also a common term for a prostitute.

94–5 take . . . mouth both (a) believe what you have been told *by*, and (b) perform oral sex *on*, anyone else.

105 moyles mule's.

133 'Wonders an asseveration.

143 gage guarantee.

149 in . . . ye in her private parts.

2.2

40 a wise . . . shot The proverb says that a *fool's* bolt is soon shot (Tilley, F.515); with a bawdy secondary meaning (bolt = penis).

54 *Mars* and *Venus* Roman god of war and goddess of love, respectively; in astrology, the planets were thought to influence human behaviour in accordance with the deities after whom they were named.

66 finde . . . follies consider it foolish to be dominated by sensual appetites.

71 but two women i.e. Venus and the Moon (Diana, goddess of chastity).

72–3 as good . . . boy and therefore unavailable for (heterosexual) fun.

104 hard to hand very imminent.

143 plurisie of lust also used in *'Tis Pity She's a Whore* (4.3.8).

149 *Phaeton* son of the classical sun-god, who misappropriated his father's solar chariot, but lost control and scorched the earth.

152–3 I'll . . . there Alphonso imagines dishonourable regal behaviour in terms of the weak kings of late 1580s and early 1590s tragedy: Mycetes of Persia, who hides his crown in a hole (Marlowe, *1 Tamburlaine*, 2.4) and Henry VI, who sits on a molehill and wishes he were a shepherd instead (Shakespeare, *3 Henry VI*, 2.5), both during battles.

166–7 to whose . . . Dad compare with *'Tis Pity She's a Whore*, in which Soranzo protests that he 'must be the Dad' (4.3.12) to Annabella's unborn bastard.

197 Willow wreath traditionally worn by forsaken women.

199 Ingrayn'd in tawny dyed an orange-brown colour worn by broken-hearted women; see *The Fancies, Chaste and Noble*: 'Tawny? Heigh-ho! The pretty heart is wounded' (3.3).

210 do present, proffer, perform.

2.3

1–3 Velasco is advised to make a quick approach, not giving Salassa time to evaluate, rather than pussy-foot about with polite preliminaries.

76 **thus . . . warrant** Sedge inserts a stage direction to the effect that she kisses him here; but 'thus' more likely refers to the permission to kiss she grants in her next speech, after the eager Velasco has cut in.

3.1

25–6 **Wee'll . . . measures** they will revel and drink so hard that they will end up flat on their backs looking upwards; alcoholic hallucination will make the sky appear to bustle and the stars to dance.

25 **bussle** bustle. Bang points out that the compositor had a habit of inserting an otiose *l* into words (as in 'flabled' for *fabled* at 4.2 . . ., and 'lustly' for *lusty* at 4.3 . . .).

26 **fixt Stars** in modern terms, the stars as distinct from the planets, which were understood to be moving 'stars', whereas in Renaissance cosmology the others were affixed to the outermost celestial sphere.

26 **old measures** old-fashioned dances; the term was more specifically used of the social dances performed at the Inns of Court Christmas revels in the late sixteenth century. See David R. Wilson, 'The Old Measures and the Inns of Court: A Note', *Historical Dance* 3.3 (1994), 24.

27 **Caraoch** a stately or luxurious type of coach.

45 **luxury** lechery.

48–9 **Princelike . . . again** the Queen magnanimously reciprocates Petrucci's boldness with toleration, or even encouragement.

53 **grafting** of cuckold's horns.

61 **lady in ordinary** regular lady-in-waiting.

64 **Usher** an unfortunate choice of word, since 'usher' not only meant an officer who goes before a person of dignity, but also had a sexual connotation: 'For 'tis the usher's office still to cover | His lady's private meetings with her lover' (William Barksted and Lewis Machin, *The Insatiate Countess*, in *Four Jacobean Sex Tragedies*, ed. Martin Wiggins (Oxford, 1998), 3.4.16–17).

95 **ump** a drunken belch.

99 **a side blow** Sedge proposes that Bufo strikes Velasco, but the 'blow' could as well be his (perhaps noxious?) eructation.

112 **Mahound** corrupted form of Muhammad, but here implying the worshipper rather than the object of worship.

114 **woman–woman–woman** perhaps the worst insult Velasco can summon by way of rejoinder, consistent with his perceived obligation to tolerate the beating?

122–34 **twelve dozen . . . bills and all** a fantastical passage full of references to London and its local government. 'Eastward ho' was the cry of the city watermen travelling downstream. The Corporation of London was made up of twelve livery companies, including the Drapers, whose arms featured Aries the ram; each company had its own 'grand hall'. In the Stillyard was a drinking-house by the Thames, just upstream of London Bridge. Each of the twenty-six wards of the city elected an alderman, who was entitled to be addressed as 'right worshipful'. Constables armed with halberds ('brown bills') were responsible for policing the city.

123 **black Jack** a large leather beer-jug, coated with tar.

125 *Aries . . . Taurus* signs of the Zodiac, appropriate for cuckolds because they are horned.

126 **recognizances** an identifying badge or emblem enabling a person to be recognized (*OED, n* 5).

128 *Mercury* messenger of the gods, known for his criminal cunning.

130 **beaver** a between-meals snack (*OED, n* 3).

131 **holland** linen; either sheets or his underwear.

133 **both the *Indies*** the West Indies, known for tobacco, and the East Indies, known for spices.

137 **maligo** a fortified Spanish wine.

137 **have . . . here** the only surviving line of George Peele's tragedy *The Turkish Muhammad and Irene the Fair Greek* (1588); 'Hiren' is a form of the name Irene. The line was quoted in five earlier plays: Shakespeare, *2 Henry IV* (1597; 2.4); Dekker, *Satiromastix* (1601; sc.9); Day, *Law-Tricks* (1604; 5.2); Jonson, Chapman, and Marston, *Eastward Ho* (1605; 2.1); and Rowley and Middleton, *The Old Law* (1618; 4.1).

137–8 **What . . . calf?** are you mad or merely foolish?

139 **Stock-fish** salted, air-dried cod which needed to be tenderized (and soaked) before cooking.

141 **Saturn** the father of the classical gods; Pynto is calling Velasco old (and saturnine).

141–2 *Charles* **his wayn** the constellation now known as the Plough, which points to the North Star.

145 **Clubs** the rallying cry of the London apprentices, calling their fellows to take up blunt instruments in their own defence.

146–7 **two . . . knaves** making up a jury of twelve.

151 **Armado** naval fleet; the 'Invincible Armada' was specifically the one sent by Spain against England in 1588.

157 **Bilbo** a fine sword from Bilbao.

157 **foxes tayl** sword blade; compare 'English fox' (Webster, *The White Devil*, 5.6.231). OED *fox n* 6 conjectures that the sense originated because some blades were stamped with an apparently vulpine figure (but which was, in

fact, a running wolf, the widely counterfeited trademark of German sword-makers in Passau and Solingen).

160 **the sign is mortal** the astrological conditions make fighting inauspicious.

162 **booth** fairground sideshow.

186 **Gleek** a set of three (*OED*, *n*¹ 2b); hence, three people in the marriage when one partner commits adultery.

3.2

87 **prov'd . . . man** because they were beaten by Velasco in the battle before the start of the action.

92–5 Petrucci intends to give the King back his ring, but instead the Queen swaps it for one of her own rings, which is just as valuable; for her, however, the ring she receives in exchange is more valuable than the one she gives, because Alfonso sent it.

127 **woodden daggers** children's toys; no longer carrying prominent associations of the morality-play vice of two or three generations before.

127 **play a prize** take part in a competitive fencing match.

130–1 **a hundred ducates** if golden ducats, the equivalent of £45; if silver ducats, £17.10s.

136–7 **brains . . . manchet** Manchet was a loaf of bread of fine quality (and therefore usually white), such as would be served at court. The 'heel' of a loaf was the crust (*OED*, *n*¹ 8), a source of breadcrumbs which were used to polish objects. The brains of Mopas and company obviously need a lot of polishing.

3.3

39 **Keep . . . chaps** keep your mouth shut.

56–7 **fast . . . now** the same phrase appears, word for word, in *Love's Sacrifice* (5.1.27–8).

61 **natural Soveraign** whose title rests on inheritance rather than, like Alfonso's, marriage.

4.1

6 **bread-eaters** heavy and dull.

15 **Present . . . attendance** the money will be paid instantly, whereas more often the court took years to pay its bills, forcing tradesmen to keep asking. This was a topical concern: in the late 1620s, Charles I's exchequer was

running awkwardly and unprecedentedly low, and bills for court festivities of the 1625–6 revels season went unpaid for ten years.

27–8 time was, . . . time is past the words of the brazen head in *Friar Bacon and Friar Bungay* (1589; ll. 1595, 1604), aptly applied to Chaperon because, as a bawd, she has passed the age of being a practitioner in the sex industry and can only be a manager.

28 forwards and backwards Ford wrote a similar parody of an epistolary valediction in *'Tis Pity She's a Whore*, 2.4.26–7: 'Yours upwards and downwards, or you may choose'.

34 cue sense.

4.2

22 to compared with.

37 beauty The Q reading, *beau*, is first recorded as a noun in 1687, and first in the relevant sense of a wooer or lover (*OED*, *n* 2) in *c.*1720.

58 creatures created things, subject to human frailty, rather than supernatural or divine beings (as he himself previously said).

63 recognizance identification (close to, but not identical with the sense *OED*, *n* 2a).

82–3 chair . . . stool marks of relative status. In the second scene of Middleton and Dekker's *The Roaring Girl* (1611), the knights visiting Sir Alexander are given chairs, the gentlemen only stools.

124 whips of steel wielded by the avenging Furies in classical mythology.

129 Basilisk fabled serpent whose gaze struck the object dead (rather than blind, as Alfonso seems to suppose).

155–6 Eaglet . . . Sun eagles were thought to be able to look directly at the sun without risk of ocular impairment.

167 leave . . . another 'she must die, else she'll betray more men' (*Othello*, 5.2.6).

4.3

36 very authentic.

97 Genius guardian spirit.

143 an old proverb Tilley L.173 (in which this is the only example cited).

145 shift for one look after myself.

145 lustly both pleasure-giving (*OED*, *adj.* 1) and lustful (*OED*, *adj.* 2).

171 **stranger** foreigner, outsider.

175 **run at charges** cost themselves money.

175–6 **never . . . Horn-book** they only need elementary education to do their accounts, and so save themselves the expense of advanced schooling.

177 **proctor** legal representative in a church court; the equivalent of a solicitor or attorney.

178 **consistory** ecclesiastical court, with jurisdiction over moral rather than criminal matters.

179 **be . . . longtayle** whatever kind of person they are; deriving from terms for animals, such as dogs or horses, with docked and undocked tails.

191–3 There is a legal foundation for Mopas's comic confusion here. English law differentiated between murder and manslaughter as types of homicide: both were capital offences, but a person convicted of manslaughter was permitted to claim benefit of clergy, which waived the death penalty for a first offence by those who could pass a literacy test. Self-defence was an admissible extenuation.

196 **old . . . twang** a term of contempt (*OED, twang n* 3).

196–7 **dog dayes** the hottest part of the year, usually understood to be the forty days following 11 August, and often associated with increased sexual activity.

197–8 **way . . . flesh** Joshua 23.14 (Douai translation).

207 **dudgion** the wooden hilt of a sword or dagger.

5.1

4 **Craven** a non-fighting cock, or a human coward.

73 an unmetrical, nine-syllable line, covering her ascent up the stairs of the scaffold.

76 **O women** there are no other women on stage; Salassa is addressing the women in the audience, like Anne Frankford in Heywood's *A Woman Killed with Kindness* (1603; sc.13, 140–3).

78–9 **'less . . . frailties** i.e. unless my advice is supererogatory.

89 **a sword** to act in her defence as her champion (90).

118–20 **let Snakes . . . life** alluding to Aesop's fable of the man who warmed a frozen snake in his bosom, and received a fatal bite for his kindness; used as a byword for ingratitude.

5.2

17 **upon the castaway** at the point of becoming spiritually reprobate.

25 **erected** exalted, noble (*OED,* 2).

43–4 **They . . . eyes** his tears bear witness, in public, to the view of those present.

66 **medley** (a) combative (adjectival usage from *OED*, *n* 1); (b) motley, incongruously mixed (*OED*, *adj.* 2).

118 **mettall men** men of mettle, punning on the suits of armour worn by Velasco, Alfonso, and Petrucci.

215 **Suresby** an appellation for a dependable person.

235 **loose-bodied** promiscuous; but (since a pair of bodies is a corset) perhaps also implying pregnant.

240 **this lady** Herophil.

241 *quietus est* formal discharge of a debt; referring to Bufo's mock-marriage to Mopas.

276 SD **white rod** carried by a person doing penance for a serious sexual misdemeanour.

311–13 riffing on Luke 15.7: 'joy shall be in heaven over one sinner that repenteth, more than over ninety and nine just persons, which need no repentance'.

Appendix: Paratexts

Title Page

Greek quotation: Hesiod, *Works and Days*, 157–60: 'Upon the fruitful earth Zeus, the son of Cronos, made another generation, the fourth, which was nobler and more virtuous, a god-like race of men called demi-gods'.

Latin quotation: 'Now let Greek antiquity, which marvelled at the young shield-bearing women, give place; let Volscian Camilla give place. Be silent, Fame, about the woman who ruled Assyria; I sing of greater things.' The source of the lines, if they have one, is untraced, but, like much neo-Latin writing, the passage is partly a compilation of phrases from classical Latin authors: 'Graia vetustas' is from Claudian, *Panegyric on the Fourth Consulship of Honorius*, 398; 'flectit habenas' is from various classical Latin poets, including Virgil, *Aeneid* (12.471), Statius, *Silvae* (5.1.37), and Valerius Flaccus, *Argonautica* (5.436); 'Fama tace' is from Statius, *Sylvae* (1.2.28). The historic women referred to are probably the warrior Amazons of Greek mythology; Camilla, who assisted Aeneas against Turnus in the battle for Italy (Virgil, *Aeneid* 11); and Semiramis, the tyrant Queen of Assyria who murdered her husband, dressed as a man in order to rule in her own right, and was killed after conceiving an incestuous passion for her son.

Dedication

Lady Catherine Mohun née Welles, wife of Lord Warwick, 2nd Baron Mohun of Okehampton (1620–67); she was a Roman Catholic.

the Thunder-shocks . . . age the English Revolution; plays in particular were endangered after the antitheatrical legislation of 1648.

wreath it was believed that a laurel wreath protected the wearer from being struck by lightning.

waxed . . . fall referring to the classical myth of Icarus, who escaped from Crete with artificial wings held together with wax, but flew too close to the sun and melted them.

Alexander Goughe born 1614, a former boy actor associated with the King's Men, who played a woman's part in *The Lover's Melancholy*. During the interregnum he was reportedly responsible for notifying 'persons of quality' of the time and venue for surreptitious performances. See Bentley, *JCS*, ii.446–7.

Commendatory Verses

Mr. Alexander Goughe:

15 In *Q*, a marginal note to 'Presbiters' reads: 'in the originall it is Puritans.' The Blackfriars precinct, where the King's Men's indoor playhouse was situated, had a strongly Puritan element among its residents; the church in the precinct fell down during a sermon in the autumn of 1625. The note seems to be drawing attention to, and thereby subverting, censorship of the poem in the light of the current ascendancy of the Puritans.

22 Jack Fletcher less familiarly, John Fletcher (1579–1625), son of Richard Fletcher, Bishop of London; a prolific and popular Jacobean playwright whose works included a small contribution to *The Fair Maid of the Inn*.

23 that order is condemn'd Parliament abolished the temporal power of the bishops in 1642.

26–7 where no . . . strip't illegal performances in London were frequently raided by government troops in the 1640s. The specific referent is the last performance by the King's Men, at the Cockpit on 1 January 1649, was broken up by soldiers; the actors were arrested and stripped of their costumes, which were confiscated as theatrical apparel.

28 No . . . whip't the printer's copy, substituting for the actors, is not subject to the penal laws which defined actors as vagrants and so liable to be whipped; *Histriomastix* (literally a whip for players) was the title of William Prynne's interminable antitheatrical tract of 1633.

29 No . . . cloth's transvestism, one of the standard antitheatrical objections, founded on Deuteronomy 22.5.

29–30 **the guiltles . . . garments** a common trope; see Catherine Richardson (ed.), *Clothing Culture, 1350–1650* (Aldershot, 2004), 209–21.

R. C. Bang suggests that the author might be the minor dramatist Robert Chamberlain (b. 1607), author of *The Swaggering Damsel*, acquaintance of the dramatists Thomas Nabbes, Thomas Rawlins, and John Tatham, and clerk to John Ball, Queen Henrietta Maria's Solicitor General.

For Plays:

Edmond Rookwood probably a member of the Lincolnshire Roman Catholic family whose most prominent member, Ambrose Rookwood, was executed for his part in the Gunpowder Plot.

To Mr *Gough*:

7 *Eastern Prophet's Dove* Muhammad was reputed to keep a tame dove, representing the Holy Ghost, which appeared to whisper in his ear, but was actually pecking corn from it; see Samuel Butler's note to *Hudibras*, Part 1, 1. 230 (ed. John Wilders (Oxford, 1967)).